1 MONTH OF FREE READ

CW01500670

at
www.ForgottenBooks.com

By purchasing this book you are eligible for one month membership to ForgottenBooks.com, giving you unlimited access to our entire collection of over 1,000,000 titles via our web site and mobile apps.

To claim your free month visit:

www.forgottenbooks.com/free847959

ISBN 978-0-282-36073-3
PIBN 10847959

HISTORY *of the* MONGOLS

FROM THE 9th TO THE 19th CENTURY.

PART II.

THE SO-CALLED TARTARS OF RUSSIA AND CENTRAL ASIA.

DIVISION II.

BY

HENRY H. HOWORTH, F.S.A.

LONDON:

LONGMANS, GREEN, AND CO.

1880.

CONTENTS.

CHAPTER VIII.

THE WHITE HORDE AND THE KIRGHIZ KAZAKS.

BORRAK KHAN.

WE have now traced out the various lines of princes who ruled at Astrakhan, Kazan, Kasimof, and in the Krim until their final overthrow and absorption by Russia, and we must turn once more to the White Horde, which held sway in the eastern parts of the Kipchak.

We traced its history down to the death of Borrak Khan in the year 831 (*i.e.*, 1427-8). He was, as I have shown,[*] a constant candidate for the throne of Serai, and not only had a considerable struggle for it with Ulugh Muhammed, but he also strove to disposses the Timurids of Sighnak, the ancient capital of his horde, and which Timur had annexed. On his death in 831 his children were apparently very young, and Abulkhair Khan, of the house of Sheiban, acquired supreme authority in the country east of the Yemba.[†]

GIRAI KHAN AND JANIBEG KHAN.

Borrak Khan, it would seem, left two sons called Girai and Janibeg, who apparently shared their father's throne. Of these Girai was probably the elder, since his son succeeded Janibeg. Girai is not mentioned by Abulghazi, who calls his brother Janibeg, "Abusaid surnamed Janibeg Khan."[‡] They are both mentioned in the Tarikhi Rashidi of Haidar and in the Sheibaneh Nameh. The latter work expressly calls Janibeg the son of Borrak, the brother of Girai.[§] We do not hear of them until the year 1451, when we are told by Haidar that Abulkhair, the representative of the house of Sheiban[||] had gained great authority in the Kipchak, and that Janibeg and Girai fled from him, and sought refuge in Mongolistan (*i.e.*, the country of Issikul and Kashgar) with Issanbugha, who was Khan there. By the latter they were well received and given the district of Chu (*i.e.*, of the river Chu), Bashi Kuzi (?), which lies on the western limit of Mongolistan. There, we are told, they enjoyed themselves in quiet until Abulkhair's death, which took place in 1469. Many then repaired to Girai and Janibeg, so that their number increased to 200,000 persons, and they got the name of Uzbeg *Kazaks*. This name of Kazaks they got no

---

[*] *Ante*, chapter v.   [‡] See next chapter.
[†] Op. cit., 188.   [§] Vol. Zora., 263.   [||] See next chapter.

doubt, as I have shown in the introduction, from their being fugitives *par excellence*. This was the beginning then of the history of the Kazaks, who are called improperly Kirghiz Kazaks by most writers.

The sons of Abulkhair carried on the strife with Girai and Janibeg Khan, and when Mahmud Khan of Mongolistan in 893 hej. (*i.e.*, 1488) granted Turkestan to Sheibani, the grandson of Abulkhair, we are told he incurred the enmity of Girai and Janibeg. "Sheibani was their enemy," they said, "and why was he sent to be in collision with them?"* In consequence of this two battles took place between Mahmud Khan and the brothers, and the former, who had made himself unpopular among the amirs by his arbitrary ways, was defeated. Ahmed Khan, the brother of Mahmud, subsequently repaired this misfortune, and defeated the Kazaks three times.† We do not again read of either Girai or Janibeg, nor do we know when either of them died. M. Veliaminof Zernof‡ has shown how Von Hammer was led astray in regard to the genealogy of Janibeg, and what confusion has been created by the author of the Golden Horde identifying him with Seyid Ahmed, who died at Kovno in Lithuania, and whose history has already occupied us.§

BERENDUK KHAN.

Haidar tells us that both Girai and Janibeg left many sons. Girai, it would seem, was succeeded by his son Berenduk, who became the over-chief of the Kazaks, and we are told that the famous Kasim Khan, son of Janibeg, was in all respects submissive to him, as his father before him had been.‖ During his reign the Kazaks and Sheibanids or Uzbegs continued their former strife. We are told by Khuandemir that when at Sighnak on one occasion an envoy went to Sheibani, the great chief of the Uzbegs, from Musa, the leader of the Nogais, offering him the throne of Desht Kipchak if he would go there. Sheibani accordingly went, and was well received by Musa. Meanwhile Berenduk Khan, who was the real ruler of the country, set out with a large army against him. Sheibani won the victory and Berenduk fled, but Musa refused to fulfil his promise on the ground that his amirs were not agreeable.¶ Khuandemir also reports that about the year 1494 Sheibani and his brother Mahmud, having subdued all Turkestan, Berenduk Khan appeared at Sabran, and at the request of the amir Muhammed Terkhan the people of the town seized Mahmud and handed him over to Kasim. The latter sent him with an escort to Suzak, but he escaped on the way, and joined his brother at Otrar. Berenduk was not long in beleaguring that town, and had several fierce fights with its garrison, but at length agreed to a peace and returned home. Presently the Kazaks allied themselves with the Khan of Mongolistan, and again made a demon-

* Tar. Rash.　　† *Id.*　　‡ ii. 263-268.　　§ *Ante*, 292, &c.
‖ Tar. Rash.　　¶ Vel. Zern., II, 242.

stration against Otrar, from which they once more retired. Shahibeg then marched against the Kazaks, whose chief camp was in the Ala tagh mountains (probably Ala Tau near Vernoe). Peace was again made between them, and Berenduk made Sheibani's son Muhammed Timur Sultan his brother-in-law.

In the winter of 912 (i.e., 1507) we again find the Kazaks molesting Mavera un nehr,[*] and Sheibani marching against them.[†] Two years later, namely, in 1509, he again went against them. We are told that at this time, although Berenduk Khan was the *de jure* ruler of Kipchak, that all the authority was virtually in the hands of Kasim, and that the Kazaks could muster a force of two hundred thousand men. Sheibani took up his winter quarters at Kuruk, whence he sent a force into the enemy's country, but on hearing a report that Kasim Khan was coming, this division retired, and created quite a panic in Sheibani's army, and he beat the drum for retreat. "Nothing was attended to," says Haidar. The army, broken and scattered, reached Samarkand in the end of the winter, whence Sheibani withdrew to Khorasan. As I have said, nothing was left to Berenduk but the semblance of authority, and this was now to end, for we read in the Tarikhi Rashidi that he was at length expelled and retired to Samarkand, where he died in exile.[‡]

KASIM KHAN.

The throne of the Kazaks now passed to the family of Janibeg Khan. The latter, according to Abulghazi, had nine sons, Iranchi or Iraiji, Mahmud, Kasim, Itik or Aitek (perhaps rightly Aibek), Janish, Kanbar, Tanish (called Benish by Haidar), Uziak, and Jauk, Yadik, or Jadik.[§] Iranchi is called Iranji Khan on one occasion by Khuandemir, who names him as the ruler of Sabran, where he punished Sheibani,[‖] but it would seem from Haidar's positive statement and other facts, that Berenduk was in fact succeeded by Kasim, who had long previously been the real ruler of the Desht. We are told that during Berenduk's reign he would not live near him, for if he should not pay him due regard he would resent it, and if he did he could not in his heart submit to him. Berenduk then lived at Seraichuk (? Sighnak) and Kainu on the borders of Mongolistan. Haidar says he subdued the whole of Desht Kipchak, and his army was more than a thousand thousand in number. After Juchi Khan none was ever more powerful in that yurt than he.[¶] The Turkish biographer of Uraz Makhmet tells us the mother of Kasim was Jaghun Berkin, and that he ruled for some time in his father's ulus.[**] The most famous of Kasim Khan's brothers was Yadik, who is called Uzbeg in Erskine's translation of the Tarikhi Rashidi, but Yadik by Vel. Zernof in his extracts from that work. He is no doubt the "Uzbeg Sultan," one of the sultans of the Kazaks mentioned

* *Id.*, 251, 252.   † Tar. Rash.   ‡ *Id.*   § Op cit.. 188. Vel. Zern., ii, 267, 268.
‖ Vel. Zern., ii. 240.   ¶ Tar. Rash.   ** Vel. Zern., ii. 295.

by Baber, and who Erskine says in a note was called Awik Sultan in the
Persian text.* He married Sultan Nigar Khanum, the fourth daughter of
Yunis Khan of Mongolistan, the widow of Mahmud Murza, son of Sultan
Abusaid,† who after his death married his brother Kasim,‡ which shows
the latter outlived him. The biographer of Uraz Makhmet tells us he
was killed with one of his sons at Ilianli Tuk, fighting against the Nogai
Sheikh Murza. He was buried at Bakirghan Ata, in the district of
Urgenj or Khiva.§ This place is mentioned by Abulghazi, and was the
burial place of a famous Mussulman saint named Suliman Hakim.‖ Kanbar,
another son of Janibeg, was all his life in the service of Kasim Khan, and
was constantly in the front of the army.¶ But to return to Kasim.

We are told that in the year 918 (i.e., 1512), when the Uzbegs had
acquired great influence in Mavera un nehr, news arrived of the approach
of Kasim Khan. The latter marching from his quarters near Mongolistan
went to Tarez, the keys of Sairam were given up to him by Ketch Beg, its
governor, and thence he went on to Tashkend, but again retired. The
Khan Sultan Said went after him and overtook him at the river Chu.
Kasim was then past sixty and going on towards seventy, and did not go
to meet the Khan, but sent some of his sultans, such as Janish Khan,
Benish Khan, &c., to the number of thirty or forty, with orders to
bend the knee to the Khan. Of this number Janish Khan and
Benish Khan were very aged. When they kneeled the Khan rose, and
he remained seated while the others did obeisance. Kasim treated the
Khan with a courtesy the latter never forgot, and he always described
him as a man of worth.

After they had met he approached the Khan and said, "I am a
man of the desert. Here we have neither form nor ceremony in our
friendship. Our only valuable property is our horse ; our best food is its
flesh, our best drink its milk and what is made of it. In my country
there is neither palace nor garden. My great recreation is to inspect my
herds. Let us go and pass an hour in looking at them." They accordingly went. He then showed the Khan two horses which he said were
worth all the herd besides. The Khan assented. "We people of the
desert depend for our lives on our horses. These are my choicest ones.
You are an incomparable guest. Do me the favour of choosing which
you like and leave me the other." He at the same time pointed out the
good points of each. The Khan chose one, which he called Oghlan
Turuk, and surely, says Haidar, such a horse was never seen. With it
he joined a number of other horses and offered them to the Khan with a
cup of kumiz, saying, "This is the way we greet our guests, oblige me
by drinking." The Khan had previously renounced all intoxicating
drinks, and replied, "I have foresworn such things as this, how can I

* Erskine's Baber, 13. Note, 4.   † Baber, 13.   ‡ Tar. Rash.
§ Vol. Zernof, ii. 125.   ‖ Id., 127.   ¶ Id., 125.

break my vow?" Kasim urged that he had nothing else to offer him, as mare's milk and what was made of it was the best drink he had. Years must elapse before I can entertain such a guest as you again, and here I am deprived of the power of showing you hospitality. Thereupon he held down his head and seemed much crestfallen. Upon this we are told that the Khan, to please him, drank it up, to the great joy of Kasim. For twenty-one days they continued to feast together and exchange cups of kumiz. It was now the end of summer, and the Kazaks began to retire to their winter quarters without Kasim's permission. He apologised for them, and said it was not convenient to make an attack on Turkestan till the spring. Next year (*i.e.*, in 920) Kasim seems to have made an unimportant attack on the Uzbegs.[*] This is the last notice I can find of Kasim Khan, of whom Baber reports that it was said none of the Khans or Sultans of the Kazaks ever kept the horde in such complete order as he did, and that his army amounted to nearly three hundred thousand men. Haidar says he died in the year 924 (*i.e.*, 1518).

MIMASH OR BIBASH KHAN.

Kasim was succeeded by Mimash, who Haidar apparently in one place makes his son, but he was probably a son of Yadik Sultan, for Haidar mentions a son of Yadik called Bibash or Mimash, who married the sister of Muhammed Rashid Khan. Haidar says Bibash fell in one of the wars.

TAGIR OR TAHIR KHAN.

Mimash was succeeded by Tagir, who was unquestionably the son of Yadik. Of him we read that in the year 929, after carrying on an intercourse with the Khan of Mongolistan by envoys, he went to him in person and took with him Sultan Nigar Khanum. He was very fond of her, but she complained that her old age prevented her attending him in his migratory life, and that she wished to go to her brother's son, Sultan Said Khan to end her days. He agreed to go with her. The Khan, out of gratitude to him for taking his aunt, rose to meet him, which was contrary to etiquette, but Tagir would not be outdone in courtesy, and duly bent his forehead to the ground in the prescribed way. His sister, the Khanum's daughter, says Haidar, was married to Rashid Khan, and was still in his harem when he wrote.[†] At this time, we are told, Tagir Khan's power was on the decline. He once controlled one million of men, but now only two hundred thousand. He was of a harsh and severe disposition,[‡] and became embroiled with the neighbouring Sultans. He slew his brother Abul Kasim Sultan with his own hand. His people deserted him and dispersed, and being left alone with his son he took refuge with the Kirghiz (*i.e.*, the Buruts). They also apparently got weary of him, for we read that in the year 936 (*i.e.*, 1530) the Kirghiz as well as his own people deserted him.[*] In another place Haidar says he died miserably among the Kirghizes, and that nearly thirty thousand Kazaks collected in Mongolistan and raised his brother Buidash to the throne. " Such has been the change in fortune's wheel," says Haidar, " that of these tribes for the last four years not a trace remains. In the year 930 they were a million of men, in 944 not a trace of them remained."[†] This is probably an exaggeration, but there can be no doubt that at this time the Kazak confederacy was much disintegrated.

UZIAK AHMED KHAN.

The biographer of Uraz Makhmet tells us that in this time of con- fusion several chieftains are mentioned as leaders of the Kazaks. He says of one of them : There was also an Ahmed Khan, sometimes called Uzbeg and sometimes Ahmed. He did not rule long, and fell in a fight with Seidiak the Nogai prince, by the hand of Urak Murza.[‡] This is no doubt the same Seidiak who in 1535 wrote to the Emperor Ivan Vasili- vitch to tell him how his neighbours had submitted to him, and he adds, " the Kazak Tzar Uzian Mahmed Tzar is living with us with fifteen sons."[§] As M. Vel. Zernof says, this seems clearly to be the same person as the Ahmed Khan above named. But we may perhaps go a step further, and identify this Uzian with the Uziak who is made a brother of Yadik by the biographer of Uraz Makhmet. This author says he had a son named Bulat Sultan, who with his sons died in battle against the Nogais.[ǁ] Levchine, in his genealogical table of the Kazak chiefs, also makes Yadik and Uziak brothers, and makes them the stem- fathers of the Royal race of the Kazaks. He also names his son Bulak, thus showing he was the same Uziak as the one mentioned in the biography just cited. Uziak was the ancestor of Abulkhair Khan, the famous chief of the Little Horde. At this time the Nogais were very active and enterprising. Haidar tells us that in 932 hej. they drove a large number of the Kazaks from Uzbegistan (*i.e.*, from the Kazak steppes). In 1535 we are told, however, that they were strong enough to capture and conquer the princes of Tashkend. They also seem to have defeated the Kalmuks.[¶] In 1537 the Nogai prince Yusuf wrote to the Emperor to tell him how he had defeated the Kazaks.

AK NAZAR KHAN.

The person who apparently restored the prosperity of the Kazaks was Ak Nazar, the son of Kasim, whose fame had spread beyond the borders

---

* Tar. Rash.   † Op. cit.   ‡ Vel. Zernof, 275.
    § *Id.*, 235.   ǁ *Id.*, 125.   ¶ *Id.*, 330.

of his own people, and is still alive among the Bashkirs and Nogais.
The biographer of Uraz Makhmet tells us Ak Nazar was the son of
Kasim by his wife Khanik Sultan Khanime.* Haidar Razi calls Ak
Nazar lord of the Kazaks and the Kirghises, and says that the ruler of
Aksu and Mongolistan fell in a struggle with him. This was Abdul
Latif Sultan, son of Abdur Rashid Khan, and grandson of Sultan Said
Khan.† He is mentioned also in the Abdullah Nameh, where in relating
the struggle between the Sheibani Khan Abdulla and his rival Baba
Sultan,‡ the author tells us how a spy came and reported that the latter
had fled to the Kazaks on the river Talas, who had done homage to him.
The Khan sent messengers to inquire, who brought word that the chiefs
of the Kazaks, such as Ak Nazar Khan, Jalim Sultan, Shigai Sultan (the
son of Yadik), and Dustai Sultan, with others their brothers and sons, were
settled on the banks of the river Taras, and that one of them, Ondan
Sultan (the son of Shigai), had married the wife of Abdul Kerim Sultan,
and had made captive her sister for Jalim Sultan. They also reported
that the story told by the spy about Baba Sultan having taken refuge
with the Kazaks was untrue. The spy was accordingly put to death.
Thereupon the Khan himself set out for the Talas, where envoys came to
him from the Kazak chiefs with greeting, and in the inflated language of
the Abdulla Nameh, "put the head of submission in the yoke of
obedience," and declared that the treaty they had made with him they
were willing to keep, and reported that one of Baba Sultan's children
and some of his dependents having taken refuge with them, they wished
to know whether they were to be sent alive or whether their heads alone
were to be sent. The Khan, we are told, gave the envoy a robe of
honour and presents, and ordered the amir Sukhum Atalik to accompany him back to the Kazak camp. The Khan bade the Kazaks send
the captives to him, and he also made over four towns in Turkestan
to them as a token of his good will.§

Some time after we read how the Kazaks, who it seems were not
content with their foothold in Turkestan, were making raids on the
Khan's territory. Baba Sultan, the ruler of Tashkend, being unable
to resist them, had surrendered Yassy (i.e., Turkestan) and Sabran
to them. He seems then to have conspired with them, and it was
arranged that Saiban Sultan Kazak, who had for some time been
obedient to the Khan, should cross the Sihun and invade the district of
Bukhara, while Baba and his people similarly ravaged Samarkand.
Both parties seem to have made a successful harrying. The allies of
Baba Sultan were apparently only a small section of the Kazaks, and we
now find him sending Jan Kuli beg as his envoy to his father-in-law
Jalim Sultan, to ask him and the other Kazak chiefs to come to a

---

* Vel. Zernof, ii. 125.   † Id, 333.   ‡ See chapter on Bukhara.
§ Vel. Zern,, ii. 279-283.

3 H

conference, where they could arrange a common policy against the Khan. He was evidently no favourite of theirs, for the Kazaks determined to kill his envoy Jan Kuli, and to send Jalim Sultan with some troops to try and surprise him. Jan Kuli was allowed to escape by his executioner, and hastened to acquaint his master.

Meanwhile Jalim Sultan and two sons of Ak Nazar Khan, unaware of this escape, marched with a considerable force to surprise Baba Sultan. They met on the banks of the river Shirab khani (i.e., the wine cellar), and it was agreed that Baba Sultan should accompany them to Ak Nazar Khan. Baba Sultan, who had been forewarned, as I have shown, ordered his warriors to draw their swords and fall upon the treacherous chiefs. Thereupon we are told the valley " blossomed forth in tulips with their blood." He then ordered his brother Buzakhur to ride on in all haste and endeavour to surprise and destroy Ak Nazar Khan.* We are not told what the issue was, but it would seem that Ak Nazar was in fact killed. On turning to the Russian archives we find him mentioned in them more than once. Simeon Malkhof, who was sent on a mission to the Nogais in 1569, mentions the Kazak hordes of Ak Nazar, of Shigai Tzarevitch, and of Chelim (i.e., Jalim) Tzarevitch,† and eight years later, namely, in 1577, we find the son of the boyard Boris Tomoshirof reporting that the Kazaks, who were then ruled over by Akak Nazar (i.e., Ak Nazar), were at war with the Nogais, but desired to be on friendly terms with the Russians.‡ The death of the Kazak princes took place in 1580.§

SHIGAI KHAN.

Ak Nazar Khan was immediately succeeded by Shigai, the son of Yadik, who is mentioned above as Shigai Sultan, and who occurs in Levchine's tables. The biographer of Uraz Makhmet says that Yadik had many wives and concubines, and also many sons. The best known of whom were Tugum Khan, Bukei Sultan, Shigai Sultan, and Malik Sultan. The mother of the last two was Abaikan-Bikem.║ This Tugum Khan I have very little doubt was the Tagir Khan already named, and this exactly agrees with the note in the biography just named, that he with Bashibeg, son of Malik, died on the borders of the Jagatai ulus. Bukei Sultan will occupy us presently. He was probably dead at this time, which explains why Shigai acquired the supremacy.

Yadik, according to the Tarikhi Rashidi, died about the year 1503, and as Hafiztanish mentions Shigai as late as 1582, it is clear that he must have lived to a very old age. The latter author says in the Abdulla Nameh that he was well versed in affairs, and had had many experiences

* Id., 292-296.   † Op. cit., 323.   ‡ Id., 334.   § Id., 292.
║ Vel. Zernof, op. cit., ii. 274.

of life.* Some time after the plot against Baba Sultan above mentioned Shigai seems to have tried to surprise the latter on the Talas, but failed and had to retire.† In 1581 Abdulla Khan, who was still struggling with Baba Sultan, found himself at Kara tau, near the river Sir Daria. There came to meet him Shigai Khan, with his son Tevkel and others. The two chiefs had a friendly meeting, and it seems Abdulla appointed Shigai governor of Khojend, where he left him on his return home, and took Tevkel Sultan with him. The latter distinguished himself at a grand shooting match held in the outskirts of the Khan's garden, where the competitors fired at a number of glistening silver and gold balls hung on the end of a pole. Soon after this Abdulla undertook his famous expedition to the Ulugh Tagh in pursuit of Baba Sultan. He set out from Bukhara in January, 1582. He crossed the Jaxartes, and on the river Aris he learnt that Baba had retired to the Desht Kipchak, leaving a part of his army at Kara saman, a place mentioned in the accounts of Timur's campaigns, and identified by M. Vel. Zernof with Kara asman on the Arish,‡ and over the rivers Bugan, Chayan, and Arslanlik to Ikan, now a village near the town of Turkestan, and thence on to the river Sari su. This he crossed in April, and advanced to the Ulugh Tagh mountains, where he learnt that Baba had taken shelter with the Manguts or Nogais. He sent a body of troops in pursuit of him, and himself returned towards home, and laid siege to Sabran, where he was delayed for two months.

On one occasion when Abdulla was hunting on the river Sabran his son Abdul Mumin Sultan was lost, but the following day he came into the camp with Yan Behadur Sultan, the younger brother of Shigai Khan, who was handsomely rewarded by the Khan. The latter once more entered the Kipchak in pursuit of his indefatigable enemy, and ordered the Kazaks under Tevkel to lead the way, crossing the two lost rivers called Kenderlik.§ Here we are told that one of the commanders with a body of scouts, near *the grave of Juchi Khan*, came upon some of Baba Sultan's people and were made prisoners. These spies Baba Sultan put to death, and being thus duly warned he fled to the Nogais. Some of his people were overtaken and plundered by Shigai Khan. Abdulla Khan now advanced to the Ulugh Tagh, and thence to the Ilanchik or Jilanchik, where Shigai Khan went to meet him.‖ This is the last mention I can find of the latter, and he probably died about this time at a very advanced age. Muller in his account of Siberia mentions an old Tartar tradition that Ahmed Girai, the brother of Kuchum, the famous Khan of Siberia, had married a daughter of Shigai Khan, a prince of Bukhara, whom he treated badly. Shigai marched against him to punish him, and slew him on the banks of the Irtish. I quite agree

---

* Id., 325.   † Id., 294.   ‡ Op. cit., ii. 302.
§ See notes at the end of the chapter.   ‖ Op. cit., ii. 309.

with M. Vel. Zernof that by this prince of Bukhara none other than our
Shigai Khan is meant. The Russians sometimes used the name Bukhara
for Central Asia.* The biographer of Uraz Makhmet, so often quoted,
tells us Shigai had many wives, of whom three are well known. By
Yashem Bekem, of the race of Jagatai, he had Tukai Khan, Ishim Sultan,
and Sultan-Sabir-bek-Khanim; by Baim Bekem, Seyid kul Sultan, Ondan
Sultan, and Altin Khanim; and by Dadim Khanim, the daughter of
Berenduk Khan, Ali Sultan, Selim Sultan, Ibrahim Sultan, and Shagim
Sultan.†

The Tukai Khan of this list is no doubt the Tevkel Khan who will
next occupy us.‡ We shall also have more to say of Ishim, who afterwards became Khan. The only other name in the list of much interest
is Ondan Sultan, of whom we are told he was very brave and shot
superbly with the bow, and during Shigai Khan's reign led the van
of the army. The Kalmuks killed him at the age of thirty, and his
grave is still to be seen near Ahmed Issevi in Turkestan. He had
a number of wives and concubines, of these two were pre-eminent. By
Altin Khanim, the daughter of Bulat Sultan, son of Uziak Khan, he had
Uraz Makhmet Khan and Tatli Khanim, and by Chuyum Khanim
daughter of Kemsen Sultan, son of Berenduk Khan, Kuchak Sultan, who
was a favourite and *protegé* of Tevkel Khan.§ The Uraz Makhmet here
named was the well-known Khan of Kasimof.‖

TEVKEL KHAN.

Shigai Khan was succeeded by his son Tevkel, whose name has
already been mentioned in the account of the struggle between Abdulla
Khan and Baba Sultan, when Tevkel Sultan is named among the active
supporters of the former. When Abdulla returned from his famous
expedition to the Ulugh Tagh,¶ Tevkel, who was in charge of some
herds at Ak kurgan, heard that Sultan Tagir, Baba Sultan's brother, had
got through the pass Sungluk. He went in pursuit of him, captured
him, and handed him over to Abdulla. Abdulla rewarded Tevkel with a
robe of golden tissue and other presents. This was about 1582-3. Soon
after he presented Abdulla with the head of Baba Sultan, Jan Muhammed
Atalik, Latif Sultan, son of Baba, &c., and the latter again rewarded him
with presents, and made him governor of Aferinkend, the best post in
Samarkand, and which had been filled by Abdulla's own father.**

The capture of Baba is described in the Abdulla Nameh. That restless
intriguer having taken refuge among the Nogais had proved treacherous
to them, and was forced to fly. He first thought of going to Tura (*i.e.*,

* Op. cit., ii. 324.   † Id., 362-365.   ‡ On this see Vel. Zernof, op. cit., ii. 367, 368.
§ Id., 365.   ‖ Ante, 436.   ¶ Vide Ante, 635.   ** Vel. Zern., ii. 310-312.

Siberia), but eventually resolved to return to Turkestan, in the hope of raising his own people. He stopped *en route* at Sighnak, whence he sent on two Kalmuks who had supported him to report. They fell into Tevkel's hands and acted as guides to him. With their assistance he found out Baba's encampment, killed him, and captured his son Latif, Jan Muhammed Atalik the head of the amirs, &c.[*]

There is an interesting reference to Tevkel in the extracts from Seify, translated by M. Schefer in his edition of Abdul Kerim. He says the Kazaks, who numbered two hundred thousand families, had a Khan called Tevkel. That on one occasion these Kazaks invaded the country of the Kalmuks. The chief of the latter ordered one of his officers to go against him, and not to return without taking either Tevkel or his head. When Tevkel discovered the enormous strength of the enemy he fled towards Tashkend. The Kalmuks pursued and carried off one-half of his people. The other half remained with him at Tashkend. This town was then governed by Nauruz Ahmed Khan, who was also called Borrak Khan.[†] Tevkel sent a messenger to him with the message: "I have come to your country and have put myself under your protection. We are both descended from Jingis Khan, and are therefore related. Besides, we are both Mussulmans, and therefore of the same faith. Help me and let us march together against the Kalmuks." Borrak Khan replied, "If ten princes like you and I were leagued together, we could not overcome the Kalmuks, who are as numerous as the hordes of Yajuj."[‡]

In 1583 Tevkel took part in Abdulla's campaign against Andijan and Ferghana. Suddenly suspecting that Abdulla was unfriendly to him, he retired to the Desht Kipchak. In 1586, having learnt that Abdulla and his people were occupied on a distant campaign, Tevkel suddenly appeared in the north of the kingdom, and threatened Turkestan, Tashkend, and even Samarkand. A small force was sent against him, and a fight ensued at Shirab Khani, a dependency of Tashkend. The Kazaks were badly armed. They had only fur coats and yirgaks for armour. This circumstance made the Uzbegs over confident, and they were badly beaten. News was at once sent to Samarkand to Ibeidulla Sultan, the brother of Abdulla Khan, who crossed the Sir Daria and reached Tashkend. Tevkel was encamped near Sairam, whence he now hastily retreated. Ibeidulla pursued him into the steppe, but could not overtake him.[§]

In 1588 a revolt against Abdulla and his brother-in-law, Uzbek, the son of Rustem, the son of Janibeg, whom he had appointed ruler of that district, took place at Tashkend. The people of Tashkend, Shahrukhia, and Khojend proclaimed Jan Ali, one of the Kazak Sultans, as Khan. Things were unsettled for some months,

---

[*] *Id.* Note, 45.   [†] See next chapter.   [‡] Op. cit., 294, 295.   [§] Vol. Zernof, op. cit., ii. 339, 340.

and we are told that the sons of Ak Nazar Khan, Mungatai, and Din Muhammed took part in the disturbances.* When we next read of Tevkel it is in connection with Russia. We are told that in 1594 he sent his envoy Kul Muhammed to the Tzar Feodor Ivanovitch offering to consider himself and his tribe as subjects of the Tzar, and asking the latter to liberate his nephew Uraz Makhmet.† In March, 1595, the Tzar wrote him a reply accepting his suggestion to treat him as his suzerain, and sent him some firearms, but requiring him to keep Abdulla, the Khan of Bukhara, quiet !!! and to reduce the Siberian Khan Kuchum to obedience. In regard to Uraz Makhmet he undertook to liberate him if he (Tevkel) would send his own son Hussein in his place. This note was sent back by Tevkel's envoy, who was accompanied by Veliamin Stepanof.‡

Iskander Munshi mentions Tevkel in 1597. He says that when the news of the quarrel of Abdulla Khan and his son Abdul Mumin spread in Turkestan, the various Kazak Sultans, who had up to then feared the power of Abdulla and lived at peace, broke out into rebellion, and among them Tevkel, who had assumed the title of Khan, and who approached Tashkend with a numerous army. Not deeming Tevkel a foeman worthy of his steel, Abdulla contented himself with sending some of the sultans of his house, the neighbouring amirs, and a portion of his troops. A severe battle was fought between Tashkend and Samarkand, in which Abdulla's army was beaten, and a large number of its chiefs perished. The survivors fled to Bukhara in a sad plight. Abdulla collected his people to exact revenge and marched towards Samarkand, but he there fell ill and died. His death was succeeded by confusion. Tevkel determined to take advantage of this. Collecting a large army, he marched into Turkestan, where and in Mavera un nehr some of the more important towns, namely, Aksi, Andijan, Tashkend, Samarkand, and the country as far as Miankal, submitted to him. He left his brother Ishim Sultan with twenty thousand men in Samarkand, while he advanced with seventy or eighty thousand on Bukhara, which was defended by a garrison of fifteen thousand men under Pir Muhammed. The latter made daily sorties from the various gates. These continued for eleven days. At length on the twelfth the whole garrison came out, and a fierce battle was fought from dawn to sunset. The Kazaks were defeated and most of their men scattered. Tevkel now determined to raise the siege. Having lighted a number of fires in the camp to deceive the enemy, he withdrew during the night. Meanwhile some of the fugitives reached Samarkand and informed Ishim of his brother's defeat. The latter sent off a messenger with the following message : " You should be very much ashamed that your numerous army has been defeated by a handful of Bukharians. If you appear here, it may well be the people of Samarkand will not receive you. Let the Khan return and I will join him with my

* Id., 341.   † L'ide ante, 436.   ‡ Vel. Zernof, op. cit., ii. 106.   Levchine, 141. 142.

troops." Tevkel accordingly turned back in company with his brother
Meanwhile Pir Muhammed had set out in pursuit, and was joined by
many of the people from the country round. The hostile forces faced
one another at Uzun Sukal in Miankal. For a month there were almost
continuous skirmishes between them. At length Tevkel losing patience
determined upon a general attack. The fight was a fierce one. Said
Muhammed Sultan, a, relative of Pir Muhammed, and Muhammed Baki
Atalik were both killed; but on the other hand Tevkel was wounded,
and did not gain any marked success. He fell back on Tashkend, where
he died. This was in 1598.[*]

ISHIM KHAN.

Tevkel was succeeded as over-chief of the Kazaks by his brother
Ishim, already named. After the events just mentioned, we first hear of
him in the year 1020 hej. (i.e., 1611), when with five thousand Kazaks he
is mentioned as mixed up in the. civil strife which arose between Vali
Muhammed, the banished Khan of Bukhara, and his nephew Imaum
kuli. This strife ended with the death of Vali. In this struggle Said Bi,
the brother of Ishim, also took part.[†] We next read of him in Abulghazi.
The latter when a fugitive from Urgenj, about the year 1625, took refuge
with Ishim Khan at Turkestan, with whom he lived for three months. He
tells us that when Tursun Khan of Tashkend visited Turkestan, Ishim
presented him to him, saying, "Here is Abulghazi, a descendant of
Yadigar Khan, never before has a prince of this house sought shelter
with us, while many of our princes have sought shelter with them."
Tursun Khan took him to Tashkend. Two years later (i.e., in 1627) the
latter was killed by Ishim Khan, and Abulghazi received permission to
go to Imaum kuli Khan at Bukhara.[‡]
   This Tursun Khan of Tashkend is called Tursun Muhammed Sultan,
son of Mehdi Sultan, in one of M. Desmaison's notes.[§] That is, he
identifies him with the Uzbeg prince of this name, who a hundred years
before is mentioned by Baber.[||] This seems quite inadmissible chrono-
logically. Was he the Tursun Khan, son of Khodai Mendi, mentioned
by Levchine in his second genealogical table, and whom he makes a
descendant of Bukei Khan, who was probably the Bukei Sultan, son of
Yadik, mentioned by the biographer of Uraz Mahkmet.[¶] It is true that
author says Bukei left no sons, but this may well be a mistake since the
family of Bukei was more or less obscure, and it is almost certain that
the Kazaks at this time would be found obeying no chief who was not
descended from Yadik. Bukei Khan, according to Levchine, had a son
Kuchuk, whose son was called Khudai Mendi, whose son was Tursun

[*] Vel. Zernof, ii. 345-351.　　[†] Id., 371, 372.　　[‡] Op. cit., 328, 329.
[§] Abulghazi, 328. Note, 3.　　[||] Baber's Memoirs, 399.　　[¶] Vel. Zernof, ii. 274.

Khan. This view also has chronological difficulties. I am rather disposed to identify him with Tursunbi, who was with Tevkel at Bukhara, and who in the feast already described distinguished himself by his dexterity, and we are told was rewarded by Abdulla with a present of a large sum of money, a horse, and the gold and silver balls he had knocked down in the shooting.* He was not improbably a son of Ak Nazar Khan. Iskander Munshi tells us how in 1621 Imaum kuli of Bukhara, having been twice beaten by the Kazaks, was compelled to make peace ; the negotiations for which were chiefly carried on with the Khan of the Kazaks Tursun Muhammed.† Tursun, as I have said, was killed by Ishim Khan in 1627.

In 1635 we find Ishim Khan at war with Baatur Khungtaidshi of the Sungars, a war which ended disastrously for the Kazaks. Yangir or Yehangir Sultan, the son of Ishim, who commanded his troops, was captured.‡ This is the last mention I can find of Ishim Khan, and he probably died about this time.

YEHANGIR KHAN.

I have mentioned how Yehangir was made prisoner by Baatur. We are told that having recovered his freedom, he molested the Kalmuks with continual attacks, and at length Baatur the Sungar chief, in the summer of 1643, marched against him with fifty thousand men, and carried off the two tribes of Alat Kirghiz and Tokmani (i.e., the people of Alatau and Togmak). Yehangir had only six hundred men with him, but he posted them well, dug some trenches between the hills, and when the Kalmuks attacked him fell on them in rear, and his fire-arms created such a panic that they lost ten thousand men killed!§ Yehangir was soon after joined by another Tartar prince named Yalantush with twenty thousand men, and Baatur thought it prudent to retire.∥ In 1644 Baatur again summoned his people, and again resolved to fight the Kazaks, but the Khoshote Kundelung Taishi, who was a friend of Yehangir, intervened, and the strife was apparently postponed.¶ This is the last mention I can find of Yehangir, who according to Levchine lived, like his forefathers, at Turkestan.**

TIAVKA KHAN.

Yehangir was succeeded by his son Tiavka, who is one of the most famous of the Kazak Khans. Levchine grows rhetorical in speaking of him and the veneration in which he is held by his compatriots.

----

* Vel. Zern., ii. 299.   † Id., 374.   ‡ Fischer, Sib. Ges., 608.610.   § Vide ante, vol. i. 618 619.   ∥ Fischer, Sib. Ges., 608-610.   ¶ Fischer, op. cit., 610, 611.   ** Op. cit., 149.

According to him he was the Lycurgus and Draco of the Kazaks. He introduced peace among them and put an end to the quarrels of their clans. His sagacity and equity gained him great influence. He united the weak tribes with one another, and compelled the strong ones to respect them. It is to him that may most reasonably be traced the division of the Kazaks into three hordes. These were at first probably merely administrative divisions. It may be that as such they were of very old date, for we find the Oghuz Turks, from whom the Kazaks are in fact descended, divided into three similar sections, but Tiavka seems to have given them their present organisation. He appointed three vice-gerents to control their affairs, Tiul for the Great Horde, Kazbek for the Middle Horde, and Aitiak for the Little one. But during his reign the Kazaks remained a tolerably homogeneous race and directly subject to him, as they had been to his ancestors. He reigned like them at Turkestan.* Muhammed Amin tells us that in the year 1688 Subhan kuli, son of Imaum kuli, sent two of his officers to Tashkend to interview and negotiate with the Kazak Khan Tiavka.† This shows that the Kazaks were still supreme at Tashkend. Tiavka spent all his life in fighting the Kalmuks. In 1698, at the beginning of his reign, we find the Sungar chief Tse wang Arabtan writing to the Chinese Emperor and giving him the reasons for his strife with the Kazaks. How Galdan, having captured the son of Tiavka, had sent him to the Dalai Lama, whereupon Tiavka had asked him (Tse wang Arabtan) to intercede with the Dalai Lama on his behalf. That he had done so, and sent Tiavka's son to his father escorted by five hundred men, who had basely put them to death, together with a Sungar grandee, with his wife, children, and people, appropriating one hundred kibitkas to himself. This was in the district of Huliyan han (? the Ulugh Tagh range, which was apparently at this time the camping ground of some of the Kalmuks), how he had further waylaid the son of the Torgut chief Ayuka, who was going to him with his sister; and, lastly, how he had pillaged a Russian caravan which was returning home again after visiting his country‡ This war was very disastrous for the Kazaks. They were very hard pressed and driven from their old quarters, and largely disintegrated. In the later years of Tiavka his authority seems to have grown weaker, and the administrative officers he put over the hordes began to assert them-selves in a more independent fashion, and it is from this time that I date the division of the Kazaks into three more or less independent and substantive hordes, governed by their own princes. Of the three divisions the Middle Horde was the most powerful and numerous, and was the direct heir of the White Horde, with whose line of princes its rulers was continuous, and I shall therefore begin the separate histories with that of the Middle Horde.

---

* Levchine, 149.   † Vel. Zern., ii. Note, 53.   ‡ Ante, i. 642. Vel. Zern., ii. Note, 53.

3 I

In 1718, when he was evidently driven to great straits, we find Tiavka (or Tefki, as Muller calls him), Khaip, and Abulkhair, who are all styled Khan, appealing to Prince Matthew Petrovitz Gagarin, the governor of Siberia, offering to put themselves under Russian protection, no doubt in the hopes of receiving assistance against the Kalmuks.[*] Tiavka died about the year 1718.

THE MIDDLE HORDE

BULAT KHAN OR SHEMIAKA.

In Levchine's genealogical table Tiavka's son is called Bulat Khan. The use of this title Khan shows that he actually ruled. Now it is strange that his name does not occur, so far as I know, elsewhere, nor is it known to the Russian chroniclers. On the other hand, they mention at this time or shortly after a Shemiaka Khan, who was the ruler of the Middle Horde, and who is made the immediate predecessor of Abul Makhmet. Now Abul Makhmet was the son of Bulat Khan according to Levchine's table, and this Shemiaka, who was so famous, does not occur in that table at all. These facts have driven me to the conclusion that Bulat Khan and Shemiaka were in fact synonyms for the same person. It is a curious fact that one of the Russian princes, who acted a very turbulent part in the history of Russia in the fourteenth century, was called Shemiaka.

We have reached a very critical stage in Kazak history. The terrible power of the Sungarian Kalmuks, which was at this time dominating over Central Asia, crushed them to powder, and drove them largely out of their old quarters and largely disintegrated them. The Sungarian Khan, after inflicting several defeats upon them, had in 1723 captured Turkestan, the old capital of their Khans, and where most of them were buried. He had also appropriated Tashkend and Sairam, and reduced the Great Horde and a section of the Middle Horde to obedience.[†] The greater part of the Middle Horde retired towards Samarkand, part of the Great Horde and a small section of the Middle towards Khojend, and the Little one to Bukhara and Khiva. Famine and want pursued the unhappy fugitives.

These disasters pieced up for a while their internal quarrels, and it was determined at a general assembly to make a united effort to eject their enemies from the old Kazak country. Abulkhair, the chief of the Little Horde, who will occupy us at some length presently, was appointed generalissimo, and a white horse was sacrificed as a gauge of mutual fidelity. They thereupon advanced against their old enemies, and

---

[*] Muller, Saml. Hist. Nach., iv. 254.   Vel. Zernof, ii. Note, 53.   [†] Levchine, 151, 152.

defeated them in several encounters, but afraid that the Sungar chief would exact terrible vengeance upon them, they determined finally to withdraw from their old land. The Great Horde alone remained behind. The Little Horde advanced westwards, driving before it the Kalmuks of the Volga, and settled down between the Yemba and the Ural or Jaik, while the Middle Horde went northward as far as the rivers Ori and Ui, whence they ejected a large number of Bashkirs. This invited and in fact secured ample reprisals in after days, and the dispossessed Bashkirs, with the Cossacks of the Ural, formed a continual thorn in the flank of the Kazaks; and in view of the many dangers which surrounded them, the latter determined to submit to Russia. We accordingly find that in 1732 Shemiaka took the oath of allegiance to the Empress. This was apparently resented by his people, and disturbances broke out in the Middle Horde.* They attacked the Bashkirs unsuccessfully, and afterwards repeated the venture with similar results. This second raid was led by Shemiaka, notwithstanding the oath he had sworn to the Russians,† but he afterwards sent envoys to apologise for his behaviour.‡ At this time Abulkhair of the Little Horde, who was the most important of the Kazak chiefs, seems to have used his influence to induce the Middle Horde to submit to Russia, and in the year 1734 Kirilof, the Russian frontier commander, was intrusted with patents of investiture for Shemiaka. These were not presented as he in the meantime died. The document is still extant, and has been translated by Levchine. It was addressed by Anne, the Empress and autocratrix of all the Russias, &c., "to our subject Shemiaka Khan and the elders and army of the Kirghiz Kazaks of the Middle Horde." It recited his recent oath and backslidings, and offered him pardon.§

ABUL MAKHMET KHAN.

Levchine says that on the death of Shemiaka the Middle Horde was ruled by Abul Makhmet and Ablai. The latter did not become Khan, however, till much later. Abul Makhmet was, according to the first of his genealogical tables, the son of the Pulad Khan (that is in my view of Shemiaka), and he there says that he submitted to Russia in 1730. Ablai will occupy us further later on. When Tatischef was appointed governor of Orenburgh, in the place of Kirilof, in 1737, he sent a summons to Abul Makhmet Khan and Ablai to go and meet him at Orenburgh. They did not obey this summons, and on the return of the envoy, in August, 1738, explained that it was because they lived a long way off on the river Irtish, but that they would go the following spring and duly swear fealty.‖

* Levchine, 170.　† Id., 171.　‡ Id., 180.　§ Id., 180, 181.　‖ Id., 189.

This did not come about, however, for Tatischef was recalled in the beginning of 1739 and replaced by Prince Urussof. Hitherto the Middle Horde had not apparently elected a definite Khan, but Abul Makhmet at this time acquired that position, and a feud arose between him and Abulkhair of the Little Horde, who claimed some kind of suzerainty over him. In 1740 Abul Makhmet Khan, accompanied by Ablai Sultan, and by many chiefs, elders, and ordinary Kazaks of the Middle Horde, arrived at Orenburgh, and had an interview with Prince Urussof, by whom they were received with the same honours as he had previously received Abulkhair. They presented courteous letters of submission, which were read out by an interpreter, after which Abul Makhmet and Ablai knelt down on a piece of golden tissue and swore fealty They kissed the koran, put it on their heads, and attached their tamghas or seals to the documents containing the oath. One hundred and twenty eight grandees of the Middle Horde took a similar oath in an adjoining tent, and the commonalty out of doors, and the ceremony was followed by a feast, the firing of salvoes of artillery, &c. The following day an interview took place between them and the Russian commander, at which he urged upon them that they should protect the Russian caravans traversing their country, endeavour to restore the things which had been pillaged by the Great Horde from Müller's caravan (vide infra), and endeavour to restore peace between the Kazaks and the Volga Kalmuks. These requests were hardly in the power of the two chiefs to comply with. The plunder of caravans was too old a perquisite of the Kazaks to be given up at the instance of their chiefs, while they had no authority near the Volga, where the disputes with the Kalmuks chiefly arose. Abulkhair's two sons Nurali and Erali happened to be at Orenburgh at the same time as the chiefs of the Middle Horde, but they refused to meet them, and took their departure hastily, for fear of being imprisoned at the instance of Abul Makhmet.*

In 1741 Karasakal (i.e., Blackbeard), the leader of the rebellious Bashkirs, sought refuge among the Kazaks, and led a plundering band of the latter (doubtless of the Middle Horde) against the Sungars, who pursued them, ravaging the Kazak encampments they met with en route. They were stopped by a message of Prince Urussof, who warned them not to disturb the peace which subsisted between their masters and the Russians. They protested they did not know the Kazaks were Russian subjects, and did not seem to understand the diplomatic language of the prince, who told them to remit their complaints against the Kazaks to St. Petersburg, and not to take the law into their own hands.†

Abul Makhmet now wrote to ask the Russians to build a strong fortress in his country.‡ The Kazaks continued to molest the Sungarian frontiers, and in 1741 the Sungar chief Galdan Chereng sent two armies

---

* Id., 190-193.   † Id., 193, 194.   ‡ Id., 194.

to punish the Middle and the Little Horde respectively. The result of this was that Ablai was captured and carried off as a prisoner, and in 1742 we find the Russian Major Müller being despatched to Galdan Chereng to negotiate his surrender. Abul Makhmet was also constrained to send the Sungar chief an embassy and to give up his own son to him as a hostage.* The Russian authorities now protested against this intercourse, and objected strongly to their new clients the Kazaks having direct negotiations with the Kalmuks, and undertook to restrain their raids, but the Sungars, who knew their neighbours well, refused to rely on Kazak promises, and insisted upon hostages.† Abul Makhmet was warned to restrain his people. The latter was an object of jealousy to Abulkhair of the Little Horde, who sent him word when he was on his way to Orenburgh that the Russians meant to detain him. This caused his speedy return home, but Nepluief, the border Russian commander, having sent the interpreter Urazlin to him, he willingly took the oath of allegiance to the Empress Elizabeth. It would seem that at this time a large number of the Kazaks of the Middle Horde obeyed Borrak, the son of Tursun Khan, and he was even styled Khan. He took the oath of allegiance at the same time as Abul Makhmet. A letter and a golden sabre were presented to him in 1743, but he was indignant that these presents were sent him by only a simple messenger and not an envoy, and he returned them with a rude answer. In 1742 Ablai Sultan was released by the Sungars, at the instance of the Russian officer Müller.‡

In 1744 the Sungars made a demonstration towards the Russian frontiers in Siberia. Abul Makhmet and his people retired towards Turkestan, and sought a closer alliance with Galdan Chereng, who still kept his son as a hostage, and from whom he hoped to get a grant of the town of Turkestan itself, which was then in his hands.§ Borrak Sultan had also surrendered his son as a hostage to the Sungars, and intrigued busily to win over the grandees of the Middle Horde to his side. But the old hatred of the Kalmuks and the Kazaks was so great that there can be small doubt that if war had broken out between the former and the Russians, the Kazaks would have been found on the side of the latter; but this war did not take place, the Sungars in fact returned homewards. We then find the Middle Horde, after an estrangement of two years, once more drawing near the Russian frontier, and both Abul Makhmet and Borrak renewing their oath of allegiance.∥ In 1746 the Sungars made a raid on the Kazaks, and carried off many horses. The same year their chief Galdan Chereng died.

In 1748 Abulkhair of the Little Horde was defeated by Borrak, as I shall describe later on. He afterwards pillaged the Karakalpaks, who

* Id., 196. † Id., 196, 197. ‡ Id., 200.
§ Id., 203. Id., 206.

were subjects of Russia, and fearing the latter's vengeance, withdrew eastwards and occupied the towns of Ikan, Otrar, and Sighnak, where he pitched his camp, but the following year he and his two sons were poisoned while living with a khoja. This was apparently by order of the Sungars, to whom Nurali, the son of Abulkhair, had complained of his father's murder.* At this time the greater part of the sultans and chiefs of the Middle Horde had given hostages to the Sungars, who began to claim this branch of the Kazaks as their subjects,† and we find its Khan Abul Makhmet retiring to Turkestan, where he lived until his death.‡ His authority in the larger part of the horde, however, seems to have been lost, and Ablai succeeded as its *de facto* ruler.

ABLAI KHAN.

On the withdrawal of Abul Makhmet, Sultan Kuchuk, brother of Borrak, was nominated as their chief by some clans of the Middle Horde, but his appointment was not confirmed by the Russians, and he leaned for support on the Sungars. Ablai, whose genealogy has not been preserved in full, but who was probably descended from Shigai Khan, followed a different policy. As most of his people lived close to the frontier of the the Russians, he naturally drew nearer to them. This was hastened by a defeat sustained by the Middle Horde at the Ulugh Tagh mountains in 1751 on the part of the Sungars.§ In 1754 they were again so pressed by the latter people that many of them asked permission from the Russians to allow their wives and children to take shelter within their lines and to give them lands on the frontier, which they promised to till and to build villages there.‖ A number of them were allowed to settle near the lines of Uisk, while permission was given others to retire in case of necessity behind the lines on giving suitable hostages; but about this time, as I showed in the former volume, the Sungar empire was entirely destroyed.¶

Ablai took a prominent part in the revolutions which brought about this end. The downfall of the empire, as I have shown, was chiefly caused by the quarrel between Amursana and Tawatsi.** The former having been put on the throne by the Chinese, afterwards rebelled, and a large Chinese army was sent against him.†† He thereupon took refuge with the Kazaks, whose Khan Ablai furnished him with horses and an escort, hoodwinked the Chinese generals as to his whereabouts ;‡‡ and having promised to arrest him, excused himself on the ground that he had slipped through his hands and found refuge among the Russians.§§

---

* Id., 211. † Id., 212. ‡ Id., 221. § Id., 223. ‖ Id., 227. ¶ Ante, i. 651-654.
** Ante, i. 651, 652. †† Ante, i. 656. ‡‡ Memoires sur la Chine, 351, 352. Notes.
§§ Id., 399. Note.

The Chinese general Taltanga pursued him into the Kazak country, where he allowed himself to be beguiled by the promises of the Kazaks, and halted a while. This conduct disgusted the Mongol and Manchu soldiery who were with him, and many of them abandoned him, and he was consequently constrained to retire. Hoki, one of his bravest generals, was killed, and the same fate seems to have overtaken Nima, Payar, Sila, Mangalik, and other Kalmuk chiefs who had taken part against Amursana.[*] Fresh armies were thereupon prepared by the Chinese, and despatched under the generals Fute and Chao hoei. The former was sent into the country of the Kazaks. He punished severely those tribes who dared to resist, subdued the rest, and captured many prisoners, the chief of whom were sent to Peking, and there executed for having been false to their allegiance.[†]

According to Levchine, when the Chinese arms began to be successful Ablai sided with them and helped them to subdue the Sungars, and afterwards acknowledged himself a vassal of the Chinese Emperor Kien lung, who sent him a patent as prince and a calendar reciting the conditions on which he was accepted as a subject.[‡] It was in 1756 that he first received overtures from the Chinese, and the following year he was approached by an envoy who wished his horde to declare itself subject to China; but to this he demurred, his relations with Russia making it dangerous for him to openly change his allegiance in this fashion, and his crafty policy urging him to play off one of his powerful neighbours against the other.

In 1758 a part of the Middle Horde made a raid on the Russian frontiers, and carried off two hundred and twenty Tartars from the district of Kuznetz, who were known as Dvoedantry (i.e., those who paid a double tribute), which name is explained by the fact that, being borderers both of the Sungars and Russians, they had to pay tribute to both. The other portion of the Middle Horde migrated eastwards, and occupied a part of the country formerly held by the Sungars.[§]

While we find the Chinese Imperial authorities inscribing Ablai in the list of their tributary princes, we read how the latter wrote to the Russians to inform them that his submission to the Chinese was involuntary, and that he was ready to fight against them when thought necessary. He was rewarded accordingly with the Empress's praises and the gift of a precious sabre.[|] Hitherto it would seem that Ablai continued to be styled Sultan, but a large part of the Middle Horde now began to give him the title of Khan, and he began to adopt the style himself without the authorisation of the Russians. The latter were not pleased at this, as they looked upon the Middle Horde as their subjects. They approached him diplomatically to induce him to apply for the

* Mem. con. la Chine, &c., i. 350-358.   † Id., 370. Note, 40.   ‡ Op. cit., 229, 230.
§ Id., 237. | Id., 229.

dignity, and to surrender his son as a hostage, as Nurali of the Little Horde had done, and he was granted a douceur in the shape of an annual pension. These advances were coldly received by Ablai. The Russians at the same time learnt that Abul Makhmet was still living.[*] In 1760 the Kazaks of the Middle Horde attacked the Buruts or Wild Kirghises, and severely punished them. They also committed some ravages in Sungaria. The Chinese complained to Ablai of this, and sent an army to compel restitution. This frightened the Kazaks, who not only behaved submissively to the Chinese, but also returned to the Russians a number of Bashkirs and Barabinski Tartars whom they had carried off as prisoners.[†]

The policy of the Russians was to detach Ablai from his dependence on China, and in 1762 orders were issued to distribute presents among his grandees, to build stables and cart-sheds near the frontier, while a small palace with shops round it and enclosed by a rampart was ordered to be built for the Khan himself. This was apparently erected opposite the fort of Petropaulofsk.[‡] On the accession of the Empress Catherine II., Ablai, and Aichuvak with Nurali of the Little Horde, took the oath of allegiance. He still remained dependent on the Chinese, however, so that he leaned on both empires.

Meanwhile the Chinese continued their victorious course, and now assailed the districts of Khokand and Tashkend, whose rulers appealed to Ahmed, the ruler of the Afghans, as a good Mussulman, to go to the assistance of his co-religionists. He was also appealed to by the people of Kashgar, Yarkand, &c., and he accordingly sent a considerable army, which entered into a parley with the Chinese between Tashkend and Khokand. Meanwhile a sort of jehad or holy war was preached, and the neighbouring Mussulman powers received invitations to go and help them. Abul Makhmet, as legitimate sovereign of the Middle Horde, received such an invitation, but as he no longer had any authority among the Kazaks, he sent on the invitation to Ablai. Meanwhile the Chinese had sent the latter a diploma and given him permission to settle on the river Ili, promising him their protection, while they took his father-in-law Sultan Ahmed and some grandees and their children as hostages.[§] This, it would seem, prevented him joining the Muhammedan league. The Russians now ordered a small town to be built on the river Kolchakli, to be a kind of rendezvous to the Kazaks, and in 1764 the fort of Semipalatinsk was constituted an entrepot of trade for them. This was at the instance of Abulfeiz (son of the Khan Abul Makhmet, and brother of Pulad Khan of Turkestan), who was the chief of the Naimans, the most powerful tribe of the Middle Horde. He lived in Sungaria, and was more or less dependent on the Chinese. His request that the people might be allowed to trade at Semipalatinsk was

* Id., 241.　　† Id.　　‡ Id., 243.　　§ Id., 245, 246

immediately granted.* Ablai at the same time asked the Russians to send him ten cültivators to teach his people agriculture. This also was granted on his giving hostages for their safety.

We now (*i.e.*, 1770) reach the period of the famous flight of the Torguts, which occupied us in our former volume. The passage of the Kalmuks across the lands of their ancient enemies the Kazaks was an opportunity the latter were not likely to neglect, and as they were duly warned and incited by the Russians, their policy was safe as well as profitable. Ablai and his people inflicted severe losses on them, as did Sultan Abulfeiz, and their united forces captured a large number of prisoners from them.†

In 1775 some chiefs of the Middle Horde, including Abulfeiz, together with the son and nephew of Ablai, went to the Russian authorities on the Siberian frontier and asked to be admitted as Russian subjects. This was apparently a move to secure annual pensions and gifts, and was not reciprocated by the Russian authorities, who replied that the Kazaks were already subjects of Russia.‡

Ablai, by his sagacity and experience, had become very powerful. He played his cards well between China and Russia, with a leaning towards the former power, whose language he is said to have spoken. After the year 1771 he openly adopted the style of Khan, and we find Sultan Dair, son of Borrak, protesting to the Orenburgh authorities against his doing so.§ On being asked by the Russians how he had acquired the title of Khan he replied proudly, he had done so by his victories over the Torguts, and after the death of Abul Makhmet by the suffrages of the Kazaks and of the people of Turkestan and Tashkend, and added that, like his predecessors, he wished to live at Turkestan, near the tomb of Khoja Akhmed, who was looked upon by the Kazaks as their greatest saint. The Russians pressed him to ask for the title, and he promised to do so, and also to send his son Tugum to the court with the request, and in 1777 Tugum went to St. Petersburg with a letter asking for the dignity of Khan on behalf of his father. He was well received there, and on the 22nd of October, 1778, a diploma constituting him Khan was sent to Orenburgh with a state-pelisse, a sabre, and cap. He was invited to go to Troitsk, or some post in Siberia to receive them. This he refused to do, and the oath of allegiance was sworn at his camp in the presence of a Russian officer. As he did not wish to offend the Chinese, he would not accept the presents the Empress sent him, which were detained at the fort of Petropaulofsk, close to his usual residence, and as the Russians refused to assist him against the Buruts, he in turn refused to restore the Russian prisoners in his hands, and the Turkomans who had been carried off by the Torguts and left behind in his country. The Russians, much irritated, withdrew the pension they paid him and incited some sultans against him. They also had a design to carry him off to

---

* *Id.*, 248. † *Id.*, 257. ‡ *Id.*, 259. § *Id.*, 260.

Russia, but this he frustrated, and we find him carrying on a successful campaign against the Buruts and then retiring to Turkestan. He also built a house surrounded with a rampart for his son Hadil on the river Talas, and at the instance of the Kazaks of the Great Horde, who were subject to him, he founded a small town close by, which he peopled with Karakalpaks, who were practised in agriculture. The Buruts whom he captured he transported to the north of the country of the Middle Horde, where Levchine says they continued to live in his day, and were known as Jany or Yany Kirghiz (*i.e.*, the New Kirghiz). In 1781 he returned towards the Russian frontier, but died on the way at the age of seventy. He was buried at Turkestan. When the news reached Peking the Chinese sent an officer, who assembled his family and performed a stately funeral service in its presence.*

VALI KHAN.

According to tradition, after the death of Ablai the southern portion of the Middle Horde suffered a terrible reverse at the hands of the Great Horde, which carried off a great quantity of cattle, a disaster which was revenged by subsequent reprisals. The northern part of the horde chose Vali, the son of Ablai, as Khan, who asked for a confirmation of his dignity from the Russians. This was granted, and in 1782 he was proclaimed Khan of the Middle Horde by the lieutenant-general Jacobs at Petropaulofsk with the usual ceremonies.

Meanwhile the Naimans elected another chief, and he was confirmed by the Chinese authorities. Abulfeiz, the son of Abul Makhmet, died in 1783, leaving a son named Bupu and a son-in-law, namely the Khan Khoja, son of Borrak. These two princes each claimed the succession, and thus divided the allegiance of the Naimans. The majority sided with Khoja, and to him the Chinese Emperor sent a diploma.

With the exception of Vali, none of the other relatives of Ablai had intercourse with Russia, but leaned rather upon China. One of his brothers named Jingis levied an army in the steppes in 1784, and with it quelled a revolt in Tashkend. Another named Sultan Tiz is famous from his animosity to the Buruts, against whom the various Kazaks who lived on the Chinese frontier, and who inherited the feud from Ablai, carried on a fierce war. The Buruts are a warlike race. They defeated the Chinese more than once. Sultan Tiz was also beaten and captured by them, and had to surrender some of his slaves. The Elder Berdi Khoja, who governed part of the Middle Horde on the Chinese frontier, fought frequently against the Buruts and defeated them. In 1785 he won a signal victory over them, but this was his last. This was

---

on the banks of the Aiaguz, and when acting as an auxiliary to the Chinese. Encouraged by his success, he advanced with a small body of men and halted for reinforcements on the Yidisse. The Buruts surprised him there during the night and captured him. Knowing his captors well, and feeling how little he had to expect from them, he killed one of the Buruts who was escorting him. The rest of the party set upon him, decapitated him, cut off his feet and hands, slit open his stomach, and placed these grim trophies inside his body. Ak kiak, the brother of Berdi Khoja, and his sons Lepes and Choka had a successful fight subsequently with the Buruts, and captured their chief's son. They took him home with them to their aul, where he was set upon by the wives of Berdi Khoja, and he died under their blows.*

In 1786 the Russian authorities determined to reinstate the dignity of Khan in the Little Horde (where it had been in abeyance for some time), in favour of Nurali, the son of Abulkhair, and we are told he was largely supported by the most powerful chiefs of the Middle Horde, among whom the Sultan Khudai Mendi held a prominent place for power and resources.† He was also supported by Vali Khan.‡ In 1786 Khudai Mendi asked for a grant of land on the frontier. This was conceded, and he was also given a present of some money.§

Meanwhile peace and tranquillity reigned in the northern portion of the Middle Horde. Having as its neighbours the closely allied tribes of the Great and Little Horde, the Russians, and the inhabitants of the Khanates of Tashkend and Turkestan, who were not very warlike, these Kazaks had no predatory neighbours except the Bashkirs, who bordered upon them near Troitsk, and the Buruts at the other extremity of their country. Their position was therefore much more favourable than those of the Great and Little Hordes. This led to the people being more settled, more civilised, and more amenable to their princes than in the Great and Little Hordes, a position strengthened by the long reign of Ablai. Vali, his son, retained a large measure of his father's authority, although he was not so conciliatory to the Russions as they wished. He refused to surrender the Turkomans already mentioned, who had been carried off from Astrakhan by the Kalmuks, and he persecuted the elders who sided with the Russians, and in 1789 a large number of his subjects passed into Russia with Tugum, a sultan of the Great Horde, and received a grant of lands near the fort of Ust Kamenogorsk.‖ In 1793 the Turkomans who had been detained¶ were released by a Russian detachment sent by General Strandman, the commander of the Siberian line. Vali complained of this to the Empress, and was told to go to St. Petersburg with his grievances; but this he deemed imprudent, and on the death of his brother Jingis, which followed shortly after, he laid on him the blame of

* Id., 265, 266.   † Id., 277, 278.   ‡ Id., 278.   § Id., 283.
‖ Id., 294, 295.   ¶ Vide ante, 649.

his tortuous conduct,* but he continued to have intercourse with the Chinese Emperor, to whom he, in. the winter of 1794-5, sent his son to offer him his submission. He also oppressed his own people, and in consequence in 1795 two sultans, nineteen elders, and 43,360 of his followers, with 79,000 other Kazaks, sent to ask the Empress to deliver them from the power of Vali, and to accept them as Russian subjects. The opportune repentan e of the Khan induced the authorities to look coldly on this proposal. Meanwhile the section of the Middle Horde bordering on the Bashkirs made, in 1795, a raid on the districts of Chelia-binsk and Verkhni Uralsk, and committed depredations in revenge for the previous attacks by the Bashkirs.

In 1798 a tribunal for the settlement of Kazak disputes, composed of Russians and Kazaks, was founded at Petropaulofsk, but it did not begin its real labours till 1806. Vali continued to reign for some years longer, and died in 1818. In his later years his authority was disputed by several other chiefs, and at the request of the Kazaks themselves, the Emperor Alexander in 1816 nominated Bukei, the son of Borrak, as a second Khan of the horde. He also died in 1818. With him ended the dignity of Khan in the Middle Horde,† which now became entirely subject to Russia and controlled by a special administration.

THE LITTLE HORDE.

ABULKHAIR KHAN.

We have seen how on the death of Tiavka Khan the power of the Kazaks became much disintegrated. It was then apparently that the three divisions of the race became separated from one another, and each began to have a substantive history of its own. We will now turn to that of the so-called Little Horde.

The princes of the Little Horde were descended from Uziak Sultan, the brother of Yadik Khan, both of whom were sons, as I have shown, of Janibeg Khan. Uziak's son, according to the information furnished to Levchine by Tevkelef, was Buliakai Kuyan, whose son was Aichuvak, whose son was Irish, whose son was Adia. Adia and Tiavka Khan were descended by equal steps from their common ancestor Janibeg Khan, and I believe he was the same person who, according to Levchine, was nominated as the administrator of the Little Horde by Tiavka, and was by him called Aitiak.‡ The son of Adia was Abulkhair, who is men-tioned for the first time in 1717, when with Tiavka and Kaip he sent to Russia to ask assistance against the Kalmuks.§ On the death of Tiavka he had a struggle for supremacy with Kaip. Kiap was the son of Sultan

---

* Id., 295.　† Id., 297.　‡ Op. cit., 149.　§ Id., 150.

Kosref, the son of Sultan Syrdak, the son of another Sultan Syrdak, the son of Ishim Khan, and as representing the family of Yadik, doubtless resented the inferior pretensions of Abulkhair, who was descended from the latter's brother Uziak. Abulkhair in 1717 came into conflict with the Russians, and made an incursion into the province of Kazan as far as Novosheshminsk, which he destroyed, and where he captured many prisoners.* The continual attacks of his Kazaks at length aroused their neighbours, and we are told the Kalmuks drove them out of Turkestan, Tashkend, and Sairam in 1723. According to Neplouief and Rytschkof, Abulkhair lived at Turkestan until 1723,† and it would appear that he was in fact the most powerful of the Kazak rulers at this time. Feeling that they were being exterminated by their mutual strife, the various Kazak chiefs had a general meeting, where they agreed to acknowledge Abulkhair as their head, and sacrificed a white horse as a gauge of future peace.‡

They now turned again upon the Kalmuks, and won several victories over them, but Tse wang Arabtan was too powerful for them to hope to make much impression on him, and the three great sections of the race separated, as I have mentioned.§ The Little Horde migrated westwards. It crossed the Yemba, which was formerly the western limit of the Kazaks, drove the Torguts before it, and took possession of the country as far as the Jaik.‖ This naturally aroused the Torguts against them, and they were also speedily at issue with the Cossacks of the Ural. In 1726 we find that a Kazak envoy named Kaibakar was deputed by the elders Sungur, Yedikbey, Khajibey, Tiak-Kulibey, &c., to ask the protection of Russia. They were not very important chiefs apparently, and we certainly miss the name of Abulkhair Khan. This negotiation came to nothing.¶ At length Abulkhair was satisfied that the best policy was to submit to Russia himself, and although the greater part of his people disapproved of it, he in 1730 sent certain envoys escorted by the Bashkir chief Aldara to Buturlin, the voivode of Ufa, with a letter tendering his obedience. They arrived at Ufa in July, 1730, and were sent on to St. Petersburg. In his letter he gave his reasons for the step he had taken. He set out the difficulties he had with his neighbours, the Kalmuks, the Bashkirs, and the Cossacks of the Ural, and promised to help Russia against its enemies. He asked for troops to help him to subdue the Khivans, Karakalpaks, and Aralians, and finally acknowledged himself and his people as subjects of Russia. Abulkhair's envoys were well received, and their arrival caused considerable rejoicings at St. Petersburg, since Russia had acquired a number of new subjects without striking a blow, while there was a promise that the unruly Bashkirs would now have a thorn in their side,

---

* Levchine, 151. † *Id.*, 152. Note, 1. ‡ *Id.*, 152, 153. § *Ante*, 645.
‖ *Id.*, 153. ¶ *Id.*, 154.

and the ruler of Khiva, who had so lately killed Prince Bekovitch
Cherkaski and his companions, would be duly punished. They returned
to their master with a letter from the Empress Anne accepting his
submission, and promising him the aid and protection which he asked.
With them went the murza Tevkelef, interpreter in the College of Foreign
Affairs, some notables from Ufa, Bashkirs, and Russian Cossacks. They
were also accompanied by two engineer officers charged with making a
map of the Kazak country.* Meanwhile the news of the negotiation was by
no means welcome at the horde, and the Russian officers on arriving there
were treated with some contumely. Tevkelef would probably have been
killed but for his eloquence and the fact that he was a Mussulman, and also
for the intervention of the Khan, who was himself assailed, and asked by
what right he had entered into communication with foreign powers and
pledged the obedience of the horde without its consent. The eloquence
of Tevkelef and the counsels of the renowned Bashkir elder Batir Taima
were apparently urged in vain, and it was decided to summon a general
meeting of the horde to discuss the question of submission. To this
Tevkelef was invited. Having bought over some of the chiefs, he faced
the dangerous meeting, which was presided over by Abulkhair. His
language was more than usually persuasive, and he was supported by
Bukenbey, who was much respected both in the Little and Middle
Horde. The result was that both Abulkhair and also Shemiaka Khan of
the Middle Horde took the oath of allegiance to Russia. This took place
in 1732, and soon after Tevkelef sent off his suite to report the result of
his mission, while he himself stayed with Abulkhair. This result was not
so promising as it seemed. He had secured the chiefs, but the sturdier
spirits among the commonalty, whose heritage of freedom was of very
old date, chafed at what they deemed a modified servitude, and the
hands of Shemiaka Khan of the Middle Horde, who was more independent, were strengthened. Abulkhair at length left his more turbulent
subjects in the desert, and with the remainder fixed his camp at the
mouth of the Sir or Jaxartes, where he subdued the Karakalpaks and
brought them also under the protection of Russia.

After this Abulkhair returned once more towards Russia. When
he reached the frontier he despatched his son Erali Sultan, his step-
brother Niyas Sultan, some Kazak elders, and Aralbey and Arasgheldi
Batir, two elders of the Great Horde, on a mission to the Empress.
They were accompanied by Tevkelef, and arrived at Ufa in January,
1733. The Kazak envoys did not reach St. Petersburg till the January
following. They were presented a month later, and Erali on behalf of
his father and his people offered submission to Russia. The Empress
listened graciously, and ordered presents to be distributed among the
members of the mission, and they were largely feted during their stay in

* *Id.*, 268.

the capital. Two Kazaks were sent back to thank Abulkhair for the pains he had taken to secure the submission of the Middle and the Great Horde, to tell him how well his son had been received, and to bid him treat his neighbours and the Karakalpaks well. Meanwhile negotiations continued between Erali and the Russian authorities. The former asked that the dignity of Khan might be settled upon Abulkhair's family, and that the Russians would build a fortress at the confluence of the Ori and the Ural. The latter that Abulkhair would guard the Russian frontiers near his own, would convoy and protect the caravans of merchants which crossed his country, and would supply, like the Kalmuks and Bashkirs, contingents of troops when needed, and pay a tribute or yassak of skins.* These conditions could be more easily promised than carried out, for the constitution of the Kazaks was an exceedingly democratic one, and the chiefs had always a very weak hold on their subjects. At length the embassy returned, and the famous geographer Kirilof was intrusted with the duty of carrying out the views of the Russian Government. He was accompanied by some engineers to build forts, by some surveyors to draw maps, and by three officers and some artificers and sailors to build boats on the rivers; a mining engineer, some artillery officers, an historiographer, a botanist, an apothecary, a painter, a doctor, some young students to study the language, &c. At Kazan he was joined by a regiment and some artillery, and at Ufa by a battalion of infantry, Cossacks, &c. Tevkelef was appointed interpreter, with the rank of colonel, and the revenues of Ufa were assigned for the expenses of his expedition.† He was ordered to build a town at the mouth of the Ori, and to attract inhabitants to it, to deliver letters patent for Abulkhair, Shemiaka, the chiefs of the Great Horde and the Karakalpaks; to invite these chiefs to meet him, and to persuade those of the Middle and Great Horde to swear allegiance, to send back Erali well escorted to his father, to keep the Kazaks quiet by bribes, and either use tenderness or a strong hand, as policy required; to allow the chiefs to build houses and mosques at the new town, and to pasture their cattle near it; to assign the river Ural as the frontier, and to forbid the Kazaks passing it; and to appoint a mixed court of Russians and Kazak grandees to try disputes, which were to be settled according to the custom of the country. After matters had been arranged with the Kazaks to despatch a caravan to Bukhara or further, so as to attract commerce to Russia, and to send surveyors with the first caravan to draw maps; to make a search for mines, and especially for gold; to try and establish a port on the Sea of Aral, and for this purpose to build some boats on the Ural, and to transport them across the steppe in the winter with the consent of the Kazaks and the Karakalpaks; to buy some Kazak horses for the cavalry, and to work the mines, if found, except

---

* Levchine, 173, 174.   † Id., 176.

those of gold and silver. Kirilof was also the bearer of letters for the
Khans. He set out from St. Petersburg with the envoys on the 15th of
July, 1734.

In 1734 Abulkhair sent another important embassy to Moscow, at the
head of which was his son Erali. This embassy was sumptuously treated.
It agreed on the part of the Kazaks to respect the Russian frontiers, to
defend the caravans crossing the steppes, to furnish contingents of troops
when necessary, like the Bashkirs and the Kalmuks, and to pay a yassak
or tribute of hides. In return the Russians promised to confirm the
Khanate in the family of Abulkhair, and to build a fort at the confluence
of the Ori and the Ural, where the Kazak Khan might take refuge when
hard pressed. By the advice of Kirilof a body of artisans was sent to
complete this last work. He was chosen to superintend it, and took with
him a considerable body of soldiers, and in 1735 the foundations of the
city of Orenburg were laid. This colony and the increasing interference of
the Russians were naturally very jealously regarded by the surrounding
tribes. When Kirilof arrived on the frontier he found the Bashkirs
in full revolt. They had become frightened at the gradual advance
of Russian settlements, and they determined to oppose his project.
He, however, reached the mouth of the Ori in safety, and on
the 15th of August, 1735, laid the foundation of the famous town of
Orenburg. As soon as the walls arose somewhat, a message was sent to
Abulkhair to announce to him that one part of his request was fulfilled,
and asking him with the other chiefs of the horde to go there in the
spring of 1736, while some Tashkend merchants who had been in Russia
were sent home with presents and invited to return and traffic at Orenburg. Meanwhile the disturbances continued among the Bashkirs, and
a number of fresh forts were founded to restrain them, namely, those of
Guberlinsk and Ozernaia on the Ural, which still remain, and three
others of less importance on the same river, namely, those of Sredny,
Berdskoi, and Krilof. Others were also built on the Samara and in the
interior of the country of the Bashkirs, afterwards known as the
Orenburg line, which for a long time marked the Russian frontier. We
now find the Kazaks under Russian countenance attacking the Kalmuks
of the Volga. This licence was more easily given than withdrawn, and,
not satisfied with carrying off a large number of prisoners in 1736, they
made another raid in 1737, in which they captured much booty. Kirilof
was ordered to tell Abulkhair to refrain in future from these attacks, but
unfortunately he died in April, 1737. At this time a caravan of Russian
merchants, accompanied by Captain Elton, who afterwards entered the
service of Nadir Shah of Persia, was about to set out for Tashkend.
Elton was commissioned to report on the navigation of the Sea of Aral,
and it was also proposed to build a town at the mouth of the Sir or
Jaxartes, and to people it with criminals.

Tatischef, the famous Russian historian, was appointed in the place of Kirilof. He commenced his administration by giving Abulkhair permission to waste the lands of the rebellious Bashkirs, with orders to spare those who were peaceable. Abulkhair's people did not discriminate, and he even ventured to form the project of putting his son at the head of the Bashkirs. He was now ordered to withdraw. Meanwhile his son Erali was retained as a hostage at Orenburgh. While Abulkhair was plundering the Bashkirs another section of his people molested the Kalmuks and carried off some Russians as prisoners. Fearing punishment for this, Abulkhair delayed repairing to Orenburgh, and did not go until he had sent on his faithful friend Bukenbey to reconnoitre the state of affairs. He at length determined to go, and the interview was fixed for August, 1738. A company of dragoons, two sections of grenadiers, a military band, and some led horses were sent out to escort him to the town. The road along which he passed was lined with troops, while a salvo of nine guns greeted him when he arrived. In the tent of audience was placed a portrait of the Empress. He then addressed Tatischef: "Her Majesty the Empress," he says, "excels other sovereigns as the light of the sun does that of the stars. Although she is too distant for me to see her, I feel her beneficent influence in my heart, while I deem you as illumined by her reflected light. I declare my submission to her and my obedience as a faithful subject. I congratulate you on your victories over your enemies, and hope you may win others in the future. I put myself, my family, and horde under her Majesty's protection as under the wing of a powerful eagle, and promise an eternal submission, while I extend the hand of friendship to yourself, great general." After this Tatischef addressed to him a few cordial words, and then the oldest of the Muhammedan clergy entered the tent with a koran and a piece of gold tissue. On the latter the Khan knelt down, and having heard the oath of allegiance read, he kissed the book. He was then decked with a rich sabre with a golden haft. Meanwhile the elders and commonalty swore similar allegiance to Tevkelef in other tents. The ceremony ended with a feast, where the health of the Emperor and Empress was drunk amidst salvoes of artillery. The following day Abulkhair's son Nurali arrived, and also took the oath, and was presented with a silver-handled sabre. Several mutual visits now took place between Abulkhair and Tatischef, and it was agreed that Erali Sultan should return to his father, and be replaced as a hostage at Orenburgh by his brother Khoja Ahmed. Abulkhair undertook to restore all the Russian prisoners at the horde or in its neighbourhood. He also asked that his wife Papai might visit the Imperial court. This was partly due to curiosity and partly to the hope of getting some rich presents. Ho also undertook to protect the Russian caravans, and accordingly the first one on record set out under Lieutenant Müller for

3 L

Tashkend. It traversed the Little and Middle Hordes in safety, but was plundered by the Great Horde at two days' journey from Tashkend.[*] Before Abulkhair's departure rich presents were given him and his people.

In the spring of 1739 Tatischef returned to St. Petersburg, and was replaced by Prince Urussof, and the first news he heard on reaching Orenburgh was that two Russian caravans had been pillaged by the people of the Little Horde.

The following year the rebel Bashkir, Karasakal fled beyond the river Jaik with his accomplices, and the Khan and sultans refused to surrender him. For these reasons, and in order not to meet Abul Makhmet of the Middle Horde, over whom he claimed some suzerainty, Abulkhair would not go to meet Prince Urussof, but sent his sons Nurali and Erali. They were well received. Seventy-five elders dined at the prince's table, and food and drink were distributed in the open air to the ordinary Kazaks. Nurali was accompanied by his governor or atabeg Baatur Janibeg, who was also well received. They promised to restore the merchandise recently captured from the caravans and to send back the Russian prisoners at the horde. They asked for some cannon to be used in a campaign against Khiva, and that the Russians would build a town on the Sir or Jaxartes. In this year Abulkhair became for a short time Khan of Khiva, as I shall show in a future chapter. He was accompanied by the surveyor Muravine and the engineer Nazimof, who made the first map of the Kazak steppes and the district of Khiva. The Russians positively refused, however, to supply Abulkhair with any artillery.[†] In 1740 Abulkhair sent about three thousand Kazaks to plunder the Volga Kalmuks. After they had been forced to retire from. Khiva by Nadir Shah,[‡] Abulkhair and Nurali returned once more to the horde.

We now find the chief of the Sungar Kalmuks, weary of their constant attacks, sending two armies, one against the Middle the other against the Little Horde. Abulkhair applied to Russia for help, and received permission in case of danger to shelter with his family at Orenburgh.[§] This was no great boon, since he lived generally near the mouth of the Sir, and in the midst of the Kirghiz steppe, and the Sungars, who overran the northern parts of these steppes, could cut him off from Orenburgh. We now find the crafty Kazak ruler sending submissive messages to Galdan Chereng of the Sungars, and offering to submit to him, but when the latter's envoys went to receive hostages he moved with them towards Orenburgh, where he had been invited by the new governor Nepluief. The latter speedily told the envoys that Abulkhair was a subject of Russia, and could not treat with a foreign power nor give hostages. The Sungars raised objections to this, and

* Id., 187-189.   † Id., 191.   ‡ Vide infra, chapter x.   § Id., 195.

complained that they were constantly being molested by the Kazaks, and said they had come to treat with Abulkhair and not the Russians, and expected him to do what the chiefs of the Great Horde had done, namely, give their master hostages. They had to leave, however, without any more satisfactory answer, and were accompanied by Müller, who had commanded the plundered caravan as a Russian envoy.

In August, 1742, Abulkhair, Erali, Baatur Janibeg, and other Kazak chiefs renewed their oath of allegiance to Russia, and Abulkhair promised to desist from molesting the Sungars. He also endeavoured to persuade Nepluief to accept as a hostage, in lieu of his son Khoja Ahmed, another son by a concubine who was named Jingis, but this the Russians refused, and he was so enraged that he began to instigate the Kazaks to attack the frontier towns of Russia, and we accordingly find that in 1743 bands of these plunderers, from one to two thousand strong, fell on the newly-founded settlements, and carried their inhabitants beyond the Jaik. In one day eighty-two men were carried off from the small town of Iletzk, &c. The leader of the marauders was Derbeshali Sultan, a relative of Abulkhair, and his chief aim was to capture the fort of Saraschinsk, where Khoja Ahmed was imprisoned, and to carry him off. This was prevented by the Russian troops, who could not, however, stop the marauding, and many of their horses were captured. Abulkhair professed to disavow these acts, and even asked the Russians to put the robbers to death.[*] As it was a difficult task for the border commander to suppress the outrages, and the risks of a campaign in the steppe were very considerable, it was determined to arm the Kalmuks against them, and to seize several important Kazaks as hostages. This was momentarily effective, and a number of Russian prisoners were returned. During 1744 Abulkhair threw off the mask more completely. His people plundered a Russian caravan on its way to Khiva, while he arrested Lieutenant Gladyshef, a Russian envoy to the Karakalpaks. Gladyshef mentions in his journal having met an English merchant named Djake (Jack) in the Little Horde, and that he bought some things from him to dispose of to the Karakalpaks. The Russians at length issued a patent, dated the 24th of April, 1744, to Donduk Taishi,[†] the Kalmuk leader, in which he was ordered to collect his people, was given powder and lead, and told to march against the Kazaks. Any booty he might capture was to be his own. This was sent to Nepluief, but was apparently never used, and it is supposed the Russians changed their minds in consequence of the impending attack of the Sungarian Kalmuks on the Siberian district of Kolyvano-Voscressensk,[‡] which made it necessary to gain the Kazaks over to repel them. The Sungar attack did not, however, come off, and we next read of the removal of Abulkhair's son to St. Petersburg, of the renewed oath

---

* *Id.*, 201.   † *Vide ante*, vol. i. 572, &c.   ‡ *Id.*, 203.

which Abulkhair himself took in his aul or camp to the Emperor
Peter III., the successor of Elizabeth, when he returned thirty prisoners,
Russians and Kalmuks, and of his complaints against Neplnief, whom he
personally disliked because he would not allow him to replace his legiti
mate son as hostage by a bastard.* In 1746 we find the Volga Kalmuks
attacking the Kazaks and carrying off a large number of horses. This
raid was punished by the Russians, and it was strictly forbidden to the
Kazaks and Kalmuks to cross the Jaik, and new forts were built
on that river, but the ingenious Kazaks were not to be thus foiled.
In February, 1746, they crossed over the frozen Caspian, and attacked
the unprepared Kalmuks at Krasnoyar so vigorously that they carried off
nearly seven hundred prisoners of both sexes, killed about a hundred
men, and secured much plunder. They then made some small raids
on the Russian borders. Abulkhair was at the bottom of these attacks,
and we now find him detaining for a year an interpreter sent to him by
the Russians and subjecting him to torture, while he tried, but in vain, to
persuade his people to migrate further away from Russia into the
southern steppes, and revenged himself on such of his compatriots who
opposed his plan. In January, 1747, the Kazaks once more traversed the
northern part of the Caspian on the ice, and attacked the Kalmuks, but
the latter had withdrawn to the western portion of their territory, where
it was unsafe to follow them, and their assailants returned with empty
hands. Meanwhile there came on a thaw, and they were obliged to return
home by the country of the Cossacks of the Ural or Jaik, who attacked
them mercilessly. They lost the greater part of their horses, and many
of them were drowned, by the ice on the river giving way. Abulkhair's
rage was still further increased by this accident, and we now find him
allying himself with Persia To appease him Tevkelef, who was a
Mussulman and knew the Kazaks well, was ordered to go to him and to
offer to exchange his son Khoja Ahmed for another son of legitimate
birth. Abulkhair seemed to relent, and went in the summer of 1748 to
Orsk or Old Orenburgh to meet his old friend, and agreed to give his son
Aichuvak in place of Khoja Ahmed, and also some of the children of his
Kazak subjects; he also undertook to return the Russian prisoners in his
hands, and that the Little Horde should not again attack the empire.
Meanwhile he secretly offered his daughter in marriage to the Khung
taidshi of the Sungars.

But his adventurous career was nearing its close. On his return home
he collected his people and marched against the Karakalpaks. The
Karakalpaks were claimed as his subjects by Borrak, who was an old
enemy and rival of Abulkhair's.† Rytschkof calls him one of the most
powerful princes of the Naimans, and says he had at this time the
chief authority in the Middle Horde.‡ Borrak in his contention with

---

* Id., 205.   † Levchine, 210.   ‡ Topog. of Orenburgh, i. 124.

Abulkhair, as is shown by M. Vel. Zernof, claimed to be descended from
Shigai, or perhaps rather from Yadik, whose family he declared to be a
more worthy stock than that of his rival.* In Levchine's table he and his
brother Kuchuk are made the sons of Tursun Khan, who we are told
occupied Ikan and the neighbouring towns.† Tursun Khan was the son
of Khodai Mendi, the son of Kuchuk, the son of Bukei Khan.‡ Bukei Khan
was probably, as M. Vel. Zernof suggests, the Bukei Sultan, son of Yadik
mentioned by the Turkish biographer of Uras Makhmet, whom he
quotes §

Borrak was jealous of the favours which Abulkhair had received from
the Russians, and annoyed that his rival had intercepted the presents
sent to him by the Khan of Khiva. He had an encounter with him, in
which his own people, who were in a majority, were successful, and
Abulkhair and his party took to flight. Shigai, the son of Borrak,
overtook Abulkhair and dismounted him with a lance thrust, and Borrak,
having himself shortly after come up, completed the work by putting his
old enemy to death with his own hands, and then proceeded to plunder
the Karakalpaks.‖ Afraid of the vengeance of the Russians, whose
protégés the Karakalpaks were, he then retired towards Turkestan, and
took possession of the towns of Ikan, Otrar, and Sighnak, but the year
following he and his two sons, when on a visit to a Khoja, were poisoned.
This was apparently at the instance of the Khungtaidshi of the Sungars,
to whom Nurali, the son of Abulkhair, had complained of his father's
assassination.

The tomb of Abulkhair is marked on the maps as situated near the
river Kodir, one of the tributaries of the Ulkia, about 50.30 N. latitude
and 80.10 E. longitude.

NURALI KHAN.

On the death of Abulkhair, Neplulef, after a consultation with Tevkelef,
sent an officer to the Little Horde to secure the throne for a son of the
late Khan, and to induce him to send an embassy to St. Petersburg to
ask for the confirmation of the Empress.¶ He was successful, and
Nurali was duly elected Khan, and sent Janibeg and other Kazaks to
inform the authorities at Orenburgh. They pretended to have been
deputed by both the Middle and the Little Horde, and asked that he
might be declared Khan of both. The fact was that Janibeg Baatur,
who had long lived with Abulkhair, was the only grandee of the Middle
Horde who had taken part in the election. The difficulty was got over
by his being simply named "Khan of the Khirghiz Kazaks." The patent
of office was sent to him on the 26th of February, 1749, and he was

* Vel. Zernof, ii. 369.   † Id., 368.   ‡ Levchine's table.
Op. cit., ii. 274 and 368.   ‖ Levchine, 210, 211.   ¶ Id., 211, 212.

invited to go to Orenburgh, there to be duly installed. Nurali's mother Papai, who had considerable influence in the horde and was a good friend to Russia, was mainly instrumental in the election of Nurali, and she now received some presents from the Empress. In July, 1749, Nurali set out for his installation, which took place amidst music and the firing of cannon, in a special camp erected on the banks of the Jaik. The pageant commenced with the reading of the letters patent, after which the Khan was presented with a state robe, cap, and sword, and then took the oath of allegiance on his knees. He asked for some Russian troops to help him against his neighbours, and for the surrender of fugitives. Both requests were declined. He then asked for one thousand men to build his father a suitable tomb. Negotiations about this ensued, and the plans were prepared, and are still preserved among the archives of Oren-burgh, but the matter broke down as the Russians insisted he should be buried near their frontiers, which was interpreted as an intention to annex the Kazak country. On his return to his horde Nurali met the envoys of the Khungtaidshi of the Sungars, who went to ask his sister in marriage for their sovereign, and offering to make over to him Turkestan, where the bones of his ancestors were buried, in lieu of Kalym. This request was very embarrassing, for his sultans and principal people wished him to comply while he dared not offend the Russians. The latter were duly informed of what was going on, and were well aware of the dangerous power which the Sungarian chief, who already dominated over the Great and Middle Hordes, was acquiring in Central Asia, and they determined to prevent the match. The opportune death of the young lady, which took place in 1750, perhaps not altogether naturally, was a relief to both parties. In 1749 Nurali sent his brother Adil to replace another brother (Aichuvak) as hostage at Russian head-quarters, and the following year he was changed for his son Pirali, who was only five years old.

I have described the rivalry between Abulkhair and Kaip in the former's early days. Kaip's son Batyr, who kept alive his father's feud, was now proclaimed Khan by a section of the Little Horde, and his son Kaip was elected as ruler of Khiva. Batyr now sent envoys to Oren-burgh, and asked that his people might be allowed to escort the Russian caravans to Khiva and Bukhara, a request which was supported by his son Kaip. This was refused on the ground that it would be a grievance to Nurali, with whom he was ordered to live amicably. Nurali was as unable as any other ruler of the Kazaks to restrain his turbulent people, and Levchine says that after much consideration, and on the advice of Tevkelef, it was determined to adopt towards them the practice fol-lowed by the rulers of Bukhara, Khiva, &c., namely, to make reprisals, technically known as barantas.* In case of a frontier robbery it was

* Id., 221.

ordered that immediate reparation should be asked from the Khan, and if satisfaction was not given, that a relative of the plunderer or one of his tribe should be seized and detained until the objects or person carried off were restored. It was also determined to make Nurali some handsome presents when he restored the Russian and Kalmuk prisoners in his hands.

In the spring of 1750 Aichuvak, with a number of his friends and a body of Kazaks, made a raid upon an inoffensive tribe called Aralians, who were dependent on the Khan of Khiva, and carried off many prisoners, horses, and other objects. By way of reprisal Kaip seized a number of Nurali's subjects who were at Khiva trading, and also his envoy, and in consequence a part of the booty and the prisoners were returned to the Aralians. Aichuvak's brother Erali tried a similar venture against the Karakalpaks, but his people were too weak, most of them were killed, and he himself was made prisoner and detained for some months.[*]

In 1752 Nurali exchanged his son Pirali for a younger one only three years old. He still nursed his hatred for Batyr, and as the Khivan caravans were in the habit of traversing the latter's country and paying to him the usual dues, he was much irritated. In 1753 he ordered a caravan which was travelling between Russia and Khiva to be plundered. The same year some Kazaks of the clan of Alimul and tribe of Kara Kitin robbed at Saghiz some Khivan and Turkoman merchants who were being escorted by Kazaks of the tribe Chiklin. On the Russians sending to complain, Nurali took the blame to himself, and excused the act on the ground of the hostility of Batyr and his son Kaip towards him; he also suggested that the latter meditated an attack on Russia, and offered to subdue him in a few days if the Russians would supply him with ten thousand men and some artillery.[†] He at length consented to restore the plundered merchandise to the Khivans, but the latter behaved badly, and a feud arose between them and the Russians.[‡] Nurali and his brother Erali were therefore encouraged to make an attack on Khiva. They called an assembly of their people to sanction the campaign, which was, however, prohibited and prevented by the interdiction of a Khoja who had been asked to give it his blessing.[§]

In 1755 the Bashkirs again broke out in rebellion and killed the Russians resident among them. This outbreak was excited by a certain mollah named Batyr Sha, who summoned the Kazan Tartars and Kazaks to aid their co-religionists. Some of the latter accordingly began to plunder the Russian settlements. Things were growing critical, for the line of Orenburgh was then very weak, and its detached forts ill fortified. Nepluief, the Russian commander, however, showed great vigour. He summoned the Cossacks of the Don, the Kalmuks, the Meshkeriaks, and

* Id., 222.   † Id., 225.   ‡ Vide infra, chapter x.   § Id., 227.

the Teptiars to his assistance, while he distributed among the Kazaks a proclamation of the akhun of Orenburgh, who was the head of the Muhammedan clergy of the district, in which, while approving of the revolt of the Bashkirs, he ended up by suggesting that after defeating the Russians the Bashkirs should subjugate the Kazaks. To prevent an alliance between the two tribes, Nepluief, who knew the Kazaks well, with the consent of the Imperial authorities, sent word to the Khan and Sultans of the Kazaks that the Russians made over to them all the Bashkir women and children who were then living among them, on condition that they drove out the men from their frontiers. At this time a vast crowd of Bashkirs had fled across the Jaik. The voluptuous Kazaks greedily sacrificed all other considerations to seize upon these unfortunate Russian subjects, for such they were, although rebels. The Bashkir men were too weak to resist, some were killed, some restored to the Russians, and some returned home to prepare a revenge, and under the covert patronage of the Russian authorities, large bands of Bashkirs crossed the Jaik and savagely attacked their tormentors. Thus was sown between the two races a strife which subsists to our own day. It was certainly an extraordinary method of defending their frontiers thus to arouse a malignant conflict between the border tribes, and was only excused by the weakness of the Russians and their imminent peril. Nurali complained of the Bashkir raids, but was told that it was a just punishment for having sheltered Bashkir deserters, and the two races mutually ravaged each other until Nepluief thought they had been sufficiently punished. The Jaik or Ural was then fixed as the boundary between the tribes, and both sides were forbidden to cross it.[*]

The bloodshed for a while ceased, but the feud lived on. The Kazak chiefs restored to the Russians the Bashkirs who had sought refuge among them, and were duly rewarded *inter alia* by being allowed to send to the Russian court every two or three years some of their more distinguished relatives, who naturally did not return home with their hands empty. Meanwhile, notwithstanding the prohibition, Kazaks and Bashkirs continued to make mutual raids into each other's country, and when the chiefs of the former interfered to prevent them, they were accused by the commonalty of being creatures of Russia, and of an intention to subject the tribes to that power. The Russian authorities therefore determined to make a vigorous display of their power, but their plans had to be postponed in consequence of the Seven Years' War with Prussia.[†] A curious instance of how events apparently remotely connected affect each other.

In 1757 Donduk Taishi, the Kalmuk ruler, tried to persuade Nurali to join with him and the Krim Khan in a campaign against Russia. This was probably a treacherous proposal, and he doubtless wished to embroil

---

[*] *Id.*, 233.   [†] *Id.*, 235.

the Kazaks with the Russians. In 1758 the Chinese army which had
destroyed the Sungarian empire threatened the Russian frontier, and
Nurali received orders to assist in repelling it.[*] Although the
Chinese retired, Nurali's loyalty on this occasion was rewarded by
presents. In 1759 the new Russian governor, who replaced Nepluief
having treated Nurali with scant courtesy and the Kalmuks having
pillaged his subjects, they made reprisals. These raids were renewed the
following year, and were duly punished by the Russians.[t] The Sultans
Aichuvak and Erali, irritated at the discourtesy of the Orenburgh
authorities, began to pillage the Russian caravans, and the former also
proposed to migrate with the tribe Semirodsk to Sungaria. They were
pacified by the central authorities at St. Petersburg assigning them
annual stipends, and orders were issued to the people at Orenburgh
to treat the Kazaks with every consideration, to distribute presents
generously to them, and to build cattle sheds and stables where they
might winter their cattle, the chief fear of the Russians being that the
Kazaks might leave their pastures for the Chinese borders, and thus
depopulate the important country through which the trade routes to
Central Asia inevitably passed. On the advent of Catherine II. to the
throne Nurali, Aichuavak, and Ablai Khan of the Middle Horde all sent
their homage.[‡] In 1762 Nurali sent an embassy to Peking. It was
well received, and he in consequence became so elated that he took
no more notice of the complaints of Russia. His people again began to
molest the Kalmuks, and made another attack on them over the frozen
Caspian, while they pressed a demand for winter quarters west of the
Jaik. This same year two hundred Turkoman families, who had long
lived among the Kalmuks, took refuge with the Kazaks, who "suo more"
reduced them to slavery and partitioned them.

At this time the various Mussulman states of Central Asia drew nearer
together, in order to oppose a common front against the dreaded
approach of the Chinese, and we find Nurali Khan entering into
negotiations with the Afghans. In 1764 he wrote to the Empress
Catherine to acquaint her with the result of the mission to Peking, and
that he had been invited by all the Mussulmans of Asia to take part in a
war against China. His people continued their raids upon the Kalmuks
and the border Russian provinces, and were duly punished. Such
attacks are mentioned in 1765, 1766, and 1767. In 1769 Nurali's son,
who was a hostage at Orenburgh, died, being the second who had ended his
days there. He suspected that they had not been duly looked after, and
refused to send another. He was also annoyed at the attentions shown
by the Russian court to his brothers, whom he wished to displace from
the succession in favour of his own son Ishim. His irritation was met

---

* *Id.*, 238.   † *Id.*, 242.   ‡ *Id.*, 244.

3 M

by increased coolness on the part of the Russian authorities, and the presentation of fresh sabres to his brothers.*

We now reach the period of the famous flight of the Torguts, which I described in the first volume.† The Russian authorities had authorised Nurali to oppose them and drive them back. Such encouragement was unnecessary, as each Kazak deemed it a privilege to attack the Kalmuks, who occupied such a wide extent of the country where their ancestors had lived. All were on the *qui vive;* Nurali, his brother Aichuvak, and Kaip, the late Khan of Khiva, who was now living with the Little Horde, &c., and they had to run the gauntlet of these waspish foes right up to the Chinese frontier, and lost a great number of prisoners. Aichuvak defeated one section of them on the Saghiz, Nurali gained an advantage over them further east, and the Kazaks were successful in encounters near Mount Mugajar and on the Ishim. This famous flight took place in 1771. In 1773 and 1774 the country of the Jaik and the Volga were agitated by the revolt of the famous impostor Pugachef.‡ The latter's supporters were the Cossacks of the Jaik and the Bashkirs, both enemies of the Kazaks, who did not accordingly join him, but fished in the troubled waters and made raids on the Russian settlements. For this they were duly punished in 1774, and had to surrender the prisoners and booty they had made. At this time some of the Turkomans living between Khiva and Seraichuk elected Pirali, a son of Nurali, as their chief, who levied dues on the caravans which traded with Khiva.§

In 1776 we again find the Kazaks molesting the Russian outposts, and Nurali soliciting assistance to restrain his own turbulent people,‖ a request which was repeated, and orders were issued in 1779 that the Russian guards should make reprisals, which were frequent in the interval between 1781 and 1791. In 1784 we are told that a body of 3,462 Russian soldiers having pursued some plunderers beyond the Jaik, and being unable to catch them seized forty-three Kazaks who had taken no part in the raid. Their relatives made reprisals, and other bodies of Kazaks, whose leading spirit was a famous freebooter named Sirim Batir harried the frontiers. In 1785 two divisions of troops were sent towards the Yemba. They carried off 230 women and children, who were duly exchanged against a number of Russian prisoners. The same year there was founded at Orenburgh a new tribunal, consisting of the commandant of Orenburgh, two Government employés, two merchants, two Russian peasants, a sultan, six Kazak elders, and a deputy each from the Bashkirs and the Meshkeriaks. This tribunal was to try matters of dispute among the frontagers of the empire. In 1785 mosques and schools for the young Kazaks were opened at Orenburgh and Troitsk, and caravanseras were also ordered to be built. These well-meant efforts Levchine attributes to the far-sighted policy of the

* *Id.*, 251.   † *Ante,* i. 575, &c.   ‡ Levchine, 257.   § *Id.*, 259.   ‖ *Id.*, 620.

Empress, who not only could excuse the raids of a naturally nomade race, but who also knew well that many of their attacks were amply justified as reprisals for attacks made by the Russians and Bashkirs.[*]

In 1784 Batir Sirim with his three thousand followers caused much trouble to the garrisons on the Orenburgh line, made a successful attack on the fort of Tanalitskoi, and tried to raise a rebellion against the Khan Nurali, whose excuses for his own weakness and want of authority were only accepted as so much chicanery by the Russians.

At length in 1785 the new Russian governor, Baron Igelstrom, determined to introduce a new system altogether of dealing with these pestilent neighbours. He proposed to divide the Little Horde into three sections, according to its chief clans, Semirodsk, Baiulin, and Alimul, to give each of them a Khan, to make these Khans in fact Russian administrators,[†] and to abolish altogether the office of "Khan of the Little Horde." He issued an order, not to the Khan, but to the sultans and elders, to summon a general assembly of the horde, and bade them abandon their habits of pillage, and arrange a method of keeping order. This summons, we are told, destroyed the little remaining influence of the Khan. The assembly met; not a single sultan was present, and the robber leader Sirim Batir presided. Ambitious and crafty, he was a declared enemy of the Khan, whose hereditary claims he envied. He urged that there was no need of a Khan, and that merit ought to weigh before birth. He persuaded his hearers that their best policy was to swear allegiance to Russia. From the latter he demanded that the family of Abulkhair should for ever be deprived of the right to the Khanship. The Russians partially consented. This was in 1786, and the immediate result was satisfactory; a greater quantity of cattle was brought for sale at the frontier fairs in 1786 and 1787 than had hitherto been the case, and fewer Russian prisoners were made, while a large number were released; and during the winter of 1786 forty-five thousand Kazak families passed the season west of the Jaik without committing any depredations there.[‡] Batir Sirim became a confidential correspondent of Baron Igelstrom, notwithstanding Nurali's warning that he was treacherous and hated Russia in his heart. Nurali himself was very conciliatory, offered to give up his children as hostages, returned such prisoners as he had control over, and put himself at the disposition of Russia. He was sent to live at Ufa and Aichuvak at Uralsk.

Erali, Nurali's eldest son, had been living on the Sir for some years, and as early as 1781 had ruled over the Karakalpaks there. He now marched against Batir Sirim with but a small force. At the same time some clans of the Little Horde which were not attached to the family of Abulkhair nor were friends of Sirim raised Kaip, who had reigned at

Khiva, to the dignity of Khan. Another section of them petitioned for the restoration of Nurali or some one else in his place. Baron Igelstrom was inclined to favour the pretensions of Kaip, and to have him proclaimed Khan of the Little Horde, but the Empress would not consent, and wished to insist on the dignity of Khan being abolished, as had been arranged.

Meanwhile the claims of Nurali to reinstatement were pressed by the chiefs of the Middle Horde, and their view was endorsed in 1787 at a general assembly; but the Russians would not listen, and Batir Sirim, having regained his liberty, seems to have seconded their efforts to Russianise the Kazaks. Special tribunals, called raspravas, were constituted to control their affairs. Two of these were planted in each of the tribes Alimul and Baiulin, and one in that of Semirodsk. These courts sat daily, and consisted of a president and two members, together with a mollah or secretary, who kept the records; from them there was an appeal to Orenburgh. An old chief and two subordinates were selected to control each of the tribes, Batir Sirim being put over that of Baiulin. These officials were granted salaries, paid in corn and money, and took the oath of allegiance to the Empress. For a few months tranquillity prevailed, but it was short-lived, the respective partisans of Nurali, Kaip, and Batir Sirim intrigued against one another. Those of Sirim were the most powerful, and the Russian nominees were mere creatures in their hands.

At this time the Turks were at war with Russia. They sought an ally in the Khan of Bukhara, who in turn incited the Kazaks to rebel, and offered to help Erali to release Nurali, and also intrigued with Sirim. He issued a proclamation addressed to the brave warriors, begs, and elders, Saritai bey, Sirim Batir, Shukurali bey, Sadirbek, Borrak Batir, Dajdane Batir, &c., stating how he had heard from the sovereign of Turkey, the vicar of God, that the infidel Russians had allied themselves with seven Christian states against the Turks, and bidding the Kazaks join with the other true believers in punishing them. In view of their general ignorance of the faith and of letters, there not being a scholar among them, he, whose schools were frequented by the Uzbegs, Tajiks, Arabs, and Turkomans, invited them to send two or three representatives from each tribe for instruction. He promised to defray the expense of their education, and to send them home well versed in the law and able to conduct the services, and ended by threatening them with the pains of eternal fire if they neglected the opportunity thus offered to them. This letter was written in the year 1788, and was sealed with the tamgha of the atalik of the Bukharian ruler Shah Murad. Sirim wrote to say that he and his people were ready to obey the summons, and only awaited the time when the Bukharian and other Asiatic peoples should invade Russia. This duplicity came to the ears of the Russian authorities. Meanwhile the Kazaks continued their attacks. The elders who had been nominated by the Russians lost control over the people, and only went to Orenburgh to receive their salaries, and a section of the Kazaks with their chief sultans demanded the re-appointment of a Khan. This was at length deemed advisable by the Russian authorities. Their decision on this point was naturally gall and wormwood to Sirim, who declared himself an enemy of Russia, began to make raids across the Jaik, and to seek assistance at Bukhara, which was promised him in due time. This latter intrigue was disclosed by one of his envoys, who had been captured by the Cossacks of the Jaik. Nurali, it appears, died in the year 1790, while still detained at Ufa, and enjoined his children on his death to remain faithful to Russia.

ERALI KHAN.

In 1791 Sirim, in the hopes of persuading the whole of the Little Horde to attack Russia, called a general meeting at the mouth of the Yemba, but his purpose was frustrated by the descendants of Abulkhair, who warned the Empress, and it ended in a number of detached raids by his own people, which continued without intermission for seven or eight years. Meanwhile, in the January of the same year, the Empress, having learnt the death of Nurali, had nominated his brother Erali· as his successor, and sent him a patent of office as Khan of the Little Horde. In the autumn he approached the banks of the Jaik, and was solemnly proclaimed Khan on the 4th of September, at a place situated about fifteen versts from Orsk. The Imperial diploma proclaimed that he owed his position to his merits as well as to the fact of his being the senior member of Abulkhair's family. At the assembly envoys arrived from Batir Sirim and Abulghazi, the son of Kaip, and several elders, declaring their non-concurrence in the election. They were told what was done was with the consent of the Empress, and when the election was complete six deputies were sent to St. Petersburg for its con. firmation.

On the 6th of September a letter arrived from Pirali, the son of Nurali, who was then Khan of Turkestan, asking to be allowed to acknowledge the suzerainty of Russia. By an ukaze dated the 31st of October of the same year this was duly accepted. Kaip, the rival of the family of Abulkhair was now dead. He left three sons, Abulghazi, Burkan, and Shirgazy. The latter of these lived for a long time at the court of Catherine, but eventually returned again to the horde. His two elder brothers allied themselves with Sirim, whose superior skill put them entirely at his command. He intrigued with all his might against the Russians, denounced the election of Erali as irregular, and quoted the

Koran to show that it was illegal for Mussulmans to be subject to Christians. He tried to persuade the Kazaks to retire from the Russian frontiers, and boasted of his alliance with the Khan of Bukhara. He sent his son to Khiva in 1793, to try and secure an ally there, and wrote a letter to the governor of Ufa, couched in most insolent and insulting language. This was followed by another series of raids upon Ilezhoi-gorodok, the Kalmuk fort, and some other points on the line of Iletzk.[*]

The Khan Erali asked the Russians to send some troops to punish the marauders, but the request was refused. Erali died in June, 1794.

ISHIM KHAN.

On the death of Erali the Little Horde was divided in its allegiance, one section obeyed the Abulghazi above named and Sirim, and the other Ishim Sultan, the son of Nurali, whose hereditary position, friendship for Russia, and good character entitled him to the general succession ; but his people were not disposed to submit to Russian tutelage, and insisted if he were elected Khan that he should be one in reality, and urged him to retire towards the Sir Daria. In informing the Orenburgh authorities of this, he also complained to them how the partisans of Sirim forbade him to punish marauders, and had even inflicted a fine or "kun" of two thousand sheep on him for having surrendered two noted bandits to the Russians. Notwithstanding this his partisans met near Orenburgh in September, 1795, and on the 17th of the same month he was duly elected, and his people swore to live peaceably together and not to molest Russia. He continued to be faithful to his patrons and to repress disorders in the horde. This created him many enemies, and especially aroused the hatred of Sirim, who attacked him suddenly near the fortified post of Krasnoiar in November, 1797, killed him, and pillaged his property.[†] Sirim's people continued to harass the outposts, and in 1797 and 1798 the Cossacks of the Jaik made reprisals upon them, and carried off several thousand horses, an example shortly after followed by the Bashkirs, who harried their herds in a similar manner. These attacks were followed by counter attacks, and so on.[‡]

AICHUVAK KHAN.

After the death of Ishim the government of the Little Horde was confided to a council, composed of two representatives from each of its tribes, and presided over by Aichuvak Sultan, a son of Abulkhair. This

---

* Id., 286.   † Id., 289.   ‡ Id.

council was selected by Baron Igelstrom, who was again governor of Orenburgh, and its seat of government was fixed on the river Khobda. But the Kazaks grew weary of it and demanded a Khan. A meeting was called in 1797. The two candidates were the Aichuvak just named and Karatai, the son of Nurali The Russians supported the former, who was accordingly elected, and shortly after he was confirmed by the Emperor Paul. He was an old man, however, and could not keep his people under control. The attacks of the Buruts and the raids made by the Kazaks on the Bashkirs and on the Russian caravans, which were duly punished by reprisals, reduced matters to great confusion ; anarchy increased daily, and the Khan had neither the power to punish the guilty nor to protect the innocent. The horde became partially disintegrated, some retired to the Middle Horde, others to the Sir Daria, where, having subdued the Karakalpaks, they elected the sultan Abulghazi, son of Kaip, as their ruler. Another section attacked the Turkomans, and made them surrender the greater part of the Ust Urt to them, and Aichuvak with some sultans took refuge in Russia until the fermentation had ceased.

Meanwhile Bukei, a son of Nurali, who had been the president of Aichuvak's council, applied to General Knorring, the governor-general of Georgia and Astrakhan, to be allowed to settle with his people in the district called Rin Peski, between the Jaik and the Volga, which had recently been abandoned by the Kalmuks, and asked him to assign him a hundred Cossacks to enable him to keep order. Knorring having reported this to the central authorities, a ukase permitting the settlement was issued on the 11th of March, 1801. Bukei's followers belonged chiefly to the tribe Baiulin, and altogether the emigrants numbered about ten thousand tents. This emigration had a wonderful effect. The emigrants became so prosperous that their flocks increased tenfold in seven or eight years, while their brethren beyond the Jaik, torn by dissensions, were fain to sell their children to the Russians.*

Aichuvak continued to rule the Little Horde till the year 1805, when he abdicated on account of old age and infirmity.

JANTIURA KHAN.

Aichuvak was succeeded by his son Jantiura, who was assassinated in 1809 by his cousins, the sons of Nurali, after which the Little Horde was two years without a Khan.† It was at this time, and in the year 1810, that a large area known as the Iletsk district, and containing rich salt mines, was enclosed within the Orenburgh line and peopled with Russians.

----

* Id., 292. 293.   † Id., 297.

SHIRGAZY KHAN.

In 1712 Shirgazy, the brother of Jantiura, was raised to the dignity, while at the same time Bukei was given the title of Khan over those Kazaks who had migrated to the neighbourhood of Astrakhan, and were known as the Horde of Bukei. The latter died in 1815, leaving several sons, of whom the eldest, called Yehanghir, was nominated Khan in 1824, and continued to rule this section of the Kazaks when Levchine wrote. Of Shirgazy he says, "He still lives, but no longer governs the Little Horde, which is divided into three districts, whose chiefs are independent of the Khan." Of these three divisions Schuyler says they were controlled by three Sultans Regent, but the divisions were carelessly made, tribal distinctions and rights to land not having been recognised, and the difficulties of the situation were not removed.

"The Kirghiz had great respect for their aristocracy, and the common people (black bone) were led by the white bone* or the descendants of the old Khans and ruling families. These men stood up for their tribes and families, in defence of the honour and safety of their members. Recognising at the same time bravery, dash, and boldness, and loving their freedom, they were always ready to follow the standard of any batir or hero, such as Sirim, Arunhazi, or Kenisar, who might appear in the steppe. The Sultans-Regent were either mere Russian creatures entirely destitute of influence, or they were themselves inclined to revolt at times, and neither they nor the annual military expeditions from Orenburgh sould maintain order in the steppe."†

In 1833 Novo Alexandrofski, afterwards called the fort of Mangushlak, was erected on the Eastern Caspian, to protect the Yemba fishermen from marauders.‡ In 1835 a new military line was established between the Ural and the Ui, and the territory enclosed within it was added to that of the Orenburgh Cossacks. A few years later a famous chieftain named Kenisar Kasimof, who apparently belonged to the Middle Horde, aroused a wide insurrection among the Siberian Kazaks, who were joined by a section of the Little Horde. For six years he kept the Russian authorities in continual alarm, until in 1844, being pursued by the Russian forces, he was compelled to take refuge among the Buruts or Kara Kirghiz, and was killed in a fight with them.§ In consequence of this insurrection the Orenburgh fort on the river Turgai, and the Ural fort on the Irgiz were built in 1847, and in 1848 the Karabulat fort on the Karabut.

In 1847 the fort of Raimsk, afterwards called Aralsk, was built on the Lower Sir, as an outpost and menace to the Khokandians and Khivans,‖ who had begun to molest the Kazaks within the Russian borders. This

---

* The Kazak term for blue blood.   † Schuyler's Turkestan, i. 31.
‡ Michell's Asia, 320.   § Grigorief, see Schuyler, ii. 412.   ‖ Michell, op. cit , 320-322.

gradual encroachment of the Russians at last brought order and submission to the turbulent Kazaks, "but it was not," says Schuyler, "till the final overthrow of the bandit Iset Kutebarof and the death of the celebrated batir Jan Khoja that the steppe became quiet and safe, and the Russians really gained the position of *protectors* of the Kazaks." Even then all danger was not removed. Some years ago an attempt was made to abolish as far as possible the tribal distinctions of the Kazak aristocracy, and the so-called reform was introduced into the Orenburgh steppe in 1869. By this all the Little Horde was divided into two large districts, that of Uralsk and that of Turgai, each under a Russian military commander, district prefects, and *volost* or aul-elders, the last only being elected by the Kazaks. This caused much dissatisfaction; it was interpreted as the surrender of the Kazak government to the Russian Cossacks, whom were cordially hated. Disturbances accordingly arose, which were fomented by the Khan of Khiva, and during 1869 and 1870 the steppe was in great commotion. The postal route was blockaded, stations destroyed, and travellers captured, some being killed and others sold into slavery. Peace was at length restored, and, according to Schuyler, the Kazaks are getting reconciled to the new state of things, and their old clannish feeling for members of the same tribe and family is being transferred to the members of the same volost and district.[*]

When Schuyler went to Turkestan in 1873 he travelled part of the way with a Kazak prince named Chingis, the son of the last Khan of the Bukeief horde, who on the death of his father was given the Russian title of Prince. He was a good Mussulman, and had just returned from a pilgrimage to Mecca, and was going to spend the summer on his estates in the government of Samara. He says he seemed a cultivated gentleman, and was most of his time deep in a French novel.

THE GREAT HORDE.

The Middle and the Little Hordes lived in close neighbourhood and also had regular intercourse with Russia. We consequently know their history in some detail. The Great Horde, on the contrary, lived in a remote and largely inaccessible district, and had few communications with Russia, so that its history is only known to us in a fragmentary form. This is perhaps not much to be deplored, for it is perfectly clear that it had not a continuous and homogeneous status like the other two hordes, but was broken into a number of sections, governed by princes of the Middle or Little Hordes, or by begs and sultans, and was for the most part subject to the Sungars and the Chinese. Its name of "Great Horde"

---

[*] Schuyler, op. cit., 33. 34.

is somewhat misleading. Neither in numbers nor power could it compare with the other two hordes, and its name seems to me to have arisen chiefly from the fact that it continued to live in the old country of the Kazaks, and was thus the real heir of the original undivided Kazak horde, to which the name of Great probably belonged, and by which it was distinguished from the many predatory bands of other origin, all of whom as vagabonds and plunderers could claim the name of Kazak. ·I will now collect the few scattered facts I have been able to meet with relating to the history of the Great Horde. When Tiavka Khan, as I have mentioned, nominated three administrators to manage the three hordes, we are told he appointed Tiul to control the Great Horde.* He does not occur in any of the genealogical tables, and I do not know his origin.

In 1723, when the Sungars took Turkestan and overran the Kazak country, they completely subdued some branches of the Great and Middle Hordes. The rest of the Great Horde and a small section of the Middle one retired towards Khojend.† Eventually, as I have shown, the Kazaks returned northwards, and the Middle and Little Hordes found their way to their more recent quarters. The Great Horde meanwhile remained in its old country, and was there subjected by the Sungars.‡ In 1734 Aralbey and Arasgheldy Batir, who belonged to the Great Horde, but who were apparently subject to Abulkhair Khan, accompanied the latter's son Erali on his mission to Russia, and offered their submission to the Empress Anne.§ In 1738 we meet for the first time in the Russian annals with a notice of a Khan of the Great Horde. We are told that having heard of the foundation of a town on the river Ori, and of the opening of traffic between the Russians and the Middle and Little Hordes, Yolbars Khan, of the Great Horde, wrote to offer to make his people and his neighbours subjects of Russia if they were allowed to trade with Orenburgh. It would seem that trade and not submission was what he really meant, and the patent of investiture which the Russian officials prepared for him was never delivered, and still remains in the archives at Orenburgh.‖ At this time the Sungar chief Galdan drew a tax of a skin of a korsak (?) per head from the Kazaks of the Great Horde.¶ In 1739 Tatischef, the governor of Orenburgh, sent a caravan to Tash-kend, which was commanded by Lieutenant Müller, who was accompanied by the engineer officer Kushelef. M. Khanikof has abstracted a portion of their journal, in which we have some notices of Yolbars Khan. The caravan was plundered by the Kazaks of the Great Horde before it reached its destination. Müller tells us he arrived at Tashkend on the 9th of November, 1739, presented his credentials to Yolbars, and asked for the return of the stolen articles. The Khan told him he had

* Levchine, 140.   † Id., 152.   ‡ Id.   § Id., 155.   ‖ Id., 156, 157.
¶ Id., 158.

already heard of his misfortune, and he bade him thank God that
he had arrived alive. He told him he had sent to demand the
restoration of the property from Kogilde, who commanded the predatory
band, and had threatened unless he complied not to surrender his
(Kogilde's) son to the Sungar chief Galdan Chereng; but Yolbars seems
to have held out small hopes of reparation. While at Tashkend Müller
stayed in the house of a Tashkend merchant named Mamaia Usupof.
He had travelled with him from Orenburgh, had several interviews with
the Khan, who secured the release of the prisoners taken with the
caravan. At this time Turkestan was governed by Seyid Sultan, whose
relations with Yolbars are not clear, he did not, at all events, use the
title of Khan, and it is not improbable he was the representative of the
Khan of the Middle Horde, who shortly after is found ruling at
Turkestan. It would seem from the notes of Chulpanof that the Kazaks
and their Khan Yolbars were really only permanently encamped in the
district of Tashkend, and that they plundered the Tashkendians at their
will. We accordingly find that four days after Müller left, the Sarts or
citizens broke out in revolt and killed Yolbars Khan. This was in April
1740. The Kazaks revenged themselves by again sacking the town and
also the caravan.*

Levchine reports that in 1742 Shubai, Arslanof, and Mansur, three
natives of Viatka, returned from Tashkend to Orenburgh. Their account
confirms that of Müller. They add that during the reign of Yolbars
Khan a powerful elder named Tiul bi divided the authority with him,
and levied black-mail from the town. On the death of Yolbars he
became the sole ruler of the horde. It is very probable that he was the
same person as the Tiul who was appointed administrator of the Great
Horde by Tiavka Khan. His authority was very short lived, and he was
driven away by Kusiak bi, who was apparently a vicegerent of Galdan
Chereng. Some years after, namely, in 1749, Tiul bi, who had become
very weak, sent to offer to become a subject of the Russians, but the
proposal came to nothing.†

Kusiak bi was the ruler of Tashkend in 1742, when Shubai and
Mansur left there, but the tribute was then paid to the Sungarians. They
report that the Kazaks no longer dominated in the town, but that they
encamped all around it, kept up a state of virtually permanent siege,
and were ready to fall upon it on any convenient opportunity. Turkestan
was for some time in a similar position, although they allowed the
Sungars to trade there. The small villages between these two important
towns were more or less in the permanent occupation of the Kazaks.
The latter seem in fact to have been at this time a nomadic army settled
in Ferghana, and domineering over the old inhabitants without being the
undisputed rulers of the country, and they were in permanent dread of

* Vestnik, Imp. Geog. Soc. of St. Petersburg, 1851.   † Levchine, 158, 159.

the Sungars, who in effect were their suzerains. When, as I described
in the former volume, the Sungar power began to fall to pieces, the
Kazaks eagerly took part in the intrigues. They took the part of one
chief against another, and sided with Amursana, the last of the Sungarian
rulers, against the Chinese. In 1756 the Sungars were finally crushed
and dispersed, and a large portion of their country was laid waste. As
Levchine says, this was a boon to the Kazaks in two ways, it destroyed
their most potent enemy and enabled them to get new pastures for their
cattle. The Chinese seem to have encouraged their migration. The
Chinese occupied Tashkend in 1758.

The Great Horde seems now to have broken up into fragments. One
section migrated to Sungaria, where it had several conflicts with the
Chinese authorities. One portion of this division became subject to the
empire while another retained its independence These two sections
had continual and fierce fights with their neighbours the Buruts, and
severely punished the Torguts in their famous flight in 1771. The most
distinguished leader in these attacks was Erali Sultan, who was probably
Erali Sultan, the son of Abulkhair Khan of the Little Horde. M.
Levchine says that for his valour he received from the Chinese Emperor
the title of knight or paladin of the court. He had proposed a plan for
overwhelming the Torguts, but the leaders of the Middle Horde did not
fulfil their part. ⸙He nevertheless so alarmed Ubasha, the Torgut chief,
that instead of overwhelming him with his superior numbers, the latter
halted for eighteen days. Meanwhile Erali collected a great number of
allies, whose cupidity he excited by pointing out to them the wealth of
the retreating Kalmuks, and also the booty of fair women that might be
made. Ubasha grew so timid that he even asked permission from Erali
to be allowed to pass freely into the valley of the Ili. Erali pretended to
consent, but with a treacherous motive, and as soon as the Torguts had
passed on, and were unsuspectingly encamped, he attacked them, committing great slaughter and captured an immense booty in prisoners
and treasure.

Another section of the Kazaks of the Great Horde remained in the
district of Tashkend, where they adopted a more settled life, but preyed
freely on the towns there, especially Tashkend itself, and also laid waste
the surrounding country. Although not subject to the Kazaks, the
miserable inhabitants had to pay them black-mail for every privilege.
In 1760 this section of the Great Horde was joined by a large body of
Karakalpaks, who had been driven away from the mouths of the Sir
Daria by the Little Horde. After suffering great tyranny for many years
the people of Tashkend, under their ruler Yunus Khoja, at length
attacked the Great Horde in 1798. They defeated them severely more
than once, and proceeded in turn to cruelly revenge themselves upon
them. We are told they cut off the heads of their prisoners, and made

pyramids of them, in the well-known Central Asiatic fashion, in view of the Kazaks. The latter were frightened at the spectacle. Robbers and marauders, they lacked both the discipline and courage of trained soldiers, and were now embarrassed between their fear of punishment and their dread of being subjugated and reduced to slavery by Yunus Khan.[*] The latter deprived them of the various towns where they had so long dominated, and exacted from them not only absolute submission, but also made them make restitution for the many wrongs they had inflicted on Tashkend, &c.; he made laws, and levied a tax of a sheep on every hundred of them; he in fact subjugated and compelled them to enter his armies. These Kazaks passed in 1814 with Tashkend under the authority of the Khan of Khokand, but a number of them who had been living near Chimkent left their gardens and fields there and withdrew towards the Chinese frontier; another section had before this found the restraints of a settled life too much for them, and retired to the banks of the Irtish to the Middle Horde; others withdrew to the Aktagh mountains, &c.

A section consisting of several thousand tents still remained independent, and encamped on the Semrek, the Kuk su, and the Kara tal. They acknowledged their dependence on Russia in 1819. At this time they were governed by Siuk, son of Ablai Khan, of the Middle Horde. Veniukoff, whose account of Sungaria was translated by Messrs. John and Robert Michell, visited and described Vernoe, now the metropolis of the Great Horde. He says Sultan Ali was then at the head of the largest division of the horde (i.e., of those known as the Dulats or Doghlats). "This old man," he says, "has seen a great deal of adventure in his day, and having at various times been subject to three States, he has learnt to adapt himself to the customs of different countries." This chief was descended, he says, from Ablai Khan, and was probably the son of the Siuk just named. He received an allowance of three hundred and fifty silver roubles (i.e., £52. 10s.) from the Russian Government. In his youth, we are told, he went to Peking to be presented to the Chinese Emperor. For a long time after the whole of his tribe acknowledged the power of Khokand, although deputies from the horde had previously sworn allegiance to Russia. As the Khokandians were determined to abolish even the nominal dependence of the Great Horde on Russia, the latter determined to attack Kopal, which was then subject to Khokand, and Sultan Ali was chosen to lead them. He and his people then nomadised on the river Kuk su. The artful politician, after calculating the probabilities of success, held aloof. Enraged at this, the sultans and bis reproached him with cowardice. "Most worthy sultans and bis," Ali wrote, "the serpent when on its way to its nest winds and trails along slowly; it is only at the entrance that it exerts itself and quickly glides in." This answer disarmed their wrath and delayed the enterprise, which was ultimately abandoned.*

Veniukof paid the old chief a visit. " I do not doubt," said the diplomatic traveller, "that your people are happy in having you for a ruler. Your fame had reached me even at St. Petersburg, and now I see that it represented only half your merits."

" Do not say so," answered the old man. " I govern my people according to the decrees of the Padishah. May Heaven protect him and his dignity the Pristaf. As you must know, a piece of timber is a rude block at first, but becomes seemly and serviceable as this arm-chair under the skilful hands of the joiner. Were it not for him and the Padishah, we should always remain blocks."

"You are too modest, Sultan. Can he thus speak whose wit is as sharp as the well stropped razor, and whose will inclined to good is as hard as steel ? All of us certainly fulfil the wishes of the Emperor, and everyone in Vernoe should obey the Pristaf ; but you, Sultan, are of high degree in the horde. The allegiance of your people to the Padishah depends on you."

" My people cannot but be faithful to the Padishah and obedient to those he sets over us We live together here as two hands. You Russians are the right hand, we the left, and the Pristaf is the head." (He here joined hands, making the fingers of one fit between those of the other.) " It were indeed bad if the left hand disobeyed the right, and if both did not fulfil the orders of the head."†

I may add that a certain number of the Kazaks of the Great Horde settled in Russia, many years ago. Thus in 1789 the Empress Catherine issued an ukaze authorising the Sultan Churighei with four thousand families, partly of the Middle and partly of the Great Horde, to settle near the fort of Ust Kamenogorsk. In 1793 Tugum, a sultan of the Great Horde, with his people was allowed to settle in a similar manner within the frontiers of Siberia.‡

The Chinese, it seems, received a nominal tribute from the Kazaks of the Great Horde within their borders, consisting of a head of cattle for every hundred and a sheep for every thousand ; but this cost much more in presents than its value, and the various journeys made by the Kazaks to Peking, under pretence of doing homage, were really to receive gifts, and directly they had left the borders of the empire they destroyed the Imperial diplomas and other marks of distinction they had received. They treated the Russian gifts in the same way, except the money and robes, which had an intrinsic value. The Kazaks told a Chinese official, who asked for tribute for the first time, that grass and water were the products of heaven and cattle its gift, and that they pastured them themselves ; why then should they pay tribute to anyone ?§

---

* Michell's Russians in Central Asia, 245, 246.   † Id., 243-245.   ‡ Levchine, 164, 165.
§ Id., 394, 395.

The subjugation of the Kazaks by the strong arm of Russia can only be looked upon as a great gain for civilisation. However we may write idylls about the virtues of freedom and of untutored man; however we may indulge in pleasant romances, about independence, it is inevitable that a nation of robbers by profession, who occupy the border lands of a great empire, who prevent its trade and its culture from having their natural outlets, who make perpetual raids into its borders, and who hold no treaty and no promise sacred, should be crushed and subdued. As was said of such tribes long ago, "Swearing allegiance is regarded by nomades as a bargain which binds to nothing, but in which they expect to gain four to one, and for a mistake in their calculations they revenge themselves by pillage and incursions." No one not blinded by perversity would deny that the present condition of the steppes is very far in advance of what it was in the last century, or in any century since the Mongols were really a strong power and insisted upon robbers being repressed; and the result has followed from the wise policy adopted by Russia of late years, under such distinguished guidance as that of my friend M. Grigorief and others.

Note 1.—In the notes to Chapter IV. I have collected a number of facts about the topography of the country occupied by the White Horde. I will now supplement them by some other information which I then overlooked. This is contained in a famous document written, according to Karamzin, during the reign of Feodor Ivanovitch (*i.e.*, at the end of the sixteenth century), and copied out in the military bureau in 1627.* It is known as the Bolshomu, Chersteyu or Grand Survey, and gives a very curious and detailed account of Russia and its borders. In this we read, " 300 versts from the Blue Sea is the mountain Uruk. The Uruk mountain is 90 versts long. From it flow three rivers; the river Vor, which flows into the Jaik on the right side (*i.e.*, the north), the Irghiz, which flows into lake Akbashly on the east, and the river Ghem, which flows southwards towards the Sea of Khualimak, and falls into a lake before reaching that sea, and from Irghiz to the Blue Sea are the sands of Barsuk Kum, stretching over 25 versts, and those of Karakum 200 versts from the sea. The Karakum sands are 250 versts long and 130 versts wide. Into the Blue Sea on the east falls the Sir, and into the Sir falls the Kenderlik, and the river Kenderlik flows from the Ulugh Tagh mountains in two channels, and runs for a distance of 330 versts, and another river Kenderlik springs from the same mountain and falls into the Sarisu."

" The Sarisu ends in a lake before reaching the Sir, at 150 versts from the outfall of the Kenderlik and 70 versts from the mountain Karachat (*i.e.*, Karatau), and this mountain is 250 versts long, and is distant 80 versts from the Sir.

---

* Karamzin, x. 345. Note, 241.

"At 150 versts from the outfall of the Kenderlik, on the left bank of the Sir, is the town of Sunak. Opposite the mountain Karachat and between the lake Akbashly and the river Sauk and the lake Ankul, and on the two banks of the Zelenchik, and of the rivers Kenderlik and Sarisu, and on the sands of Karakum and their environs, over a space of 600 versts are the pasturages of the Kazaks."*

Again, in another place, in speaking of the Sir we read, "On this same river Sir, at 90 versts from the town of Sunak, is the town of Yasirvan, and 100 versts from Yasirvan is the town of Turkestan, situated 20 versts from the river Sir, and 140 versts from Turkestan. On the Sir, is the town of Arkan, and 60 versts from Arkan, on the south bank, is the town of Yangurgan, 10 versts from the Sir."† He also mentions the towns of Akkurgan, Sairim, and Tashbkur (i.e., Tashkend), near the Sir.‡

This account is singularly interesting and accurate, and we must devote a short space to its examination.

The Blue Sea is the well-known name by which the Aral was known formerly to the Russians. The mountains Uruk are clearly, as Levchine has shown, the branch of the well-known Mugojar range which are still called Airuk or Airuruk. Hence, as the survey says, spring the Vor (now called the Or or Ori), the Irghiz, and the Ghem or Yemba. The lake Akbashly, into which the Irghiz is said to flow, is now called Aksakal Barbi. When Rytschkof wrote his account of Orenburgh, in the latter half of the last century, this was still one sheet of water about 200 versts in circumference, and was the receptacle of the many streams called Turgai, Ulkiaki, and Irghiz. He adds that the lake then formed the division between the camping ground of the Middle and Little Hordes.§ It now seems to have shrunk considerably, and like the other lakes in the steppe, is broken into several pieces and much choked with reeds.| It is curious to read that the Yemba did not reach the Caspian when the Grand Survey was made, as it does now, and as it did when Rytschkof wrote. He says the Little Horde then often had its winter quarters on its banks.¶ The sands of Barsuk and Karakum are too well known to detain us, and we will pass on to the Sir or Jaxartes. First of its tributary the Kenderlik, described so pointedly in the Grand Survey. No such river exists now, nor does the Sir receive any tributary in its lower course, and it is quite clear that we have here another case of the gradual drying up of a river in that rapidly desiccating area the steppe of the Kazaks.

The Grand Survey speaks of two rivers Kenderlik, one of them flowing into the Sarisu and the other into the Sir. Of the former there can be small doubt, as Makshieff argued,** that we have the head stream still remaining in the rivulet Kara Kungur, which takes its rise in the Ulugh Tagh mountains and falls into the Sarisu on its right bank. The other Kenderlik, which rose by two streams from the Ulugh Tagh, I can hardly doubt is still represented by the Jizli Kungur and the Jilanli Kungur, which spring in the same mountains, and once apparently joined the Belanti.†† The Kenderlik and the Tira Kenderlik are mentioned in the Abdulla Nameh, in the account of Abdulla's campaign to the Ulugh Tagh,* so that the Grand Survey is confirmed by a contemporary document. When the Kenderlik was a tributary of the Sir a much larger quantity of water must have fallen into the Sea of Aral, and it was perhaps the drying up of this great feeder which caused the shrinkage of that sea, which, according to the statement of the Kazaks, extended forty years before Meyendorf wrote as far as the sand hills of Sari bulak and Kuk Tornak, while they were then 60 versts distant from it.† The Sarisu, when the Grand Survey was made, did not reach the Sir, but fell into a lake before reaching it, namely, the Telekul. The Sarisu was formerly the boundary between the Sungarian Kalmuks and the Kazaks.‡

The Sauk of the Grand Survey is clearly the river Sauk mentioned in the account of Abdulla's campaign, and whose site Makshief says it is very hard to fix.§ It seems from the account in the Abdulla Nameh to have been several days' journey to the west of the Ulugh Tagh, and it may not improbably be identified with the Suouk su, one of the upper streams of the Ilek, a tributary of the Jaik mentioned by Levchine.‖

The Ak gul or white lake of the account we are illustrating was not improbably the Ak tash gul or white stone lake marked on the map to the east of the Mugojar mountains, and not far west of the burial-place of Abulkhair Khan. The Zelenchik of the Grand Survey is no doubt the Jelanchik of the Abdulla Nameh. It is a well-known river issuing from the Ulugh Tagh and falling into the lake Yakan Ak, situated 100 versts south-east of lake Aksakal Barbi.¶

On turning to the Sir we find the Grand Survey mentioning several interesting towns. In regard to Sighnak, the first capital of the White Horde,** it seems very probable that it is the Sunak of the Grand Survey, which it places on the Sir, but, as Levchine has argued with some reason, on the wrong bank of the river.†† Ninety versts from Sunak on the river, it names Yasirvan, identified by Levchine with great probability with Sabran. One hundred versts further was the town of Turkestan. This as the later capital of the Kazaks must delay us a short time.

It has been recently visited and described by my friend Mr. Schuyler, who tells us " its only important building is the famous mosque built over the tomb of Hasret Khoja Ahmed Yasavi, whose construction was begun by Timur in 1397, when he went on a pilgrimage to Turkestan, or Yassy, as it was then called, while waiting for his new bride, Tukel-Khanim. Sheikh Ahmed Yasavi, who was the founder of the sect Jahria, and died about 1120, is one of the most celebrated saints of Central Asia, and is the especial patron of the Kazaks. The mausoleum is an immense building, crowned by a huge dome, and having annexed to the rear another small mosque, with a melon-shaped dome. The front consists of an immense arched portal, at least a hundred feet high, flanked by two round windowless towers with crenelated tops, which reminded me in some indefinite way of the front of Peterborough cathedral. In the archway there is a large double door of finely carved wood, and over this a small oriel window, dating from the last reconstruction by

---

* Vel. Zernof, op. cit., 305.　　† Levchine, 45.　　‡ Rytschkof, i. 182.
§ Vel. Zern., ii. 310.　‖ Levchine, 64.　¶ Id., 67.　** Ante, 289.　†† Op. cit., 461, 462.

3 o

Abdulla Khan. The walls are of large square-pressed bricks, well burnt, and carefully put together. Only the rear and side still bear the mosaic facings of enamelled tiles, though in a very injured condition. The blue tiles which covered the dome have nearly all fallen off, and of the inscriptions in large Cufic letters which surround it only the end can now be deciphered. It reads thus: 'The work of Khoja Hussein, a native of the city Shiraz.' Similar inscriptions—gigantic ornamental texts from the Koran, in blue on a white ground—run round the frieze, and the building, which is still grand in its decay, was evidently once wondrously beautiful. Earthquakes and despoilers have ruined it, leaving large cracks, now filled up in many places with coarse plaster. The front was apparently never completed, for the old beams which once served as scaffolding, remain standing in the walls, occupied now by immense storks' nests. These birds, which seem to be regarded with reverence, are frequently seen perched on one leg upon the top of Mussulman mosques. In the middle of the mosque is an enormous hall, under the lofty dome which rises to a height of over a hundred feet, and is richly ornamented within with alabaster work in the style common in Moorish buildings, and especially seen in the Alhambra. On the right and left are rooms filled with tombs of various Kazak sultans of the Middle and Lesser Hordes, among them the celebrated Ablai Khan. One room answers for a mosque, where the Friday prayers alone are said, while under the small dome at the back of the building are the tombs of Ahmed Yasavi and his family; and opening out of a long corridor full of tombs is a large room with a sacred well. Next to the tomb of the saint the most interesting monuments are those erected to a great-granddaughter of Timur, Rabiga-Sultan-Begim, daughter of the famous Ulugh-Bek. She was married to Abulkhair-Khan, and died in 1485. One of her sons lies next to her.

" The walls of the first room are covered with numbers of inscriptions, chiefly short prayers or verses from the Koran, one of which is said to have been written by Muhammed Ali Khan of Khokand, who was killed by the Amir of Bukhara in 1842; and in the middle, standing on a pedestal, there is a large brass vessel like a kettle, which would contain at least fifty gallons of water, for the use of the persons who live in the mosque and the pilgrims and students who come there. It is said to have been cast at Churnak, now in ruins, about fifty miles from Turkestan. Around this vessel there are several lines of Arabic inscription, in different characters; the first and longest reads: 'The highest and Almighty God said, " Do ye place those bearing water to pilgrims and visiting the sacred temple." '* He (i.e., the Prophet) said, 'May peace be on him ! Whoso sets a vessel of water for the sake of God, the Highest, him will God the Highest reward doubly in Paradise. By command of the great Amir, the ruler of nations chosen by the care of the most merciful God, the Amir Timur Gurgan. May God prolong his reign !' This water-vessel was made for the tomb of the Sheikh-ul-Islam, chief of all Sheikhs in the world, the Sheikh Ahmed of Yassy. ' May God give repose to his worthy soul ! The twelfth of Shavval, in the year 801 (1399).' The other inscription is: ' The

---

* This is the beginning of the 19th verse of the 9th Sura of the Koran, and ought to proceed, on the same level with him who believeth in God,' &c. (Schuyler op. cit., i. 71. Note.)

work of the servant, striving Godward, the Abul-aziz, son of the master Sheref-uddin, native of Tabriz.'

"There are besides in the mosque four large candlesticks, but the inscriptions are so defaced that one can only read the name of Timur, and that of the maker, a Persian from Ispahan, with the date 799 (1397). The Sheikh-ul-Islam has several documents from various rulers of Central Asia in whose possession Turkestan has been, conferring privileges on the shrine, one of them of the year 1591, signed by Abdulla Khan.

"This mosque is considered the holiest in all Central Asia, and had very great religious importance, as previous to the capture of the city by the Russians, pilgrims of all ranks, even khans and amirs, assembled there from all quarters.

"The mosque is entirely supported by property which has been given to it by various worshippers, including the revenues from several caravanserais and shops in the city, and very large amounts from land. Before the capture of the city the Khan of Khokand used to send five hundred tillas a year, and even now pilgrims are in the habit of offering sheep every Friday, the meat of which is distributed to the poor of the city.

"In the little enclosure in front of the portal are numerous tombs bearing inscriptions, and in a corner of the large court-yard is a small and very elegant mosque, with a lemon-shaped cupola, covered with blue tiles. The local legend runs that this was the temporary resting-place of the body of Rabiga-Begim, whose early death caused Timur such grief that he built the great mosque. Unfortunately history shows that she died some eighty years after him, and it is very doubtful if he ever saw her.

"The termination of the great mosque called Hazret was almost contemporaneous with Timur's death. The word *Hazret*, an Arabic word, meaning literally 'presence,' is used in the sense of 'majesty' for rulers, and with the meaning 'sanctity' is frequently applied to saints, especially to those most reverenced, and in this case the celebrity of the saint has given a name to the town, which is often called 'Hazreti-Turkestan,' or even simply 'Hazret.'

"Besides the mosque there is little in Turkestan to interest one. The city has much fallen off, and barely numbers six thousand souls. Everything looks dilapidated and desolate, though I found the straggling bazaar very curious, as it was the first really genuine Oriental bazaar which I had seen, that at Perovsky being half-Russian.

"I wandered for a long time, in spite of the heat, past the little rows of shops, looking at the silversmiths plying their trades, and seeing the general idleness and listlessness of the shopkeepers, for there seemed almost no business going on. The central point of interest was a raised platform, where stood a man with a little mountain of snow, which he was dealing out to the little boys in small portions, with a sauce of sugary syrup. The eyes of the boys were big and greedy, yet their timidity or their hatred of a Kafir was such that I had some difficulty in inducing them to allow me to treat them.'"[*]

One hundred and forty versts from Turkestan, on the Sir, the Grand Survey mentions the town of Arkan, which is probably the Ikan mentioned in the

---

[*] Schuyler, i. 70-73.

Abdulla Nameh, and which still remains as a small village not far from
Turkestan.* Sixty versts from Arkan, on the opposite side of the river, he
mentions Yankurgan, a well known town which still survives. It also
mentions, as situated. on the Sir, Akkurgan, Sairam, and Tashkend, which
are also well known.

In the Kazak steppe there are numerous ruins of towns, whose descriptions
I will remit to the notes of a later chapter.

Note 2.—I have overlooked in the text any reference to the early European
travellers who mention the Kazaks. The first to do so was Anthony Jenkinson,
who went to Bukhara in 1558, and whose account was published by Hackluyt.
He merely says that when he was at Bukhara the caravans from Cathay had
ceased to go there, *inter alia* because of the attacks of a certain people called
"Cassaks of the law of Mahomet, who warred against Tashkend."† Herberstein,
Miechof, and Guagnini merely mention the Kazaks as forming one of the
hordes beyond the Volga. The English merchants Hogg and Thompson, who
went to Bukhara in 1746, crossed the Kazak steppes. They call the Kazaks
Kirgeese Tartars. Setting out from the Jaik on the 26th of June, they reached
the camp of their friend Jean beek Batir (*i.e.*, Janibeg Batir), who sent his son
to meet them on the 16th of the next month. This camp was 800 versts from
the Jaik. The chief sat in his tent on a carpet, and taking a bowl of kumiz
he drank and offered them some. They gave him some presents, and informed
him they wished to open a trade with Khiva which would be very profitable to
him. He promised to assist them in every way, and insisted on their staying
with him during the extreme heat to refresh their cattle. Our travellers
describe the Kazak country as bounded on the north by the Bashkirs, on the
east by the Black Kalmuks and Tashkend, on the south by the Karakalpaks
and the Sea of Aral, and on the west by the Jaik. They say they were divided
into three hordes, of which the one nearest to Russia was governed by Jean
beek, always styled Batir. They add that what little religion there was among
them was Muhammedanism, and they describe some of their manners and
customs. *Inter alia* we are told they were very civil to strangers while
they continued under their protection, for they esteemed it the greatest
dishonour to affront a guest, but no sooner was he departed than his professed
friend and protector would sometimes be the first person to rob him, and he
would be fortunate if he escaped without being made a slave. They had no
money, and their wealth consisted in cattle and furs.

Having travelled in Jean beek's company for some days, they went on
towards Urgenj under the guidance of one of his brothers. On the return
journey Mr. Hogg was set upon by a party of seventeen Kazaks and plundered.
Having found his way back to his friend Jean beek, who had gone on an
expedition against the Black Kalmuks, he had some part of the plundered
property restored to him.‡ The Jean beek Batir of this account was no doubt the
Janibeg Baatur, a chief of the Middle Horde, who long lived with Abulkhair.§
Hogg is clearly mistaken in making him the chief of the Little Horde.

Vel. *Zernof*, ii. 302.   † Hackluyt, London, 1809, i. 372.
‡ Hanway's Travels, i. 238-242.   § *Vide ante*, 661.

Note 3.—In the following genealogical table I have marked two conjectural links by dots.

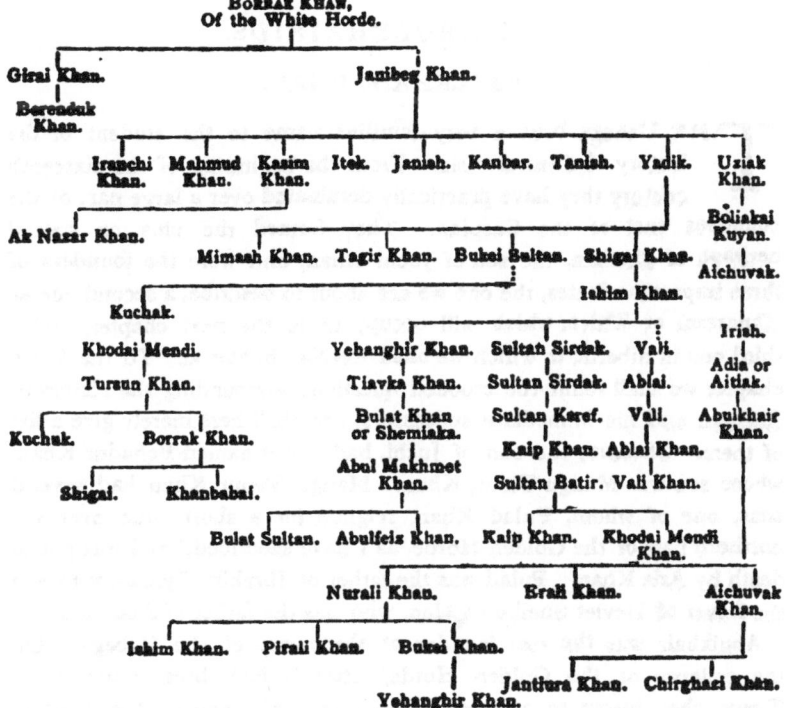

CHAPTER IX.

THE UZBEGS IN MAVERA UN NEHR, BALKH, AND KHOKAND.

THE ABULKHAIRIDS.

ABULKHAIR KHAN.

THE Uzbegs bear a very familiar name to the student of the history of Central Asia. From the beginning of the sixteenth century they have practically dominated over a large part of the countries east of the Caspian. They formed the ulus or special heritage of Sheiban, the son of Juchi Khan, and were the founders of three important States, the one we are about to describe, a second one at Khuarezm or Khiva, which will occupy us in the next chapter, and a third one in Siberia, to which we shall devote chapter xi. To the latter chapter we shall remit the crooked questions surrounding the history of Sheiban and his immediate successors, and shall here merely give a list of them. Sheiban, the son of Juchi, had a son named Behadur Khan, whose son was Mangu Timur Khan. Mangu Timur Khan had several sons, one of whom, Pulad Khan, reigned for a short time over the northern part of the Golden Horde, as I have described,* and was put to death by Aziz Khan. Pulad was the father of Ibrahim Oghlan, who was the father of Devlet Sheikh Oghlan, who was the father of Abulkhair.

Abulkhair was the real founder of the power of the Uzbegs. On the collapse of the Golden Horde, after it had been crushed by Timur, they began to assume an important *rôle,* and on the death of Borrak Khan, Abulkair became the real master of the steppe of Turan. From him were descended the rulers of Mavera un Nehr, whose history will occupy us in this chapter. It is true his grandson Sheibani was the conqueror of that district whence the dynasty has been styled that of the Sheibanids, but none of Sheibani's own descendants ever ruled there, and the dynasty, as M. Grigorief has already argued, should be styled that of the Abulkhairids.

Abulkhair was born in the year 816 (1413).† Munshi tells us that before he was twenty he conquered Khuarezm from Murza Shah Rukh, the son of Timur, and immediately after mounted the throne of the Uzbegs. He says he had a particular affection for Mevlana Hussein of

---

* *Ante*, chapter iv.   † Abulghasi, 192. Note, 1.

Khuarezm, a descendant of the celebrated Nejmeddin Kubarai, executed by the Mongols at Urgenj, a pious and wise person, from whom he learnt the lessons in religion and politics for which he was famous.[*] In his early days he was doubtless subordinate and subject to Borrak Khan of the White Horde, who was killed in 831 (i.e., 1427-8).[†] The Tarikhi-Abulkhair, for an abstract of which I am greatly indebted to my friend Dr. Rieu, begins its account of his life abruptly with the notice of his return from an expedition against Mustapha Khan, by whom, I have little doubt, the same person is meant who acted a prominent part in the history of the Golden Horde, and who was killed in an invasion of Russia in 1445.[‡] Abulkhair defeated this chief with the loss of four thousand five hundred men, and returning home victorious divided the booty among his amirs. After this, and when the sun was in the constellation Libra, he prepared to attack Sighnak, and sent several of his principal amirs in advance. The governor of the fortress, which then doubtless formed a part of the dominions of Shah Rukh, seeing the strength of the invaders surrendered it, and the Uzbegs took possession of it with Kard (?), Ak kurgan, Aruk, Suzak, and Uzkend.[§] Abulkhair bestowed the fort of Suzak upon Bakhtiar Sultan, Sighnak upon Manahdan Oghlan, and Uzkend upon Vakhas bi Mangut. He spent the winter there. On the return of spring he was preparing to return to his summer quarters at Ilak, when news arrived of the death of Shah Rukh and the march of his son Ulugh Beg to Khorassan. This was therefore in 1448. Ulugh Beg had been the governor of Mavera un Nehr and Turkestan, and when he thus withdrew south of the Oxus to secure the important province of Khorassan, Abulkhair summoned his captains and pointed out to them that Samarkand was left defenceless. He accordingly marched his troops thither, and the inhabitants on the way submitted. The governor of the city, the amir Jelal ud din Bayazid, sent some notables with presents to sue for peace, and to say that Ulugh Beg was well disposed towards the Khan, and that the latter would do best to retire homewards, which he accordingly did.[∥]

This is probably the event referred to by Abdurrezak, who tells us that while Ulugh Beg was absent in Western Khorassan pursuing his rival Ala ud Daulat, the son of Baisongkhor Murza, the Uzbegs advanced to the suburbs of Samarkand; which they plundered. That author tells us "the beautiful mosaic pictures, brought expressly from China, were shattered on the walls of the picture gallery (Chinikhaneh) by the clubs of the Uzbegs, the rich gilding was scraped off, and the works of art, which had cost many years of labour to make, were utterly destroyed in a few hours."[¶] Ulugh Beg was murdered by his son Abdul Latif in

---

[*] Senkofski, 18. Vambery, Bokhara, 238. [†] Ante, 274. [‡] Golden Horde, 392. Ante, 300.
[§] This enumeration is another proof that the Uzkend of the White Horde was, as I have argued (ante, notes to chapter iv.), a different place to the eastern Uzkend.
[∥] Tar. Abul, 322-354. [¶] Vambery, op. cit., 222.

1449. The latter succeeded to the throne, and then marched against
Abusaid, a great-grandson of Miranshah, who had seized upon authority
in Samarkand. Abusaid was beaten and taken prisoner, but escaped to
Bukhara.* There he was arrested. Abdul Latif was himself assassinated
in 854 (i.e., 1450), whereupon Abusaid was released. Not content with
the authority he had at Bukhara, he marched against Samarkand, where
Abdul Latif's successor Abdulla Murza, a grandson of Shah Rukh,
reigned. Being beaten in this attempt, he fled to Turkestan and seized
the fortress of Yassy (i.e., the modern town of Turkestan).† Thence he
repaired to the camp of Abulkhair, by whom he was received with the
greatest honour, and he undertook to restore Samarkand to him. The
Uzbegs thereupon marched, the van of the army being led by Bakhtiar
Sultan, and the main body by a number of amirs, whose names are
enumerated in the Tarikhi Abulkhair. It is curious to read that as it
was the hot season, the Yedehchis or rain bringers were ordered to
perform their incantations, when there came abundant rain, and the
army easily traversed the desert of Jizak. Abdulla, who was master of
Turkestan, Mavera un Nehr, Kabul, and Badakhshan, collected his
troops, and the two armies met at Shiraz in the plain of Kanvan, on the
banks of the Bulalghur. The Uzbegs won a bloody victory, and Abdulla
himself was pursued and slain. This was in the latter part of 855 (i.e.,
1452). Abulkhair released the prisoners he had taken, ordered his men
to refrain from pillage, and held a grand durbar. We are told he alighted
in the Bagh i Maidan and the amirs on the lawn of Kangul.‡ Abusaid
was reinstated at Samarkand, and the Sheikh ul Islam, then Khoja
Fazlulla, had an interview with Abulkhair, and engaged in pious conversation with him. Abusaid sent daily presents to the Khan. He also
sent him Ulugh Beg's daughter Rabiga Sultan Begim, to whom he was
immediately married. After firmly establishing Abusaid and pacifying
the district he returned to Desht Kipchak.§ We next read in the
Tarikhi Abulkhair that Uz Timur Taishi, the ruler of the Kalmuks, who
was jealous of Abulkhair, having summoned his amirs, announced to
them that that Khan, after securing great wealth and possessions, was
now taking his ease in his summer quarters (Ilak) .He easily persuaded
them to march against him. Abulkhair, on his side, also advanced. The
probability is the latter was in fact the assailant. On reaching Chubui (i.e.,
the well-known river Chu), his men left their baggage behind and went
on in light order. Bakhtiar Sultan and Ahmed Sultan went on with the
vanguard, and the main body followed under a number of the chief
amirs. The two armies met at Kuk Kashanah (?) in the Chir of Kili
Kiyat (?) in the Nur tukai (?). The Kalmuk chief, in spite of the
number of his men, sent to offer peace, "but Bakhtiar Sultan, Ahmed, and
their companions, forgetting the aphorism that peace is best, insisted on

fighting." The two sultans were killed. The main body of the Uzbegs then fought against the Kalmuks, but was also defeated, whereupon Abulkhair retired to Sighnak. The Kalmuks went on and ravaged Turkestan, Shahrukhia, and the tract of Tashkend. Uz Timur again offered peace, which was now accepted, and he then returned by Sairam to the river Chu, where he had left his baggage, and thence home again.[*]

This campaign of Abulkhair against the Kalmuks is very interesting. Uz Timur Khan was, as I believe, the Timur, Chingsang or vicegerent of the Segon Gar or right wing of the Uirads, mentioned by Ssanang Setzen,[†] and who seems to have succeeded Essen Khan. Abulkhair's name occurs in the traditions of the Kalmuks as Bolghari Khan, and it would seem that it was in this very campaign that the Khoshotes first acquired their name. Pallas, in reporting the traditions of this tribe, says one of their chiefs named Aksugaldai had two sons, Arrak Timur and Oerrok Timur,[‡] who jointly ruled the tribe, and allied themselves with Toghon Taishi,[§] in whose army they fought very bravely against a famous Bolghari Khan, and thence derived the name of Khoshotes.[‖] After his fight with the Kalmuks, Abulkhair devoted himself to the affairs of Desht Kipchak, which greatly prospered in his hands.

We next read that about the year 1455 Abusaid, being engaged in a campaign in Khorassan and Mazanderan, Muhammed Chuki Murza, the son of Abdul Latif Khan, whom he had defeated, fled to Abulkhair, by whom he was well received, as well as by his father's sister Rabiga Sultan Begim. He asked Abulkhair for assistance with which to recover his ancestral dominions. Abulkhair assented, and despatched an army under Bereke Sultan, Bishikda Oghlan, and other amirs, which marched towards Samarkand. They were joined by some Jagatai amirs, who were discontented with Abusaid Khan, and by the partisans of Ulugh Beg. They speedily captured Tashkend and Shahrukhia, and then crossed the Sihun. The governor of Samarkand, the amir Masid Arghun, marched out to Sistan to meet them, but he was defeated after a terrible struggle, and withdrew to Samarkand, whence he dispatched messengers to Abusaid for assistance. The Uzbegs overran the open country of Mavera un Nehr, and encamped at Kufin (?) and Kermineh. On hearing of the approach of Abusaid, Bereke Sultan and the other Kipchak officers were for defending the passage of the Amu or Oxus, the Jagatai officers for withdrawing behind the Sihun or upon Shah rukhia. Chuki having supported the latter course, a large number of his men deserted to Abusaid, while the Uzbegs began to plunder. His people were disorganised, and he was speedily beleagured at Shah rukhia, where he was compelled by famine to surrender. The Tarikhi

---

[*] *Id.*, 357-359. [†] Op. cit., 169.
[‡] Probably to be identified with the Alak Chingsang and Timur Chingsang of Ssanang Setzen, and one of them with the above-named Uz Timur.
[§] Probably a mistake for his son Essen Khan. [‖] Pallas, Saml. Hist. Nach., 25.

3 P

Abulkhair says he was treated kindly by Abusaid, who took him with
him to Herat and confined him in the fort of Ikhtiyaruddin, where he
died.[*]

We are told the Desht Kipchak greatly flourished under the beneficent
rule of Abulkhair. He died at the age of fifty-seven, in the year of the
rat A.H. 874 (*i.e.*, A.D. 1489). According to Abulghazi there were none
of his relations who had not felt the weight of his hand, and whom he
had not forced to submit to him. In consequence of this they rebelled
against him, and killed him with several of his sons, while his people
were scattered.[†] According to the Abdulla Nameh of Hafiztanish,
Abulkhair had eleven sons. By Aghanak, of the tribe Burgut, he had
Shah Budagh Sultan and Khoja Muhammed Sultan; by a second wife
of the Mangut tribe, Muhammed Sultan and Makhmet Sultan; by a
third of the Kungrad tribe, Sheikh Haidar Khan, Sanjar Sultan, and
Ibrahim Sultan; by Rabiga Sultan Begim, the daughter of Ulugh Beg
Gurkhan, Kuchkunji Khan and Suiunich Khan; and by a concubine
Ak Buyuk and Seyid Baba.[‡] In the Tarikhi Abulkhair Muhammed
Sultan, the brother of Makhmet Sultan, is not mentioned, and instead we
have the name of Abul Mansur, who is apparently made the whole
brother of Kuchkunji. It also calls Ak Buruk, Ak Burun.[§]

The strife that arose on the death of Abulkhair was chiefly between
his descendants and those of Yadigar, the head of a collateral branch of
his family which founded the Khanate of Khuarezm, and which will
occupy us in the next chapter. The story is a complicated one. On
turning to the Tarikhi Rashidi we find its author stating that on the
death of Abulkhair Khan his people acknowledged his eldest son Baruj
Oghlan, who, to avoid Girai and Janibeg Khan of the Kazaks, who were
becoming very powerful, lived in the territory of Turkestan. It seems
that Yunus Khan of Mongolistan had marched to the assistance of his
protégés the Kazaks, and was attacked in Kara tuga by Baruj, who came
upon him by surprise with twenty thousand men. The Khan had sixty
thousand families with him. The fighting men had crossed the Sihun to
hunt, and Baruj found the camp defenceless, and his people immediately
began to plunder. The Khan having learnt what had happened, did
not wait to collect his men, but instantly returned. He crossed
the river on the ice with only six companions, one of whom carried the
Shesh tugha or Grand Standard. He also had the great trumpet with
him, which none could blow like himself. When he came near the camp
he gave a loud blast, and the standard coming in sight, a general panic
seized the Uzbegs. Baruj Oghlan tried to mount his horse, but he was
seized, and the Khan ordered him to be beheaded and his head to be put
on a spear, while few of his followers escaped.[|] It was long ago noticed

---

[*] Op. cit., 345-349.   [†] Op. cit., 202, 203.   [‡] Vel. Zern., Coins of Bukhara, 359.
[§] Op. cit., 350.   [|] Tarikhi Rashidi.

by Hafiztanish, who refers to this passage, that no such name as Baruj occurs among the lists of Abulkhair's sons;* but as he is so distinctly called the eldest son of Abulkhair, and was apparently succeeded by Sheibani, I am disposed to think he was the same person as Shah Budagh Sultan, the father of Sheibani. Abulkhair's second son was named Khoja Muhammed, who was own brother to Shah Budagh. As he was only half-witted, the Uzbegs named him Khoju 'am Tintek (*i.e.*, the idiot). "He was such a fool," says Abulghazi, "that he used to prophecy to the women of the aul by the sputterings of fat in the fire whether they would have boys or girls, yet he could not tell whether the boy his wife presented him with was his own or another's." It seems he had married Malai Khanzadeh, the widow of Bereke Sultan, the leader of the rival house of Uzbegs. She was already *enceinte* when he married her, and seven months later gave birth to a son, who was called Janibeg, and who filled an important *rôle* in Uzbeg history.†

MUHAMMED ABULFATH SHEIBANI KHAN.

When Shah Budagh died he left an infant son named Muhammed, who was called Sheibani, after the original founder of the Khanate, Sheibah, the son of Juchi. He was given the title of Shahbakht (*i.e.*, the fortunate prince) by his grandfather, which was corrupted by some Persian writers into Shaibek. While we find the additional name Abulfath on his coins (Fræhn Res., 437; Vel. Zern., Coins of Bukh, &c., 333). He was born in 1451 of the hejira, and his mother's name was Ak kuzi Begim.‡ On his father's death his grandfather Abulkhair ordered Uighur Sheikh, who had been Shah Budagh's atabeg, to look after him, and on Abulkhair's death, Karachin beg, one of the most powerful amirs among the Uzbegs, undertook to take charge of him and of his brother Mahmud Sultan. At this time, we are told in the Sheibani Nameh, there came forward many enemies of the house of Abulkhair, such as Seidiak and Ibak, the sons of Haji Muhammed Khan of the horde of Sheiban; the descendants of Arab Bereke Sultan (probably Arabshah the Sheibanid is meant); Janibeg and Girai, the sons of Borrak of the White Horde; and the Manguts or Nogais, Abbas, Musa and Yamgurchi.§ The heritage of Abulkhair was now in the feeble hands of his son Sheikh Haidar, who was presently defeated by the Ibak just named. Karachin repaired with his two charges to Kasim, the Khan of Astrakhan, who appointed his own amir el umera Timurbeg (who was a Nogai) to look after them. When Kasim was beleagured in Astrakhan by Ibak and Ahmed Khan of the Golden Horde, the two young princes and Karachin fought their way through the enemy after a desperate struggle.‖ Sheibani now seems to have repaired to his old

* Vel. Zernof, ii., Khans of Kasimof, 146.　　† Abulghazi, 206.

‡ Senkofski, 20. Vel. Zernof, ii. 234.　§ Vel. Zernof, op. cit., ii. 235.　‖ Id., Ante, 350.

country about the Lower Sir, where he gathered some people about him, but having been defeated near Sabran by Iranchi, the son of Janibeg Khan of the Kazaks, he went to Bukhara, where he was well received and entertained by the amir Abdul Ali Terkhan, who governed that town for Ahmed Murza. The latter sent for him to Samarkand, where he treated him hospitably, and he afterwards returned again to Bukhara.* After spending two years with Abdul Ali he returned homewards. When he approached the fort of Artak the Khoja Begchik and the oldest of the amirs with the chief people went out to meet him with the keys of the place. Thence he went on to Sighnak. There envoys met him from Musa, the chief of the Manguts or Nogais, inviting him to go to the Desht Kipchak, and promising to make him Khan there if he went. He accepted the invitation and had an interview with Musa, who treated him well. Berenduk Khan of the Kazaks, whose authority was being thus questioned, marched against him, but was defeated and fled. Sheibani having asked Musa to fulfil his promise, the latter evaded the proposal, on the ground that the Manguts were unfavourable.† Sheibani now withdrew from the Desht Kipchak, and fought several times with the Kazak chief Mahmud Sultan, the son of Janibeg, who was the ruler of Suzak. Being at length defeated by him, he went to Mangushlak on the Caspian, and thence to Khuarezm, where the amir Nasir ud din Abd ul Kalik Firoz Shah, who ruled in the name of Sultan Hussein Murza of Khorassan, presented him with lordly gifts. Thence he went to Karakul and Bukhara to his old patron Ali Terkhan, who again accompanied him to Samarkand.‡ At this time the ruler of Mavera un Nehr, Sultan Ahmed Murza, was in conflict with the Khan of Mongolistan, Sultan Mahmud Khan, who ruled also at Tashkend and Shahrukhia. He led an army against Tashkend, which was joined by Sheibani. This was in the year 893 (*i.e.*, 1488).§ The two armies opposed one another on the river Chirr, a tributary of the Sir Daria. Sheibani treacherously made secret overtures to the enemy, and offered to throw his allies into confusion and to fly at a critical moment. The following day the army of Mongolistan crossed the Chirr, the foot soldiers leading and the cavalry following, when Sheibani carried out his purpose. Sultan Ahmed Murza was defeated, and many of his men were drowned.‖ Sheibani now seems to have transferred his services to Mahmud Khan, who having shortly after captured the town of Turkestan, which was at this time subject to Sultan Ahmed Murza, made it over to Sheibani as a reward for his services at the battle of the Chirr.

This greatly exasperated Janibeg and Girai, the chiefs of the White Horde, to whose ancient heritage Turkestan apparently belonged, and who thereupon quarrelled with Mahmud Khan, as I have mentioned.¶

---

* Vol. Zernof, ii. 240.   † Khuandemir, quoted by Vol. Zernof, ii. 240, 242.   ‡ *Id.*, 245, 246.
§ Vol. Zernof, ii. Note, 33.   ‖ Tarikhi Rashidi.   ¶ *Ante*, 608. Tar. Rashidi.

Mahmud Khan assisted him with troops, and there also joineo him a large number of his grandfather's retainers. Now happened the romantic incident described by Abulghazi, in which Bereke Sultan met his end, and to which I shall refer more at length in the next chapter. Sheibani also had several encounters with the Kazaks; thus we read that, having secured all the surrounding fortresses, he moved upon Sighnak, where he struggled with Berendul Khan of the Kazaks.* He then marched into Khuarezm, seizing the opportunity when its governor Firoz Shah was in Khorasan with his master Sultan Hussein Murza. After several days' attack on the capital, Firoz Shah having marched to the rescue, he raised the siege and went to the fortress of Buldum, whose ruins still remain about 88 versts north-east of Khiva. There he was well received, and passed on to the town of Vestr, where he was defeated by the troops of Khorasan, and passed on first to Alak and then to Asterabad, plundering several places in the neighbourhood.† After this, by the invitation of Mahmud Khan, he went to Otrar, where they formed a league, and where the Khan gave up Otrar to him. At this time the people of Sabran expelled their darugha or governor Kul Muhammed Terkhan, and gave up the keys to Mahmud Sultan, the brother of Sheibani, and we are told the people of all Turkestan acknowledged the authority of the two brothers. The Kazaks having marched against Sabran, the citizens treacherously seized Mahmud and surrendered him to Kasim, the Kazak chief, whose mother, according to the Sheibani Nameh, was sister to Mahmud's mother. He kept him for some time, and then sent him under escort to Suzak. On the way Mahmud escaped. He sent to inform his brother, and they had an interview on the mountain Ugusman, whence they both returned to Otrar. Soon after Berenduk Khan of the Kazaks attacked him at Otrar, but after some days agreed to a peace. Sheibani then went to Yassi (i.e., the town of Turkestan), which was governed by Muhammed Mezid Terkhan, who was captured and sent prisoner to Otrar. Thereupon Mahmud Khan of Mongolistan marched to his assistance, released him, and sent him to Samarkand. That chief now began to see what a dangerous person he had been patronising, and allied himself with the Kazaks against him. They feared to attack Sheibani at |Yassi, but beleagured his son Muhammed Timur Sultan at Otrar. The attack was unsuccessful, and not long after we find Berenduk Khan giving his sisters in marriage to Sheibani's son Muhammed Timur and his brother Mahmud. Sheibani was a very unscrupulous person. As Erskine says he habitually aimed at extending his territory, and never scrupled as to means. He was totally without faith, and bound by no promise or engagement, and frequent misunderstandings occurred between him and Mahmud Khan. Notwithstanding, the latter continued to countenance

---

* Vol. Zera., ii. 247.   † Id., 248, 249.

him and to employ him in his designs upon Samarkand and Bukhara. This policy was naturally grateful to the wily Sheibani, whose power increased daily.

It would seem that in 1497 he had been called to his assistance by Baisongkhor Murza, the ruler of Samarkand, when attacked by Baber, but finding the latter's army well prepared, he drew off again.* This was doubtless the invasion mentioned in the Sheibani Nameh, where we are told that Sheibani's brother, Sultan Mahmud penetrated as far as Jizak and was there repulsed, and that Sheibani, to revenge him, crossed the Sihun with an auxiliary force of one thousand Jetes, by whom he was betrayed, whereupon he retired.† He now prepared a more elaborate plan.

Vambery relates how his future strategy was guided by an aphorism of his spiritual adviser Sheikh Mansur, who, having asked him to a feast, said to him, when the viands were taken away, "Dost thou see that this tablecloth is removed, not by snatching it in the centre but by folding up each corner, and so the country must be taken, not by seizing the capital but by securing the frontiers."‡

More of the old supporters of his house hastened to him. "He led them," says Erskine, "into the rich fields of Transoxiana, which he and his followers had had ample opportunities of surveying as fugitives and exiles." These provinces they now found a prey to faction and torn with civil war. Their forces, which at first consisted only of Uzbegs, had been recruited by adventurers from all parts of the Desht Kipchak. *Inter alia* we are told Sheibani went to Khiva, where he borrowed some Mangut auxiliaries. He was also joined by several Uzbeg chiefs who had hitherto stood aloof from him, such as his two uncles, Kuchkunji Sultan and Suiunich Sultan, and his relatives Hamza Sultan and Mehdi Sultan.§

At this time the various princes of the house of Timur were engaged in civil strife, and there was great confusion in Mavera un Nehr. The famous Baber was among the chief offenders. Having captured Samarkand from Baisongkhor in 1497, he had afterwards been constrained to withdraw, and the nominal ruler of Mavera un Nehr at this time was Sultan Ali Murza, the son of Sultan Mahmud Murza, by Zureh Beghi Aga, who Baber says was an Uzbeg and a concubine.‖ Although Sultan Ali was the nominal ruler of Samarkand, it would seem that the real authority was in the hands of Khoja Yahia, whose ancestors had held the post of Sheikh ul Islam there for four hundred years.¶ Sheibani having appeared before the town, beleaguered it for ten days, and repulsed a sortie from the gate Sheikhzade; he then entered it by the gate Tshihar rah, and penetrated unresisted to the summer palace of Baghi No. We are told "he had to fight the garrison inside the town itself. The

* Memoirs of Baber, 47, 48.　　† Vambery, History of Bukhara, 250, 251.
‡ Id. Note, 251.　　§ Vambery, op. cit., 251.　　‖ Op. cit., 29.　　¶ Vambery, 25.

struggle began at noon and lasted till midnight, Sheibani displaying reckless courage during its progress. The next day news arrived that Baki Terkhan, a son of the Abdul Ali Terkhan, under whom Sheibani had commenced his career, was coming from Bukhara to the help of Samarkand, and was already besieging the fort of Dabusi."* The Uzbegs thereupon desisted from their attack, and turned upon and defeated Baki Terkhan, and leaving a force to beleaguer Samarkand, itself went on towards Bukhara. This was speedily captured. Sheibani having put his harem there, attacked Karakul. The inhabitants of that place rose against the garrison and murdered them. The Uzbegs speedily recaptured it, and exacted vengeance. They then returned to continue their attack on Samarkand.† Baber tells us that Ali Murza's mother, who, as we have seen, was an Uzbeg, "was led by her stupidity and folly to send a messenger privately to Sheibani Khan, proposing that if he would marry her, her son should surrender Samarkand into his hands on condition that, when he recovered his own paternal dominions he should restore that town to Sultan Ali "‡ We are further told that Abu Yusuf Arghun was the originator of this plan. When Sheibani reached Bagh e Meidan (i.e., the Garden of the Plain), Sultan Ali Murza, without acquainting anyone, left the town by the Char raheh gate, accompanied by only a few insignificant individuals of his personal attendants, and went to meet him. Sheibani did not give him a very flattering reception, and as soon as the ceremonies of meeting were over made him sit down lower than himself. Khoja Yahia, finding the murza had left the town, was alarmed and left it in turn. He also waited on Sheibani, who did not rise to greet him, but said some severe things to him. The Khoja's example was followed by Jan Ali, the son, of Khoja Ali bi, who was at Rabat Khoja, "so that," says Baber, "the wretched and weak woman, to get herself a husband, gave the family and honour of her son to the winds, nor was she well treated, for Sheibani did not value her as much as his own wives and concubines."§

Another account attributes the fall of the place to the quarrels between Sultan Ali and his patron the Khoja, and tells us how Sheibani, who knew of them, "wrote to the princely puppet asking him whether he was not tired of the guardianship of the Khoja, and bade him do homage to the star of Abulkhair, now in the ascendant, and also proposed to his mother; and accordingly one Friday Sultan Ali left the city furtively on one side, while the Khoja, ignorant of what was going on, was at prayer in a mosque on the other side."∥

This capture of Samarkand took place in 906 (i.e., 1500), and it is from this date that the Tarikhi Timuri and the Tarikhi Abulkhair Khani date Sheibani's accession to the throne.¶ After his surrender Sultan Ali

---

* Vambery, op. cit., 252.   † Id.   ‡ Baber, 83.   § Id., 84.
∥ Vambery, 253.   ¶ Abulghasi, 203. Note, 2. 206, 200. Note, 1.

Murza had quarters assigned to him near Timur Sultan. Some of his friends wished him to escape, but he refused. According to Baber he was put to death three or four days after in the meadow of Kalbeh.[*] The author of the Sheibani Nameh, who was a panegyrist of the Uzbegs, says he was accidentally drowned while riding along the banks of the Kohek or Zarefshan.[†] The Tarikhi Timuri says he died at Kan i Gul, on the banks of the same river.[‡] The Khoja Yahia was soon after killed with his two sons, while on their way to Khorasan. He was probably privy to the murder, although he denied it and laid the blame on Kamber bi and Kepek bi.[§] Sheibani was now master of Samarkand. His followers were no friends of city life, and after occupying the city for some time, he encamped with seven or eight thousand troops near Khoja Didar, two thousand others were posted near Samarkand, under Hamza Sultan and Mehdi Sultan, while the city was only garrisoned by from five to six hundred men. It was under these circumstances that Baber ventured on the dashing exploit of surprising it with a force of only two hundred and forty men. He naturally boasts of the skill and daring of this feat, which was performed when he was only nineteen, while Sheibani was very skilful and experienced.[‖]

He has himself described the capture. He had previously tried to surprise the town, but found the garrison on the alert. He was now accompanied by the Khoja Abdal Makaram. They reached the bridge of the Moghak (i.e., the hollow) at the Khiavan or public pleasure grounds, whence he detached seventy or eighty men, with orders to scale the wall opposite the Lover's Cave, to pass round and surprise the troops stationed at the Firozeh Gate, which they were to seize, and then to apprise him of the result. They were successful, killed Fazil Terkhan, who commanded the guard at the gate, and while some of his men broke its lock with axes, and threw it open, Baber came up at the very time and immediately entered. "The citisens were fast asleep," he says, "but the shopkeepers, peeping out of their shops and discovering what had happened, offered up prayers of thanksgiving. The rest of the citisens were soon on the alert, and having sided with his people, pursued the Uzbegs in every street and corner with sticks and stones, hunting them down and killing them like mad dogs." They slaughtered about four or five hundred in this way, the governor of the city Jan Vafa, however, escaped and joined Sheibani.[¶] Baber proceeded to the college of Ulugh Beg and Kanekah, and on reaching the latter sat down under the Grand Tak or arched hall, where he received the congratulations of the citizens. In the morning he heard that the Uzbegs still held the Iron gate, he immediately mounted his horse and galloped to the place, accompanied by only fifteen or twenty men, but the rabble of the

---

* Op. cit., 84.   † Vambery, 253. Note, 2.   ‡ Abulghasi, 203 Note, 2.
§ Baber, 84.   ‖ Id., 88, 89.   ¶ Id., 88.

town who were prowling about in every lane and corner had already driven the Uzbegs away. Sheibani Khan, "the foreign robber," as Baber-calls him, on hearing what had happened, went hurriedly to the Iron gate with a hundred or a hundred and fifty horse, but seeing he could effect nothing, hastily retired. The capture of Samarkand was followed by the flight of the Uzbegs from many of the surrounding districts. Sogd and Miankal submitted to Baber, the districts of Khozar and Karshi to Baki Terkhan, the late governor of Bukhara, while Karakul was seized by a force from Merv. Bukhara alone and its surrounding district remained in the possession of the Uzbegs. Baber was too weak, however, and the surrounding princes too unwilling to assist him to enable him to retain his conquest long.

The following spring the Uzbegs again captured Karakul and took the fort of Dabusi by storm, slaughtering the garrison. At length in April or May, 1501, Baber marched out to join battle with Sheibani, and encamped near Sir e pul (*i.e.*, Bridge end). He fortified his camp with a palisade and ditch. Sheibani went to meet him and encamped about four miles away. Skirmishes took place during four or five days, and in one Sheibani and his people advanced to the very edge of the ditch and discharged a volley of arrows, but finding the place too well protected withdrew. The struggle was precipitated by the impatience of Baber who ascribes it to following an astrological conclusion. The stars Sahziulduz (*i.e.*, the eight stars), he says, were exactly between the two armies, while for thirteen or fourteen days afterwards they would have been favourable to the enemy Without waiting, therefore, for the reinforcements which were at hand, he moved out in battle array, his horses being defended by cloth of mail. Sheibani was not loth to meet him. His right wing was commanded by Mahmud Sultan, Janibeg Sultan, and Muhammed Timur Sultan, and his left by Hamza Sultan, Mehdi Sultan, &c. The Uzbegs, says Baber, in fighting placed great reliance on the Tulghmeh (*i.e.*, turning the enemy's flank), and never engaged without practising this manoeuvre; another of their practices was to advance and charge in front and rear, discharging their arrows at full gallop pell mell, chiefs and common soldiers, and if repulsed in like manner retiring at full gallop. As they greatly outnumbered Baber's people, the Uzbegs had no difficulty in outflanking them on the left, and his forces being pressed in front and rear, and being at the same time deserted by the contingent from Mongolistan, which began marauding, were completely routed, only ten or fifteen people remained with their chief, with whom he plunged into the river Kohik close by. When half way over the ford their horses sank beyond their depth, and they were forced to swim them for upwards of a bow-shot, both horses and men being encumbered with armour, but they plunged through and reached Samarkand before nightfall.[*] In regard to his impetuosity, which had

---

[*] *Id.*, 93, 94.

brought on this disastrous battle, Baber wrote a couplet which is good
philosophy even now—

> He who impatient haste lays his hand on his sword
> Will afterwards gnaw that hand with his teeth from regret.

Baber was now deserted by his relatives and fairweather friends, who
were scattered in various directions. He was not daunted, however, but
summoned a council of such Begs and officers as stood by him, and it
was determined to put the place in a state of defence, and to resist to
the death. He had a public tent (chader sefid) pitched for himself in the
arched portal of Ulugh Beg's College, in the midst of the city, and
assigned his various officers their posts at the gates. In two or three
days Sheibani arrived and posted himself some distance from the city.
Thereupon, says Baber, the idle and worthless rabble assembling from
every district and street of Samarkand came in large bodies to the gate
of the College, shouting aloud, "Glory to the Prophet!" and clamorously
marched out for battle, in spite of the old and experienced veterans, who
were only abused for counselling prudence. On one occasion when they
had thus gone out in their bravado they were assailed by a body of
Uzbegs. Baber had sent some of his troops to cover the retreat. When
the mob was broken and scattered the brunt of the fight fell on these
soldiers. The Uzbegs seem to have pursued their advantage closely, and
Baber describes how he and his companions eventually stopped them by
discharging their crossbows from the top of the gateway.* On another
occasion the Uzbegs made a false attack, which divided the attention of the
garrison, while they made a real assault between the Washing-green
Gate and the Needlemakers' Gate. They planted twenty-five or twenty-
six scaling ladders, on which two or three men could mount abreast,
and were already clambering on the ramparts when the vigour of a few
of the garrison threw them over, and repelled the attack. The Prince-
historian also describes as an incident of the siege a sortie in which
some of his men succeeded in dismounting some of the enemy, and in
bringing back several heads. The distress in Samarkand became very
great. The harvest was ripe and had not been gathered, and the poor
were driven to eat the flesh of dogs and asses, a great degradation for
Muhammedans. Horses had to be fed on the leaves of trees, and it
was ascertained from experience, says the historian naively, that the
leaves of the mulberry and black wood (Kara ighaj) answered best.

Sheibani meanwhile blockaded the town from a distance, and sent at
nights a force, with drums beating, to alarm the garrison. Baber complains that he was not assisted by his relatives, especially by Sultan
Hussein Murza of Khorassan, and cites an aphorism to show the hope-
lessness of resistance, to the effect that to maintain a fortress, a head
(i.e., a good captain), two hands (i.e., two relieving armies), and two feet

---

* Memoirs, 95

(*i.e.*, water and stores) are needed.* His soldiers and even his immediate attendants began to desert him, while the provisions were exhausted. Sheibani thereupon proposed terms, a capitulation was agreed upon, and he left the town at midnight with his mother and some other ladies. His elder sister, Khanzadeh Begim, was, however, captured by the Uzbegs. Baber hastened away, and at length reached Jizak, where he says he found nice fat flesh, bread of fine flour well baked, sweet melons, and excellent grapes in great abundance, thus passing from the extreme of famine to plenty, and from danger to peace and ease.† It would seem from the Tarikhi Rashidi that Baber's sister, in fact, married Sheibani, and that this was a condition of the treaty. By her he had a son, Khurram, to whom he gave Balkh, but he died young. He afterwards divorced her, being jealous of her partiality for the interests of Baber, whose favourite sister she was.‡ The second capture of Samarkand by the Uzbegs took place about September, 1501.

Sheibani, who was now master of the beautiful country of Sogd, seems to have quarrelled with his old patron Mahmud, the Khan of Tashkend and Shahrukhia, and we read that in the winter he crossed the river of Khojend on the ice and ravaged the district of Shahrukhia and Tashkent. Baber, who was at Dehkat, one of the hill districts of Uratippa, marched against him. He describes how the violent icy wind Haderwish was then blowing, and how in consequence some of his people perished from cold. When he arrived at Beshkent he found that Sheibani had retired.§ In the spring of 1502 Sheibani made a raid upon Uratippa.‖ At this time Sultan Ahmed Tambol having become rebellious, or in the words of Haidar, having begun to shoot the arrows of discord at the target of sovereignty, broke out into revolt against Mahmud Khan. The latter and his brother Ahmed, who was joint-Khan of Mongolistan, marched against him. The Khans' army numbered about 30,000 men, and they ordered Baber to make a diversion by way of Akhsi. The details of the strategy on either side are described in some detail by Baber, but do not concern us at present. The result was that Tambol was very hard pressed, and sent to Sheibani for help against his suzerains, offering to hold Ferghana as an appanage under him.¶

Sheibani was not loth to accept the invitation. The two Khans had not time to assemble their various contingents, and had only 15,000 men with them, with whom they rapidly retired. They were also accompanied by their nephew Baber. They had recrossed the river of Khojend, and were loitering near Akhsi, when Sheibani came up, having evaded two covering armies which the Khans had planted, one at Tashkend, and the other at Uratippa. He had marched by way of the latter place, which

---

* *Id.*, 97. † *Id.*, 98. ‡ Erskine's India, 157. Note. § *Id.*, 200.
  ‖ *Id.*, 101. ¶ Baber's Memoirs, 114.

he made a show of attacking, but at nightfall he raised his camp and went on. The expresses who were sent with the news reached the Khans concurrently with Sheibani. The latter had 30,000 men with him, together with his relatives Kuchkunji Sultan, Suiunich Sultan, Janibeg Sultan, &c. The enemy had barely time to draw up in confusion. They offered but slight opposition, and were completely routed. Both Khans, their horses being wearied out, were captured, while Baber escaped to the hills south of Ferghana. On the news reaching Tashkend, its garrison under Muhammed Sultan, the son of Mahmud Khan, made all haste to withdraw to Mongolistan, while Muhammed Hussein, the father of Haidar, retired with the forces of Uratippa towards Karatigin.* Sheibani behaved with considerable generosity to his illustrious prisoners, but he seems to have insisted on three intermarriages with his own family as the price of their release. For his son Muhammed Timur Sultan he claimed the hand of Doghlat Sultan Khanum, the sister of the two Khans; for himself the hand of Anba Sultan Khanum ; and for Janibeg Sultan Kuruz Khanum. He also incorporated 30,000 of the Khans' followers in his own army.† Sheibani also insisted on the surrender of Tashkend and of Shahrukhia, in which latter town the mother of the two Khans was commanding.‡ The famous transactions which I have just described took place apparently in June, 1503.§ Haidar tells us that the younger Khan on reaching his house in Mongolistan was taken ill and died. Haidar himself was told by the Khoja Taj ud din Muhammed, whose family held the post of hereditary Sheikh ul Islam there, that when the Khan was very ill with dysentery, the Khoja having told him that it was reported that Sheibani had mixed noxious herbs with his food, and that if so he would procure the precious teriak or antidote against poison from Khita or China, he replied, " Sheibani has indeed poisoned me. He has raised himself from the lowest state of abasement to such a height that he has taken us two brothers prisoners and then set us at liberty. This disgrace is the cause of the disease in my frame. If you have any antidote for this it may be useful."‖ Sheibani seems to have treated one of his prisoners with harshness, this was Baber's friend the Khoja Abul Mokaram. Having been thrown into prison at Tashkend he made his escape, and as a disguise consented to have his beard cut off, a great disgrace in Mussulman eyes. He was discovered dining in a cottage and taken before Sheibani. The latter on seeing him inquired " Where is your beard," to which the Khoja answered in two Persian verses, "He who puffs at the lamp which God has lighted singes his beard." The graceful allusion availed him nothing and he was put to death.¶ Having placed Uzbeg garrisons in the chief towns of

---

* Tar. Rash.   † Tar. Rash. Erskine, op. cit., i. 185, 186.
‡ Id. Vambery, 258.   § Erskine, 184. Note.   ‖ Tar. Rash. Erskine, 190.
¶ Erskine, 185, 186.

Ferghana Sheibani, returned. When he had prostrated his rivals in the north, the Uzbeg chief turned his arms to the south of Mavera un Nehr, where Khosru Shah, a Turk of Kipchak, had in these times of confusion seized upon Hissar, Khatlan, Kunduz, and Badakshan.* Sheibani during the winter of 909, probably in October or November, 1503, made a raid into his dominions and then turned upon Balkh, which was governed by Badiezzeman, the son of Murza Hussein, of Herat. Having besieged Balkh during the winter he returned once more to Samarkand, and then proceeded to attack Andijan where his former *protégé*, Tambol, who had probably aroused his jealousy, still ruled.† When Sheibani reached Marghinan Tambol concentrated himself at Andijan. He had 2,000 men with him.

The siege had lasted forty days, when one day he perceived in Sheibani's trenches Muhammed Hussein Doghlat, of Uratippa, the father of Haidar, who had been his foster-brother, and who had recently been driven away from Hissar by Khosru. He thus addressed him from the wall :—" My Murza, do not forget me, and think of the times when we sucked milk from the same breast   Tell me what I should do, and I will do it." The Murza sorrowfully counselled him to surrender. He accordingly came out accompanied by his brothers. They were all put to death by the Uzbegs, while it was forbidden to plunder.Andijan.‡ Sheibani now settled at Samarkand, gave Tashkend, with the provinces ruled over by the elder Khan, to his paternal uncles, Kuchkunji Sultan and Suiunich Sultan. He appointed his cousin Janibeg Sultan governor of Andijan, his brother Mahmud Sultan governor of Bukhara, while the office of darugha of Shahrukhia he gave to the amir Yakub, one of his chief nobles.§

Sheibani himself, who was getting very inflated with his success, and in the rhetorical phrases of Haidar, "had put the foot of ambition in the stirrup of daring," returned to Samarkand, where he prepared to attack Hissar. " He would have little trouble with Khosru, the ruler of that land," he said " he would drive him away like a fly from a dish, with a wave of his hand." He marched, and Khosru, according to Baber,‖ without battle, or effort, abandoned his territories and fled. Hissar, the capital of the country, held out bravely under one of his officers named Shirim Chihrih, but it was surrendered after a while on honourable terms. Sheibani, meanwhile, despatched his brother Mahmud against Kunduz, the principal fortress of the country, where Khosru had laid up stores and provisions to serve for a twenty years' siege. As I have said, he did not wait to test the fortress, but fled precipitately, and it was surrendered to the Uzbegs. Sheibani gave the command of Hissar to

* Vambery, 231 and 256.   † Erskine's India, 186-188.
‡ Tar. Rash. Erskine's Hist. of India, i. 189.
§ Baber's Memoirs, 125. Hist. of India, i. 189.   ‖ Memoirs, 188.

Hamza Sultan, and of Cheghanian, to Mehdi Sultan, and retired leisurely home.* "After we reached Buyeh," says the princely narrator, Haidar, "I was sitting one day about noon in the audience pavilion. Only a few were present, when a man arrived in great haste, with a face of terror and dismay, and laid a letter at the foot of the throne. After reading it, a great change came over Sheibani; he retired to pray, and then mounted. It became known that Mahmud Sultan (Sheibani's brother) had died at Kunduz, and that they were bringing his body. After advancing some distance, we saw a great crowd as of mourners covered with black, drowned in grief and lamentation, who had laid down the bier, and were standing behind it in rows. Both sides raised cries of mourning. On a sign from him, the sultans dismounted, and on another the people with him formed themselves into a line and stood still while he rode alone till his horse's head was over the bier; on another sign all ceased weeping, tearing their clothes and beards, and having asked some questions from one of Mahmud's Amirs, he remained silent for an hour, showing no alteration in his visage, and uttering no groan or sigh. He then said, "'Twas well that Mahmud should die; men said the power of Sheibani was supported by Mahmud. Now let it be known that Sheibani depends on no man. Carry him away and bury him.' All were filled with astonishment at his sternness and composure."†
Sheibani returned to Samarkand and commenced at once to prepare for the invasion of Khuarezm, which was subject to Khorassan. He had now about 30,000 so-called Mongols in his service; they were the subjects of the elder Khan Mahmud, and were undoubtedly Turks by blood. They were turbulent and dangerous subjects, and Sheibani determined to disintegrate them by destroying their chiefs. He seems to have given timely warning to two of them, namely, to Haidar's father Muhammed Hussein and to Sultan Seyid, the third son of the younger Khan. "The rest of the Mongol chiefs," says Haidar, "he sent to their eternal home, or to hopeless imprisonment." Such was the strong hand and iron grip of the Uzbeg chief. Having incorporated the Mongols with his army, he now laid siege to Urgenj or Khiva, the capital of Khuarezm, which was defended with great bravery for ten or eleven months by its governor, Chin Sufi, who governed it for Sultan Hussein Murza, of Herat or Khorassan. As no succour came, the inhabitants apparently grew wearied of the siege, and treacherously surrendered the walls. Chin Sufi was killed by an arrow, which put an end to the struggle, and the place was taken. Baber calls him Hussein Sufi.‡ It would seem that Chin Safi's chief hope of succour had been from the fugitive Khosru Shah who was about this time, however, made prisoner and put to death, with 700 of his followers. Mirkhond says he fell alive into Sheibani's hands,

*Tar. Rash. Erskine's Hist of India, i. 203, 204.   † Id., 204-205.
‡ Tar. Rash. Erskine, op. cit., 237, 238. Baber, 176.

and having been dragged at a donkey's tail through the streets of Kunduz, was then executed. He describes him as severe and just as a ruler, pious as a Muhammedan, but cruel and ungrateful as a man.[*] When he had put Khuarezm under the control of Kuchuk bi, Sheibani returned to Samarkand. This campaign took place in the year 1505. Having spent the winter at Samarkand, and being now master of all the country between the Oxus and the Jaxartes, as well as of Ferghana, Khuarezm, and Hissar, &c., he now determined to conquer Khorassan, ruled by the famous Hussein-Murza, who was then a very old man. He first made an attack on Balkh, which he captured, and then withdrew again to Samarkand. Hussein thereupon summoned the neighbouring princes to his assistance, but he almost immediately afterwards died.

This news did not stop preparations. Baber continued his march from Kabul to assist his relatives, and after a progress of 800 miles joined the sons of Sultan Hussein Murza at their camp on the river Murghab. Two of these sons had been jointly raised to the throne, a subject of cynical comment, by Baber, who quotes the passage from the Gulistan, that "although ten dervishes can sleep on one rug, a whole division of the world is too small for two kings." He was not long in quitting the murzas, who were given up to luxury and dissipation, and returned to his own dominions. Meanwhile (*i.e.*, in the spring of 1507) Sheibani once more crossed the Oxus. Baber tells us that Shah Mansur Bakhshi, who governed Andikhud, was treacherous, and sent to tell Sheibani to hasten his approach, and when the latter came near that place "he dressed himself very fine, put a plume on his head, and taking along with him a peshkent and a present of his choicest curiosities, issued forth. The Uzbegs, who had no officer of rank with them, flocked round him and quickly plundered him and his people of all their finery."[†] Having captured Andikhud, Sheibani advanced to Baba Khaki, where the army of Khorassan lay under the joint rulers of that province, Badiaez zeman Murza and Mozaffer Murza, but indecision, uncertainty, discord and intrigue reigned in the camp. In June, 1507, Sheibani crossed the Murghab, and advanced against Baba Khaki, where the army of Khorassan lay. Having crossed the river and marched to Siraks he attacked the camp of Murzas. No preparations were made. When Sheibani arrived a stampede ensued. One old chief, named Zulnun Arghun, who, infatuated by the statements of certain astrologers, firmly believed he was to win the title of Huzeberulla, or Lion of God, and to defeat the Uzbegs, kept his ground at Kara Rebat against 50,000 Uzbegs, with 100 or 150 men." He was captured and beheaded.[‡] The Murzas fled to Herat, where they rested only a few hours and then fled again, leaving their mothers, sisters, and families to find shelter as they could in the adjoining fort of Ekhtiar ud din. Sheibani pursued and at once took possession of

---

* Vambery, 259. Note. † Baber's Memoirs, 221, 222. ‡ Baber, 222.

the city (Haidar says it is not known how it fell). Two or three weeks
after the fort also surrendered, and with it the harems, treasures, &c.,
of the murzas. "More generous than the former conquerors of the city,"
says Vambery, "Sheibani contented himself with levying a contribution
of 100,000 tengas, and spared this celebrated seat of science and art the
infliction of a visit from his plundering Uzbegs. He took up his abode
outside the city; the members of his fugitive adversary's family were
presented to him, and although himself at that time fifty-eight years old,
he fell so violently in love at first sight with the bride of Muzaffar
Hussein Murza, that in spite of all representations and the assurance
that she was already the legal wife of the above-named Timurid, he
determined to marry her. The treasures of the family, including an
enormous quantity of gold and silver plate and valuable rubies, onyxes,
pearls, and diamonds, were brought out to the camp. The family of
Bediaezzeman was treated with every mark of respect and consideration,
and all the people who from fear of the Uzbegs had hidden among the
rocky defiles of the Badgiz hills gradually returned and resumed their
ordinary occupations.*

After the capture of Herat; each of the Timurid princes retired to his
own government. Sheibani sent detachments of his army against them.
The contest was not prolonged, though several battles were fought in
different provinces. The victorious Uzbegs marched in every direction over Khorassan which was soon prostrate before them. All
the murzas fell in action, or were put to death when prisoners in
the course of the next year or two, except Badia-ez-zeman Murza,
the eldest, who fled to Shah Ismael, of Persia, and after various
adventures died at Constantinople about ten years later.† Baber
thus describes Sheibani's doings when at Herat: "In spite of his
supreme ignorance he had the vanity to deliver lectures in explanation
of the Koran to Kazi Ekhtiar and Muhammed Mir Yusuf, who were
among the most celebrated Mollas in Khorassan and Herat. He also
took a pen and corrected the writing and drawings of Mollah Sultan Ali,
and Behzad, the painter. When at any time he happened to have composed any of his dull couplets he read it from the pulpit, hung it up in
the charsu (or public market), and levied a benevolence from the people
on the joyful occasion. He did know something of the reading the
Koran, but he was guilty of a number of stupid absurd presumptions,
infidel words and deeds, such as I have mentioned."‡ This is the
testimony of an enemy. Vambery, judging from such of his compositions as are stil extant, says, that both for ideas and language
they are among the best productions of eastern Turkish literature, and
show a thorough knowledge of Turkish, Persian, and Arabic. Sheibani
was now master of the whole country, from the deserts of Jitteh to the

* Vambery, op. cit., 262.   † Erskine's Hist. of India, i. 260.   ‡ Memoirs, 224.

Hindu Kush and Paramisan mountains, and the farthest limits of Khorasan. He now turned his attention to Kandahar which had only recently been conquered by Baber. At this time Muhammed Hussein, the father of Haidar, who had escaped from Uratippa, as I have mentioned, had afterwards stirred up a rebellion against Baber at Kabul, was pardoned by the latter, and allowed to return to Khorasan. Before he reached Farrah he met crowds of fugitives, who reported how Sheibani had scattered the murzas. Having halted there three months, Sheibani sent for him, and treated him with great distinction, and he afterwards accompanied him to Samarkand.*

Meanwhile Sheibani marched rapidly upon Kandahar, which at once surrendered, its garrison retiring under Baber's brother Nasir Murza, into the citadel. Here they were hard pressed by the Uzbegs, who ran mines in various directions, and Nasir Murza was wounded in the neck with an arrow; but when the fort was on the point of surrendering Sheibani hastily retired, the cause being that his harem, which he had sent to the strong fort of Nirehtu, east of Herat, had been surprised by some hill tribes and captured.† He now employed himself in hunting down the remaining members of the family of Sultan Hussein Murza. Spreading his forces over Khorasan, he fought actions during the summer of 1507, at Meshed Nishapur, Asterabad and Turshiz, in which the armies of the Timurid princes were uniformly beaten and completely scattered. He then returned to Mavera un Nehr to repel an invasion of the Kazaks.‡

During the summer of 1508 we find him putting an end to Mahmud Khan, of Tashkend. After his brother's death, Mahmud surrendered all the country, from Kashgar to the borders of China, over which he had a joint authority to the latter's children and himself, nomadized in the deserts of Mongolistan. After spending five years in this way he was persuaded (finding himself hard pressed) to trust himself in Ferghana, where Sheibani then was. The latter ordered him to be seized at Khojend. where he was put to death, with five of his sons. He was buried in the mausoleum of Sheikh Masilek uddin. Khojendi.§ According to the Tarikhi Seyid Rakein, Mahmud Khan had made an invasion of Sheibani's dominions, with the intention of capturing Andijan and even Samarkand, when he fell with his five sons in a fierce battle on the banks of the Khojend. This was in 914 hej. (i.e., 1508).‖

About the same time another unruly person, namely, Haidar's father, Muhammed Hussein Murza, was summoned to Sheibani's presence, and his escort it seems received orders to put him to death. He was buried in the mausoleum of Amii Seyid Husseini. Sheibani also ordered Haidar to be drowned, but he escaped.¶ Vambery says the province of Jorjan fell into Sheibani's power this same year. The year following we find him

---

* Erskine, op. cit., 257.   † Baber's Memoirs, 233.   ‡ Tar Rash. Erskine, 295, 296.
§ Erskine, 291, 102   ‖ Vambery, op cit., 263. Note, 1   ¶ Tar. Rash

3 R

crossing swords with a more potent enemy, namely, the Kazaks of Berenduk Khan, who were so closely related in blood to his own Uzbegs.

At this time, as I have shown, Kassim was the *de facto* ruler of the Kazaks, and his army numbered 200,000 warriors. Haidar tells us that on the approach of winter each took up his quarters where there was food for his cattle. Sheibani planted himself at Kuruk, whence he sent people to explore. One day they learned that Kasim Khan was close at hand. The rumour was a false one, and had been spread by Pulun Sirkhas, one of the Kazak amirs. The Uzbeg detachment did not wait, but abandoning the booty it had captured, hurried back to inform Sheibani, who thereupon beat the drum for retreat. " Nothing was attended to," says Haidar. " He that stayed stayed, and he that went went," and the Uzbegs reached Samarkand in disorder in the end of winter. Sheibani went on to Khorasan, where he waited till the spring. These events happened in the winter of 1509-10.[*] This was the first serious break in the hitherto triumphant career of Sheibani, and was the harbinger of much more serious disaster at hand. In the beginning of the summer of 1510, he marched against the Hazarahs, robber tribes, who were descendants of the Mongols of Khulagu Khan, and who lived in North-western Afghanistan. They were not to be found, having withdrawn into the recesses of the mountains. He, therefore, withdrew. His retreat lay through the precipitous defiles through which the river Helmund flows. There his people suffered terribly and lost many cattle. It was difficult to descend to the stream at all, and even where a descent was practicable the paths were so narrow that it was impossible to bring water up by them to supply such an army, and it accordingly returned in a shattered state to Khorasan. As winter was approaching and his two divisions had suffered severely, he gave a general leave of absence to his men from the frontier of Irak to those of Turkestan to return to their homes.[†]

Shah Ismael, according to his flatterers, was a descendant of the seventh Imaum, but, according to Vambery, he was of Turkish descent. He had created by his prowess a considerable power in Persia proper, Kerman and Irak, and had inherited the blood as well as the position of the Great Turkoman, chief Uzan Hassan. His mother was that chieftain's daughter. When Sheibani ravaged Khorasan, he was imprudent enough in his wantonness to pillage Shah Ismael's borders, and especially the province of Kerman. His arrogance was sharpened by religious zeal, for Shah Ismael was a Shia, and had given that sect a great ascendancy in Persia, while Sheibani was a Sunni. The Shah remonstrated with Sheibani for this attack upon what he called his hereditary dominions. To this he received the jeering answer, that sovereignty descended through the father and not the mother, through males and not females. That the unequal match between his family and the females of Uzan

* Tar. Rash. Erskine, op. cit., i. 296.   † Tar. Rash., 208.   Erskine, op. cit., 297.

Hassan could confer no right. He reminded him of the saying, the son should follow his father's trade, the daughter her mother's, and insultingly sent him as a present a beggar's staff and keshkul (*i.e.*, a dish made of half a cocoanut in which the dervishes collected alms), adding, " If thou hast forgotten thy father's trade this may serve to recall it to thy memory, but if thou would'st place thy foot on the steps of the throne remember

> He that would clasp to his breast royalty as his bride
> Must woo her in the battle fray athwart sharp scimiters."

In conclusion, he remarked that he intended shortly to make a pilgrimage to Mekka and would visit him on the way. Shah Ismael sent a dignified answer which concluded with some spirit.

> Boast not thyself, O vain youth, of thy father who is dead,
> Pride not thyself on bones as if thou wert a dog.

He said he too meditated a pilgrimage to Meshed, and would there wait on the Khan. In return for his present he sent him a spindle and distaff, and, alluding to the quotation about the wooing of royalty, he said, " I have tightened my girdle for a deadly contest, and placed the foot of determination in the stirrup of victory. If thou wilt meet me face to face in fight like a man our quarrel will at once be decided. But if thou would'st rather shirk into a corner then thou mayest find what I have sent of some use.".

> We have sparred long enough let us now exchange hard blows in the field,
> He who falls borne down in the combat let him fall.*

This answer was quickly followed by the march of the Shah. The scattered Uzbeg detachments retired and concentrated at Herat. Sheibani did not feel strong enough to oppose him having so recently disbanded his army. He therefore retired to Merv, in Northern Khorasan, leaving a garrison in Herat which was soon obliged to follow him. Shah Ismael first visited Meshed and the tomb of the Imaum Riza, and then pursued the Uzbegs. Near Tukerabad a well-contested battle was fought in which they were defeated and driven under the walls of Merv. Shah Ismael pitched his camp close to the city. Meanwhile Sheibani sent messengers to summon forces from Mavera un Nehr and Turkestan. Fearful of having to keep up a long blockade in a desert country, fearful also that effective aid might come to his enemy, Shah Ismael wrote a scornful letter to the latter saying he had been more punctual in his visit to Meshed, than the latter to Irak ; but that Sheibani had shut the door in the face of his guest, that he was now returning home but should still be glad to meet him when he went to Mekka. He then drew off his forces which were 40,000 strong. Sheibani, stung with these scornful words, followed him with 20,000 horsemen and a number of the chiefs and grandees, who had joined him, nor would he take the advice of those who wished him to await the arrival of the contingents on their way from

---

* Erskine's India, i. 300.   Vambery, op. cit., 266-268.

beyond the Oxus. He would not, he said, let them share in the evening's plunder, to do so would be a loss both here and hereafter. Shah Ismael's retreat was apparently only a ruse; for he set his forces in battle array at Mahmudabad of Merv. The Uzbegs were attacked both in rear and front. They fought with great bravery, but were broken. Sheibani with his retreat cut off, attended by about 500 men, chiefly the sons of sultans, heads of tribes, &c., was obliged to take shelter in a cattle-pound. This had no gate on the further side. When all hope seemed gone of retrieving the day, he and the other fugitives attempted to escape by leaping over the wall of the enclosure towards the bank of the river, but they fell in heaps on each other, and the Khan was overlaid and smothered by the numbers who crowded after him. After the contest his body was disentangled from the heaps of slain by which it was covered. His head was cut off and presented to Shah Ismael, who ordered the lifeless trunk to be dismembered, and the limbs to be sent to different parts of the empire to be exposed to the popular gaze. The skin of the head stuffed with hay, was sent in scorn to Sultan Bajazet, the Turkish emperor of Constantinople, who was an ally of his brother Sunni, the great Uzbeg leader. The skull set in gold was made into a drinking cup, which the Shah was proud of displaying at his great entertainments.* The same author tells us a ghastly anecdote about the end of the great Uzbeg leader. One Aga Rustam Rozefzun, the ruler of Mazanderan, and who still held out against Shah Ismael, had been in the habit of saying that his hand was on the skirts of Sheibani's garment, an idiom meaning that he clung to him for assistance and protection. One day, when he was sitting in state at a grand festival, a special messenger from Shah Ismael advanced fearlessly into his presence, and with a loud voice, delivered a message from the Shah. "Though thy hand was never on the hem of Sheibani Khan's robe, yet his is now on thine," and with these words he flung the rigid hand of the Uzbeg chief on the skirt of the prince's robe and withdrew uninjured through the midst of the stupefied assembly.† In Central Asia Vambery says the story is current that Sheibani's remains were buried in the splendid college he had built at Samarkand, where his grave is held in great reverence as that of a martyr. Such was the tragic and perhaps becoming end of the adventurous chieftain; the Turkish Ishmael, whose life was a long and bitter struggle against his neighbours, and whose administrative skill had so far made compact his robber subjects that they easily survived the disaster when he was killed, and are found still ruling in the border lands of Persia. Vambery justly remarks that Sheibani was the last of the great desert leaders who succeeded in forming a formidable power in Central Asia, and that henceforth the Sunnis of the West and those of the East were effectually separated, the Safi dynasty

---

* Erskine's Hist. of India, i. 304.   † Id.

having driven a wedge of Shias between them, while the Oxus became once more the boundary between Iran and Turan. Sheibani was notable patron of learned men, and built mosques and colleges at Samarkand, Bukhara, and Tashkend. He took into his service many cultivated men who were left homeless and destitute by the death of Sultan Hussein Murza, and gave them liberal salaries, and he was always accompanied even in his campaigns by various learned men who exercised great influence over him, and we are told that when the Mollah Binai, Sheibani's poet laureate, handed to the philosophers of Herat the summons for the surrender of the town, they went to Sheibani's camp, and it was entirely by their influence that he contented himself with imposing only a money contribution upon them. In these respects he whs sharply contrasted with his rude unsophisticated nomad followers.[*]

When the news of Sheibani's death arrived at Merv, every man who was able fled with his wife and family, while many who had no means of transport left them to their fate. Ubeidulla Sultan of Bukhara, and Muhammed Timur Sultan of Samarkand, the nephew and son of Sheibani, who had arrived at Merv with the troops of Mavera un Nehr, which were still upbroken, entered the fort, carried off the dead chief's harem and what valuables they could hurriedly collect, and hasted away the same night. Numbers, however, were left behind. All the Uzbegs found in the place were put to the sword by the Persians, and the women were carried into bondage. The inhabitants of Merv were included in the general massacre.[†] The Mongol auxiliaries in Sheibani's service, by whom we must understand the recent subjects of the elder Khan Mahmud, now separated from the Uzbegs and set out for Kundus, plundering as they went. The Uzbegs abandoned Khorasan, and Shah Ismael took possession of Herat, and commenced a severe persecution of the Sunnis. Haidar tells us how he ordered the chief men to assemble in the Melkan mosque, and there to read the Khutbeh in his name, and to pour curses on the companions of the Prophet and the faithful Aisha: They assembled, but remained dumb till Hafiz Zems ed din, who was the preacher (Khalib), was placed in the pulpit. Having poured out praise and thanksgiving to the Giver of all good, when he came to the commemoration of the holy companions of Muhammed, "the hand of zeal and faithfulness to Islam, seizing the collar of manhood of Hafiz, made him spurn all regard for the deceitful life of this world, and press forward to the real and substantial enjoyment of the world that is to be, and he said, 'For many years have I read the prayers for the prince in the legal and orthodox fashion ; shall I change it now, when the sun of my life is about to set, and my old years have come. If I hesitated doing so in the morning of life, what could I benefit by becoming an apostate when its evening draws near. God forbid that I should do it,' and so saying he

---

[*] Vambery, 271.   [†] Tar. Rash. Erskine's Hist. of India, i. 505.

repeated the formula in praise of the Prophet and his companions in the orthodox fashion. The accursed Kizilbashis—God curse them"—says Haidar, "all rose, and dragging him down from the pulpit cut the hoary old man to pieces."

Shah Ismael then summoned the Sheikh ul Islam, and bade him also curse the Prophet's companions. He replied in scornful terms, whereupon Ismael shot an arrow at him. Dragging it out of his body, the old man rubbed his face and beard with blood from the wound, saying "Praise be to God, that after a life of eighty years, at length, because of my defence of the faith, and opposition to false religion, I have been able to see my white hair bathed red in the blood of martyrdom." Ismael, unmoved, drew another arrow, shot it at him, and ordered his people to hang him on a tree and then to cut the tree down. They did so, and then took him and burnt him on the Malik Bazaar. The persecution of the Sunnis lasted as long as Shah Ismael was in Khorasan.*

Directly after the fatal battle of Merv the Uzbegs withdrew, as I have said, across the Amu Daria or Oxus, and abandoned Khorasan. For some time there was an interregnum, and Janibeg Sultan apparently acted as regent. A few days after the battle a messenger with the news reached Kabul, with his feet frostbitten and his strength exhausted by crossing the snowy mountains. When Baber heard the news he deemed it a good opportunity to recover his ancient dominions, and to dissipate the broken power of the Uzbegs, and made an immediate advance upon Hissar. The Uzbegs were, however, by no means crushed. Under Janibeg Sultan, who held a kind of interim authority, they put to death a number of so-called Mongols (i.e., Kashgarians) in Mavera un Nehr, and gathered themselves together. Hamza Sultan and Mehdi Sultan, who were in command of the district, leaving a garrison at Hissar, advanced on Waksh, Baber having reached Desht Kulak, one of the chief towns of the Khutlan, he and Hamza Sultan tried respectively to surprise each other, and each occupied the ground abandoned by the other. Both, it seems, expected to find his enemy weaker than he was, and when the truth dawned on them they withdrew from one another, Baber towards Kunduz and Hamza to Hissar. Both at the moment believed they had made a great escape, and each in a few days heard of the flight of the other.† While Baber was at Kunduz an embassy was sent to him from Shah Ismael, escorting his sister Khanzada Begim, who after marrying and being divorced from Sheibani, had been married to Seyid Hadé, a member of a religious family who had been killed at Merv Baber received her very gladly. He took the opportunity to despatch an embassy in turn to Shah Ismael to congratulate him on his victory and to ask for his assistance to reconquer Mavera un Nehr. This was granted, and a contingent of Persians soon joined his forces. Notwith-

* Tar. Rash., 266, &c.   † Brskine, op. cit., 307, 308.

standing which, however, the Uzbegs were not daunted, and when Baber reached Pul Sangin, or the stone bridge, on the Surghab, Hamza Sultan from Hissar had already occupied it. He found the enemy very powerful and venturesome, for they crossed the river lower down by swimming, and tried to turn his position. He therefore retired in all haste by very arduous roads towards Abdera, and reached a position which was deemed very strong. About midnight news reached his camp that the Uzbegs were advancing in force. Baber rode out to reconnoitre, and noticed there was only one narrow road by which the enemy could march on his position. The Uzbegs, nevertheless, made a determined assault and continued tlie struggle till nightfall, when, having to withdraw for water, Baber's people were encouraged, made a general charge, and routed the enemy. Hamza Sultan and Mehdi Sultan were captured and taken before Baber. Their fate is condensed in Haidar's graphic phrase, "What they had done to the khakan of the Mongols, and the sultans of the Jagatais, that did he to them." The Uzbegs were pursued unceasingly as far as Derbend Ahinein.* By this victory the country of Hissar, together with Kunduz, Khutlan, and Khozar, apparently fell into Baber's hands, fresh troops now joined him from Shah Ismael and the neighbouring tribes, and his prestige grew so rapidly that his army soon numbered 60,000 men.† He determined to follow up his victory quickly. The Persian detachment was commanded by Ahmed Sultan Sefi (who was related to the Shah Ali Khan Istijlu) and Shahrukk Khan Afshar, of whom the two former had served with distinction against the Turks.‡ Baber marched on Karshi where Ubeidulla Sultan, who held the appanage of Bukhara, had fortified himself. By the advice of his officers he determined to pass the fortress by, and to hasten on to Bukhara: Ubeidulla, when he learnt this, also left in haste for the same place, but Baber forestalled him and arrived there first, whereupon the Uzbegs passed by and retired towards Turkestan, plundering *en route*. The Uzbeg sultans who were at Samarkand being alarmed also withdrew towards Turkestan, and thus Mavera un Nehr was once more clear of these marauders after they had occupied it nine years.§

Meanwhile they were equally unfortunate elsewhere, for Sultan Said Khan and Haidar's uncle Syed Muhammed Murza seized Andijan and secured Ferghana. The Uzbegs who had marched against them, having learnt of Baber's victory were discouraged and withdrew.

Baber was received at Samarkand with great rejoicings, and duly mounted the throne there on the 8th of October, 1571. The dominions of Baber now stretched from "the deserts of Tartary to the farthest limits of Ghazni, and comprehended Ghazni, Kunduz and Hissar, Samarkand and Bukhara, Ferghana, Tashkend, and Sairam."‖ He pro-

---

* Tar. Rash. † Tar. Rash. Baber's Memoirs, 242. ‡ Erskine, op. cit., 315.
§ Tar. Rash. Erskine's India, L 315, 316. ‖ Erskine, op. cit., 316 and 319.

ceeded to carve out appanages for his relatives, little aware of the short
tenure he was to have of the greater part of that wide tract.

After his victory Baber seems to have dismissed his Persian auxiliaries,
but he did not withdraw from under the shadow of his patron. One
authority, the Mirza Bokander, says the Khutbeh was actually said in the
Shah's name. He is said to have adopted the Persian dress, and ordered
his troops to adopt it also, and particularly the Persian cap, distinguished
by twelve points emblematic of the twelve Imaums, and by a long
strip of red cloth issuing from the centre and hanging down the back,
whence the Persian soubriquet of Kizilbashis or Red Heads. This com-
placency towards the Shias aroused bitter animosity in those centres of
orthodoxy, Samarkand and Bukhara, and Baber speedily lost his popularity.
His position was an awkward one, for he could hardly hope to oppose
the Uzbegs successfully without the help of his patron, Shah Ismael·
This state of things greatly facilitated the campaign which the Uzbegs
now renewed. In the spring of 1512 one of their armies marched
towards Tashkend, while another under their famous leader, Ubeidulla,
went towards Bukhara. Baber having sent a contingent to the assistance of Tashkend massed his remaining forces to crush Ubeidulla, who
thereupon withdrew. He was overtaken at Kul Malik, where a fierce
and important battle ensued. The candid Haidar, who was Baber's
cousin and Ubeidulla's brother-in-law, and was a Sunni, says the
Uzbegs only numbered 3,000 men, while Baber had 40,000 with him, and
he adds, "God raises whom he pleases and depresses whom he pleases
without regard to numbers." Baber was in fact defeated, and fell back
on Samarkand. This battle was fought on the 18th of April, 1512. To
Samarkand Baber was quickly followed, and as the granaries there
were empty and the people ill-disposed to him he withdrew and retired
to Hissar, whence he sent messengers to Shah Ismael to tell him of his
misfortune and to ask assistance. Meanwhile a number of Uzbeg
sultans and chieftains set out from Derbend to assail him there. He
seemed to have barricaded the streets and prepared to defend himself
bravely. When the Uzbegs saw this they withdrew again.* Shah Ismael,
on hearing of his *protégé's* position, ordered the Amir Yar Muhammed
styled Nejim Sani (*i.e.*, the second star), his Minister of Finance, whom
he had intrusted with the settlement of Khorasan, to march to his
assistance. These combined forces amounted to about 60,000 men.

This army overran Khozar, then attacked Karshi, which the Nejim
called Ubeidulla's lair, and which was strongly fortified. It was besieged
and carried by storm; the governor, with all in the place, whether Uzbegs
or citizens, to the number of 15,000, were slaughtered without reference
to age, sex, or sanctity. Among the victims was Mevlana Binai, the poet,
who was a great wit; with him fell many Seyids and holy men, "and from

---

* Baber's Memoirs, 305.

that time forward Murza Sekander Amir Nejim prospered in none of his undertakings."* This act of Shia fanaticism disgusted Baber, who detached himself from his ally. The Persians continued their advance and approached the fort of Gijuvan, into which Ubeidulla and Muhammed Timur Sultan, the Uzbeg chiefs, threw themselves. A fierce battle ensued, intensified in its bitterness by the religious fury of the combatants. In an hour, says the Sunni narrator, Mirza Haidar, "the influence of Islam began to prevail over heresy and infidelity, victory declared for the true faith; the invaders were routed, and most of them fell in the field, and the arrows of Gijuvan revenged the sabre of Karshi ; Mir Nejim and all the chief officers of the Turkomans were sent to hell fire."† The Persian historian, who wielded a friendly pen, in describing Nejim's luxury says, " 100 sheep, an innumerable number of chickens, ducks, and geese, and 40 cwt. of cinnamon, saffron, and other spices, were used daily in his kitchen, and the dishes were all either of gold, or the richest porcelain."‡ By this famous battle, one of the most important in its consequences in the world's history, Baber was finally excluded from Mavera un Nehr, and had to turn his ambitious view elsewhere. It is said, the Persians, disgusted by the insolence and haughtiness of the Amir Nejim, did not assist him cordially—whence his capture. The defeat was a great blow to Persian prestige, and it was ascribed by their partisans to the treachery of Baber, who is even reported to have shot an arrow into the town with one of his caustic couplets attached to it, in which he intimated his hatred of his allies.§

KUCHKUNJI KHAN.

The internal history of the Uzbegs, after the death of Sheibani, is complicated, and has been much misunderstood. We are greatly indebted to M. Veliaminof Zernof for the light he has thrown upon it. In the first place their government was not an absolute sovereignty, but, as in Russia, in medieval times, it was broken up into a number of appanages, each under its own Khan, and all subservient to an over-chief, who was styled Khakan, and answered to the Grand Prince in Russia, who had a similar feudal authority over the appanaged princes. On the death of a Khakan the appanaged princes met together to choose a successor ; and their choice, as is usual in the East, generally fell upon the senior representative of the house, not necessarily the heir by right of primogeniture, but the oldest living representative of the senior line. It has followed, in consequence, that in many notices of Bukhara there has not been a sufficient discrimination between the line of Khakans, or chief Khans, and those of the appanaged princes, and the two lists have been confused

* Erskine, op. cit., 324.
† Erskine, 324, 325.   ‡ Vambery's Bokharah, 276.   § Erskine, op. cit., 325, 326.

3 8

together. I will try and steer more clearly, with my very learned friend M. Veliaminof Zernof for a guide.

The victory of Gijuvan secured for the Uzbegs the control of Mavera un Nehr, and we are told by Hafiztanish, in the Abdulla Nameh, that a meeting of the various Uzbeg chiefs was held, and Janibeg, who had beer a quasi regent, redistributed the appanages. Kuchkunji received Samarkand, and Muhammed Timur, the son of Sheibani, was given joint authority with him; Kuchkunji's brother Suiunich, was given Tashkend. Ubeidulla, the son of Mahmud Sultan, and nephew of Sheibani, was given his father's appanage of Bukhara, together with Karakul and Karshi, while Janibeg reserved for himself Miankal (which in Sheibani's reign had belonged to his own son Muhammed Timur) and the Soghd of Samarkand, with the towns of Kermineh and Nur.* The same author goes on to say that this same year (i.e., in 918) the Sultans proceeded to elect Kuchkunji as Khakan of the Uzbegs. Kuchkunji, according to Vambery, means nomad or vagrant.† He was also called Kuchum.‡ Although Kuchkunji was de jure ruler, Ubeidulla, the prince of Bukhara, had the chief authority, and was the most famous leader of the Uzbegs at this time. When Baber retired from Samarkand he had with him a number of the turbulent eastern Turks, called Mongols by Haidar. Having some grievance against him they attempted to waylay and kill him. He, however, escaped to the fort of Hissar. They then took up a position on the hills of Karatigin, whence they wasted the district round Hissar. Their exactions and ravage were so great that a famine followed in the city of Hissar. This was succeeded by a pestilence, and thousands of women and children were sold into captivity among the Uzbegs. To add to the general horrors the winter was very severe.§ On hearing of this Ubeidulla marched from Bukhara to punish the marauders. Knowing they could expect no help from Baber they took up a strong position on the hills of Surghab and Waksh, where they were protected by mountains on either flank, and by deep snow in front. A sudden thaw opened a way for the Uzbegs. Many of the so-called Mongols rushed into the river, and "thus reached the flames of hell through water," says Haidar, while many who escaped this went in the same direction by the sword. Some were captured, and others retired to Andijan. Hissar thus fell again into the hands of the Uzbegs, and Baber, leaving Khan Murza in Badakhshan, withdrew towards Kabul.‖

We must now revert, somewhat. When Ubeidulla marched against Baber at Bukhara, his great uncle, Suiunich, moved against Tashkend, which he besieged and captured. As we have seen it was assigned to him as an appanage. In the summer of 1512 Sultan Said Khan, who still ruled in

---

* Vel. Zernof, Coins of Bukhara, &c., 353-355.   † Op. cit., 274. Note, 1.
‡ Vel. Zernof, Coins of Bukhara, 338 and 358.   § Erskine, op. cit., 327, 328.   ‖ Tar. Rash.

Ferghana, marched against Suiunich with 5,000 men. The Uzbegs met him with 7,000, and a struggle ensued at Beshkend, in which he was defeated and wounded, and then retired to Andijan. After the battle of Gijuvan Suiunich advanced against him, Sultan Said thereupon put strong garrisons in Andijan, Akhsi, and Marghinan, and then repaired to the hill country to the south, so as to be prepared to harass him should he lay siege to any place.* Sultan Said, in his distress, now appealed to Kasim, the powerful Khan of the Kazaks, who controlled an enormous force in the deserts of Kipchak. He was eager to accept the offer. The governor of Sairam surrendered the keys of that fortress, and he then marched on towards Tashkend, plundering the country on the way, after which he withdrew. The attack, however, and the fear of its repetition kept Suiunich quiet during 1513 and 1514. During the summer of 1514, when Kasim Khan was absent on a distant expedition, the Uzbegs proceeded to assail Ferghana in force. Sultan Said Khan and his amirs deemed it hopeless to resist them, and determined to cross the mountains towards Kashgar, and to carve a new kingdom for themselves there, which they accordingly did, and he ruled over Kashgar for many years. Thus was Ferghana added to the dominions of the Uzbegs.†

Let us now turn our attention to Khorasan. According to the Tarikhi, Alem arai, Ismael, after his victory over Sheibani, in which the latter fell, intended to invade Mavera un Nehr in person, and had advanced as far as Meimeneh and Kara Robat, when he was met by envoys from Muhammed Timur Sultan, Sheibani's son, and other chiefs, bearing rich presents and offers of peace. As Shah Ismael wished to repair to Ajerbaidjan and the frontiers of Turkey, where he had important business, he readily agreed to this, and it was arranged that all the land south of the Oxus, including Khuarezm or Khiva, should belong to the Shah.‡ When Shah Ismael sent Nejim Sani to the help of Baber, this pact was clearly broken, and we accordingly find that after the battle of Gijuvan, Ubeidulla crossed the Oxus, near Charjui, with Janibeg, the chief of Kermineb, and being joined at Murghab by Muhammed Timur Sultan, Sheibani's son, who had advanced from Samarkand, by way of Kerki, they proceeded to attack Meshed. Other bodies of them advanced by way of Termes as far as Balkh, devastating the country.§ Shah Ismael now marched to the rescue, whereupon the Uzbegs retired. He caused several officers to be executed for having deserted Nejim in the late battle, while he laid a heavy hand on some of his Sunni subjects, who were accused of encouraging the Uzbegs and of persecuting the Shias This was in 1513 ‖ For some years the Uzbegs seem to have remained quiet. They were probably restrained by fear of the famous Shah. That potent chief died in 1523, and was succeeded by his infant son, Shah

* Erskine, op. cit., 330.   † Erskine, 331, 332.   ‡ Erskine, op. cit., 309, 310.
§ Vambery, 177.   ‖ Erskine, op. cit., 326, 327.

Tahmasp. This favourable opportunity was not neglected by Ubeidulla, who crossed the Oxus, and entered Khorasan. Durmish Khan Shamlu, beglerbeg or governor of that province, took shelter in Herat, where the Uzbegs besieged him for several months, but finally raised the siege.[*] Durmish Khan died in the following year. The governor of Meshed having been killed in a civil strife, and a sharp contention having arisen among the Amirs, there was confusion in Khorasan, and we accordingly find that in 1525, Ubeidulla crossed the Oxus at Charjui, and captured Merv, where ten or fifteen peasants were killed. Passing on to Sirakhs, he found thirty or forty Kizilbashis, who refused to surrender the place, but the inhabitants, being divided in their affections, a friendly band opened one of the gates ; the Uzbegs entered, and put the Persians there to the sword. They then advanced to Meshed, the sacred city of the Shias, which being defenceless, submitted. Tus was now blockaded for eight months, and then, in spite of the capitulation entered into, all the men in the place were massacred, and the women carried off into slavery.[†]

Vambery adds that concurrently with this attack, Abusaid, the son of Kuchkunji, made an attack on Herat, which failed.[‡] The Uzbegs were more successful in another direction. Under Kara Kitin they laid siege to Balkh, which still belonged to the Persians. Two officers in Baber's service went over to the enemy, who soon afterwards captured the city, and then made a raid upon Baber's own dominions, reduced Ibak, Sarabagh, and Khuram, places situated in the valley of the river Khulm, while the garrison of Ghuri, on the river of the same name, panic-stricken at the fall of Balkh, also surrendered.[§] This was in 1525. After capturing Meshed and Tus, Ubeidulla advanced and secured Asterabad, where he left his son, Abdul Aziz, as governor, and himself went towards Balkh. The Persians having received large reinforcements from Azerbaidjan, the young prince withdrew, and joined his father. The combined forces gave the Persians a severe defeat near Bostam, which again put Asterabad in his power. He now confided it to Renish or Zinish Behadur Khan, and went to spend the winter of 933 at Ghurian.[||] During 934 Ubeidulla pressed the siege of Herat, which resisted bravely for seven months under its governor, Hussein Khan Shamlu, when news arrived that Zinish Behadur had been defeated. We are told that the governors of Sebsevar and Asterabad attacked him near Damghan. At first they were successful, but he afterwards won a complete victory, when both of them were killed. Meanwhile Shah Tahmasp, at the head of forty thousand men, came to the rescue of his people, utterly defeated the Uzbegs at Damghan, and killed Zinish. In their sweeping course, says Erskine, they routed a second Uzbeg detachment, which accordingly fell back on Ubeidulla,

[*] Erskine, i. 457.   [†] Erskine, i. 457. Baber's Memoirs, 342-344.   [‡] Op. cit., 278.
    [§] Baber, 350. Erskine, op. cit., 458.   [||] Erskine, 489.

who was still besieging Herat. He raised the siege, and withdrew towards Merv, where he summoned the various Uzbeg princes of Mavera un Nehr, &c., to a general rendezvous. Kuchkunji Khan came from Samarkand, and with him his sons, Abusaid Sultan and Pulad Sultan, and the sons of Janibeg Khan; Suiunich Khan from Tashkend, the sons of Hamza Sultan and Mehdi Sultan from Hissar, and Kitin Kara Sultan from Balkh. Thus was collected the largest army hitherto assembled by the Uzbegs. Baber says they numbered one hundred and fifty thousand, Mir Yahia Saifi, the author of the "Leb al Towarik," one hundred and twenty-one thousand, and the "Alim-arai Abasi," eighty thousand veterans, exclusive of other troops.* So great an army, says the Persian historian, had not crossed the Amu since the days of Jingis Khan. The Persians, according to Baber, numbered forty thousand men, but they were veterans, disciplined in the Turkish fashion, and had seen hard service against the Ottomans. They also had a body of two thousand artillerymen, and six thousand matchlock men,† while the Uzbegs were armed with their primitive weapons, and this difference was no doubt an immense moral as well as physical advantage.

Shah Tahmasp having visited Meshed and other holy places, intrenched himself strongly in a position near Jam, on the way to Herat. The Uzbegs, who interpreted this as a sign of weakness, advanced to attack Meshed. Their plan, says Erskine, was singularly illustrative of the superstition of their age and tribe. While the main army encamped at Meshed, twenty thousand horsemen were to scour the country round the enemy's camp, and not to allow a man to show outside his trenches. Meanwhile their magicians were to work their enchantments and to make the enemy spell-bound, so that not one of them was to escape. But Shah Tahmasp did not wait for these preparations to be complete.‡ He advanced to meet them, and the two armies met on the 25th of September, 1529, at Jam. Vambery says it as on the vigil of the ninth Muharrem, on which the Shia Muhammedans keep the anniversary of the tragic end of Hussein near Kerbela with every demonstration of woe. He tells us Jam is now the first place one enters on Persian territory in coming from Herat, and is a miserable village, whose inhabitants live in mortal terror of the Turkomans.§ The Persians had their guns in the centre, protected by twenty thousand chosen troops under the personal command of the king. The Uzbegs, as usual with them, outflanked the Persian army, and having turned both flanks, got into the rear and began to plunder the camp, but the Persian centre stood firm, and at a favourable moment, the chains connecting their guns being dropped, the troops stationed behind rushed forward. A furious

* Id., 490. Note. † Erskine, i. 491. ‡ Baber's Memoirs, 390. Erskine, op. cit., 490, 491.
§ Op. cit., 279.

hand-to-hand fight ensued, in which a body of three thousand Persian cuirassiers greatly distinguished themselves. The struggle terminated in the defeat of the Uzbegs with a dreadful slaughter, fifty thousand of them are said to have lain on the field of battle. Twenty thousand Persians lay beside them. Erskine says these numbers are probably much exaggerated. Several of the leading Uzbegs were slain. Kuch-kunji, the Grand Khan, and Ubeidulla escaped, but the latter was wounded. "Janibeg Khan, who had pursued the flying troops of the Persian wings to a great distance supposing the victory secure, returned back the same night, and guided by the fires and lights of the camp, which he thought were those of Ubeidulla, came upon the encampment of Tahmasp. The Persians pursued him but he escaped. Tahmasp shortly after his victory had to turn his attention to his western dominions,"* where the Osmanlis, own brothers of the Uzbegs, were a constant menace to Persia. That the defeat was not overwhelming we gather from the fact that directly Tahmasp retired, Ubeidulla prepared to revenge himself. He crossed the Amu and went to Meshed. This town he blockaded for two months, and then went to Herat, which capitulated after a seven months' siege. Erskine says that in the invasion Ubeidulla did not fail to pay back the Shias for their cruelties to his co-religionists.† Next year his people advanced to Farra, which he attacked for some time, but was eventually obliged to raise the siege, and on hearing that the Persians were advancing in force he abandoned Herat and withdrew to Merv.

Let us now turn elsewhere for a short time. Shah Tahmasp's victory revived Baber's hopes of recovering Mavera un Nehr, and he encouraged his son, Humayun, who governed Badakhshan, to make the attempt. The scare produced by the defeat of Ubeidulla had it seems caused the Uzbeg sultans, who were ruling at Hissar, to abandon that place, where they left Chalmeh, the son of Ibrahim Jani, as governor.‡ Humayun having collected an army of fifty thousand men, and accompanied by Sultan Weis, now marched towards Samarkand, while the latter's brother, Shah Kuli, occupied Hissar, and Tursun Muhammed Sultan marched from Termez and captured Kabadian.§ It is curious that while his son was thus invading the Uzbeg country with Baber's connivance, he himself was entertaining the ambassadors of Kuchkunji in India. They were present at a grand feast he gave at Agra. We are told the Kizilbash or Persian envoys were housed in a tent to the right of his own, and Yunis Ali was selected from the Amirs to sit amongst them, while the Uzbegs were housed in a similar tent on the left, and Abdalla was told off to look after them. At the feast, which is described in great detail, the ambassador of Kuchkunji was presented with Sirkamash robes of muslin, with rich buttons, and a dress of honour suited to his rank.

* Erskine, i. 491.   † Op. cit., ii. 98.   ‡ Baber, 390.   § Id., 399.

He was also presented with a certain weight of gold.* This embassy left Baber on the 31st of January, 1529. He tells us he presented Amin Murza, the envoy of Kuchkunji, with a dagger and belt, an elephant knife, a milek of brocade, and seventy thousand tangas (i.e., small silver coins of the value of a penny). To the Mollah Taghai, the representative of Abusaid Sultan (i.e., the Khakan's son), and to the servants of Meherban Khanim (i.e., his wife) and her son Pulad, vests richly ornamented with buttons, kaftans of rich cloth, &c.† He sent Chapak back with them, as his envoy to the Uzbeg chiefs.‡ Baber's health was at this time failing, and Humayun, who did not wish to be far away from the capital, does not seem to have prosecuted his campaign further. Kuchkunji died in 1530, his death preceding that of Baber, whose career ended at Agra, in the December of the same year, by only a few months. Kuchkunji, according to Vambery, spent most of his life in the society of ascetics and dervishes.§ He left three sons, all of whom afterwards became Khans of Bukhara. They were Abusaid, Abdulla, and Abdul Latif. Coins struck during his reign are extant. They bear no Khan's name, but are dated within the period of his rule, and were struck at Samarkand and Bukhara.‖

ABUSAID KHAN.

According to Hafiztanish, when Kuchkunji was nominated Khakan, his brother Suiunich was appointed kalga or next heir, and his nephew Janibeg Sultan, the son of Khoja Muhammed, the next after him, but both these princes died before Kuchkunji.¶ On the latter's death the eldest of his sons, Abusaid, was elected Khakan. This is what Kazvini says,** in which he is confirmed by Hafiztanish.†† The seat of the Uzbeg empire during his reign, as during his father's, was at Samarkand, and Ubeidulla, the ruler of Bukhara, continued to control the forces of the empire. I have described how the latter retired before Shah Tahmasp. Having arrived at Merv he summoned a council of the Uzbeg chiefs to prepare measures of defence. At this, opinions were divided, and Abusaid, who was now on the throne, set his face against the war, and advised Ubeidulla not to undertake it. The Khakan was supported by some other chieftains. Ubeidulla thereupon withdrew from Khorasan and "the fish standard of Persia once more gleamed over the whole province." Tahmasp put his brother Behram Murza there as his viceroy, and then returned to Irak.‡‡ In 1531, although unsupported by the other sultans, Ubeidulla made a raid towards Meshed, but was driven back by the local

* Id., 395.　　　† Id., 399, 400.　　　‡ Id.　　　§ Op. cit., 280.
‖ Frahn Res., 438.　Vel. Zernof, Coins of Bukhara, 334, 335.
¶ Vel. Zernof, Coins of Bukhara, 348.　　** Id., 339 and 344.　　†† Id., 346.
‡‡ Erskine, ii. 99.

forces. In 1532 he renewed the invasion with a larger army. He marched himself on Herat, his son Abdul Aziz on Meshed, Kamish-oghlan (the Boy of the Bushes) on Asterabad, and Khankeldi Behadur on Sebsevar.* The country was wasted in various directions for a year and a half, during which the Uzbegs pressed the siege of Herat, where terrible distress ensued. Impure food, the flesh of dogs and cats was eaten, and the distress was so great that overtures for a surrender were made to Ubeidulla, on condition that he withdrew his troops a march or two so as to let the garrison escape unmolested. This he refused, and insisted that it must defile under his tent ropes, and in consequence the siege proceeded. Meanwhile, Shah Tahmasp having quelled the revolt in Azerbaijan, hastened by forced marches towards Herat. A party he sent out surprised the Uzbegs at Asterabad when bathing, put them to death with little resistance, and sent him five hundred heads. The Uzbegs at Sebsevar retired fighting to Nishapur and then to Meshed. Abdul Aziz hurried from the latter place with seven thousand men to help his father at Herat. Ubeidulla dared not meet Tahmasp in the field; he was probably not very cordially supported by the other Uzbeg chiefs. At all events he retired to Bukhara, and for two years Khorasan was free from Uzbeg attack. Abusaid Khan died in 839 (i.e., 1532-3), after a very short reign. Perhaps Ubeidulla had a hand in his death, as Vambery suggests. None of his coins are apparently known.

UBEIDULLA KHAN.

On the death of Abusaid Khan the overkhanship of the Uzbeg princes did not pass to his brother, who was his heir, but to Ubeidulla, the son of Mahmud and nephew of Sheibani, whose prowess in the Persian wars had doubtless secured him the position. His private appanage, as I have said, was Bukhara, and that city during his reign was the capital of the Uzbegs. He mounted the throne about the year 1533. Shah Tahmasp had appointed his brother Sam Murza to be governor of Khorasan, and for two years there was peace there. In 1535, Sam Murza having marched against Kandahar, Ubeidulla deemed it a good opportunity to renew his incursions. A body of five or six thousand Uzbegs entered and laid waste Northern Khorasan, but they were defeated by Sufian Khalifa, the governor of Meshed. Further east another attack was made upon Gurjistan. Khalifa Sultan Shamlu, who governed Herat in Sam Murza's absence, having marched to meet the latter with a motley and ill-assorted army, was attacked, defeated, and killed, upon which the people of Herat summoned Sufian, who had so lately been successful, to the rescue.

* Vambery, 380.

The attacks just named were mere desultory raids, but they encouraged Ubeidulla, who the next year crossed the Amu Daria with an immense army, and threatened Meshed. Sufian was sent for hastily from Herat. He affected to despise the enemy, promised to be soon at the holy city and to send Ubeidulla's skin to the King stuffed with straw, and set out from Herat with only three thousand horse, and on the road, says Erskine, filled a bag with hay, lest the Uzbegs, by not leaving a blade of grass around Meshed, might defeat his boast. He routed the first detachment he met, but on getting near the town was obliged to shelter in an old ruin, where he obstinately defended himself for several days, subsisting his followers on the flesh of their horses, but was eventually taken and put to death.*

The deputy whom Sufian had left at Herat behaved so harshly there that some of the people summoned the Uzbegs to their relief. Ubeidulla went and besieged the place for five months, during which the inhabitants suffered terribly. At length 300 Uzbegs having gained access to a bastion, probably by treachery, the city was taken, and the garrison retired to the fortress of Ekhtiar ed din. The city was plundered, and the citadel was afterwards surrendered on condition that the garrison was to be allowed to march out with its property, but as they left the fort they were all stripped naked and sent to Bukhara, the greater part perishing miserably on the way. Ubeidulla retained possession of Herat for four months, and persecuted the Shias severely. At length Shah Tahmasp, having his hands more free, went to the assistance of the much-suffering province of Khorasan. Ubeidulla wished to resist him, but the other Uzbeg chiefs counselled a retreat, and, although it was winter, they set out on their return by way of Balkh, and Tahmasp took possession of Herat unopposed.† Ubeidulla seems to have made two or three other inroads into Khorasan during his life, but none of any importance, and the province remained in possession of the Persians, and enjoyed comparative tranquillity.‡

Meanwhile the Uzbegs had founded an independent principality at Khuarezm, or Khiva, whose history will occupy us in the next chapter. At this time matters were in a state of confusion there, and Ubeidulla determined to fish in the troubled waters. We are told he was joined by Borrak Khan, of Tashkend, otherwise known as Nauruz Ahmed Khan,§ by Jevan Mard Ali Behadur, the son of Abusaid Khan, and now Khan of Samarkand, his father's appanage, and by the grandsons of Hamza and Mehdi Sultan of Hissar, and that they marched upon Urgenj. The princes of Khuarezm, too weak to resist this invasion, retired towards Kir. On arriving at Urgenj, Ubeidulla sent in pursuit of them, and Avanek Khan, the ruler of Khuarezm, with all his people, were captured at a place called Begat Kiri, north of Vesir. The Khan was handed over

---

* Erskine, ii. 103.　　† Id., 103, 104.　　‡ Id., 106.　　§ Vide infra.

3 T

to Omar Gazi, whose father he had killed, and who now put him to death in turn. Ubeidulla gave Urgenj to his son Abdul Azis, who took up his residence there. The Sarts and Turkomans were not disturbed, but the Uzbegs were divided into four sections, of which one was assigned to Ubeidulla ; a second to the princes of Hissar; a third to the princes of Samarkand; and a fourth to the princes of Tashkend. When they retired from the country these several princes, who had placed deputies in charge of these various contingents, took the latter home again with them.*

Meanwhile Din Muhammed Sultan, the son of the Avanek Khan above mentioned, continued to hold authority at Derun, which he had received as an appanage. A number of fugitives from Urgenj repaired to him, and it was at length determined to recover possession of the Khanate. They marched against the town of Khiva, which was captured, and its darugha, with a few of his men, were put to death. The darugha of Hazarasp fled. On hearing this news Abdul Azis retired from Urgenj and went to his father. Ubeidulla was not long in taking up arms, and advanced with some four thousand men. Din Muhammed, who had only three thousand, determined to risk an encounter. Three times his beks urged upon him the reckless nature of the enterprise. Twice he took no notice of them, but the third time, having dismounted, he took some earth in his hands, and scattering it on the collar of his shirt, he said, " My God, I confide my soul to thee and my body to the ground." Then, turning to the beks, he said, "I myself am dead; as to you, if your lives are more precious to you than mine do not go forth with me; if the contrary, then go." He then mounted his horse, and was followed by his enthusiastic people, and took up a position at Guerdin Khast, west of a lake which was afterwards known as Shikest Kuli (i.e., the lake of the defeat). It was night when news arrived that the enemy was approaching. Din Muhammed divided his men into two divisions, and placed them in ambush. Presently the van of Ubeidulla's army appeared, preceded by forty men carrying flambeaux. This division was suddenly attacked on either side and routed, several beks being killed and others captured. The slaughter was terrible ; Kun Tughar Behadur of the Kungrat tribe, boasted he had himself killed sixty. After the battle the beks who had been captured were presented to Din Muhammed one by one. One of these, named Hafiz, was charged with having openly said that the people of Urgenj were infidels, and not Mussulmans. Being asked to explain this, he replied, "We are about to test which are infidels and which Muhammedans," a happy phrase under difficult circumstances, which afterwards passed into a proverb among the Uzbegs. Din Muhammed now proposed an exchange of prisoners against those who had been captured by Ubeidulla in the previous campaign. This was accepted,

* Abulghazi 238-240.

and they were allowed to return to Bukhara with Hajim Khan, who was charged with negotiating the exchange. He was well received by Ubeidulla, who restored him the prisoners in his charge, as well as those belonging to the princes of Samarkand and Hissar.* This campaign took place in 946 (*i.e.*, 1539-40), and was almost immediately followed by the death of Ubeidulla, who died, according to Kazvini, from chagrin, in the fifty-sixth year of his age, and was buried in the chapel of a college he had himself built.† Coins of Ubeidulla, struck at Bukhara, are extant, but most of them apparently do not bear the Khan's name.‡

Haidar says of him that during the previous one hundred years no prince had equalled him. He adds that he was pious, meek, religious, abstinent, and just, pre-eminent for generosity and valour. He could write seven hands, but especially excelled in the Naski. He copied out the Koran more than once. He possessed divans of the Turkish, Arabic, and Persian poets, and was a good musician. During his reign his capital Bukhara recalled to mind Herat during the reign of Sultan Hussein Murza.§

ABDULLA KHAN I.

Ubeidulla was more or less an usurper, and on his death the throne was again occupied by a son of Kuchkunji, namely, by Abdulla Khan. This is expressly stated by Kazvini,‖ and also by Muhammed Effendi.¶ D'Herbelot and De Guignes have confused this prince with the great Abdulla, son of Iskander, who will occupy us presently. Abdulla, the son of Kuchkunji, only reigned six months. Apparently no coins of his are known. He doubtless held his court at Samarkand.

ABDUL LATIF KHAN.

Abdulla was succeeded by his brother Abdul Latif, who also ruled from Samarkand. He began to reign in 947 (*i.e.*, 1540-1), and according to M. Vel. Zernof continued to do so till 959 (*i.e.*, 1551-2).

I have described how in 1526 Balkh was captured by the Uzbegs. It was afterwards constituted an appanage, and given to Pir Muhammed the son of Janibeg. Kamran, the brother of "the Great Moghul' Humayun, having rebelled against the latter in 1547, fled to Balkh, where he was well received by Pir Muhammed, who entertained him in his palace, and supplied him with troops, with which he recovered Ghuri and took Baklan. Pir Muhammed accompanied him on this expedition, and when his *protégé* was master of the open country, he

---

* Abulghazi, 241-245.   † Id., 245. Note, 1. Vambery, 281.
‡ Vel. Zernof, Coins of Bukhara, &c., 336. Frœhn Ræ., 438.   § Tarikhi Rashidi.
‖ Vel. Zernof, Coins of Bukhara, 368.   ¶ Id., 369.

returned to Balkh, leaving a contingent of Uzbegs with him.[*] This naturally aroused the animosity of Humayun, and in 1549 we find him, while professing other objects, really setting out on a campaign against Balkh. We are told that when he reached Istalif, Abbas Sultan, a young Uzbeg, who had married Humayun's youngest sister (Gulshehreh Begim), suspecting that the expedition was directed against his people, disappeared without taking leave. Humayun went on by Anderab and Talikan to Nari, and crossing by the pass of Nari, reached the beautiful valley of Nilber, where he was met by several dependents, but not by Kamran, who had made friends with him, and had promised to assist. Having arrived at Baklan, he ordered an attack to be made on Eibek, a fertile and populous district in the territory of Balkh, which was defended by a strong castle. Pir Muhammed's Atalik, with a number of officials, on hearing of the invasion, had hastily thrown themselves into the fort, which was not provided either with provisions or water for a prolonged siege, and which surrendered to Humayun, after a short attack. At a feast, given on this occasion, he asked the Atalik Khoja Bagh what was the best way to conquer Balkh. The latter, embarrassed, replied that "he was but a poor judge, as he was an enemy." But on Humayun's praising the honesty of the Uzbegs, and his honesty in particular, he replied, "If you would conquer Balkh, cut off our heads, hasten on to the capital, and it will be yours." When objection was made to thus killing good Mussulmans, he said there was yet another alternative. "I have much influence with Pir Muhammed. I will undertake that the country on your side of Khulm shall be yours, that the Khutbeh shall be said there in your name, and that Pir Muhammed shall send one thousand of his best men to accompany you when you go to Hindostan." This advice was also rejected, and Humayun, keeping the Atalik with him, sent the other Uzbeg chiefs back to Kabul.[†]

After a few days halt he went on by way of Khulm. On reaching Astaneh (where was the shrine of Shah Avlia), and while the audience hall was still disarranged, and the people in the bazaar were busy with their loads, and the Emperor, who had been visiting the shrine, was in his private tent, a sudden attack was made in the direction of the camp bazaar by a party of Uzbegs, under Shah Muhammed, Sultan of Hissar, the son of Berenduk Sultan, which captured a chief officer, named Kabuli, whose head was carried off as a trophy to Balkh. This warned Humayun that the Uzbegs, from beyond the Amu, were arriving.[‡] When they neared Balkh, he also began to suspect that his brother, Kamran, as he did not come, was meditating some attack on Kabul in his absence. Nevertheless his people attacked the van of the Uzbeg army, under Abdulla Sultan and Khosru Sultan, the sons of Iskander Sultan, near the Takteh pul, and drove them across the bridge to the Balkh side of the

* Erskine, ii. 346, 347.   † Id., 370, 371.   ‡ Id., 370-372.

stream. When they neared the city a council was summoned, and in
view of the possible treachery of Kamran and the reported approach of
Abdul Aziz, the son of Ubeidulla, with the troops of Bukhara, it was
determined to retreat, and take up a position near the entrance of the hills
at Dera-Gez, a valley with narrow defiles, easily defended, and whence
both Kabul and Balkh could be watched. The council broke up at midnight, and orders were given for a retreat, which instantly commenced.*

This is the account given by Bayezid, who was present with Humayun's
forces. Abulfazl, who is followed by Ferishta and others, makes Abdul
Aziz join the Uzbegs before the retreat, and describes a general action in
which the latter were defeated and driven into the town, although they
had thirty thousand men ; and Abulfazl adds that Humayun proposed to
improve the advantage by an immediate advance, which was not, however, done.† To return to Bayezid's story. At dawn the retiring army
reached the broken ground on the banks of the river flowing through
the Dera-Gez. Here a panic seems to have seized it (as it often seizes an
irregular force), caused partially by the rumours that Kamran had attacked
Kabul. The Uzbegs were quick in pursuit. The rear-guard was broken
and dispersed, an arrow even struck Humayun's horse in the chest, and
all attempts to effect a rally were unavailing. The Emperor's adventures,
says Erskine, for some succeeding days, when he sought to repass the
mountains by unknown or little-frequented roads a prey to thirst, hunger,
and fatigue, and guided by the barbarous inhabitants, are related in the
liveliest and most picturesque manner by Bayezid, who was a sharer in
his flight. He at length reached Kabul on the 23rd of September, 1549.‡
In the rout many of the amirs, including Shah Bidagh, fell into the hands
of the Uzbegs. The Atalik and his companions, who had been allowed
to return to Balkh, gave such a favourable account of the handsome
treatment they had received, that Pir Muhammed returned these prisoners
in a most handsome manner.§ Although Kamran had not seized on
Kabul, he tried to improve his fortune in these troublous times, and on
Humayun's retreat he made an unsuccessful attack on Badakhshan and
Kunduz. He then turned to the Uzbegs for assistance, and entered into
a treaty with them. They supplied him with a contingent which helped
him in the siege of Kunduz. Its commander Hindal Murza thereupon
forged a letter in Kamran's name, in which suggestions were made for
overreaching the Uzbegs. It was contrived that this should fall into the
latters' hands. Whereupon they abandoned him, and returned home.
He (Kamran) now raised the siege and marched against Suliman Murza,
the governor of Badakhshan. When he reached Rostak a large body of
Uzbegs, who were plundering in the neighbourhood, under Said, attacked
and plundered his camp without inquiring whose it was. When Said learnt
what had happened he apologised for the mistake, but the blow was a

---

* Id., 372, 373.   † Id., 373. Note.   ‡ Id., 376.   § Id.

erushing one for Kamran nevertheless.* According to Bayezid, the Uzbeg
commander on this occasion was Mir Taulon Uzbeg, and not Said.† This
fight took place in 1550. Kazvini tells us that after the accession of Abdul
Latif the Uzbegs did not cross the Oxus, and Khorasan enjoyed comparative tranquillity.‡   The fact is, they were too much occupied at
home. The system of appanages was bearing its natural fruit in internecine struggles among the different princes.   In these struggles the
descendants of Janibeg, who, as I have said, was regent on Sheibani's
death, were pitted against the other Uzbeg princes.   In 956 or 957 Abdul
Aziz, the son of Ubeidulla, who held the appanage of Bukhara, died, and
was succeeded by Muhammed Yar Sultan, the son of Suiunich Muhammed
Sultan, the son of Sheibani Khan.

On the latter's accession, Pir Muhammed of Balkh, son of Janibeg, went
to Bukhara on pretence of paying the last debt of respect to Abdul Aziz,
but in reality to secure the place for himself. Thereupon the Khakan
Abdul Latif, Nauruz Ahmed, of Tashkend, and Burgan Sultan, the grand-
son of Ubeidulla Khan, with other princes, marched to the assistance of
Yar Muhammed, and invaded Miankal, which belonged to the family of
Janibeg. The princes of Janibeg's family thereupon dispersed. Rustem
Khan, with his son Uzbeg Sultan, fled to Bukhara ; Izkander Khan left
Kermineh and went to Andkhud ; Kermineh itself resisted, and after a
siege of twelve days, terms were agreed upon, and Abdul Latif and
Nauruz retired respectively to Samarkand and Tashkend, and during the
next year (i.e., 958) Pir Muhammed gave up Bukhara to Yar Muhammed
and withdrew once more to Balkh. Soon after Burgan Sultan was
nominated joint ruler of Bukhara with Yar Muhammed. Abdul Latif
died in 959 (i.e., 1551-2).§ Coins struck by him at Samarkand, and
bearing his name, are well known.|

NAURUZ AHMED KHAN.

According to the Abdulla Nameh, on the death of Abdul Latif his
special appanage of Samarkand fell to Sultan Said Sultan, the son of
Abusaid Khan, while the empire of Mavera un Nehr (i.e., the khakanship)
fell to Nauruz Ahmed Khan.¶ He was the son of Suiuinich Khoja Khan,
who, as we have seen, held the appanage of Tashkend. At this time
Abdulla, the son of Izkander, the son of Janibeg, who afterwards became
so famous, had already begun to show his prowess. Having inherited
the small district of Kermineh, he first took Kesvi from Khudai berdi
Sultan, the son of Abusaid Khan, and then began to molest the district
of Karshi. Thereupon, to prevent a struggle, Khudai berdi exchanged

* Id., 377, 378.   † Id., 379. Note.   ‡ Id., 377, 378.
§ Vel. Zernof, Coins of Bukhara, 366, 367. Fre ha Res., 439, 400.
| Vel. Zernof, Coins of Bukhara, 373.   ¶ Id., 379, &c.

appanages with Kilish Kara Sultan, the son of Kisten Kara Sultan and cousin of Abdulla, who had previously ruled at Sagraj. Abdulla had as little respect for his cousin as for his more distant relative, and occupied Karshi and also deprived Gashim Sultan, the son of Berenduk Sultan (who ruled at Hissar) of the town of Kesh or Shehr i Sebz.* When Nauruz Ahmed mounted the throne, having collected a large army from Tashkend, Turkestan, and Khojend, he marched against Abdulla and his partisans. He made an ineffectual attempt to seize Samarkand, and then laid siege to Kesh, whence he summoned Burgan Sultan and Yar Muhammed Sultan, who ruled jointly at Bukhara, to his help. Abdulla appealed to his uncle Pir Muhammed, but before the latter could arrive with the contingent of Balkh, Burgan had reached Kasan and was plundering the district of Karshi. Abdulla went out to meet him, and as a portion of Pir Muhammed's men came up at a critical moment, the battle was decided against the Bukharians, who withdrew. Abdulla and his uncle now marched to the relief of Shehr i Sebz. Nauruz did not wait for their arrival, but having raised the siege of Karshi went home again to Tashkend. Abdulla returned to Karshi and Pir Muhammed to Kilef, the capital of Balkh.† This campaign took place in 960 hej.

Next year Nauruz Ahmed renewed the struggle, and captured Samarkand from Sultan Said, who was apparently a partisan of Abdulla. Through the intervention of Muhammed Sadik he afterwards made peace with the young prince, to whom he promised that he would deprive his late ally Burgan Sultan of Bukhara and give it to him. It would seem that Burgan had incurred his displeasure by the murder of Muhammed Yar, his co-ruler at Bukhara. He first, however, punished the descendants of Janibeg, and invaded their appanage of Miankal. Iskander Khan, the father of Abdulla, fled to Balkh, while the other sultans of the house of Janibeg gathered round Abdulla at Karshi. Miankal was speedily conquered, and Nauruz Ahmed proceeded to divide it among his relatives. Kermineh he gave to his son Dost Muhammed Sultan; Dabusi to Abdul Sultan, son of Abdul Latif Khan; and Shehr i Sebz to Gashim Sultan, son of Berenduk Sultan of Hissar. He then ordered his son Baba Sultan to march against Abdulla at Karshi. He fought with the latter and won a battle, in which Abdulla's uncle Rustem Khan was killed, while he himself with his troops was forced to cross the Oxus and take shelter at Balkh. After this and in the year 962 Nauruz went against Bukhara. After sustaining a three months' siege, Burgan Sultan appealed to Abdulla, who was then living at Andkhud and Shabirgan, for help. The latter was delighted, and although it was very sultry went with three hundred companions, and soon reached Farab on the Oxus, which belonged to Burgan. There he was shortly after beleagured by Sultan Said Khan and Dost Muhammed

Sultan, the son of Nauruz, with 22,000 men. Although his force was so ridiculously small he ventured on a sortie, which was successful. His opponents were beaten, and the fugitives on reaching the camp of the Khakan Nauruz, so disturbed his men that he broke up the siege of Bukhara and returned to Samarkand,* where he ordered Sultan Said to be arrested and to be sent prisoner to Rashid Khan at Karaigutak (? in Kashgar). Abdulla after his victory went to Bukhara. Burgan Sultan went to Shehr i Sebz to meet him, and conducted him to the city, which he gave up to him according to his agreement, and himself went to Karakul. He was not long content there, however, and having made a demonstration against Bukhara, Abdulla marched against him, but the latter's army left him and went over to Burgan. Abdulla had once more to seek shelter at Balkh.

In the spring of 963 Khalkman bi of the Durmans, having quarrelled with Burgan, incited the amirs at Karakul to rebel. They did so, and invited Abdulla to go to them. Burgan thereupon again appealed to Nauruz Ahmed, who we are told collected a vast army. He was joined by Burgan, and the two went on to Bukhara, which they beleagured. Terms were at length conceded to Abdulla, who was allowed to withdraw to Chechket and Meimineh. Burgan now returned to Bukhara and his patron to Samarkand, and thence to Rabat Khoja, at the sources of the river Dirgem, where he gave himself up to debauchery, fell ill, and died.† This was in 963 hej. (i.e., 1556). Nauruz Ahmed was surnamed Borrak, as is clear from Hafistanish.‡ Vambery calls him Borrak Khan and makes him a son of the Jagatai Khan Mahmud. His account of Bukhara at this period, like that of all other authors except M. Vel. Zernof, is very confused. Herberstein calls him Borrak Sultan, and makes him the Khan of Urgenj and brother of Ubeidulla ;§ both of which are mistakes. Nauruz Ahmed has left coins struck at Bukhara.‖

It was in the reign of Nauruz Ahmed that the intercourse between the Turks of Constantinople and their very near relatives the Uzbegs became more cordial. They were both Sunnis, and had therefore a common grievance against the Persians. In a letter of Sultan Suliman, written to Nauruz, he says he was on terms of close friendship with the latter's predecessors Ubeidulla and Abdulla. During the reign of Abdul Latif, Suliman, it seems, sent a body of three hundred janissaries and some artillery to his assistance. This arrived after the accession of Nauruz. The latter wrote to his friend to tell him how the sultans of his family who n led at Dabusi, Kufin, Kermineh, Kesh, Karshi, and Khazar had been rebellious, and had occupied his time in suppressing them, which accounted for his not having made a diversion in his favour, and he promised that when he had taken Bukhara, which still held out, that

---

* Id., 381-383.   † Id., 383-386.   ‡ Id., 383.   § Op. cit., ii. 75.
‖ Vol. Zernof, op. cit., 376.

he would invade Khorasan. Two months later, namely, in February, 1556, his envoy Nisameddin Ahmed Chaushbeg went to announce to Suliman the capture of Bukhara. This was followed by a third letter. The Sultan wrote in cordial terms, but said it would be impossible for him to unite in a campaign against Persia then, as the two countries had made peace.*

PIR MUHAMMED KHAN.

On the death of Nauruz, Pir Muhammed of Balkh, the son of Janibeg, who was the oldest of the appanaged princes, was nominated Khakan, and his name was duly put on the coins. On the accession of his uncle, Abdulla left Chechket and Meimineh, where he had taken shelter, and moved upon Miankal. Dost Muhammed, the son of Naurus, who reigned at Kerminek, fled, and presently Abdulla also captured Shehr i Sebz from Gashim Sultan, and assisted Kedai Sultan, son of Abdul Latif, and Jivan merdi Ali Khar the son of Abusaid, to take Samarkand from the sons of Nauruz Khan. The next year, i.e., in 964, he began a campaign against Burgan Sultan, the ruler of Bukhara. The latter, feeling himself too weak to resist, sent the holy Khoja Juibareh to sue for peace. The same evening that the Khoja left Bukhara, Burgan was entertained at the house of the Murza Eke bi, where he was treacherously assassinated, and at dawn his head was put upon a pike and sent to Abdulla.† Vambery calls the assassin Murzaki Kushji (the bird catcher).‡ Abdulla now went to Bukara with the Khoja, where he speedily overcame all resistance. This victory made him one of the most powerful princes of Mavera un Nehr, and increased his ambition. He now prepared to invade Khorasan, and first went to visit his uncle, Pir Muhammed, who was at Shabirgan. An exchange of territory was agreed upon between them, Abdulla surrendering Bukhara and accepting Balkh (which was nearer Khorasan), in lieu of it. They had already commenced the mutual surrender, when Din Muhammed, the son of Pir, rose in revolt and seized upon Balkh. While Pir Muhammed went to repress the rebellion, Abdulla ordered his brother Ibeidulla not to give up Bukhara. Having hastened there, he summoned his father Iskander from Kerminek, and had him thereupon proclaimed, to use the inflated language of Hafiztanish, "Khakan of the whole world." Pir Muhammed, thus dethroned, retired to his own appanage, made peace with his son, and died in 974. The ruler of the appanage of Balkh was styled Kalkhan, which Senkofski suggests may be a corruption of the Turkish, Mongol, and Manchu, Kalkan a buckler, Balkh being looked upon as a kind of buckler to Mavera un Nehr. One of the rulers of Khuarezm, as we shall see presently, was called Kalkhan Khan.§

* Von Hammer, Osm. Ges., ii. 255, 256. † Vol. Zernof, 388, 389. ‡ Op. cit., 284. Note. Senkofski, op. cit., 79, 80.

3 U

A coin of Pir Muhammed, struck no doubt when he was Khakan, is described by M. Vel. Zernof.* Pir Muhammed, like his predecessor, had intercourse with the Turkish Sultan Suliman.†

IZKANDER KHAN.

Izkander Khan was only nominally the ruler of Mavera un Nehr, and his son Abdulla had the virtual control of the State. Izkander became Khakan in 968 (*i.e.*, 1561). It would seem that Abdulla had made some raids or razzias,—"alamans," as the Turkomans call them—into Persia ; but while Shah Tahmasp lived the Uzbegs were restrained from venturing on more ambitious schemes. On his death anarchy ensued in Khorasan under the disorderly rule of his sons, and the Uzbegs accordingly poured over the frontiers. In 974 (*i.e.*, 1566), Muhammed Murza, the son of Tahmasp, narrowly escaped capture by them, while on his way to Herat with 15,000 men.‡ Abdulla was in command of these plunderers. Meanwhile he was hampered by a pressing danger nearer home. On the death of Nauruz Ahmed, he was succeeded in his appanage of Tashkend and Turkestan by his son Baba Sultan, who also inherited his father's animosity against the house of Janibeg. When Abdulla was absent in Khorasan, Baba Sultan invaded Mavera un Nehr, and advanced to Samarkand, whence he carried away Khosru Sultan, the son of Yar Muhammed, and grandson of Janibeg, who ruled there, and whom he put to death. This was in 975 (*i.e.*, 1567).§

In an inscription, which still remains on a slab of rock in the Pass of Jilan uti, on the way from Jizakh to Samarkand, we have the following record of a victory gained by Abdulla over Baba Sultan in 1571. It reads thus : " Let passers in the waste, and travellers on land and water, know that in the year 979 hej. (*i.e.*, 1571), there was a conflict between the army of the lieutenant of the Khalifate, the Shadow of the Almighty the great Khakan Abdulla Khan, son of Izkander Khan, consisting of 30,000 men of war, and the army of Dervish Khan, Baba Khan, and other sons of Borrak Khan. In this army there were fifty relatives of the Sultan, and 400,000 fighting men from Turkestan, Tashkend, Ferghana, and Desht Kipchak. The army of the Sovereign, by the fortunate conjunction of the stars, gained the victory, having conquered the above-mentioned Sultans, and gave to death so many of them that from the people who were killed in the fight, and after being taken prisoners during the course of one month, blood ran on the surface of the water in the river of Jizakh. Let this be known."‖

Pir Muhammed, the ruler of Balkh, died, as I have mentioned, in 975,

---

* Op. cit., 386.   † Von Hammer, Osm. Ges., ii. 271.   ‡ Vambery, 286.
§ *Id.*, 284.   ‖ Schuyler's Turkestan, i. 321, 322.

and was succeeded in his appanage by his son Din Muhammed, who reigned till 980, when Abdulla, having some grievance, marched against him, and captured Balkh after a siege of ten months. Abdulla appointed the Atalik Nazarbi of the Naiman tribe its governor. Din Muhammed was pardoned, and given the district of Shehr i Sebz as an appanage. Nazarbi ruled at Balkh for ten years, when he was recalled, and Abdulla put his own son Abdul Mumin there, and the latter ruled Balkh till Abdulla's death, in 1006.[*]

At this time Juvanmerdi, the brother of Sultan Said, and the son of Abusaid Khan, held the appanage of Samarkand. He had two sons, Abulkhair Sultan and Muzzaffar Sultan, who were constantly at feud with one another. The former allied himself with Baba Sultan against the latter, who was the *protégé* of Abdulla. He was defeated, whereupon his father Juvanmerdi took his side, and we are told Abdulla determined to rid himself of both father and sons. Juvanmerdi and Muzaffar were taken prisoners, and executed at Samarkand, and a similar fate soon after overtook Abulkhair.[†] Abdul Sultan, a son of Abdul Latif Khan, also raised a revolt at Zamin. He likewise was defeated by Abdulla, and took shelter in the hill country of Hissar, whence he continued to harass his opponent till he was taken prisoner and executed, in 988 (*i.e.*, 1580).[‡]

In 983 Baba Sultan was severely punished and driven across the Sihun.[§] Abdulla apparently installed his elder brother Dervish Sultan as ruler of Tashkend.

In 987 (*i.e.*, 1579), Baba having occupied Tashkend and killed his brother Dervish, Abdulla, who was then living on the confines of Khokand, attacked and defeated him near Tashkend.[|] Baba fled. Shortly after a spy came to report that he and his brother Buzakhur and his nephews, the sons of Khuarezm Shah Sultan, had taken shelter among the Kazaks, who had done homage to them on the banks of the river Talas. Abdulla sent an exploring party, consisting of Isfandiar Sultan, Abdul Baki bi Durman, and others, to Sairam to inquire. Having found that the story was not true, and spent some days in the delightful neighbourhood of Sairam hunting, he went to the Talas, had an interview with the Kazak chiefs, as I have described,[¶] and rewarded them with presents. They surrendered to him Ubeid Sultan, a son of Baba Sultan, whom they had captured, together with Jan Muhammed Atalik Naiman, and Shah Gazi bi Durman, with a number of leading men.[**]

Baba Sultan now apparently made terms with Abdulla; who returned again to Bukhara, but matters were at peace for only a short time. Baba Sultan, it would seem, made a demand for the district of Andijan,

[*] Vel. Zernof, Coins of Bukhara, &c., 594.   [†] Vambery, 291.   [‡] Id. Note 1.
[§] Id., 284.   [|] Vel. Zernof, Khans of Kasimof, ii. 279.   [¶] Ante, 633.
[**] Vel. Zernof, Khans of Kasimof, 279-283.

and at the same time, probably aware that this would not be granted, allied himself with the Kazaks, to whom he surrendered Yassy and Sabran, and concerted common measures against Mavera un Nehr. The Kazaks under Sarban Sultan were to cross the Jaxartes and to make for Bukhara, while Baba Sultan and his brother Buzakhur were to devastate the district of Samarkand. The plan was carried out, and both divisions retired carrying off large stores of plunder.* This took place in 1579 and 1580.

We now find Baba Sultan having a bitter feud with the Kazaks, in which he killed several of their chiefs, as I have described. He shortly after defeated their leader Shigai Khan, and returned with the booty he had made to Tashkend.†

In 1581 Abdulla again marched against his inveterate rival. He set out from Samarkand, and went as far as Uzkend. While encamped at Karatau, near the Sir Daria or Jaxartes, he was visited by Shigai, whom he rewarded with the town of Khojend. He then returned to Bukhara.‡ There he held a grand feast, in which his son Abdul Mumin and Tevkel, the son of Shigai, engaged in athletic sports, in which the latter distinguished himself.

In the spring of the following year Abdulla, having determined to crush Baba Sultan, pursued him into the deserts of Kipchak as far as the Ulugh Tagh Mountains, as I have mentioned.§ On this occasion Abdulla erected a memorial pillar opposite the one put up by Timur.‖ Finding that Baba Sultan had withdrawn among the Nogais, he returned homeward, again crossed the Sarisu, and then laid siege to Sabran. Meanwhile he had sent an advanced body of troops in pursuit of his indefatigable enemy. Shigai and his Kazaks defeated a body of them near Seraili and Turaili.¶ They also defeated one of their chiefs named Kuliah bi Durman, and captured an enormous number of sheep, horses, and camels. This was a very welcome supply to the main body of Abdulla's army, which had begun to suffer want.

At length, after much fatiguing manœuvring, Isfendiar Sultan, son of Khosru Sultan, Abdulla's cousin, with the Kazak chief Tevkel and others, fell upon the spoor or footprints of a large force. After six or seven days' march they reached the river Sauka, where they came up with the enemy. One of the Kazak chiefs asked that the Khan's army might advance first, for the enemy would fear it most, while they would fight desperately against the Kazaks. They attacked and completely defeated them, and Baba again took refuge among the Manguts. I have already described his subsequent career and end.** His brother

---

*Id., 286, &c.　　　† Id., 292-294. Antis, 635.　　　‡ Id.　　　§ Id.
‖ Senkofski, 27. Vambery, 285.

¶ Three rivers Serili spring in the Ulugh Tagh range. One of them falls into the Ishim and the other two into the Tobol. (Vol. Zernof, ii. 308.)

** Antis. 637 and 7.

Burakhur found refuge at Sairam, where he seems to have died. Let us now revert to Abdulla. After a two months' attack Sabran was captured. During the siege Tagir Sultan, another of Baba Sultan's brothers, was surprised by the Kazak Tevkel, who was pasturing his cattle at Ak Kurgan. He captured him and handed him over to Ibeidulla, the brother of Abdulla.* Abdulla now speedily conquered Suzak, Shahrukhia, and other towns, together with Turkestan or Yassy.

Next year (i.e., in 1583) he apparently conquered Ferghana and Andijan, in which he was assisted by the Kazak Tevkel. We are expressly told that after the fall of Baba Sultan the towns of Turkestan and Tashkend acknowledged the authority of Abdulla, who appointed and removed their rulers.† Thus the appanage of Suiunich Khan was annexed to Mavera un Nehr, and the line of Uzbeg princes who had so long reigned north of the Sihun was suppressed. The name of Abdulla occurs so prominently in all these transactions, that it quite puts in the shade that of his father the Khakan Izkander, who died in 1583. His capital was doubtless Bukhara. Several of his coins are extant.‡ He was a mere puppet in the hands of his son Abdulla. We are told he was a skilful falconer and devoted to religious exercises.§

ABDULLA KHAN II.

Abdulla was the greatest of the Abulkhairids. He was born in the year 940 (i.e., 1533).‖ The Khoja Kasani is said to have foretold a great career for him, and to make his predictions more efficacious he bound the camel's-hair girdle he wore round his own waist round that of the child Abdulla.¶ We have already described the earlier part of his adventurous career. On the death of his father he determined to be de jure as well as de facto Khan.

When Izkander died Abdulla was not at home, and we are told the Khoja Kalian, the head of the clergy, with others, after burying the Khakan, repaired to Khojend, where Abdulla then was, and whom they met en route. He summoned them to a council (the Mongol kuriltai) to consider the question of the succession. The Khoja was not long in proclaiming him as the fittest for the post of Khakan. Thereupon they took a piece of white felt, which had been dipped at Mekka in the waters of Zemzema, upon which he was raised aloft. The amirs having presented their congratulations and presents, they went to Zamin, whence news of Abdulla's accession was sent in various directions.** Thus the apple which had been so long in ripening fell on his knees. Under cover of

* Vel. Zernof, il. 311, 312.
† Vel. Zernof, op. cit., il. 339.   ‡ Vel. Zernof, Coins of Bukhara, &c., 395-397.
§ Vambery, 283.   ‖ Abulghazi, 193. Note, 2.   ¶ Vambery, 263.
** Vel. Zernof, Coins of Bukhara, 399, 400.

his father's shield, he had crushed or displaced all his various rivals from
the deserts of the Kazaks to the frontiers of Kabul, and the Uzbegs were
for the first time subject to a single strong grasp, instead of being broken
in pieces among a number of appanages.

Abdulla having consolidated a homogeneous power, was now in a
position to threaten Khuarezm and Khorasan. His campaigns against
the former I shall notice in the next chapter. In regard to Khorasan,
after the death of Tahmasp, the province was torn by internal dissensions,
which were only terminated on the final success of the great Shah Abbas,
the greatest of the Persian rulers of modern times. This state of confusion in Persia was naturally inviting to the Uzbegs, who made very
profitable raids across the frontier and retired again at the approach of
the Persian forces. In 1585 they made a very famous attack while Shah
Abbas was engaged in a war with the Turks. Herat fell after a siege of
nine months, and its Governor Ali Kuli Khan Shamlu, and several
other chiefs, were put to death, while the city was plundered.* A large
number of prisoners were carried off to Bukhara, and the north-eastern
part of Khorasan was laid waste. What follows is well told by
Vambery, and I shall abstract his notice. He says that "it was on this
occasion that the guardians of the tomb of Imaum Riza, who were at
this time wardens of the numerous benefices, fields, gardens, and other
possessions of the venerable Alid, addressed a letter to Abdulla,
inquiring how he made it accord with his religious feelings to destroy the
goods of Imaum Riza, and thus to waste the substance by which so many
thousand pious pilgrims, including many Sunni, were supported? The
Transoxianian mollahs present in Abdulla's camp replied by a long controversy on Shiaism in general, alleging that according to their principles
and their faith, the disciples of Shia were worse than the unbelievers,
whose destruction was ordained by God himself. If it was the duty of
every Moslem to wage war on unbelievers, how much more was it his
duty to fight against those who had wandered from the right path, and,
in spite of their connection with the saint whose bones rested in the
midst of them, had fallen into grievous sin. As regarded the reproach
cast on them for destroying Imaum Riza's fields and gardens, they were
well aware that they were devoted to pious uses, connected with the
shrine of Imaum Riza. But it was an open question who had most right
to the enjoyment of them—the warriors fighting for the cause of God
and right, and deprived of all means of subsistence, or those who had
sinned against Allah and treated with contempt the most exalted
guardians of the faith. The Shia mollahs were of course ready enough
with a rejoinder. They had the tact to begin by proposing a sort of
general council of an equal number of Sunni and Shia philosophers,
who were to decide whether the Shias were traitors to the faith for

---

declaring the three first khalifs usurpers, and asserting the hereditary
rights of Ali. Shiaism was as old as Islamism itself, and if the adherents
of this sect were really so abhorred, how came Imaum Riza to settle
down in the midst of them? why did he not rather go to Transoxania?
&c. These discussions had no more definite results than the council
of Sunni and Shia philosophers, convoked 150 years later by Nadir
Shah at Bagdad.* Whilst the two parties were thus striving to settle by
the pen a schism which the sword had for centuries failed to quell,
young Shah Abbas advanced with an army from Kasvin, and Abdulla
retired by Merv to Bukhara. Abbas, as is rightly observed by Malcolm
in his History of Persia, effected this diversion rather with the object of
increasing his own prestige than with any definite intention of driving
out or conquering the Uzbegs, for he only remained a short time at
Meshed, and then hurried to Georgia, where the Osmanlis threatened him
with hostilities, and soon after defeated him. As had often before been
the case, the echo of the Ottoman victory in the West resounded in the
East, and Abdulla had no sooner received the intelligence than he made
a second attempt to conquer Meshed, and intrusted the vanguard of his
army to his son Abdulmumin Khan, the viceroy of Balkh.

"Abdulmumin, a savage warrior, and a cruel and ambitious man,
hurried forwards with Din Muhammed and a large force, to which Kul
Baba Kukeltash, the faithful servant of Abdulla and governor of Herat,
had attached himself. Their first attack was directed against Nishapur. A
few Uzbegs were taken prisoners in an affair of outposts, and set at
liberty again in order that they might let their young commander know
that Nishapur was simply a part of Meshed, and that if the latter were
taken the former would be sure to submit. In consequence of this
information Abdulmumin now directed all his efforts against Meshed,
sparing no sacrifices and no pains to subdue it. The commandant of the
fortress, Ummet Khan Ustajlu, had done all in his power to repel the
attack, but the panic became general; many of the people from the
surrounding country took refuge in the city, which was but imperfectly
provisioned, and the consequence was that famine came to the assistance
of the Uzbegs, and finally, at the first assault, caused the surrender of
this holy city of the Shias into their hands, with all its treasures,
monuments, and wealthy bazaars. When Abdulmumin's troops entered
the town, they found that the inhabitants of both sexes, and the numerous
holy and learned men, had all congregated in the outer court of the
shrine of Imaum Riza, in the hope that they might be protected there by
the sanctity of the spot; but the Uzbegs, in their blind fury, cut down
and destroyed everything that came in their way; even the supposed

---

* Nadir is supposed by modern Persians to have been himself a Sunnite at heart. He was
clear-sighted enough to perceive the danger threatening all Islam from this schism, and
wished to bring about a settlement. He summoned a sort of council at Bagdad, but it came
to no result, in consequence of the bitterness on both sides. (Vambery, Hist. of Bukhara, 287.)

descendants of Imaum Riza, who were clinging to the holy shrine of their ancestor, were there pitilessly massacred. ft is said that Abdulmumin himself looked on from the court of Mir Ali Shir, whilst his soldiers were murdering children and old men, common people and learned philosophers indiscriminately, and that even the shrieks of a thousand victims and their dying groans were unavailing to move his pity. Not only the public streets but the holiest precincts of the mosque and the shrine itself were deluged with blood, and in the general sack of the town the grave of the Alid suffered more than most parts, costly offerings of pious pilgrims, which had been accumulating there for three centuries, falling into the hands of the conquerors. Amongst them were enormous massive gold and silver candelabra, whole suits of armour in precious metals, splendid single stones, buttons, studs, and other articles of jewellery richly ornamented, and, most valuable of all, the magnificent library with its celebrated copies of the Keran, marvels of the art of ealigraphy, the gifts of the former Sultans : all these were dragged away, torn up, and completely destroyed. The vengeance of the Sunni conquerors did not even spare the very dead, for the ashes of Tahmasp were torn from their grave by the side of Imaum Riza's and scattered to the winds with curses and execrations. In order to gratify another Sunni enemy of the Sefids by the report of this deed, Abdulmumin despatched his chamberlain Muhammed Kuli to Constantinople to Sultan Murad III. with a letter, in which, after describing in the most bombastic style his victories in Khorasan, he gives an account of scattering the ashes of Tahmasp, and goes on to say that, in order completely to annihilate the godless set of Shia heretics, he should soon march upon Irak, and solicits the assistance of the Sultan in this enterprise. This plan came to nothing, for two reasons. In the first place, the Ottomans not only declined to help their co-religionists in the extreme East, but did precisely the contrary, promising assistance to the Persians, as they began to be uneasy at Abdulla's victories, and to think that his further successes might prove inconvenient to themselves. In the second place, Shah Abbas, who had been detained at Teheran by illness during the sack of Meshed, had now recovered, and was taking the most energetic measures of defence. For the moment, however, Abdulla was completely victorious, and had got possession of a great part of Khorasan, including the towns of Herat, Meshed, Sirakhs, Merv, Khaf, Jam, Fusheng, and Ghurian, all which he retained very nearly till his death."*

In 1586 the Kazaks, having heard that Abdulla and the main body of his army were absent in Khorasan, invaded Mavera un Nehr under Tevkel Khan and his brother Ishim, as I have described.† After defeating the army of the Uzbegs, Tevkel was alarmed by the prepara-

---

* Vambery, Hist. of Bukhara, 286-290.　　† Ante, 637.

tions made by Ibeidulla, brother of Abdulla, whom he had left in command at Samarkand, and when the latter marched against him, and reached the district of Tashkend, he withdrew once more to the steppes.*

The latter years of Abdulla's reign were disturbed by the ambition and recklessness of his son Abdul Mumin. · I have described how the latter was made governor of Balkh. It was half in ruins when he took possession of it, but in six months it was in great part rebuilt. The beautiful domes covered with kashi or enamelled tiles, the fine portal of the palace, the bazaar Babajanbaz, and the tomb of Ali, are all attributed to him.† Abdulla had allowed him, as heir to the throne, to assume the title of Khan, the father being known as Ulugh Khan, or the great Khan, and the son as Kuchuk Khan, or the little Khan. We are told he was of a ruthless and adventurous disposition, and scoured the country round with his predatory bands. He apparently subdued a large part of Badakhshan, Akbar, the Emperor of India, having withdrawn any attempts at ruling the country north of the Indian Caucasus.‡

He was ambitious to control all the Uzbeg possessions south of the Oxus, and wished to turn Kul Baba Kukeltash, the governor of Herat and a faithful retainer of Abdulla's, out of that post. He had just defeated Nur Muhammed Khan of Khuarezm (see next chapter), and now marched against Kul Baba. Abdulla ordered him to lay aside all scruples, and to resist the prince as he would any foreign enemy.§ This aroused Abdul Mumin's hatred against his father, and while the latter was hunting on the upper Oxus, in 1595, he was warned that his son was marching against him with hostile intentions. He accordingly hurried back to Bukhara, and Abdul Mumin withdrew to his appanage of Balkh; after which some bloody encounters took place between the two princes.|| When news of these dissensions reached the Steppes of Kipchak, we are told by Izkander Munshi that the Kasak Sultans, who had hitherto feared the power of Abdulla, and lived peaceably, began their aggressions again. Their great chief Tevkel advanced upon Tashkend. Abdulla, despising him, sent an insufficient army to oppose him, which was defeated in a sanguinary struggle between Tashkend and Samarkand, and a large number of chiefs were killed. The rest fled to Bukhara in a very broken condition. This defeat greatly distressed the Khan, who had been weighed down by his son's ill-conduct; but he summoned his people and advanced to Samarkand to meet the Kazaks; his health, however, failed.¶ To add to his other misfortunes, Shah Abbas, in alliance with the Uzbegs of Khuarezm, re-conquered Meshed, Merv, and Herat.** Thus borne down by disaster, Abdulla, at the end of his career, saw the greater part of his life-work undone. He died, according to

* Vol. Zernof, op. cit., ii. 399. † Vambery, 297. Note, 1.
‡ Yule's Cathay and the Way Thither, ii. 542. § Vambery, 293.
¶ Vol. Zernof, Khans of Kasimof, ii. 342. ** Vambery, 294.

Vambery, on the 6th of February, 1597. Munshi says he died, in the sixty-eighth year of his age, on the last day of 1006, which would be in 1598. His tomb still remains at Kermineh, which was the chief town of the appanage of his family.

He was a bigoted Sunni, and with his Uzbegs had caused terrible devastation in Khorasan, and Munshi, who is a panegyrist of his, speaks also of his cruelty and vindictiveness, and reports a story of him which ought perhaps to be assigned to his son, that when the walls of Balkh were being constructed (which work was completed in six months), he seized the sluggards and built their bodies into the walls with the bricks, and that some of their bones were still visible when he wrote.

ABDUL MUMIN KHAN.

Abdulla was succeeded by his son Abdul Mumin, one of whose first acts was to seize on the venerable Kul Baba Kukeltash, universally honoured for his many virtues, and who had been the governor of Herat. We are told he took him prisoner there, and dragged him about on foot after him, heavily laden with chains. He then hastened to Bukhara, where he was proclaimed Khan. Many did homage to him from terror, and few from real regard. Having taken possession of his father's treasures there and at Samarkand, he set off to visit personally all the places where any of his father's old servants were filling posts in the government; to reward their services by death under the hand of the executioner. This he did at Uratippa, Khojend, and Tashkend, in which last place Kukeltash was put to death, with his nearest relatives. He then went to Andijan and Akhsi to get hold of Uzbeg, the son of his great uncle, Rustem Sultan, who had acted as governor there for some time. Uzbeg resisted, but died a few days after the beginning of the siege. As Abdul Mumin did not make any mystery of his murderous intentions, a report soon spread that he would never rest until he had killed off all his father's servants and friends.‡ A conspiracy was formed against him. Its object was tersely expressed in an ambiguous phrase by an old Kazak soldier, named Abulvasi bi, "Words are useless, we must have deeds." Lots were cast for who should do the deed. It was July, and Abdul Mumin, to avoid the heat, travelled in the night. As he was going through a narrow pass, between Uratippa and Zamin, with his torchbearers, where there was only room for two horsemen to ride abreast, a shower of arrows met him and he fell. His head was immediately cut off. All passed on so rapidly that it was not discovered till daybreak, when some of the stragglers in the

* Schuyler's Turkestan, ii. 114.   † Senkofski, 28.   ‡ Vambery, op. cit., 296.

rear of the army coming up tumbled over the bodies of himself and a companion, who had shared his fate, and recognised the headless body of their chief by his clothes.* Abdul Mumin had reigned but six months. No coins of his are apparently known.

PIR MUHAMMED KHAN II.

On Abdul Mumin's death matters were left in terrible confusion. As Munshi says, most of the royal princes of the Uzbegs had perished in Abdulla's various wars, had been executed as rebels, or died in obscurity, and there was no one among the survivors fit to occupy the throne.†

It was reported, says Vambery, that Abdulla's widow had brought forward a second son, whom she had always kept in girls' clothes, and that one party was disposed to recognise him as prince, others wished to proclaim an infant son of Abdul Mumin's, who was but two years old. Another section of the Uzbegs at Bukhara set up Pir Muhammed, the son of Suliman Sultan, who was brother of Izkander, and who was, therefore, Abdulla Khan's first cousin.‡ At Balkh, Abul Amin, who was given out to be the son of Ibeidulla, the brother of Abdulla, was produced by Ibeidulla's widow, who with the assistance of the Amirs, assumed authority in his name. He seems to have acknowledged Pir Muhammed's right to the Khutbeh, and to have put his name on the coins. At Herat and in Khorasan Din Muhammed, the son of Abdulla's sister, and of a famous emigrant from Astrakhan, called Janibeg, who will occupy us further presently, and who was also named Tilim Sultan, was nominated as Khan. Din Muhammed, during Abdulla's reign, had ruled several towns in Khorasan. On Abdulla's death, Abdul Mumin having put his father Janibeg in prison, he revolted, and planned the seizure of Herat. That town was then governed by Khaji Bi, a lieutenant of Abdul Mumin, who refused to surrender. When the news arrived that Abdul Mumin had been murdered, and that the Persians were determined to reconquer Khorasm, and had invaded the country, Khaji Bi, and the others with him, opened the gates of the town, and admitted Din Muhammed, whom they proclaimed Khan there. Meanwhile Yar Muhammed, styled Kari, or the Grey, on account of his great age, who was Din Muhammed's grandfather, having returned from a pilgrimage to Mekka and Medina, Din Muhammed wished that the Khutbeh should be said in the latter's name, which was also to be stamped on the coins. At Merv, Kasim Sultan, who is called a relative of Abdulla's, had set up authority. He was speedily put to death, and the government of the town was assumed by Vali Muhammed, a younger brother of Din Muhammed, in the name of Yar Muhammed. Fortune did not long

---

* Vambery, 296.   † Senkofski, 30.   ‡ Vel. Zernof, Khans of Kasimof, &c., ii. 345, 346.

favour Din Muhammed. The Persians, who invaded Khorasan, under Shah Abbas, in July, 1598, defeated him near Puli Salar, in the neighbourhood of Herat,* and he escaped wounded to the Turkomans. In this campaign Abbas reconquered Sebsevar and Meshed and captured Herat.† When the news of Abdul Mumin's death reached the Kazak Steppes, Tevkel Khan deemed it a good opportunity to invade Mavera un Nehr. Matters were utterly confused, and there was no one to make head against him. He speedily conquered Turkestan, Akhsi, Andijan, Tashkend and Samarkand, and marched with seventy or eighty thousand men on Bukhara. Pir Muhammed and his Amirs, who had only fifteen thousand men with them, fortified the town, which was duly beleagured by the Kazaks. For eleven days the garrison made repeated sorties. On the twelfth they came out and gave the Kazaks battle, completely routing them as I have mentioned.‡ Tevkel retired to his brother Ishim, at Samarkand. Meanwhile Pir Muhammed and his adherents proceeded to recapture the various towns which had been taken by the Kazaks. A general muster of the warriors of Mavera un Nehr took place to aid him in expelling the hated robbers. They met the enemy at Uzun Sakal, in Miankal. After the beginning of the fight, Baki, the brother of Din Muhammed, arrived with the news of the terrible disaster at Puli Salar, and reported how his brother had perished in his flight.§ It would seem that the latter having found his way, after the battle, among the Karai Nomads, near Andkhoi, he was recognised by his royal dress and slain.∥ Baki, who became a famous person in later days, and was apparently a brave warrior, now had several struggles with the Kazaks, in one of which he captured Abdul vasi bi, one of the con spirators against Abdul Mumin, who had joined the Kazaks, and who had encouraged Tevkel to invade the country. After a month's unimportant skirmishing, matters came to a crisis, and a sanguinary battle was fought, in which Said Muhammed Sultan, a relative of Pir Muhammed's, and Muhammed Baki Atalik were killed, and Tevkel himself was wounded. He, thereupon, fell back on Tashkend, where he died. Pir Muhammed rewarded Baki Sultan with the government of the district of Samarkand, and then returned to Bukhara. Soon after, through the intercession of the Sheikh of Nakshbendief, peace was concluded with the Kazaks.¶

Baki Sultan was received with great rejoicings by the people of Samarkand, who went out to meet him, and cheerfully submitted to his authority. He seems not long after this to have quarrelled with Pir Muhammed, and to have had ambitious views in regard to the throne. His principal supporters were his uncles Rakhman Kuli and Abbas Kuli, and his brother Tursun Muhammed Sultan. He presently rebelled,

---

* Vol. Zernof, Khans of Kasimof, ii. 345-347.   † Vambery, 298.   ‡ Ante, 638.
§ Vol. Zernof, ii. 350.   ∥ Vambery, 306.   Note.   ¶ Vol Zernof, ii. 350, 351.

invaded Miankal, and captured the fortress of Dabusi, and killed its
governor Muhammed Sherif Sultan, a relative of the Khan. The latter
now appealed for aid to his deputy at Balkh, Abdul Amin. The two
thereupon went to Samarkand with 40,000 men, and besieged it, but the
Khan was defeated and killed. His army dispersed. Baki Muhammed now
repaired to Bukhara where he seated himself on the throne.* Thus was
an end put to the dynasty of the Abulkhairids, which had reigned so long in
Mavera un Nehr. Before we continue this history it will be convenient to
survey with Vambery the condition of Mavera un Nehr during the epoch
we have been describing. I shall abstract the following passage from his
work on Bukhara. He says, "During the epoch of the Sheibanids (i.e.,
the Abulkhairids) the process of separation of the east Islamite world
from western Islam was completed and Muhammedanism assumed the
character in which it is met with up to the present day between the
eastern frontier of Iran and China. There was naturally nothing like the
amount of culture existing under the Timurids to be found under the
Sheibanids. These rough warriors, who believed in the powers of their
Yada tashi (magic stone) to control the elements, cure diseases, and
insure victory in battle, were sincerely devoted to their religion and to its
priests. In the time of the Mongolian occupation, a few remarkable
mollahs, in virtue of their spiritual powers, had been practically rulers
of the land, controlling by their veto the will of the most imperious
despots, and this experience was repeated under the Sheibanids. The
teachers of godly wisdom not only enjoyed the complete devotion of the
people, but the princes vied with each other for their favour, and, whether
we ascribe it to superstition or to fear of popular opinion, it remains
equally a most remarkable manifestation, how the mightiest princes of
this dynasty invariably bore themselves towards the mollahs, not only
with respect but with all the marks of the most abject humility. Two
of these mollahs were most especially honoured, and invested in their
lifetime with the odour of sanctity.

"Makhdum Aazam, more usually called Mevlana Khojhaki Kasani,
a pupil, under the Timurids, of the celebrated ascetic Khoja Ahrar, is
said to have distinguished himself by a most holy life, to have been
endued with miraculous power, and to have been treated by all the
princes of his time with a respect bordering on fear. He died at
Samarkand on the 21st Muharrem 949 (1542), and his tomb, a league off
at Dehbid, is to this day a much frequented place of pilgrimage. Kasim
Sheikh Azizan, a pupil of Khudadad's, celebrated like the former for
sanctity of life rather than for any profound learning, was held in high
respect, as is best illustrated by the following anecdote :—Sheikh Azizan
was living at Kermineh and heard that Abdulla Khan, then at war with
Juvanmerd Ali of Samarkand, intended to pay him a visit. The sheikh

was friendly disposed to the prince, and went a little way out of the town to meet him. He soon saw a long train approaching headed by a man walking bareheaded, with a cord round his neck, the other end of which was held by a horseman. To his great astonishment he recognised in this abject creature the mighty Abdulla, the ruler of so many countries. He asked why he appeared thus in the garb of a penitent; and Abdulla replied, ' I have imposed on myself as a penance to go in this fashion from the Kham Rabat to the khankah (convent) of the Sheikh.' Sheikh Azizan was deeply affected by this, himself placed the prince on horseback and put his mantle on him, and the two returned thus together to Kermineh. Abdulla of course desired by this act of humility to implore the help of the Sheikh in his enterprise against Samarkand; he obtained it and got possession of the place. Sheikh Azizan died about three years afterwards, in 989 (1581).

"Theological studies were alone pursued at this time with any ardour. Amongst the most distinguished scholars were Mevlana Isam-eddin, the son of Arabshah, who first lived at the court of Sultan Husein Murza at Herat, and afterwards went to Bukhara; he was much in favour with Ubeidulla Khan. This prince, notwithstanding his warlike propensities, was not averse to poetry, and tried himself to make verses. Being doubtful as to the right interpretation of an Arabic quatrain, he one day asked Isam-eddin to explain it to him, and received from him in the course of a few hours 656 different readings of each line of the quatrain in question. This story is told by his panegyrist Seyid Rakim. He died in 943 (1536), at Samarkand; his best known works are: Marginal Annotations on Tefsir i Kazi, and on Jami's exegetical works. Mevlana Sadik, a learned exegetical scholar of Samarkand, who made two pilgrimages to Mekka and wrote valuable commentaries on theological works and glossaries of some abstruse poetical compositions. In his later years he lived at Kabul at the court of Hakim Shah, where he died in the year 1007 (1597). Amongst other equally distinguished men we may further mention Mollah Zia-eddin, a learned theologian who died in 973 (1565); and Khoja Jelal Juibari, a pupil of Makhdum Aazam's, who was held in high honour both as an ascetic and as a learned theologian and exegetical teacher. Turkish had now become the popular language, so that the poets from this time forward were all exclusively Turks; the most distinguished of them seems to have been the Uzbeg prince Muhammed Salih, whose father was deprived of the government of Khuarezm by the Timurids, and who entered whilst very young into the service of Sheibani. He was the author of the 'Sheibani Nameh' (Sheibaniade), a masterly epos which raises him even above Newai. The other poets of this period were mostly mere rhymesters and concoctors of chronograms, but history has preserved the names of Amir Ali Kiatib and Molla Mirek, poets laureate to the first Sheibanids. Also that of Mollah Mushfiki, who wrote chronograms on the various buildings of Abdulla, and also a few sonnets, kassids, and epigrams. He died in 994 (1585). Kazi Payende of Zamin, a perfect master of language, left a work especially deserving of notice, a poem of eighteen strophees in praise of the Vizier Kul Baba Kukeltash, in which there is not a single dotted letter. This is equivalent to a poem written in a European language without using the letters b, kh, f, j, k, n, p, sh, t, tch, or z. Finally, Shirin Khoja, a poet of the time of Ubeidulla and Khair Hafiz, a popular singer and musician at the court of Abdulla, who died in 981 (1573). The architectural monuments of the time of the Sheibanids owe their origin in addition to the public spirit of Abdulla Khan, chiefly to the theological and Suffi tendencies of the spirit of the times. Numerous mosques, convents, colleges, halls, and mausoleums were built in memory of deceased saints. Amongst'them may be mentioned, a mosque built at Samarkand by the Vizier Kukeltash in 934 (1527), to which Kuchkunji Khan gave a pulpit of white marble. The college of Abdulla Khan, which is in good preservation to this day, has a high portico, and over it a text of the Koran inlaid in enamelled tiles with letters more than two feet long, so that it can be read at an enormous distance. Abdul Aziz Khan restored the Mesjidi Mogak, formerly a Parsi temple, and built the convent at the tomb of Khoja Bahaeddin, a short league from Bukhara. Finally, Abusaid built a college at Samarkand, and the millionaire Mir Arab another at Bukhara, which is to this day the most richly-endowed school in all Central Asia."[*]

The period of the Abulkhairid domination in Mavera uń Nehr was contemporary with the domination of the famous Sefid dynasty in Persia, during whose rule Persia reached its culminating point of prosperity and culture, and with that of the great and famous Moghul emperor of India, Akbar. We will now continue our story.

THE JANIDS OR ASTRAKHANIDS.

BAKI MUHAMMED KHAN.

With the accession of Baki Muhammed we make a fresh start in the history of Mavera un Nehr. He introduced another royal race there. The change was not so great as is generally supposed, for the new stock seems to have acquired its rights to the throne through intermarriage with the family of Abulkhair. We will make a short retrospect in order to make the matter clearer. Kuchuk Muhammed, the famous Khan of the Golden Horde, the father of the Khan Ahmed, had, besides the children I have mentioned,[†] another son named Chuvak Sultan who was the father of

---

* Vambery, History of Bukhara, 299-30a.   † Aŭŝte, 305

Maagushlak, whose son was Muhammed Sultan, called Yar Muhammed
Sultan by Abulghazi, whose son was Jan or Janibeg Sultan.* This Jan
may be looked upon as the founder of the new royal race of Mavera
un Nehr.

A few years after the capture of Astrakhan by the Russians, Yar Muhammed, who like his ancestors had lived there, removed to Bukhara,
where he took shelter with Iskander Khan, who gave his daughter Zehra
Khanum in marriage to his son Jan Sultan. This settlement took place
apparently in 975 (*i.e.*, 1567). Yar Muhammed, on account of his advanced
age, was called Kari (*i.e.*, the Grey). I have described how in his old age,
when returning from Mekka, he was proclaimed at Herat by his grandson
Din Muhammed, who had been intrusted by Abdulla with Nissa and
Baverd.† His authority was limited to Herat and the district in Khorasan
dependent on it, and he was a mere tool in the hands of his grandson Din
Muhammed. Yar Muhammed with his son Jan probably perished at or
after the terrible battle of Puli Salar, in which the Uzbegs were so badly
beaten by the Persians. I have described how Din Muhammed himself
fell into the hands of the Karai Turkomans, by whom he was put to death.
His wife only escaped by the self-sacrifice of a brave servant named
Khaki Yasaul. He had placed her and her two sons, Imaum Kuli and
Nadir or Nasr Muhammed, in bags on either side of his saddle, and then
galloped away. A bullet struck Nadir Muhammed in the foot which
lamed him for life.‡ Din Muhammed has been numbered among the
Khans of the Jani dynasty, but he only had authority over Herat and its
neighbourhood. On his death his brothers, Baki Muhammed and Vali
Muhammed, escaped to Mavera un Nehr, the former at length
succeeded in securing the throne of Bukhara, the Uzbegs no doubt
looking kindly upon him because his mother was the sister of their
great chief Abdulla. He was in reality the first Khan of Bukhara of
the new dynasty.

I have mentioned how on the death of Abdul Mumin, Balkh was
seized by the widow of Ibeidulla, the brother of Abdulla Khan, who put
her son Abdul Amin on the throne, and how he recognised the suzerainty of Pir Muhammed of Bukhara.§ I have also mentioned how he
went to the succour of his suzerain against Baki. When the latter had
mounted the throne of Bukhara he marched towards Balkh. Meanwhile
his nephew Sultan Muhammed Ibrahim, the son of his brother Tursun
Muhammed Sultan, who had lived for some time at the court of Shah
Abbas of Persia, made an alliance with Abdul Amin, and marched
to his assistance with a Persian army, the two having agreed to
divide Mavera un Nehr between them. But the very day Ibrahim entered
Balkh, Abdul Amin was given up to him by his people, who did not

---

* Vel. Zernof, i. Note, 83.   † Senkofski, 32.   ‡ *Id.*, 33.
§ *Ante*, 739. Vel. Zernof, ii. 346.

care for him, and he put him to death, and sent his mother, the widow of
Ibeidulla, to Mekka.* Ibrahim's religious views were not those of his
subjects, for he belonged to the Persian sect of the Rifzis, and he seems
to have behaved in a ruthless fashion, and some months after his
accession men were found hanging in the principal streets and squares.
These clandestine murders were attributed to him.† Izkander Munshi
tells us that he died of drunkenness. Thereupon the people of
Balkh seem to have set up a prince named Sultan Ubeidulla. Meanwhile Baki, who was besieging Hissar, sent his brother Vali against
Balkh. Ubeidulla came out to meet him at the head of his soldiers, who
were defeated and dispersed, and he was not again heard of. His chief
tributaries, the Sultan Yehanghir Murza, son of Seyid Muhammed Sultan,
from Shaburghan, and Muhammed Selim Sultan, son of Pir Muhammed
Khan, from Andkhud, fled to Shah Abbas, and Baki entered Balkh
in triumph, which was added to the dominions of Bukhara.‡ The
fugitives, it seems, took with them the famous diamond which Abdul
Mumin had stolen from the monument of the Imaum Riza, where it was
once more solemnly placed.§

In 1602 Baki Muhammed marched against the Karai Turkomans, in
Kunduz, with the avowed object of revenging the murder of his brother
Din Muhammed. The Uzbegs attacked their ancient enemies mercilessly. Many of them shut themselves up in the fort of Kunduz. "It
was not till large portions of the walls had been undermined and blown
into the air, together with hundreds of the garrison, that the fortress
could be taken by storm. None of the prisoners were taken alive. The
power of the Karai tribe of the Turkomans was broken in this war, and
it has never recovered itself."‖ These Turkomans were the allies of
Shah Abbas, who marched hastily to punish the invaders. He captured
the towns of Shaburghan and Andkhud, and wasted the country with
fire and sword as far as Biluk Akchi, devastating that part of Khorasan
claimed by the Uzbegs.¶ When the Persians neared the tomb of
Baber Abdul, near Balkh, their army was attacked by an epidemic.
While thus suffering it was assailed on both sides by the Uzbegs and
badly beaten, and Shah Abbas barely escaped with a few thousand
followers. Vambery remarks that the usually diplomatic Persian
chronicles confess to this defeat; stating that the extraordinary heat and
thirst so tried the Persian troops that it was difficult to resist the
Nomads, who broke in upon them from every side.** The same year
Baki Muhammed's nephew, Bediuz Zeman rebelled and retired into
Karategin, but his strong fortress Mesdia was captured, and he himself
was put to death. This rebellion was followed by that of Muhammed
Zeman, the governor of Badakhshan, whose father had had Bediuz

* Vol. Zernof, ii. 562.　† Senkofski, 34.　‡ Vol. Zernof, op. cit., ii. 362.
§ Vambery, 308.　‖ Id., 309.　¶ Senkofski, 35.　** Op. cit., 309. Note.

3 X

Zeman executed, but that was also repressed. At length, after a reign of seven years, namely in 1605, Baki Muhammed fell ill. No sooner was this known than the Kazaks began to ravage the land. Everybody turned to the saint Sheikh Alim Azizan "whose miraculous powers were expected to restore the prince to health" "As the Sheikh prescribed the fresh breezes of the Oxus, Baki Muhammed Khan was carried in a litter on board ship, in which he floated for several days on the river. The pious man had, however, failed in his diagnosis, for the patient died soon after, towards the end of Redjeb, 1605."[*] Fræhn has published one of his coins struck in 1602-3 at Bukhara, on which he styles himself Baki Muhammed Behadur Khan.[†]

VALI MUHAMMED KHAN.

Vali Muhammed went from Balkh to visit his sick brother. When the latter died, he mounted the throne, after defeating two of Baki's sons near Termez.[‡] We are told he gave himself up to drinking and the most scandalous debauchery, and made himself detested by his cruelty, injustice, and exactions. He confided the government of Balkh to a bey of the house of Fuladchi (Vambery says to his vizier, Shahbeg Kukeltash), and also gave him charge of Imaum Kuli and Nadir, the young sons of Din Muhammed. His cruelty was revolting. We are told he made small embrasures in the walls, through which he had his victims drawn by oxen. Others were put in cauldrons of boiling oil, or had their skin scraped off with woollen cards.[§] Dostum Argun, Shah Kuchuk, and Haji Naiman, three viziers of Baki Muhammed, were among the victims of the monster.[||] A powerful party now rose against him, headed by Imaum Kuli, who seized on Balkh. Kukeltash was put to death with the same torments he had inflicted on others, and Imaum Kuli then marched on Bukhara. His brother Nadir, with another body of troops, marched there by a different route. Vali, who was hunting in the beautiful neighbourhood of Karshi, knowing that he had few friends on whom he could rely, fled to Persia,[¶] where he was received by Shah Abbas with great distinction. The latter went three days' journey to Dauletabad to meet him. About 20,000 musketeers formed the lane through which the refugee entered the city. The houses and shops in the bazaar which he passed were adorned with costly carpets. Poets celebrated his entry in kasids. Not long after the Shah sent him towards the Oxus, escorted by 80,000 Persians. Imaum Kuli sought counsel from the saintly Khoja Muhammed Amin, a descendant of Makhdum Aazam. Vambery graphically relates how little disconcerted the holy man was at

---

* Vambery, 310.   † Frahn Res., 441.   ‡ Vambery, 310.
† Senkofski, 36, 37.   ‖ Vambery, 310. Note.   ¶ Senkofski, 57, 58.

the size of the opposing force. "Hanging his bow and quiver on his clerical robes, he himself shot the first arrow, and, after he had thrown a handful of dust against the enemy, which had the effect of enveloping them in darkness, he gave the signal for the general assault; a fierce combat began, and the chronicler gravely describes how the darkness defended the Uzbegs as it were with a wall, while it rendered the hostile camp, pitched beside the lake of Maghian, indefensible." As a fact the Uzbegs were successful in the battle, Vali Muhammed fell alive into Imaum Kuli's hands, and, after a reign of six years, was beheaded by order of the enthusiastic Sheikh.[*] Vali's two sons, Rustem and Muhammed Rahim, escaped to Persia, where their descendants, Munshi tells us, still ruled when he wrote over Ubé and Shiflan, which the Persian king had assigned to them.[†] Vali Muhammed's death took place, according to Vambery, in the beginning of 1020 (i.e., 1611).[‡] Senkofski and Vel Zernof date it in 1608.[§]

SEYID IMAUM KULI BEHADUR KHAN.

The mother of Imaum was the daughter of the murza Abu Talib, the last of the descendants of Ali, whence the rulers of Bukhara now began to add the title Seyid to their names.[||]

The first act of Imaum Kuli's reign was to nominate his brother Nadir, or Nazr, as he is otherwise called, as governor of Balkh.[¶]

The young prince proved himself an admirable ruler. He is described by his panegyrist, as just, disinterested, active, and pious, and both his public and private life were exemplary, he loved the society of literary men and poets, and distributed in largess the presents he received from his grandees and people, while his personal habits and expenditure were simple. He kept few horses in his stables, and when he went to war his people, who were much attached to him, readily supplied him with the necessary horses.[**]

On the side of Persia there was peace for many years, the strong arm of Abbas restraining both Uzbegs and Turkomans from making their predatory raids.[††] Imaum Kuli's hands were not, however, altogether idle, for he was kept busy in watching his northern neighbours the Kazaks.

Yusuf Munshi tells us how in 1021 (i.e., 1612), Imaum Kuli advanced into Turkestan against the Kazaks and Kalmuks, and marched as far as Ashghara and Karatagh where he defeated these hordes, and forced them to withdraw to the most sterile mountains, and left his only son Izkander in charge of Tashkend, but the latter having committed some indiscre-

---

* Vambery, 312.　　　† Senkofski, 38.　　　‡ Op. cit., 312.
§ Senkofski, 38. Vel. Zernof, Coins of Bukhara, 403.　　　|| Vel. Zernof, id., 403.
¶ Senkofski, 38.　　　** Id., 38, 39.　　　†† Vambery, 312.

tions, there was a revolt against him, and he was killed. He thereupon marched with all his troops against Tashkend and summoned his brother Nadir to join him from Balkh. The inhabitants prepared to resist him, and he swore, in hyperbolic language, not to stay the carnage till the blood of the Tashkendians reached as high as his stirrups. He ordered a general assault. The town was captured and given up to pillage. After some hours of slaughter, his officers who knew him well, went to intercede for the lives of the rest of the inhabitants. Wavering between his oath and his kindly feelings, he hesitated what to do, when his embarrassment was solved by a fetva of the Imaums. These interpreters of the law, who like others of their craft were great casuists, declared that the oath would be satisfied if he made his horse enter a tank where the water was red with the victims of his vengeance, and that his conscience would then be purged since in fact the blood of the Tashkendians would reach his stirrups. The Khan gladly seized upon the subterfuge and ordered the slaughter to cease.* The Tarikhi Alim ari Abbasi reports, on the contrary, that Imaum Kuli was beaten on this occasion,† but the story of Munshi is too circumstantial to be doubted, and it would seem that the former author has confused the account with one of a later campaign. The Kazaks apparently succeeded during the next few years in gaining possession of Tashkend, and we find Imaum Kuli negotiating in 1621 with the Kazak Khan Tursun for peace. It was then, apparently, that he conceded Tashkend and its district to them.‡

The greater part of Imaum Kuli's reign, however, was free from such disturbing elements, and the historian of the times fills it up with more interesting anecdotes. Vambery has translated several of these which I will relate. He tells us, " he often exchanged the robe of the prince for the mantle of a dervish. He wandered about the city, accompanied by his vizier, Nezr Divanbegi, and his favourite Abdulvasi, so that he might learn how things were going on. Of the learned men of the time he chiefly associated with the Mollah Turabi and the Mollah Nakhli. He once rewarded a kasid composed by the latter with its weight in gold. Several successful poems of his own have been preserved." The following anecdote regarding his adventures when incognito is worth relating. "The young mollah of a college was madly in love with a beautiful creature, but he was poor, and the object of his affections required a decisive proof of his passion in the form of a new dress for an approaching festival. The mollah's sorrow and melancholy knew no bounds, and in his desperation he called to mind the Muhammedan principle, ' The property of the unbelievers belongs to the believers.' He determined to break into the shop of an Indian jeweller by night and so procure the

---

* Senkofski, 39-41.   † Vel. Zernof, Khans of Kasimof, ii. 375.
‡ Id., 574, 575. Is it possible that this Tursun Khan, whom we previously noticed (ante, 639), was the Tursun Muhammed, brother of Baki, already named ? (Ante, 744.)

money, which he so urgently needed. *Dictum factum*. The mollah went to the bazaar accompanied by two trustworthy servants and forced his way in through the door, imperfectly secured on account of the much vaunted security of property. He had regained the street with a casket of jewels in his hand, when the Hindu, awakened by the noise, raised an alarm, and caught the mollah by the collar just as the watchman came up with a torch in his hand. The mollah hastily knocked the torch out of his hand, and then, concealed by the darkness, exclaimed, 'Ah ! Nazr Divasbegi thou hast made a foolish joke.' To this came the answer, 'Your Majesty, it was not me but Abdulvasi Kurji.' As it was well known that Imaum Kuli wandered incognito with persons bearing these names, the terrified watchman supposing he had spoiled some jest of his prince, ran off as fast as he could. What followed is easily told. The injured Hindu appealed to the justice of the prince, and complained of neglect of duty on the part of the watchman. The latter, when summoned, supposed he was going to be punished for too much zeal. The whole affair came to light. The mollah was called on to return the stolen property, did so, and on his appearance before the Prince, was not only pardoned his offence but withal received a present."[*]

In 1620 the Russian Tsar, Michael Feodorovitch sent Ivan Khokhlof on a mission to Imaum Kuli. He had strict orders how to conduct himself. If any dues or payments were demanded of him in order that he should be admitted, he was not to pay them, but to return, and if invited to the Khan's table he was only to accept the invitation on condition of no other envoys being there, or if any should be there that they should sit below him. He went to Samarkand, where he was received by the Khan. On entering the palace, one of the officials wished to take the Tsar's letter from his hand, but he refused to give it up. On presenting the Tsar's compliments, and noticing that the Khan did not rise at the mention of his name, he observed that on such occasions it was usual for all kings to rise. Imaum Kuli complied, excusing himself for not doing so before on the ground that it was so long since a Russian envoy had been there that he had forgotten, and declaring that he meant no incivility.[†]

At this time the throne of Delhi was occupied by the famous Emperor Yehanghir, to whom Imaum Kuli sent envoys to announce his own accession. Yehanghir was much devoted to love making with his charming spouse Nurjihan (*i.e.*, light of the world), and he condescended to ask after the fair ones of Imaum Kuli, which is deemed a great breach of Muhammedan good manners. The offended envoy replied that his master was free from earthly passions, and did not concern himself with the things of this world. Yehanghir replied, "When has thy prince seen the world, that it has inspired him with so much disgust?" This speech, when reported to Imaum Kuli, greatly displeased him, and Yehanghir having presently sent a skilled physician as his envoy to Bukhara, bearing a rich tent broidered with gold and precious stones, the khan, who disliked luxury, in the first place kept the envoy waiting a long time for an audience, telling his courtiers that if he received him and his presents he should put himself under an obligation to him, while if he received him and declined the presents he should be guilty of incivility; but, as the vizier continued to press him to grant an audience, he at length consented to do so on some informal occasion as on a hunt. The envoy accordingly dressed his tent with the other presents, and had it placed so that Imaum Kuli must see it on his return. The Spartan Khan barely deigned to look, and then turning to Rahim Pervaneji he said, "Take them. All these have I given to thee." The astonished envoy still had a present in reserve, however, and on getting an audience the following day he said, "Two remarkable swords have been left behind by Akbar Shah. One my emperor has kept for himself, the other he sendeth thee, his brother, as a token of friendship." The Uzbeg prince could not well refuse this present. When, however, he attempted to draw the sword from its sheath, and found it somewhat difficult to do so, he remarked, with a reference to Yehanghir's former project of conquering Badakhshan, which was never carried into execution, "Your swords are too difficult to draw." "Only this one," answered the envoy, with ready wit, "because it is a sword of peace; were it a weapon of war it would leap readily from its scabbard." History has preserved another witty remark of this ambassador, who afterwards gained the favour of Imaum Kuli, and was by him graciously dismissed. On one occasion the two poets, Nakhli (the Palmy) and Turabi (the Earthy), competed with one another in poetical composition at the court of the prince of Bukhara. The prudent physician was asked to which he gave the preference. "O prince," he answered, "out of the earth grows the palm." In consequence of this decision, the last-named poet was treated with greater distinction. Yehanghir's embassy returned home in 1036 (1626). A year later he died, and was succeeded by his son Shahjihan.* The latter collected a large army with the intention of invading Balkh and Badakhshan, and advanced as far as Kabul. Having been informed by his brother Nadir of what was going on, Imaum raised a large force, and himself went to Balkh. His brother Nadir, accompanied by his ten sons and the principal people of the place, with a vast crowd, went out to meet him. They all, including Nadir and his sons, followed him on foot. Imaum Kuli alone went on horseback, and the road was carpeted with brocades, &c., which the people had spread out. When he reached the city he busied himself with preparing to resist the invader. Meanwhile he sent the Dadkhah, Haji Mansur, as his envoy to Kabul. Shahjihan, who now realised what a difficult venture he had entered upon, professed to the ambassador that he had no

* Vambery, 315-317.

warlike intentions, and had only gone to inspect his provinces.* Imaum
Kuli's friendly relations with Persia were chiefly secured by his brother
Nadir, who was on friendly terms with the Shias. He had one campaign
there, however, during the government of Shah Sefi, when, we are told, that
in consequence of numerous executions, disturbances broke out at Merv,
and this tempted the Uzbegs to make an attack. Imaum Kuli is said
to have sent fifteen thousand men from Bukhara, and Nadir twenty
thousand from Balkh, under the leadership of the latter's son Abdul Aziz,
but after a prolonged defence they were obliged to retire on the approach
of a large Persian army.† Nadir in 1621 sent a present of fifty horses of
Turkestan to Shah Abbas, by his envoy Payende Murza.‡

Imaum Kuli, after his visit to Balkh, returned to Bukhara, where he
reigned in peace and prosperity for some years, when he was seized by
an attack of opthalmia, from which he speedily became blind. He
thereupon summoned his brother. They went together to the mosque to
hear the Friday prayer, and when the khatib, after reading the praises
of the Prophet, was about to proclaim the titles of the reigning sovereign
he ordered the name of his brother Nadir to be substituted for his own.
This was received with great consternation and trouble by his people,
but he insisted, and Nadir was duly proclaimed Khan.§ This was in the
year 1050 (i.e., 1640).‖ He then determined to repair to Mekka. On his
way he was received with great honour by Shah Abbas II. Fifteen
thousand horsemen accompanied him from Karshi to the capital, and the
Shah went out from Ispahan with his grandees to meet him, and the two
sovereigns rode together over silken tissues into the town. This was in
1052 (i.e., 1642).¶ Imaum Kuli died in his sixty-second year, at Medina,
where a public garden and bath founded by him still remain.**

SEYID NADIR MUHAMMED BEHADUR KHAN.

The new Khan was a great contrast to his brother, and the austerity
of manners which had prevailed at Bukhara rapidly altered. Nadir was
master of immense treasures. According to Vambery, it required six
thousand strong camels to transport them, and he had eight thousand
horses in his stables, without counting brood mares. He also had
eighty thousand sheep of the breed which produced the blue lambs (i.e.,
the lambs for making Astrakhan skins of), and four hundred chests filled
with orange-coloured Frengish satin.

Having set out to try and conquer Izfendiar Khan of Khuarezm, a
revolt broke out in his northern dominions, headed by Baki Yaz (?). His
son Abdul Aziz, who was sent against him, sided with the rebel, and was
proclaimed in his father's stead. Nadir, who was at Karshi, and knowing

---

* Senkofski, 41, 42.   Vambery, 317.   † Vambery, 317. Note, 2.   ‖ Id.
§ Senkofski, 42.   ‖ Vambery, 319.   ¶ Malcolm, i. 580.   ** Vambery, 319.

his son's energy, retired to Balkh. There he conferred the appanage of Gar on Khosru Sultan, Meimeneh and Andhud on Kasim Sultan, Gulab on Behram Sultan, Salu Chiharjui (the ford over the Oxus now known as Khoja Salu) on Subhan Kuli, and Kunduz on Kutlan Sultan.* This was in 1647.

SEYID ABDUL AZIS KHAN.

After Nadir Muhammed retired beyond the Oxus Abdul Azis was duly proclaimed at Bukhara. He then wrote to his father a penitent letter, and asked that Kutluk Sultan might go to him to receive further explanations. When the latter arrived he was persuaded to rebel. Thereupon his brother Subhan Kuli was sent to recall him to his duty, and was promised, if successful, the title of Kali Khani (i.e., commander of the forces). Kutluk shut himself up in Kunduz, which was speedily captured, whereupon Subhan had him executed. Nadir was outraged by this act, and said he had sent him to correct his brother, not to kill him, and having delayed the promised promotion, Subhan Kuli also rebelled. Nadir, under these trying circumstances, appealed to Shahjihan, the Emperor of Hindostan, for assistance, who greedily seized the opportunity. He sent his sons Aurengzib and Murad Bakhshi with a large army towards Balkh. They traversed the defile leading from Kabul to Balkh. Khosru Sultan, who resisted them, was captured and sent prisoner to India. Meanwhile Nadir was made aware by a secret missive from some one in the invaders' army that their real purpose was not to aid him but to seize Balkh. Having collected his treasure, he escaped in the night by a hole in the garden wall of his palace, and retired toward Shaburgan and Andkhud. He was pursued, but having been joined by his grandson Kasim Sultan from Meimeneh with some hundreds of men, beat off the pursuers. Having repaired to Shah Abbas II., by whom he was looked upon as a more or less sacred person, his mother having been a descendant of the Imaum Riza,† he was in consequence well received and treated with princely hospitality. Meanwhile the Jagatai troops, as they are called (i.e., the troops of the Great Moghul), continued their advance, and placed governors in the various towns south of the Oxus, while the Uzbegs retired beyond that river to Mavera un Nehr. For two years they remained in possession of Balkh.

At length Abdul Azis prepared to drive them out, and when the campaign opened it was a savage and severe one. During four months there were continual fights, in which the troops of "the Great Moghul" were great sufferers. The devastation caused such a famine that an ass's load of corn cost one thousand florins. This was aggravated by a terrible winter, during which, in the inflated language of Munshi, "those

---

* Vambery, 320.   † Senkofski, 44, 45. Vambery, 221, 222.

who went out of their houses were frozen to death, and those who remained in had to scorch themselves on the fire to keep warm."*

Thereupon Shah Jihan sent to invite Nadir to return, while he withdrew his forces southwards, and most of them perished from cold and hunger on the way. The author of the Tarikhi Mekim Khani reports how the next year, when he went on a mission to India, he saw piles of human bones on the highways.† Nadir Muhammed, whose reign reminds one of the latter part of that of Louis, the son of Charlemagne, now returned, but the feud with his sons continued, and he at length determined to adopt a religious life and to withdraw from Balkh. We are told he wished to be reconciled with his sons and to give them his blessing, but Subhan Kuli refused to accept this paternal gift. He thereupon set off for Mekka, but died *en route* in 1061 (*i.e.*, 1657). His body was taken to Medina and buried beside that of Imaum Kuli.‡ When the news reached Mavera un Nehr his sons put on mourning and distributed gifts, while readers of the Koran recited the holy book day and night for the repose of his soul, a form of conventional regret which has not been unfrequent further west. But almost directly after Abdul Azis sent Kasim Sultan, the favourite son of Nadir, to occupy Balkh, which was governed by Subhan Kuli. The latter naturally resisted, and the town was assailed for forty days and its environs devastated. He then retired to Hissar for the winter. In the spring he went to Khulm biluk, where a parley ensued. It was agreed he should become governor of the town, and that Subhan Kuli should succeed him there, but he was shortly after assassinated. The author of the Tarikhi Mekim Khani says none of the Astrakanids was braver, wiser, more generous, and courageous than he. He was a good poet and prose writer, and he left behind a divan of one thousand couplets, in some of which he imitated Saib Ispahani.§ In 1665 Abulghazi, the famous ruler of Khuarezm, invaded the dominions of Abdul Azis, and commenced a bloody strife, which was continued by his son Anusha. Its details will occupy us in the next chapter.

Vambery has graphically condensed the notice of the latter days of Abdul Azis contained in the Tariki Mekim Khani, and I shall take the liberty of appropriating his account. He says :

" In the meantime, however, Abdul Azis, worn out with constant feuds with his enemies and sick of the cares of government, owing to the quarrels with his brothers, determined to follow the example of his two predecessors. He resolved to abdicate in favour of Subhan Kuli, to take up the pilgrim staff and go to Mecca. When Subhan Kuli was summoned to come to Bukhara and assume the sovereignty, he sent the Atalik Imaumkuli and the Pervaneji Tangriberdi to say that he would willingly comply with the request when Abdul Azis had himself left the capital.

---

* *Id.*, 46.   † Vambery, 322   ‡ Senkofski, 46.   § *Id.* Note, 24.

3 Y

This message did not produce a good impression on Abdul Azis, and the men of Bukhara took advantage of it to dissuade their sovereign from carrying out his intention of resigning. But Tangriberdi, who saw that the interests of his master were in danger, went to Abdul Azis Khan and spoke as follows: 'Lord, with thy permission I will relate a story of which I am now reminded. When Sultan Ibrahim from Balkh passed through Nishapur on his way to Mekka, he visited Ferid-eddin Attar, the wisest man of his times, and stayed with him to supper. But the highly honoured was, as is well known, very poor. So when evening was come he prayed to God, and O wonder! a dish full of good food was suddenly placed upon the table from which both his guest and himself ate and were satisfied. The Sultan invited the holy man to return the visit on the following day, when he also prayed, and in answer to his prayer several dishes full of dainty meats were served before them. Ferid-eddin, marvelling at the diversity of the heavenly blessing, exclaimed : "O God, why have I obtained but one dish, but the Sultan several?" Thereupon a voice answered, "Ye are verily both my servants, but Ibrahim hath given up for my way sceptre and throne, but thou only a shop; as his merit is greater, so is also his reward." And so too is it with thee,' continued the crafty Tangriberdi ; 'thy pilgrimage is really worth all the trouble it will cost thee, for it has a thousand times more merits than that of another.' Abdul Azis, moved to tears by this parable, was confirmed in his previous resolution. He at once began to prepare for his journey, for which he started in the year 1091 (1680), accompanied by more than three thousand pilgrims, who had attached themselves to his caravan. Like his predecessors, he enjoyed on his way through Persia the hospitality of Iran. Shah Suliman, the son of Abbas II., treated him with royal honours. In Ispahan he was lodged in the charming palace of Chil Sutun. As the festival of Noruz was at that time being celebrated with all the festivities customary on that occasion in Iran, the Uzbeg prince could take his farewell of the pomps and glories of the world amid the delightful gardens of Ispahan, then in the full bloom of spring, and amid all the magnificent splendour of the Persian court. Thence he took his way by Hamadan and Baghdad through the desert, where he had the misfortune to be attacked by a large band of Bedouin robbers. They demanded forty thousand ducats as his ransom, threatening in case of refusal to proceed to extremities. Not wishing to defile his hands with blood on his pious journey, Abdul Azis promised them half the sum, but as the Arabs would not abate their demands he at last became enraged. 'Have I reigned for forty years to be now dictated to by robbers?' he exclaimed, 'Up to battle ; if I fall it is in the service of God.' Fortunately the struggle terminated in favour of the pilgrim prince. He reached in safety the goal of his wishes, and died soon after in the seventy-fourth year of his life. He was buried at Medina near his father and his uncle.

"Abdul Azis was a man of remarkable corpulence, and indeed is said to have been the stoutest man of his time. One of his historians avows that a child of four years old could find room in one of the legs of his boots. A poet was daring enough to make his corpulence the butt of his wit. Abdul Azis heard of it, and sent for the satirist, who appeared before him trembling for his life. The prince addressed him in the following terms : ' O Mollah, I am told that thou hast composed a poem in ridicule of me ; do not the like to others or thou may'st see reason to repent such conduct.' With that he presented him with ten thousand dinars and a robe of honour. The poet replied, ' Lord, better had'st thou had me hewn into ten thousand pieces than thus disgrace me by thy magnanimity.' And indeed he left Bukhara and emigrated into India. Abdul Azis, who had proved so heartless in his conduct towards his father, displayed similar magnanimity on several other occasions. He himself was by no means wanting in culture ; he wrote good verses, and during his pilgrimage is said to have written some beautiful hymns. He is also said to have been remarkably familiar with the celebrated work 'Bukhari.' Learned men had always free access to him, and caligraphers he so greatly esteemed that he supported for seven years the celebrated caligrapher Mollah Haji, whom he employed to make a single copy of ' Hafiz.' The artist only wrote a couplet a day, and when on his journey Abdul Azis presented this copy of ' Hafiz' to Shah Suliman, the latter was much more delighted with this one present than with all the jewels and costly stuffs given him by the ex-prince of Transoxiania. Daring in battle, calm in danger, Abdul Azis was often inaccessible for days to the impressions of the outer world. This was attributed by many to his practice of continued meditation ; for the princes of Bukhara, who took part in bloody battles, and strove with their fathers and brothers for objects of worldly ambition, were obliged, by way of propitiating popular favour, to spend hours in the society of holy men, meditating on the greatness of God, and reflecting that all earthly activity is but mere trifling."*

SEYID SUBHAN KULI KHAN.

Subhan Kuli, on his brother's departure, became the ruler of Bukhara. This was in the beginning of Muharem 1091 (*i.e.*, 1680). Directly after his accession he appointed his son Izkander, Kalkhan of Balkh, but after retaining the post for two years he was poisoned by his brother Mansur Sultan. Subhan Kuli thereupon nominated his third son Ibeidulla Sultan to the post,† but Mansur contrived to have him assassinated also, and retained his hold on Balkh for four months in spite of his father. During

---

* Vambery, Hist. of Bukhara, 325-328.   † Senkofski, 50.

this interval he gave a grand feast, for which we are told in the Tariki Mekim Khani his ministers levied contributions on the merchants and artists there, so that a collection of rich stuffs, of broidered tents, and other works of art "as beautiful as the work of the Chinese or the Europeans," was brought together.* After controlling Balkh for four months a conspiracy was formed against him, and he was murdered while going to visit his aunt. A fourth son of Subhan Kuli, named Sadik Sultan, was now proclaimed governor of Balkh. He was a debauchee like his brother, whose murderers he had flayed alive and torn limb from limb. This caused an outbreak and great disorder in Balkh.† In the beginning of 1684 the "Great Moghul" Aurengzeb sent one of his grandees named Zeberdest Khan with elephants and other presents to Bukhara. In his letter he recited to him his victories and exploits, and solicited his alliance as a good Sunni against the hated Shias of Persia, whom he suspected of inciting the Afghan tribes of the Sulimani mountains to their continual restlessness. He wished to induce the Uzbegs to invade Khorasan.‡

At this time the Uzbegs of Khuarezm, under their chief Anusha, continued their perennial ravages, and had even plundered the environs of Bukhara. Subhan Kuli, who found it difficult to resist them single-handed, summoned Sadik to his help from Balkh. The latter set out, but learning *en route* how successful Anusha had been, that several of the Bukharian amirs secretly favoured him, and that others had broken out into rebellion at Hissar and Khojend, he thought it more prudent to return home again and shut himself up in Balkh. Subhan Kuli thereupon summoned to his aid Mahmud bi Atalik, whom he had appointed governor of Badakshan. The latter having marched at the head of his troops, defeated Anusha in a battle on the plains of Gijuvan, compelled him to abandon Samarkand and return home, and then subdued the rebel amirs at Khojend.§

Subhan Kuli was determined to punish his son who had treated him so badly, and Sadik, aware of this, prepared to resist. He first killed his two brothers Abdul Ghani and Abdul Kaiyum, and then sent an envoy to negotiate an alliance with Aurengzeb. Thereupon in 1685 Subhan Kuli marched against him. He advanced as far as Khan Abad, whence he wrote an affectionate letter, bidding him go to him and promising him pardon. He accordingly went, and was cordially received by his father, but when they entered the city he ordered him to be seized and to be chained in a dark and noisome prison. He put to death his accomplices with terrible torments, and kept his son a prisoner for three months, when the young fratricide, whose hands were soiled with so many crimes, died. This was apparently in 1098 (*i.e.*, 1686).¶

While the Khan had his hands full at Balkh, the Khuarezmians under

---

* *Id.* Note 31.   † *Id.*, 50, 51. Vambery, 330.
‡ Vambery, 332, 333. Senkofski, 51.   § *Id.*, 51, 52.   ¶ Senkofski. Note, 34.

their chief Anusha, made another raid on Mavera un Nehr, and carried destruction to the very gates of the capital. The Khan sent Mahmud Jan Atalik, of the tribe of Yuz, against them who utterly defeated them. The faithful Mahmud Atalik was rewarded with the government of Balkh which was added to his former charge of Badakhshan. Leaving Jan Atalik in charge of Balkh, the latter now marched against a very stubborn rebel who for seven years had harassed the district of Hissar. He is called Kara Alchin bey, by Senkofski, and Bayat Kara the chief of the tribe Bayat, by Vambery. This sturdy chief was besieged in the strong fortress of Badakhshan, called Nasman or Jebel.* The siege lasted for several months, during which we are told, the rebel communicated with Yar bi, the governor of Jurgun, who twice ravaged Kundus and Kashim, part of the appanage of Mahmud bi, but at length, after several assaults, the town was taken, the rebel perished fighting, and his head was sent to Bukhara.† At this time a civil strife seems to have been carried on between the Uzbeg tribes of Ming and Kipchak, the former of which lived in Meimeneh and Andkhud, and the latter near Balkh.‡ Meanwhile Subhan Kuli having gone on a pilgrimage to Meshed, Anusha Khan of Khuarezm seized the opportunity and made another savage raid towards Bukhara. This was his last venture, however, for having been badly beaten, his people put him to death, and raised his son Erenk Sultan to the throne.§ Subhan Kuli now sent an army into Khurasan as he had promised the envoy of Aurungzeb. This was commanded by Mahmud Jan bi. He ravaged the country and carried off many women and children prisoners. The most important place he captured was Bala Murghab, but meanwhile Erenk Khan of Khuarezm, continuing his father's policy, again crossed the borders. Bukhara being denuded of troops, Subhan Kuli sent in haste to Badakhshan to the Atalik for assistance. After the Khan had defended himself vigorously for ten days the Atalik arrived, and a terrible battle was fought under the walls of Bukhara, in which the Khuarezmians were defeated and pursued to their borders. After the war several begs rose in revolt against Subhan Kuli, but were repressed by the Atalik, who took them to Bukhara, and added another laurel to his others in obtaining their pardon, except that of their leader.| Meanwhile the partisans of Subhan Kuli at Urgenj created a revolution there in his favour, Erenk Khan was put to death, and in 1687 a deputation went to the Khan of Bukhara with the offer to have the money struck and the Khutbeh proclaimed in his name, and asking him to appoint a governor. This he accordingly did, and nominated Shahniaz-Ishik-Aka to the post.¶ During the rest of his reign Khuarezm apparently remained subject to Bukhara.

Subhan Kuli also had diplomatic relations with Ahmed II., Sultan

---

* Senkofski, 54. Note, 35.   † Id., 54.   ‡ Vambery, 351.   § See next chapter.
| Senkofski, 50.   ¶ Id.

of Turkey, who reigned from 1691 to 1695, and the latter sent him a
special envoy named Mustapha Chaush with presents of Arab horses,
jewels, rich garments, &c. He also sent him a letter which has been
preserved in the Tarikhi Mekim Khani. It has been translated at length
by Vambery. It was written in answer to a letter of congratulation,
whose receipt is acknowledged in the inflated phrases dear to Eastern
writers. " He boasts of having held it an eminently godly occupation to
exterminate from the face of the earth the Frankish unbelievers and the
miserable heretics, the Kizilbashis." He boasts of many victories over
the Franks which we know were all imaginary, since his reign was a
disastrous one for the Ottomans. He then goes on to tell his friend to
make a levy of his Uzbegs, and in unison with himself " to extirpate the
sinners against religion, and clear away thorns and thistles from the fair
valleys of Irak."* There are some suspicious circumstances about
this letter. Although professing to be sent by Ahmed II., it is dated in
1102, and therefore before his accession. It is not mentioned apparently
in the Turkish archives, and it is scarcely credible that Ahmed II., whose
career was an unfortunate one, should have boasted of victories over the
Franks, unless he transferred to himself the glories of the campaign
fought in his predecessor's reign by Kuprili Mustapha Pasha, the Grand
Vizier, against a coalition of Christian princes.†

Besides envoys from Turkey, we are told others went to him from
Kerim, which was a part of Cathay, where there lived Mussulmans and
heathens, and the former of whom had acknowledged the supremacy of
Bukhara, and had proclaimed Subhan Kuli in their mosques.‡ I do not
know where this country of Kerim was, but it was clearly not Krim, as
M. Vambery says. Senkofaki has discussed the question, and makes out
that Kerim was a name for North China,§ which is not impossible.
Was it a part of Kashgar? Envoys also went to him from Muhammed
Amin, the ruler of Kashgar, who reported that the Kirghises or Buruts
had occupied his country, that he had put himself under Subhan Kuli,
and had also had the Khutbeh said in the latter's name. The envoys
from Turkey, Kerim, and Kashgar were presented the same day.

In 1099 (i.e., 1687) Mahmud Jan, the governor of Balkh, died, and
Mahmud bi Atalik, whose deputy the former seems to have been, and
who was entitled Umdetul devlet, or the supporter of the empire, took
the government into his own hands. His rigorous justice and strong
hand were not grateful to the Uzbegs, but they caused great prosperity
at Balkh, and grain became very cheap there. He was constantly
engaged, however, in small expeditions for repressing the turbulent, and
among others defeated and punished Yar bi, the governor of Juzgun, who
had appropriated the mines of Badakhshan; but the amirs grew weary

---

* Vambery, 353-356.   † Senkofaki. Note, 36.   ‡ Senkofaki, 57.
                          Op. cit. Note, 38.

of his Cato-like virtues, and to bring him into disrepute, even organised bands of robbers to plunder the environs of Balkh. Weary of his pestilent companions, he wrote to Subhan Kuli asking him to send his young grandson Mekim, son of Iskander Sultan, to undertake the control of the place. The Khan at first refused, alleging that the prince was too young, but the amirs grew more turbulent. Some of them seized the citadel, others drew a certain Khoja Salih, whose mother was the daughter of Nadir Khan, from a monastery of dervishes, and put him on the throne. They also wrote to Subhan Kuli to complain of the Atalik. The Khan apparently listened to them, and even denounced his conduct, and they accordingly incited the tribes of Kuhistan, the mountainous part of Badakhshan, to ravage Kunduz, which was part of the Atalik's appanage. Mahmud bı thereupon, leaving Balkh in charge of two of his friends, went to quiet his own appanage. This retreat from his post seems to have disgusted the Khan, who fancied he was in league with Salih Sultan. He therefore collected an army of two hundred thousand men, crossed the Oxus, and marched upon Balkh. Thereupon Salih, who was in great trepidation, wrote to the Atalik to say he had not supplanted him wilfully at Balkh, but had been forced into his present position by others, and begging him to come to his succour. The Atalik, indignant at the Khan, who had so misinterpreted his actions, left Kunduz with seventy men, and in three days managed to reach Balkh, escaping the cordon Subhan Kuli had placed round it. He entered the citadel and was received with great joy, for the Khan had imprudently taken with him bands of " Kazaks, Karakalpaks, and other unknown tribes," whose main object was rapine, and who in fact plundered the town. During the siege of the citadel the Atalik displayed his great military capacity, and defeated the unwieldy army of the besiegers in several sorties. His men were still more encouraged to resist by the cruelties practised by the Bukharians on those whom they captured. At length Mahmud gave the besiegers a decisive blow, he engaged the Turkomans, the Bedouins (Arabs) and other nomads of those parts to make a night attack on Subhan Kuli's camp and to carry off his horses and camels, which they effectually did. The Khan being driven into a corner asked for peace, the terms of which were that he was to abandon the siege and return home again. On his departure the Atalik returned to Kunduz, where he exercised his former zeal and energy.* Salih Sultan, who was a mere dervish, could not keep order at Balkh, and the Atalik once more appealed to the Khan by his friends Shah niaz and Adil bi to send his grandson Mekim to the town, which he promised to secure for him. The Khan insisted that he must first displace Salih Sultan. This he did with little difficulty, and sent him off with all honour to Hindostan.†

Mekim thereupon repaired to Balkh with the title of Kalkhan, with

---

* Senkofski, 58-61. † Id., 61.

Adil bi as Atalik and Shah niaz as divan bégi. These two favourites, forgetting what they owed to Mahmud bi, succeeded in the course of twelve months in excluding him from the counsels of their master, and allied themselves with his deadly enemies, the family of Kurma beg. Having complained to Mekim and only received an evasive answer, couched in hyberbolic compliments, he marched on Balkh. Civil war was on the point of breaking out when Shah niaz died suddenly, and Adil lost his influence. Peace was thus restored, and the old Atalik returned once more to Badakhshan. Mekim Sultan's rule at Balkh was a difficult one, and troubled by the continual turbulence and outbreaks of his feudal soldiery.* In the midst of these disturbances the Persians of Khorasan invaded the province, and advanced as far as Meimeneh and Jijektef. Mahmud was once more summoned to the rescue. He scattered and crushed the rebels, and was rewarded by Mekim with magnificent presents, and returned home again to Kunduz loaded with laurels and the blessings of the people of Balkh. He was a person of remarkable courage, and did not scruple to enter a hostile town alone, where the force of his character reduced matters to order. On one occasion one of the Khan's sons having been made prisoner by the tribe of Kunkurat, which encamped at Termuz. Although these Uzbegs were his deadly enemies, he went and lived among them for a month, and did not retire till he had released the young prince. He was not only a very skilful soldier but loved the society of men of letters, and could himself write a beautiful hand. He was also a person of exemplary piety, and courted the friendship of a famous theologian named Sufi Haji Ali.†

Subhan Kuli Khan died in the year 1114 (i.e., 1702), at the age of eighty, after reigning thirty-one years at Bukhara, beside the twenty-three years during which he lived at Balkh,‡ which has been well styled the Dauphiné of Bukhara. Although personally brave, Subhan Kuli had no military capacity. To a crafty and cunning temper he added a strong devotion to Islam, and liked to discuss Mussulman casuistry with dervishes and others, and was also fond of improvising poetry. He built several palaces and mosques, and was the founder of one of the most beautiful medresis or colleges at Bukhara. He composed a medical work, of which Vambery obtained a copy at Herat. It was apparently the first book on medicine written in Turkish, and was founded chiefly on Arabic translations of Galen, Hippocrates, and Avicenna, with a quantity of lore on the use of incantations, talismans, &c.§

SEYID UBEIDULLA KHAN.

On the death of Subhan Kuli the grandees at Bukhara put his young son Ubeidulla on the throne of Bukhara, apparently to the disgust of his

---

* Id., 62, 63.   † Id., 64, 65.   ‡ Id., 65.   § Vambery, 357. Note, 1.

grandson Mekim, who had expected to succeed, and who still ruled at Balkh, and it was only after an interval of five months that he wrote to condole with him on his father's death, as prescribed by Eastern etiquette. He afterwards wrote a second letter, in which he treated Ubeidulla as an equal instead of as his suzerain. His envoys were consequently detained for six months at Bukhara, and they were only allowed to return when Ubeidulla, having collected an army, had marched against his nephew, and had already reached Karshi. Thereupon Mekim determined to gain over the famous Atalik Mahmud to go to his support. Ubeidulla did the same, and the envoys of the two princes reached Kunduz on the same day. The Atalik, who looked upon Mekim in some measure as his foster son, took his part, and went to Balkh, where he was received with great rejoicings, and Ubeidulla, by the advice of his officers, deemed it prudent to retire.* But he did not slacken his animosity. In 1115 (i.e., 1703) a body of marauders inspired by him made a raid upon Khan abad. The Atalik Mahmud bi marched against them and pursued them, but his brother Abdulla unfortunately fell into the hands of the Kunkurats, who killed him. Mahmud asked permission to punish this turbulent tribe, which had for many years infested the borders of the Oxus. Having obtained Mekim's permission, he in three days reached the fort of Kubadiyan, occupied by the Durmans, close allies of the Kunkurats. They submitted and gave up the fort, upon which, leaving a garrison there, he advanced against the Kunkurats, who abandoned their homes and withdrew. They were attacked and many of them killed among their own baggage, while others escaped to the mountains. The Atalik secured their property, but he released their women and children. The men he pursued as far as Tenki Divan and Bendi Harem, and making the fort of Kakai his headquarters, he scoured the country in various directions, and almost exterminated the tribe. On his return to Balkh, Mekim presented all his companions with rich robes.

The same year Utkan bi, governor of Hissar, having rebelled against the Khan of Bukhara, the latter sent his Atalik Rahim bi and his divan begi Maasum bi against him. En route they endeavoured to effect a reconciliation with Mekim bi, and suggested a conference on an island of the Oxus called Orta Erel, but Mekim distrusting them, argued rather that they should be attacked while besieging Hissar. This counsel was adopted, and Mahmud bi, in concert with Utkan bi, the rebel governor of Hissar, inflicted a terrible defeat on them, so that few succeeded in regaining Bukhara.† After his return Mahmud fell ill at Kunduz. The opportunity was tempting, and we find bands of marauders immediately disturbing the districts of Ishkmish and Talikan, but the old chief was soon aroused from his bed, and once more restored tran-

---

* Senkofski, 67-69. † Id., 71.

762 HISTORY OF THE MONGOLS.

quillity. Utkan bi having been drawn away from Hissar, Ubeidulla momentarily occupied it, but in 1116 (i.e., 1705-6) Mahmud bi re-occupied it and put Kush begi there as governor on behalf of Mekim Khan.* At this point we lose the guidance of the Tarikhi Mekim Khani, and for the next quarter of a century the history of Mavera un Nehr is very obscure. The point which is chiefly in debate among students is as to whether Abulfaiz Khan, against whom Nadir Shah of Persia marched about 1739, was the same person as the Ubeidulla just named or not. M. Vel. Zernof has discussed the question at some length.† Senkofski identifies the two names as those of the same ruler, but the weight of evidence seems to me to be strongly in favour of the other view. I believe they were brothers.

The date of Ubeidulla's death is uncertain. Izzetulla, who calls him Abdulla, says he reigned fourteen years. Frazer, that he reigned twelve, but as Fræhn has published a coin of Abulfaiz, dated in 1711, this is not possible unless he mounted the throne earlier than Munshi says.‡ It is not improbable that Ubeidulla died about 1705. According to the tradition reported by Vambery, he quarrelled with his Atalik Rahim bi, and was consequently put to death violently.§

SEYID ABULFAIZ MUHAMMED KHAN.

The title just given is the one we find on coins dated in 1711, 1716, and 1718, given by Fræhn,‖ and on which he styles himself son of Subhan Kuli Muhammed Behadur Khan. He was a mere puppet in the hands of Rahim bi, and is described as having had the religious mildness and character of a dervish. He lost Balkh and the Uzbeg country south of the Oxus, except Andkhud, Meimeneh, and the country of the Ersari or Lebal (i.e., river side Turkomans) which had been, as I have shown, governed by Salih Khoja, and remained subject to the latter's son, Seyid Abul Hassan.¶

We know little of the earlier part of his reign. The Uzbegs apparently continued to make their raids upon Khorasan, in one of which they captured Nadir, who afterwards became so famous as Nadir Shah. He made his escape four years after.** About 1718 the Uzbegs again invaded Khorasan, and in alliance with Azadulla, the chief of the Abdali Afghans, ravaged the greater part of the province. An army of thirty thousand men sent against them marched towards Herat, under Sefi Kuli Khan, and defeated twelve thousand Uzbegs, but it was in turn defeated by the Afghans.†† We do not again read of the Uzbegs until the reign of Nadir Shah.

* Id., 71, 72. † Coins of Bukhara and Khiva, 409, &c. ‡ Vel. Zernof, op. cit., 409. § Op. cit., 398. ‖ Res. 441, 442. ¶ Vambery, 339, 340. ** Malcolm, ii. 5. †† Id., i. 624. Ferrier's Afghans, 36.

While the latter was besieging Kandahar in 1736-8, he sent his son Riza Kuli by way of Badghiz, and Marcha or Mervichak to punish Alimerdan Khan, the ruler of Andkhud, who it seems was in league with the Afghans. He was deserted by the nomad tribes of the neighbourhood, was defeated, and sent prisoner to Nadir. He then captured Akshi and Shaburgan, and then advanced upon Balkh, which was governed by Abul Hassan, as we have seen. The road to this famous city was barred says Vambery by several ditches, which could not, however, prevent Riza Kuli's powerful artillery train from approaching; and after a short bombardment the town capitulated. Nadir Shah rewarded his son with a present of twelve thousand ducats in gold, three hundred dresses of honour, and some high bred norses, with their saddles and bridles decorated with gold and jewels. Riza Kuli now crossed the Oxus and assailed Abulfaiz, who allied himself with Ilbars, the Khan of Khiva, and although he succeeded in mastering the fort of Shelduk he seems to have been defeated by the united forces.* Malcolm says he won a signal victory over the Uzbegs. Both are agreed that he was recalled by his father, who wrote to the Uzbeg chiefs to tell them he had withdrawn his son, and ordered him not to disturb "countries which were the inheritance of the race of Jingis Khan, and of high Turkoman families."†

On his return from India, Nadir Shah was met at Peshawur by a stately embassy from Abulfaiz bearing rich presents and a message thus couched : " I am the last of an ancient royal stock. I have not the power to join issue with such a redoubtable monarch. I hold myself at his service. If he will deign to pay me a visit I will treat him as an honoured guest." Nadir Shah was much pleased and sent the envoys back with another missive in which he acknowledged his civility ; told him he intended to punish Ilbars Khan, of Khuarezm. He said he coveted neither the state nor the treasures of Abulfaiz, and after visiting Herat he intended to accept his invitation to go to Bukhara by way of Balkh. With the letter he sent some of the products of Hindostan as presents.‡ Abulfaiz in vain tried to persuade his neighbour Ilbars to propitiate Nadir. He only got some insults for his pains, and proceeded with his preparations for giving the great conqueror a fitting reception. He laid in a large stock of wheat, barley, and rice, and collected many sheep. Nadir arrived at Herat with three hundred elephants, a tent embroidered with pearls, and the famous peacock throne of the Emperors of Delhi. Having stayed a while in Kuhistan, east of Herat, whence he sent off some rich presents to the Sultan and the Russian Empress, he then set out and was joined at Badghiz by his son and heir, Riza Kuli Murza, with whom he went on to Meimeneh, Fariab, and Balkh.§ He sent word to Abulfaiz of his

---

* Vambery, 340, 341. † Malcolm, ii. 70. ‡ Schefer's Abdul Kerim, 95, 96.
§ Id., 96-99.

approach and transported one half his army across the Oxus, leaving the
other half with his artillery and a flotilla of a thousand boats containing
provisions on the left bank.* He crossed the river himself in a boat
artistically carved and adorned with Mosaics (? tiles), which had been made
for him by the artificers of Bukhara.† At Kerkhi, four stations from
Bukhara, Muhammed Rahim bi the Mangut, the famous Atalik of
Abulfaiz, who it would seem was a partisan of Nadir, went to meet him
with presents and provisions, and had the honour of an audience. There
also went the governors of Karshi and Hissar. Thence Nadir went on
to Charjui and Karakul, where Abulfaiz Khan with the Seyids Ulemas
and the other notables welcomed him and offered him some Arab
horses and other presents of high value. This was on the 12th of
September, 1740.‡ Nadir made Abulfaiz sit beside him. He gave him
a royal robe and a crown (? a girdle), adorned with precious stones, and
an Arab horse with a gilded saddle. In addressing him; he styled him
Shah. The next day Abulfaiz returned to Bukhara. He had some
beautiful daughters. Nadir married one himself, and gave a second one
to his nephew Adil Shah, the son of his brother Ibrahim.§ Vambery
says, he also exacted the cession of the Uzbeg possessions, south of the
Oxus, and made the Khan promise to supply him with a contingent of
Uzbeg and Turkoman troops.‖ He conferred the title of Khan (i.e.,
among the Persians of prince) on Muhammed Rahim bi, together with
the command of six thousand troops of Turkestan, which, doubtless,
formed the contingent just named, and with which that chief returned to
Khorasan, and afterwards took part in Nadir's campaign against
Daghestan. Nadir now withdrew to Charbekr. Thence at the instance of
Abulfaiz, he sent an embassy to recall Ilbars Khan to his senses. I shall
describe in the next chapter the intercourse that ensued between Nadir
and the recalcitrant Khan, which ended in the submission and execution
of Ilbars. Returning to Charjui, he sent back the daughter of Abulfaiz,
whom he had married, to her father, and gave him authority in all
Turkestan (i.e., the country beyond the Oxus). He also left him some
cannons and returned to Meshed. Some time after we read how Ibeidulla Uzbeg coming from Ferghana and Tashkend pillaged Samarkand
and Miankal, and advanced as far as the tomb of Shah Nakshbend, near
Bukhara. Abulfaiz accordingly sent to Nadir Shah to ask assistance.
The latter sent him twelve thousand men under Hassan Khan Beyath,
and Behbud Khan Jindaul. At their approach he beat a hasty retreat,
and they pursued him. Nadir Shah also authorised Muhammed Rahim
bi, who was still with him, to go to Bukhara to assist his former
master. The latter had long had ambitious views about the Khanate to
which he returned with alacrity. Meanwhile, Nadir Shah was assas-

---

* Id., 99.   † Vambery, 341, 342.   ‡ Abdul Karim, 100. Vambery, 342.
§ Abdul Karim, 101.   ‖ Op. cit., 342.

sinated. This was on the 23rd of June, 1747. The news reached Muhammed Rahim at Charjui. He kept it secret and hurried on to Bukhara, and still begrimed with dust went to the palace and demanded an interview with Abulfaiz. He immediately had him seized and then occupied the throne, and beat the drums in token of sovereignty. He also confiscated the treasure of the Khan. The latter, who ought to have been a dervish, sought shelter among the Khojas of Juibar, but his relatives there did not dare to oppose the usurper. Leaving Bukhara by the gate Namazgah he retired to the monastery of Kalender Khaneh, and asked his late Atalik to supply him with sufficient money to pay for his journey to Mekka. Meanwhile, Hassan Khan and Behbud Khan who had pursued and killed Ibeidulla, returned to Bukhara with his head and unaware of Nadir Shah's death. Their approach induced Muhammed Rahim to imprison his late sovereign in the Medresseh of Mir Arab at Pai Menar. The Persians were indignant at his conduct, but he replied that if he was only an ordinary Uzbeg, what was Nadir Shah, who had despoiled so many kings? As they began to besiege the town he made overtures to the Ghiljai Afghans, who to the number of fifteen hundred were in the Persian camp. He told them how Nadir had given their country of Kandahar to the Abdalis and promising to reward them with land, wives, and pay. They accepted his offer, and secretly entered the town at night, under Abdul hai Khoja. The same night Abulfaiz was put to death. The following day the Persians made peace with Muhammed Rahim, and abandoning their artillery, tents, and baggage, were rewarded in return with rich presents, and returned home.*

SEYID ABDUL MUMIN MUHAMMED KHAN.

Abulfaiz was killed in 1747. Muhammed Rahim, it seems, did not at once mount the throne, but he put a puppet on it in the shape of Abdul Mumin, the son of the murdered Khan, who had married his daughter. One day, we are told, the young prince presented himself to her carrying a melon in a handkerchief. "What have you there?" she said. "The head of your father," he replied, "for he killed mine and has taken possession of the country." His wife having reported this to Rahim, the latter said, "The wolf's whelp will end by becoming a wolf," and a few days later, having taken him on a pleasure excursion, some of his people took the opportunity while he was looking into a well to push him in.† Malcolm tells the story differently, saying the young prince had shot in play at a melon which he thought resembled Rahim beg,‡ while Izzetulla says that some conspirators having determined to put Rahim to death, he was invited to a dinner by the prince, when one of the latter's attendants shot

---

* Abdul Kerim, 107-114.   † Id., 116.   ‡ Op. cit., ii. 242. Note.

at him, but the ball lodged in his cap and he escaped. He thereupon had the young prince drowned.[*]

UBEIDULLA KHAN III.

Muhammed Rahim now put another puppet on the throne, in the person of Ubeidulla. A Greek named Nikólai Grigorief, who had lived at Bukhara about ten years, and went to Russia about 1752, calls him a son of Shah Timur Khan of the Aralsk people.[†] Negri and Meyendorf call him a son of Abulfaiz.[‡] We are told he was only sixteen years old, and was feeble in mind and body. He was reigning when Grigorief left Bukhara, but was apparently soon displaced by Muhammed Rahim, who then mounted the throne himself. It was during his feeble reign, namely, in 1751-2, that the founder of the Durani empire in Afghanistan, after making peace with Shah Rukh Murza, the ruler of Khorasan, sent Beghi Khan, one of his viziers, with an army to subdue the Uzbeg possessions south of the Oxus. After some unimportant struggles, he conquered Meimeneh, Andkhud, Akshi, Shaburgan, Serpul, Balkh, Khulm, Badakhshan, and Bamian. He organised these various districts, and having appointed governors and left garrisons there, returned to Kandahar, where he was given the title of Sedre Azem.[§]

MUHAMMED RAHIM BEHADUR KHAN.

Muhammed Rahim, although not a descendant of Jingis Khan, and only the bi or chief of the Mangut tribe, was not quite the usurper generally supposed. As far as the throne of Mavera un Nehr, his claims were probably as good as those of Baki Muhammed, the founder of the Janid dynasty, for his wife was the daughter of the Khan Abulfaiz.[‖] Rahim Khan confided the government of Miankal to Danial bi, who is called his uncle by Abdul Kerim and Izzetulla, and his nephew by the Russian traveller Yefremof,[¶] while he retained Bukhara, Samarkand, Miankal as far as Karshi, Khazar, Kerki, Charjui, and other towns. He is also said to have lost Sher i Sebz, Hissar, and Tashkend.[**] He was on terms of friendship with Shah Ahmed, ruler of the Afghans, and rewarded the Ghiljais who had helped him to gain the throne with grants of land. Danial bi seems to have chiefly administered his affairs. Having met one day with a dervish who spoke lugubriously to him on the ephemeral

* Journ. Asiat. Soc., vii. 341.   † Vel. Zernof, op. cit., 411.
‡ Senkofski, 120 and 129.   § Ferrier's History of the Afghans, 81.
‖ Abdul Kerim, 116. Senkofski, 120 and 129.
¶ Abdul Kerim, 116. Vel. Zernof, Melanges Asiatiques, iii. 580.
** Abdul Kerim, 118 and 116. The last of these towns was assuredly never his at all.

nature of life, he became melancholy, fell ill, and died. He was buried
at Bukhara, in the street of the gate of Mezar. He had lived a life of
luxury recalling that of the Persians, and left no sons; only two daughters.[*]
One of his coins is published by M. Vel. Zernof.[†]

SEYID ABULGHAZI KHAN.

On the death of Rahim Khan, Devlet bi, a Persian by origin who had
been his prime minister, summoned Rahim's uncle Danial bi, the son
of Khudayar bi, to Bukhara ; the latter went, but he would not take the
title of Khan, contenting himself with that of Atalik, while he put Abulghazi, who belonged to the Janid family, on the throne. Izzetulla says
he was the son of Ibrahim, sultan, the son of Rejib Muhammed Khan,
who was an enemy of Abulfaiz.[‡] Gregorief calls him a son of a cousin-
german of Abulfaiz; Vambery, the latter's grandson; while Yefremof says he
belonged to the family of the Khojas, and was a shepherd ; and Malcolm
that his father was called Abdul Rahim Chakbuti, or "Old Clothes,"
alluding to this habit of picking up old clothes, washing them and making
them up again in order to give them to the poor, or to use as garments
for himself.[§] Abulghazi was a mere puppet, while Danial bi seems to
have been a dissolute and feeble person, the chief authority resting in
the hands of Devlet bi, the late vizier. During his rule the habit of
smoking kalian (or tobacco) in the Persian fashion spread over the
town and bazaars, a house of ill fame was opened at Kafir Rubat,
while the police were powerless to repress these scandals. Danial bi's
eldest son Amir Maasum, familiarly styled Beggi Jan, and afterwards
entitled Shah Murad, was much scandalised by this, and repaired to a
famous acetic, the Sheikh Sefer, to ask his advice. He remarked, How
can the son of a tyrant perform good works, and obey the Sheikhs ? He
bade him if he wished to show his humility to go and exercise the office
of a porter for some months. He accordingly repaired to the bazaars in
sordid clothes and did so. His father having reproved him he spoke
out bravely in reply, how in Bukhara "the asylum of science and the
faith," injustice and debauchery were being practised by his sons, while
Devlet Kushbegi, a mere slave, was made master of the country, and he
declared he meant to devote himself to a life of mendicity. After a
year thus spent, Sheikh Sefer accepted him as his disciple, and he
devoted all his time to the Ulemas. Determined to put aside Devlet bi
who dominated over his father, he summoned him to an interview to
make preparations for the reception of some envoys from Khokand. The
Kushbegi was met at the door of audience by the executioners who put an

---

* Id., 116-119.   † Coins of Bukhara, 409.   ‡ Journ. Asiat. Soc., vii. 341.
§ Schuyler, op. cit., i. 383, 384. Vambery, 347. Vel. Zernof, Mel. Asiat., iii. 380. Malcolm,
ii. 243. Note.

end to him. His goods and wealth were confiscated.* He next revenged himself on the Kazhi who, while he still performed the duties of a porter and carried sacks of charcoal, had dared in revenge for Murad bi's not very civil treatment of him, and for his opposition to the smoking of kalian, to suggest to his father that he should be deprived of his virility. Shah Murad gave him twelve months' grace, in which, as he said, he might abandon his evil practices, and cease smoking kalian; then summoning him to his house, although he pleaded he was an old man, and asked to be forgiven if he had wronged him, and although Danial bi also interceded for him, he was put to death.† Shah Murad's brothers, whose lives were given up to rapacity and ill doing, now began, says the chronicler, to grow fearful for their fate like the brothers of Joseph. Murad bi put to death several of their accomplices, and speedily enacted good behaviour from themselves. The houses of ill fame were repressed, and "Bukhara again became the image of paradise."‡ Danial bi, meanwhile, did not interfere with his son Shah Murad. The latter's brother called Sultan Murad bi was granted the appanage of Kermineh, while a third one, Toktamish, ruled at Karshi, but having been rebellious, was afterwards deposed.

Soon after this Danial bi fell ill, and summoned Shah Murad to his couch. He made him promise not to exile or put to death his brothers, nor to give his widows in marriage; to treat with every consideration the chief of the eunuchs Khoja Sadik; to assign decent sums to his brothers and sisters, and to bury him near the tomb of Shah Nakshbend. Shah Murad swore by his head and his eyes, and an hour later Danial bi died. The latter is described as a brave and unostentatious man. He lived on terms of friendship with the rulers of Urgenj, Khokand, and Merv,§ and has been numbered by some among the sovereigns of Bukhara, but he was nothing of the kind. He neither struck money nor was the Khutbeh said in his name. He continued to his death, which apparently took place in 1770,‖ to fill the post of Atalik merely, and was no more a ruler than the mayors of the palace in Merovingian times. Abulghazi Khan filled the post, although a mere puppet and recluse, till long after the Atalik's death.

Shah Murad succeeded his father as Atalik. One author says he went about Bukhara imploring forgiveness from the people for Danial bi's ill-doings, and offering his own life in expiation. We also read that he refused to share in his father's inheritance, and bade them take his share to the public charities, so that those from whom it had been extorted might in part be recompensed.¶ One man, a fanatical Mussulman, refused to join in the prayers for Danial bi. "He extorted money from me, and I cannot make his act lawful by forgiving him," he said, and

---

* Schefer, Abdul Kerim, 123.   † Id., 124, 125.   ‡ Id., 125.   § Id., 127, 128.
‖ Id., 135. Note, 2.   ¶ Malcolm, ii. 244.

although the sum was large, Shah Murad's enthusiastic followers found it.[*]
He was a fanatical Mussulman, and his accession to power was the signal
for increased tension in the religious atmosphere of the Khanate, where
asceticism prevailed widely. He appointed his brother Sultan Murad as
governor of Kermineh, while his other brothers remained at Bukhara.
One of these, Toktamish, who has already been named, conceived a
violent hatred for Shah Murad, and hired a slave to assassinate him.
The latter, named Feridun, stole into his chamber at night, and struck
him with his sword as he lay asleep. The blow made a gash from his
mouth to his ear, but was not fatal. Being thus suddenly awakened, he
seized the assassin by the beard. The latter, terribly frightened, did not
finish his work, and fled to Toktamish, who inquired how he had fared.
He said he had killed Murad. Where then was his head. He replied he
had not had time to cut it off. Toktamish and his creatures waited about
until morning, when, suspecting that Murad had not in fact been killed,
he withdrew furtively, fancying suspicion would not rest on him.[†]

When in the morning Shah Murad gave audience to the amirs he
appeared with his head and face in bandages. Feridun was arrested and
executed, but Toktamish was only exiled, Shah Murad not wishing to break
his promise to his father. He afterwards went to Mekka.[‡] Some time after
Sultan Murad bi rebelled. He was defeated and removed as a prisoner
to Bukhara. Shah Murad, who had a very martial turn for a dervish,
was now determined to capture Merv, which was a stronghold of the
hated Shias, and governed by the famous tribe of the Kajars, which
gave a dynasty to Persia. Its chiefs were related to the Astrakhanids.
At this time it was ruled by Bairam Ali Khan, who had for a
long time been a terror to the nomadic robbers of the district.[§]
He had sent envoys with letters of condolence to Bukhara on hearing
of the death of Danial bi, and had caused the Koran to be read, and
water and provisions to be distributed at Merv, for the repose of his soul,
but this did not conciliate the Sunni spirit of Murad. He sent a
body of Turkomans from the Oxus and some Uzbegs to harry his borders.
Although at the head of a much inferior body, Bairam, "like a wolf
among a flock of sheep," killed and captured those whom he attacked, and
became a terror to the Turkomans. Shah Murad thereupon determined
upon a ruse. He encamped with six thousand Uzbegs at Charjui, a fact
which was duly reported to Bairam, but immediately after he left with
a few officers for Bukhara. This was also reported to him as a proof of
his timidity. Bairam was thus thrown off his guard. Shah Murad,
however, hastened back to Charjui, whence he reached Merv by a forced
march and having planted four thousand horsemen in ambush he sent
one thousand more ahead to forage. The news of the raid reached

* Id., 265.   † Schefer, Abdul Kerim, 129-131.   ‡ Id., 131.
§ Vambery, 351, 352.

4 A

Bairam at midnight, and, notwithstanding the warning of his mother who declared she had had an unpropitious dream, and wished him to wait till morning, he would not listen, but, putting himself at the head of but one hundred and fifty expert horsemen, he set out to cut off the invaders' retreat to Bukhara while the rest of the troops took another way. As usual he had an immediate success, and among his prisoners was Kara Khoja, relative of Shah Murad, who warned him of the ambush the latter had planted, and of the fewness of his men. His ruthless answer was to tell the Khoja he lied, and to cut off his head with his sabre, " thus admitting him," the chronicler says, " among the martyrs." He went on and was suddenly surrounded by overwhelming numbers, was shot and decapitated, and his head taken to Bukhara, where it was exposed for a week at the place where executions took place. His men who asked for quarter were made prisoners. A poet wrote a piece distich on the event. " The head of Bairam Ali has become the ear-ring of power."[*] The environs of Merv were laid waste. The body of Bairam Ali was sent back to his mother. This happened in 1785.[†] Seven of his followers who had been carried off to Bukhara, having become Sunnis at the request of Shah Murad, asked permission to be allowed to return to Merv, which they promised they would persuade Muhammed Kerim Khan to give up to him. They went and addressed themselves accordingly to the notables of the town, but were apparently treated as renegades and traitors, for they were cruelly massacred.[‡] Muhammed Kuli Khan, who had instigated their murder, was afterwards exiled by Kerim Khan's brother, who succeeded him as governor of Merv, but Shah Murad exacted further revenge. He levied an army and again marched on Merv. The river was crossed close to the town by a fine weir made of stones, cemented with bitumen and hydraulic cement, the work of Sultan Sanjar, which was guarded by a fort. The governor of this fort had fallen desperately in love with a courtesan. Hussein Khan, the governor of Merv, having heard of her attractions, sent a body of men who carried her off forcibly and treated the governor of the fort with contumely. He accordingly, "like a falcon but half gorged," appealed to Shah Murad, offering to surrender the fort to him.[§] The latter, who had been ravaging the environs of Merv and had returned home, made a forced march of four days with four thousand men, and the citadel was duly surrendered to him. He thereupon transported its garrison to Bukhara, and ordered the weir to be cut. The town was deprived of water for irrigation, and the crops could not of course grow, so that a famine was impending. The Afghan Timur Shan now sent an army and provisions to the rescue. The commander of this force was an Afghan called Leshkery Khan, whose son Khanjer Khan

---

fell in love with a sister of the governor of Merv. The amorous pair seem to have committed themselves, and were surprised by Hussein Khan under ambiguous circumstances. He struck the young prince a blow from which he died, and then ordered his sister to be also put to death. Leshkery Khan was outraged by all this, and withdrew with his forces and two thousand families from Merv to Herat. Matters were in a serious position in the former town, and Hussein deemed it prudent to send envoys to Bukhara with a submissive message. These were received with great satisfaction by Shah Murad, who showered presents on them. Thereupon Hussein with some of his principal notables went in person to Bukhara, which they entered in state, and he was assigned suitable quarters at the Cheharbagh. Soon after his brother Muhammed Kerim Khan, who had retired to Meshed, also went to Bukhara. Hussein now sent messengers to summon his family to go to him, while Shah Murad ordered a division of troops to occupy the place and to transport some of the inhabitants of Merv to his own capital. The families of Bairam Ali, of Hussein Khan, and of his brother Kerim were accordingly removed, as well as a large number of the inhabitants. There only remained behind in fact three thousand Sunni and two thousand Shia families, while seventeen thousand others were transported.[*] Merv has since rapidly decayed, and now nothing remains of it but a few mounds, the camping place of the Turkomans who have occupied the wasted site.

The Uzbeg possessions south of the Oxus had been ruled by the Afghans since they were conquered by them in 1751-2, as I have described. Shah Murad viewed this with impatience, and when the Afghan ruler Timur, the son of Shah Ahmed, in 1786 was embarrassed by a campaign in Scinde, a revolt broke out at Balkh and Akhshi, instigated by the Uzbeg chief. He sent a force to their assistance, and these towns drove out the governors that ruled them.[†] Timur thereupon wrote a letter to Shah Murad, complaining of his constant aggressions under the cloak of humility, of his attack on Merv, which he had defended on the plea not recognised in the laws of nations, that he wished to convert its Shia inhabitants to the true faith, and contrasting his zeal on this occasion with the impediments he threw in the way of the Afghans, who wished to clear India of Hindoos, Jews, Christians, and other unbelievers, and with his wars against the people of Shehr i Sebz, Khojend, and the Turkomans, who were Sunnis. Having been appealed to by these peoples, he said he had determined to march to Turkestan, and ordered Shah Murad to go and meet him to arrange their differences. In the spring of 1789 he accordingly left Kabul with an army reckoned by some at one hundred thousand men, and by others at one hundred and fifty thousand.[‡] He first went towards Kunduz, and

---

* Id., 142. . † Ferrier, op. cit., 100. ‡ Elphinstone, ii. 308. Schefer, 22.

then to Akhshi. Meanwhile Shah Murad summoned his people and
crossed the Oxus at Kilif. His army, according to Abdul Kerim,
numbered about thirty thousand men. He despatched his brother Omar
Kushbegi with a light armed force towards Akhshi, and another officer
was ordered to molest the communications of the Afghans. But he
speedily saw that his force was too weak to resist them, and at
once adopted a policy of humility. He professed to give Timur the
credit of the victory, and a battle was avoided by the intervention of the
mollahs, who did not care to see two orthodox sovereigns destroying one
another while the Persian Shias looked on. Shah Murad sent his son to
the Afghan camp, and there was peace between the two countries till
Timur's death.* Murad had appointed his brothers Omar bi and
Fazil bi governors of Merv, where, incited by the Turkomans, they soon
rebelled, but as they leaned on the truculent nomads the citizens
beleagured them in the citadel, and compelled them to sue for terms, and
they were allowed to retire to Shehr i Sebz. Three hundred of their
followers, who had been locked up as a precautionary measure, seem to
have been placed in a kind of Black Hole of Calcutta, for on the doors
being opened only one was found alive. The citizens again submitted
to Shah Murad, who forgave the action last mentioned as one which was
necessitated by the place being in revolt.†

In 1796 the famous Turkoman chief Aga Muhammed, who was a
eunuch and the real founder of the dynasty of the Kajars, captured Meshed
from Shah Rukh the Blind, the grandson of Nadir. Shah Rukh's eldest
son Nadir went to Kabul, and sent his brothers Imaum Kuli Murza and
Haidar Murza and some other chiefs to Bukhara with a letter, reminding
Shah Murad how through his marriage with a daughter of Abulfaiz he
was related to him, reminding him also of their common Sunni faith, and
of the obligations that Rahim Khan had been under to Nadir. They
ended up by asking him for a contingent of troops with which to recover
Meshed, and promising that the Khutbeh there should be read in his
name.‡ The princes were lodged in a palace in the Pai Menar, and
treated with courtesy, but they waited in vain for twelve months in hope
of getting some help, and at last obtained permission to return to Herat ;
but meanwhile Shah Murad had commissioned Muhammed Amin
Topchi with five thousand men to waylay them on their way and to
drown them in the Oxus. He caused them to be ferried over the river
in a rotten boat by two old men, who had received due orders. When
the boat was half way over it was accordingly filled with water. The
young princes succeeded, however, in reaching Charjui.

When Shah Murad heard of this, not to be baffled of his prey, he
summoned Tureh Kazak, the grandson of Ilbars Khan of Khiva, who had

---

* Elphinstone, *id.* Schefer, *id.*   † Schefer, 143, 144.
‡ *Id.*, 145-148.

been killed by Nadir.* He reminded him that he had his grandfather's blood to avenge, and that he might now do it on Nadir's grandsons. He also promised to give him a part of their property. The Kazak went to Charjui, where he put up at the house of Balta Kuli Bek, governor of the town. There the princes were summoned to a feast. They speedily learnt what their fate was to be. In vain they pleaded that they were Sunnis, and moreover guests. Their prayers for mercy were not listened to, but the Kazak proceeded to decapitate them.† There seems no adequate motive for this brutal crime on the part of Shah Murad, and we are told the people and the Ulemas of Bukhara were disgusted with it, and compared it to the murder of Siavash, the son of Kaikaus, who, having gone to Turkestan in all confidence, was put to death there by Afrasiab.‡ The assigned reason was that they were accused of being addicted to wine and other debauchery.§ Perhaps it was done in some way to conciliate Aga Muhammed. The intercourse between the latter and Bukhara is differently told by two Persian writers. One of Aga Muhammed's letters, as reported in the Rauzat es Sefa, is thus translated by Vambery. . . . "It is unnecessary to recapitulate the history of the Sefids and of the contemporaries of Muhammed Sheibani Khan down to Afshar Nadir Shah. I well know, and it is sufficiently well known to thee also, that Balkh, Merv, Zemindaver, Seistan, Kandahar, and Kabul were from the earliest times integral portions of the Iranian empire. Well, then, how has it occurred to thee to conquer Balkh and Merv, and in the last-named place to slay Bairam Ali Khan, the kinsman of his illustrious house? Dost thou perchance wish to renew the old wars between Iran and Turan? For such a task thou art verily not sufficient. To play with the tail of the lion, to tickle the tiger in the ear, is not the part of a prudent man. Yet all men are descended from Adam and Eve, and if thou art proud of thy relationship to Turanian princes, know that my descent is also the same. The origin and the derivation of Kajar Noyan is not only nobler and more distinguished than that of the family of Mangut and Kungrat, but even surpasses in glory the renowned houses of Sulduz and Jelair. We all of us owe thanks to God the Almighty that he hath given the dominion over Turan and Iran, over Rum, Rus, China, and India to the exalted family of Turk. Let each be content with the position which hath fallen to him, and not stretch out his hand over the frontier of his own kingdom. I also will dwell in peace within the ancient boundaries of Iran, and none of us will pass over the Oxus."‖

Another account, which was followed by Malcolm, makes the letter be written not to Shah Murad but to Abulghazi, proving that the latter was still living. In it the writer says he had heard of the usurpation of Danial bi's son, and how in consequence true believers, who were made prisoners in Persia,

* See next chapter. † Schefer, 149, 150. ‡ Id., 150. § Id., 151.
‖ Vambery, 354, 355.

were sold like cattle in the market-place of Bukhara. He called upon Abulghazi to at once restore all captives, and to beware how he behaved in future. The Dervish Khan wrote to his Eunuch brother in equally peremptory phrases. "I have heard," he says in a circular letter which he addressed to the chiefs of Khorasan, "that Achta Khan* is come among you: seize him if you can: if not inform me and I shall proceed to your quarter to punish him."† The two chiefs, however, never met, for Aga Muhammed was now summoned westwards.

The letter above quoted contains the last notice I can find of Abulghazi, who continued to be a mere nominal ruler, his family being kept in seclusion and supported from the produce of the Royal estates.‡ Coins struck by him are known as late as 1200 hej. (i.e., 1785-6).§ Until his death it is probable the Khutbeh was said in his name, and Shah Murad apparently contented himself with the style of Naib and the honourable appellation Vali-n-niam, and never took the title of Khan.‖

No coins with Shah Murad's name on them are known, nor do we know the year when Abulghazi died. It is singular that certain coins struck in 1791-2 and 1793-4, at Bukhara, have the name of Murad's dead father Danial bi upon them.¶ Izzetulla says that Murad applied for a sened to the Sultan of Rum, probably as the successor of the Khalif, who nominated him his viceroy, and gave him the title of Vali Niamat with the style of Kurshi Bashi.**

In the latter part of his life he lived on bad terms with his son, the Amir Haidar Tura, who was governor of Karshi. He died in rejeb 1214 (i.e., 1799), at the age of sixty-three.††

Shah Murad was one of the most remarkable characters in Asiatic history, and was the hero of many stories. When he held an open durbar with the doctors of the law, &c., the party sat on goatskins, which were ranged round the room, and the Shah took any seat, to show he did not esteem himself above his fellows. He performed the most menial offices. His kitchen establishment consisted of a wooden bowl, an iron cauldron, and some earthen pots. He made his own market, cooked his own *pot au feu*, and when he had guests, went round himself to pour water on their hands, and ate from the same bowl with them. He had a donkey of no price which he would ride without saddle through the streets of Bukhara.‡‡ Among other stories of him, we are told he was one day riding on his ass through the bazaar, followed by a cortége of Uzbeg, Afghan, and Kizilbash nobles, when he stopped at a coppersmith's shop, and thus addressed him: "Salaam Alekum," "Alekum Salaam." "Your health is good." By your condescension and favour I am concerned

---

* Malcolm says My Lord Eunuch is a very delicate translation of this phrase.
† Malcolm, ii. 291, 292.   ‡ Id., 250.
§ Frœhn Rec., 443.   Vel. Zernof, Coins of Bukhara, &c., 413.
‖ Grigorief, cited by Schuyler, op. cit., i. 385.   ¶ Vel. Zernof, Coins of Bukhara, &c., 419.
** Journ. Asiat. Soc., vii. 341.   †† Schefer, 150, 151.   ‡‡ Conolly, i. 159.

to see you, born a gentleman, toiling in an occupation that is beneath you, rather abandon this profession and come and live in the town as befits a man of your birth : fear not to write to your friends all that goes on here : God be thanked, our actions are not such as we are ashamed should be known, but what you *do* write, write *truly*, and send it openly and worthily." The explanation of this was, that the supposed copper-smith was really an Afghan spy, and Shah Murad thus obtained credit both for mildness and for knowing all that was going on.[*] He used to style himself the fakir, though he allowed himself to be addressed by the title Huzzurut i Vali Naiami (His Excellency the Lord of Beneficence). One day he came into the court with the lower part of his upper garment lopped, and explained that he had cut it off to make stockings for a poor man. He was very methodical in his punishments, and, although he seldom forgave an offence against his sovereign power, he generally managed to bring it within the Muhammedan code. This was made tolerably elastic, however, to suit his friends. Thus, a man taken as a slave to Bukhara and professing himself a Sunni had to prove himself so by four witnesses, whom he was hardly likely to find among strangers. As some of the more scrupulous Bukharians were averse to buying orthodox slaves, the Turkomans were in the habit of pricking their tongues till they could not articulate, or beating them so unmercifully that they were willing to deny their faith as the lesser of two evils, and to be sold as infidels.[†]

He carried out on the throne the rigid and austere virtues of a religious recluse. He replaced the magnificent court of Bukhara by one of a very sordid nature. He himself drew from the Imperial treasury but a tenga, *i.e.*, five pence (being the fee allowed to the poorest student), a day each, for himself, his cook, his servant, and his tutor ; and his wife, ho was of Royal blood, only took three tengas. "Learn, lady," he used to say, "to be content with little that thy God may be content with thee." His joy at the birth of a son so overcame his penuriousness that he actually allotted five gold pieces daily for the subsistence of the mother and child, and a similar amount was allotted for two other sons directly they were born. While his family lived in comparative affluence he himself occupied a small unfurnished room, where persons of all classes were admitted at all hours. He was generally clad in a coarse garment, like that of a mendicant, which was seldom changed, but when he went to see his family he threw over it a skin of a deer. He sat regularly as president of his court of justice, and was assisted by forty mollahs. All who had any complaints could come there, but the prosecutor might not speak unless the accused was present. No one could refuse a summons to attend, and even a slave might cite his master there. Shah Murad listened carefully to both sides. If it was not a criminal offence he gene-

---

* *Id.*, 160, 161.   † *Id.*, 161-163.

rally advised an amicable settlement. If this was impracticable, he took notes of the evidence, which were given with his opinion to the mollahs, who were directed to prepare a fetva or decision according to holy law. After this proceeding the parties had a week's respite to arrange the matter when sentence was passed, which was irrevocable. Criminal justice was administered according to the Koran. Robbers were punished with death, thieves with the loss of their right hands; drunkards were publicly whipped, and the smoking of tobacco was forbidden under severe penalties. The police officers were cohtinually employed driving the inhabitants to the mosques to hear the prescribed prayers. They carried small books by which they·could catechise whom they met and see if they were ignorant of the prayers, when they might punish them with the whips they carried, which were also used to awaken the devotion of the negligent. Anyone who wished to improve himself could enter the colleges, and received daily sustenance, and we are told the number of students at one time was thirty thousand.* Shah Murad abolished all duties except upon foreign goods. No monopolies were allowed, and revenue was only collected from the Crown lands. "But the Jiziat or 'regulated tax upon infidels' was regularly exacted, and the Zukat or 'established charity' was levied upon all believers, even upon the soldiers who had been exempted formerly. This, with one-fifth of the captured booty, went into the State exchequer.† His rigid conduct and asceticism made him an object of superstitious veneration on the part of the Uzbegs, and enabled him to grasp in his strong hand the hitherto dishevelled reins of power among that sturdy race. As Malcolm says, "they were easily persuaded that a leader who contemned the worldly pleasures which they prized, and who preferred the patched mantle and crooked staff of a mendicant priest to a Royal robe and sceptre, must act under the immediate direction of the Divine being."‡

His army is said to have numbered sixty thousand, but he was seldom attended by more than half that number. In his barantas or plundering raids into Khorasan he left his heavy baggage with a part of the army several marches in rear, while the advance, consisting entirely of cavalry, spread over the country. Every man took seven days' provisions with him for himself and his horse, and they would pounce suddenly on forts or walled villages, or carry off all travellers, and those working in the fields who if not ransomed were reduced to slavery. They usually exacted black-mail from places they did not take, for as their invasions took place before harvest, a refusal involved the destruction of all the crops around. A fifth part of the plunder went to the exchequer. Shah Murad always led his men. He generally went in front of the army, dressed like a mendicant and mounted on a small pony. He exacted strict obedience and discipline, and the duties of religion were duly

---

* Malcolm, ii. 249. † Id., 330. ‡ Id., 332.

attended to, even when on a campaign, a number of mollahs attending with every division. They also acted as envoys. Although himself very spare, he liked to be surrounded with magnificence, and his nobles and principal officers were profuse enough.* Malcolm has translated a notice of the Khan and his surroundings, given by an envoy of Mameish Khan, chief of Chinnaran, who visited Shah Murad's camp on one of his invasions of Khorasan. He was intrusted with letters both for the Khan and for his nephew Ishan Nukib, the son of Ishan Mukdum, chief of Jizakh, who had married a daughter of Danial bi. This notice is so graphic and interesting that I shall abstract it.

" I was introduced," he observes, " to Ishan Nukib, who was seated at the further end of a magnificent tent. He was a man of handsome appearance, uncommonly fair, but had a thin beard. He asked after my health, and then after that of Mameish Khan, adding, ' Why has he not come himself?' On my making some excuse, he added, ' I understand the reason; had I been alone he would have paid me a visit, but he is afraid of Beggi Jan.' After these observations he arose and retired to another tent, desiring me to repose myself where I was. A rich sleeping dress was brought, and every person went away; but I had hardly laid down when I was sent for to attend Ishan Nukib, who very graciously insisted upon my dining with him. The repast was luxurious, and an hour after dinner tea was brought. The favourite drank his in a cup of pure gold, ornamented with jewels. The cup given me was of silver, inlaid with gold. Three hours after noon he carried me to a large tent with five poles, where a number of persons were saying their prayers. We did the same, and afterwards returned to his tent, which he had hardly entered when a servant in waiting announced Utkhur Sufi. This religious person, for such he was, from the moment he entered occupied all the attention of Ishan Nukib, who appeared to treat him with the profoundest respect, and when tea and coffee was served, he held the cup while Utkhur Sufi drank. We had not sat long when an officer came into the tent and told Ishan Nukib that Beggi Jan desired that he would wait upon him and bring his guest. The moment this intimation was made we arose, mounted our horses, and proceeded with him. After riding a short distance we came to a one-pole tent, which I judged from its size and tattered appearance to belong to some cooks or water-carriers. An old man was seated on the grass so near it as to be protected from the sun by its shade. Here all dismounted and advanced towards the old man, who was clothed in green, but very dirty. When near him they stood with their hands crossed in a respectful posture, and made their salutation. He returned that of each person, and desired us to sit down opposite to him. He appeared to show great kindness to Ishan Nukib, but chiefly addressed his conversation to Utkhur Sufi.

* Malcolm, ii. 254, 255.

After some time the subject of my mission was introduced. I gave my letter to Ishan Nukib; he presented it to the old man in green, who I now discovered was Beggi Jan. That ruler opened, read it, and put it in his pocket. After a short pause he said, ' No doubt Mameish Khan has sent me a good horse,' and desired him to be brought. After looking attentively at the animal, he began to whisper and laugh with those near him, then addressing himself to me, said, ' Why has not your master sent the horse Kara Goz (*i.e.*, Black Eye), as I desired?' 'That horse has defects,' I replied, ' or he would have been sent.' 'With all his defects,' said Beggi Jan, smiling, ' he is twenty times better than the one you have brought.'

"While we were conversing a great number of nobles came in, and I could not help observing the extraordinary richness and splendour of their arms and dresses. Beggi Jan returned the salute to every one of these in a kind and affable manner, and bade them be seated ; but the shade of this small tent did not protect one half of them from the rays of the sun. Soon after their arrival their chief fell into a deep reverie, and till evening prayers were announced he appeared wholly absorbed in religious contemplation. At the time of prayer all arose and retired. I slept that night at the tent of Ishan Nukib. At daylight the army marched, and passed within a few miles of the fort of Chinnaran. After Beggi Jan had reached his encampment he sent for me, and honoured me with a private audience, at which he was very affable. ' Your master Mameish Khan is, I hear, always drinking wine.' 'I have not seen him drink,' I replied, ' and cannot speak to that point.' ' You are right,' said he, ' not to state what you have not seen. Tell Mameish Khan,' he continued, ' I have a regard for him ; but as for Nadir Murza (the ruler of Meshed) he is a fool. Bid Mameish Khan,' he added, ' write to Jaaffer Khan of Nishapur, and advise that chief to solicit my friendship if he wishes to save his country from destruction.' After this observation a handsome dress was brought for me, with a present of money. Every article of the dress was good except the turban, which was of little or no value. This, however, Beggi Jan took to himself, giving me his own in exchange, which was a great deal worse than the one brought for me. I took my leave and returned to the tent of Ishan Nukib, to whom I repeated all that had passed. He laughed very heartily at the account, made me a handsome present, and I was on the point of retiring when two men came at full gallop with a letter from Mameish Khan, stating that, notwithstanding the protection he had received, some of his followers had been taken by the Uzbegs. Ishan Nukib took me again to Beggi Jan, whom we found seated in a small tent upon a goat's skin. He directed the captives to be brought, and made them over to me. He had before written a letter to Mameish Khan, which he reopened, wrote what he had done, and again committed it to my charge. As this affair was settling, his cook, a diminutive person with weak eyes, came into the tent. 'Why do not you think of dinner?' said Beggi Jan. 'It will soon be time for prayer.' The little cook immediately brought a large black pot, and, making a fire-place with stones, put four or five kinds of grains and a little dried meat into it. He then nearly filled it with water, and having kindled a fire, left it to boil while he prepared the .dishes; these were wooden platters of the same kind as are used by the lowest orders. He put down three and poured out the mess. Beggi Jan watched him, and the cook evidently understood from his looks when more or less was to be put into a dish. After all was ready he spread a dirty cloth, and laid down a piece of stale barley bread (about which the author ejaculates, 'God knows in what year of the hejirah it had been baked),' and which Beggi Jan put into a cup of water to moisten. The first dish was given to the ruler of the Uzbegs, the second was placed between Ishan Nukib and me, and the cook took the third for himself, sitting down to eat it opposite to his master. As I had dined I merely tasted what was put before me. It was very nauseous, the meat in it being almost putrid, yet several nobles who came in ate the whole of our unfinished share, and with an apparent relish that could only have been derived from the pleasure they had in partaking of the same fare with their holy leader.

"After dinner I obtained leave to depart on my return to Chinnaran. Mameish Khan was pleased with the result of my mission, but he afterwards informed me that, notwithstanding the fair promises of Beggi Ian, eighty-two of his people were during the season carried away by the Uzbegs."*

On the seal which he generally used the inscription, "Amir Maassum, the son of Amir Danial," was written in the centre, and round it "Power and dignity, when founded on justice, are from God; when not, from the devil."†

We may here give from Vambery a short account of the state of culture at Bukhara during the rule of the Astrakhanids. He justly remarks that while the fortunes of Bukhara were then at a very low ebb, the courts of Constantinople, Lahore, and Ispahan had been brought into contact with the West by the visits of Europeans, in the garb of the diplomatist, the merchant, or the missionary. Shut out from intercourse with the outer world by the deserts and nomads which bounded it, Mavera un Nehr retained chiefly its fanaticism and religious zeal. The chief culture that survived there was devoted to the exegesis of the Koran and dogmatic theology. The ideal of human perfection was the life of a sufi spent in contempt of human exertion, and the confession of the worthlessness of all human objects. A few poets and writers of chronograms survived, and Imaum Kuli Khan, Kasim Muhammed Sultan, and Subhan Kuli Khan have left proofs of considerable culture. Half-ruined canals still bear the name of the first, a divan that of the second, and a book on

* Malcolm, op. cit., ii. 256-260.   † Id., 261.

medicine that of the third; but the best proof that pietism and religious extravagance predominated is to be found in the fact of three successive Khans abdicating the throne for the pilgrim's staff. Among the buildings dating from this period is the college of Yelenktosh, built in 1611, opposite the already ruined colleges of Ulugh beg; a mosque and college at Bukhara, raised by the wealthy Nezr Divanbegi in 1029 (1620); and two korunush khani or reception rooms, which Baki Muhammed built at Bukhara and Samarkand in 1014 (1605).[*]

THE HAIDARIDS OR MANGUTS.

SEYID AMİR HAIDAR.

On the death of Shah Murad, the dynasty of the Astrakhanids was finally displaced, in name as well as in fact, and was replaced by another dynasty, namely, that of the Manguts. The revolution, as in the case of the former dynasty, was not, however, so great as many suppose, and Haidar, who succeeded to the throne, had through his mother the Imperial blood of Jingis Khan in his veins. The old family was not extinct, and Burnes reports that when he was at Bukhara some members of it were still living there in obscurity.

According to Izzetulla, Haidar was descended from Khudayar, a famous warrior, who first got the title of Atalik He was the father of Danial bi, the father of Shah Murad. Shah Murad married Shems-ban-aim, the widow of Rahim Khan and the daughter of Abulfaiz, who was the mother of his eldest son Haidar.[†] Besides him he had two other sons, Seyid Muhammed Hussein and Nasr ud din Turek.[‡] On Shah Murad's death the Kushbegi Utkhur, who governed Bukhara, sent to fetch Haidar from Karshi. Meanwhile Shah Murad's brothers, Omar bi, Mahmud bi, and Fazil bi, who had claims to the throne, collected some troops, entered Bukhara, and posted themselves in the open square of Righistan, opposite the great gate of the citadel, where several suspected amirs were put under arrest, and the citadel itself was prepared for a siege. The citizens having been ordered to fall upon Omar's people and to pillage their property, did so, and he was constrained to escape by the gate of Samarkand, and to retire towards Miankal. The houses of himself and his brothers were pillaged, the wooden pillars supporting the upper chambers being broken. Some of those found inside, according to Abdul Kerim, "had their souls intrusted to the hands of the master of hell," while the wives and children of Omar bi were stripped of their clothes and left naked. The corpse of the Khan remained for three days in the palace. Haidar now entered the town with a brilliant *cortège*, and having said

* Vambery, 344. 345.   † Journ. Royal Asiat. Soc., vii. 341.   ‡ Fraser, Suppl., 79.

the customary prayers over his father's body, returned to the palace and received the oath of fealty from his retainers. Utkhur Kushbegi retained the post of vizier, the latter's son Muhammed Hakim bi was appointed governor of Karshi, while Haidar's brothers, Nasr ud din and Muhammed Hussein bi, were nominated governors of Merv and Samarkand respectively.[*]

Meanwhile Omar bi and his brothers occupied Miankal, Penjenbeh, and Ketteh Kurgan, and were joined by the Khoja Keya, the governor of Kermineh. Amir Haidar marched against them and dispersed their forces. We are told his people killed or made prisoners about one thousand men of Shehr i Sebz, and orders were given to put the prisoners to death. Omar bi and Fazil bi, with their children, were soon after captured in a village, and were both executed. Their brother Mahmud bi escaped to Khokand, and Khoja Keya to Shehr i Sebz. After crushing this rebellion Haidar returned once more to Bukhara. Soon after, his brother Muhammed Hussein was accused of being in league with the rebels of Shehr i Sebz and Khokand, and was deprived of Samarkand, which was given to a Persian named Devlet Kush begi. Haidar gave him a pension, and apparently kept him under surveillance.[†]

The next victims of his suspicion were the sons of Haji Muhammed Khan, the former ruler of Merv, and of his relatives Kerim Khan and Bairam Ali Khan. " Twelve of these princes were seized and killed like sheep," says Abdul Kerim. " Their wives and little ones were given away as presents, and no one ever knew what crime they had committed."

This succession of executions frightened Nasr ud din, Haidar's other brother, who deemed it prudent to withdraw from Merv, and to go with his family to Meshed. The Shah assigned him an annual stipend, and gave him the title of Amir Din Nasr Murza, and he visited Teheran annually.[‡] He seems to have afterwards become somewhat needy,[§] and we are told he went to Constantinople in 1829, and the next year to Russia, where he lived when Abdul Kerim wrote. He describes him as an able archer, who could send a beechwood arrow through an iron plate.

Haidar now marched against Uratippa. Although its governor was submissive and came out with rich presents, he was handed over to some one who had a blood feud against him, and was put to death. Kabilbek, son of Utkhur Kush begi was nominated governor of Uratippa, and the country as far as Khojend and Tashkend was put under the authority of Bukhara.[||] The same year (i.e., 1804) Haidar married the daughter of the Prince of Shehr i Sebz. At this time Haidar sent an embassy to St. Petersburg, which was accompanied by Abdul Kerim, who tells us he saw many wonders there, and returned by way of Moscow, Astrakhan,

* Schefer, Abul Kerim, 154, 155.   † Id., 156, 157.   ‡ Id., 157-159.   § Fraser, Suppl., &c.
|| Schefer 157.

Khuarezm, Khiva, and Urgenj. While on his way he learnt that the Khivan Khan was meditating a raid upon Bukhara. This was carried out, and we shall say more about it in the next chapter. Here it will suffice that he carried off fifty thousand sheep and several thousands of camels. Muhammed Niaz bi was ordered to take the troops of Bukhara and to march against him. After some doubtful skirmishes the Khivan army was routed, and Iltazer, the Khan of Khuarezm, was drowned in crossing the Oxus. The Bukharians captured a large treasure, *inter alia* a tuk or tugh (*i.e.*, a horse-tail standard), whose shaft was plated with gold, and had cost one thousand miskals.* The man who carried the news of the victory to Bukhara was rewarded with one thousand tillas. The army now returned with its prisoners to Bukhara. The latter were stripped of their irons, pardoned, and set at liberty, while their officers were presented with robes of honour. Kutli Murad Bek, the Khivan Khan's brother, was nominated governor of Khiva, with the title of Inak. Before his arrival at home, however, the people had raised his younger brother to the position of Khan. He acquiesced in this, and wrote to the Khan of Bukhara to say it had been done by force, and that he was obliged to agree, and could not therefore carry out his promise to hold the place as his (Haidar's) deputy.† A cold and platonic truce continued to subsist for some time between the two countries, varied by Turkoman raids upon the Bukharian caravans.

Frazer describes Haidar as of a mild, pacific, unambitious character, charitable, just, and religious even to bigotry. He was in fact more of a dervish or devotee than a king, and although not so austere as his father, his mode of life was very simple. His dress was generally of white or buff colour, and his food mainly vegetables and bread. His privy purse, it is said, was supplied by the money raised by the conversion of Jews to Muhammedanism, which was surely no mean test of his economy. He spent many hours and even days in seclusion, and it was remarked that at his court it was far better to be a dervish or a mollah than a soldier or a noble. He held open assemblies, like his father, for the administration of justice, but chiefly delighted in haranguing his people from the pulpit on religious subjects. In person he was tall and handsome, with a fair and florid complexion, somewhat tinged with yellow, and having a full round beard. He wore an Uzbeg cap on his head with an Uzbeg turban wrapt round it like an Arab imaum, a short jacket on his body, and above it a jameh or robe, a knife at his waist, and Uzbeg boots on his feet.

Rising at midnight he repeated supernumerary prayers for some time. After the morning prayers he read and lectured to forty or fifty scholars on the Tufseer and traditions, after which he knelt on his knees on a green velvet musnud, while the various chiefs came in turn, made

---

* *Id.*, 166.   † *Id.*, 167.

obeisance and greeted him with the words, Salaam Alekum, or " Peace
be with you," which greeting was duly returned by the naib or deputy.
The Seyids and Ulemas then sat down on the right, and the civil chiefs
and dignitaries on the left, all being dressed in uniform fashion and
colour. Everyone presented to the Khan for the first time had to don
the Uzbeg dress.* A stranger on being presented was conducted to his
presence, and saluted him with the Salaam Alekum ; he then advanced
again, a servant holding up each of his arms, and either kissed the
Khan's hand or seated himself as the Khan directed. In the latter case
he lifted his hands with the *al khyr* or blessing. He then stated his
business or presented his petition. If he was an envoy a fixed allowance
was made him from that day, if a holy person or the descendant of a saint
he received two hundred tengas on taking leave. These introductions
over, those who had complaints were summoned, and the Khan decided
their cases according to the Koran. At noon five or six eminent
expositors engaged in literary controversy before him, the Khan joining
with them, and then as peish imaum said the noon-day prayer. Similar
business fills up the afternoon until within an hour of sunset, when he
decided affairs of State and justice. He then again recited the afternoon
prayers and what belongs to penitence and fasts until evening. After this
he broke fast with some sweetmeats and light food, then recited evening
prayers, then took his principal meal, again recited prayers, and then only
went for a short repose to his palace.† It will thus be seen that his position
was anything but a sinecure. On Wednesday mornings he went to visit
the tomb of Hazrat Khoja Beha ud din Nagsbaud, where he repeated the
due form of prayer, distributed alms, and again returned to spend the
evening with his mother. When anyone died he went to his house as
imaum to recite the funeral prayers. He always, as peish imaum, recited
the Khutbeh on the Friday in the Great Mosque himself, his return from
the mosque being made with great state. Among the holy people who
were so influential at the Bukharian court we are told that the Khojas of
Juibaur, who claimed to descend from the Khalif Abubekhr, were the most
powerful, and had great possessions. They were not, however, the first
in official rank. This post was filled by the nukib or head of the Seyids,
who sat on the Khan's right hand on a musnud or elevated seat. The
highest civil official was the hakim beg or vizier, who acted as viceroy
in the Khan's absence, and had charge of the collection of the taxes.‡
The court was splendid in its surroundings, the amirs wearing rich gold
brocade and embroidered broadcloth dresses, but no jewels. The
Ulemas and Seyids wore gowns with hanging sleeves, made chiefly
from a cloth brought from Benares, called nohri-khab and sal i abreshim,
one kind being blue, the other very white, like silver, whence its name.
The chief men wore turbans and slippers, the common people often

---

* Fraser, op. cit., App., 80, 81.   † Id., 81, 82.   ‡ Id., 82, 83.

boots. Some, instead of a turban, had a Kerman or Herat shawl wrapt round the head.

The district round Bukhara was divided into seven tumans, each governed by a nakim, assisted by a vizier, both appointed by the crown. A tuman contained many villages. Each of which was governed by an aksakal, white-beard, or elder, elected by the villagers, whose office was permanent, and even hereditary, except when charged with misconduct. He settled disputes, collected revenue, and levied the militia. Every man in the village on marrying made the ak sakal a present or khelut, and at harvest-time each one gave him a portion of grain. The revenue he collected consisted of the deh-yek or tithe of the produce of the land and the zikhaut or fortieth of flocks and herds, with the fortieth of merchandise. The land belonging to charities paid no tax. Customs duty was collected on the entry and exit of goods from the village. In making levies for the militia, *i.e.*, kara mairghan, each man in the village paid a sum of money or a quantity of grain proportioned to the number of his family, and with this the ak sakal paid a stipendiary body of men, who were generally hanging about him. Conjointly with the ak sakals there were also in the villages Imperial officers, who acted as deputies of the nakim, and were known as naibs. They were always mollahs. The richer and more influential Uzbegs were styled begs. A force of from thirty to forty thousand cavalry was apparently kept in constant pay, which could be increased very largely by a body of the country militia. The troops were armed with lances, swords and shields, and some with matchlocks. All wore long knives or daggers, some individuals having two or three at their waist.[*]

In 1820 Bukhara was visited by a famous mission from Russia, headed by the envoy Negri, and accompanied by Baron Meyendorf, who has left us an account of his journey. The embassy was sent in answer to requests made in 1816 and 1820, on the part of some Bukharians who visited St. Petersburg as representatives of the Khan.

The mission was escorted by a small force of Cossacks, and took with it several hundred camels carrying provisions and presents. They left Orenburgh on the 10th of October, 1820, and duly crossed the Kazak steppes and reached Aghatma. After they entered the Bukharian territory they found themselves welcomed at the various villages by great crowds, who turned out on foot and horseback in gala style to see them, and among the white-turbaned Bukharians they noticed several old Russians who had long been slaves. The Kushbegi went to meet them, and the Russians visited him at his camp of gaily-coloured tents, bright also with richly-caparisoned horses, which were picketed about. At the interview the Kushbegi suggested that they should present the Khan with the two cannons or the carriage which they had with them,

---

[*] *Id.*, 80-84.

a new thing they did not accept.* He was a stately-looking person, with a long beard, and spoke Persian with facility. Continuing their advance, they still had to make their way through the crowd, and their Cossacks marched in full uniform. Other officers came to welcome them, dressed in red and blue silks, bordered with gold. At length they entered Bukhara. This was on the 20th of December. A thirty-six hours' discussion had already taken place on that most critical matter in Eastern diplomacy, the ceremony to be gone through on presentation. The Russian presents consisted of furs, porcelain, cut glass, watches, and guns. They entered through one of the city gates in military order, and, having traversed a narrow street, reached a wide square surrounded with mosques and colleges, and also containing the palace. Having dismounted, they passed through a vaulted passage, lined with about four hundred soldiers carrying guns, then into a small court, through a second passage, past a number of unlimbered guns, and into a court-yard, where three or four hundred Bukharians in white turbans were collected, and eventually reached the hall of reception, where the Khan was seated on some red cushions, bordered with gold. Beside him, on his left, sat two of his sons, the eldest being about fifteen years old; on his right was the Kushbegi, and on each side of the door five grandees. After the presentation of the envoy's credentials in due form, some of the soldiers (who first left their arms behind), were called in, as the Khan wished to see them. He laughed childishly when they entered. Meyendorf describes him as about forty-five years old, with black eyes and a fine beard, but enervated by the pleasures of the harem. He wore a khalat of black velvet, decorated with gems, and a muslin turban surmounted by an aigrette of herons' feathers. The turban was crossed diagonally by a gold braid like those of the chief officers of the Ottoman court. The Kushbegi and three other grandees did not wear turbans, but cylindrical caps made of sable. The master of the ceremonies carried a kind of halbard having a silver axe at the top. The audience lasted about twenty minutes, after which the envoys and their escort returned. The former lodged at Bukhara itself, in a large house belonging to the Kushbegi, but the latter encamped at Bazarchi.†

Meyendorf describes the Bukharian villages as half hidden by orchards and sometimes protected by crenellated walls. Each of them consisted generally of about a hundred houses made of earth, clustering round a tank, and they were generally situated on a canal, so that the gardens might be watered. He assigns to Haidar the final removal of the inhabitants of Merv when it became deserted, and attributes it to his jealousy for his brother Nasr ud din, who governed it. It was afterwards treated as a penal settlement, and contained a garrison of five hundred soldiers and a population of about the same number. To prevent its becoming

---

* Meyendorf's Voyage, 81, 82.   † Id., 83, 87.

4 C

again peopled, the Khan forbade the irrigating canals being used.* The Jews at Bukhara were numerous. They were only allowed to live in three streets, and were chiefly artisans, manufacturers, dyers, and silk merchants. About eighty thousand roubles a year were drawn from them in taxes. They were not allowed to ride on horseback in the city nor to wear silk robes, and had to have a border of black lambskin round their caps, which was of a prescribed width. They could not build a new synagogue, and were only allowed to repair the old one. Their chief rabbi had come from Algeria. The trade between Russia and Bukhara is of long standing. The great Eastern Russian marke in former days was Makarief, whence the famous annual fair was removed in 1818 to Nijni Novgorod. This Orenburgh and Troitsk were the main goals of the Bukharian traders, who were the continual victims of the Kazaks.

The details of this trade are described in graphic fashion by Meyendorf. In speaking of the despotism of the Government, he remarks how it was qualified by the ease with which the population of Bukhara could migrate and transfer its allegiance to Khiva or Khokand. The smallness of the country made it easy also to control the hakims or provincial governors, and prevented them becoming satraps.† Nevertheless the tyranny was terrible. The grandees were not ashamed of styling themselves slaves of the Khan, which really meant of his favourites for the time being.‡ Gross venality prevailed everywhere, and it was dangerous for any person to display his wealth, as it was a temptation to plunder him. This again prevented very luxurious living. The Khan was a libertine in his private life, and was imitated by those about him. Fear and distrust were the necessary compliments of tyranny. The dishes prepared for the Khan's dinner were tasted by the cook and Kushbegi, and then duly covered and sealed by the latter, and we are told that every time the Khan left the city he made his son do so also. The Khan had about two hundred women in his harem, but, as a good Mussulman, only four wives, one a daughter of the Khan of Hissar, a second of a Khoja at Samarkand, and a third of Zeman the Afghan Shah.§

The rigid ceremonial which was exacted at state interviews was dispensed with at other times, and the Khan spoke to Meyendorf and others in a friendly fashion on meeting them in the street. Anyone meeting the Khan stopped and made the salaam, which was answered by one of the Khan's officers. When he went to the mosque on Friday he alone was mounted, his companions walked. Although the clergy were so powerful, we are told that no man of position became a mollah. Meyendorf has collected a great mass of reliable information about the internal economy of the Khanate and the manners and customs of its people, to which I must refer my readers, and again pass on to the history of Mir Haidar.

---

* Id., 255.   † Id., 254, 255.   ‡ Id., 255.   § Id., 261.

His character, as before described, was clearly not likely to impress his turbulent dependents, and we find in fact that the greater feudatories became more or less independent, and the Khanate was greatly disintegrated during his reign. We are told by Izzetulla that on his accession he applied to the Sultan of Constantinople for a confirmation of his authority, and was given the title of Mir Akhor Bashi, but at the end of two years he imitated the unpretending style of his father, and assumed the title of Amir al Mumin.* The Murza Shems tells us that in the year 1242 (i.e., 1826) Mir Haidar went to Karshi, where his son Nasrulla was living. On his return homewards, he fell ill on the way, and died on reaching Bukhara. His death took place on the 6th of October, 1826.† Many of his coins are known, on which he styles himself Padishah Mir Haidar and Seyid Mir Haidar. On some of them the name of his father Maasum and of his grandfather Danial also occur.‡

Vambery sums up his character in· some graphic phrases. Having spoken of his ascetic life, he continues : " When his western neighbour Muhammed Rahim of Khiva would avenge the death of his father Iltazar Khan and, plundering and burning, advanced by way of Charjui and K tkul to the very gates of Bukhara, even then Amir Said did not allow himself to be disturbed in his pious mode of life, as he exclaimed, ' Akhir Rigistan amandur,' i.e., The Righistan (the place where the palace is situated) is still safe. In the absence of any great or glorious achievements, the Bukharians praise highly the strict clerical character of their prince. The servile herd of the capital on the Zerefshan are said to have wept with joy when the Amir passed through the streets with his head bowed low and supported on a stick, not from any weakness but by way of acting the mollah. Nay, they even attributed to him miraculous powers, although it is known of this living saint that he violated in the most flagrant manner the holiest of Asiatic laws, to wit, those of hospitality, by violently carrying off the beautiful daughter of the blind fugitive at his court, Shah Zeman, and when the blind father broke out in just complaints, would have had him put to death."§ The high pressure at which morality was enforced produced its natural effects. Wine and tobacco, being forbidden by the letter of the law, were replaced by opium, and the draconic laws about the separation of the sexes led to the most revolting immorality.

MIR HUSSEIN.

While Mir Haidar lay ill the Hakim Kushbegi, who was a partisan of Nasrulla, sent to Karshi to tell him the news, and on the Amir's death

* Journ. Asiat. Soc., vii. 341.
† Mems. Imp. Arch. Soc. of St. Petersburg, Orient. Sec., vii. 336.   Melanges Asiatiques, iii. 643.
‡ Vel. Zeraof, Coins of Bukhara, &c., 419-424.   § Op. cit., 363.

he even secured the oath of allegiance from seventy or eighty chieftains
for his *protégé*. His brother Hussein, who was living at Bukhara, was
the people's favourite however. He had not been on good terms with
his father, who had intrusted him successively with the government of
Kermineh and Samarkand, and had afterwards removed him to Bukhara,
and he was now living there with only a few dependents. Having been
informed of the Kushbegi's doings, and fearing for his personal safety,
he determined to brave matters out, and rode up to the gates of the
citadel with barely a dozen followers. He asked the guard for permission to pass in, the latter said Mir Haidar was still living. " If he
still lives," he said, " I have come to visit him, while if he is dead I wish to
possess myself of the inheritance." " The garrison," says Murza Shems,
who was one of the party, " began to stone us, but we knocked a panel
out of the gate and crept in, whereupon those in charge fled." Hussein
made his way to his father's bedroom, followed by the people. He then
summoned the Kushbegi, who was penitent, and pardoned him. In the
morning a circular letter was despatched to the various surrounding
towns, including Karshi, with the news of his accession. When
Nasrulla heard of his father's death he set off with seven or eight
hundred followers and rode towards Bukhara, and received his brother's
letter on the road. He thereupon returned crest-fallen to Karshi. Great
festivities took place at Bukhara, and congratulations poured in upon
Hussein, including those of the Persian Shah.*

Meanwhile Nasrulla intrigued with the grandees to create himself a
party to enable him to displace his brother. The chief of those he won
over was Mumin bey Dodkha, who had been named chief of Hissar by
Amir Hussein, but he had scarcely begun preparations in earnest when
he heard that the latter had died. It was suspected that the Kushbegi
had poisoned him. He only reigned seventy-five days. A gold coin of
his is extant, struck at Bukhara in 1242 (*i.e.*, 1826).†

MIR OMAR.

The throne was now seized by Hussein's brother Omar, who was
younger than Nasrulla, and whose mother had been a slave of the
mother of Hussein. The latter, who dreaded that the accession of
Nasrulla would be the signal for the destruction of his own adherents,
summoned Omar from Kermineh, to be near Bukhara in case his illness
should prove fatal. He accordingly set out with five or six thousand
followers, and on Hussein's death encamped at Sherbudineh, near the

* Mems. of Murza Shems, op. cit., 337-340.
† Khanikof, Hist. of Bukhara, 296-298. Vel. Zernof, Melanges Asiatiques, St. Petersburg
Academy, iii. 635, &c.

city.* Among his chief supporters were Ismet Ulla bi, Taghai Khan the
Kazak, and Khudai Nazar the Shaghaul (i.e., the chamberlain). On the
death of Hussein he entered the capital and seized the throne. Nasrulla
persuaded the Kazi Kalen of Karshi to address a letter to the clergy and
people of Samarkand, inviting them to recognise him as lawful Khan,
and he also sent envoys to the Prince of Shehr i Sebz to secure his
alliance.† At length, having mustered a small force, he left Karshi and
marched over the snow-covered desert towards Samarkand, by whose
governor he was admitted with the concurrence of the citizens, and was
seated on the famous blue stone. Notwithstanding this friendly act, the
governor was deposed and replaced by Muhammed Alim bey. Nasrulla
continued his advance towards Ketta Kurgan. Omar Khan thereupon
marched to Kermineh with fifteen thousand men, and sent troops to
secure Ketta Kurgan and the adjacent towns. These troops, on hearing
of Nasrulla's success at Samarkand, submitted to him, and this was
followed by the surrender of Ketta Kurgan, Penj Shambeh, Chelek,
Yanghi Kurgan, and Nurata, whose governors were displaced and had
to accompany the victors; other troops also deserted, and the Murza
Shems confesses that he behaved like the rest. Omar now shut himself
up in Bukhara, and put Kermineh in charge of Abdulla Khan, son of
Hakim Kushbegi, who by his father's advice also surrendered his charge.
Nasrulla marched on, and planted ramparts about the capital and
beleagured it, one account says for fifty-one days, another for forty-four.
Food speedily became scarce, meat was sold at four, or as others
affirmed, at seven tengas a pound, and flour was introduced into the city
in coffins under pretence that they contained dead bodies, while the
drinking water became very fœtid. The Kushbegi and Ayaz the
Topchibashi now sent to the Amir offering to surrender the place if he
would spare the inhabitants, and on his asking for some proof of their
sincerity, he offered to blow up a huge cannon, which, according to the
native accounts, weighed one hundred batmans, and he kept his word.
Nasrulla at length entered the town by the Imaum and Saleh-Khan
gates, Ayaz not resisting his entrance.‡ Ismet Ulla bi the Kalmuk,
Toghai Khan the Kazak, and some others, as well as the astrologer Gul
Makhdum and Murza Asim, son of Rahman Kul, were put to death.
The houses of Omar Khan were ordered to be plundered. One account
says he went on a pilgrimage to Mekka, another that having been
imprisoned he escaped, and went first to Meshed and then to Balkh, and
that he ended by dying of cholera at Khokand, whence his body was
taken to Bukhara to be buried.§ The capture of Bukhara took place on
the 24th April, 1827.

---

* Murza Shems, 341.

† Khanikof, op. cit., 298.   ‡ Khanikof, 301, 302.   § Melanges Asiat., III. 641.

MIR NASRULLA.

The early part of Nasrulla's reign was marked by prudence and justice, and after he had put aside his immediate rivals he seems to have been a tolerably exemplary ruler. He styled himself Amir ul Mumin, and was called Hazret by his subjects, a name used by the Turkestan Muhammedans when speaking of their prophets. He was proud also of holding the official position of bowbearer to the Sultan of Rum.* He devoted himself very strictly to his religious observances, and Burnes tells us that when he wrote he was drifting into the bigoted attitude of his father, which the nature of his government made it difficult to avoid. On his accession he divested himself of all his own and his father's wealth, which gained him great reputation. He guided his conduct strictly by law, and it was reported that his privy purse was supported entirely by the capitation tax levied on Jews, Hindoos, and other unbelievers. He was ambitious and warlike, and conciliated his army by profuse largess. Meanwhile the laws were very draconic and rigidly executed. The chief adviser of the Amir was the Kushbegi, and Burnes says he never quitted the citadel till the Kushbegi was ready to take his place, nor would he receive food from other hands than his. This officer was a Mangut and about sixty years of age, and was unremitting to business. His father had held the office before him, and his two brothers and thirteen sons were all employed in the Government. He was a crafty person and conciliated the priesthood. He was also attached to Europeans.†

Dr Wolff confirms this account, and adds that so long as Nasrulla was under the influence of Hakim beg as his Kushbegi he ruled very wisely, was on good terms with his neighbours, and Bukhara was adorned with beautiful mosques and its environs with gardens and country houses.‡

The change in his character which afterwards came on, he affirms, was the work of Abdul Samut Khan, who arrived at Bukhara about 1832, and began to intrigue against the Kushbegi (who had introduced him to the Amir), and to accuse him of having a correspondence with England.

Abdul Samut was born at Tabriz in 1784, and having learnt something of military science from General Court, was employed for some time by Muhammed Ali Murza at Kermanshah. There his ears were cut off for some offence. He then went to India, thence to Peshawur, where he joined the service of Dost Muhammed Khan, whence he repaired to Bukhara with a bitter hatred for the English. Patronised by the Kushbegi Hakim beg, he was employed in organising the Bukharian army, and was appointed his naib or lieutenant by his patron. He lived

---

* Burnes, ii. 364.   † Id., 364, &c.   ‡ Wolff, op. cit., 324.

outside Bukhara in great pomp, and accumulated a fortune of sixty
thousand tillas. He visited the Amir every Sunday, and liked to pass
himself off as a European by birth and a disciple of English officers.*
At this time a rumour reached the Amir that Lieutenant Wyburt was on
his way to Khiva. He ordered him to be waylaid, and he was imprisoned
in the Siah chah, *i.e.*, black hole, of which more presently. Wyburt was
treated with contumely by Abdul Samut, and on the Amir bidding him
become a Mussulman and enter his service he refused, and was
accordingly beheaded and his body thrown into a well.† This was about
a year before the arrival of Stoddart.‡

The Kushbegi now began to lose favour. He warned the Amir of the
danger of quarrelling with such a powerful nation as England when he
had so many dangerous nations round him. This was probably
ungrateful advice. Presently the Chief Mollah, with a sycophancy not
often to be found among the proud priests of Islam, proclaimed to the
people that the Amir was a shepherd and that they were his sheep, and
that he could use any man's wife as he pleased. He then, according to
Dr. Wolff, became the greatest profligate in Bukhara, and the Kushbegi
having reproved him, again incurred his displeasure.

At length, about 1837, he determined to crush the latter.§ He had
amassed great riches. Vambery says he was reported to have a thousand
slaves, and camels, horses, and sheep innumerable. He is also said to
have trafficked with caravans of his own to Russia.‖ He was banished
first to Karshi and then to Nurata, whence he was recalled to Bukhara and
imprisoned. Meanwhile the Topchibashi Ayaz, who was father-in-law
of the Kushbegi, was given the command of Samarkand, but this was
only to quiet his suspicions. He too was rich, and his wealth would
be useful. The pantomime went on for a while. Being at length
summoned to Bukhara, he was presented by the Amir with a khalat
or dress of honour of gold brocade and a turban of the same stuff,
while a beautiful arghamak, richly caparisoned, was furnished him
to ride upon. The Amir himself came out and helped him to
mount. Ayaz was frightened at this suspicious condescension, and asked
to be punished at once, but Nasrulla embraced him, as Khanikof says,
"with the subtle caresses of the snake," and lulled his suspicion. He
returned accordingly to Samarkand, where he began to think all danger
was over, when he was once more summoned back again and thrown into
the same prison with the Kushbegi, where they were both put to death in
the spring of 1840.¶ The Khan then banished several of the Kushbei's
relatives and put others to death, and proceeded to stamp with a heavy
foot on the sipahis or feudal soldiery, whose turbulence was perhaps a
sufficient excuse for his ruthless policy. His most efficient instrument

* Burnes, op. cit., 340, 341.   † Wolff, 326.   ‡ Vide infra.
§ Khanikof, 303.   ‖ Vambery, 367.   ¶ Khanikof, 302-305.

in the work was the Turkoman Rahim Birdi Maazum, who had already
befriended him sixteen years before at Shehr i Sebz, and who hated and
despised the Bukharians. "The common people were beaten with sticks
to induce them to say their prayers, the sipahis were butchered or forced
to seek safety in flight, and the people execrated the Reis or chief of
police."*

The latter ended his days in 1839, and the Amir determined to
dispense in future with any chief functionaries, but as it was necessary
to have some one to fill the office of vizier, he conferred that dignity
during the short space of three or four years on the favourites of his
male harem, after which they were replaced by others, and themselves
stripped of their wealth, and as they might prove dangerous or not, were
made away with or consigned to want.†

Vambery reports how the city, its bazaars, schools, mosques, and baths
became tenanted with spies, who sometimes used to sit with their arms
crossed before them, and took advantage of their loose wide sleeves to
write unseen what they heard. Whoever sought to protect his property,
slaves, or children from the tyrant, was accused of rebellion against the
" Prince of True Believers," the "Shadow of God upon Earth," and was
confined in the foul prison, known as the Siah chah or black hole, or the
kenne khane or house of ticks, from its swarming with the latter animals,
which in lieu of human victims were fed on the offal of slaughtered
animals. Into this place the victims were placed bound; others were
flayed alive, roasted in ovens, thrown down from high towers, &c.‡

At this time the Amir introduced a revolution in the military organisation of Bukhara, which enabled him to fight his neighbours on more
than equal terms. With the assistance of Abdul Samut he organised a
body of regular troops or Sarbasis, and had a number of new cannons
cast. Nasrulla first used his new army against the stiff-necked people
of Shehr i Sebz, who had long been practically independent of Bukhara.
This invasion led to an intermittent struggle, in which the little secluded
district continued more or less to secure its liberty. I shall refer to it
again presently.

Nasrulla now turned upon Khokand. The chief pretext for this war was
that the Khan of Khokand had in 1839 built the fort of Pishagar so close
to the land of Bukhara that the Amir declared it was actually built on
his ground, and insisted on having it dismantled, and as his request was
refused he marched against Pishagar. The Khan of Khokand, having
united his forces with those of the Beglerbeg of Khojend, marched to
meet the Amir, but, intimidated by a sharp attack from some Bukharians
who made a sortie from a fort, he withdrew and left the besieged town to
its fate. The Amir's army of Uzbegs had a contingent of three hundred
Sarbasis with it, and also some cannons cast by the Naib Abdul Samut.

---

* Id., 303.   † Id., 307.   ‡ Op. cit., 308, 309

The latter, after a vigorous cannonade, compelled the place to surrender. This was in August, 1840. The Khokandians were not cowed however. The very same winter they plundered several frontier villages of Bukhara. The Amir meanwhile busied himself in increasing the number of his Serbasis, and in the autumn of 1841 found himself master of one thousand of them, as well as of eleven cannons and two mortars. With this army he again advanced, and captured Yom on the 21st September of the same year. After putting his uncle, who had some time before sought refuge at Khokand and been nominated governor of this fort, to death, he marched to Zamin, which surrendered on the 27th of the same month. He then captured and plundered Uratippa, and entered Khojend as a conqueror on the 8th of October. On reaching Mahram he received proposals from the Khan of Khokand, who offered to surrender to him all the country as far as Khojend, pay a large sum, to acknowledge the Amir as his liege lord, and to have his name introduced into the Khutbeh and on the coins. As his Uzbegs were growing discontented, Nasrulla gladly accepted this offer, and after appointing Sultan Mahmud, the brother and rival of the Khokand Khan, governor of Khojend, he once more returned to Bukhara.

The two brothers having been reconciled, now united their forces and recaptured all the country taken by the Bukharians, as far as Uratippa. To revenge this, the Amir once more set out on the 2nd of April, 1842, and, although fifteen thousand Khokandians were close by, he speedily conquered Khojend, and was equally successful when he reached Khokand, which also fell into his hands.* Muhammed Ali, the Khan of Khokand, was overtaken at Marghilan, and being accused of having committed incest with his own mother, was ten days after put to death, with his brother and two sons. Even his wife and her unborn child were not spared. Having caused his principal adherents to be executed, and also confiscated their property, he returned to Bukhara, leaving Ibrahim bi, a native of Merv, with two thousand men to garrison the capital.† It was not long before there was an outbreak at Khokand, which once more recovered its liberty, and defied all the efforts of the Amir to annex it. I shall have more to say of this struggle presently.

We have now reached a time when the mutual rivalries of England and Russia in Asia give the affairs of Bukhara a much wider political interest. Russia, for purposes of trade and to secure a useful ally against its persistent enemies of Khiva and the Kazak steppes, had carried on an intermittent intercourse with Bukhara since the seventeenth century, and had sent several missions there, as well as more confidential agents. One of these, Dr. Demaisons, went in 1834 in the guise of a mollah, and a second, Vitkovitch, disguised as a Kazak, in 1835.‡ The first Englishman who visited Bukhara in the last century was

* Khanikof, 312-314. † Vambery, 374, 375. ‡ Schuyler, L 367.

4 D

Captain. Burnes, whose journey was more that of a pioneer and to gain information about Central Asia than with any political motive. It created considerable feeling in Russia, however, and the two travellers just named probably went to learn what he had been about. In 1836 we find the Russian governor of Orenburgh addressing a long letter to the Amir, who is styled " the esteemed, all perfect, glorious, and Great Amir, descendant of the benignant Hakim, the centre of learning, order, and glory, and the disseminator of glory." It calls attention to the persistent ill-conduct of the Khivans. How they kept in bondage a great number of Russians and interfered with the Kazaks, who were their subjects, and telling him how the Emperor had determined to detain all Khivans in his dominions until his subjects were released. The letter asked for the friendship of the Bukharians, and also that if any Russian prisoners should exist at Bukhara, they might be released.* In 1836 Kurban beg Ashurbek arrived at the fortress of Orsk as an envoy from the Amir. He went on to St. Petersburg, and reported his master's wish to be on friendly terms with the Russians. That the English had sent agents to try and open trade with Bukhara, and that the ruler of Kabul, threatened by Runjeet Singh, had also sent to ask for his alliance.† The English and Russians had for some time been intriguing at the Persian court, and the ambassador of the former at Teheran deemed it a prudent thing to send an envoy in the person of Colonel Stoddart to Bukhara. This was in 1838. His proud and austere demeanour irritated the Amir, who two days after his interview with him put him in prison. There can be small doubt that whatever the Naib Abdul Samut could do to incite him against the English, who had virtually expelled him from India for his crimes, would be done.

In August of the same year another envoy from Bukhara appeared at Orsk, escorting an elephant and some arghamaks, and taking some Cash-mere shawls with him, as well as some Russian prisoners. His retinue consisted of twenty men. Two silver roubles a day, or about six shillings, were allowed him by the Russian authorities for his maintenance, others of his retinue had about one shilling and sixpence a day allowed them, and the rest ninepence. The envoy went on to St. Petersburg, where he made devoted promises of friendship and goodwill, and asked the Russians to send an engineer officer to explore his territory for gold and precious metals. He returned home with some handsome presents of brocade, cloth, crystal, &c. The cost of maintaining and conveying this embassy, exclusive of presents, was about nine thousand silver roubles, while the charge for the elephant was three thousand more.‡

In April, 1839, in accordance with the Amir's invitation, Captain Kovalefski, of the mining engineers, with Captain Herrngros, an interpreter, a head miner, two viewers, and four Cossacks, set out for

Bukhara, with instructions to inquire into its mineral wealth, product of precious metals, method of manufacturing Khorasan steel, &c. ; to get information as to Asiatic trade, and to endeavour to procure a reduction of the duties on Russian goods ; to inquire how far English articles competed with them, to obtain the release of Russian prisoners, and to try and secure that a Russian consul should reside at Bukhara. Being threatened on the way by the Kazaks, the Russian officers abandoned the caravan on the way, and returned home in great haste. The caravan, notwithstanding, reached Bukhara in safety, and the abandoned articles were afterwards given up to the Russians.*

At this time the English were engaged in that struggle in Afghanistan which ended so disastrously. The real cause of this war was the rivalry between Russia and England. Dost Muhammed, the ruler of the Afghans, was accused of carrying on secret intrigues with the Russians, whose agent Vitkovitch arrived in Kabul in December, 1837.† Dost Muhammed was at this time the ruler of Afghanistan, and the English supported a claimant to the throne in the person of Shah Shuja, and also encouraged the Sikhs in their campaign against the Afghans. In the spring of 1839 they entered Afghanistan, and Kabul on the 7th of August of that year, when they put Shah Shuja on the throne. Dost Muhammed, with his family and three hundred and fifty devoted followers, retired and took refuge with Nasrulla at Bukhara.‡ He at first received them hospitably, but presently behaved in his usual fashion, and is accused of having committed the grossest indecencies upon Dost Muhammed's beautiful son Sultan Jan. Nasrulla, who wished to conciliate the English, now began to act in a very threatening manner towards his guest, and entered into a plot with his brother, Shah Shuja, to undo him. The Shah of Persia, who was Dost Muhammed's patron, warned the Amir that he would hold him responsible for any harm that might befall his *protégé;* he also ordered him to set him and his family at liberty, so that he might go on a pilgrimage to Mekka, and threatened war if he refused to comply. As Nasrulla did not care to openly beard the Shah, he released the Afghan chief, but, with characteristic duplicity, he ordered the ferryman who was to take him over the Oxus to upset the boat midway, and to take care he did not reach the other bank ; but having been warned in time, he disguised himself as a woman and escaped in a litter, making his way to Shehr i Sebz, by whose ruler he was well received. Thence he passed on to Khulm, and after a while returned to Kabul, where he made a hollow peace, and where he was joined by several of his sons.§

Meanwhile Colonel Stoddart continued in durance at Bukhara. As I have said, he was a proud soldier, attached to the habits and religion of his childhood and his country, and inflexible to

---

* *Id.,* 418-420. † Ferrier's Afghans, 263. ‡ *Id.,* 330. § *Id.,* 338, 339.

everything but military discipline.   He entered Bukhara two days
before the feast of Ramazan, when Muhammedan fanaticism is at its
height, and he bore a letter of introduction from the ruler of Herat, which
proved to be a treacherous document.   The Amir grew suspicious, and
sought every means to humiliate him, which was haughtily resented by
Stoddart.   One day when the vizier Mahram Berdi Reis entered his
room with the violent apostrophe, "Do you know I have destroyed all
the Amir's enemies?" he replied ironically, "I rejoice to hear the Amir
has no more enemies."*   On being told to go on foot to meet the Amir
in the Great Square of Bukhara, he replied that he would ride on
horseback as if he was in London.   This was really an affront.   Neither
Jew nor Christian might appear on horseback in Bukhara, and no one at
all but the Amir in the Righistan or Great Square.   Stoddart was told to
do as he pleased, and, much to the scandal of the populace, he in full
European costume caracolled his horse on the forbidden ground, and
more so when at the approach of the Amir himself he did not dismount,
but received him with a mere military salute.   The Amir, who felt
himself defied, gave him a long look and passed on in silence.   He was
then summoned to the palace.   The chamberlain was about to use the
ordinary phrase of presentation at Bukhara, *erz bendeguiani*, the
"supplication of his slave," but Stoddart objected.   As Ferrier says,
he might as well have been offended at the words, "Your Majesty,"
which scarcely belongs to anyone but God, or have objected to the
ordinary phrase, "Your very humble servant," which means nothing.†
Stoddart refused, however, to comply.   Nor would he allow himself to be
supported on either hand by two officials, in the Eastern custom derived
from a diplomatic fiction, that "a stranger before the sovereign is so overcome by the effulgence of his rays that he cannot stand without support.".

The master of the ceremonies having presumed to feel if he had any
concealed arms, was knocked down by a blow from the Colonel's fist.
Instead of repeating, as was customary, a silent invocation for the
sovereign on entering, he began reciting a loud prayer to God in Persian,
upon which the Amir, seated in his royal chair, "stroked his beard,
full of hatred for this arrogant stranger, and disgusted by his coarse
and domineering behaviour."‡   The Amir having asked for his credentials, he could produce none save a letter from Sir John M'Neil,
the ambassador to Persia, and on his offering *vivâ voce*, on behalf of the
East India Company, to pay him a subsidy if he would resist the
entreachments of Russia, he replied ironically, "Very good, I see that it
is your intention to make me your slave ; it is well, I will serve you.   In
the meantime withdraw."§   Being summoned two days later to the vizier's
house, he was seized by a body of men, thrown down, and tied hand and
feet.   The vizier then approached him, put a sword to his throat, and said,

---

* Ferrier, op. cit., 441, 442.   † Id., 443.   ‡ Id., 444.   § Id., 445.

" Miserable spy, infidel dog ! You come here, do you, from your English employers to buy Bukhara as you have bought Kabul? You will not succeed. I will kill you," and he pressed his sabre on the grim old Colonel, whose eye did not flinch. Soon after the men were ordered to remove him, and he was carried like a corpse, still bound, through the driving rain, with his bearers carrying torches, amidst profound silence, through the deserted streets of the city. " Sometimes they let him fall on the ground, or drew tighter the cords that confined his bruised limbs, and sometimes they stopped and insulted him with savage gestures and laughter." When he asked them to kill him and end his misery, they said he was either a devil or a sorcerer, since he seemed to have no fear. Having confined him in a dark room and barred the door, presently the latter was opened, some lights appeared, and some servants entered, preceded by a man enveloped in woollen drapery, which allowed his eyes only to be seen. This figure, which from the deference paid to it, was clearly a person of consequence, having set itself on a divan, Stoddart reproached it with the indignities he had suffered, and said he should not have been allowed to enter Bukhara if it was intended to treat him thus, and he asked leave to be allowed to depart. The figure, who was the Mir Cheb or Prince of the Night (i.e., the chief of police), promised to communicate his wishes to the Amir. He seized and burnt all his papers, and sold his effects and horses, and then removed him to the Siah chah or black well, a dungeon pit, twenty-one feet deep, where the worst malefactors were confined. He was let down into it by a rope, and there found himself with two thieves and a murderer for his companions. There he remained for two months, covered with vermin and surrounded by reptiles. His food was passed down to him by a rope, and he spent the most of his time in smoking. He was then taken out and offered his life on condition of his becoming a Mussulman. To this alternative, says Ferrier, "borne down by the dreadful sufferings he had endured, and the exhaustion of his mental and bodily powers, he gave a reluctant consent, repeating the Muhammedan Confession of Faith, after which he was taken to the public square and circumcised, in the presence of an immense crowd, who had been attracted there by the novelty of the event."*

The Russian officials endeavoured to get his release, and this was apparently secured, whereupon he resumed his intrepidity. The Amir was so struck by it, that he took off his own fur cloak and gave it to him, and ordered him to be led in triumph through the streets of Bukhara. He now renounced Muhammedanism, to which he had only conformed through force.

The Amir and his officials had quite altered their conduct to him. The British successes in Afghanistan had perhaps frightened them, but besides

---

* Ferrier, op. cit., 447.

this "he hoped," says Ferrier, "that he should attach him to his interests, as Runjeet Singh had done other Englishmen." "Those Feringhis," said the Amir, "so powerful and clever in the arts and diplomacy, so talented in organising an army, bring everywhere success in their train." Stoddart was next offered the chance of accompanying an embassy to St. Petersburg, where he might have been free again, but, with a singular perversity in his devotion to his duty, he declared that he would not do so, as he had not yet received orders from his Government to withdraw from Bukhara. This devotion was misunderstood, and only increased the suspicions that he was a spy. The Amir issued orders that he should be poisoned, but he saved his life by exciting the cupidity of Samut Khan, who hoped to get a large ransom for him. At other times the Amir was better disposed towards him, and sent him tobacco and other presents, requesting him in turn to replace the quicksilver on his mirrors, and to make him a thermometer, and candles that would burn without smoke, and if he had had as much tact as courage, he might have availed himself of these circumstances. Some letters he wrote at this time, which were intrusted to Khorasanis, Kurds, Persians, and Jews, who sewed them in the hems of their robes, reached their destination. They breathe the spirit of the Puritans of Cromwell's days, and in them, says our guide Ferrier, "diplomatic interests and the feelings of the soldier take their place far below the religious sen iment which governed the mind and destiny of Stoddart, whose character they invest with real grandeur."* The Sultan of Turkey, the Tzar, and the Khan of Khiva in turn pleaded for his release. To the two former the Amir returned ambiguous answers. To the latter he used these whimsical words, " You have an Englishman and so have I. Why do you wish to take mine ?"† This Englishman at Khiva was Captain Conolly.

The rivalries of England and Russia in Central Asia at this time brought about strange combinations. Thus we find that in 1840 several English officers reached Khiva.‡ One of these, Captain Conolly, was ordered to visit Khokand, to explore that district, and apparently also to attempt to checkmate the Russian advance thither. Khiva and Khokand, and especially the latter, were looked upon by the Amir of Bukhara as in some measure dependent on him, and as Captain Conolly's visit was coincident with the obduracy of the Khokand Khan, which led to a fierce campaign I have already mentioned, he was deemed its instigator. At this time he received a letter from Stoddart, inviting him to go to Bukhara, and he determined, notwithstanding the advice of his Khivan and Khokandian friends, to go to Nasrulla's camp, and to try and persuade him to join with the other Uzbeg princes in a league against Russia, and having applied for a firman speedily received one, the Amir wishing to gain possession of him. He reached the camp at

---

Jizakh, and having brought about a parley between the Amir and his vassal, he went on to Bukhara under escort, and took up his residence in the house of Abdul Samut, already so often mentioned,* and who now worked on the capricious mind of Nasrulla, and persuaded him to forbid the two officers from communicating with one another. Stoddart was at this time lodging with the Russian envoy Butenief. In order to be able to see his friend, he consented to move his quarters to the house of the notorious Abdul Samut. On his return to his capital the Amir, who had grown very hostile to the English, began to show marked incivility to the two officers. Although three tillas, or forty shillings, a day were assigned for their maintenance, they were kept under restraint. At an interview he had with them, he told them Bukhara would not be so easily conquered as Afghanistan, and said he intended putting them both in prison, and the English Government might go and take them out if it liked. They had similar interviews with him on three successive days.

The last time they were taken to the citadel with seven of their pich khetmets or upper servants. Their house was ransacked, and their other servants, forty-three in number, were thrown into the Siah chah. Conolly had been accompanied to Bukhara by Allah Dad Khan, the envoy of the recent ruler of Afghanistan. The Amir hated the Afghans bitterly, but he did not care to arouse the moollahs by imprisoning the envoy of an orthodox sovereign. He therefore let him leave the city, but he was arrested at Karshi and sent back to Bukhara, and taken to a place called Ab Khaneh or the water-house, so cold that no person could be left in it two nights in succession and live. After a few hours he was removed and confined in a dungeon adjoining that of the English officers. The Russian envoy interceded for the latter, but was met by such a rebuf in consequence, that, afraid he might suffer their fate, he determined to withdraw.

Meanwhile Akhud Zadek, the son of Hassan Muhammed, the former Kazi of Herat, who had accompanied Conolly to Khiva, and had thence been sent to Kabul, having received a letter from that English officer whose fate he did not know, went to him at Bukhara. Having said openly he was in the service of the English, he was arrested and imprisoned in the same prison as Allah Dad Khan. At this time the disastrous campaign in Afghanistan had reached its dismal climax in the massacre of Kabul. No longer afraid of the English, hating the officers who had gone to him empty-handed, and who were a source of embarrassment to him, their release being urged from Persia, Khiva, Constantinople, Kabul, and Herat, as well as by the Russians, he determined to put an end to them. When the Grand Mollah of Herat pleaded for Colonel Stoddart, he denounced him as a

---

disgrace to Islam for interceding for the infidels, while the pressure put upon him by the European Governments made him exaggerate the importance of his prisoners.

Their servants, after remaining forty-four days in the Siah chah, bound hand and foot to each other, with only a small ration of bad bread, were taken out, chained by the neck, eleven to a chain, in four parties, and marched at daybreak to the public square, where they remained all night, exposed to the deep snow and piercing cold. One who died remained chained to the rest. The greater number of his comrades had their feet and hands frost-bitten, and were awaiting their fate impatiently, when they were suddenly set at liberty. This was at the intercession of the mollahs, who declared them to be Mussulmans like themselves, and threatened the Amir with the wrath of Allah if he shed their blood.* They thereupon returned to Kabul, and some of them were afterwards in Ferrier's service, and it was from them he learnt the graphic details he reports. The release of the servants was followed by the incarceration of Allah Dad Khan and Akhud Zadek in the Siah chah, where there still remained a Greek from Constantinople in Conolly's service, named Joseph, and the seven pich khetmets already named. The mollahs succeeded in getting the release of the latter, as well as of Allah Dad Khan and Akhud Zadek, and the former made his way to Kabul, while the latter went to join his father at Meshed in Khorasan. Joseph claimed to be a subject of the Sultan, but as he was not circumcised he was not believed, and was remitted back to his loathsome prison. He now became a renegade, but this did not save him, for on the 17th of June, 1842, he was duly executed with the three malefactors who had been Colonel Stoddart's companions. Three days after, the two officers having been stripped and searched, there were found, sewn up in the sleeve of Colonel Stoddart's choka or Bukharian robe, a pencil, some steel pens, a small phial filled with ink, and some sheets of paper, which were taken to the Amir.† A few days before the police had seized on the frontier a letter which the Colonel had written to the English embassy at Teheran. This the Amir wished him to translate, as well as to explain the use of the articles that had been found on him. The obstinate Colonel refused to translate the letter, although beaten with rods on the soles of his feet for three days in succession. He simply declared that it contained nothing hostile to himself. The suspicious Amir would not believe him, and insisted it was meant to incite the Khivan Khan to make war on him, and he condemned the two officers to death. "Not a word of weakness," says Ferrier, "escaped Colonel Stoddart when he was informed of the fate that awaited him, but he completely gave way to the violence of his disposition, exhausting the whole vocabulary of personal abuse, in Persian, against the Amir and his

* Id., 456.   † Id., 458.

executioners, and ceased not to apostrophise them but in yielding his latest breath. He was put to death like a sheep in some ruins at the back of his prison, and in the presence of a few passers-by, who had been attracted to the spot by his cries and his invectives." The officer charged with the execution offered Conolly his life if he would become a Mussulman, but this he firmly refused to do, and was accordingly also put to death, and the two Englishmen were laid in the same grave, which had been dug before their eyes.* This tragedy took place on June 24th, 1842, "some days after the first apricots," says Akhud Zadeh.† It created a great sensation in Europe when it became known, which it did chiefly through the indefatigable and brave journey of the famous traveller Dr. Wolff and the narrative of General Ferrier.

Let us now revert again to the intercourse between Bukhara and Russia. The advance of the English in Afghanistan naturally made the Bukharian ruler look out for allies elsewhere. Mukin beg, a distinguished person, together with his two sons and other persons, set out accordingly on a mission to Russia, bearing a letter and a present of six shawls and two arghamaks or horses for the Emperor. The professed motive of the embassy was to complain of Khivan treachery, to obtain protection for Bukharian merchants, and for pilgrims who wished to pass through Russia to Mekka; but there were clearly more potent reasons for the journey. It reached St. Petersburg on the 30th of October, 1840, and returned again a few months later, but Mukin beg died of dropsy of the chest at Nijni Novgorod on his his way home. His body was embalmed at the expense of the Russians, and was sent to Bukhara. It was determined to send a mission in return, and Major Butenef was charged with its conduct. He was told to make inquiries about the Khanate of Bukhara and the neighbouring counties, to endeavour to strengthen Russian influence, and to develope Russian trade there. He was further to try and obtain the Amir's consent to certain definite proposals. 1. Neither openly nor secretly to show hostility against Russia. 2. Not to keep in slavery or in any way to obtain Russian prisoners, and to guarantee the personal safety and property of every Russian travelling in his territory. 3. The property of Russians dying at Bukhara to be returned intact. 4. To prohibit Bukharians robbing and imposing arbitrary laws on Russians and to punish those who did so. 5. To impose a single duty, not exceeding 5 per cent. on all Russian goods. 6. To protect Russian traders at Bukhara as Bukharians were protected in Russia. In return for these privileges, safety of person and property were accorded to the Amir's subjects in Russia; they were to be allowed similar privileges as other Asiatics trading there; the Kazaks and Turkomans subject to Russia were to be punished when they plundered Bukharian caravans;

* Id., 458, 459. † Id., 460.

4 E

and pilgrims to Mekka were to have permission to traverse Russia on conforming to its police regulations.* The envoy was also to try and arrange that a Russian agent should either be allowed to pay an annual visit or to reside at Bukhara, to obtain the release of all Russians held in bondage, and also to secure, if possible, the release of Stoddart, and to forward him to Russia.

Butenef was accompanied by the mining engineer Captain Bogos-lofski, the naturalist Lehmann, the archæologist and Eastern scholar Khanikof, an interpreter, a biographer, three miners, two stuffers of animals, ten Cossacks, and five Kazaks. They were ordered to secrete the gold pieces necessary for their expenses in their sword cases or leathern belts, so as not to excite the cupidity of the Bukharians, who would examine their luggage. The party was transported by fifty-five camels,† and entered Bukhara on the 17th of August, 1841, dressed in their uniforms, and were granted the unusual privilege, enjoyed only by the vizier, of riding into the palace on horseback.‡ They then passed on through a row of officials into a court-yard in which, wearing a white turban and robes (khalat), and seated on cushions, was the Amir himself. Having surveyed them a long time, he bade the vizier take the Emperor's letter from Butenef's hands, and then dismissed them. They were assigned the former palace of the Amir's brother Mir Hussein, the best residence in Bukhara, to live in. A large retinue of servants and one hundred and four tengas a month were also set aside for their main-tenance, &c. Exchanges of presents took place, and Butenef was ordered to go weekly to the palace on Fridays for prayers. Some of the party went to Samarkand and Karshi for mineralogical explorations, &c. Butenef visited Stoddart at the house of the naib Abdul Samut, and delivered to him a letter from Lord Clanricarde.§ At this time, having had a successful campaign in Khokand, and having ceased to fear the English, the Amir had become much inflated. " He was a thorough Asiatic; his concessions and friendships were governed by fear and cupidity," and there was now no necessity for showing any warmth towards Russia,‖ nor would he give Butenef an audience before he left for a second campaign against Khokand. As I have said, Stoddart at this time lodged with the Russian envoy, who describes him as a very clever, well educated, and agreeable man.¶ On his return from his campaign, the Amir continued to treat the Russian envoy with great coldness. He refused to release the Russian prisoners without compensation, and Butenef was convinced he avoided him on purpose. At length, early in April, he was summoned to hear "*the gracious words of the Amir,*" but he only received a curt answer. Nasrulla told him he had instructed his Dostrakhanshi or vizier to tell

* Michell, op. cit., 424-490.   † Id., 434.   ‡ Id., 439.   § Id., 441.
‖ Id., 443.   ¶ Id., 444.

him what his views were, and then rode off for Khokand. The end of the matter was, that he promised to ratify a treaty of peace with Russia if such a treaty was sent him. When this treaty was ratified the Russian slaves would be sent home. The customs duties would be reduced when the Russians reduced theirs on Bukharian articles. As to the Englishmen, he had written to the Queen of England, who wished to be on friendly terms with Bukhara, and on receiving her answer he would send them both *direct to England.*

These unsatisfactory and dilatory answers were naturally very irritating to the Russian envoy, who returned home again, after securing a valuable collection of topographical and other facts about the Khanate, but in regard to political matters the result was practically nothing. Butenef had scarcely left the Khanate when he was followed by a fresh envoy from the Amir, named Khudayar Karaulbeg, who duly arrived at Orenburgh with presents of shawls and arghamaks, and large expectations of presents in return. He was not allowed, however, to go on to St. Petersburg. The authorities pointedly told him they wanted some thing more than assurances of friendship, nor was Russia going to submit to such treatment as the Amir had served out to her envoy Butenef. Thus ended for many years the intercourse between Russia and Bukhara.*

Meanwhile the Amir did not alter his character, and Bukhara continued to be a most dangerous residence for Europeans. In 1842 a young Neapolitan named Nasseli Flores foolishly ventured there. He met Akhud Zadek at Charjui on the Oxus, who tried in vain to persuade him not to go, speaking to him by signs, as the Italian understood no Eastern language. He had scarcely been an hour in Bukhara when he was seized, stripped, and committed to the Siah chah. At a subsequent interview with the Amir, Giovanni Orlandi, a renegade from his own country, acted as interpreter, while Abdul Samut was present. The latter was jealous of Nasseli's supposed military knowledge, and determined to compass his death. He was accordingly executed.†

We must now turn to Dr. Wolff's famous journey to Bukhara in 1844, to ascertain the fate of the English officers. He went supported by letters from the Sultan of Turkey and others. The Russian envoy in Persia, wrote on his behalf to the Amir, and introduced him as a Christian priest of great celebrity, a dervish exclusively occupied with religious and scientific meditations, and completely indifferent to worldly affairs, and explained his object as being to obtain the release of Stoddart, Conolly, and Nasseli.‡ The Shah also wrote a letter, phrased in most inflated language, commending Dr. Wolff and his object, and asking for a renewal of the old intercourse between the two courts. Nearly ten lines are occupied by the fulsome titles found in this note

* *Id.,* 454 455.   † Ferrier, 465-467.   ‡ Wolff's Bukhara, i. 213.

to the notorious Amir.* At Shahr Islam, the Amir's chamberlain (Makhram) went to meet him, and took him sweetmeats and a kind message from Nasrulla. Wolff was dressed as a mollah, carried the Bible in his hand, and was viewed by the populace as a sacred being. They greeted him as· he went along with the words, " Peace be unto you."† and he describes his entry into Bukhara through the motley crowd as a triumphant march. He had to dismount before entering the palace, for only the grandees of the empire and the envoys of the Sultan and the Shah, and no Christians, heathens, or others are allowed to ride in. He was asked if he would submit to do the salaam three times in regular order, with the Shagaul holding his shoulders and meanwhile to stroke his beard five times, saying, " Allah Akbar," *i.e.*, " Peace to the King." He replied he would do it thirty times if necessary. Having sent in his letter of introduction, he and his people were then admitted. The Amir was seated in the balcony of the palace looking down upon them, thousands of people in the distance. " The Western dervish" not only made the salaam three times, but, as he tells us, exclaimed unceasingly " Peace to the King," until the Amir burst out laughing, as well as those about him, and cried "enough." He was duly informed the terrible ruler had smiled on him. He tells us he was about five feet six inches high, rather stout, with small black eyes, had a dark complexion with a convulsive twitching of the muscles of his face. He had a rapid intonation and a forced smile, and the looks of a *bon vivant*. His dress was without pomp or decoration, and like that of a mollah.‡ He had four wives, by one of whom he had an only son, who had a sickly disposition. His wives were Persian slaves, and creatures of Abdul Samut. His mother had also been a Persian, whence the caustic remark of a Turkoman, "As a horse paired with a donkey produces a mule, so an Uzbeg married to a Persian must produce a monster."§ He had been nursed by a Kazak woman, and this it was therefore said accounted for his being such a bloodhound since he had drunk the milk of a man-eater, the Kazaks being accused of eating the bodies of dead men.‖ His brutal cruelty was easily excused, however, in the Bukharian atmosphere of rigid divine right, and the people eagerly went near him to touch his clothes or hands and to be cured of their diseases, as they did in Western Europe in mediæval times.¶ As a curious instance of the modes of thought in Bukhara, it may be mentioned that the Amir sent expressly to ask Dr. Wolff two questions, " Are you able to awake the dead? When will the day of resurrection be ?" The Doctor gave answers as judicious, and as lacking in information, as those of the Delphic oracle.** In an interview with the famous naib Abdul Samut, the latter described the latter days of Stoddart and Conolly, and tried to evade any responsibility for their death, and when he got the

---

* *Id.*, 217.   † *Id.*, 312, 313.   ‡ *Id.*, 322, 323.   § *Id.*, 331, 332.
‖ *Id.*, 352.   ¶ *Id.*, 331.   ** *Id.*, 338, 339.

Doctor by himself he denounced his master without stint, accusing him of the intention of putting an end to him, and said he wished the English to send an officer to Khokand, Khulm, and Khiva to incite them against Bukhara, and promised to join them himself if they granted him twenty or thirty thousand tillas, while he undertook to invite the Amir to sit down on an undermined seat and to blow him up. In the evening Dr. Wolff was surprised to hear "God save the Queen" played by some Hindoos from Lahore, formerly in Runjeet Singh's service.[*] Among other curious adventures, the missionary was asked to write a life of Muhammed as reported among the Europeans. This he did, and he tells us the document was remitted to the library of the Great Mosque, and that copies of it were sent to Balkh, Khulm, and Mazar, to Samarkand and Uratippa, to Kabul and Cashmere. The Doctor had to answer many questions about the customs of the English. He tells us all the letters that went in and out of Bukhara, except those written by the chief of Merv, were opened and read by the authorities. Everybody was encouraged to be a spy upon his neighbour for the edification of the Amir, while Abdul Samut was in turn duly informed of what took place in Nasrulla's private apartments.

Every pretext was put forward for delaying the Doctor's departure. When he offered to redeem some Russian slaves he found they were unwilling to go back, many of them having been deserters, and exorbitant sums were asked from him by the naib on various pretences. The latter, who was a most treacherous villain, was evidently wishful to do for him what he had done for Stoddart and Conolly. Of this he was warned by many. He was most avaricious, like the greater part of Eastern officials, and with his creatures, was constantly asking the missionary for money. The following remarks made to him by two of these human limpets is very characteristic: "Mollah Yusuf Wolff, tillas (i.e., ducats) are sweet. We dream of tillas day and night, and we dreamt last night that you, on your return to England, sat near your monarch, and all the grandees of your country kissed the hem of your garment. The most beautiful women crowded around you and desired to become your wives, and you took the daughter of the Queen as your lawful wife. You will live in the finest palace, except the Queen's, and fanned by dancing girls; and if you shall say to her, 'Oh my Queen, cut off the head of this or that person,' she shall immediately follow your advice. Both of us, Kahir Kuli and I, Amir Saroj, dreamt this at one and the same time, and therefore it will become true."[†] The naib, who had dissembled greatly in his intercourse with Dr. Wolff, now began to show himself in his true colours. He acknowledged that he had been the cause of Stoddart's and Conolly's death, and he was evidently prepared to go any length with the missionary. On one occasion as he sat in his room a beautiful girl unveiled

---

[*] Id., ii. 7-25.   [†] Id., ii. 57, 58.

entered it. This was at the naib's suggestion, to entrap him into an indiscretion.* The Amir having said he would send an Uzbeg envoy back with him as his representative to the English Queen, the naib coolly suggested that his English guest should poison him *en route*.† On his return from his second expedition to Khokand, Nasrulla sent a mollah to ask him if he would become a Mussulman. He replied "Never." He then sent his executioner, the one who had put Stoddart and Conolly to death, threatening him with the same fate. Meanwhile the Persian ambassador, at the instance of his master, seems to have interested himself greatly in the English missionary, and he now obtained permission for him to accompany him on his return, and the Amir actually sent him a present of ninety tillas, a horse with a silver saddle, a shawl, and also a Persian MS. of the Tavarikh Tabari, on which the Amir put his tamgha or seal. Before he set out Abdul Samut extorted a promissory note for six thousand tillas from him, and he tells he wrote thus:—

"In the garden of the infamous Naib Abdul Samut Khan, surrounded by his banditti and compelled by him, I write that he forced from me a note of hand for six thousand tillas.

"JOSEPH WOLFF, Prisoner."‡

He at length left Bukhara, taking with him four slaves whom he had redeemed, while Abbas Kuli, the Persian envoy, took twenty whom he had bought with his own money, and a thousand who had redeemed themselves.§ He was also accompanied by Amir Abul Kasim, who was sent as an envoy from the Amir to the Queen, and a large number of persons, merchants, dervishes, fakirs, &c., altogether a caravan of quite two thousand camels. Crowds turned out to see their departure. A veiled woman as he passed exclaimed, "What joy your wife will have ! How will she sing ! You have been *born again*. Such a favour has not been shown for a long time by the Padishah."‖ This anecdote proves well what a tiger's den Bukhara then was. Cruel and dissolute as the Amir was, however, Dr. Wolff says he had some good points. He did not tyrannise over the poor, but protected them; he was not avaricious, while he hated bribery. His great model was Timur, and he adopted a similar motto on his seal, "Hakan Adalat," "Truth and Equity," as his own.¶ Although very passionate, he was singularly inquisitive and anxious for information and knowledge. "He put down," says Dr. Wolff, "by the simple word 'Hukum' (order) the most ancient customs, and overthrew entirely the power of the mollahs." He liked to hear that people were frightened of him, and was jealous of the reputation of the famous Muhammed Ali of Egypt, of whose exploits he had heard.** Abdul Samut had organised a plot for Dr. Wolff's assassination *en route*,

---

* Id., 80, 81.   † Id., 79.   ‡ Id., 115.   § Id., 118.   ‖ Id., 133, 134.
¶ Id., 123, 124.   ** Id., 123-125.

but this was happily frustrated, and he reached home in safety. I will conclude my extracts from his narrative with a curious discussion on the rivalry between England and Russia, he reports as having taken place at Merv. It was started by a dervish, who having related the exploits of Timur, suddenly broke off, and turning to Dr. Wolff, said, "The English people are now Timur, for they are the descendants of Jingis Khan. The Inglees will be the conquerors of the world. On my pilgrimage to Mekka I came to Aden, where they keep a strong force, and from whence they may march to Mekka whenever they please, and walk towards Mekka they shall."

A Turkoman thereupon said, "The Russians shall be the conquerors of the world. They have now built a strong castle in the midst of the sea, not far from Khiva. The people of Khiva have once burnt it down, but they soon built it up again. All is over with Islam."

A dervish sitting among them confirmed this with the following observation: "The great mollahs of Samarkand assert that Russia is the Jaj Majaj (i.e., Gog and Magog), and this has been already predicted by Amir Sultan, the great dervish of Rum."

We must now return once more to our immediate subject. A few years after Dr. Wolff's visit the infamous Abdul Samut met with a fitting punishment. Knowing his master well, he determined to send the money he had accumulated by foul and fair means, and which in 1847 amounted to £40,000, to his brother, a merchant at Meshed. He himself wished to return to Persia, but found it difficult to leave, hampered as he was with heavy baggage and a large family, whom he dared not send away for fear of arousing the suspicions of the Amir, who he knew hated him, although he found him too useful to put him away. At length he determined to try treachery. When in 1847 Nasrulla was at war with Shehr i Sebz, he sent the ruler of the latter notice that he might charge the artillery without any anxiety, as he would have the guns loaded with powder only, and when once he had broken the lines, he promised to turn the same guns upon his master, and thus crush him. The letter, having been confided to a Persian artilleryman, was conveyed to the Amir himself, whereupon "the naib was immediately sent for and put to death in his presence," and his wives and children were surrendered to the merciless soldiery, under whose cruelties many of them lost their lives.[*]

Somewhat later we read of another European who fell a victim to the Amir's temper. This was the Giovanni Orlandi already mentioned. He had been by trade a watchmaker, and was living at Teheran in 1839. Thence he found his way to Khokand, and from Khokand was carried off a prisoner by the Amir,[†] who spared his life on his promising to make him a machine for measuring time. He accordingly made the clock

---

* Id., 467, 468.　　　† Ferrier, 468.

with Arabic numerals placed in the tower above the palace gateway at Bukhara. This gained for him the appointment of artificer, and also his liberty. He afterwards made a telescope for the Amir, who unfortunately one day let it fall from the top of a minaret. Being sent for to repair it, he went somewhat intoxicated, when he was again imprisoned and ordered to become a Mussulman. This he refused to do. The executioner, to frighten him, cut the skin of his throat, promising to complete the work the following day, and as he still remained obdurate, he was duly executed. This was in 1851.* We know little of the later years of Nasrulla beyond his campaigns in Shehr i Sebz and Khokand, which will occupy us presently, and a long quarrel he had with Dost Muhammed, the Afghan ruler. He at length died in 1860. His sobriquet of "The Butcher" well befits him. He was one of the most brutal and utterly bad characters who ever disgraced a throne. All who came in contact with him seem to agree in this, and Ferrier has summed up his character in graphic lines. He says:

"The Amir of Bukhara, Nasrulla Khan Behadur, Malik el Mumin, is a monster of ferocity. The titles he bears are thus translated: Nasrulla Khan, the Victory of God; Behadur, the Victorious; Malik el Mumin, Prince of Believers. He raised himself to the throne by a series of frightful murders amongst his kindred, and other crimes from which even Bukharians recoiled with horror; his bad faith became proverbial amongst them, and his name was pronounced with terror by the people. The Bukharians, however, are now apparently indifferent to the atrocities committed by the Amir, or the disgusting character of his vices, the extent of which is beyond all that can be imagined, and they consider that he is justified by his position in gratifying every passion in any way that he pleases. An increase in the taxation is the only thing upon which they are at all sensitive; but as on that point Nasrulla keeps strictly within the commands of the Koran, and generally speaking the duties are rarely above 2½ per cent., which is fixed by the Zekiat, the Bukharians are satisfied, and do not think the virtue of their wives and daughters of any importance so far as the sovereign is concerned. Besides, the mollahs were the first to set the example of base submission, and the Kazi of Bukhara issued a *fetva* proclaiming that Nasrulla was by the will of God the absolute master of all the women in his territory, that he had a right to do what he liked with them, and that it would be a crime to oppose his wishes; singularly enough, the Kazi was the first person to feel the effects of the doctrine he preached, for his daughter fell a victim to the Amir's brutal passions. One must, therefore, conclude from all this that the inhabitants, though so perfidious and cruel, are in regard to their prince the most easy-going people in existence; of this he seems so perfectly convinced, that when he leaves his palace he never has any escort to attend him, and two or three times a week the Amir may be seen walking through the bazaars in the dress of a dervish, accompanied only by one servant. The shopkeepers are aware of the order he has given that no one shall pay him the least respect, or treat him otherwise than as one of the public, and for this reason nobody moves away at his approach : he walks from one shop to another inquiring the price of grain or other merchandise for sale; makes here and there a purchase; and, if he finds a tradesman playing tricks, he never offers a remark at the time, but on the following day sends for the delinquent at his public audience, and inflicts the punishment that he thinks he merits."[*]

MIR MUZAFFAR UD DIN.

Nasrulla was succeeded by his son Muzaffar ud din, who had spent his early youth at Karshi, the metropolis of the Mangut possessions. Vambery says he was early remarkable for his industry and capacity, and that he was a thoroughly cultivated Muhammedan in the Turkestan sense of the word.[†] His father was jealous of him, and to keep him more under supervision, removed him to Kermineh, of which he was appointed governor, and where he lived from 1842 till his father's death. One of his first ventures after his accession was an attempt to subdue the obstinate district of Shehr i Sebz, where he gained a very transient success.[‡] He was engaged in besieging Chirakchi, one of the fortresses of that little state, when he was summoned away to Khokand by a pressing invitation from Khudayar Khan, who had been recently hard pressed by other claimants for the throne.[§] Khudayar had sent Sultan Murad Bek to solicit assistance from the Amir of Bukhara, who marched accordingly at the head of a large army. Alim Kul was at this time the most potent person at Khokand. On the approach of the Bukharians he withdrew to the defiles of Kara Kulja, where he was besieged for a long time. Growing weary with the want of success the Amir showed his anger towards Khudayar by sending his rival a golden staff, a belt, and a fine Koran, and withdrew to Bukhara, where he was speedily followed as a fugitive by Khudayar himself.[‖] For some time Alim Kul reigned supreme in Khokand, but his foot was heavy on the people there and they once more invited Khudayar to go to them. He again appealed to the Amir for help. The latter was not loath to go, and in 1865, the very same year when the Russians made their first attack upon Tashkend he captured Khojend and thence went to Khokand, where he reinstated Khudayar as Khan. [¶] Inflated by his success, and doubtless afraid of the menacing encroachments of the Russians, Muzaffar now sent them a letter ordering them to evacuate the portion of Khokand

---

* 468, 469   † Op. cit., 392.   ‡ Vide infra.   § Id.
‖ Schuyler, op. cit., 352, 353.   ¶ Id., 353, 354.

which they had appropriated,* and threatening them if they refused with
a holy war. He also confiscated the property of the Russian merchants
at Bukhara, an act followed by reprisals at Ozenburgh. His hands were
tied however by the hostilities in Shehr i Sebz which still continued, and
he determined to send an embassy to St. Petersburg. The Khoja
Nejm ud din was chosen to lead the mission, and its professed object
was to announce the Amir's accession to the Emperor. This envoy was
detained at Ozenburgh. Thereupon the Amir complained to General
Chernaief and requested him to send some one to Bukhara, to confer
about and settle the disputed boundaries between the two countries. An
officer named Struve with a number of engineers were accordingly
despatched. On their arrival they were arrested, a stroke apparently
meant as a counterblast to the Russians' detention of the Bukharian
envoy. Thereupon General Chernaief on the 11th of February, 1866,
crossed the Jaxartes with about 2,000 men, and marched straight upon
Samarkand, with the intention of releasing his imprisoned countrymen.
After seven forced marches across the arid desert he reached Jizakh.
There he found himself confronted by a very superior force, and having
apparently tried in vain to obtain his way by a parley, he had to retire
once more across the desert assailed by the hordes of the enemy.
The retreat was conducted in an orderly fashion, and whenever the
Uzbegs ventured to join arms they suffered severely.† This somewhat
untoward campaign, which had not apparently been sanctioned by the
authorities, and was apparently carried out entirely at the instance of
General Chernaief, was followed by his supersession by Major-General
Dimitri Ilyich Romanofski. The Bukharians encouraged by the Russian
retreat now crossed the Jaxartes. On the 5th of April, Romanofski
encountered and defeated a large body of them towards Khojend,
and captured from them their cannons and the booty they had made,
together with 14,000 sheep. The Russian commander then sent two
steamers up the river provisioned for ten days, which advanced as far as
Chinaz. Muzaffar had meanwhile collected an army of 40,000 men,
consisting of 5,000 drilled Bukharians and 25,000 Kazaks, with twenty
cannons, and had set out to attack Tashkend. The Russian General
although he only had about 3,600 men with him determined to risk a
battle, and after a preliminary skirmish a fierce fight took place on the
20th May, at Irjar, on the Jaxartes, a few miles N.W. of Khojend.‡

Hellwald has given a detailed account of this battle, in which
the Bukharians were completely defeated. Muzaffar with 1,000 sarbasis
and two cannons escaped to Jizakh, but his camp, where we are
told "the food and tea were steaming, and the pipes already lit !! for the
the begs," was sacked. The Amir's tent and park of artillery were

---

* Vide infra.   † Hellwald, Die. Russen in Central Asien, 95-98.
‡ Op. cit., 99.   Vambery, 403.

captured, with a large quantity of provisions and munitions of war. Of the Bukharians about 1,000 perished, while the Russians lost but about fifty wounded, proving as on many other occasions what havoc modern weapons make when opposed to the rude ones which preceded them.* Vambery well calls this the Cannæ of Central Asia, which broke the power and prestige of Bukhara. The Russians might easily have marched upon Samarkand, but contented themselves with occupying the fort of Nau which intercepted the road from Bukhara to Khojend. Khojend from its trade and strategical position is one of the most important sites in Central Asia. It was garrisoned by a Bukharian army commanded by a dependent of Muzaffar, and surrounded by a famous wall except towards the river. On the 29th of May, the Russians appeared before the place with two divisions. The dykes had apparently been cut and the surrounding districts laid under water, the woods had been levelled, and the people of the environs been accommodated in the town. The latter was at length beleagured, and on the 1st of June the Russians began to bombard it, when a deputation of merchants went out to offer to surrender; meanwhile, however, the more fanatical part of the citizens having got the upper hand determined to resist. The bombardment recommenced, and on the 5th of June orders were given for the assault. It was bravely carried out. The Russians lost from 100 to 150 men, while that of the Bukharians was about 2,500 killed and wounded.† The fortunes of the Uzbegs were indeed growing desperate, and it was a forlorn hope that induced Muzaffar to send an embassy to the Great Sultan of the West, Abdul Aziz the Ottoman ruler, (who was deemed in Central Asia to be the suzerain of the Christian kings of Europe), to implore his help.‡ Muzaffar we are told was openly accused at Bukhara of cowardice before the enemy, and of having precipitated the catastrophe by his flight from the battle-field of Irjar. He was also accused of replenishing the treasury by the questionable means of lowering the standard value of corn and confiscating the secular property of the clergy. He was also charged with selling Bukhara itself, and could only go out at night, or in disguise, for fear of the insults of the people, who were egged on by the mollahs, and amidst the curses and abuses of the women.§ Nothing could apparently crush the vanity and self-conceit of the citizens, a Jihad or Holy War was proclaimed, old and young, mollahs and soldiers joined in it, and the Amir was forced to comply.‖ Romanofski was succeeded as Russian commander by Prince Dashkof, who was not sorry to find this spirit at Bukhara. On the 2nd of October, 1866, he captured Uratippa, where he secured sixteen cannons, six standards, and many prisoners, the Russian loss being three officers and 200 soldiers killed and wounded.¶

---

* Hellwald, 101.   † Id., 101, 102.   ‡ Id., 102, 103.   § Vambery, 407.
‖ Id., 408.   ¶ Hellwald, 103.

On the 18th of October the Russians captured the fortress of Jizakh, which was garrisoned by the Amir's best troops, and where they obtained twenty-six standards and fifty-three cannons. This was the last foothold of the Amir in the valley of the Sir Daria. He now turned hither and thither for help. He proposed an alliance with the ruler of Kabul against England and Russia. Then he sent his envoy Belisar to Calcutta, and another named Muhammed to Constantinople for help, but all in vain. The stubborn people of Shehr i Sebz meanwhile secured a greater degree of independence, while he was worried by the outbreaks of the Kitai Kipchaks, an Uzbeg tribe which pastured the lands on the Zarafshan, between Samarkand and Kermineh.*

After the capture of Jizakh a kind of armed truce subsisted between Bukhara and Russia for some months, but both sides prepared for a final struggle. At length a Russian officer, named Slushenko, and three privates having been carried off, General Kaufmann attacked the village of Ummy, which was apparently the nest of the robbers, and destroyed it. This was on the 12th of October, 1867.† Two months later a Bukharian envoy appeared at Tashkend, but no *modus vivendi* between the rival powers was discovered. The Amir, however, released Slushenko and his three companions. We are told that while a prisoner he had been put in a grave, near which were some gallows, and was given the option of becoming a Mussulman and marrying two Bukharian damsels, or of remaining a Christian and being executed. He gave way to these threats. According to the report of the Bukharians, he was circumcised, married, and given command of a regiment of Sarabasis.‡ General Kaufmann was too ambitious to be restrained by any peaceful overtures. Whatever the Russian authorities might desire he had his reputation to make with his sword, and he was a Proconsul too far removed from the capital to be easily controlled thence. He, therefore, continued to advance. On the 13th of May, 1868, he set out from Tash Kupruk, half way between Yanghi Kurgan and Samarkand. Near the Zarafshan, Petrushefski, who commanded the advance guard, was met by the Amir's envoy, Medjm ud din, proposing peace, and asking, meanwhile, that the Russians would not advance any further. The two armies were separated by the Zarafshan, and General Kaufmann insisted that before he could listen to the Amir's proposals the latter must withdraw his forces, and threatened that unless they were so withdrawn in three hours he should order their positions to be stormed. His army consisted of about eight thousand men. That of the Bukharians outnumbered it four or fivefold. The truce having elapsed, the Russians proceeded with their attack. They forded the Zarafshan (which reached up to their breasts) in the face of the enemy, made their way through the swampy ground beyond, and stormed their positions. They speedily fled, leaving twenty-one

* Hellwald, op. cit., 103, 104.   † Id., 106.   ‡ Id., 108. Note.

guns in the hands of the victors, whose loss was incredibly small, only three officers and under fifty men being injured.[*] More afraid of their returning countrymen than of the Russians, the citizens of Samarkand, which was situated near the battle-field, closed their gates to the fugitives, while they sent a deputation of the chief Mollahs and Aksakals to invite the latter into the town, and professing their devotion to the Emperor. Some of the deputation were retained, while others were told to return and tell the inhabitants to open the gates, and to let the troops pass in. General Kaufmann was received with at least an outward appearance of cordiality. He took possession of the town in the name of the Emperor, and ordered the citizens to resume their occupations, open their shops, and to recall any fugitives who had gone away, and he then secured the citadel.[†] Thus, as Vambery says, did an Alexander of the nineteenth century A.D. (Alexander II. of Russia) rival the feat of another and more famous Alexander of the fourth century B.C., who also captured "Maracanda," and thus did the capital of Timur, the metropolis of Mussulman culture, fall into the hands of the hated Franks.

Meanwhile Muzaffar ud din had found shelter at Kermineh, and his eldest son, Abdul Malik Murza, who had escaped from the battle returned to Bukhara. The Amir was more penitent, but had to receive another blow before he submitted finally.

General Kaufmann having left Major Baron von Stempel with a garrison of under a thousand men to guard Samarkand, himself advanced on the road to Bukhara. Samarkand was well provided, and contained twenty-four cannons captured from the enemy, ninety puds of powder and a large quantity of ammunition with provisions for two months. It was well that it was so furnished for it was now assailed by a great force of 25,000 from Shehr i Sebz, under Jura Beg and Baba Beg, 15,000 Kitai Kipchaks under Abdul Taj, and 15,000 Samarkanders under Hassan Beg, Abdul Gafda Beg, and Omar Beg. Through the treachery of some Aksakals, a body of the enemy forced its way into the town, but the Russians occupied the citadel and bravely resisted all efforts to capture it. Night and day the attacks were renewed, and when the gates were fired, a rampart of sacks of earth was made. For six days the terrible struggle was kept up, the sick men leaving their beds to fight, and all acting heroically. It was fortunate for the garrison that General Kaufmann having heard of what had taken place retraced his steps and at length rescued his people, but not until they had lost forty-nine in killed and 172 in wounded out of their small numbers. This heroic defence brought the Amir to his knees. He agreed to pay a sum of 125,000 tilas or 500,000 thalers, to surrender the country on the Middle Zarafshan, including Samarkand and Katti Kurgan to the Russians, and to allow them to put cantonments at Kermineh, Karshi, and Charjui.

---

* Id., 112, 113. † Id., 113. Vambery, 410.

The district thus ceded forms the province of Sir Daria, the eastern province of Turkestan. Besides this the Amir agreed to allow Russians of all creeds to trade freely in all parts of Bukhara, to have agents in the Bukharian towns to protect them and their property, to charge a maximum customs duty of 2½ per cent. on Russian products, and to allow Russian merchants a free transit across Bukharian soil to the neighbouring districts.*

This peace was very distasteful to the Mussulmans of Bukhara. "All their defeats," says Vambery, "all their disasters, the loss of so many fortresses, and of so many lives, all had failed to bring the vain fanatical, half insane mollahs of the capital on the Zarafshan to a true understanding of the state of things." They could not realise how their famous army and proud faith should have to stoop to a few infidels, and in their chagrin they readily charged their ruler with treachery, and a party rapidly gathered round his eldest son Abdul Malik, called Ketti Tureh, or the Great Prince.† He was supported by the begs of Shehr i Sebz and the steppe nomades under their confederate Sadik. He went to Karshi where he had himself proclaimed Khan of Bukhara, and began a vigorous war against his father. The latter who was being driven into a corner appealed to the Russians for help. They determined to protect their *protegé*, and sent a strong contingent under General Abramof to attack Karshi. In October, 1868, he defeated the army of the young prince, which was eight thousand strong, and a few days later captured Karshi, and handed it over to the Amir, after which he returned once more to Jam. Abdul Malik fled to the begs of Shehr i Sebz and thence to Hissar.

In 1870 the Russians conquered Shehr i Sebz, and made it over, much against the will of the inhabitants, to the Amir,‡ and in 1873 they also made over to him a strip of territory on the right bank of the Oxus, from Kukertli to Meshekli, and thence to the Russian boundary, which was taken from Khiva, and a new treaty was made, securing their rights to navigate the Oxus, and to build piers and warehouses on the Bukharian bank, and opening all the towns of the Khanate to Russian traders and travellers; fixing a maximum duty of 2½ per cent. on Russian merchandise, and that no transit dues should be charged for goods which were to pass through the Khanate; that Russians should be allowed to found caravanserais and agents there, to practice any trade allowed by the Shariat, and to buy real property. No one was to be allowed to enter the country from Russia without a proper passport, while the Amir was to have a resident agent at Tash-kend, and the Russians one at Bukhara.§ The Khanate had, in fact, become a Russian dependency, as much as Cashmere is a British one.

---

* Hellwald, 116.   † Vambery, 414, Hellwald, 120.   ‡ *Vide infra.*
                              § Schuyler, ii., 321.

As to the future, Mr. Schuyler has some very just remarks. He says, " The conquest of Bukhara, except for the purpose of getting control over the greatest market in Central Asia, and of putting an end to an independent and sometimes troublesome Mohammedan state, will probably not have for the Russians the same advantages as that of Khokand. The agriculture of the country is in poor condition, and M. Sobolef brings up weighty reasons to prove that the area of cultivable land is being gradually and rapidly diminished by the encroachments of the desert. There is probably no reason to look for the occupation of Bukhara by Russia before the death of the Amir, whom the Russians, in spite of the complaints of his people, will probably continue to maintain upon the throne."[*]

Muzaffer ud din was visited both by Mr. Schuyler and Vambery, the former describes him as a tall stout man, with sallow complexion, and small dark uneasy eyes, which he moved in all directions; his flesh looked flabby and unhealthy, and his hands trembled constantly from a too frequent use of aphrodisiacs ; his beard was very dark and thin, and he wore a plain grey silk gown, and a white turban.[†] Vambery describes him as a rigid Mussulman, and in his capacity as Mollah as the declared enemy of every innovation, even when convinced of its utility ; his love of strict justice was proverbial, and he was especially severe against the grandees while he was lenient towards the poor—hence, why his people reported that "he is a killer of elephants and a protector of mice." Luxury of all kinds was rigidly suppressed. Thus we read that his serdari kul, or commander-in-chief, Shahkukh Khan, ordered a grand house to be built for himself at Bukhara like those at Teheran, in which, besides other articles of luxury, glass windows were introduced, and the place is said to have cost 15,000 tillas. The Amir waited till it was furnished when he had him apprehended and exiled, and the house confiscated, and although an offer was made to purchase it at twice its cost price he ordered it to be demolished. The ruins themselves looking too ornamental were further destroyed, except the timber, which was sold to a baker for 200 tillas.

The Amir, when Vambery was at Bukhara, had four wives and about twenty concubines ; he had sixteen daughters and ten sons ; the two eldest daughters were married to the governors of Serpul and Akshi, but as these two towns had been conquered by the Afghans his two sons-in-law lived as the Amir's guests at Bukhara. His mother and grandmother presided over the harem, and it bore a high character for chastity and orderly training, only pious sheikhs were allowed to enter, or throw a glance thither, and our traveller mentions how one of these, named Haji Salih, was allowed access to it, to administer a dose of the khaki shifa, or health powder, from Medina. The cost of the harem was very

* Op. cit., ii., 312.   † Op. cit., ii., 83, 84.

small, the ladies making their own clothes, and often also those of the
Amir; his kitchen expenses were said to be only from sixteen to twenty
tengas daily, chief dish consisting of pilaf boiled with mutton fat.[*]

We will now turn to the history of the district north of the Jaxartes,
which had for more than a century been independent of Bukhara.

KHOKAND AND TASHKEND.

At the beginning of the last century, when the power of the Astrakhanids was growing feeble, the greater part of the valley of the Jaxartes
passed out of their control. The Kazaks planted themselves firmly, as I
have shown, in the western part of the country, and until the year 1740
were virtual masters of Tashkend and Turkestan, owning a certain
allegiance to the Sungar Kalmuks. In the eastern part of the country,
known as Ferghana, we have a state of things very like that in Kashgar,
further east. The heads of the Khoja or Seyid families were apparently
appointed rulers of the various towns, and thus acquired an independent
status, and the community was broken up into a number of fragments.
The early history of this movement is obscure. In the case of Khokand
we are remitted to certain traditions preserved by Mahsum Khoja, which
however unsatisfactory are the only materials available. According to
him a certain Shah Rukh bek, who was of noble but not royal birth,
went, at the beginning of the last century, from the neighbourhood of the
Volga and settled in Ferghana, where he married the daughter of Yadigar
Khoja, the ruler of the town of Khurram Serai, and then settled with his
people in Kurkan, twelve miles west of the present Khokand, and probably the Khuakend of Ibn Hauknl. If this be reliable Shah Rukh bek
was probably a Mangut prince, and it may be that the tribe of Ming,
which dominated over Khokand, was in effect of the same race as the
Manguts. We are told that Shah Rukh, who is mentioned by an independent authority, as a descendant of Jingis Khan,[†] murdered his father-
in-law, made himself master of the district, and soon extended his sway.
He was succeeded by his eldest son Rahim bek, and he by his brother,
Abdul Kerim bek, who built the present city of Khokand, to which he
moved his residence.[‡]

This is the account of the origin of the Khanate as given by Mahsum
Khoja; while Vambery[§] makes its chief descend from Kaidu, the
famous rival of Khubilai Khan, who occupied us in the former volume,[||]
and whose family he elsewhere strangely confuses with that of the
Jagatai rulers of Kashgar. We will now resume our story.

---

* Vambery, Travels, 187-190.		† Wathen. Journ. Asiat. Soc., Beng., iii., 373.
I Ritter's West Asien, vii., 770.		§ Op. cit., 372.		|| Ante, vol. i., 173, &c.

Abdul Kerim was succeeded by Erdeni Bek, who is made his son by some, and the son of Rahim by others : I prefer the former view. The great Chinese Geography, translated by Klaproth,* says that the Beks of all the other towns of Ferghana were subject to him, and obeyed his orders. In 1759 the Chinese general, Chaohoei was in pursuit of Khozi-jan, and detached some officers to subdue the Buruts. They were enter-tained by Erdeni at Khokand with mutton and wine, and when they departed he sent back one of his officials to tender his submission to the Emperor Kien Lung. The other Beks *inter alios* Toktu Muhammed of Andijan and Ilas Ping li † of Marghilan also sent officers with tribute, and in 1760 the former went to Peking in person. Among the presents sent to the Emperor were arghamaks, great eagles, falcons for hunting, and "plates of the fountain of the dragon" (?). Tashkend had submitted to China in 1758. In 1762 Erdeni invaded the country of Ush, which belonged to Adzi bi, but was ordered to withdraw by the Chinese general. In 1763 there was another invasion of the Burut country, which was blamed by an Imperial decree. Erdeni died in 1770.‡

NARBUTEH BI.

Mahsum Khoja makes Erdeni be succeeded by Suliman beg, and he by Shah Rukh beg, the last of whom only reigned three months. He was then followed by Narbuteh bi, the grandson of Abdul Kerim.§ Nar-buteh, according to local tradition, was the son of Abdur Rahman Batir, an Uzbeg of the Ming tribe, who ruled over the town and district of Isfara, and who married Erdeni bek's sister.‖ Khanikof and others call him Yamchi bi or Jamchi bi, and tell us he was descended from the famous Baber.¶

Abdur Rahman was treacherously killed by Erdeni, who wished to possess himself of Isfara, but his son Narbuteh who was then but a child was spared, and when on Erdeni's death his heirs were killed or dispersed he was chosen by the Khokandians to succeed him.** By Wathen, Narbuteh is made a grandson of Shah Rukh Beg.†† He ruled over Khokand during the domination of the Amir Shah Murad, at Bukhara, and was doubtless more or less subordinate to him, for he neither struck coins nor had the Khutbeh said in his own name.‡‡ He had an army of fifty thousand men, lived at Khokand, and was styled his son by the Emperor of China, to whom he sent envoys every one or two years, with presents of horses, sable skins, &c., and received in return red gold, &c., amounting in value to several

---

* Mag. Asiat., i., &c. † (? Kuli.) ‡ Mag. Asiat., i., &c. Schuyler, i., 398.
§ Schuyler, i., 299. ‖ Id. Note 2.
¶ Savillef, Coins of Khokand, Mems. Imp. Arch. Societ., St. Peters., ii., 129, 120. Russische Revue, viii., 330.
** Schuyler, i., 339. †† Journ. Asiat. Soc., Beng., iii., 375. ‖‖ Schefer, Abdul Kerim, 220, 221.

laks of rupees.* The Afghan ruler, Zeman Shah, sent an ambassador in 1794 to Khokand, who describes one of these embassies to China. The representative of Khokand was met at the Chinese frontier by a carriage, shaped like a box, drawn by two horses, and as it was wintry-cold they put a hot stone before him to warm him, while the carriage itself contained all necessary food and drink. He dined *en route*, while he stayed to sleep at some post station. These were garrisoned by 500 men. He saw nowhere on the way any well peopled district. It took him a month and a few days to reach Peking from the frontier. He was admitted to an audience in the palace, whose grandeur greatly surprised him; the walls and ceiling being coated with gold and glass, and in the midst was a kiosk, also richly gilded and glazed. He prostrated himself in the prescribed way, and then saw a hand issue from the top of the kiosk and heard a voice speaking in "the Turkish of Kitai," which said, "The Emperor deigns to ask, does my son Narbuteh bi enjoy good health and contentment?" The envoy prostrated himself again, and replied, as he was told, "Narbuteh has no other wish than to satisfy the behests of his majesty." Afterwards the Emperor gave him presents for the Khan to the value of ten laks of rupees, which were put into the carriage in which he once more returned to Khokand.†

The Afghan envoy speaks in high terms of the qualities of Narbuteh bi, he says, "He had built himself a palace of singular beauty, whose walls were covered with encrusted glass (? porcelain). No one was allowed to approach him; and fifty or sixty soldiers mounted guard at his gate, who carried the requests of suppliants into the palace, and returned with written answers. Every Friday he went to the Mosque, escorted by about 10,000 soldiers. There he met the Ulemas and Seyids, and heard disputes. The easier matters he decided himself, remitting the more difficult ones to the Muftis. He then went to his palace, which held a vast crowd of people, where he gave a feast. His food was the same as that of the other Uzbegs, but he ate little rice. Envoys were received by him with the usual ceremonies practised by sovereign rulers, and he had by him, representatives of the different Uzbeg states."‡ Mahsum Khoja says Narbuteh conquered all Ferghana except Khojend, and we elsewhere read that he subdued Andijan, Namangan, Ush, and other places. His latter days were spent in a struggle for Khojend with Fazil bi and his son Khudayar, the governor of Uratippa. It seems that, in alliance with the Amir of Bukhara, he tried to take Uratippa, but was completely routed by Khudayar, who is said to have killed twenty thousand men, and made a pyramid of their heads.§ In 1799 he undertook an expedition against Tashkend, which was governed by Yunus Khoja.

Here we must divert a little. Soon after Yolbars, Khan of the Kazaks, was killed at Tashkend in 1740, as I have described, Tashkend passed under the domination of the Sungar Kalmuks, and was ruled for some time by Kusiak bi, who was probably little more than the deputy of the Sungarian sovereign.* He still governed the town in 1749.† A few years later the Sungarian empire was overthrown by the Chinese, who in 1750 occupied Tashkend. Like Ferghana this district seems to have passed under the control of various Khojas, each of whom ruled over a town and its surrounding district. We do not read of Tashkend again till the end of the century when we find it subject to Yunus Khoja, who is called a descendant of the famous Khalif Abubekhr, by Abdul Kerim.‡ He reduced the surrounding districts to order, and in 1798 severely punished the Kazaks of the Great Horde, who had so long harassed his borders, and at length completely subdued them.§ Yunus Khoja was now master of Tashkend, Turkestan, and of a wide district in the neighbourhood, and in 1797 came into conflict with Narbuteh bi, of Khokand, as I have mentioned. The latter was defeated and captured, and was put to death at Tashkend in 1800.| He left three sons, Alim, Omar, and Shahrukh.

ALIM KHAN.

Narbuteh bi was succeeded by his eldest son Alim Khan, who on his accession put his brother Rustem Beg and several of his other relations who had opposed him to death. He had the Khutbeh said in his own name, and also struck money.¶ Meanwhile, Yunus Khoja of Tashkend marched with the Kazaks who were subject to him against Khokand, and allied himself with Bek Murad, the son of Khudayar Bek, who was then ruling at Khojend. The armies of Khokand and Tashkend fired at one another across the Sir Daria but they did not come together, and afterwards retired. Subsequently we find Yunus Khoja and his ally trying in vain to capture Uratippa, which was governed by Khudayar's brother Baba Bek. The latter thereupon went against Khojend, whence he drove away Bek Murad bek. Baba was subsequently murdered by his nephew Bek Murad, in return for which Bek Murad was himself killed by the children of Baba Bek in Samarkand, whither he had been invited by the Bukharian Amir, Haidar. Yunus Khoja was finally unsuccessful and obliged to retreat to Tashkend, which was captured by Alim Khan in 1803 or 1805,** but it was apparently not finally conquered till the reign of Omar Khan his brother, who we are told took it from the sons of Yunus Khoja.†† Alim then subjected the Kazaks, turned his arms against Bukhara, and tried unsuccessfully to

---

* Ante, 675, 676.   † Levchine, 139.   ‡ Schefer, 221.   § Levchine, 269.
| Travels of Pospialof, &c., Mem. Geog. Soc. of St. Peters., 1851-52, &c. Note 5.
¶ Schefer's Abdul Kerim, 211.   ** Schuyler, i., 220, 221.
†† Wathen, Journ. Asiat. Soc., Beng., lii., 371.

capture Uratippa, which fell however in a second campaign.* It was afterwards retaken by Mahmud Khan a nephew of Khudayar Bek.† Alim Khan seems to have been a self-willed obstinate person, and he paid no heed to the Sheikhs and Sufis. On one occasion a Sheikh of Khokand who had a great number of disciples, pretended that he possessed the power of doing miracles. He was summoned by Alim Khan who was seated near a pond over which he had suspended a rope, and who thus addressed him, O Sheikh, on the day of resurrection you will no doubt conduct your disciples over the gulf of hell by the bridge of Sirath. I now wish you to cross over the pond by this rope, that I may witness one of your miracles. The Sheikh began to make excuses and to cite the Koran, but the Khan was inflexible. Hardly had he set foot on the rope when he fell into the pond, whereupon they beat him with sticks till he died. He had all the dervishes and professed religious arrested and converted into camel drivers.‡ When the Chinese conquered Altishehr or Eastern Turkestan, the sons of the famous Khoja Serim Sak fled to Bukhara. Thenceforward it seems the Imperial Court of China paid an annual sum of money to the governor of Khokand, in consideration of his looking after the young princes, and preventing them from returning to Kashgar, and an envoy accordingly went every two or three years from Khokand to China. This pension having on one occasion failed to go, Alim Khan forbade the caravans of Bukhara and Khokand visiting Kashgar, which speedily brought the Chinese to terms and they remitted the arrears of pension in one sum.§

Latterly Alim Khan became very tyrannical and cruel. He disposed of the daughters of his subjects as he liked, and put to death many innocent people, and his subjects prayed for his death. On one occasion, during the Khokand fair, he went to Tashkend with a large army, which was commanded by his brother, Omar bek, and his maternal uncle, and he ordered them to lay waste the country of the Kazaks. Notwithstanding the rigour of the season this order was carried out. The Kazaks submitted, and Omar thereupon returned to Tashkend, and reported how he had slain some of the nomades, and secured the submission of the rest. Alim abused him for having shown any mercy, and ordered him to return, and slaughter them without mercy. Omar went outside the city, where his troops to the number of ten thousand lay, and he reported to Taghai and the other officers what had taken place. They all agreed that their horses could not then march, that the season was too severe, and that the Kazaks, besides being Mussulmans and innocent, were scattered over the desert, and that it would be impossible to find them. Omar thereupon asked what was to be done. Taghai, his uncle, replied, " Omar Bek must be Khan; we cannot obey a tyrant like Alim Khan," and he swore the oath of fealty to him. The army then marched

---

* Schefer, 211.   † Schuyler, i., 341.   ‡ Schefer, 211, 212.   § Id., 217, 218.

to Khokand, where Omar Khan was duly proclaimed. Alim soon found himself with only three hundred followers, among whom he liberally distributed largess. He marched towards Khokand with his treasures, his harem, and his son, Shah Rukh Murza, whose mother was a Kazak. En route he came to a fort, which refused to surrender, and having halted for the night, even his three hundred followers deserted him and went into Khokand. He thereupon, with tears in his eyes, summoned his son, gave him one thousand tillas, and bade him go to the Amir Haidar, at Bukhara. Then leaving his wives and treasures in a village, to whose chief men he intrusted them, he set out with twenty horsemen and his Divan begi Muhammed Zuhur, for Derahkuh, whence he could see Khokand. The Divan begi asked him not to trust himself further, but to go to Khojend, where there were four thousand men who would probably support him. He insisted upon going near the town, and was abandoned by his remaining followers, except three only. When the patrols, who were outside the walls, saw him they gave chase, whereupon the Khan's horse became bogged in a marsh. He then asked the Divan begi to give him his, but the latter replied that he had not heeded his counsel, and he was not prepared to sacrifice his life for him. He thereupon put his horse to the gallop, and went towards the town. The soldiers of Omar Khan having now come up one of them shot him in the back, and they buried him at night. This was in 1224 of the hej, i.e., 1809. Muhammed Zuhur was at first well received by Omar Khan, but was afterwards stripped of his wealth, and eventually devoted himself to a religious life.[*] Mahsum Khoja says Alim Khan was the first of the Khokand rulers to strike money in his own name, and that these coins, which were of bronze silvered over, were made from old cannons left by Nadir Shah at the time of his conquest.[†] One of his coins has been published by Savilief. It was struck in 1216 hej, i.e., 1801-2, and on it he styles himself Alim bek.[‡]

OMAR KHAN.

The young prince, Shah Rukh Murza, instead of going to Bukhara as his father had counselled him went to Tashkend, where he was well received, but news having arrived there of the death of Alim Khan, the Kush begi seized him, and had him conveyed towards Khokand. He was killed en route. Omar Khan seated himself on the throne, and confided the administration of the country to his maternal uncle, Muhammed Riza bek.[§] The rule of Omar Khan was a beneficent one, and Khokand became a great resort of merchants.

---

[*] Schefer, 219-223.　　[†] Schuyler, i., 341.
[‡] Mems. Imp. Arch. Soc., Eastern Section, II., 121.　　[§] Schefer, 223, 224.

We are told he captured Mahmud Khan, of Uratippa, and sent him prisoner to Khokand, replacing him by one of his adherents, and although the latter was soon after driven away, Uratippa, in fact, remained subject to Khokand. Omar also conquered Turkestan and several surrounding towns, and Tozai Khan, who, Schuyler says, was the last descendant of the Kazak Khans, fled to Bukhara, where he was afterwards killed.*

A dependent of Alim Khan, named Muhammed Rejeb Karajeh, who had been a fugitive at Bukhara, having repaired to Khokand, secured the hatred of Muhammed Riza bek, and of his friend Kitaki, who was a Karakalpak and a famous commander. The two latter plotted together to seize the throne. Their scheme having been disclosed by a slave, Omar Khan and Muhammed Rejeb concerted measures for defeating it. They were invited to a feast at the palace, where Muhammed Riza was arrested, put in prison, and then strangled, his friend Kitaki was cut in pieces, their property was confiscated, and Rejeb Karajeh was appointed governor of Khojend. Omar Khan sent an envoy to Russia to arrange for the visits of caravans to Khokand, and he proposed that when they were pillaged on his side of the half-way line, he would recompense the merchants, if the Emperor did the same on his side. This was accepted, Abdul Kerim says, that when he wrote, many such caravans passed to and fro. He reports how an envoy from Khokand having been killed by a Russian soldier at Kiziljar, the Russians paid a fine of 1,000 tillas.†

This intercourse with Russia led to the famous visit to Khokand, of Colonel Nazarof, in 1813-14. He went to explain the death of the Khokandian envoys on the Russian frontier, one of whom had been killed by an outlaw on the frontier, which was doubtless the event referred to by Abdul Kerim. He took an escort of Cossacks, and merchandise to the value of 20,000 roubles. On arriving at Khokand they were assigned a place to camp in, in the garden of the palace, and were there kept strictly guarded, but themselves and cattle were supplied freely with food, their own consisting of white bread, rice, tea, and melons.‡ Twelve days after his arrival Nazarof had an interview with the Khan, whom he calls Amir Vali Niami. They were escorted by some of his guards riding arghamaks, who were richly dressed, and wore red turbans. The envoy rode, and his Cossacks followed on foot. On approaching the palace all dismounted. The streets and roofs were crowded with people. The Khan sat at a window, and Nazarof was told to salute him as he did his sovereign, whereupon he uncovered himself which was deemed a solecism. The Khan was about twenty-five years old, he was seated on his throne, and richly dressed; at the audience there were also envoys from Bukhara, Khiva, the Sarsans (?), and China—the last, probably, from the Chinese governor of Ili. After the presentation, at which

---

* Op. cit., i., 341, 342.   † Schefer, 225-229.   ‡ Ritter, West Asien, vii., 763.

Nazarof placed the imperial letters on his own head ; they were feasted with horseflesh, and rice stained of a rose colour ; Nazarof refused to eat this as contrary to his religion. Several of the Cossack officers were presented with state robes, and allowed to return home, but Nazarof himself was detained ; he was closely confined, and told he must either pay the blood penalty for the lives of the two envoys, turn Mussulman, or be hanged on a gallows ; but this was a barren threat, and he was, in fact, kindly treated and taken to many festivals, musical entertainments, &c. In order that he might not try to escape he was invited by the Khan to go with him on a hunting excursion to Marghilan, where he stayed for some time, and where the devoted Mussulmans threw stones at him as a Kaffir ; he afterwards returned home again.*

Izzetulla also visited Khokand ; he tells us Omar Khan maintained a standing army of 10,000 horse, which he paid by grants of villages and lands. The troops could not keep the field for longer than two months as their provisions then became exhausted ; besides them the tribes could raise 30,000 men, who served for a month, and that once a year. The services of these last were not paid for by the Khan ; most of them were armed with spears, but some had matchlocks.† Omar Khan died in 1822 ; according to some he was killed by his brother, Muhammed Ali ;‡ on his coins he is styled Seyid Muhammed Omar Sultan, and Muhammed Khan Seyid Omar.§

MUHAMMED ALI OR MADALI KHAN.

Muhammed Ali, who now succeeded, was also called Madali, which is a contraction of the former name. On his accession he exiled several of his relatives, and among them his brother Mahmud Sultan, who went to Shehr i Sebz, where he married the daughter of the ruler. He was afterwards patronised by Nasrulla of Bukhara, by whom he was appointed successively governor of Urmitan and Khojend.‖ Schuyler reports that a disagreement with Bukhara, which broke out at the beginning of Madali Khan's reign ended peaceably in 1825.¶ This probably arose out of the shelter which Madali offered to Nasrulla's brother Omar Khan. Some time after the Bukharian Khan seems to have conquered Jizakh, which was his when Burnes wrote. In 1826 Yehanghir Khoja, a descendant of the former rulers of Kashgar, rose in revolt against the Chinese, but having been defeated by them he fell into the hands of the Kirghises, and eventually into those of Madali, who kept him in restraint for a while, when he again took shelter with the Kirghises, and persuaded them to march with him against the Chinese.

* Id., 763. Univers Pittoresque, Asia, vi., 111, 112.　† Jour. Roy. Asiat. Soc., vii., 325.
‡ Schuyler, i., 342.　§ Savilief, op. cit., 182.　‖ Schuyler, i., 342.　¶ Op. cit., i., 342.

Madali, who was irritated at the treatment the Mussulmans had received, also marched an army there, and surprised and cut up the Chinese. The Khoja secured possession of Kashgar, and the Khan's cavalry overran the whole of Chinese Tartary, and got possession of Yarkand, Aksu, and Khoten, which victories secured for Madali the title of Ghazi. Presently the Khoja grew jealous of Madali, and drew off his people, and, as the Chinese advanced in force, the latter withdrew. Yehanghir himself was captured, and was sent to Peking to be executed. The Chinese now sent an envoy to Khokand to negotiate for peace, which was agreed upon on condition of the Khan retaining a deputy at Kashgar to superintend the religion of the Muhammedans there. He was granted a share in the transit dues, and Madali agreed to restrain the Kirghises, and to assist the Chinese in maintaining order in Chinese Tartary.*

In 1828-9, while Murza Shems was living at Khokand, Yusuf Khoja, the brother of Yehanghir, who was also living there, asked permission from Madali to reconquer his fatherland. The Khan gave him some royal robes, and a contingent of twenty-five thousand men, which he accompanied himself as far as Ush. Twenty days after leaving Ush they reached one of the Chinese frontier stations, garrisoned by about one hundred and fifty men, which they assaulted for some time, when the garrison blew the place up. Murza Shems tells us how when they despaired of success and thus committed "the happy despatch" wholesale the Chinese dressed themselves in their best clothes, drank much wine, and then fired the powder magazine. When the Khokandians entered the fort they found the bodies of fifty or sixty Chinamen charred and swollen, and others who had shot themselves. Fourteen were found alive in a well, and were sent back as trophies to Madali Khan. The Khokandians then went on about fifteen versts further, and came to another fort, with a garrison of about five hundred Chinese, where the neighbouring heights were covered with a larger force. One report making it seven thousand eight hundred and another thirteen thousand strong. After a terrible struggle the Khokandians won the day, and most of the Chinese were either killed or committed suicide. Leaving the fort to be invested they continued their advance by way of Mushi and Liangar, about ten versts from Kashgar. There the feud was still in progress between the Black and White Khojas, of whom the latter were the partisans of Yusuf, while the Black Khojas were the partisans of the Chinese. The former now came out with great joy to welcome their champion, who entered Kashgar to the sound of trumpets and drums. Meanwhile Ishak beg, who belonged to the other faction, withdrew with his supporters to another Chinese fort, apparently called Gul bagh, with a garrison of some thirteen hundred men. This was beleagured by the Khokandians, while Yusuf himself

---

went to Yanghi Hissar, one hundred and fifty versts off, and thence to
Yarkand, leaving his son at Kashgar in charge of the Murza Shems.
Four months after Yusuf had left the capital, news arrived that a large
Chinese army one hundred thousand strong was marching to the rescue,
and had already reached Faizabad. Murza Shems at once packed up
the valuables he had charge of in sixty boxes, and prepared to depart,
but this baggage was plundered by the Black Khojas. The Khokandians
retired in all haste, and were accompanied by a great crowd of
Kashgarians of the White Khoja faction; one account says twelve
thousand, and another from fifty to sixty thousand. It was a regular
migration of men, women, and children on foot, on horses and
donkeys, and the weather being very cold many of them perished on the
way. Yusuf himself died at Khokand, about five months later.* The
fugitives from Kashgar were settled in the city of Shehri Khana, built by
Omar Khan, and on the Sir Daria, below Khojend.

In 1831 a treaty was concluded at Peking between the empire and
Khokand, by which the ruler of the latter country was "to receive the
duties on all foreign goods imported into Aksu, Ush Turfan, Kashgar,
Yanghi Hissar, Yarkand, and Khoten, and was allowed to maintain
aksakals in all those towns to collect the duties, and to protect the Muhammedans, while he bound himself to prevent the Khojas leaving his
dominions, and to punish them if they did so. In this way Khokand
acquired great influence in Kashgar.†

On another side it began to have more regular intercourse with its
more dangerous neighbour Russia.

At this time a large number of Kazaks, notably those of the Great
Horde were, as we have seen, subject to Khokand, and much difficulty
arose in consequence of the uncertain limits of the territory over which
rights were claimed by Russia and Khokand respectively. About
1827 or 1828, envoys were sent from Orenburgh to settle the matter, who
took with them as presents from the Tzar several mirrors of very large
size, a musical clock, and guns and pistols. It was finally agreed that
the river Kuk Su should be the boundary of the two countries, the subjects of Russia keeping to the north, and those of Khokand to the south
of it. Beacons were also erected along the frontier, but it would seem
the Russians were not long in encroaching on these limits, and built some
forts south of the river; whereupon the Khan sent another envoy to
St. Petersburg with an elephant, and some Chinese slaves, as a present
for the Emperor.‡

Madali Khan was a martial person in his young days, and *inter alia*,
conquered Karategin, and compelled Kulab, Darwaz, and Shugnan to
recognise his authority.§

---

* Mems. of Murza Shems, op. cit., 344-250. † Schuyler, i. 343.
‡ Wathen, op. cit., 374. § Schuyler, I, 343.

I have described how at this time the English and Russians were trying to checkmate one another in Central Asia, and each endeavouring to secure the assistance of the Uzbeg Khanates. When Colonel Stoddart went to Bukhara, Captain Conolly, who had had considerable experience, was sent on a mission to Khiva, and told to go on from thence to Khokand, and to explore the road between the two Khanates, leading by way of Altun Kaleh, Ak Musjid, and Achkian. He was six weeks on this journey and ingratiated himself into the favour of Madali Khan and his supporters by the rich presents of expensive firearms, inlaid and ornamented, and Cashmere shawls which he lavishly distributed. He travelled we are told with a train of eighty servants and an immense quantity of baggage, and the chief people of the country he passed through shared his liberality as well as the Government officials, however low or high might be their rank.[*] This created him many partisans. It seems that at this time the feud between Khokand and Bukhara had recommenced, for although Madali had in 1839 submitted to the Amir of the latter country, the presence and attentions of Conolly seem to have made him more arrogant, and the Amir had once more to march against him. Meanwhile Nasrulla, who knew of Conolly's visit, attributed this altered conduct of his dependent to his instigation. Having been promised a safe conduct by the Amir, Conolly determined to trust himself at Bukhara, notwithstanding the advice of his friends at Khokand. He was received in a cold and haughty manner by the Amir at Jizakh. There he brought about negotiations between the two rulers which ended in a short peace.[†] He then went on to Bukhara where he joined Stoddart, and where he was put to death as I have mentioned.[‡]

Let us now revert to Madali Khan. About 1840 a great change came over him, and from being a vigorous warrior he degenerated into a debauchee. The change was attributed to the remorse he felt at the execution of Hak Kuli, by whose counsels he had generally been guided. Weakness at head-quarters had its usual effects, and we find a conspiracy was started by the Kushbegi Leshker of Tashkend, the Kazi Kalian, the commander-in-chief, Isa Khoja, and others.[§] They determined to displace Madali and to put Shere Ali, the son of Alim Khan or Murad bi the son of Haji bi, the brother of Narbuteh bi, on the throne. The former had lived for many years among the Kipchaks, and the latter at Khiva where he had given his daughter in marriage to Allah Kuli Khan. The conspirators sent an invitation to Nasrulla Khan of Bukhara to go and assist them. The latter was only too willing to go, but so rash did the proceeding seem on the part of the Khokandians that he fancied there was some sinister motive behind it, and it was only on

* Ferrier's Afghans, 437, 438.   † Id., 438-440.   ‡ Anis, 800, 801.
§ Vel. Zern Hist. Notices of Khokand., Mems. Russ. Arch. Soc. Orient. Sect., ii., 329-331.

the receipt of a second invitation that he set out in April, 1842, with an army of 18,000 men, and encamped fifteen or sixteen miles from Khokand. Frightened by this demonstration Madali sent out his son Muhammed Amin with the Kushbegi Leshker and the Kazi Kalian to offer humble terms, *inter alia* that he would acknowledge himself a vassal of Bukhara and have Nasrulla's name inserted in the Khutbeh and on the coins. These envoys were amicably received and two of them were sent back but the Kushbegi Lesker was detained, and at a private audience he informed the Amir that the Khokand chiefs and people were ready to surrender the place to him. Nasrulla thereupon sent to summon Madali to his presence. The latter was naturally afraid nor could he get any assistance from his usual counsellors. He then discovered how unpopular he had become, and packing up his valuables in 100 arabas and taking with him but 1,000 men he set off for Namangan. The grandees now sent to invite Nasrulla to enter Khokand which he did in state, and deeming it good policy to be feared rather than loved, and by striking terror to overawe his other neighbours, he ordered the town to be pillaged, and it was given up to plunder for about four hours, the mollahs themselves being robbed of their books, and the women and children subjected to great outrage.* The next day the captured property was resold to the citizens, except the gold, silver, and other valuables which went into the treasury. The Amir now ordered Madali to be searched for.

The latter was gradually deserted by his escort which carried of his baggage, and at last he was left with but three followers, and deemed it best to return to Khokand and throw himself on the clemency of the victor. He had scarcely reached the town however, when he was seized with his mother, wives, sons, and brother. His harem was transported to Bukhara in forty arabas. Nasrulla now summoned a grand council to try his captive, and he let it be known that he intended to kill him, to appropriate the Khanate, and to put his own deputy there. The grandees who had conspired were now disenchanted, the Kushbegi Lesker and the Kazi Kalian, with an old noble called Erdineh raised their voice against this policy,† and begged of him to appoint as their chief (subordinate to himself) some prince of the family of Narbuteh. This news was not welcome to Nasrulla, who gave a hint to his own subject the Kazi Kalian of Bukhara, and the latter like a good courtier pressed his master's wish, and urged that Madali was a criminal for having married his own mother-in-law, the widow of Omar Khan, and deserved death together with his family. Nasrulla adopted this view and the unfortunate Khan, his mother and brother, and his eldest son Muhammed Amin were brought into the hall and executed in the presence of the council.

Two hundred and fifty of the principal Khokandian chiefs, with their families, were arrested and sent to Bukhara as hostages.‡ We are told

* *Id.*, 332-334. † *Id.*, 334-336. ‡ *Id.*, 336-338.

that a second son of Madali, named Muzaffer, was also killed by
Nasrulla's order, and a third son by another wife, named Ashula, was put
to death long after, namely in 1866-7, near Chusta, by Khudayar Khan.[*]
Nasrulla sent to announce his victory to the various towns of the empire,
and he appointed Ibrahim Datkha, the former governor of Samarkand,
as his deputy, with a force of 600 soldiers to control the newly conquered
city.

SHERE ALI KHAN.

The Bukharian Khan was greatly puffed up by his success, but
his triumph was only short lived.   About three months after the
capture of Khokand an insurrection broke out there, and the Bukharian
sway came to an end.   The new governor had oppressed the citizens
and forced them to pay one-fourth of their produce, besides the usual
taxes levied at Bukhara, into the treasury.   The people thereupon sent
to the Kipchaks to ask them to assist in putting their guest Shere Ali
on the throne.   After some hesitation they consented, and on their
approach the Khokandians fell on the Amir's garrison and killed nearly
all of them.   Ibrahim Datkha with difficulty escaped, and Shere Ali
was speedily proclaimed Khan.   Nasrulla was greatly enraged, he
ordered his late deputy to be killed, and prepared an army of 20,000
men, with which and the 250 hostages he had with him he marched for
Khokand.[†]   He pressed the siege for some days.   One of the hostages,
a Kipchak, named Mussulman Kul surnamed Chulak, or the Cripple, who
had formerly commanded a company of 100 men in Madali's service
gained great influence over the Amir, who was so artless on this occasion
as to allow him to ride into Khokand on his pretending that he could
secure the town for him.   On getting inside he speedily roused the
enthusiasm of the garrison to whom he was well known, and they built
themselves great ramparts of wood and earth and made several successful sorties.   He also wrote a letter to some of the Bukharian nobles
pretending that they had promised him to put their master to death.
Chulak took good care this should fall into the Amir's hands, who at the
same time heard that the Khivan Khan had invaded the Bukharian
territory, and carried off many of its people.   He was much moved
by all this, released his hostages, raised the siege, and returned home.[‡]

Schuyler tells us that Shere Ali was simple and good-natured, and was a
kind and mild ruler, and so weak as to get the nickname of pustiak (*i.e.*,
mat or rag).   He distinguished the beginning of his reign by disinterring
the body of Madali Khan and burying it again with great funeral ceremonies conducted by all the clergy.[§]

Shere Ali virtually owed his throne to the efforts of his friends

* Schuyler, i., 344, 345.   † Vel. Zern., op. cit., 338-340.   ‡ Id., 341-342.   § Op. cit., i., 346.

the Kipchaks, who now claimed their reward and to control the chief departments of the State, displacing the Sarts from their former supremacy. Their leader Yusuf Mingbashi was placed at the head of affairs at Khokand, and Mussulman Kul held authority at Andijan. Meanwhile, Shere Ali behaved with clemency. One of the sons of Muhammed bi, a descendant of Narbuteh, was put to death, and his brothers expatriated, but otherwise he did not in the usual Eastern fashion lay violent hands on his relatives.*

The jealousy between the Kipchaks and Sarts continued. The latter were headed by Shadi, who was a favourite of the Khan, and who secured the death of Yusuf Mingbashi, and ordered his adherents to be executed. He now summoned Mussulman Kul to Khokand. The latter judiciously professed to be pleased at the death of Yusuf, whom he styled his enemy, but he nevertheless collected a considerable force, and incorporated a number of Yusuf's fugitive retainers in it. When Shadi heard of this he sent some assassins to Andijan to kill Mussulman Kul, who, however, caught and hanged them. Matters now came to open war; a struggle ensued at Tuz, in which the Sarts were defeated, Shadi killed, and the Khan himself captured. As he found some difficulty in securing another person of royal lineage to fill his place he reinstated Shere Ali as Khan, and himself took the post formerly filled by Yusuf and Shadi. Mussulman Kul was a Kipchak, and naturally favoured his own people, which again aroused the jealousy of the Sarts, and we accordingly find that Rahmet Ulla and Mehmed Kerim, two leaders of the latter, repaired to Shehr i Sebz to invite Murad, the son of Alim Khan, to occupy the throne.† Having received assistance from the Khan of Bukhara, he accordingly, in 1845, marched there. Unfortunately Mussulman Kul was then absent with the army collecting tribute from the Kirghises, and Murad had no difficulty in securing the town. He put Shere Ali to death, and proclaimed himself viceroy of the Bukharian Khan.‡ No coins of Shere Ali are apparently known.

MURAD BEK KHAN.

The citizens, who hated Nasrulla, with good reason, were disgusted at this subserviency, and at once sent off for Mussulman Kul, who speedily returned and occupied the town. According to one account, Murad Bek was put to death, while another says he retired to Shehr i Sebz.§

KHUDAYAR KHAN.

Murad had five sons; by Jarkin, the daughter of the Kipchak Tokhta Nazar, Sarimsak then twenty-two, and Bek of Tashkend; Khuda-yar, then sixteen, Bek of Marghilan and Sultan Murad; and, by

* Vol. Zern., op. cit., 343. † Schuyler, op. cit., I., 346, 347. ‡ Russische Revue, viii., 333.
§ Vol. Zern., op. cit., 345.

another wife, Suna Aim, also a Kipchak, Malla, then seventeen, Bek of
Andijan and Sufi.* Mussulman Kul, having a feud with Sarimsak,
summoned him to Khokand by a letter sealed with Khudayar's seal, and
he was put to death on the way there. The next day his death was
announced, and Khudayar was proclaimed Khan.† Khudayar was
Mussulman Kul's son-in-law, and was kept by him under strict
surveillance, being allowed very little money lest he should buy himself
friends. Meanwhile, his father-in-law concentrated the power in his
own hands, and as he was a good-natured and benevolent person, he could
not restrain the rapacity of the Kipchaks, whom he naturally employed as
his subordinates, nor was he strongly supported by some of the latter, and
we find the governors of Marghilan, Uratippa, and Khojend conspiring
with Nur Muhammed, who held authority at Tashkend against him.
The latter, who was an important personage, and had been offered the
post of Mingbashi by the other conspirators, marched to meet Utenbi,
the Bek of Marghilan, but Mussulman Kul having heard of their
manœuvres, planted himself between them and cut off their communication with one another. Nur Muhammed thereupon retired to Tashkend,
while his ally feigned that he had gone really to the Mingbashi's help.
This excuse was not accepted, and he was deposed. This was in 1851.‡
The following year there broke out a fresh dissension between Mussulman
Kul and Nur Muhammed. The latter had paid a large sum of money
into the treasury, but had taken no receipt for it. The man in charge
thereupon appropriated some of it, and distributed it among his
friends, Nur Muhammed himself apparently sharing. Mussulman Kul
having heard of this, summoned the Khokand council, and then
demanded from the treasurer an account of the dues payable by
Tashkend. The implicated officials lost their temper, and even drew
their swords on the Mingbashi, who, however, escaped, and reported the
matter to the Khan. Meanwhile, they fled to Tashkend, as did the Bek
of Khojend. Mussulman Kul now, in the Khan's name, summoned Nur
Muhammed to surrender the fugitives, and to go in person to Khokand.§
On refusin to do either, the Khokand army, 40,000 strong, with eight
guns, laid siege to Tashkend. Through the treachery of the Bek of
Marghilan, who deserted with 600 men, and the incessant rains, the
siege had to be raised, and Mussulman Kul returned to Khokand
with his prestige greatly reduced, so much so that his enemies
rapidly increased in numbers, secretly supported no doubt by the
Khan, who was weary of his father-in-law's surveillance, and in June,
1852, in order to recover his position he was obliged once more to march
against Tashkend with 30,000 men. This second campaign was fatal
to him. Nur Muhammed had put Tashkend in a good state of defence,
and installed his creatures as governors of the surrounding towns.

---

* Schuyler, 348.   † Vel. Zern., op. cit., 347.   ‡ Schuyler, 349.   § Vel· Zern., 348, 349.

As he found it impossible to take the place by storm, Mussulman Kul sent a detachment to Turkestan while he himself went to the fortress of Niazbek, situated at the sources of the Chirchik which supplied Tashkend with water, and which he apparently cut off. He then went north and captured Chimkent. Meanwhile the Tashkendians made a sortie, defeated the garrison he had left near Niazbek, and recovered their water. Marching speedily to the rescue he encountered the army of his rivals, but at the very beginning of the fight the Khan Khudayar, who was with him, went over to the enemy, and so disconcerted his men that they fled. Many of them were killed and about 1,000 drowned in the Chirchik. Mussulman Kul with difficulty escaped to the Black Kirghises, his mother's people. His partisans were duly punished. Meanwhile he was succeeded in authority by the conspirators, who were themselves Kipchaks. The Khan had not freed himself from one patron to fall into the hands of another, nor were the Sarts content to be again under the heel of their enemies ; and about two months after the revolution just described a conspiracy broke out against the Kipchaks. Utenbi and his chief adherents were killed, and their places given to Sarts. Nur Muhammed was replaced at Tashkend by the Khan's brother Mallabek. "General orders were now given for the massacre of all the Kipchaks in the Khanate from Ak Musjid (Port Perofski) to the mountains separating Khokand from Kashgar, and they were killed everywhere, in the bazaars, in the streets, and on the steppe wherever they were found." Twenty thousand men are said to have been thus slaughtered. Khudayar was himself a Kipchak on his mother's side, and this act of carnage was never forgiven nor forgotten.* Safarbi, who had been commander-in-chief, was bastinadoed, he had his hands and feet broken, his head was then placed under leaden weights till his eyes protruded out, his body was then coated with paste over which hot oil was poured, and lastly he was cut to pieces. At length, in the beginning of 1853, Mussulman Kul was himself captured and taken to Khokand for punishment. They chained him to a high seat on a wooden platform in an open space with a tall cap on his head. There he was kept for three days, during which time they killed six hundred Kipchaks before his face. He was then hanged. Thus ended the life of a famous Uzbeg, who had twice saved his country from the Bukharians, and had ruled Khokand for ten years.†

It was now the turn of the Sarts and their leaders Kasim and Murza Ahmed. Mallabek having quarrelled with Khudayar was deprived of his government at Tashkend, was defeated and had to fly to Bukhara, and Murza Ahmed was put in his place. He severely aroused the animosity of the nomad Kazaks living about Chimkent and Avlie Ala, with whom he had eventually to make terms and to satisfy their demands.‡ This was in 1857. At the same time Mallabek, who had returned and

* Schuyler, L, 350.   † Vel. Zern., 352.   Schuyler, op. cit., L, 350.   ‡ Id.

settled at Khokand, formed himself a party out of such of the Kipchaks
as remained and of the Black Kirghises, and was also supported by a
leading Uzbeg named Alim Kul.

MALLA KHAN.

The rebels proclaimed him as Malla Khan, and marched towards
Khokand. A decisive battle was fought at Samanchi, in which Khudayar
was defeated, and had to retire to Bukhara.* We must now divert
somewhat to consider the intercourse between Khokand and Russia.
At the beginning of this century the Khokandians had no settlement on
the lower Sir, but after the capture of Turkestan in 1814 they began to
claim tribute from the Kazaks there, and as this claim was resisted a
bitter and prolonged struggle ensued between the two powers. To
further their ends the Khokandians built a number of forts on the Sir
below Turkestan, at Jany Kurgan, Julek Ak Musjid, Kumish Kurgan, Chim
Kurgan, Kosh Kurgan, &c. The most important of these, Ak Musjid
was built, according to the Kazaks, about the year 1817, on the left bank
of the Sir, but removed a year later to the right bank. The other forts were
subject to the beg of Ak Musjid, who was himself subordinate to the
governor of Tashkend.† The Khokandians were very rapacious, and
now levied exorbitant taxes on the Kazaks. Six sheep were taken from
each kibitka, beside a tax of one-third of the crop of corn and the usual
presents to the siakschiks or tax-gatherers; a tax on wood, charcoal,
and hay, each kibitka having to furnish twenty-four bags of charcoal
annually, four ox loads of saksaul for fuel, and 1,000 sheaves of reeds.
Those Kazaks who were too far off compounded for their taxes
in cattle and corn. The Kazaks had also to furnish one man and his
keep for every kibitka, and to work in the gardens of the Khokandians,
at the repair of the forts, and for cleaning out the stables, &c., in the
forts, which took place six times a year; while in time of war every
able-bodied Kazak had to serve, and also to supply himself with
his own horse and provisions. The Khokandians behaved otherwise
brutally, carrying off the women from the Kazak auls without giving the
customary kalim or payment for a wife, and violated them, marrying
them in opposition to the Shariat.‡ Although they kept the country of
the lower Sir under their control, their garrisons there were very small.
At Musjid but fifty sipahis and 100 Bukharians and Khokand traders ; at
Kumish Kurgan, twenty-five ; at Kosh Kurgan, four ; at Julek, in 1853,
there were forty ; and at Jany Kurgan, a small quadrangular entrench-
ment of a spear's height, but two or three.§ In order to protect their
caravans and the Kazaks subject to them, the Russians, in 1846, sent
Captain Schulz to survey the mouths of the Sir, and plant a small fort,

* Id., 351.   † Michell's Russians in Asia, 324. 315.   ‡ Id., 317.   § Id., 318.

there. The following year saw the foundation of the fort of Raimsk, afterwards called Aralsk. At first this only aroused the jealousy of the Khivans, but in 1850 the Khokandians attacked the Kazaks under Russian protection, and carried off in one raid 26,000 head of cattle, and in another 30,000. In 1851, they captured 75,000, whereupon the commander of Fort Aralsk attacked and took Kosh Kurgan.* In May, 1852, two steamers, built in Sweden, were forwarded in pieces, and put together again at Fort Aralsk. During the summer of that year Colonel Blaramberg was sent up the river to survey it as far as Ak Musjid, and to insist on the removal of that post. He had between 400 and 500 men with him, and two nine-pounders. As they neared Ak Musjid the environs were laid under water by the citizens ; nevertheless, the river was safely crossed on rafts and by wading.† Two envoys, one a tax-collector and the other a Bukharian merchant, now went to their camp to inquire the reason for their going. Blaramberg replied that he and his men were marching on the Russian side of the river where no Khokandian settlements would be permitted. On reaching the fortress it was reconnoitred ; the enemy now reappeared and asked for a respite of four days with the motive of giving time for his reinforcements to come up. As the place could not be stormed they having no ladders, the Russians threw some grenades into it which were answered by musketry and the cannons on the walls. The latter were speedily silenced, the wooden gate battered in, and the outer fortification stormed. The citadel, however, with its walls four fathoms high made of clay, proved impregnable. All inside the fortification was burnt and the Russians then retired, having lost fifteen killed and seventy-five wounded. Their retreat was conducted under great difficulties, but they destroyed the small forts of Kumish Kurgan, Chin Kurgan, and Kosh Kurgan on their way down. In 1853 a larger force consisting of 2,138 men, 2,442 horses, 2,038 camels, and 2,280 sumpter oxen with twelve guns, and carrying moveable pontoons, &c., marched from Fort Aralsk. To preserve the herbage for the cattle the Kazaks had been ordered not to encamp during the summer between the frontier and Fort Aralsk. The expedition arrived safely at the latter fort and again set out, the steamer Perofski co-operating on the river. The route lay across a terrible country, with bad water, increased heat, &c., to contend against, but the Russians duly arrived at Kara Uziak and reached Ak Musjid on the 2nd of July. The fort had been greatly strengthened, the outer wall having been demolished, and the ditch enlarged, so that it was one and a half fathoms wide and ten deep. The walls were four fathoms high, protected by crenelated battlements and a breast-work skilfully constructed of cemented lumps of clay. There was a garrison of 300 men inside with a month's provisions, three guns were on the ramparts, besides heavy missiles to hurl down on the assailants with the

---

* *Id.*, 324. † *Id.*, 333.

hand. The place was speedily beleagured and a bombardment commenced. A summons was sent to its commander to tell him the Russians were firmly determined to definitely appropriate the fort, and bidding him surrender.. He asked for fifteen days' grace, and if this were not granted replied that he should continue to resist so long as his weapons and stock of Kisiak hand-balls of hard clay held out. After the siege had lasted three weeks an expedition was sent to reconnoitre the country towards Tashkend. The defenders of the fort of Julek abandoned it and fled on the Russian approach. The fort was dismantled and its buildings destroyed, and the Russians returned to Ak Musjid with twenty guns, falconets, and stores of powder and lead as trophies. At length a mine having been prepared was successfully fired and a wide breach opened. Twice the assaulting party was repulsed, but the third charge was successful. Muhammed Vali, the governor, with 230 of his followers were killed, two horsetail standards, two spear flags, two brass guns, several falconets, sixty-six pieces of artillery mostly broken and shattered, one hundred and fifty sabres, and two coats of mail were captured. The place had been deemed impregnable, having withstood several sieges. A Russian fort was now built at the headwaters of the Kazala and was named Fort Number One, another was built at Karmakchi and called Fort Number Two, a third one at Kumish Kurgan called Fort Number Three, and Ak Musjid was renamed Fort Perofski.

The Khokandians did not submit quietly to their defeat. In the autumn of 1853 a large body of 7,000 men set out for Tashkend under Sabdan Khoja and advanced towards Fort Perofski. A force of 275 men and two field pieces was sent against them. The enemy speedily attacked this contingent and kept up a violent assault all day, but without avail. They lost very severely, and although they camped all around at nightfall, they made off at dawn, ninety-two camels carrying their wounded. They left 193 corpses behind. At the approach of winter fhey again.advanced, and on the 14th of December appeared before Fort Perofski with 12,000 to 13,000 men and seventeen brass guns. The Russians made a vigorous sortie, and surprised and fired the Khokandian camp. A terrible struggle ensued, with the usual story as to results, where arms of precision are pitted against savage weapons. Two thousand Khokandians were killed, while the Russian loss was only eighteen dead and forty-nine wounded. Four horse-tail standards, seven flags, seventeen guns, and 130 pounds of gunpowder were captured.[*]

In the spring of 1854 the Khokandians began to prepare even a larger expedition. A gun founder was sent to Turkestan, and to supply him with materials all the utensils of brass were seized by the Beg of Tashkend, and a large body of men was made ready. In order to resist them Perofski determined to strengthen the fort called after his name, and to

---

[*] Id., 363-5.

abandon Fort No. 2, which was not strong enough to hold out against a strong force. The Khokandian advance meanwhile was delayed by the threatening attitude of Bukhara.* They incited the Kazaks, however, to make continual raids, and also negotiated with the Khivans for a common policy against Russia. The internal disorders in the Khanate, however, which were not diminished by the recent victories of the hated Kaffirs, prevented any active hostilities for some time, and we must now revert more immediately to Khokand itself.

I have described Khudayar Khan's flight to Bukhara; there he was well received by the Amir, who hoped, doubtless through him, to regain his hold upon Khokand. He gave him a post at his court, and allowed him to live at Samarkand, but presently growing suspicious he sent him to live at Jizakh, where he ordered him to be kept in seclusion, and where no one was to see him. Schuyler says, he lived with two personal adherents in a little hut made of mud outside the walls. Afraid to appear in public himself, his attendants gathered reeds and roots which could be used as fuel, and disguising themselves, sold them in the town, and with the money thus obtained purchased provisions, while his mother sent him a little money, with which and under an assumed name, he bought two or three camels, and began to traffic as a merchant.†

Malla Khan, after a reign of two years, which is described as benevolent, was murdered by the Kipchak grandees; they had expected great favours from him, but the authority was monopolised by Alim Kul, who allowed no one to approach the Khan. Their leader was Shadiman Khoja, and during the absence of Alim Kul, who had been appointed bek of Andijan, they gained access to his chamber and killed him while sleeping.

Schuyler met at Tashkend with a person named Asudulla, who had been doctor to various Khans of Khokand; he described to him how during the night of the murder he occupied the next room to the Khan and that he suspected something was wrong, but was unable to fix upon anything definite so as to warn his master. Malla Khan was sleeping soundly, having taken several love-potions during the day. Presently he heard the door being unbolted, and some one say, "The Khan is here." A crowd then rushed into the room and beat and stabbed him with their knives; he defended himself bravely but was at last cut almost to bits.‡

SHAH MURAD KHAN.

The conspirators now proclaimed as Khan, Shah Murad, the son of Sarimsak, and therefore a nephew of the two last Khans, who was only fifteen years old. Seyid Sultan, the son of Malla Khan, escaped to Alim

---

* *Id.*, 368.   † Op. cit., i., 351.   ‡ Schuyler, i., 92.

Kul at Andijan. The latter took him under his protection and made profession at least of a loyal attachment to the new Khan Murad. Meanwhile an important revolut on occurred at Tashkend. Shadiman Khoja, the chief conspirator against Malla Khan, with Khamayat Shah, the bek of Turkestan, recalled Khudayar from Jizakh, and the latter with his adherents took possession of Tashkend. Murad with the army of Khokand marched against him, but after besieging Tashkend for thirty-one days retired. As the army was retreating Alim Kul came up from Andijan, seized four of the late conspirators against Malla Khan who were contemplating desertion, and put them to death, and the following day he ordered another of them named Alim bi to be executed. Alim Kul was now made regent of the Khanate. Khudayar followed the retreating army, seized Khojend and then Khokand, while Alim Kul retired to Marghilan, and then to the mountains. Shah Murad fell into Khudayar's hands, and was killed by him.*

KHUDAYAR KHAN (RESTORED).

There were now two parties in the Khanate. Khudayar Khan was supported by the Sarts and the townsfolk, and Alim Kul, the regent, by the Uzbegs and Karakalpaks, and a violent struggle ensued between them, in which not only the armies but also the individuals of each party murdered each other whenever they had an opportunity.† The Uzbeg party was somewhat distracted by the appearance of three pretenders, descendants of former khans, namely, Shah Rukh, Sadik bek, and Haji bek. Alim Kul got possession of all three and had them executed at Ush, where they are buried on the side of the hill called Solomon's Throne. He now proclaimed Sultan Seyid as Khan, and began a vigorous campaign. He captured Marghilan and Andijan, and twice defeated Khudayar's army. The latter appealed to the Amir of Bukhara, Muzaffar ulla, who had succeeded his father, and on his approach with a large army Alim Kul withdrew to the defiles of Kara Kulja. Presently the Amir quarrelled with Khudayar, sent Alim Kul a present of a golden staff, a cap, belt, and a fine koran, and withdrew to Bukhara. Alim Kul now speedily re-occupied Khokand, and Khudayar had once more to find refuge in Mavera un Nehr.‡

SEYID SULTAN KHAN.

Alim Kul again placed Seyid Sultan on the throne, but his rule was only nominal, and his powerful patron retained control of affairs and proceeded to restore order in the Khanate by a series of executions, which it is said caused as many as 4,000 victims. Presently his

---

* Schuyler, op. cit., i., 392. Russ. Revue, viii., 317. † Schuyler, L, 332, 353. ‡ Id., 353.

rigid sway caused many in the Khanate to turn once more to Khudayar, who had been living at Jizakh. He was preparing an expedition to recover his dominions when Alim Kul died, apparently of a wound received in an attack made on Tashkend by the Russians in 1865.[*] We must now turn shortly to the encroachments of the latter. In 1859 they captured Fort Julek, which, in the opinion of the Russian Governor of Orenburgh Katenin, was a menace to Fort Perofski; and two years later they built a new fort on its site, and also demolished that of Yany Kurgan.[†]

Further north they had gradually encroached upon the area subject to the Kazaks under Khokandian rule, and had some years before captured the Khokandian forts of Pishpek, Tokmak, &c.[‡] We now find a plan organised for a double attack upon the Khanate. While one division was to advance upon Avlie Ata or Talas from the north, the other marched upon the ancient city of Turkestan or Yassy from the west. The outbreak in Poland and the danger of a war with Western Europe caused this plan to be postponed till the next year, i.e., 1864. The forts built by the Khokandians along the Kara Tau and Boroldai Tau ranges fell one after another into the hands of the Russians. The Khokandians were soon on the move, and proceeded to strongly fortify the fortress of Chimkent, on the road between Turkestan and Avlie Ata, and threatening both positions. This was not to be tolerated, and General Chernaief, who was in command on the Lower Sir, having learnt that it was only garrisoned by about 10,000 men, advanced upon it in September, 1864, from two points. In a very few days the siege was so hardly pressed that the outer wall was stormed and the citadel surprised, a number of soldiers having forced their way in through a water conduit. Its garrison of 10,000 men, four standards, twenty-three cannons, eight mortars, and many other trophies fell into the hands of the victors.[§] By this victory the whole route from Ak Musjid to Vernoie was secured, and a large and important section of the Khanate was irretrievably lost.

The Khokandians under Alim Kul prepared to revenge their serious loss. General Chernaief fought a battle against them on the 9th of May, 1865, near Tashkend, in which Alim Kul was wounded; Asudulla, the doctor already mentioned, was close by; we are told he took off the warrior's clothes one by one and gave them to the bystanders to hold, so as to give some fresh air to the dying man; these were carried off by the Uzbegs, so that by the time Alim Kul died, his body was quite naked, and the doctor had to cover him with his own khalat.[‖] After their victory the Russians beleaguered Tashkend itself, that famous centre of wealth and of Mussulman culture, the central point where the caravans of Bukhara, Khiva, and Russia met, which speedily surrendered;

---

* Id., 353.   † Michell's Central Asia, 389.   ‡ Schuyler, i., 351.
§ Hellwald, op. cit., 85, 86.   ‖ Schuyler, i., 93.

its wealthy merchants preferring to be under the strong hand of Russia
than to be made the victims of Khokandian and Bukharian tyranny.
The Russians guaranteed the town its autonomy and freedom of
worship to its inhabitants, and in August, 1865, General Kryschanofski
having summoned its grandees and clergy to a conference, they
gave him bread and salt on a silver salver, and presented him
with an address, in which they declared themselves subjects of the
White Tzar—"You cannot split a sea in twain, nor have a kingdom
within a kingdom," they said, and Tashkend was accordingly annexed to
the Russian crown, and the conquered districts were erected into a new
province, to which the name of Turkestan was given.

While the Russians were thus conquering Western Khokand, Khu-
dayar, the expatriated khan, again marched to recover his own under the
ægis of Bukhara. Alim Kul, as I have said, fell in the battle near
Tashkend, and the Bukharians had little difficulty in conquering
Khojend. They then marched on Khokand; where they reinstated
Khudayar, retaining Khojend as the reward of their services. Seyid
Sultan Khan escaped for a while, but was eventually taken to Khokand,
and executed in Isfara in 1871.[*]

KHUDAYAR KHAN (Third Reign).

I have described how in 1866 the Russians quarrelled with the Amir
of Bukhara, and how they captured Khojend.[†] Khudayar, although
secretly hating the Russians, judiciously sent to congratulate them on
this victory, and for some years he retained possession of what remained
of his Khanate by subservience to the White Tzar, under whose
patronage he became very avaricious and arbitrary in the seizure of his
subjects' wealth and in the taxes he levied on them, and the nomad
Kazaks and Kipchaks for the first time for many years were in sympathy
with the Sarts and townsfolk. Mr. Schuyler has translated a native account
of the taxes levied from the unfortunate Khokandians, and as it is a good
specimen of the tyrannical way in which Central Asiatic Khanates were
trodden under by their rulers, I will take the liberty of extracting it.

" To keep the roads in repair, to build houses for the Khan, to cultivate
his gardens and to clean out the canals, men are seized in all parts of
the country and forced to work. These get no pay, not even their food ;
and besides this, when half a village is forced to work, the other half is
compelled to pay a tax of two *tengas* (11d.) a day for each man during
his work. Anyone who runs away or who refuses to pay is whipped.
Sometimes people have been whipped to death, and others have been
buried alive in the place of work. This same forced labour existed under
previous Khans, but with less cruelty, and the workmen at least received

---

their daily food. Formerly, the inhabitants had the right of collecting without pay grass, reeds, and brushwood; now, everyone is obliged to deliver to the Khan the half of what he collects, and these articles are then sold by the *Serkar* at fixed prices. Besides this, every cart load of reeds or brushwood must pay at the entrance of the town half a *tenga* (2¼d.), and at the bazaar a *tenga* (5½d.) more. Leeches were formerly free, but now the Khan makes people pay for them four *cheka* (½d.) a piece to the official who lives near the pond where they are. When cattle are sold, besides the ordinary *zekat* there must be paid to the Khan one *tenga* each on horned beasts, half a *tenga* on sheep, two *tengas* on camels, and one *tenga* on horses and asses. All imported merchandise besides the *zekat* of one-fortieth part, or 2½ per cent., pays in addition 5 per cent. of the price to the Khan; this is called *aminiana*. Silk and cotton, when exported, pay 10 *tengas* per camel-load. In sales on the bazaar, men's and women's clothing, beds and silk stuffs and other valuable objects pay half a *tenga* a piece; things of less value, from one-eighth to one-quarter of a *tenga*. Soldiers of the Khan are set every night to guard the shops, and for this each shop must pay from two to ten *tengas* every four months. On grain sold at the bazaar four *chekas* (½d.) a *charik* (180 lbs.) must be paid. Vegetables and melons and fruit pay from one to three *tengas* a load. This tax is called *tek-jai*, or right of selling at the bazaar, and is in addition to the *haradj* and *tanap* (*land tax*). Milk, sour cream, &c., must pay a farthing a cup. Of every pair of ducks or wild geese sold at the bazaar, the Khan takes one. On domestic fowls a farthing each is paid; and a *cheka* (½ farthing) for every ten eggs. From time immemorial the tribe of Liuli (*i.e.*, gipsies) has got its living by amusing the people, and leading monkeys, bears, and goats through the streets and villages. This means of earning their livelihood has now been taken from them by the Khan, who has made it a source of revenue for himself. Khudayar has set his agents over them, and has increased the number of animals. On every bazaar day, in the large towns three times a week, his showmen go through the bazaar with bears, wolves, hogs, goats, and foxes; every shop must pay four *chekas*. The buffoons of the Khan also go through the bazaars, and all that they get goes to pay his kitchen expenses. When an Imaum is appointed to a mosque, he must pay the Khan ten *tengas;* and a Sufi must pay five *tengas*, or neither of them will be permitted to perform his functions. If the Khan learns that there is a family feast, or a circumcision, or a wedding, he sends his musicians there. The master of the house must give each of them a gown, and besides, from two to five *tillas* (18s. to 45s.) for the Khan. Every spring, outside of Khokand, there is a popular festival, called *Dervishkhana;* and then every guild must felicitate the Khan and make a gift of money, according to its means, from 100 to 1,000 *tillas* (£45 to £450). If this were not done the leaders would be beaten and tortured. If the Khan desires a

piece of ground, or a garden, belonging to a private person, he forces
him to sell it, only paying him the price at which it was originally
bought, and taking no account of the present improvements made
on it. Every person wishing to leave the Khanate presents a petition
and obtains a pass, for which he pays two *tengas*. This pass is
then presented to the Makhram, who receives one *tenga*, and at
every station on the road an additional tax must be paid. The receipt
of the taxes on grass, brushwood, and leeches, as well as on pasturage,
which is 1½d. per month, for every head of cattle, is intrusted to
Sidik Kuichi, who pays to the Khan annually 20,000 *tillas* (£9,000).
The *karaj*, or harvest tax, gives yearly 300,000 *chariks* (a million
bushels) of grain which are sold by the Khan. In each district there is
a special officer for this. The district of Sharikana gives 9,000 *chariks*,
Balikichi 100,000, Sokh 14,000, Nerkent 12,000, &c. The *tanap*, or
tax on gardens and orchards, produces 60,000 *tillas* (£27,000). The
Serkar receives the tolls on the Sir Darya, between Balikichi and
Chil-Makhram, the taxes on provision sales in the bazaar, on the regis-
tration of marriages, which comes to half a *tilla* (4s. 6d.), the tax on
inheritance, one-fortieth part, and the tax on making salt ; and he pays
annually to the Khan 20,000 *tillas* (£9,000). The *sekat* on the country
people and the nomad tribes, intrusted to the Cherchi-Bashi, gives 11,000
tillas (£4,950). The Mekhter who collects the *sekat* from the merchants,
pays over 35,000 *tillas* (£15,750) The caravanserais and shops built by
the Khan, which number over a thousand, are farmed out to a man
named Issaie, and bring into the treasury 30,000 *tillas* (£13,500). The
cotton tax and the brokers' tax bring in 10,000 *tillas* (£4,500). The oil-
presses, grain markets, silk markets, hay markets, and milk markets
bring 5,000 *tillas* (£2,250). The exactions from marriages and ecclesiastical nominations bring in also 5,000 *tillas*."[*]

We will now return to our story. The Khan had become little more
than a Viceroy of Russia. Russians traded freely in his towns and
dominated his policy. Discontent soon appeared. In 1871 a revolt
broke out, which was quickly suppressed. In 1873 a more serious
insurrection took place. Khudayar wished to impose new taxes on the
Black Kirghises as much as three sheep instead of one from a family,
and also a new impost on the cultivated land in the mountains.
This they refused to pay, beat the tax collectors, and when troops were
sent against them they retired into the recesses of the mountains.
At this time the Aftobacha Abdur Rahman Haji, the son of Mussulman
Kul, and brother-in-law to the Khan, who had been to Mekka, and had
visited Constantinople to ask the Sultan's aid against the Russians, was
sent at the head of the troops against the Kirghises. He persuaded
the latter to send forty of their number as a deputation to put their

* Schuyler, ii., 57-60.

grievances before the Khan, whom he at the same time advised that he should retain them as hostages but not harm them. Khudayar in the most ruthless way put them to death, and the Aftobacha, who was compromised, had to leave the Kirghiz country and to retire to Khokand. The Kirghises now took up arms, captured Uzkend and Suk, a small fort in the mountains where the Khan kept part of his treasure. In the open country they made little way, many of them were made prisoners and 500 executed in the bazaar at Khokand, and Muzaffar the son of Madali, whom they had apparently set up as Khan, was impaled alive. The Khan applied to the Russians for help but they would not move. As many of his people secretly sympathised with the rebels, he became very suspicious, and was jealous even of his son, the Khan Zada Nasruddin, Bek of Andijan, who at length quitted that post with his family and treasure, saying he no longer wished to hold a public position.[*] Ush and Andijan, Suzak, Uch Kurgan, and Balikchi speedily fell into the hands of the insurgents. The bek of the last town was put to death by being pinned to the ground with a stake driven through his mouth. Many of the Khan's soldiers passed over to the enemy, and their commander the Aftobacha shut himself up in the fort of Tiura Kurgan near Namangan, and refused to take any further action.[†] During the cold weather of the autumn of 1873, there was a lull in the insurrection, and the Khan recovered some of his towns. It broke out again however in the spring of 1874, and it was proposed to put Muhammed Amin, Khudayar's second son, on the throne. The plot was disclosed it is said by the young prince's too great talkativeness, and his uncle Batir Khan Tiura, who was his chief supporter, being summoned to the palace with sixteen other conspirators never returned, and it is supposed that they were all drowned in a pond within its precincts, while the young prince was placed under surveillance. Another victim was the Mekhter Mollah Mir Kamil, who was poisoned by order of the Khan for not having warned him. He had previously, on being charged with embezzlement, been made to gallop his horse several times over a thin lattice bridge suspended over a ravine, from which ordeal he had escaped in safety and been therefore deemed innocent.[‡]

Another plot was now formed in favour of Abdul Kerim bek, a grandson of Fazil bek, Khudayar's uncle, who was only sixteen years old, and was living at Khojend, but the Russians removed him for safe custody to Tashkend, and his chief adviser Abdul Kerim to Chimkend. The Khan now became more suspicious than ever, he distrusted even his body guards or prætorians. For a long time he did not leave the palace, and had the door guarded by a black slave much attached to him, named Nasim Toga, who was told to allow no one, not even his wives and children, to enter without consulting him. His eldest son was closely watched, and an elaborate system of espionage was organised. Meanwhile other revolts occurred and were put down. In 1875 General Kaufmann contrary to all the laws of Eastern hospitality and asylum, without being asked to do so, and with the mere object of conciliating the Khan and getting permission for a Russian contingent to march through Khokand to Kashgar, surrendered Abdul Kerim and sent him to Khokand. This discreditable transaction injured the prestige of Russia considerably.[*]

The Aftobacha it would seem had long been preparing to revenge his father's cruel death, and now put himself at the head of a fresh rebellion. The army deserted to him *en masse*, as did Khudayar's brothers and sons. The Khan accordingly fled with all his treasures to Tashkend, where he was well received by the Russians, who were perhaps not altogether guiltless of the manifold outbreaks which had recently occurred, and whose policy has often been to sow internal discord amongst their neighbours and then annex them. He was accompanied by the Russian merchants and their families. Their exit through an angry and excited mob, says Schuyler, was attended with considerable difficulty. The Khan's soldiers deserted him, and always fired at the Russians in doing so, but he at length reached Tashkend in safety with his harem and about 650 attendants of whom some were women. He also carried off treasure to the amount of 1,000,000 sterling. The Khan was well received at Tashkend. This welcome, with the patronage the Russians had constantly extended to him, and their surrender of Abdul Kerim, naturally created a bitter feeling among the insurgents against them.[†] Khudayar was sent to live at Orenburgh. No coins of his immediate predecessors are known. Savilief has published several of Khudayar, in which he calls himself Seyid Khudayar Khan and Seyid Muhammed Khudayar Khan.[‡]

NASRUDDIN KHAN.

On the withdrawal of Khudayar, the insurgents proclaimed his son Nasruddin as Khan. The young Khan and his chief supporters Abdur Rahman Aftobacha (*i.e.*, holder of the washing can), Mollah Issa Avlia, and Halik Nazar Parmanachi deemed it prudent to send conciliatory letters to General Kaufmann, setting out the late Khan's ill-doings and asking for his friendship. This he promised on condition that the young prince would carry out his father's engagements, and would recompense Russian subjects for their losses in the late rebellion.[§] The Russians hoped much from the weakness of the young prince, who, among other Russian tastes, was very fond of vodka.

Meanwhile the Khokandians prepared a holy war against the hated

* *Id.*, ii., 280.   † *Id.*, 282.
‡ Mems. Imp. Arch. Institution, Eastern Section, ii., 124-127.   § Schuyler, ii., 282, 283.

Kaffirs, and a proclamation was issued calling upon the Russians to accept the faith or the consequences of refusing to do so.* This proclamation led to outbreaks on the frontier. Three stations on the post-road from Tashkend to Khojend, as well as that of Nau between Khojend and Samarkand, were burnt and sacked, and the station masters and post boys either killed or carried off. Travellers shared the same fate.† Khojend itself was sharply attacked and was for some time in danger. Mr. Schuyler has told the story in graphic fashion.‡

Meanwhile General Kaufmann prepared a formidable force to crush the threatening enemy, his lieutenants being General Golovachef, who had succeeded in clearing the district of Kurama of marauders and inflicted a severe defeat on them, and Colonel Skobelef, the last of whom has latterly become so famous. He accompanied the expedition in person, as did Jura bek and Baba bek, two princes of Shehr i Sebz and Farab, who we are told proved themselves of great use.§ The expedition reached Khojend on the 31st of August, and found that the enemy had already retired. After waiting a day they reached Makhram, the only fortified post between the frontier and the city of Khokand, where the Khokandians had collected in force. The fort was captured in less than an hour, its wooden doors being broken in by the soldiers who gave repeated thrusts with their shoulders, beating time meanwhile. The main body of the enemy outside were now attacked and routed. The victory was complete, and there was the usual disparity in the casualties. The Russians lost but six killed and eight wounded. Eleven hundred of the enemy's bodies were buried, and this does not include those who were drowned or fell at a distance. Thirty-nine cannons and other trophies were also captured.‖ The district was duly annexed and a proclamation issued recalling the people who had fled to their homes. On the 7th of September, the advance was continued towards Khokand. Issa Avlia was now sent by Nasruddin with apologies and protestations of amity. He was detained and his overtures were not received. The advance was continued in a triumphant fashion, the people on the route presenting the victorious General with dosturkhans, i.e., bread and salt. Another mission was sent to the General from the Khan with presents, and with the prisoners captured at Nau, &c., including the daughter of Dr. Petrof, who had himself been beheaded there. They had had their heads shaved, but reported that they had been otherwise well treated, the women and children having been given quarters in the Khan's harem.¶ On reaching Khokand no resistance was offered. The Khan came out to meet General Kaufmann, who rode into the place for some distance with his staff, and then returned with him to the camp. The troops remained encamped there for some time and were marched

---

* Id., 283.   † Id., 285.   ‡ Op. cit., i., 316-319.   § Id., ii., 286.
‖ Id., 288, 289.   ¶ Id., 289, 290.

through the town. The General issued a proclamation calling upon the other places in the Khanate to surrender, but although Muzzaffer himself went daily to his camp, these towns made no sign of giving in. In fact the Aftobacha began to collect a considerable force at Marghilan, and the people of Khokand itself seemed uneasy, the bazaars being largely deserted.* General Kaufmann therefore on the 17th of September advanced on Marghilan, whereupon the Aftobacha lost heart and retired with the Kipchaks who stood by him. Marghilan submitted, and Colonel Skobelef went in pursuit. He went as far as Ush, which also surrendered, as did Andijan, Balikchi, Sharikhana, Assaki, &c., while Halik Nazar, one of the three insurgent leaders, was given up to him. Nasruddin was now invited to Marghilan to make peace. The district north of the Sir, dependent on Namangan, was to be given up to Russia, an indemnity of 3,000,000 roubles or £410,000 was to be paid in six years, and a general pardon issued. The Russians succeeded afterwards in excepting from this last clause three of the most vigorous and patriotic of the Khokandian leaders, Issa Avlia, Zulfukar bi, and Muhammed Khan Tiura, who were transported to Siberia, a measure which was doubtless dictated by proper prudence in the very disturbed condition of the country. They now retired and their new subjects, the people of Namangan, presented them with 120 carts of provisions and 40,000 cakes of bread, a grand tent was prepared for the General and he walked to it from the river over silk, while silver coins were showered on him.† It was not long before disturbances again broke out, and a fresh expedition consisting of 14,000 men and eight guns was sent to quell an outbreak at Andijan, where it was said that the Aftobacha had collected from 60,000 to 70,000 men, while the Kirghises had proclaimed Pulad bek as Khan and gathered round him to the number of 15,000. He professed to be the son of Atalik Khan, son of Alim Khan, but was in reality a tobacco seller of Piskent named Mollah Iskak, whom the Kirghises had chosen the previous year to personate the real Pulad bek, who was then living with his mother at Samarkand.‡ The city had to be stormed and the streets were found to be barricaded. The barricades were forced and the bazaar and other chief buildings fired; the Russians then withdrew to their camp outside and afterwards to Namangan, burning and ravaging the villages *en route* and closely pursued by the enemy. The whole matter, as Schuyler says, looks very much like an unsuccessful attempt at occupying the city and a forced retreat ; nevertheless honours were duly showered on General Trotzki who commanded. When the Khokandians learnt the terms which their Khan had accepted they drove him out of the city and he arrived alone at Khojend, while the partizans of Pulad bek and Abul Gaffar the former bek of Uratippa occupied the capital. The people of Namangan, who had so lately become

* *Id.*, 291.   † *Id.*, 294.   ‡ *Id.*, 295.

Russian subjects, also revolted, and General Skobelef did not scruple to bombard and almost destroy the place in order to punish the Kipchaks who had seized it* Anarchy now reigned in the Khanate, large bands of Khokandians appeared in various directions, nor did the burning and devastating of the country break their spirit. Skobelef defeated them in the field and was ordered to waste the district between the Narin and the Sir, the head-quarters of the Kipchaks. He accordingly set out in January when the nomades were all collected in their winter quarters. Following the north bank of the Sir he destroyed Paita, the chief Kipchak settlement, defeated the Kipchaks, and destroyed everything as far as Sarkhaba. Andijan was then approached and summoned, but as it refused to submit it was bombarded and captured with terrible loss to the enemy. Another victory was won at Assaki, which led to the submission of Shahrikhana and Marghilan, and at length on the 1st of February the indefatigable Aftobacha, who had been the soul of the opposition, gave in. He surrendered unconditionally, together with Batir Tiura, Isfendiar, and other chiefs.[†]

The people of Khokand having grown weary of Pulad bek, sent to Khojend to Nasruddin to ask him to return, but on his way thither he was attacked by Pulad bek's supporters and his force scattered, and he barely escaped with his life to Makhram. Pulad bek meanwhile took refuge in the Alai mountains near Uch Kurgan, which was shortly after taken and many of his followers captured. Nasruddin then returned to Khokand, but the Russians had made up their minds to annex the Khanate, and General Skobelef was ordered to occupy the city, which he did on the 20th of February. Nasruddin, the Aftobacha, and other prominent persons were sent prisoners to Tashkend, and on the anniversary of his accession, March 2nd, 1876, the Emperor issued an order by which the whole district was annexed to Russia under its old name of Ferghana. Pulad bek was soon after captured by a Kirghiz and taken to Marghilan, where he was hanged on a charge of having killed twelve Russian soldiers whom he had taken prisoners.[‡] Thus was the famous country of Baber, which he has described in such picturesque language in his Memoirs, added to the dominions of the White Tzar.

We must now describe the history of the other small principalities which arose on the decay of the central power at Bukhara.

URATIPPA AND JIZAKH.

These two well-known towns—one on the road from Khokand and Khojend to Samarkand, and the other on that from Tashkend to the same place—were the camping ground of the Yuz tribe of Uzbegs. In the last century, when the feeble sovereigns of Bukhara lost control of so

many of its dependencies, it would seem that Fazil bi set up authority at
Uratippa. I have mentioned how Narbuteh bi of Khokand and Rahim bi
of Bukhara marched against him, and how he routed them with great
loss, and made a pyramid of their skulls at Uratippa.* He was succeeded
at Uratippa by his son Khudayar bek. M. Schefer has given an account
of Khudayar bek from the relation of Shah Ghafran ulla Serhindi, who
visited Khokand in 1794. He calls him Khudai Nazar bi and he says he
ruled at Uratippa, and had control over 10,000 families. He once
defeated Shah Murad bi and pursued him to the gates of Bukhara.
Every year he spent 10,000 tillas upon the Ulemas, officers of the law,
the sheikhs and students ; and Timur Shah of Afghanistan, out of hatred
for Shah Murad bi, sent him presents of silver and vestments. His
authority extended to the neighbourhood of Balkh. One of Khudayar's
dependents reported that, notwithstanding his age, he ate a sheep daily.
He slept during the day, and at night a ragout comprising a whole
sheep which had been cooking a long time was produced, and two large
deep plates were filled with it and placed before him, and although he ate
all night, yet he complained that his appetite had decayed. He was
reputed to be very brave, and his lance was so heavy that no one could
carry it but himself.†

On the death of Khudayar he was apparently succeeded at Uratippa
by his brother Baba bek, while his son Bek Murad bek held Khojend.
The former, in alliance with Omar Khan of Khokand, succeeded in
driving out his nephew Bek Murad from Khojend, but he was afterwards
murdered by him. The latter was in turn killed by the sons of Baba bek
at Samarkand, where he had been invited by Mir Haidar of Bukhara, and
Uratippa was for a short time reunited to Bukhara.‡ It was shortly after
captured by Alim Khan of Khokand, but the latter having left a feeble
garrison there, the place was surprised by Khoja Mahmud Khan, a sister's
son of Khudayar bek. Izzet ulla says that through his mother's side he
was related to Abulfaiz, Khan of Bukhara ; he was also descended from
the Khoja Ahrar of Herat. He was assisted in his enterprise by the ruler
of Bukhara, and took possession of the place in the latter's name, which
was also mentioned in the Khutbeh and on the coins, but the Amir's
authority extended no further. The Uzbegs in the district could supply
Mahmud Khan with a force of from 15,000 to 20,000 men.§ Mahmud
Khan was ruling at Uratippa when Izzet ulla travelled in these parts in
1812. Omar Khan, the successor of Alim at Khokand, marched against
Uratippa, which he captured, and carried off Mahmud to Khokand,
appointing one of his followers its governor. The latter was turned out
in three months, and the struggle renewed. Schuyler says it ended by
Jizakh being added to Bukhara and Uratippa to Khokand, while

* Ante, 818. Schuyler, i., 339.   † Schefer's Abdul Kerim, 284, 285.
    ‡ Schuyler, i., 340, 341.   § Journ. Roy. Asiat. Soc., vii., 327, 328.

Mahmud's son Tiura bek Yirua went to Khokand, and was given a post at the Court there.[*]   A large portion of its Uzbeg inhabitants of the Yuz tribe seem now to have migrated to the valley of the Lafir Nahan.[†] Thus ended the independent history of Uratippa, which now became a part of the Khanate of Khokand.

SHEHR I SEBZ.

Shehr i Sebz, *i.e.*, the green city, is a famous site.   It is widely known under its former name of Kesh, as the birthplace and original patrimony of the great Timurlenk. Mr. Schuyler has collected its later history, and to his admirable narrative I am chiefly indebted for this sketch.

Separated from Bukhara by a desert, and from Samarkand by a mountain range, the passes of which are easily defensible, it offered a good area for the formation of an independent government, and we find that it early asserted itself. It was subdued by Rahim bi of Bukhara in the middle of the last century, and he held it for five years, when it again rebelled and fell into the power of the Chief of the Kairosali Uzbegs who encamped there.

From 1811 to 1836 it was gove ned by Daniar Atalik, one of its most noted rulers. He took the title of Vali n niam and successfully resisted the attempts of Mir Haidar and his son Nasrulla to conquer him. He was succeeded by his two sons Khoja Kul at Shehr i Sebz and Baba Datkha at Kitab. The two brothers quarrelled, and Nasrulla took ad- vantage of the circumstance to invade the counary, but before he arrived the Khoja had driven out his brother, and he then succeeded in defeating the Bukharians. "Angry at this, Nasrulla sent his cavalry twice a year to devastate the meadows of Shehr i Sebz, and each time a truce was made, which lasted till the following foray."[‡] Khoja Kul died in 1846. His brother Izkander then took Kitab, and his son Ashur Kuli bek Shehr i Sebz, but the latter was speedily driven away, and Izkander adopted the title of Vali n niam.[§]

This title he retained till 1856, when, after a persistent struggle of ten years, Nasrulla captured Shehr i Sebz, having first blockaded and reduced it by famine. Izkander defended himself at Kitab, but shortly after surrendered to the Amir on favourable terms. He was sent to live at Bukhara, and given the revenues of Karakul for his support. Izkander's sister Aim Keninghez was a remarkable beauty. She was already married, but the Amir sent her husband to Charjui and appropriated her for his own harem, while the chief families of Shehr i Sebz were colonised in Charjui, Karshi, and other places. The Amir seems to have grown jealous of his exiled brother-in-law, and just before his death ordered him and his sister, whom he had married, to be killed.[‖]

[*] Schuyler, op. cit., i., 341, 342.   [†] Mayef, Geog. Mag., iii., 329.
[‡] Schuyler, op. cit., ii., 73.   [§] *Id.*   [‖] *Id.*, 73.

The account of the execution, as told by an eye-witness, is thus translated by Schuyler :—"Every day people made salaam to the Amir. Iskander and his brother, Chumchu Khan, came once to the salaam, bowed, and went away. As soon as they had gone the Amir called me and ordered me to call them back and make them sit in a little court in a separate room. I went after them and brought them back, as they had not yet got as far as their houses. They were put into the separate room. They asked what was the matter, and said, ' It cannot be that they have called us to the council. This is something bad. Our affairs are wretched.' I said to them, ' I know nothing about it. They probably call you to some council.'

" That same day Murza Abdullah, who lived in the fortress, received an order from the Amir not to leave his house. We were very much frightened, since we thought that something bad would happen to Abdullah, because in Bukhara nobody knows what is going to be done : to-day you are alive, to-morrow they behead you. We were for a long time unquiet, then said our midday prayer, and sat still and waited.

" Suddenly another message came from the Amir, ' from above,' to let all our people go home for the night, and to have only three trustworthy men stay, and after sunset prayers to be in the fortress at the drum-beat, and to send for the executioner and a woman to wash the dead and to prepare two shirts.

" We began to guess that they were going to punish Iskander, but could not understand what woman was to be punished with him, because we knew nothing about it before.

" After this a badacha came from the Amir ordering us to execute Iskander and the woman he would send to us.

" A badacha is a small seal like an almond, which the Amir uses when he orders some one to be executed. For other matters the Amir has a large seal.

" As soon as we received the order we immediately sent for Iskander and brought him to the place of execution. In the Amir's fortress there is a place like a well, deep, and covered with boards. As soon as they execute them they throw the body there. There are many corpses there.

" The executioner was already waiting for us. He immediately seized Iskander, threw him on the ground, and as Iskander had no beard he put his fingers in his nostrils, and, taking hold of his head, cut his throat. After this they brought a woman from the Amir. As soon as she saw the dead body of Iskander she immediately began to weep and to abuse the Amir. We then saw that the woman was the sister of Iskander, the wife of the Amir. She was of the family of Keneghez, and all called her ' My moon of Keneghez.' The executioner tied her hands, and shot her with a pistol in the back of her head.

" With us they do not cut the throats of women, but shoot them.

" He did not kill her at once. She fell and struggled for some time. The executioner kicked her twelve times on her breasts and back till she died.

" They say that she was punished because she, according to the order of her brother, poured mercury into the ear of · the Amir when he was asleep."[*]

On Nasrulla's death Shehr i Sebz revolted. One of the chiefs of the family Keninghez (which with the other families has the hereditary duty of raising the Amir on his throne), called Kalentar bek or the Dervish bek, had a son named Baba, who had entered the service of the Amir as one of the youths in waiting. On Nasrulla's death he escaped to Shehr i Sebz. When, six months later, Nasrulla's son, the Amir Muzaffar visited that district, the very same night the dissolute chief demanded the sister of Baba bek who had already been forced to serve the passions of his father † This aroused a great outcry, and he withdrew to Bukhara, and many important persons were imprisoned. They were released by the populace, however. Baba bek was appointed ruler of Shehr i Sebz, and Jura bek of Kitab, whence they expelled the Amir's officials. Muzaffar marched against them, but was obliged to raise the siege and hastily withdraw by a diversion caused by the Khan of Khokand. The beks afterwards sent him yearly presents and helped him with contingents of troops, but did not allow him to interfere with the internal affairs of the country.‡

After the defeat of Muzaffar by the Russians in 1866, two parties of rebels arose in Bukhara, one of them supported his son Ketta Tiura, and the other his nephew Seyid Khan. Among the chief supporters of the latter was Jura beg, who afterwards said of him, " the more stupid he was the better for us, we should have been more independent."§ One of the conspirators Omar bek, of Chilek, was ordered to fall on the Russians, who were allies of the Amir. He was easily defeated and escaped to Shehr i Sebz, afraid the Amir would punish him.‖ This attack was misinterpreted by the Russians, who revenged themselves on the Amir and captured Samarkand. When he showed a bold front against them, the begs of Shehr i Sebz, changing their tactics, came to his assistance with a force of 20,000 men, and threatened Samarkand.¶ They had been intriguing with General Kaufmann, but when after the capture of Samarkand he summoned them to meet him, they grew suspicious, and made overtures to Muzaffar, and offered to help him. He in turn agreed to make over to them the frontier town of Chirakchi, about which there had been constant disputes.[**] The siege of Samarkand was duly pressed, and its defence is a very heroic chapter in the history of the

---

* Id., i., 95-97.   † Id., i., 85.   ‡ Id., ii., 73.   § Id., i., 241.
         ‖ Id., id.   ¶ Id., 243.   ** Id., 244.

Russians in Central Asia. It would doubtless have been captured, but that Jura bek, misled by a rumour that General Kaufmann was marching on his appanage, withdrew his men.[*]

It was doubtless in consequence of the arrangement above mentioned that, as we are told, the Muzaffar made a grant of 10,000 tengas to each of the beks, and also gave Jura bek the title of Datkha.[†]

In 1870, when General Abramof was absent on the Izkander Kul expedition, a band of marauders attacked Prince Urusof and his escort, who were collecting taxes. The latter insisted that this attack had been led by Haidar Khoja, a *protegé* of Jura bek's, and his surrender was demanded, and as Jura bek refused to comply, urging that Haidar Khoja was innocent, and had, in fact, been elsewhere at the time, General Kaufmann determined to suppress the Khanate. General Abramof was sent against it : Kitab was taken by storm, and Shehr i Sebz directly after surrendered. The beks fled to Khokand, and the Khanate was duly made over to their *protegé*, the Amir of Bukhara, by the Russians,[‡] and still remains his. The beks were presently treacherously given up to the Russians by the Khan of Khokand. They lived together under surveillance at Tashkend for some time, and at length obtained pensions of 2,000 roubles from the Bukharians. Jura bek has become a strong partisan of the Russians. Schuyler speaks of him as a very honourable, upright, and chivalrous person.[§]

URGUT AND KOHISTAN.

The mountainous district east of Samarkand is known as Kohistan, *i.e.*, the mountain country. Mr. Schuyler says that up to 1870 it was divided into the seven bekships of Farab, Magian, Kshtut, Fan, Yagnau, Macha, and Falgar, which paid a small tribute to Bukhara, but were otherwise independent.

Urgut was formerly governed by some independent beks of its own, who held its office of governor hereditarily, and we are told the three petty chiefs of Magian, Kshtut, and Farab acknowledged them as their suzerains. In the early part of the century Mir Haidar of Bukhara subdued Urgut, and sent its ruler, Yuldash Parmanachi, a prisoner to Bukhara, whereupon the three districts just named submitted to the latter Khanate. Some time after Katta bek, son of Yuldash, recovered possession of Urgut, and put his brother Sultan bek over Magian and Kshtut. He had a struggle with Haidar, and even threatened Samarkand, and peace was at length made by his giving his daughter in marriage to Haidar's son Nasrulla, whereupon he retained his possessions as a fief of Bukhara, and on his death they passed to his sons Adil Parmanachi, who had Urgut, and Allayar Datkha, Magian.[||]

---

* *Id*, 245, 246.   † *Id.*, ii., 74.   ‡ *Id.*, i., 74.   § *Id.*, i., 86.
|| Schuyler, i., 279.

Shortly before his death Nasrulla summoned these chiefs to Bukhara, and then exiled them with their families to Charjui where most of them died, and he appointed new beks to the mountain districts. The nominees of the Amir fled when Samarkand was captured by the Russians. Meanwhile Hussein bek, one of the princes who had been exiled to Charjui, escaped to Khokand and thence to Urgut, which, on the flight of the Bukharian beks, he occupied. Driven thence by the Russians, he went to Magian, where he planted himself, and put his brother Shadi in charge of Kshtut, and his cousin Seyid at Farab.[*]

In regard to the other petty districts of Eastern Kohistan we are told that their annals are crowded with internecine struggles, with the adventures of Bukharian tax collectors, and notices of incursions from the neighbouring countries beyond the mountains. The memory is still green, says Schuyler, of a bek of Falgar, Abdush Kur Datkha, who in the beginning of this century united all the districts under his rule, and built roads and bridges through some of the hitherto inaccessible defiles. In the time of Mir Haidar, Bukharian begs were established in these districts and forts built. Thus matters remained till the close of Nasrulla's reign. On the capture of Samarkand, the Bukharian beks having fled, Abdul Gaffar, formerly bek of Uratippa, occupied Urmitan, and made himself bek of Falgar.[†] The people of Macha submitted however to Muzaffar Shah of Karatigin, who sent his nephew Rahim Khan there as his deputy. The latter drove out Abdul Gaffar from Falgar, defeated Shadi beg, of Kshtut, who had gone to his assistance, subdued Yagnau and Fan, and marched towards Hissar, but on the way thither his troops rebelled, drove him out, and put Pacha Khoja in his place. The people of Falgar, who deemed themselves more cultured than those of Macha, again recalled Abdul Gaffar, but he was beaten and fled to Samarkand, where he submitted to the Russians.[‡] The disordered state of the country tempted the latter to intervene, and in May, 1870, General Abramof set out with a small division. On the 12th he occupied Urmitan, and on the 21st, Varsaminor, both in the bekship of Falgar, then subject to Macha. Pacha Khoja, bek of Macha, who was very unpopular, retired and contented himself with sending threatening letters. The Russians now approached the bekship of Macha, forced one of its defile-approaches, and on May 28th captured Oburdan. Pacha Khoja fled, and the Russian General much to the joy of the inhabitants razed the forts at Paldorak, and advanced to the very fountains of the Zarafshan in a glacier of the Alai range.[§] Returning again down the Zarafshan valley as far as Varsaminor, he captured Sarvada, on the river Fan, subdued the valley of the Yagnau, and went as far as lake Iskander Kul.[‖] Turning

* Id., 280.   † Schuyler, i., 280.   ‡ Id., 280, 281.   § Id., 281.
‖ Id., 282.

new to Western Kohistan, he crossed over the pass of Kshtut, 10,000 feet above the sea level. In descending from this pass, the Russians fought a severe engagement in the defiles on the western side. They were victorious, however, and having occupied and destroyed Kshtut returned to Penjakend and Samarkand.[*]

After the conquest of Shehr i Sebz, a detachment was sent up the valley of the Kashka Daria to Farab and Magian, whose beks had been implicated in the recent attacks on the Russians. The two fortresses were destroyed, and Seyid and Shadi beg surrendered. Hussein bek of Magian was not captured for some months after. Farab and Magian were at once annexed to the Russian district of Urgut, and the remaining mountain districts in 1871. The country seems since to have been in a very unsettled and disturbed condition.[†]

HISSAR, KULAB, &c.

South of the Karatau range, and between it and the Oxus, are a number of small states, whose history is very obscure. The head waters of the Surkhab, one of the main feeders of the Oxus, flows through the country of Karatigin, a Tajik state, whose sovereigns claim like those of several neighbouring districts, to descend from Alexander. Wathen tells us that when he wrote it had been conquered by the ruler of Darwaz,[‡] but the old dynasty afterwards recovered its position. It was subdued by the Khan of Khokand in 1839, as I have mentioned, and apparently afterwards remained subject to that power. Darwaz borders Karatigin on the south, and like other hill states in the neighbourhood, such as Wakhan, Shagnan, Roshan, &c., is peopled by Tajiks and ruled by sovereigns claiming descent from Alexander. This means, at all events, that they are not peopled by Uzbegs, nor are their princes of Uzbeg descent. When Madali, Khan of Khokand, conquered Karatigin in 1839, he also seems to have subdued or made tributary Kulab, Darwaz, and Shagnan,[§] and these states continued apparently to be tributaries of Khokand till the latter lost its independence. West of these mountain states is the important district of Hissar and Kulab, occupied by the Uzbeg tribes of Kunkurat or Kungrad and Kataghan, who have encamped among and largely driven out the old Tajik population ; so much so that we are told the whole of Hissar is known in Bukhara as Uzbegistan, *i.e.*, the land of the Uzbegs *par excellence*.[‖]

The history of the district is unfortunately almost entirely unknown. It seems to have broken loose from Bukhara in the middle of the last century, for Hissar is mentioned among the places which refused obedience to Rahim bi.[¶]

[*] *Id.*, 283. [†] *Id.*, 283, 284. [‡] Journ. Asiat. Soc., Beng., iii., 273.
[§] Schuyler, i., 343. [‖] Mayef, in Geog. Mag., iii., 329. [¶] Schefer, 9.

It became the seat of several petty principalities, and Shah Ghafran ulla says expressly that the Uzbeg chiefs were numerous in the neighbourhood of Kunduz, Hissar, and Kulab.* One of the most powerful of these was Allah Berdi Zauz of Kurghan, who at the close of the last century was a terror to his neighbours. While he was besieging Hissar, he was apparently attacked and killed by the Governor and Prince of Karshi, who thereupon took possession both of Hissar and Kurghan. His name was Allah Yar bek. "The former ruler Seyid bek," says Frazer, "still retains his rank if not his power at Hissar, probably on a friendly understanding with the ruler of Bukhara, who married his daughter." He adds that Kurghan was then attached to Hissar.†

Izzet ulla, who wrote several years before, names Seyid bi as the ruler of Hissar, and Allah Yar bek of Kurghan. He also mentions Murad Ali bek and Dost Muhammed as the chiefs of the neighbouring district of Kabadiam.‡

It would seem that the various small states were eventually swallowed up in that of Hissar.

I have however no information about its later history till the second half of the present century, when we find it subject to the Kataghan prince Sari Khan, who also ruled over Kulab.§ He was a redoubtable person, and caused the prince of Karatigin in 1869 to seek shelter at Khokand.|| In the same year the Amir of Bukhara marched against and subdued him.¶ And when Mayef wrote, i.e., in 1875, he tells us the district of Hissar consisted of seven sub-districts governed by beks, and Kulab of two such sub-districts. All these were dependent on the Amir of Bukhara. The districts were Shirabad, Baisan, Dehinau, Yurchi, Hissar, Kurghan-tube, and Kabadian in Hissar, and Baljuan and Kulab in Kulab: Besides which the Amir ruled directly over the three districts of Derbend, Sarijui, and Faizabad.**

We will now cross over to the southern bank of the Oxus.

BALKH, KHULM, AND KUNDUZ.

I have described how, about the year 1751-2, the Uzbeg possessions south of the Oxus were conquered by the Afghans.†† Shah Murad, of Bukhara, tried in 1786 to recover them, but in vain,‡‡ but about this time some of the petty chiefs who ruled over the Uzbeg tribes settled in these districts began to assert a more or less independent position. Among these the most famous was the ruler of the small district of Khulm, situated to the south-east of Balkh. He was named Kilij Ali, and held the Uzbeg title of Atalik from the Afghan ruler. He speedily annexed

* Schuler, 286.   † Frazer's Travels, Appendix, 101.   ‡ Journ. Roy. Asiat. Soc., vii., 332.
§ Mayef, op. cit., 329. || Fedschenko, Geog. Mag., i., 59.   ¶ Id., 90.
** Geog. Mag., iii., 329, 330.   †† Ante, 766.   ‡‡ Id., 771.

the neighbouring districts of Ibak, Ghuri, Mosaur, Derraguz, &c. He expelled Allah Berdi Tauz, the Uzbeg chief of Kurghan tepé, already mentioned, who had occupied the district of Hazrat Imaum, and delivered it from him. He also allied himself closely with the Uzbeg chief of Kunduz,* who, although he possessed more power and resources, was as much under his influence as one of his deputies. Kilij in fact married his daughter. He also employed his influence at Kabul to acquire an ascendancy over the Sirdar Nejib ulla Khan, son of Hukumet Khan, who governed Balkh on behalf of the ruler of Afghanistan. The latter remained in possession of the city itself and its dependencies, but was a mere *protegé* of Kilij Ali, and all the rest of the province, except Talikan, was either under his government or influence. Of its revenue of 30,000 rupees, one-third went to the treasury at Kabul, and the rest was distributed between the Kohneh nuker or old servants,† and in grants to learned and religious men, in pensions to others, and in the expenses of the Sirdar.‡ Kilij, who was loyal to the Afghan ruler, had a very wide reputation for his orderly and equitable rule. He had an army of about 12,000 horse, of whom 2,000 were in his own pay, and the rest were a feudal soldiery, returning services for grants of land. He could also draw about 5,000 men from Kunduz. His revenue, after deducting the expenses of his army, was about £19,000 a year. His eldest son had a grant of £9,000 a year, with the title of Vali of Balkh, from the Afghan ruler. Kilij was a handsome man, with a red and white complexion, with a few grey hairs on his chin in lieu of a beard, small eyes, broad forehead, and Uzbeg attire. On his head he had a cap, and over it two turbans twisted up together. He wore an Uzbeg shirt and a gown, over which was a girdle wound round his loins with a long knife stuck in it, and over the whole a robe of cotton or other cloth of sombre colour. He only used Uzbeg boots when on horseback, carried a short stick in his hand, and took a great deal of snuff. He gave audience in the public apartment for two hours after sunset every day, and sat on a carpet without pillows or cushions. His intimates and those whom he chose to honour sat on the same carpet as himself; all others sat on the bare ground. There he inquired into all the affairs of his government, but remitted legal matters to the Kazi. Thieves were not put to death, but hung to a wall with an iron pin, in the midst of the market-place. Highway robbers and murderers were always executed. He walked on foot through the bazaars and examined them every market day, checking light weights and overcharges. He walked instead of riding from a sense of humility that his feet might not be higher than the heads of other true believers.§ We are further told he was honest.

---

* Elphinstone's Cabul, ii., 196.

† The descendants of the Afghan garrison planted at Balkh by Ahmed Shah, and of the recruits which afterwards joined it. Schefer, 260. ‡ Elphinstone's Cabul, ii., 197, 198.

§ *Id.*, 188.

just, well-disposed, kind to his subjects, judicious and discriminating in his treatment of his servants, economical in his expenses, vigilant and well-informed in the affairs of his government, and that he gave bread and broth to one hundred poor persons daily.[*]

In 1814 Zeman Shah, who had been deposed from the throne of Kabul by Mahmud Shah, asked permission from the latter to visit the tomb of Ali at Balkh. He went by way of Khulm, and Kilij Ali Khan went out to meet him and treated him with sumptuous hospitality. After visiting the famous tomb, Zeman went on to Bukhara, where the Amir married his young daughter and promised to conquer Balkh and to make it over to him, but the old man was imprisoned and made his escape into Persia and thence went to Mekka.[†] Kilij Ali was the ruler of Khulm when Izzet ulla visited Turkestan in 1812.[‡] According to Schefer, he died in 1817. His death was the signal for violent intrigues in his family, which, Moorcroft says, were fomented by Murad bi, of Kunduz. Kilij had left three sons, the eldest of whom was poisoned. Khulm and Ibak were divided between the other two, Balkh being dependent on the Ibak ruler.[§] They were, however, mere feudatories of the Kunduz chief, whose origin we must now trace. Kunduz, a corruption of Kohnehdiz, i.e., the Old Castle,[‖] is the chief town of an Uzbeg tribe called Kataghan, bearing a name famous even in the days of Jingis Khan. The chief of this tribe seems to have become more or less independent towards the end of the last century. His name was Kokan beg. I know nothing of him except that he ravaged Badakhshan severely and was succeeded by his son Murad bi, who became one of the most famous rulers of Central Asia. Murad bi was the ruler of Kunduz in 1812, when Izzet ulla wrote.[¶] Until the death of Kilij Khan he would seem to have been more or less subordinate to him, but he then broke loose and speedily conquered himself a wide dominion. Moorcroft visited him in the course of his well-known journey. That traveller went from Kabul by way of Ibak, which was then governed by Muhammed Ahmed (?Amin) Bek, the son of Kilij Khan, who also styled himself Vali or protector of Balkh. He was feudally dependent, however, on two patrons: at Ibak, on Murad bi of Kunduz, and at Balkh upon the Amir of Bukhara, who it would seem had conquered that city.[**] The young prince went to see him and he describes him as about twenty-four years old, with Uzbeg features, and a not unpleasing face. Moorcroft had sent on some envoys to prepare the way, but they were met with suspicion, it being said the English never entered any part of Asia but for interested purposes and ultimately to become its masters,[††] but he determined to go on. Murad bi was

* Elphinstone, op. cit., 199, 200.   † Schefer, op. cit., 73-78.
‡ Jour. Roy. Asiat. Soc., vii., 333.   § Travels, ii., 399, 400. Schefer, op. cit., 73. Note 1
‖ Id., 262.   ¶ Journ. Roy. Asiat. Soc., vii., 333.   ** Moorcroft, ii., 399, 400.
†† Id., 408, 409.

at this time master of Khulm, Kunduz, Talikan, Anderab, Badakhshan, and Hazrat Imaum. On the way from Ibak to the mountains Moorcroft passed several towns in ruins which had been destroyed by Murad, who had made slaves of their inhabitants. At Khulm, he had an audience with Baba Beg, Kilij Khan's son and the elder brother of the ruler of Ibak. He was a short thick-set person about thirty-five years old, clothed in an outer garment of flame-coloured silk and an inner one of black satin. He received our traveller coldly, and in answer to his statement that he was a merchant he said that that country was a bad one to trade in; he jeered at one of his servants for being a Mussulman and yet serving a Kaffir, and said his master, i.e., Murad bi, had given orders that the travellers should be sent on to Kunduz with an escort.*
On reaching Kunduz they found the Amir's minister, Atma Ram, in a wooden porch in the fort. Tea was served them, and a matted chamber was assigned them to live in. Shortly after they had an interview with the grim ruler himself, whom they found in an inner room with a number of attendants, some kneeling and others standing, the latter holding white wands, but all having their heads inclined towards the ground. The visitors duly saluted the chief with the Salaam Alikum, and were then told to seat themselves on a carpet prepared for them; a prayer was said, and all stroked their beards with great gravity. The Amir sat on a cushion of Chinese damask, and wore a tunic of blue silk with a sash of the same colour, and over it an open coat of an almond colour, and long brown boots with iron tipped heels. He was about forty-five years old, of a dark complexion, and had very small eyes. His attendants were all smartly dressed in Bokharian silk. No one wore any weapons. He seemed pleased with Moorcroft's presents; asked many questions about England and the motives of his journey. He then offered him some bread and sliced melons, while he himself took pears and pomegranates and distributed them among his courtiers, and also gave Moorcroft some. In the evening he sent him a fat sheep and some rice.† At Kunduz he saw a brass gun which had been spiked and bore an inscription showing it had been made for Shah Tahmasp of Persia.‡ Moorcroft had taken a large quantity of merchandise with him in bales which he had left at Khulm. Murad bi having learnt of this suspected it was of great value, and sent his Divan begi there to examine the bales. The travellers accordingly returned to Khulm, where they had to pay an exorbitant duty on all their goods. During their absence Murad bi marched against the Hazarahs of Kamand. After which Moorcroft and his party with his merchandise were ordered to again repair to the unhealthy district of Kunduz. Murad bi now became very suspicious and uncivil and determined

* Id., 414, 415   † Id., 424.   ‡ Id., 429.

to detain his guests, who wanted to go on to Bukhara. During this detention a conspiracy was formed against the Amir, headed by the Vali of Ibak, Zulfakar Shere of Siripul, Ishan Khan of Balkh, the chief of Mazar, and others, who raised a body of 8,000 men who were better armed and equipped than Murad's men.* He set out against them, leaving his son, who was friendly to the Englishmen, in charge of Kunduz. One of Moorcroft's friends on the Amir's return having said to him that if he had any regard for his character he ought not to detain them, he replied in characteristic fashion, "What have I—what has an Uzbeg to do with character? Do not I sit here to plunder the faithful, and shall I withhold my hands from an infidel?" He then offered to let them go if another friend of his, his Pir Zadeh, or spiritual adviser, Mir Fazl Hakh, would find a ransom of 50,000 rupees, otherwise he promised that they should have a taste of the summer of Kunduz. Moorcroft replied that he had no money, and the Mir might do as he pleased. It was at length agreed they should go if a sum of 10,000 rupees was paid to the Amir and 2,000 to Atma Ram.† He then set out for Tashkurgan, where he arrived safely, and was "welcomed by Baba Beg with apparent and many of the people with unaffected cordiality."‡ The previous year the people of Khulm, which was then a very thriving place, had been threatened with compulsory removal to Kunduz, where the fever constantly reduced the inhabitants and required a perennial supply of victims to keep up the population. It only escaped by bribing the Amir. The people of Old Khulm, the capital in Kilich Ali's day, and of Sar Bagh, had been already removed.

Meanwhile, a treacherous person named Mollah Muhammed Amin, who had been in Elphinstone's service, sought an audience with Murad, threw his turban down, and pledged himself that Moorcroft was in fact a spy. Messengers were at once despatched to recall him to Kunduz.§ He thereupon determined to fly, and to escape to Kassim Jan, Khoja of Talikan, the Pir or spiritual guide and father-in-law of Murad beg.‖ Having disguised himself as an Uzbeg, he set out, and after a terrible ride, whose incidents are described with picturesqueness in his journal, he at length reached the Khoja, with whom he had an interview, and on whose generosity he threw himself to protect him.¶ The Khoja promised to do his best, and to show his disinterestedness refused to accept Moorcroft's presents. Meanwhile Baba beg arrived at Talikan and had an audience with the Pirzadeh, to which Moorcroft was invited. He commended what he had done, and advised him on no account to quit the protection of the Khoja. Soon after he had to go through the ordeal of a *tête-à-tête* in the council chamber with the Mollah Muhammed Amin already mentioned, and who had been sent by Murad

* Id., 444.   † Id., 447.   ‡ Id., 448.   § Id., 454, 455.   ‖ Id., 456.
¶ Id., 463.

4 M

to try and prejudice the Pirzadeh against him. The fierce denunciations of this person, directed to the Asiatic policy of England and the antecedents of Moorcroft, with the latter's answers, are told in detail in his narrative.* Soon after, Murad himself repaired to Talikan. At an interview with him the Khoja warmly espoused Moorcroft's part, and insisted that he should be allowed to go, on paying a suitable ransom. Khoja Jan was about forty years old, of a fair complexion, and pleasing features for an Uzbeg. Although a holy person, he was a dealer in merchandise, and especially in slaves, and the beg generally presented him with some after his forays. These he sent for sale to Yarkand, receiving back, tea, China satin, and porcelain. He also kept a large number of brood mares and many sheep, but as his character required him to exercise unbounded hospitality he was not wealthy. It reads curiously to find that Moorcroft translated for him Gibbon's account of Jingis Khan and Timur, with which he was much interested.† Moorcroft was lodged at first in a kirgah or circular tent, but afterwards in a small clay chamber, and was supplied with salted tea and wheaten bread for breakfast. At mid-day, with boiled rice and pulse, in the midst of which was above a pint of kurut or curd, made into the consistence of cream, and over which about two ounces of melted fat from a sheep's tail was poured. In the evening tea was served, and about ten broth and bread, with mutton, beef, or horseflesh. Among others, whom he met at Talikan was the brother of the last king of Badakhshan, who denied the tradition about his family being descended from Alexander, saying it had not been settled in the country more than one hundred years. He said the chief of Darwaz, however, was so descended.‡ On taking leave of Moorcroft the Pirzadeh did him the unusual honour of embracing and blessing him, and gave him two pieces of green Chinese silk, and one of crimson satin brocade with flowers of gold, the last of which he hoped he would wear in remembrance of him. Moorcroft in return left him some razors, scissors, some genuine attar of roses and musk, a telescope, and gold repeater. Murad bi had given his promise that he should freely depart. At Kundus he had another interview with him. He says he had a very repulsive face, excessively high cheek bones, with a very narrow lower jaw, leaving scarcely any room for the teeth, which were standing in all directions. He was also near-sighted. Abdul Tash, the manager of the religious establishment at Hazrat Imaum, prayed for them as they left, and the hypocritical beg held up both hands as if joining in the prayer.§ He passed through Tashkurgan and Mazar. In the latter place he was well received by Shuja ud din Khan, its chief, and by the Vali 'of Balkh, who happened to be there, and who both inveighed against Murad bi as a disgrace upon all Turkistan.‖ The

---

* *Id.,* 468-475.   † *Id.,* 480.   ‡ *Id.,* 481, 482.
          § *Id.,* 486.   ‖ *Id.,* 490-7.

Khan of Mazar held the post of Mutawali, or custodian of the Ziarat Gah, or shrine of Ali.

From Mazar Moorcroft went to Balkh, which he found a huge mass of ruins, the population having dwindled to about 1,000 families. The fort was in charge of Ishan Khoja. Thence he made his way across the Oxus to Mavera un Nehr, and died the next year at Andkhud.

Our next authority on this district is Burnes. He says Murad's government was well consolidated and his measures vigorous. On conquering a district he retained the former chiefs in authority, but stipulated for the supply of a contingent of troops, and planted a garrison of his own there. His united forces amounted to 20,000 men, all cavalry, with six pieces of artillery, including a thirty-six pounder, which I have described as having belonged to Nadir Shah. The cavalry were armed with unwieldy spears, and some with matchlocks. The soldiers were paid in grain; their commanders he retained closely by him. He was an active person and himself led his troops, and made many alamans towards Balkh and the Hazarah country, whose Shia inhabitants were sold as slaves. The chief of Chitral also paid him a tribute of human beings. His people had a considerable trade with Yarkand, and he exchanged envoys with the Chinese governor there. He was not on cordial terms with the Amir of Bukhara.

One of his campaigns in the Hindu Kush, about 1830, was not a success. The Siah Posh Kaffirs allowed his people to advance into the mountains, when they attacked them, and a snowstorm having ensued one half of their army of 4,000 horse perished.[*] The revenue was paid in grain and corn was very scarce, the money current there, when Burnes wrote, being that of an emperor of Hindostan before the time of Nadir Shah. The beautiful country of Badakhshan had been wasted, its inhabitants largely transported to Kunduz, and its ruler, who claimed to descend from Alexander, had been deposed. The Amir's affairs were managed by a Hindoo from Peshawur, named Atma Khan, who held the post of Divanbegi, and although as a rule Hindoos were despised and not allowed to wear turbans, this person had secured the privilege for himself, his servants, and his tribe. He had accumulated considerable wealth, and had about four hundred slaves.

Burnes tells us Murad styled himself Mir, and that he had conquered his neighbours on various sides. He was master of the valley of the Upper Oxus and its tributary rivers; had captured Balkh, which he sacked, and carried off great part of the people to his other conquests. He also reduced all Badakhshan, and was engaged when Burnes was there against the hill states north of the Oxus. The district of Kulab, one of these, lying between Darwaz and Shughnan, was already in his possession. His power extended southwards to Sighan, within

---

thirty miles of Bamian and across two of the passes of the Hindoo Kush.

Sighan, when Burnes passed through it, was immediately subject to Muhammed Ali bek, who he says was alternately dependent on Kabul and Kunduz. He satisfied the chief of Kabul with a few horses and his Kunduz lord with a few men captured in forays by his sons and officers. These captives were Hazarahs, who were carried off on the plea that they were Shias, and it would be well to convert them to orthodoxy. He was a tyrannical person and had shortly before laid his hand on some Jewesses, excusing himself by saying their progeny would become Muhammedans. Burnes satisfied him with a present of a nankeen pelisse, and a present of eight or nine rupees, being the usual tax paid by a caravan, and received a present of a leg of venison from the Khan, who was under the impression that the travellers were Armenians.*

North of the Sighan, and separated from it by a ridge called Dundan Shikun, or the tooth breaker, was the small principality of Kamard, governed by Rahmut ulla Khan, another dependent of Murad bi's. He was addicted to wine, and having been some time without it he pathetically exclaimed to Burnes that heaven and earth were the same to him without his dose.† As an instance of the tyrannical rule of these petty princes, Burnes mentions that not being able to make forays and alamans like his neighbour of Sighan, he, in order to satisfy his suzerain, deliberately seized the whole of the inhabitants of one village, and sent them all, men, women, and children, as slaves to Kunduz. Murad bi duly rewarded him with three additional villages.‡ Let us now return to the latter's history.

Speaking of his character, Burnes says he was at once cruel and indulgent; he encouraged all the plunderers who left his country and shared their spoil. His policy of removing whole populations from one province to another, and especially from a healthy to a pestilential one, and his raids on the Hazarahs and Kaffirs were the chief instances of his tyranny, otherwise traders were well treated and duties were low, those on shawls and silk being entirely remitted. He was very jealous of the English, was about fifty years of age, tall in stature, and with the features of a genuine Uzbeg; his eyes were small to deformity, his forehead broad and frowning, and his whole countenance repulsive. He was not however addicted to excesses, like his contemporary at Bukhara. He had two sons, one of whom was then eighteen.§

About two years after Burnes' visit, and in the end of October, 1836, an envoy arrived at Kabul from Murad bi, with a present of a dozen horses for Dost Muhammed. Murad bi's brother Muhammed had long been a victim to ophthalmia; shrines had been visited and charms essayed, but all in vain, when the news of a British mission being

---

* Op. cit., i., 289-291.   † Id., 193.   ‡ Id., 194.   § Id., ii., 352, 353.

at Kabul reached Kunduz. Thereupon Mirza Buddi, the confidant and physician of Murad bi, was sent to bring the Feringhi hakim, or English doctor, over the Hindu Kush.* Captain Burnes, who was then at Kabul, determined to utilise the opportunity, and accordingly sent Lieutenant Wood (to whom we owe the famous memoir on the Oxus country) and Dr. Lord on a mission thither.† On their arrival they were graciously received in durbar by Murad bi, and after a letter from Burnes had been read aloud, a piece of Russian loaf sugar was placed before the travellers, and their presents were produced. Wood says that a spying glass and some bottles of essential oils and other restoratives particularly pleased the Mir. The bottles were duly labelled in the chief's presence. In the reception room the beks were seated in rows on one side of the room, and below them, on another level, were the Mir's personal attendants and slaves. Opposite, stretched out on a coloured felt, and leaning on a large silken pillow, was Murad bi himself. All the beks present were old men.‡ Wood compares his host, who had carved such a large fortune for himself, with Muhammed Ali in Egypt, and Runjet Singh in Hindostan. His power was absolute, and his tribe was devotedly attached to him, and seldom mentioned his name without adding, *May God add to his riches.* With the Tajiks, whom he subdued, he was not so popular, but they also acknowledged his great abilities. When he conquered his neighbours he razed every hill fort which fell into his hands, reserving the Uzbeg strongholds in the plain, which he committed to members of his own family or devoted adherents. Wood speaks of the rigid equity of his proceedings among his own people, notwithstanding the desolating wars he carried on outside his borders. Offenders never escaped punishment; theft and highway robbery within their own country were invariably punished with death. In consequence of this rigid discipline crime was greatly diminished.§ He also reports the strong predestination which prevailed among his subjects. Having one day deplored the untimely end of a chief whom Murad bi had put to death, an Uzbeg called out, *His time had come, spare your pity, for nothing happens that is not ordained.*‖ Murad bi's brother's case was well nigh hopeless. The sight of one eye had entirely gone and the other was fast waning, and the doctor had to have recourse to a good Mussulman habit of supplementing his own skill by declaring that cures were in the hands of heaven.¶ Wood himself obtained permission to survey the upper country of the Oxus. He found Talikan ruled by Murad's son, who was styled Atalik. He describes him as like his father in appearance. He was charged with the surveillance over Muhammed Shah and his two brothers, the sons of the dispossessed ruler of Badakhshan.** Wood paid the Khoja who had treated Moorcroft so well, a visit. He then went on

---

* Wood's Oxus, 177. † Id., 118. ‡ Id., 137. § Id., 139, 140.
‖ Id., 142. ¶ Id., 145. ** Id., 155.

to Kila Afghan, where in 1823 the people of Badakhshan, under Miriar beg Khan, made their last stand against Murad bi. The latter had 10,000 men with him, the Badakhshis about 9,000. They were charged and dispersed, 300 of them being killed, but it was not till two years later that the country was annexed,[*] and in 1829 Murad transported a large portion of its inhabitants.[†] Wood went as far as Wakhan, which was ruled by Muhammed Rahim bek, who claimed descent from Alexander the Great, and who was nominally a subject and tributary of Murad bi.[‡] The latter was not pleased at the tone of independence he had shown, and Wood, who found him preparing to start on a visit to Kunduz, seems to have warned him of his danger, and he describes how he set out with his half-savage escort of armed, skin-clad followers.[§] On arriving at Kunduz the Wakhan chief was well treated, but when, instead of paying his arrears of tribute, he offered only a paltry present, Murad bi had him confined, and then tried. His fate was predetermined, and at a word from the Amir a courtier, whose father had been killed in Wakhan, clove him to the ground with a wooden billet, bespattering with brains those near him. " Kub kurde, kub kurde "— " Well done, well done"—shouted the savage ruler from his musnid.[‖]

Speaking of the vast transportations of people which Murad bi carried out, Wood says, " The aggregate of foreigners thus forcibly planted to these unhealthy marshes from the year 1830 to the present time (*i.e.*, 1838) is estimated by the Uzbegs at 25,000 families, or in round numbers 100,000 souls, and I question whether of these 6,000 were alive in 1838, so great had been the mortality in the space of eight years. Truly may the proverb say, ' If you wish to die, go to Kunduz.' Twelve months antecedent to our visit a great portion of the inhabitants of Kulab were brought from their own hilly country down to Hazrat Imaum. Dr. Lord and myself walked over the ground which their straw kirgahs had covered and where some still stood ; but silence, and the numerous graves around, told us the fate of their numerous inmates."[¶]

Dr. Lord's patients, Murad's brother and nephew did not recover. The Amir insisted upon the boy being handed over to a native doctor, who prescribed an oil bath, and under whose hands he perished. " His time had come," was the philosophical reflection which covered the reputation of both the native and Feringhi doctor. The death of the prince was followed, soon after Wood's departure, by that of Muhammed beg, the Mir of Hazrat Imaum, Murad's brother. He had been an incorrigible patient, and we are told that while Dr. Lord prescribed for his indigestion he continued to gorge himself with sour milk, hard boiled eggs, and rich pilaf. He set him to rights three times, and each time his indiscretion brought on a relapse.[**]

It is not known when the potent chief, who so cruelly devastated the country south of the Oxus, died, but it was probably about 1840. He was succeeded by Muhammed Amin bek, who adopted the style of Mir Vali. He was the son of Kilij Khan, and had governed Khulm during Murad bi's reign.* He is doubtless the Muhammed Ahmed mentioned by Moorcroft, and he was the ruler of these countries when Ferrier passed through them in 1845. He then had a standing army of 8,000 horse and 3,000 foot ; of the last 800 were sarbasis or regulars. He also had ten guns, served by some escaped Sepoys from India and some Imaks. Mir Vali's son, Genj Ali Beg, was governor of Badakhshan, and Mir Rustem Khan, Murad bi's son, governed Kunduz in his name.† Balkh, which had been the alternate victim of the rulers of Bukhara and Kunduz, now acknowledged Mir Vali, and was governed for him by Ishan Suddur,‡ and the ruler of Andkhud also acknowledged his supremacy.§

Ibak, when Ferrier passed through it in 1845, was occupied by the Uzbeg tribe Kankali, whose chief was subservient to the ruler of Khulm, and paid him dues under the name of presents.|| Mahmud Khan, the governor of Sirpul, was the Vali's son-in-law, and one of his best and most faithful allies.¶ He was of Uzbeg descent, but as his ancestors for several generations had allied themselves with Persian women, his countenance had largely lost its Turanian appearance. His influence extended far among the Imaks of the Paropamisus, among whom he was dreaded for his great daring and bravery. He kept up a standing army of 2,000 horse and 2,000 foot, which number he could treble when necessary.** He wished General Ferrier to mediate an alliance with the English on his behalf, only he begged " he would not do so in Asiatic fashion, by retaining half the subsidy he expected from Calcutta."††

From the facts here quoted and from the number of his dependents it will be gathered that Mir Vali was a very powerful chief, and held sway over quite as great, if not a greater breadth of country than Murad bi.

Although the Afghans had been so long deprived of authority in this district of the Upper Oxus, they had not finally abandoned hopes of recovering it, and it was at length recovered by their famous ruler Dost Muhammed.

When the latter declared war against Nasrulla, the Amir of Bukhara, he asked permission from the Vali to march through his territory, but was sharply refused, being told that to grant the request would be to surrender the sovereignty of his country, for the Afghans would ravage and keep it if they were strong enough. Dost Muhammed replied, that what was denied in friendship should be taken by force.‡‡ Besides this

---

* Ferrier's Travels, 210, 211. † Id., 211. ‡ Id., 208. § Id., 203. || Id., 215.
¶ Id., 225. ** Id. †† Id., 206, 207. ‡‡ Id., 213.

reason he was pressed on by his son Akbar Khan, who during his exile at
Khulm became enamoured of a female slave belonging to Mir Vali, whom
he carried off to Kabul, but she managed to escape and returned to her
former master, who scarcely ever allowed her out of his presence. As
he refused to surrender her, Akbar Khan was clamorous for war. The
army of Kabul was commanded by the Sirdar Akrem Khan, while
another son of Dost Muhammed occupied the hilly country in front of
Bamian. The forces of Khulm were posted in a difficult district beyond
Sighan, and several engagements were fought between the two. This
happened while Ferrier was in the country in 1845.* The war was
a protracted one, and ended in the complete victory of the Afghans,
who in 1850 crossed the Hindu Kush and conquered Balkh. In 1859
they also recovered Kunduz, and the Uzbeg possessions south of the
Oxus now became known as Afghan Turkestan. Badakhshan was also
conquered, and a descendant of its old princes, Jehandar Shah was
placed on its throne as the *protegé* of the Afghans.

On the death of Dost Muhammed, his son Afzul Khan was living at
Balkh, as governor of this district, and in 1854, he in concert with his
brother Azim rebelled against Shere Ali, their older brother, who was
the Amir of the Afghans. The rebellion was crushed, and Afzul was
reinstated in his position at Balkh : this was in 1864. His son Abdur
Rahman had meanwhile fled to Bukhara, where he married the Amir's
daughter. Suspecting this flight to be part of some organised plot,
Shere Ali seized upon Afzul and imprisoned him. Abdur Rahman now
incited the Amir of Bukhara to assist him. He corrupted Shere Ali's
representative in Afghan Turkestan, and secured the loyalty of his best
general, Muhammed Rafik. He was also joined by Azim Khan, who had
for some time been a refugee on English soil, and speedily secured Kabul
and severely defeated Shere Ali : this was in 1866. Afzul was released
and for a short time adopted the style of Amir at Kabul. Shere Ali now
repaired to Herat and raised another army, but was again defeated.
Three days after the battle Afzul died, and was succeeded at Kabul
by Azim. Meanwhile, Kandahar and Herat remained faithful to
Shere Ali, and in the spring of 1868 he once more set out. This time,
as is well known, he was successful. Azim was driven into exile and
shortly after died in Persia. Abdur Rahman was also driven away; he
fled to Meshed, whence he sent messengers to Samarkand to ask the
Russian authorities if he might shelter there, and receiving a favourable
answer went to Tashkend in March, 1870. He eventually took up his
residence at Samarkand, and received a pension of 25,000 roubles a year
from the Russians. He was visited by Schuyler, who describes him as
tall and well built, with a large head, and a marked Afghan, almost a
Jewish face. He wore long locks of hair at the side, and a full curly

---

* *Id.,* 214.

black beard, and was dressed in a long dark Kaftan, with wide silver galloon, and frogs of silver braid, a highly wrought silver belt and silver-mounted sabre, and wore a white turban striped with blue on his head. He spoke to Mr. Schuyler in bitter terms about Shere Ali.[*]

Abdur Rahman evidently has his hopes fixed still on the Afghan throne, and his future may yet be determined by the condition of Afghan Turkestan and Badakhshan, which have always been uneasy under the Afghan yoke. He is the son-in-law of the Amir of Bukhara and also of Jehander Shah, the former ruler of Badakhshan, who still aspires to recover his position there. Jehandar was driven away from Badakhshan in 1867, by his nephew, Mahmud Shah, who married Shere Ali's daughter, and who took his place and became an Afghan feudatory. The result of his intrigues will depend largely on the policy of Russia whose guest he is, but it is not very hopeful to read M. Terentief expressing a wish that there may be constant rebellions in these northern districts of Afghanistan, until the Amir of Kabul is compelled to withdraw his troops from Badakhshan.[†]

BADAKHSHAN.

A few words will suffice to relate the story of Badakhshan, so far as it concerns our present object. Like the country bordering it on the west, Badakhshan was conquered by the Uzbegs, and formed a government dependent on the Khanate of Bukhara. The old race of Kings who reigned there when Marco Polo, and still later when Baber wrote, claimed like the petty princes, further east, to descend from Alexander, but this dynasty was displaced by the Uzbegs, and its later rulers like many others who founded more or less independent principalities, on the decay of the Bukharian Khanate, were doubtless of Uzbeg descent. Colonel Yule says they were Sahib Zadahs of Samarkand who were invited to go there about the middle of the seventeenth century.[‡] I don't know on what authority this is stated, but it is very clear that it was not till much later, and after Nadir Shah's death that an independent principality arose here, and Moorcroft was expressly told by a Badakhshan prince, that his family had only been settled there about a century.[§] The first sovereign of this dynasty I find recorded was Yar bek, who is mentioned as the founder of the dynasty and the builder of Faizabad. Sultan Shah ruled there when the Chinese overthrew the domination of the Khojas at Kashgar. Khan Khoja who had been driven thence, sought refuge at Badakhshan with 40,000 of his people. His wealth and his harem attracted the cupidity of Sultan Shah, who attacked him at Reishkhan, and his people were defeated. On suing for his life in vain, he cursed Badakhshan, and prayed it might be three times depopulated, and that

* Schuyler, i., 261.   † Id., ii., 312-316.   ‡ Marco Polo, i., 168.
§ Moorcroft's Travels, 481, 482.

not even a dog might be left in it alive.* A few years later, namely, about 1765, Badakhshan with the other districts south of the Oxus was conquered by the famous Afghan ruler Ahmed. On this occasion, Sultan Shah was put to death, and the Afghans carried off from Faizabad a famous holy relic in the shirt of Muhammed.† The Munshi Faiz Buksh promised in his memoir to publish the materials he had collected for the history of Bulkh and Badakhshan,‡ but this valuable work has apparently not been done, and I have no notice of the district till about 1812, when Izzet ulla passed that way. He tells us Mir Muhammed Shah who then ruled was the son of Sultan Shah.§ A few years later, namely, 1823, Badakhshan was invaded by Murad bi of Khulm, who defeated its ruler Miriar Beg Khan, at Kila Afghan.‖ The district was finally conquered about 1829. Thereupon Miriar's brother Mir Muhammed Riza Bek went to live at Talikan, and was there visited by Moorcroft.¶ Two other fugitives were Muhammed Shah and his younger brother, the sons of the late Shah. They were also given a residence at Talikan, Wood saw them there, and says though poor and unfortunate the family was much respected by their countrymen, among whom Muhammed the head of the house was still honoured with the title of Shah or King.** For a long interval Badakhshan remained subject to the ruler of Kunduz. I have mentioned how about 1859, Jehandar Shah a descendant of the old princes was reinstated there as the dependant of the Afghans.†† His dependence was very nominal however, for he seems not to have paid tribute. Although he was a drunkard and a dissolute person, the country prospered under him. He was on friendly terms with Abdur Rahman, and jealous of the latter's rival Shere Ali. One of Major Montgomery's sappers was present at an interview between him and the ruler of Chitral, when an alliance was apparently cemented against Kabul. The former had 2,000 horsemen with him and the latter 700. The Chitral chief gave his friend twenty-one slaves and also his daughter in marriage to his son, while Jehandar presented him with sixty chogas of Bukhara manufacture, two swords and a horse.‡‡ Jehandar was displaced as ruler of Badakhshan in 1861 by his nephew Mahmud, a partisan of Shere Ali.§§ Manphul thus enumerates the various divisions of Badakhshan and its dependencies. Faizabad and Jirm directly dependent on Mahmud. Daraim, Shahr i buzurg, Gumbaz, Farakhar, Kishm, Rustak, Rushan, Shaghnan, Ish kasham, Wakhan, Zebak, Minjan, Ragh, Daung, and Asiabi. All these dependencies were either held by Mahmud's relatives, or by hereditary rulers, with a feudal tenure, conditional on fidelity to him and rendering military service.

---

* Wood's Oxus, 162.   † Id., xxxvi.   ‡ Jour. Roy. Geog. Soc., xlii., 473.
§ Journ. Asiat. Soc., vii., 304 and 333.   ‖ Wood's Oxus, 159.   ¶ Op. cit., 487.
** Wood's Oxus, 156.   †† Ante, 864.   ‡‡ Journ. Roy. Geog. Soc., xlii., 199.   §§ Id., 197.

MEIMENEH.

After the death of Nadir Shah and the elevation of Ahmed Shah to the throne of Kabul, an Uzbeg soldier of fortune named Haji Khan was appointed by the latter governor of Meimeneh, on condition of furnishing a contingent of troops. He took up his residence at Balkh, and nominated one of his relatives as his deputy at Meimeneh. He was succeeded by his son Jan Khan, who was forced to fly from Balkh by an outbreak of the inhabitants, and withdrew to Meimeneh. On his death in 1790, there was a dispute among his sons for the inheritance; one of them was blinded, another perished in an outbreak, while the youngest, named Ahmed, governed Meimeneh from 1798 to 1810. He was killed in an insurrection and his eldest son, Mizrab Khan, fled for refuge to the tomb of Ali, near Balkh, while his cousin Allah Yar Khan occupied the throne from 1810 to 1826, when he died of cholera.*

He was apparently succeeded by Mizrab Khan, who was poisoned by one of his wives. This happened shortly before Ferrier passed through the town, where he found his two sons Ukmet Khan and Shere Khan fighting for the succession. The former, who was the elder of the two, much preferred wine to business, and would have abandoned his claims, but those about him would not consent to his doing so. This struggle led to much misery, and Yar Muhammed, the Afghan ruler of Herat, and nominal suzerain of the place, interfered to settle the dispute. It was arranged that Ukmet should continue to rule over the mercantile and agricultural population, while Shere Khan should reside in the citadel and command the army, a plan by which the latter was virtually given control of the state.† Yar Muhammed, apparently, really controlled the affairs of Meimeneh till his death, in 1853, when it again became independent.‡ Ukmet Khan was by order of his brother hurled down from the walls of the citadel, "so that," as he said, "his abler son might be placed at the head of affairs." This brother was named Murza Yakub, and was still living when Vambery traversed the district. His nephew, for whose interests he was so solicitous, was named Hussein Khan, and was largely in his hands. Yakub held the post of vizier, and is described as a person of handsome presence. Instead of inflicting corporal punishment or imposing fines, he sent culprits to be sold in the slave markets of Bukhara.§ The little Khanate, although surrounded by such powerful neighbours, had very largely preserved its independence, and been especially successful against Dost Muhammed, of Afghanistan. On his death, the Amir of Bukhara sent its young Khan a subsidy of 10,000 tillas, and a request that he should join his forces with those of Bukhara, and make a common attack on the Afghans. Hussein Khan was too

* Schefer, Abdul Kerim, 262, 263.   † Ferrier's Travels, 197, 198.
‡ Id., 204. Note.   § Vambery, Travels, 249.

impatient to wait. He set out on his own account, captured several small places, and ornamented the gate of his fortress with three hundred long-haired Afghan skulls. When Vambery was there in 1863 he was preparing for another campaign.[*]

ANDKHUD OR ANDKHOI.

Andkhud is situated between Herat and Bukhara, and is accounted as belonging to Khorasan. It retained its allegiance to the Afghans for a long time, and the Khutbeh was said in the name of Timur Shah, on whose behalf it was governed by Rahmet Ulla of the tribe Afshar. He was killed in a struggle with the troops of Shah Murad bi, of Bukhara, and was succeeded by his son Ilduz Khan.[†] Ilduz was ruling there when Izzet ulla travelled in these parts.[‡] He had a body of 1,000 troops, and seems to have secured a practical independence, for, Schefer says, he paid no one tribute.[§] Andkhud remained tolerably flourishing till about the year 1840, when it was dependent on Bukhara. Yar Muhammed besieged it when on his way to Oxus, and captured it after a siege of four months. It was then plundered and reduced to a heap of ruins, and the greater part of the inhabitants who would not otherwise escape, were put to death by the Afghans. When Vambery visited it, its governor Gazanfer Khan was a *protégé* of the Afghans, and at issue with the rulers of Bukhara and Meimeneh.[‖] He says the town then contained about 2,000 houses and 3,000 tents scattered about, and its population was about 15,000, principally Turkomans. Its climate is notoriously bad, and is summed up in a Persian verse. "Andkhoi has bitter salt water, scorching sand, venomous flies, and even scorpions. Vaunt it not for it is the picture of a real hell." It was there that Moorcroft died, apparently of fever.[¶]

SHABIRGHAN.

Shabirghan was long the seat of a petty principality. Izzet ulla calls it Shirghan, and tells us that it was ruled by Iraj Khan.[**] When Ferrier was in these parts, its ruler was Rustem Khan. He had married a daughter of Misrab Khan Vali of Meimeneh, and inflated by this match proceeded to turn Kazanfer Khan Afshar, a *protégé* of the Amir of Bukhara, out of Andkhud. The Amir persuaded Mir Vali of Khulm to reinstate Kazanfer, who handed the business over to his son-in-law, Mahmud Khan, of Sirpul. The latter formed a league with the governors of Mazar, Balkh, and Akshi, and marched against Andkhud and Shabirghan. Rustem had appointed as his deputy at Andkhud, Sufi

[*] *Id.*, 245, 246.   [†] Schefer, op. cit., 246.   [‡] Journ. Roy. Asiat. Soc., vii., 333.
            [§] Op. cit., 249.   [‖] Vambery, Travels, 241.
        [¶] *Id.*, 240.   [**] Journ. Roy. Asiat. Soc., vii., 333.

Khan Afshar, the nephew of Kazanfer. This prince was made over to the enemy, while Rustem Khan himself was made by the inhabitants whose crops had been ravaged, and who were suffering from want, to surrender. Kazanfer having regained possession of Andkhud, declared himself the vassal of Mir Vali of Khulm, regardless altogether of the ruler of Bukhara. Shabirghan was surrendered to Mahmud Khan, of Sirpul, who appointed his brother Hussein its governor, and Rustem and Sufi were sent prisoners to Bukhara. The Bukharian ruler felt he had been duped, and assisted Rustem to recover his own, but shortly after the Afghan prince Yar Muhammed Khan arrived from Herat with 20,000 men, and subdued Meimeneh, Andkhud, Akshi, and Shabirghan, which remained subject to him till his death, in 1853.* They then remained independent for a short time, but except Meimeneh, were speedily conquered again by Dost Muhammed, and have since remained more or less dependent on the Afghans.

SIRPUL.

The history of the little principality of Sirful is very obscure. When Ferrier passed through it, its governor was Mahmud Khan, who was the son-in-law of the Mir Vali, of Khulm. As it is not mentioned in the notices of Izzet ulla, nor by Schefer's authorities, it had probably but recently become independent, and doubtless formed part of Khulm during the reign of Murad bi. Mahmud Khan's influence we are told extended far among the Imaks of the Paropamisus, and he controlled a force of 2,000 horse and 2,000 foot soldiers.† Sirpul fell under Afghan rule like its neighbours, in the reign of Dost Muhammed.

I have thus surveyed the meagre annals of the various Uzbeg principalities of any note, which were formed out of the ruins of the old Bukharian Empire. The greater part of them are now nominally at least subject to the Afghans, but this has been only a recent conquest on the part of the latter, and they bear their yoke uneasily. How far it is prudent or wise that England should insist as she has done, that they should be treated as an integral part of Afghanistan, is a question of politics and not of ethnography or history, but it may be pointed out as beyond question that from the point of view of both race and history, the dominant populations of these principalities are drawn towards Bukhara, rather than Kabul.

Note I.—The title Atalik occurs frequently in the later history of Bukhara. Senkofski says this title answers to the title Lala Pasha at the court of Constantinople. He says the Khans of Kipchak and the kings of Georgia also had their ataliks. Originally the duties of the Atalik consisted in super-

---

intending the education of the heir to the throne and looking after his household. Afterwards the Atalik became one of the chief dignities of the court, almost equal to those of Divan begi and Grand Visier, and eventually having become hereditary and fallen into vigorous hands, the holders of the post became the virtual rulers of the country, like the Merovingian mayors of the palace, and succeeded like them as we have seen in usurping the chief authority in the state.* It will be remembered that the recent famous ruler of Kashgar styled himself Atalik Gazi.

Note 2.—The Seyids and Khojas occupy such a prominent position in the history of Central Asia, that it is well to remember who they were. The Seyids according to M. Schefer were all who claimed descent from the Khalifs Osman and Ali, through the daughters of the Prophet. The Khojas claimed descent from the Khalifs, Abu bekhr and Omar by other women than the daughters of the Prophet. The Seyids had precedence of the Khojas. The latter were divided into two categories, the Khojas Seyid Ata who possessed deeds proving their descent, and the Khojas Juibari whose title deeds were lost and could only appeal to tradition and repute.†

Note 3.—I have by inadvertence omitted in the notice of Bukhara reference to the visits paid to it by three early English travellers. The first of these was Anthony Jenkinson, who was there in 1558. He reached Bukhara, which he calls Bogar, on the 23rd of December in that year. He describes in his quaint language the appearance and manners of the place. *Inter alia*, he tells us its king had little power or wealth, his revenue being small and being derived from the exactions he made from his subjects. Craftsmen and merchants had to pay a tax for the things they sold, "and when he lacketh money," says our traveller, "he sendeth his officers to the shops of the said merchants, to take their wares to pay his debts, and will have credit of force." The coins were of silver and copper, each of the former being worth twelve English pence, and of the latter which were called puls, one-tenth of a penny. The king caused the value of the silver money to rise and fall according to his caprice, "not caring to oppress his people, for that he looketh not to reign above two or three years before he be either slain or driven away, to the great destruction of the country and merchants."‡

Jenkinson had an audience with the Khan, to whom he presented a letter from the Tsar, and by whom he was treated "most gently, and was caused to eat in his presence, and he divers times devised with him familiarly in his secret chamber, as well of the power of the Great Turks, as of the countries laws and religions of Europe, and he caused him to shoot in handguns before him and did himself practice the use of them, but after all this great entertainment before his departure, he showed himself a very Tartar, for he went to the wars owing him money, and saw him not paid before his departure."§ He nevertheless praises him for having punished some marauders who had attacked him *en route*, and caused all four of them to be hanged at his palace gate, as he says, "because they were gentlemen, to the example of others."‖

---

* Senkofski, Supplement. Note, 33.   † Schefer's Abdul Kerim, xcv. Note, 1.
‡ Hakluyt, Voyages, i., 370, 371.   § *Id.*, 371.   ‖ *Id.*, 372.

He speaks of the rigid discipline maintained in the Khanate, especially in regard to intoxicating liquors, and draws a curious picture showing the embarrassment of on the one hand drinking water which bred the famous long worms of Bukhara, which burrow under the skin and of being beaten by the police for drinking strong drink. He tells us the Metropolitan, *i.e.*, the head of the priesthood, had more power than the Khan, and could displace him, having done so with the predecessor of the then ruler " whom he betrayed, and in the night slew him in his chamber, who was a prince that loved all Christians well."* Having been warned that he had better return as there was a danger of the city being attacked, he set out on the 8th of March, 1559, accompanied by envoys from the rulers of Bukhara and Balkh to the Russian Emperor, and by a caravan of 600 camels. Ten days after his departure he tells us the king of Samarkand went with an army and besieged the said city of Bogar, the king being absent and gone to the wars against another prince, his kinsman, " as the like chanceth in those countries once in two or three years. For it is a marvel if the king reigns there above three or four years."†

In 1746, the enterprising agents of the British factory in Russia tried to establish a trade with Khiva and Bukhara, and accordingly Messrs. Thompson & Hogg made their way to the former town, whence Mr. Thompson went to Bukhara, intending to return home through Persia and by the Caspian. He arrived there safely, and tells us the Khan had little authority beyond the city, the adjacent district being governed by several beks, independent of each other and of the Khan. He tells us how the natives imported rhubarb, musk, and castorium, and many other valuable drugs from the Black Kalmuks and Tashkend, and that formerly they received lapis lazuli and other precious stones from Badakhshan, but that the route thither was then much interrupted by robbers. Mr. Thompson tells us they used gold and copper coins of their own, but that the silver used there was Persian and Indian.‡

Burnes was at Bukhara in 1832. On arriving there he was introduced to the Kush begi, an elderly man who occupied a small room in the palace, and who desired Burnes to seat himself on the pavement outside. The latter presented him with a silver watch and Cashmere shawl, and afterwards with a valuable compass, which he explained as an instrument that would always point in the direction of Mekka. He describes the motley crowd he met in the Righistan; Persians, Turks, Russians, Tartars, Chinese, Hindoos and Afghans, Turkomans, Kalmuks and Kazaks, Jews and Armenians. Each one who visited the Khan was accompanied by a slave. His account of Bukharian life is picturesque. He saw the Khan visit the Great Mosque on a Friday, and tells us he was about thirty years of age, with a gaunt and pale face, small eyes, and forbidding look. He was dressed in a silken robe of " adrus," with a white turban, and sometimes he wore an aigrette of feathers ornamented with diamonds. The Koran was carried before him, and he was preceded and followed by two golden mace bearers, who called out in Turkish, " Pray to God that the Commander of the Faithful may act justly." His suite

* *Id.,* 371.   † *Id.,* 373.   ‡ Hanway's Travels, i., 242-244.

consisted of about 100 persons, who were dressed in robes of Russian brocade, and wore gold ornamented daggers. The people drew aside as he passed, stroked their beards and wished him peace. Suspicion surrounded his daily life. The water he drank was taken in skins from the river under the charge and seal of two officers. It was first tasted by the vizier and his men and then again sealed. The meals he ate were similarly tested, an hour being allowed to pass to see the effects before the box in which they were kept was unlocked. Of this box the Khan had one key and the vizier the other. Fruit, sweetmeats, &c., were all tasted, and Burnes remarks that it must have been difficult for him to have a hot meal. It was a recognised custom in taking food from a person to present the giver with some first as a precaution.[*]

As an instance to be added to the many previously quoted, of the rigid Muhammedanism then prevailing at Bukhara, Burnes describes how one day a Mollah who had violated the law went to the Khan, stated his crime, and demanded justice according to the Koran. Twice was he bidden to depart, but the third time having upbraided the king for his remissness in dispensing justice and entreated that it might bring him punishment in this world instead of the next, the Council of Ulemas was summoned, and he was duly condemned to be stoned to death. Turning his face towards Mekka and drawing his garments over his head he repeated the well known phrase, "There is but one God and Muhammed is his Prophet," and met his fate, the Khan throwing the first stone. When dead he wept over his corpse, ordered it to be washed and buried, and read the funeral service over the grave. On another occasion a son who had cursed his mother similarly demanded punishment, and although she entreated for him he was executed as a criminal, according to his own wish. A merchant from China having imported some pictures, they were immediately broken by order of the Government, as against the express orders of the Koran, and their value was returned to the owner. In view of this rigid adherence to the law, there is something pathetic in the exclamation of a Bukharian when told the Russians had recently found some gold veins between their country and Bukhara. "The ways of God he said are unsearchable which concealed these treasures from the true believers, and have now revealed them near the very surface of the earth to the Kaffirs."[†]

For an admirable description of the internal government and general polity of Bukhara, I must refer to Khanikof's work so often cited in the previous pages.

Note 4.—The account of the topography of Bukhara and its borders I shall remit to the next volume, which will deal more largely with this district, and now limit myself to a description of Khokand, which is a purely Uzbeg town of quite a modern date, being not much more than 100 years old. Mr. Schuyler has described it in his usual picturesque phrases. "From its being more modern it has wider streets, and is more spacious than most Asiatic towns. It is nearly square in form, and is said to contain 500 mosques, which with an average of thirty houses to a parish gives a population of about 75,000. From the roof of the caravanserai where Schuyler stayed, he tells us he could

---

see the whole city spread out, in continuous lines of broad flat clay roofs, most
of the bazaars also being covered so as to give an easy passage from one end of
the town to the other. Near by was a group of mosques and medresses, built
of reddish grey brick, with high melon-shaped domes, the cornices covered
with blue and white tiles forming texts from the Koran. In front was the bridge
Kush-kupriuk, with its bold arch over the little stream which divides the city,
while above it stood out the large Medressi Khan. To the left were the
beautiful facade and portal of the Khan's palace, glittering in all the brightness
of its fresh tiles, blue, yellow, and green, which had only recently been built.
All around were clay roofs half hidden by foliage, and surrounding all, gardens
and orchards, backed up in the distance by mountains."*

" In a large open space at the end of the bazaar are two large Medressis or
colleges, well built of burnt brick, picked out with blue tiles, and surmounted
by domes and small blue turrets. One is called Ali, and was built by
Mussulman Kul. The other which is unfinished, was begun by the Khan's
brother, Sultan Murad bek, in fulfilment of some vow. Near the bridge above
named is the spacious Medressi Khan, built by Madali Khan, and containing
accommodation for 200 Mollahs. In the eastern part of the city is the
Medressi Mir, built by Narbuteh bi, and close by a cemetery formerly containing a famous monument put up by Madali Khan to one of his wives, with
the pathetic inscription :—

> I hope to see her at the resurrection,
> Her of lovely slender form,
> If I do not see her then,
> Go look after the judgment.

This monument was destroyed by the Amir of Bukhara when he took the city,
on the ground that it was improper thus to honour a woman."† Schuyler
visited the mint, the armoury, and paper manufactory. He says the chief
Bazaar at Khokand is very well built and regular, the streets crossing at
right angles, and with many of the shops built of burnt brick. The streets
are wide, and the whole is covered by a roof supported on timbers high up
above the houses, so that the bazaar itself is shaded, while plenty of resh air
comes in at the sides. There are two bazaar days weekly, namely on Sunday
and Thursday.‡ The Khan was the owner of the bazaars and drew a large
revenue from them, thus the Cocoon bazaar, which was only open for six or
seven weeks in the summer, brought in £810 a-year. The citadel there called
the urda, while at Bukhara it is called the ark. It is a large rectangular
building with high clay walls, containing several small courts and numerous
buildings. At the further extremity beyond the large court is the new palace,
the largest and most magnificent in Central Asia. It is a building of two or
three storeys high, with towers at the corners and two in the centre, the whole
front faced with glazed tiles, white, blue, and green, and a large inscription,
" Built by Seyid Muhammed Khudayar Khan in the year 1287," running along
the cornices.‡

---

* Op. cit., ii., 11, 12. † Id., 13. ‡ Id., 10.

40

Note 5.—Genealogy of the Khans of Bukhara and Khokand.

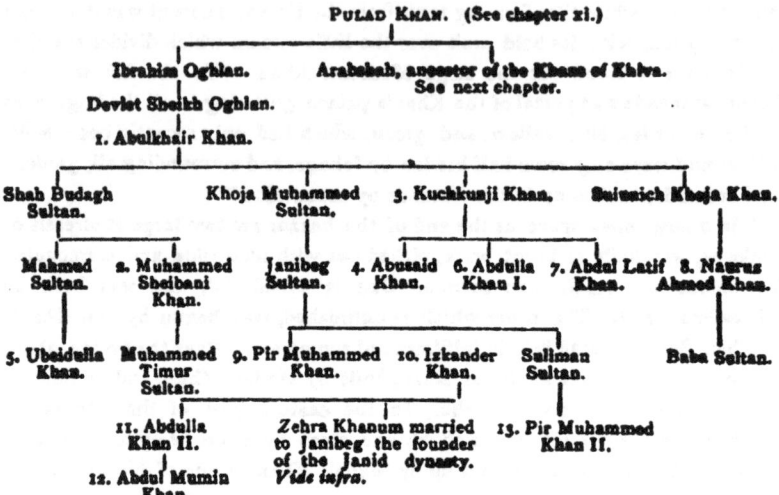

ABULKHAIRIDS.

PULAD KHAN. (See chapter xi.)

JANIDS OR MANGUTS.

Kuchuk Muhammed, Khan of the Golden Horde.

Chuvak Sultan.

Mangushlak.

Iskander, Khan of Bukhara. *Vide supra.*	Yar Muhammed Sultan.
Zehra Khanum.	Jan or Janibeg Sultan.

Dia Muhammed Sultan.   1. Baki Muhammed Khan.   2. Vali Muhammed Khan.

3. Seyid Imaum Kuli Khan.   4. Seyid Nadir Muhammed Khan.

Seyid Rejib Muhammed Sultan.   5. Seyid Abdul Asis Khan.   6. Seyid Sabhan Kuli Khan.

Seyid Ibrahim Sultan.   7. Seyid Ubeidulla Khan.   8. Seyid Abdulfais Khan.

11. Seyid Abulghasi Khan.

9. Seyid Abdul Mumin Khan.   10. Seyid Ubeidulla Khan.   Shems ban Aim married Shah Murad the father of Haidar, the founder of the Haidarid dynasty. *Vide infra.*

HAIDARIDS.

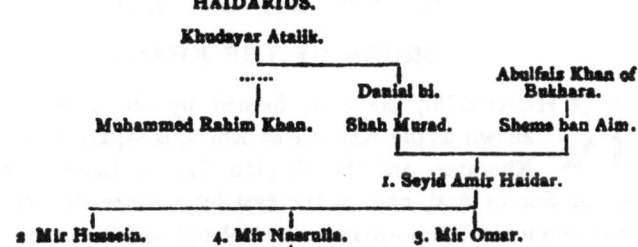

```
                      Khudayar Atalik.
         ┌──────────────┬──────────────────────────┐
      ......       Danial bi.           Abulfaiz Khan of
                                             Bukhara.
  Muhammed Rahim Khan.   Shah Murad.      Shems ban Aim.
                                   ┌──────────────┘
                          1. Seyid Amir Haidar.
         ┌─────────────────┬──────────────────────┐
    2 Mir Hussein.    4. Mir Nasrulla.        3. Mir Omar.
                    5. Mir Muzaffar eddin.
```

KHANS OF KHOKAND.

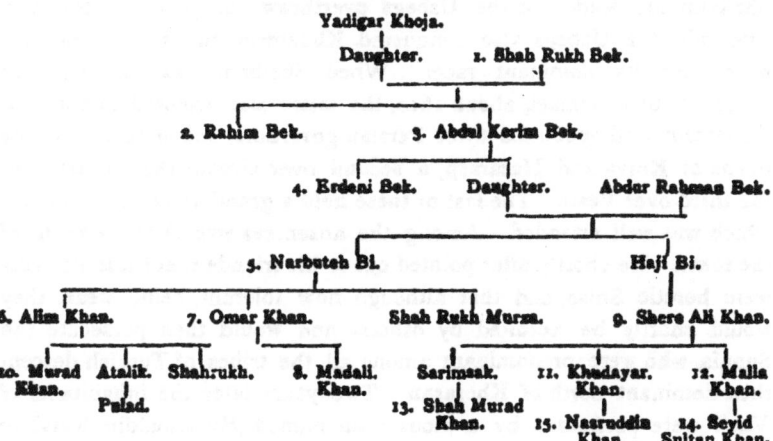

```
                  Yadigar Khoja.
              Daughter.   1. Shah Rukh Bek.
         ┌────────────────────┬──────────────┐
    2. Rahim Bek.        3. Abdul Kerim Bek.
              ┌──────────────┬────────────────────┐
        4. Erdeni Bek.   Daughter.        Abdur Rahman Bek.
         ┌──────────────────────────┐        ┌──────────┐
    5. Narbuteh Bi.                          Haji Bi.
  ┌──────────┬──────────────────────┐        ┌──────────┐
6. Alim Khan.  7. Omar Khan.   Shah Rukh Murza.   9. Shere Ali Khan.
┌────────┐  ┌──────────┐   ┌──────────┐  ┌──────────┐   ┌──────────┐
10. Murad  Atalik.  Shahrukh.   8. Madali.   Sarimsak.   11. Khudayar.   12. Malla
Khan.      Pulad.              Khan.                     Khan.          Khan.
                                    13. Shah Murad              ┌──────────┐
                                        Khan.          15. Nasruddin   14. Seyid
                                                           Khan.      Sultan Khan.
```

CHAPTER X.

KHUAREZM OR KHIVA.

ORIGIN OF THE KHANATE.

KHUAREZM, the oasis formed by the Lower Oxus and now known as the Khanate of Khiva, is separated by deserts from Khorasan and the Caspian Sea, is bounded on the north by the Sea of Aral, and on the east by another strip of desert which separates it from Transoxiana. Its isolated position has given it peculiar facilities for independence, and thus it comes about that except in the days of the early Mongol conquerors this island of verdure, surrounded by a sea of sand, has generally had a history of its own. When Sheibani the leader of the Uzbegs overthrew the power of the later Timurids, the Uzbegs also conquered Khuarezm, and since then they have been its dominant race. When Sheibani was defeated and killed by Shah Ismael, about 1610, the latter also acquired authority in Khuarezm, and appointed three Persian governors, one of them over the towns of Khiva and Hazarasp, a second over Urgenj the capital, and the third over Vesir. The last of these held a grand levée on his arrival which was well attended. Among the absentees was Omar, a kadhi of the town. He shortly after pointed out to his friends that these Persians were heretic Shias, and that although now tolerant, being weak, they would shortly be recruited by others, and would then persecute the Sunnis, who were predominant among all the tribes of Turkish descent then dominant north of Khorasan. Two years later the inhabitants of Vesir were persuaded by a pious man named Husamuddin Katal to raise Ilbars, the son of Bereke Sultan, an Uzbeg chief, to the dignity of Khan. Thus was founded a second Uzbeg state, largely conterminous in boundary and rival in policy to that of Bukhara. We will now revert somewhat in order to trace out the lineage of Ilbars Khan.

Ibrahim Oghlan, the grandfather of Abulkhair, ancestor of the Khans of Bukhara, had a brother named Arabshah, who occurs among the Khans of the Golden Horde. These two brothers we are told divided their father's heritage between them. Arabshah left a son Haji Tuli, called Tughluk Haji in the Sheibani Nameh. He had an only son Timur Sheikh who was killed by the Kalmuks. Irritated at them for having made a raid on his camp, he pursued them before his troops had assembled in sufficient numbers, and was defeated and killed. He died without leaving brother or son and his people were scattered. The Aksakals or grey beards of the Uighurs, one of the tribes which had obeyed him, went to say good-bye to his Khanum or chief widow. "The rest of the tribe have already departed," they said, "and we are about to follow them. As the Khan had many wives and concubines, see if one of them does not bear in her person some gauge of his affection. In case this be so we will not leave until the child is born." She replied that none of the other wives or concubines were *enceinte*, but that she had been so herself for three months. The Uighurs thereupon determined to stay, and the Naimans who were already some distance away also halted, pitched their camp apart, and awaited the birth of the infant. The other tribes entered the service of other princes.[*] This naïve story gives us a singularly forcible notion of the loyal attachment of the nomads to their royal house. But to continue the saga. Six months later a boy was born, who was named Yadigar. The Uighurs thereupon sent round messengers to the other tribes to ask for a suyunji, or "present for the good news." The Naimans sent a black horse, and then returned to the Ordu. On their arrival the mother took the child in her arms, and put him on the royal seat in his father's tent. The Uighurs, who wished to treat the Naimans as the honoured guests, ceded to them the position on the left side of the throne. Among the Mongols the left was deemed the more honourable side since the Almighty had put the heart there. Thenceforward the Naimans always had precedence, and took the position on the left flank.[†] The rest of Timur Sheikh's people also now returned, but the two tribes retained the honourable title of Karachi, *i.e.*, those faithful in adversity as well as in prosperity. Yadigar had four sons, Bereke, Abulek, Aminek, and Abak. In regard to the third of these names, Abulghazi has the interesting remark that at this epoch the Mongol language had not quite fallen into desuetude, and that Amin in Mongol means the same thing as Jan in Arabic, Hush in Tajik (*i.e.*, Persian), and Tin in Uzbeg (*i.e.*, Turki).[‡] The Sheibani Nameh calls the four brothers Burka, Abka, Ablak, and Ilpanek.[§] Bereke Sultan was famous both for his strength and courage, and it was reported of him that his chest was supported by a solid breastplate of bone, there being no separate parts as with other men.[‖] At this time Abulkhair Khan was acknowledged as supreme chief of the Desht Kipchak. About 1455, he sent Bereke Sultan in command of an army to support the son of Abdul Latif Khan of Bukhara. I have already described the issue of this campaign, and how it ended in the Uzbegs quarrelling with their *protégé*.[¶] They then plundered the district of Soghd, and returned home with camels heavily laden with booty.[**] Some time after, a struggle having commenced between two chiefs named Musabeg and Kujash Murza, who were apparently

[*] Abulghazi, 194, 195.   [†] *Id.*, 195.   [‡] *Id.*, 196.   [§] *Id.* Note.
[‖] *Id.*   [¶] *Ante*, 689.   [**] Abulghazi, 200.

Nogais, the latter won the day, whereupon Musa appealed to Bereke Sultan. He offered his assistance on condition that his father Yadigar was raised to the rank of Khan, and that Musa would consent to serve under him as one of his principal beks. This was agreed upon, and all Yadigar's people having been assembled, he was raised aloft on the white felt and duly proclaimed. Bereke now prepared to assist his friend, to whom he gave the command of the advance guard. It was winter, the deep snows impeded their march, their horses began to grow thin, and their provisions to fail. In vain his followers, backed up by Musa, urged him to retire. At length, mounting a hillock, Bereke noticed a number of tents in a valley beyond the Kir, or Ust Urt, which proved to belong to the people of Kujash Murza. He was captured and put to death, and his camp was plundered. Bereke Sultan married his daughter Malai Khanzadeh, and having spent the winter there, returned home again in the spring.* Yadigar Khan died a few years after this, and was speedily followed to the grave by Abulkhair Khan.

As I have mentioned, the death of the latter was the signal for the dispersal of his people, and, as reported by Abulghazi himself, Bereke Sultan came forward and joined in the scramble.† He quotes the cynical Uzbeg proverb, that "if you see an enemy harrying your father's house, you should join him and share the plunder."

Some years later, Sheibani, the grandson of Abulkhair, finding himself in winter quarters on the Lower Sir, near the camp of Bereke Sultan, ordered his men to mount in the night, and at daybreak to fall upon the tents of that chief. They had orders to secure him, and to neglect everything else. When the raid was made, Bereke was in his tent undressed. Hearing the tramp of horses' feet, he threw a sable cloak over his shoulders, escaped barefoot, and running over the ice hid among the reeds in the river. The cold was intense, and as he ran he trod on a broken reed, which wounded his foot.

Meanwhile, Sheibani's people, not having found the Sultan, scattered about in the hopes of tracing him. Some of them overtaking one of his people, an Inak of the Uighur tribe, named Munga, asked him where his master was; he said, I am he. He was thereupon seized and taken before Sheibani, who recognised him, and asked why he had done this. "I have long eaten his salt," said the faithful retainer; "I have shared his fatigue and dangers; I thought if I could detain a number of his pursuers he would have a better chance of escaping; as to the rest, you may do with me as you choose." Sheibani, pleased with his loyalty, set him at liberty, and gave him some presents. Meanwhile, his men continued the pursuit of the Sultan, and presently he was traced by the drops of blood from his wounded foot. He was taken before Sheibani, who put him to death, and plundered his camp. His widow fell to

---

* *Id.*, 201, 202.   † *Id.*, 203.

Khoja Muhammed Sultan, the second son of Abulkhair. She was already *enceinte*, and eventually gave birth to Janibeg, the grandfather of Abdulla Khan, as I have mentioned.[*]

Bereke Sultan left two sons, Ilbars and Balbars, the latter of whom was paralysed in both legs.

ILBARS KHAN.

I have already described how Ilbars was invited to occupy the throne of Khuarezm. Messengers were sent to bring him to Vezir, and he was told to conceal himself near that town until his friends were ready to help him. He accordingly set out with his brother Balbars. Meanwhile, the conspirators seized the gates, and made a general massacre of the Persians in the town, of whom only one escaped. The following day they conducted Ilbars to the palace of the late governor of the town, issued a proclamation to the surrounding districts, and the Uzbegs and Sarts joined in grand feast, where he was duly proclaimed Khan. Abulghazi dates this in 911 hej, *i.e.*, 1505, but this is clearly a mistake, for it happened sometime after the death of Sheibani in 1510, and the date ought possibly to be 921 hej. The towns of Yanghi Shehr and Tersek, dependent on Vezir, also submitted. Ilbars appointed his brother, Balbars, styled Bilikich, to rule the former, and having nominated a governor to the latter, fixed his residence at Vezir.[†]

The Persian who escaped went to Urgenj, where he informed the governor, Sultan Kuli the Arab, of what had taken place. He summoned the inhabitants, and told them he was prepared to go if they wished, but they declared the Uzbegs had only made a passing raid, and swore to assist him in repelling them.

Three months after the taking of Vezir, Ilbars advanced upon Urgenj. Sultan Kuli gave him battle outside the town, but was defeated. Ilbars pursued him into the place, where he was put to death with all his naukers.[‡] The Persian garrisons at Hazarasp and Khiva also consulted the Sarts as to what course should be taken, and the latter insisted on their remaining. Before he attacked those towns, Ilbars convoked a meeting of his own beks, and explained to them that he had only gone to Khuarezm with a few followers, and it would be better to summon his relatives so as to strengthen his hands. All apparently agreed except an old man of the Uighur tribe, who affirmed that among the Uzbegs the future greatness of a sovereign depended on his love for his dependants, while nepotism was a presage of evil, meaning doubtless that he should reward those who had borne the brunt of the fight and not go to the desert for objects of his favour. The last view did not prevail, and it was determined to send for recruits to the Desht Kipchak. The four sons of Yadigar Khan were now dead, but his

---

[*] *Ante, 691.* Abulghazi, 206.   [†] *Id.,* 212.   [‡] *Id.,* 213, 214.

grandsons were willing enough to go, and a son of Abulek Khan and six sons of Aminek Khan duly set out with their families and tribes. They settled at Urgenj, Ilbars remaining at Vezir. They so devastated the neighbourhood of Khiva and Hazarasp that those towns, as well as Kat, were abandoned by their defenders and fell into their hands, and they then proceeded to attack Khorasan. Shah Ismal was then dead, *i.e.*, it was after 1523, and the governors of the frontier districts north of the Khorasan mountains as far as Mehineh and Derun fled. The Uzbegs were now masters of a wide district, which they made a focus whence to plunder Khorasan and the Turkomans, and we are told that Ilbars' brother Balbars, whose legs were paralysed, was placed in a chariot drawn by swift horses, and distinguished himself in these raids riding at the head of his troops, ordering their tactics, and proving himself a famous archer.* Some of the Turkomans consented to pay tribute, while others remained hostile. Balbars died after a few years of this life, and was speedily followed by Ilbars, who left seven or eight sons, to each of whom, in memory of his victories over the Kizilbashis, he gave the soubriquet of Ghazi, while all the sons of Balbars were called Haji.†

SULTAN HAJI KHAN.

On the death of Ilbars, his nephew Sultan Haji, who was the oldest of the sultans, was sent for to Vezir, and duly appointed Khan, but the real power was in the hands of his cousin, Sultan Ghazi, who was a very wealthy and avaricious person, and who only resigned to Sultan Haji the title of Khan and the first mouthful at table. The latter reigned but a year, and then died.

HASSAN KULI KHAN.

On the death of Haji Khan, Hassan Kuli, the son of Abulek, and the oldest descendant of Yadigar, was appointed Khan, with his capital at Urgenj. The sons of Ilbars Khan and Avanek Khan grew jealous of him, and marched against him with an army greatly outnumbering his, with which they beleagured him at Urgenj, then without a citadel. He gave battle to them outside the town, his people being all on foot, and theirs mounted, and successfully resisted a fierce attack they made, in which Aghanai Sultan, the youngest son of Avanek Khan perished. The blockade of the town was very rigid, and at length a famine was imminent, the head of a donkey, an unclean animal, being sold for forty or fifty tengas. After a siege of four months, the place was captured, Hassan Kuli was put to death, a blood penalty for the death of Aghanai Sultan ; with him perished his eldest son, Belal Sultan, while his widow and her other sons were sent to Samarkand.‡

---

* *Id.*, 216. † *Id.*, 217. ‡ *Id.*, 217-220.

SOFIAN KHAN.

Sofian, the son of Avanek Khan, was now appointed Khan at Urgenj, and a fresh partition was made of the appanages. Vezir, Yanghi Shehr, Tersek, Derun in Khorasan, and the Turkomans of Mangushlak, were given to the grandsons of Bereke Sultan and Khiva, Hazarasp, Kat, Baldumsaz, and Nikichi in the Su Buyi, or the district bordering the river, with Bagh-Abad, Nissa, Abiverd, Chihardi, Mehineh, and Jejeh in the Tagh Buyi, or hilly district, together with the Turkomans of the Amu, of Balkhan, and Dehistan, were made over to the four sons of Avanek Khan.*

Sofian Khan summoned the Turkoman tribe of Irsari, which then encamped near Balkhan to pay tribute, which they did for some years, when they set upon and killed some of his tax-collectors. According to Abulghazi, the Amu then had an outfall at Balkhan on the Caspian, and its course was marked by flourishing settlements. Sofian Khan, having marched to punish the wrongdoers, ravaged the place where the Irsaris were encamped in company with the Khorasan Saluris, and captured a large booty of women and children. Many of the Turkomans, meanwhile, took shelter at Chutak, a high plateau, three days' journey north of Balkhan, where there was always a dearth of water. Having been blockaded there for a short time, they were driven to ask for terms, and sent their elders to ask Aghatai Sultan, the youngest, or hearth-child of Avanek Khan, to intercede for them, promising to be always faithful to him and his descendants. He accordingly appealed to Sofian Khan and his brothers on their behalf, and they consented to pardon them. They had, however, to pay 1,000 sheep for each of the murdered tax-collectors, in all 40,000. 16,000 were paid by the Irsaris, 16,000 by the Khorasan Saluris, and 8,000 by the Tekes, Sariks, and Yomuts. This number of sheep was thenceforth paid annually to the Khan by these clans, who all formed one Uruk, distinguished as the Tashki Salur in opposition to the Itshki Salur. Some time after this a census was taken of the other Turkomans and their herds, and they were taxed in accordance with it as follows : the Itshki Salur, or Salurs of the Interior, paid 16,000 sheep, as well as 1,600 for the special table of the Khan ; the tribe of Hassan a similar number ; the Arabajis 4,000 and 400, the Guklans 12,000 and 1,200. The Adaklis of the Khizir tribe, the Alis and Tivechis, known together as the Uch Il, or the three tribes, who were agriculturists, and settled on the Amu or Oxus, paid a tithe of their produce, as well as a tax upon their herds, while the Adaks furnished a contingent of troops. Sofian Khan died after reigning several years, and his sons received Khiva as an appanage.

---

* Id., 226.

4 P

BUJUGHA KHAN.

On the death of Sofian Khan, he was succeeded by his brother Bujugha. Ubeidulla, the Khan of Bokara, was now struggling with Shah Tahmasp of Persia, and the Uzbegs of Khuarezm supplemented his attacks, and advanced as far as Pil Kupruki, and made assaults on the frontier towns of Khojend and Asferain, near Asterabad. Shah Tahmasp was also fighting the Osmanlis, and to divide his eastern enemies, he sent to ask for a daughter of Bujugha Khan in marriage. The envoy said his master wished for the honour of an alliance with the blood of Jingis Khan. Bujugha Khan had no daughters, so he offered his niece, Aisha the daughter of Sofian Khan. Her brother Aghish Sultan, was sent to arrange the treaty of marriage. He was received with distinction by Shah Tahmasp, at Kazvin, and was presented with the town of Khojend as an appanage. He also sent Bujugha Khan nine ingots of gold, nine-times-nine ingots of silver, nine richly-caparisoned horses, nine tents, with their upper parts made of silk broidered with gold, and the lower of a stuff called Chubdar, with suitable cushions, &c., 1,000 pieces of silk, and a trousseau worthy of the princess. The Uzbegs of Khuarezm now ceased for a while to plunder the borders of Persia. Bujugha Khan died after having reigned over the Khanate for many years.[*]

AVANEK KHAN.

Bujugha Khan left three sons Dost Muhammed, Ish Muhammed, and Burum; the latter two were given the appanage of Kât. He was succeeded in the Khanate by his brother Avanek. The latter married three wives, all of the Mangut tribe, two of them daughters of Murzas and the third one of a slave. By the last of these he had a son Din Muhammed who early showed a taste for a military life. We are told that like Napoleon he when quite a child built a little fortress of stones, and divided his companions into two sections, an attacking and a defending body, and spoke brave words to them, saying how he would reward those who proved themselves men. His nurse overhearing him, reproved him, saying that one who would need fortresses and towns should not waste his time with earth and stones, but he retorted happily that it was with earth and stones that towns were built. At this time the district near Asterabad was subject to the Uzbegs of Urgenj, and Din Muhammed, when in his twentieth year went there without his father's permission with but forty companions, and *en route* robbed a Turkoman bek who had refused to give him a small yellow goat he coveted, of his camels and sheep. He thence made a raid into Persian territory, and prepared to return to his father with a large number of captives. The bek whom he had plundered having reported the affair to his master Muhammed Ghazi Sultan, the son of Ilbars Khan, the latter determined to waylay him on his return, and Din Muhammed having fallen into an ambush was made prisoner and placed in confinement, while all his booty was appropriated.* Avanek Khan who was not very fond of Din Muhammed, his mother having been a slave, had recently married a sister of Muhammed Ghazi Sultan. The latter having detained the young prince for some time, had him manacled and his legs tied underneath his horse, sent him back to his father, and acquainted him with his conduct. *En route* Din Muhammed sang aloud, in the hope that some of his followers might have escaped to a neighbouring aul and hear and rescue him, and, in fact, when he reached Kurdish this took place. Some of his "kazaks" discovered him, surprised his guards at night and released him. Having buried their bodies at a distance from the route, he went on to Urgenj, and told his father that although Muhammed Ghazi had treated him harshly at first, he had released him with honour, and given him horses and robes.† The young prince then caused an engraver to forge "the tamgha" or seal of his father and step-mother, the sister of Muhammed Ghazi, and wrote letters in their names to say that she was very ill, and that they wished him to go and see her before she died. Muhammed Ghazi at once hastened to Urgenj, and went to his sister's apartments. He learned from her that he had been duped, and at once suspected a plot. Hearing the footsteps of Din Muhammed's people, he hid himself in a heap of dry dung in the stables, where he was shortly after traced by them. He was dragged out and beheaded.‡ News was speedily carried to Vezir, where Ali Sultan then was on a visit to Sultan Ghazi Sultan the murdered chief's brother. In his rage the latter fell upon Ali Sultan and killed him. Avanek Khan who had all this while been out hawking, on returning home was informed of Din Muhammed's crime, and then of Ali Sultan's death. A bloody feud immediately commenced, the family and dependants of Ilbars Khan rendezvoused at Vezir, while those of Avanek Khan clustered round Urgenj, whence in spite of the Khan's remonstrances, his relatives determined to march against Vezir. Sultan Ghazi Sultan went out to meet them as far as Kumkend, a village on the edge of the Kir. In the battle which followed, Avanek Khan won the victory, and pursued it to Vezir, where the Sultan with fifteen other princes of the family of Ilbars were put to death, and their houses were pillaged. Ulugh Tubeh, the widow of Sultan Ghazi Sultan, with her sons and daughters was allowed to go to Bukhara, where they were joined by the family of Balbars Sultan, who ruled at Yanghi Shehr, and who were their partisans. The sons of

---

* Abulghazi, 230, 231. † *Id.*, 232, 233. ‡ *Id.*, 234, 235.

Avanek Khan were now masters of all the country of Khuarezm, Avanek himself retained Urgenj, and the other provinces were redistributed among his relatives, Din Muhammed Sultan receiving Derun which had belonged to Sultan Ghazi Sultan.[*]

As I have said, the sons of Sultan Ghazi Sultan who were named Omar Ghazi Sultan and Shir Ghazi Sultan, went to Bukhara. The former urged Ubeidulla Khan the chief of Bukhara, to furnish him with troops to take his revenge. Ubeidulla who deemed it a good opportunity to enlarge his borders, prepared to march against Khuarezm. I have described the result of his campaign, and the capture and execution of Avanek Khan elsewhere.[†]

Din Muhammed, whose appanage of Derun was not molested by the Bukharians, gathered round him the fugitives from Khuarezm who had escaped, including two sons of Avanek Khan.[‡] Presently he determined to make an effort for the recovery of the Khanate. Having reached Kurdish he summoned the chiefs of the Adakli section of the Khizr tribe of Turkomans, and offered them if they would join him to give them the position of terkhans, to cede to them the post of honour on the left flank of the army, and to number the Adaklis among the Uzbeg tribes. By these offers he obtained the services of 1,000 of them, who raised his own people to 3,000. Having reached Pishgah they marched on Khiva.[§] I have already described the result of the campaign and the peace that was made with Ubeidulla.[‖]

KAL KHAN

After the victory, Kal khan the fourth son of Avanek Khan, and doubtless the senior prince of the family, was elected Khan. His reign lasted seven years, and was so prosperous that it gave rise to the proverb, "Kal khan has mounted the throne and bread can be bought for a pul."[¶]

AKATAI KHAN.

Kal khan was succeeded by his brother Akatai, who was proclaimed Khan at Vezir. The late Khan's sons received the town of Kat as an appanage, but they were shortly driven away, as were Yunus and Pehlevan Kuli, the sons of Sofian Khan, by a coalition of the sons of Bujugha Khan, of Avanek Khan and Akatai Khan. They retired to Bukhara. Akatai made Vezir his capital. Ali Sultan, son of Avanek Khan, was given Derun, his brother Mahmud, Urgenj, Hajim, Bagh Abad, Din Muhammed, Nissa and Abiverd, while Ish and Dost, the sons of Bujugha Khan took Khiva and Hazarasp.[**] Meanwhile,

---

* Id., 236-238.   † Ante, 721, 722.   ‡ Abulghazi, 240.   § Id., 241.
‖ Ante, 722, 723.   ¶ Abulghazi, 243.   ** Id., 246.

Yunus Sultan, the son of Sofian Khan, had married a daughter of Ismael, the famous chief of the Nogais. He was on his way to him with forty followers from Bukhara when he passed by way of Tuk, which was deserted, the inhabitants being then encamped near Urgenj, and he conceived the wish to secure that heritage of his father's. After halting for a day, he set out at midnight, and dismounting, drew near to the town-ditch on foot. As he neared, he saw some people bearing torches, and crying out Hazir Bash, "Be ready." This was a patrol going his rounds. Having fallen down on his stomach till they had passed, he then, with his companions, made his way on to the wall, whence he repaired to the house of its governor, the prince Sari Mahmud Sultan, which he entered without alarming any one. Having secured Mahmud, he sent him under escort to Akatai Khan at Vezir. The soldiery and citizens of Urgenj, who were weary of the tyranny of Mahmud, gladly welcomed Yunus, and he proclaimed himself Khan. Akatai marched to support Mahmud, and he encountered the forces which gathered round Yunus west of the tomb of the Sheikh Najmuddin Kubra. Akatai was defeated and fled. Kassim Sultan, the son of Yunus and of Akatai's daughter, went in pursuit of him; overtook him, and took him back to Urgenj, where he shortly after had him put to death secretly by impalement, so that, like Edward II., no wound was seen on his body, and it appeared as if he had died naturally. The corpse was then sent back to his family at Vezir.†

The sons of the dead Khan mustered their forces, and went towards Urgenj, on hearing which, Yunus hastily fled to Bukhara, but his son Kassim was treacherously surrendered by one of his followers, who informed Hajim Muhammed, where he was hiding. He was taken to Urgenj, and duly executed there.‡

We are told the sons of Sofian Khan and Kalk Khan left no issue, and that the sons of Avanek Khan resided in Khorasan. Meanwhile, Urgenj and Vezir fell to the family of Akatai Khan, and Khiva, Hazarasp, and Kât, to Ish, Dost, and Burum, the sons of Bujugha Khan.

DOST KHAN.

Dost, the son of Bujugha, was now nominated Khan. He had a mild and peaceable disposition, while his brother Ish, who was a dissolute person, was exceedingly passionate. He demanded that Urgenj should be handed over to him, while Dost Khan retained Khiva, and on this being refused, he marched against it with a considerable army, and fought against Hajim, who held it as an appanage. We are told he planted his camp on the river, and protected its other sides by a rampart

---

* Id., 249.   † Id., 250, 251.

of waggons. Here the strife continued for seven days without result. He then returned the prisoners he had made, except those belonging to the Uighur and Naiman tribes, whom he put to death with cruel punishments,[*] made peace, and returned to Khiva, whence he drove out the Uzbegs of the same tribes and replaced them by Durmans. Some time after, he again marched against Urgenj, and having fought for seven days, managed to elude its garrison which was encamped outside, and entered the town where there were only the Sarts or citizens. The sons of Akatai, with the Uzbegs of the tribes Naiman and Uighur, withdrew to Vezir. Shortly after, Hajim Muhammed, having secured some allies in his brothers, in Ali Sultan, the son of Avanek, and Abul Sultan, son of Din Muhammed Khan, who was then dead, attacked Urgenj. After a four months' siege, a general assault was delivered, during which Tin ali, of the Durman tribe, who had a grudge against Ish Sultan, fired an arrow, which struck his horse. The latter fell and hurt its rider's leg, and being deserted by most of his people, he was found in this helpless condition and put to death. Some people were now despatched to Khiva, who killed his brother Dost, while Ish Sultan's two sons were sent to Bukhara, where they died, and the posterity of Bujugha Khan became extinct. These events happened in 965 of the hej.[†]

HAJIM OR HAJI MUHAMMED KHAN.

Hajim Muhammed, who was thirty-nine years old, was now proclaimed Khan. He lived at Vezir, while Ali Sultan took Urgenj, Hazarasp, and Kût. Hajim's brother Mahmud held one half of Khiva and the Turkomans of Ulugh tubé and Kunish, while Timur, another brother took the other half of Khiva and the Turkomans of Kara Bukaul.[‡] Hajim had already distinguished himself by persuading Din Muhammed to drive the Uzbegs of Bukhara from Khuarezm, and by afterwards negotiating an exchange of prisoners with Ubeidulla Khan.[§] It seems that the brothers and sons of Hajim were in the habit of making constant attacks on Merv, which was then governed by Nur Muhammed, a grandson of Din Muhammed Khan. In order to understand his position, we must make a short digression. As we have seen, Din Muhammed had received the appanage of Nissa and Abiverd, whence he had made constant incursions upon Persia. Shah Tahmasp sent an army to punish him, which captured Abiverd, and left a governor there in the Persian ruler's name. Din Muhammed weakened by this loss went in person to Shah Tahmasp's court at Kazvin, where he lived for six months, and then contrived to forge an order in his host's name, commanding the governor of Abiverd to surrender the town to him. He then returned there. The place having been duly surrendered to him he proceeded to kill all the

---

* *Id.*, 252.   † *Id.*, 253.   ‡ *Id.*, 254.   § *Id.*, 272. *Ante*, 721.

Kizilbashis he could find. Tahmasp set out to punish him. Thereupon Din Muhammed had the effrontery to go to his camp on the Karasu with but forty or fifty men. He went straight up to the Shah and kissed his side asking him for pardon. The Shah, who was astounded, put one hand on his neck and another on his heart, and noticing that the latter did not beat more quickly than usual, he remarked that it must be made of stone. He then made a grand feast, pardoned him, and gave him Abiverd!!!

Ubeidulla, the Khan of Bukhara, had appointed a Naiman named Yolum bi as commander of Merv. The latter having proved rebellious, Ubeidulla marched against him with 30,000 men, upon which he appealed to Din Muhammed, offering to hand over the town to him if he would assist him. Din Muhammed set out from Abiverd, and arriving at the place where the Murghab loses itself in the sand, he ordered each soldier to take three branches of a tree, to fasten one to each side of his saddle and the third one to his horse's tail, and to advance in loose order, and by short stages. The black moving mass of his troops was exaggerated by the addition of the branches, and the Bukharian army afraid of being caught between them and the people of Yolum bi, hastily retreated homewards. Din Muhammed occupied Merv, where he afterwards reigned. He died there in the year 960, when he was forty years old, and was succeeded as ruler by his second son, Abul Muhammed Khan, who having been made a Kalkhan by Din Muhammed, was styled Abul Khan even in his father's life time.*

On one occasion his son Jelal made a raid into Khorasan. We are told the Persians mustered their forces at Meshed, and in a battle on the Karasu, defeated his army, and killed Jelal and 10,000 Uzbegs. The loss of his only son preyed greatly on the chief's mind, and a doctor said that only another son would be an antidote for his complaint. There was at this time at Merv a woman named Bibijeh, who gained her living by playing on a tambourine for the women of the town and in drawing pictures. She had never been married, but had a son four years old. They produced him, and declared him to be Abul Muhammed's son. The latter at all events adopted him and gave him the name of Nur Muhammed.† On the death of Abul Khan, Nur Muhammed succeeded him at Merv, and had reigned several years when, as I have mentioned, he was attacked by the sons of Hajim Muhammed from Urgenj, who said they would not acknowledge the son of a luli or prostitute. Stung by their reproaches and unable to resi t them he went to Bukhara, and offered to hold Merv as an appanage under Abdulla Khan. The latter marched to Merv which he occupied himself and ignored Nur Muhammed, who thereupon returned to Khuarezm and took refuge at Urgenj with Hajim Khan. It seems that Ali Sultan, the son

---

* *Id.,* 256, 257.　　　† *Id.,* 257, 258.

of Avanek Khan, besides Urgenj, Hazarasp, and Kât, which I have
mentioned as his appanages, had afterwards received Nissa and Abiverd,
in the Taghbuyi of Urgenj, and thence he seems to have made constant
raids in spring and summer on Khorasan, as far as Pil kupruki, Tershiz,
Terbet, Jam, and Kharkerd.* He had conquered Jurjan, Jajrum, Keraihu,
and Asterabad, and had an army of 40,000 men. He paid many of his
Uzbegs sixteen sheep annually, partially drawn from the tax on the
Turkomans, and partly from the fifth of the booty taken from the
Persians, which was his share. On one occasion when he had been to
collect tribute from the Turkomans, of the tribe Okli Kuklang, and had
3,000 men with him, he was attacked on the river Gurgan by 12,000
Persians under Badr Khan; one of Shah Tahmasp's beks. The latter
intrenched themselves with great care, and carefully spanned their camels
and horses, but after a fiercely contested struggle, in which the Turkomans fought bravely on the side of the Uzbegs, the latter won a
complete victory, pursued the Persians till nightfall and captured
nearly 5,000 horses.† Ali died on one of these expeditions into Khorasan
at the age of forty. This was in 976. He was succeeded at Nissa by
his son Sanjar Sultan, who died twenty-five years after without issue.‡

On the death of Ali Sultan, Hajim gave Vezir to his brother
Muhammed Sultan, and himself went to live at Urgenj. On one
occasion while he was absent in Khorasan, when Pulad Sultan was in
command at Khiva, and Timur Sultan at Hazarasp, Abdulla Khan of
Bukhara made an invasion of the country. When the news of this
invasion arrived, Timur Sultan and his people went to Khiva from
Hazarasp, while Urgenj and Vezir put themselves in a state of defence.
The Bukharians had already reached Yanghi Arik (i.e., the New Canal),
when news arrived that Hajim was marching to the rescue. Thereupon
Abdulla patched up a hasty peace with Pulad Sultan and Timur Sultan,
and returned home.§ Shortly after he again invaded the Khanate,
assigning several reasons for his doing so. The first being that the
Ottoman Sultan had despatched an envoy to him named Salih Shah,
to seek an alliance with him, against their common enemies the Persian
Shias. Salih Shah reached Bukhara in safety, by way of India, having
been three years on the way, and was well received there. He proposed
to return home by way of Urgenj and Mangushlak, but on his arrival at
the former town, he was attacked and plundered by Muhammed Ibrahim
Sultan, the son of Hajim Muhammed Khan, who left him barely enough
money to pay for his journey onwards.

Abdulla had another grievance. Shirvan at this time belonged to
the Turkish Sultan, and it was the custom of the hajis or pilgrims on
their way from Mavera un Nehr to Mekka, to go by way of Urgenj
and Shirvan, so as to avoid meeting the hated Kizilbashi hereticks. A

* Id., 280.   † Id., 263, 264.   ‡ Id., 265.   § Id., 273, 274.

year previous to these events, one Haji Kutas had arrived at Urgenj in charge of a large caravan and a number of pilgrims. They had been attacked, plundered, and driven back towards Bukhara, by Baba Sultan, the son of Pulad Sultan. Haji Kutas laid his complaints before Abdulla Khan, who replied that Hajim Muhammed was independent of him, and that he had no authority in Khuarezm, whereupon the irate pilgrim threatened to denounce him before the tribunal of heaven, unless he avenged him, and at last secured his aid.[*] Abdulla was further incited by Nur Muhammed of Merv, as I have mentioned. The Khan of Bukhara whose former raid on Khuarezm had not been very successful, determined to prosecute a more important campaign, and made preparations accordingly. Hajim Khan, who distrusted his Uzbegs, left Urgenj in charge of his son Muhammed Ibrahim, and retired to safer quarters, at Derun, the appanage of another son, Arab Muhammed Sultan. At the approach of the Bukharian army, the Uzbegs retired from the less defensible towns, including Khiva and Hazarasp, and mustered at Vezir, and we are told that the cavalcade that left Khiva, consisting of 2,000 families took half-a-day to file out, and looked like a procession at a festival, the very hens and the mats of the houses being hung on to the carts.[†] The town was immediately occupied by the Bukharians, who summoned the citizens and issued a friendly proclamation to them. They then hurried on towards Vezir, and *en route* scattered the followers of Pulad Sultan, who were retiring too leisurely, and captured their baggage, the princes however escaping. A dissension arose at Vezir, some of the chiefs arguing in favour of surrendering Baba Sultan, who had caused their trouble by plundering the pilgrims, but he prudently left the place and joined Hajim Khan, with his brothers Hamzah and Pehlevan Kuli, and his father Pulad Sultan. Abdulla Khan now laid siege to Vezir. After he had pressed the attack for a month he made proposals, saying he had only gone to punish Baba Sultan, and that if they went to his camp the princes might depend on his treating them well for he was their relative.[‡] They agreed to submit if he would send some of his principal people to assure them of their safety. He accordingly despatched Hassan Khoja, Nakib; his Atalik, Sarkhin bi; his divan begi, Muhammed Baki; the governor of Samarkand, Haji bi, and his pervanechi, Dostum bi Arghun, who swore before the ten princes and forty of their dependents to do them no harm. The people of Khiva who saw that they had in these men the five first citizens of Bukhara, and in the words of Abulghazi, that Abdulla would not sacrifice their very nails for all Khuarezm, were for seizing them, but the princes thought differently. They consented to go to Abdulla's camp, who thus secured the whole of Khuarezm proper without a blow. He thereupon appointed governors to the various towns of the Khanate and

---

[*] *Id.;* 274-276.			[†] *Id.,* 278.			[‡] *Id.,* 280.

returned to Bukhara. This was in 1002, *i.e.*, 1594. Hajim Khan now determined to go to Irak, to the court of Shah Abbas the First.* He was accompanied by Nur Muhammed the former governor of Merv, by his own sons Suiunich Muhammed Sultan, Arab Muhammed, and Muhammed Kuli, by several of his grandsons and others, in all eleven princes, with an escort of but 150 men. Pulad Sultan, who was half-witted, refused to go. He returned and gave himself up to Abdulla, saying, "I am seventy years old, why should I go among the infidels ; I am a fool, why should Abdulla shorten my days."

Abdulla was little careful of his oath to the princes who had given themselves up so unwarily to him, and he had them all drowned in the river Ak su. Their names were Pulad Sultan and his son Kulchi, Muhammed Ibrahim, son of Hajim Muhammed Khan; the three sons of Timur Sultan, the four sons of Mahmud Sultan, and the two sons of Muhammed Sultan, in all twelve princes capable of bearing arms, besides ten others who were young.† Having committed this atrocious act of treachery, the Bukharian Khan proceeded to crush the land with his tax collectors. The poor were forced to pay a tribute of thirty tengas, and those who were left behind were made responsible for fugitives and those who could not pay. If ten or fifteen people lived together as one family, each one had to pay as had also mere boys who had reached the age of ten years, and the people had to sell their children to meet his demands. Meanwhile, Hajim Muhammed was well received by the Shah, who we are told assisted him to dismount, and appointed him a seat beside him. Hajim's son Suiunich Muhammed with his two sons went on to Turkey, saying he could not live among infidels, but the rest of the princes remained in Persia for three years. After his conquest of Khuarezm, Abdulla prosecuted a war with Persia. This was carried out mainly by his son Abdul Mumin, the governor of Balkh, who overran the greater part of Khorasan and advanced as far as Isferan, whither the Persian Shah marched to meet him.‡

In order to supply a sufficient force for this campaign, the Bukharian Khan had largely denuded Khuarezm of troops, a fact of which Hajim Muhammed was informed by the Turkomans of Asterabad. Deeming it a good opportunity to recover possession of the Khanate, Hajim's sons, Arab Muhammed and Muhammed Kuli Sultan, with Baba Sultan, Hamzah Sultan, and Pehlevan Kuli Sultan, sons of Pulad Sultan, made a speedy journey from Persia without the Shah's permission, and setting out at night, duly reached Asterabad. They were followed by Hajim Muhammed, who had been living at Bostam, and had been advised by the Shah to postpone any venture on Khuarezm till after the death of Abdulla Khan. The Turkomans at this time acknowledged the Uzbeg princes of Khuarezm as their superior chiefs.

---

* *Id.*, 282.   † *Id.*, 283.   ‡ *Id.*, 284, 285.

From Asterabad the latter went to the mountain Kuren, and thence to Pishgah, where they separated. Hajim Muhammed and his two sons. making for Urgenj, and Baba Sultan and his brothers for Khiva. The citadel of Urgenj was captured, and its governor Sari Oghlan with its garrison of fifty men were put to death. When Baba Sultan reached Khiva, its Sart inhabitants sided with him, and he speedily secured the town and put its governor Minglish bi to death, at which news the governors of Kât and Hazarasp fled to Bukhara. The Turkomans who had assisted Hajim Muhammed and Baba Sultan in this campaign, which took place in 1004, now returned home with the prisoners they had made and with their camels laden with booty.* When the governor of Hazarasp neared Charjui, he met Khojaddin Kuli the Kalmuk, who commanded a section of Abdulla's army. This officer was ordered by Abdulla to march at once to the rescue. He succeeded in surprising the town of Khan Kah and putting Hamzah Sultan who had occupied it to death,† and immediately marched for Urgenj. *En route* they encountered Hajim's son Muhammed Kuli at the head of a small force, but he managed to cut his way through them, and escaped to the Nogais, by whom he was given up to the Russians, and died among them. Meanwhile Hajim Muhammed having heard of the approach of the Bukharians fled hastily. He was pursued, and lost his camp and half his people, and being afterwards overtaken was forced to fight at a disadvantage, and again lost severely. He reached Asterabad however in safety, and once more repaired to the Shah at Kazvin.

Abdulla Khan proceeded to besiege Hasarasp in person, and after a siege of four months captured it and put Baba Sultan to death, and Khuarezm was once more added to the Bukharian Khanate.

That powerful chief died in 1597-8. When the news arrived in Persia, the Shah raised an army and marched to Bostam, and he gave permission to Hajim Muhammed and his son Arab Muhammed to make another venture on Khuarezm.‡

They had but fifteen companions with them, with whom they made their way to the mountain Kuren, the camping ground of the Teke Turkomans. Having delayed there a while, they learned that Abdul Mumin the successor of Abdulla had been killed. Hajim Muhammed Khan now mounted his horse and rode for Urgenj, where he arrived eight days later. He gave Khiva and Kât to his son Arab Muhammed Khan, Hazarasp to his grandson Izfendiar Sultan, and retained Urgenj and Vezir for himself, and was speedily joined by the Uzbegs whom Abdulla had carried off prisoners to Bukhara.§

At this time Nur Muhammed the former ruler of Merv, who as I have said had taken refuge in Persia with Hajim Muhammed, returned to his old quarters, where he persecuted the Uzbegs, and protected the Sarts

---

* *Id.,* 286, 287. † *Id.,* 288. ‡ *Id.,* 291. § *Id.,* 293.

and Turkomans. When Shah Abbas heard of this, he marched against
Merv, which he captured after a siege of a month, as well as the towns of
Abiverd, Nissa, and Derun, which were subject to Nur Muhammed, and
where he placed governors. He himself was carried off to Persia, where
he died in prison.[*] Two years after his return home, Hajim Muhammed
was rejoined by Suiunich his eldest son, who returned from Turkey by
way of Shirvan, and to whom his father surrendered Urgenj and Vezir,
retiring himself to Khiva to his younger son Arab Muhammed. Suiunich
died the year following, and was followed to the grave the following year
by his son Ibadulla Khan.

Hajim Muhammed died in the year 1011 of the hej, i.e., 1602. The
account here given of him is taken entirely from Abulghazi, but we have
a curious light thrown on Khuarezm during his reign, by the visit paid to
it by the English traveller Jenkinson, who calls him Azim Khan.

It was on the 23rd of April, 1558, that the famous traveller left Moscow
with a cargo of merchandise. He arrived at Astrakhan on the 14th of
July, where he stayed till the 6th of August. There he bought a boat,
and in company with several Tartars and Persians set sail for the
Caspian, crept along the north coast, and passed the mouths of the
rivers Jaik and Yemba. On the 27th of August, he landed at some
distance from Mangushlak, a storm having prevented him from making
that place. There he made arrangements with the governor for
camels, &c., to transport him and his goods to Vezir. He found the
people very exacting, and paid three Russian hides and four wooden
dishes for the hire of each camel, besides presenting the governor with a
seovena or present of nine and another of twice seven objects. The
caravan numbered 1,000 camels. After a journey of five days the travellers
reached the district controlled by Timur Sultan, of Mangushlak, who
treated them well, and supplied them with flesh and mares' milk, and
although he took fifteen roubles' worth of goods as his perquisite, he
presented Jenknison with a horse and entertained him in his tent.

Setting out again Jenkinson crossed a desert twenty days' journey long,
and had to kill one of his camels and a horse for food, and drank only
brackish water, this sometimes failing for two days together. He then
reached another Gulf of the Caspian, where we paid black mail to the
Turkoman governors. He tells us the Oxus once fell into this gulf.

Leaving there on the 4th of October, he arrived three days later at the
castle of Sellizure, i.e., Shehr Vezir (Lerch Khiva Oder Kharezm, 28 & 43),
(i.e., Hajim), where Azim Khan with three of his brothers was living. With
him he on the 9th of the same month had an audience and presented his
letters from the Russian Emperor, and also some presents. The Khan
entertained him with horseflesh and milk, and gave him a safe conduct. He
tells us the castle of Sellizure was placed on a high hill, and that the king's

---

* Id., 259, 260.

palace there was built of earth, very barely and not strong, and that the people were poor. The land to the south was very fruitful. There grew a fine fruit called Dynie, large and full of moisture, which the people ate after meat instead of drink (? melons), also another fruit called carbus as big as a cucumber, yellow and sweet (*i.e.*, water melons, still called arbus by the Russians)*, and a certain corn Jegur, whose stalk was like a sugar cane, and as high, the grain like rice growing at the top of the cane like a cluster of grapes (*i.e.*, Chugara the Holcus Sorghum).† Jenkinson tells us the water for irrigation was drawn from the Oxus. This had so diminished the river that it it no longer fell into the Caspian.

Two days after leaving Sellizure he reached Urgenj where he paid the accustomed dues. There he had an audience with Ali Sultan the brother of Hajim, who had recently made a raid upon Khorasan. The town he said had been won and lost four times in seven years by civil wars, whence there were few merchants there and they poor, and he could only sell four kerseys. He tells us all the land thence to the Caspian was called the land of Turkman, and was subject to Azim Khan and his five brothers, "who being the sons of different mothers and sometimes of slaves, were jealous of one another, and tried to destroy each other, and when there was war among them, if one was defeated and escaped he and his followers generally repaired to the desert, and prowled about the watering places *en route*, where he pillaged the caravans until he was strong enough to again struggle for his own."‡

Jenkinson describes some of the habits of the people, and then goes on to say that having left Urgenj, he travelled along the Oxus for 100 miles, when reached the Ardok which was swift and rapid, and leaving the Oxus was consumed in the ground about 1,000 miles to the north, and then issuing again from under the ground entered the sea of Kitai. He then reached Káit, subject to Saramet Sultan, a brother of Hajim, to whom he paid a red Russian hide for each camel and other dues, and assigned him an escort. The latter fed heartily on his victuals, and after three days claimed a large payment for going further, which being refused they took their departure. The Khojas who were with the caravan thereupon insisted upon a halt, and upon trying their divinations with the shoulder blades of sheep. Jenkinson tells us how they burnt these bones and mixed their ashes, with which they wrote certain characters using cabalistic phrases. Meanwhile this came to pass. A banished prince with a few followers attacked them fiercely but they opposed them, and thanks to some guns Jenkinson had with him beat them off, and they made a laager of their trunks and cattle, behind which they camped. During the night overtures were made to the Mussulmans of the company to surrender their Christian companions but without avail, and they eventually purchased

---

* Lerch, op. cit., 28. † *Id.* ‡ Hackluyt, op. cit., 367, 368.

peace with a present of black mail and a camel on which to carry it. The travellers then went on to Bukhara.* Jenkinson returned home by way of Urgenj, and took with him four envoys from Hajim Khan to the Russian Emperor.†

In 1595, fresh envoys where sent from Khuarezm to solicit the friendship of the Tzar Feodor.‡

ARAB MUHAMMED KHAN.

Hajim Khan was succeeded by his son Arab Muhammed, who gave his son Izfendiar the province of Kât, in lieu of that of Hazarasp. Soon after his accession (in one place Abulghazi says, six months after, which would be in 1011, *i.e.*, 1602,§ and in another he dates it in the year of his own birth, *i.e.*, 1014 or 1015),‖ ten merchants from Khuarezm who had gone to Russia were waylaid by 100 Cossacks of the Ural or Yaik, and eight of them were killed. From one of the survivors who came from Turkestan, they learnt that the garrison of Urgenj was then encamped in summer quarters on the river, at some distance from the town, and that on one side of that city there was a desert, across which an army of 100,000 men might approach it unobserved. They accordingly determined to surprise it, and set out with 1,000 men. They arrived safely and entered the town by the gate of the Murza.¶ They killed more than 1,000 of its inhabitants and burnt much property, and having loaded 1,000 waggons with booty and prisoners they retired. Arab Muhammed meanwhile cut off their retreat, and so pressed them, that in lieu of water they had to quench their thirst with blood, and this failed on the 5th day. The Uzbegs now attacked them on all sides, penetrated behind their laager of carts into their camp, and cut them to pieces. One hundred of them succeeded in reaching the Oxus, and built a small fort near the fortress of Tuk, where they lived for a while on fish, but Arab Muhammed eventually attacked them and captured their fort.** Six months later the Kalmuks, who had begun to spread westwards as far as the Aral, made a raid upon the Khanate. They passed between Khoja Kul (*i.e.*, the lake of the Khoja) and the mountain of Sheikh Jelil, and pillaged the Uzbeg camps as far as Tuk, whence they returned by way of Burichi. Arab Muhammed pursued them and recovered the booty and prisoners they had made, but did not capture any Kalmuks.†† Soon after the Naimans formed a plot to depose Arab Muhammed Khan, and to put Khosru Sultan, a descendant of Ilbars Khan, who wandered in Mavera un nehr, in his place, but the conspiracy was frustrated, and Khosru and the leader of the Naimans were put to death.* Two years

---

* *Id.*, 369, 370.　　† *Id.*, 373.　　‡ De Guignes, iii., 490.　　§ Op. cit., 294.
‖ *Id.*, 312.　　¶ *Id.*, 312, 313.　　** Abulghazi, 295, 296.　　†† *Id.*,

later the Uighurs introduced a pretender in the person of Salih Sultan, a descendant of Hassan Kuli Khan, son of Abulik, son of Yadigar Khan; but he received only a few adherents, and the Khan had him arrested and put to death. Ten years after this, the Kalmuks made a fresh invasion by way of Bakirghan, and retired with a considerable booty.† Sixteen years after the accession of Arab Muhammed, i.e., about 1618, two of his sons named Habash Sultan and Ilbars Sultan, who were respectively sixteen and fourteen years old, and were living at Khiva, rose in revolt and marched towards Urgenj. They halted at Pishgab, a long day's journey from that town, and when summoned by the Khan to his presence with the promise of being made governors of Vezir, they refused to go until they had assembled a large force. They were speedily joined by the more adventurous spirits among the young Uzbegs,‡ and their father was too weak or too indulgent to restrain them. Having made a raid upon Khorasan, they sent their father some presents, and then drew near to Urgenj. The Khan now sent one of his chief officers, a Uighur named Kurban Ali to their camp, who on his return, reported how all the Uzbegs from Darughan Ata to Bakirghan Ata had joined them, and that he had been received with shouts of defiance. He reported that matters were going badly, and advised Arab Muhammed to retire to Khiva. The Khan was a weak person, a fact which his own son the historian Abulghazi cannot hide. He did not send to inquire how far the story was exaggerated, but at once set out for Khiva. When the young princes heard this they went and encamped at Kiran Kiri. At this time, says Abulghazi, all the district from Mizdehkan to Kuighun beyond Bakirghan was a large field of wheat. Abulghazi tells us how a year before he was born the Khan had cut a canal which passed by way of Tuk and Kuighun, and fell into the Sea of Aral. This canal was closed at the epoch of Mizan (i.e., when the sun was in Libra), and opened again after harvest; and some years later was more than a bow shot in breadth. In consequence of this wheat was very cheap. The young rebels seized the magazines which the Khan had built in various districts, and gained over the poorer people by undertaking the distribution of the grain. Arab Muhammed meanwhile by the advice of the beks ceded the town of Vezir and its dependent Turkomans to them, and we are told they paid their father a visit, escorted by 4,000 men, and then returned once more to Vezir, where they lived for five years peaceably. In the sixth year, while the Khan was at Urgenj, Ilbars seized upon Khiva, and when his father returned homewards, he sent a body of 500 men who made him prisoner. He then secured his treasures, and in the words of Abulghazi, "scattered them among the dogs and the birds," and deposed the beks. After this he returned again to Vezir. All his sons did not behave thus, and we now find Isfendiar Sultan and Abulghazi

* Id., 296.   † Id., 298.   ‡ Id., 299.

joining their forces to their father's, and marching against Ilbars Sultan, who thereupon retired towards the Kir or Ust Urt,* while they pillaged his appanage. In vain Abulghazi argued with his weak father that it was now a favourable opportunity to crush the rebels. He vacillated continually and leaned for support on his Atalik, Hussein Haji, who it would seem was a secret partisan of the rebels. Nor could Abulghazi persuade his elder brother Izfendiar to take a bold course. Meanwhile, Habash and Ilbars were duly informed of the former's plans and hated him accordingly. Arab Muhammed returned to Khiva and Izfendiar to Hazarasp, while Abulghazi was given command of Kât.† Five months later the Khan changed his mind, and determined to punish his rebellious sons, and summoned Abulghazi to his aid. He would not however adopt the latter's counsel to surprise them, but marched against them in open daylight. The rebels being duly warned were prepared, and met their father with a considerable force at the canal of Tashli Yarmish, which had been excavated by Ali Sultan. Arab Muhammed was defeated and made prisoner. He was taken to Habash Sultan, who had him blinded and sent to Khiva and thence to Kum, with his three wives and two younger sons, Habash himself went in pursuit of Izfendiar Sultan, while Abulghazi went to Kât and thence to Bukhara.

Izfendiar with two other sons of Arab Muhammed, named Sherif Sultan and Khuarezm Shah Sultan, shut themselves up in the fortress of Hazarasp, but after a siege of forty days they came to a parley, Izfendiar agreed to go to Mekka, Sherif Muhammed was given Kât, while Khuarezm Shah and a younger brother named Afghan, who were both boys, went to their mother at Khiva. This revolution took place in 1030 of the hej, i.e., 1621. The following year Ilbars put his father, his brother Khuarezm Sultan, and two sons of Izfendiar Sultan to death. His other brother Afghan he sent to Habash to be executed, but the latter sent him off to Russia, where he died in 1648, and was buried at Kasimof in a tôkie built by his widow, Altun Khanim, the daughter of Hajim Sultan.‡

IZFENDIAR KHAN.

On the deposition of their father, the two rebel princes divided the Khanate between them, Habash took Urgenj and Vezir, and Ilbars Khiva and Hazarasp.

These revolutions seem inexplicable when we consider how faithful the Uzbegs generally were to their own princes, fragile as their friendship is for strangers, but we may explain them by what followed. The Khanate of Khiva was inhabited by three races; Sarts or old indigines of the towns, harmless, and of Persian descent; the Turkomans descended from the Guz and Kankalis, the stemfathers of the Siljuks and Osmanlis, and lastly Uzbegs who came in with Sheibani, and who dominated over the rest. Between Turkomans and Uzbegs, the old masters and the new, there was very great jealousy and strife, and whenever the Khan leaned on one section, he was sure to lose the support of the other. Arab Muhammed probably suffered from this policy. When his death became known, his eldest son Izfendiar received a small contingent from Shah Abbas of Persia, who told him to repair to the borders of Khorasan, and endeavour to recover Khuarezm. He made his way to Derun and Mount Balkhan, and was joined by a few Turkomans of the tribes of Teke, Sarik, and Yomut, in all but 300 men, with whom he made a night attack on the çamp of Habash, which was planted on the Oxus, opposite the fortress of Tuk. That prince however escaped and joined his brother Ilbars, who marched to the rescue, and Izfendiar was joined by the naukers or dependents of his other brothers, Sherif Muhammed and Abulghazi.

Meanwhile, a Khoja named Nazar, whose daughter Ilbars had married, took up the latter's cause with vigour, and when he noticed how the people crowded to join Izfendiar, he planted himself and a contingent of 300 followers on the route they had to follow, and cut a deep ditch across the road so as to make it impassable. He then proceeded to frighten them, by declaring Izfendiar meant to hand them over to the Turkomans, and conjured them, Koran in hand, not to assist him. These words had their due effect. Some of those who had joined Izfendiar now deserted him, and he was defeated and escaped to Mangushlak. There he was joined by a large number of his partisans and 3,000 Turkomans, and once more marched eastwards. He approached Urgenj, and fought with Ilbars for twenty days, when he at length defeated and captured him, and had him put to death. Habash fled to the Karakalpaks, and thence to the Nogais of the Yemba, whose chief Shanik Murza was under considerable obligations to him, which he repaid *more Nogaid* by surrendering him to Izfendiar who put him also to death.

Izfendiar mounted the throne in 1032 of the hej, *i.e.*, in 1622. He became the patron of the Turkomans and Sarts against the Uzbegs.

Let us now turn to his brother Abulghazi, to whose famous History we are so indebted. He tells us he was born in 1014, *i.e.*, 1605, and was named Abulghazi because his father defeated the infidel Cossacks of the Ural about that time. I have described how he fought besides his father against Ilbars and Habash. He tells us that in this struggle he commanded the right wing and that he had three horses killed under him * After their defeat he was hotly pursued, and had only one attendant with him. He was hit in the mouth by an arrow which broke his jaw bone, but eluded his pursuers among the tall tamarisks on the banks of the river.

* Op. cit., 315.

Taking off his quiver and sword he plunged in. His horse, he tells us, was thirsty and loitered to drink, while some of his pursuers spied him from the bank and sent a flight of arrows upon him. He had no whip to urge it on, nor had he ever swam a river before on horseback, and his mouth was meanwhile filled with blood from his wound. His armour too was very heavy, and his horse sank in the water till only his ears and nose were visible; he accordingly remembered the advice of a practised soldier who had told him in such a case to slip off the saddle, keeping one foot in the stirrup and putting the other on the horse's tail, to seize the pommel of the saddle with one hand and the bridle with the other, and thus allow the water to partially support him. On his doing so, the horse at once rose in the water and got over safely and he went to Kât, where he was joined by some of his people, and having secured some fresh horses and provisions he went on to Samarkand, where he was cordially received by Imaum Kuli Khan.* It was two years after this that Izfendiar was proclaimed Khan, whereupon Abulghazi with his other brother Sherif Muhammed returned to Khuarezm. The former received Urgenj and the latter Vezir as an appanage, while the Khan reserved Khiva, Hazarasp, and Kât for himself.†

The brothers soon began to quarrel. Izfendiar became the partisan of the Turkomans and Sarts, while his brothers sided with their own people the Uzbegs. After harvest, in the year 1624, they repaired to Khiva to see Izfendiar, and after staying there three days, were saddling their horses to return when the Khan ordered all the Uighurs and Naimans to be put to death. The massacre at once commenced, and that very day 100 Uzbegs of those tribes perished, nor did the persecution stop there, but all the Uzbegs who encamped between Hazarasp and Khast Minaressi were slaughtered, while of the two devoted tribes even the infants and old people were killed, and Sherif Muhammed was sent to Urgenj with orders to kill all of those two tribes whom he found there. Abulghazi himself was detained at Khiva, apparently with the purpose of eventually putting an end to him, but as the remaining Uzbegs threatened to abandon the Khanate unless he was released, he was allowed to go. He set off for Urgenj which was then almost deserted. The river Amu which had formerly watered its environs having taken another course and deserted its old bed. He accordingly stayed at a fortress near Tuk, where he was joined by Sherif Muhammed. Having collected a large body of Uzbegs, it was determined to attack the Turkomans, but Muhammed Hussein the Turkoman leader having heard of their plot escaped with his followers from the fortress, where they had been living, and repaired to Izfendiar Khan. Meanwhile, the two brothers with their Uzbegs determined to march on Khiva. At Tash Kupruk, or the stone bridge over the canal

---

* *Id.,* 316-318.   † *Id.,* 319.

of Khaikanek, they found and put to death some wretched Turkomans, almost dead with hunger. There the Kalmuks attacked their auls and carried off a number of their people, whereupon a number of their supporters returned home again.

Meanwhile, the Turkomans of Khiva having been reinforced, offered them battle near Cheshmi.* A fierce fight ensued. At first the Uzbegs were successful, but the enemy rallied, and at length the former were obliged to withdraw to their camp, which they defended bravely for six days, when terms were proposed and each party agreed to return homewards, but Isfendiar had scarcely persuaded them to leave their camp when he ordered his Turkomans to attack them, and although they outnumbered the Uzbegs almost ten to one the battle was indecisive. Eventually Isfendiar spent the summer at Khiva, and Sherif Muhammed and Abulghazi at Urgenj.† The whole story seems more or less inexplicable, unless we are to read between the lines that Abulghazi had plotted against Isfeildiar, and been supported by the Uzbegs. The latter were apparently too weak to resist, and determined to disperse, and accordingly when the comet appeared, i.e., in 1628-9, they collected in small bands, and some went to Mavera un Nehr, and some to Turkestan; presently they formed three larger sections, one of which retired to Bukhara, one to the Manguts or Nogais, and the third to the Kazaks. Abulghazi joined these last, while Sherif Muhammed went to Bukhara. Three years after the dispersal, 2,000 families returned from exile, and were joined by 800 others who came from Bukhara. They settled about the mouth of the Oxus, where they were attacked and exterminated by Isfendiar.‡

I have already mentioned Abulghazi's visit to Ishim Khan of the Kazaks, and his introduction to Tursun, who took him with him to Tashkend, where he lived two years, until Tursun was killed by Ishim.§ He then told the latter how he had gone to him for help, but as matters were not propitious, he asked permission to visit Imaum Kali at Bukhara, which was granted him. There he received an invitation from the Turkomans of Khuaresm, who were it appears growing somewhat tired of Isfendiar, to return home. He accordingly went to Khiva, and Isfendiar retired to Hazarasp, where he was shortly joined by Sherif Muhammed. The two latter now made friends and made a joint attack on Abulghazi, who defeated them. This was followed by a series of struggles and mutual raids. Eventually Abulghazi was seized by order of Isfendiar, and conveyed under an escort to Abiverd, whose governor handed him over to the begler beg of Khorasan, who accompanied him to Hamadan to Shah Sefi, the grandson of Shah Abbas the 1st, who was then the ruler of Persia, and who sent him to Ispahan. There he was assigned quarters and a pension of 10,000 tengas, but he was also guarded.[*] Abulghazi spent ten years in Irak, viz., from about 1630-40, when he escaped. He tells us how he bought eight horses one by one, and secreted them in various quarters, and having secured some trusty servants, he disguised himself as a horse driver and his servant as a bek on whom he attended. At nightfall he got his horses ready, and was *en route* through the streets as the nakares were being sounded at midnight from the Nakareh Khaneh. On reaching the gate he shouted out loudly "Open the door." It was duly opened, and he went on. Near Bostam they passed a cemetery where three men were burying a corpse, one of them was a poor Seyid. With the latter he negotiated for some provender, and also secured his assistance in exchanging three of his horses, which were breaking down, for three better ones, his servant meanwhile duly acting the part of a bek, and seating himself on a mat in a most lordly fashion in the Seyid's house.[†] Having imprudently asked the route to Maghz by an unfrequented way, one of the bystanders, who was an old man, had his suspicions aroused, and charged him with being one of the Uzbeg prisoners attempting to escape, and he tried to persuade the bystanders to arrest him, or at least not to sell him any horses. This conversation took place in Persian which Abulghazi understood, and he was not long in concocting a story in which his servant the pretended bek paraded as Muhammed Kuli bek the Circassian, a Yuzbashi in the service of the Shah, and he himself as in his service, and that they wished to meet a famous Mollah at Maghz. This story with some embellishments passed muster, and the prince duly reached the edge of the desert, where he met some fugitive Turkomans from Mangushlak. They reported how three years before their land had been attacked by the Kalmuks, who had harried their herds. He made himself known to the refugees, who persuaded him to pass the winter with them, and in the spring to go to the Tekke tribe, which then encamped near the Balkhan mountain, on the Eastern shores of the Caspian. There he accordingly went, and passed two years, and then went on to Mangushlak, which was then subject to the Kalmuks, whose chief having heard of his arrival sent for him and having detained him for a year allowed him to return to Urgenj.[‡] This was in the year 1642. Six months later Izfendiar died ; Sherif Muhammed had died two years before.

ABULGHAZI BEHADUR KHAN.

Matters must have been in a more or less confused condition in the Khanate, for Abulghazi tells us it was not till a year after Izfendiar's death that he was proclaimed Khan in the district of Aral, where the Oxus flows into the sea, and doubtless the most thoroughly Uzbeg part of

            [*] *Id.*, 331, 332.   [†] *Id.*, 332, 333   [‡] *Id.*, 333-338.

the Khanate. Meanwhile, the Turkomans seem to have held possession
of the remainder, and to have had custody of Izfendiar's two sons,
Yushan Sultan and Ashraf Sultan. These they refused to surrender and
they also had the Khutbeh proclaimed in the name of Nadir Muhammed
the Khan of Bukhara, to whom they sent Ashraf. Abulghazi thereupon
declared war against them, and twice pillaged the environs of Khiva.
Nadir Muhammed nominated governors to Khiva and Hazarasp, and
sent the widow, son, and daughter of Izfendiar to live at Karshi.
His deputies were orly military governors, and the civil administration was retained in the hands of the amalats or civil functionaries
appointed by Izfendiar, who were Turkomans. Presently the
Bukharian Khan sent his grandson Kassim, the son of Khosru Sultan
to superintend matters, but he did not meddle with the Turkoman
deputies. When Abulghazi heard of his arrival he collected the greater
portion of his people and again marched upon Khiva. His force was
much inferior to that of the Bukharians who had ranged their men
in the form of a flight of geese, while he broke his up into several
sections. The Khivans were 1,000 strong, and 800 of them were dressed
in cuirasses, helmets, dobulghas, &c., so that only their eyes were visible.
Abulghazi had but five men, who were mailed. These numbers prove
how small and petty the importance of the Khanate was at this time-
Abulghazi describes the struggle which ensued, which he won chiefly
through the skilful disposition of his men. At this point his own
narrative of events ends and is continued by his son and successor
Anusha Muhammed.[*] After the battle Kassim was recalled to Bukhara
and replaced by Yakub Tupit, but soon Nadir himself was driven from
the throne by his beks, who proclaimed his son Abdul Aziz, whereupon
the garrison he had placed at Khiva fled, and Abulghazi set out from
Aral and occupied Khiva and the land of his fathers. This was in 1644.
He issued a general pardon to all the Turkomans who had fled and invited
them to return. Three of their chiefs named Ghulam Behadur, Din
Muhammed Un Un Begui, and Urus Begui, with a number of their
followers had escaped to the deserts near Hazarasp, and now sent some
of their aksakals or greybeards with their submission. Abulghazi promised them pardon, and summoned them to meet him at Hazarasp, and
ordered them to bring with them their airan or clotted milk and kalik or
cheese, but he had made up his mind to destroy them, and his son does
not scruple to confess it, and as soon as they had fairly arrived, and
were beginning their meal, a general massacre commenced, in which a
great number of them were killed, their goods were pillaged and their
wives and children reduced to slavery.[*] He then returned to Khiva,
and shortly after attacked and plundered another body of Turkoman
fugitives at Téyén. The fugitives from this place as well as others

---

[*] Op. cit., 340, 343.

from Khiva and Balkh took shelter at Bami Burma, where they built
themselves a stone fort and sent their families for shelter to Karakasti.
They were attacked however and destroyed to a man, while their camp
of refuge at Karakasti was also taken and sacked.†

In 1648, Abulghazi defeated the Koshote Kalmuks, as I have
mentioned,‡ and also sent home a Torgut chief named Buyan, who had
been to Khuarezm for purposes of trade. In 1651, with only a very
small body of men, and after a march involving great hardships, he
attacked the Turkomans of the Bairaj clan whom he destroyed, together
with their chief Bairaj, and harried their women and children. The
following year he did the same with the tribe of the Imirs which encamped
at Tuj, and with the Sarika.§ This same year the Torgut Kalmuks
under three of their chiefs made an attack in the neighbourhood of
Hazarasp. I have described how Abulghazi pursued them, and on their
behaving humbly pardoned them.‖

Having subdued all the Turkomans, Abulghazi had reigned for
some years in peace, when Subhan Kuli of Balkh sent to ask him for
aid against his brother Abdul Aziz, Khan of Bukhara. Subhan Kuli
had married Abulghazi's niece, the daughter of Sherif Muhammed.
The Khuarezm ruler did not forget how Abdulla Khan had slaughtered
thirty-two princes of his house, and otherwise illused his people; he
accordingly set out gladly for Bukhara, in 1064 of the hej, i.e., 1653-4.
Having arrived at Kukerdlik he despatched Bek Kuli Irnak to waste the
neighbourhood of Karakul, while he himself did the same at Suiunich
Bala and other villages near Bukhara, and thence returned to Kukerdlik,
whence he again set out the same year, encountered and defeated the
Bukharian army, and captured and burnt Karakul.¶ He then ravaged the
neighbourhood of Charjui, and a few months later the district of Yaiji as
far as Nerzem, and thence to Karakul, returning to Khiva with a large
number of prisoners; nor did the Khan Abdul Aziz venture to cross swords
with him. This was in 1065 hej, i.e., 1654-5. The same year Kermineh
was taken and sacked. As the Khuarezmian army, 15,000 strong, was
returning at daybreak escorting its plunder, it was suddenly
attacked by a Bukharian force. The Khan who had loitered behind
with only a few followers had to sustain a series of repeated attacks from
the enemy, who greatly outnumbered his people. We are told by his
successor that he would have been overwhelmed but for the timely
succour brought by himself, then only sixteen years old, who having
arrived with a fresh body of but 200 or 300 horsemen, charged the
enemy's host and routed it. There seems to have been a regular
stampede, and many of the Bukharians were drowned in crossing the

_____

* Id., 344.   † Id., 345, 346.   ‡ Ante, Vol. I., 503.   § Abulghazi, 347, 348.
‖ Ante, I., 563.   ¶ Abulghazi, 352.

river. Abulghazi returned to Bukhara in triumph, gave a grand
feast there, rewarded his son Anusha with a standard and a body of
troops, and gave him command of Hazarasp. In 1658, he ravaged
Vardanzi, and in 1661 once more wasted the neighbourhood of Bukhara
and returned heavy laden with loot. According to his son he now began
to realise that he had sufficiently ill-used his co-religionists, and
determined to devote the remainder of his days to plundering the infidel
Kizilbashis or Persians and the Kalmuks. He accordingly sent an envoy
to make peace with Abdul Aziz and handed over the cares of his
government to Anusha. He died in the year 1074 of the hej, i.e., 1663,[*]
after a turbulent and lawless reign whose ill deeds have been too
much condoned by the gratitude of students for the famous history which
we owe to his pen.

ANUSHA MUHAMMED BEHADUR KHAN.

Abulghazi was succeeded by his son Anusha Muhammed, who had
already, as I have said distinguished, himself in the great fight with the
Khan of Bukhara. On the death of his father he determined to make
an attack upon the same Khanate, notwithstanding the peace recently
concluded. He invaded Mavera un Nehr, and plundered the residence of
the Khojas of Juibar near Bukhara. It seems he was partly incited by
Sultan Kuli, the brother of the Bukharian Khan. Abdul Aziz happened to
be in Kermineh when this took place. He hurried back at once, and at
midnight arrived before the city, which was in the hands of the
Khuarezmians. Accompanied by only forty slaves he succeeded in
cutting down the guard, and forced his way, fighting as he went into the
citadel. From this place a summons went forth inciting the population
to murder the Khuarezmians that very night. All who could bear arms,
whether Uzbegs, Tajiks, or foreign merchants, fell upon the enemy,
whose retreat was cut off by barricades at the gates and other outlets
from the city. The massacre was terrible, and but a small party
of the army of Anusha escaped to Khuarezm. The catastrophe for
a long time discouraged his people from disturbing the peace
of Bukhara.[†] This invasion, although repelled, according to the
Tariki Mekim Khani, led to the abdication of Abdul Aziz, who
made way for Subhan Kuli. This was in 1680.[‡] The beginning
of Subhan Kuli's reign, as I have shown, was troubled by the
insubordination of his sons, and it was this which probably tempted
Anusha to make another venture against the Khanate. This was about
1683. He burnt the towns and villages and wasted the country around

---

[*] Id., 357.   [†] Senkofski, op. cit., 47, 48. Vambery, Hist. of Bukhara, 325.
[‡] Ante, 753.

Bukhara and carried off many prisoners. The Khan now summoned his son Sadik, who had recently rebelled against him, to the rescue, but he learned *en route* that Anusha had invaded Khorasan, had caused money to be struck there in his own name, and proclaimed himself the sovereign of that province, while several Amirs were in open revolt at Hissar and Khojend, and that others about the court secretly favoured Anusha. He thereupon determined to run no risks but to return to Balkh and to fortify himself there. The Khan thereupon turned to his faithful dependent Mahmud bi Atalik, whom he had appointed governor of Badakhshan. He marched to the rescue, and encountered the Khuarezmians at Gijuvan, where he completely defeated them and compelled Anusha to return home again.* The next year, *i.e.*, 1685, while the Khan was engaged in settling the affairs of Balkh, Anusha once more marched to the gates of Bukhara, but was met by Muhammed Jan Atalik who marched against him from Balkh and defeated him.† Sometime after Subhan Kuli having gone on a pilgrimage to Meshed, Anusha again invaded Mavera un Nehr. There was a general rally of the inhabitants and the Khuarezmians were once more beaten with great slaughter, the greater part of their leaders being killed. The turbulent ruler of Khuarezm was not likely to submit to this rebuff, and he was preparing a fresh expedition when a conspiracy broke out among some of his Amirs, who were discontented with him and were supported by Subhan Kuli. The conspirators spread a rumour that the Kalmuks were about to invade the country, and suggested that the Khan should give the command of the army to his son Erenk, who was in the plot. He was no sooner raised to this position than he had his father seized and his eyes seared with a hot iron and he then deposed him.‡

MUHAMMED ERENK KHAN.

Erenk having mounted the throne, proceeded to exile the Amirs who had been creatures of Subhan Kuli Khan, and when the army of the latter shortly after marched into Khorasan, and Bukhara was divested of troops, he seized the opportunity and invaded the district. Subhan Kuli defended his capital vigorously for ten days, and sent for his faithful Atalik Mahmud to go to the rescue, and on his arrival a savage fight took place under the walls. The Khuarezmians were beaten, and lost many prisoners. Meanwhile, the party which favoured Subhan Kuli at Urgenj, under his countenance proceeded to a new revolution there, and on his return from his unfortunate expedition Erenk was poisoned by the partizans of Bukhara among the Amirs.

---

* Senkofski, 51, 52.   † *Id.*, 53.   ‡ *Id.*, 54. 55.

SHAH NIAZ KHAN.

After this revolt the conspirators in 1099, *i.e.*, 1687, sent a deputation to Subhan Kuli, offering to coin the money and to have the khutbeh said in his name if he would choose them a ruler. The Khan thereupon nominated Shah Niaz Ishik Aka, and as the author of the Tarikhi Mekim Khani says he thus reduced to subjection a province against which he had not been able to defend himself.[*] Shah Niaz retained his authority over Khiva for many years, having been no doubt supported by Subhan Kuli Khan. In 1700 he sent an envoy to the Tzar, Peter the Great, asking him to take his country under his protection. This was answered by a letter dated on the 30th of July in the same year, in which Peter intimated his compliance with the request.[†] We do not read of him again, and it is not improbable that he withdrew or was deposed on the death of Subhan Kuli in 1702.

ARAB MUHAMMED KHAN.

On the disappearance of Shah Niaz Khan, the old royal stock of Khuarezm seems to have again occupied the throne in the person of Arab Muhammed, who was probably a son of Erenk Khan, and to whom in 1703 Peter the Great sent a confirmation of the friendly message he had already sent to Shah Niaz, and accepted him and his people as his subjects.[‡] Michell's authority has corrupted his name into Arak Ahmet.

HAJI MUHAMMED BEHADUR KHAN.

In 1714 an envoy went to St. Petersburg from Haji Muhammed Behadur Khan, who is expressly called a grandson of Abulghazi.[§] He was probably a brother of the late Khan and was speedily displaced.

YADIGAR KHAN.

He seems to have been succeeded by Yadigar, wrongly called Yadiber by Michell's authority, who was probably another brother of Arab Muhammed, and perhaps named after the stem father of the Khuarezmian Khans. Michell tells us he died in 1714, so that he must have had a very short reign.

---

[*] *Id.*, 56. [†] Michell's Central Asia, 538.
[‡] Journey of Blankennagel, by Gregorief Viesnik, Imp. Geog. Soc. for 1858. Note, 27. Michell, op. cit., 538.
[§] Senkofski, 100. De Guignes, iii., 513. Note, c.

4 s

ARANK OR EVRENK KHAN.

We now meet with a curious revolution at Khiva. We are told that the Uzbegs there grew tired of their legitimate rulers, probably in consequence of the divided allegiance which had caused so much jealous struggling, as I have shown, between them and the Turkomans. But as there was among them a singular devotion to the Imperial stock of Jingis Khan, they were in the habit of sending for a scion of this famous family from among the Kazaks, the Karakalpaks, or Bukhara, whom they made their ruler. Meanwhile, the old royal house subsisted among the Kunkurats, who had withdrawn to the Isle of Aral, by which the delta of the Oxus was known to Arabians.* The first recorded of these imported Khans was Arank or Erenk, who was a Karakalpak.† I know nothing more of him than the mere mention of his name, and he was apparently succeeded by Shirghazi Khan.

SHIRGHAZI KHAN.

Shirghazi, the successor of Arank Khan, was we are told from Bukhara.†

In 1713 there arrived at Astrakhan a Turkoman chief named Khoja Nefes, and suggested to Prince Samonof, a native of Ghilan, who had settled in Russia and become a Christian, that in alliance with the Turkomans the Russians should seize the district about the Lower Oxus, where it was reported gold was found. He stated that the Uzbegs of Khiva, from fear of the Russians, were in the habit of damming up the outlet of that river into the Caspian, but that with a little pains it could be diverted into its old channel. About the same time Peter the Great received news from Prince Gagarin that gold was to be found near Erket, i.e., Yarkand, in Little Bukharia.‡ The Khoja Nefes and Prince Samonof went to St. Petersburg, where they were presented to the Emperor by Prince Bekovich Cherkaski, a favourite of Peter's and a captain in his body guard. The report about the gold was confirmed by Ashur bek, the Khivan envoy, who was at St. Petersburg from 1713-1715. He suggested that the Russians should build a fort to hold 10,000 men at the old outlet of the Oxus, probably on Krasnovoda Spit, and he said the Khan would not oppose the removal of the dams nor the restoration of the Oxus to its old bed. Ashur bek left Russia in 1715 with a present of six guns and the necessary equipage for the Khan, but he was detained at Astrakhan, in consequence of the revolution by which Yadigar, Arang, and Shirghazi had displaced one another at Khiva.§

---

* Rytschkof, Orenburgische Topog., I., 19.   ‡ Michell, op. cit., 540.
‡ Muller. Saml. Gesb, &c., vii.. 157-159. Michell, op. cit., 538, 539.
§ Id., 539, 540.

It seems Ashur bek had also been commissioned by·Peter to visit India, and to purchase him parrots and panthers there."

Meanwhile, the reports about the gold sand seem to have stirred Peter the Great's ambition, and he determined to send an expedition to Khiva. In command of this he placed Prince Alexander Bekovitch Cherkaski, already named. He was the son of a Circassian prince who had sought refuge in Russia during the disturbed reign of Shah Hussein of Persia. On his death, his son Alexander had married the daughter of Prince Boris Alexandrovitch Galitzin, and been baptized and received a commission in the Guards. He was now chosen to head the Khivan expedition, from his supposed familiarity with the Tartars.† He was ordered to survey the old course of the Oxus, to persuade the Khan of Khuarezm to acknowledge the supremacy of Russia, and to build forts in suitable places, and especially at the mouth of the Oxus. After com-pleting this commission he was to enter into negotiation with Bukhara, and lastly to send from Khiva, Lieutenant Kojin to explore the road to India, and another officer to search out the gold mines of Yarkand.‡ He set out with letters of introduction for the Uzbeg Khans and the Great Moghul, and at the head of 4,000 men, in the summer of 1716, and built three forts on the eastern shores of the Caspian, namely, Tuk Karagun, Alexandrobaesk, and Krasnovodsk, the last being where the ancient outfall of the Oxus was supposed to be. Having left garrisons there, he despatched envoys to the Khan of Khuarezm to apprise him of his journey, among whom were a Greek called Kiriak and a gentleman of Astrakhan named Voranin.§ He then returned once more to the Volga, and having enlisted 500 of the Swedish prisoners then at Kazan as dragoons, and given command of them to Major Frankenberg, he embarked on the Volga and again set off in July, 1717, overland for Gurief with a body of Grebensk Cossacks and Nogais, and a caravan of about 300 men, people of Astrakhan, artizans, Tartars, and Bukharians. At Gurief he was joined by 1,500 Cossacks of the Ural. Two days after leaving that post he reached the Yemba, which he crossed on rafts. He also despatched the Murza Tevkelef to explore the route to India and China, but the latter was detained at Asterabad by the Persians, and when released was sent back to Astrakhan.‖

Prince Cherkaski was duly warned by Ayuka, the chief of the Kalmuks, and by letter from his envoy Voranin, that the Khivans were preparing to give him a hot reception, but he doubtless felt strong enough to cope with them. Two days after leaving the Yemba, according to Ahmedof, they reached Bagachatof, and in five days arrived at the Irkitsh hills, by which the Ust Urt or Chink is meant. Then mounting the plateau they arrived at the Aral Sea, along the margin of which they went for about seven

* Id.   † Hanway's Travels, i., 126.   ‡ Journ. Asiat., 1st Series, v., 67.
§ Id., 68. Muller, op. cit., 175-177.   ‖ Journ. Asiat., v., 69 70.

weeks, digging wells and cleaning out old ones *en route*. When they
arrived four days from Khiva, messengers met them from the Khan bearing
presents of horses, kaftans, &c., who were duly received by Cherkaski.
These friendly overtures were supplemented, however, by more than one
attack made by the Khivan cavalry, which, although disowned by the
Khan, were doubtless made with his connivance if not at his instance.
Bekovitch now rapidly approached Khiva, whose inhabitants began to
evacuate it.   Thereupon the Khuarezmians summoned a council, at
which one of their chiefs, named Dussan bi, suggested that they
should circumvent the Russians by perfidy.   The Khan entered into the
plan, and sent word to the Russian commander that he had misunderstood
the object of his mission, but having been informed by his friend the
Kalmuk Khan Ayuka that it was of a peaceful character, he expressed
his regret for what had happened, and welcomed him heartily to his
country, and to show his friendship he sent some of his principal people
to make an arrangement, and he begged him meanwhile not to enter the
town, in order that the citizens might not be alarmed. Bekovitch allowed
himself to be misled by these overtures, and with only a small following
of 500 men trusted himself in the city, while Major Frankenberg was left
in charge of the little army. As soon as they had got him in their
power, the Khuarezmians massacred his suite and made him write a
letter to the camp, ordering his soldiers to hand over their arms to the
Khivan commissaries for safe keeping, and take up their quarters in the
faubourgs of the town.   It was only when this absurd order, which was
perhaps forged, had been repeated three times, and Frankenberg had
been threatened with severe punishment, that he at length obeyed.
When the Russian force was broken up and scattered in its new quarters
it was attacked and overwhelmed.   Those who were not killed were
reduced to slavery.[†]   The Russians and some of the artillery-men
apparently joined the Khan's service.   Bekovitch himself, we are told,
was brought before the Khan's tent, and a scarlet cloth being spread out
he was ordered to kneel, and refusing, according to Hanway, instead of
suffering the easy death of losing his head with the stroke of a sabre, he
was hacked on the legs and butchered in the most barbarous manner.[‡]
His head was stuffed with straw and sent as a present to the Khan of
Bukhara, who refused to receive the trophy and drove the Khivan envoys
away, asking them if they were man eaters and drinkers of human
blood.[§]   The heads of Samonof and others were put on spikes at one of
the gates of Khiva.   Hanway was offered two slaves many years after.
They were Russians, and had been part of the prisoners captured from
Bekovitch, who had been sold by the Uzbegs to the Turkomans.[‖]   A

* Popof, Zapiski, Imp. Geog. Soc., ix., 262-265.
† Muller, op. cit., vii., 175-182.   Jour. Asiat, 1st Series, v., 70-72.
‡ Op. cit., 127.   § Journ. Asiat. Soc., i., Vol., 5, 72.   Michell's Asia 54
‖ Op. cit., 126.

memento of the expedition, in the shape of a square fort, built by the
Russians on this occasion, apparently still remains near the Gulf of Aibugir.*
Muller offers an explanation of Bekovitch's apparent want of prudence.
On his way to Khiva he received news of the drowning of his wife and
children on the Volga, which seems to have entirely disconcerted him.†
Danilofski says the Russians were killed not at Khiva but at Porsu.‡

A few years later, namely in 1725, we find the Italian Florio Beneveni,
an employé in the Russian Foreign Office, who understood Persian and
Turkish (one of those adventurous Italians who figure so often in the
politics of Central Asia), visiting Khiva. The journal of his travels has
been published in the Memoirs of the Imperial Geographical Society of
St. Petersburg. Beneveni had gone through Persia to Bukhara, where
he arrived in November, 1721, and where he had to remain for four years.
Abulfais Muhammed was then Khan, and by him he was received with
courtesy. The early years of the reign of Abulfaiz were marked by
intrigues and disturbances in the Khanate, and one party there apparently
wished to displace him, and to put Shirghazi Khan, of Khuarezm, in
his place. This plan was nipped in the bud, and a large number of the
leading Uzbegs were executed. The Khan greatly distrusted his people,
and employed the descendants of Russian prisoners and Kalmuks as his
body guards. Meanwhile, the discontented Uzbegs repaired to the
steppes and duly plundered the various caravans and convoys of food
that went to the city, which began to suffer severely. They were instigated and supported by Shirghazi Khan. The Bukharian chief, on the
other hand, entered into close relations with the Aralians, who, as I have
shown, were at issue with the Khivan ruler and partizans of the old Royal
House. They now set up Timur Sultan, the son of the late Musi Khan,
who is not named by any other author known to me, but who was probably
a descendant of Abulghazi as a rival to Shirghazi. We are told that
Musi Khan had been raised to the throne before Shirghazi, and had been
killed by the Khivans, whereupon his sons had gone to live at Bukhara.
The elder one had been appointed ruler of Balkh, and the younger one
was now elected their Khan by the Aralians. This was fourteen years
before, i.e., about 1707. A struggle now ensued between him and
Shirghazi, in which the Turkomans took a characteristic part, receiving
bribes from both sides, and returning home without doing anything.
Shirghazi then had recourse to craft. He sent the Uzbeg bi who had
instigated the murder of Cherkaski and three other Uzbegs to escort a
young damsel, to whom Timur was attached. The bi pretended he was
Timur's partizan, and wished to kill Shirghazi. Timur trusted and
rewarded him, and even consented to take his troops to a rendezvous
whence Shirgazi might be surprised. The bi now wrote to inform his
real patron of what he had done, but his letter was intercepted, and he

---

* Michell, op. cit., 24. † Op. cit., iv., 204. ‡ Popof, op. cit., 267.

paid dearly for his temerity. He was beheaded with his four companions, and the heads were sent as trophies to the Khan of Bukhara,* and we are told Timur twice attacked the town of Khiva itself.

Shirghazi lived a life of constant peril among his people, and apparently only succeeded in retaining his position by the distribution of liberal largess. He would have attacked Bukhara, but his men would not consent, and he consequently tried to break its Khan's alliance with Timur, and sent him several envoys. He was in constant fear that the Russians would march upon him to revenge the murder of Cherkaski. Peter the Great was at this time preparing a campaign against Persia. These preparations were thought by the Khivan Khan to be directed against himself, and he warned the Bukharian ruler that the Russians would not spare him if they conquered Khiva, and urged a common policy against them. Timur also informed Abulfaiz of these preparations, and was advised by him to receive the Russians kindly if they did not molest him.

To conciliate Peter, Shirghazi determined to release the Russian prisoners in his hands, and he sent pressing invitations to Beneveni to visit Khiva. Meanwhile turbulence prevailed at Bukhara. The different chiefs became mere leaders of marauders, and one of them, Atalik Ibrahim, seised on Samarkand and set up Shirghazi's cousin, whom he had married to his daughter, as ruler there, with the title of Rejim Khan. Ibrahim's influence attracted a large party to the banners of this pretender, and they laid waste the country in the neighbourhood of Bukhara. Abulfaiz appointed a new Atalik and ordered him to attack the rebels, but he complained that his soldiers would not fight and that they were clamouring for pay, and bade the Khan head his army himself. He dared not trust himself outside the town, however, and Beneveni was of opinion that if the Uzbegs had once secured his person they would have killed him. One of their grievances, it appears, was the countenance he extended to this kaffir agent of the Russians.† After Peter the Great's campaign against Persia the Uzbegs became less hostile to the Russians, but the same event seems to have increased Shirghazi's jealousy still more, and also his anxiety to have an interview with Beneveni. On the 16th of March, 1725, the latter wrote to his Government to say that Bukhara was in a precarious condition, that all the roads were occupied by robbers; and that the former ruler of Balkh had retaken that city and put the brother of Timur Sultan to death, and he complained of the terrible hardships he had suffered during the previous two years. He reported that Timur Sultan and his Aralians and Karakalpaks had twice attacked Khiva and twice pusillanimously withdrawn, and that his own efforts to leave had been frustrated by the intrigues of the officials. News now arrived that Rejim Khan

---

* *Id.*, 292.   † *Id.*, 293 and 294.

was marching on Bukhara from Samarkand, and a general panic seized the authorities, during which Beneveni left the city *en route* for Meshed.[*]

He had received several pressing invitations from Shirghazi to go to him. These he had hitherto evaded on the ground that he had no instructions from the Emperor to go to Khiva, and that he had written to St. Petersburg for them. Having heard of his approaching departure, he now sent him another messenger, and Beneveni at length consented to go, but urged that this must not be made known to the Bukharian Khan, who would otherwise detain him. He left Bukhara on the 10th of February, 1725, with a convoy of Russian slaves, merchants, and others, but he had to return again, as the Turkomans had planted an ambush to waylay him. Shortly after, he escaped secretly with but four camels, and went towards Khiva.[†] He sent on to apprize the Khan of his approach, and received a kindly message, and was offered a lodging in the house of Dostam bi, the Khan's favourite. He was told in order to avoid the suspicion that he was a spy, to dress in his European uniform, and to trim his beard in the same fashion. Negotiations were now opened for a treaty. The Khan's authorities excused the murder of Bekovitch, on the ground that he had marched on Khiva with hostile purpose, and urged that bygones should be bygones. The Khan also offered to release the Russian slaves at Khiva. A difficulty arose about the paltry value of the presents he was in a position to give, and Dostam bi, it seems, acted with the usual Uzbeg rapacity. At length Beneveni was admitted to an audience, at which the Khan complained of the ill-behaviour of the ruler of Bukhara towards himself, and how he had ill-used one of his envoys and sent him back, not to Khiva, but to his rival Timur Sultan. Beneveni replied with diplomatic tact, and seems to have created a good impression on the Khan.[‡]

The latter was suspicious of the motives of his journey, and was scarcely reassured when told the envoy had merely gone to congratulate Abulfaiz on his accession. He thought the Russians were spying out for a district producing gold. On the other hand, Dostam bi was very hostile. At this time Timur Sultan had defeated the Khivan troops, and was preparing to attack Khiva for the third time. The Khan was apparently much distressed, and Beneveni had his parting audience in the night. He left Khiva in August, accompanied by Subhan kuli as an envoy from the Khan, and duly arrived at the Russian frontier.[§]

Khuarezm was at this time the great slave market of Central Asia, and as many as 10,000 Russians and Persians were held in captivity there, and had to work in the fields and on the canals. They were sold in its markets by the Kazaks, Turkomans, and Kalmuks.[‖] In the year 1728 a plan was concerted among the Russian and Persian captives to kill the

---

[*] *Id.*, 299.   [†] *Id.*, 404.   [‡] *Id.*, 411 and 412.   [§] *Id.*, 423-424.
[‖] Muller Saml. Hist. Nach. 4, 20[6].

Khan and to replace him by the Chief of Aral (*i.e.*, by Timur Sultan). Rytschkof tells us expressly the latter was of the stock of the former Khans of Khiva.* As he could only muster 5,000 men he could not hope to conquer Khuarezm without assistance, and he apparently gladly availed himself of the offers made by the conspirators. News speedily reached the Uzbegs of how matters were drifting, and they fell upon the Russians before the Khan of Aral moved. Eighty of them sought refuge in a house, where they were beleagured, and caused the death of several of their assailants, but running short of provisions they were forced to make terms, and secured at least their lives. Two days after their surrender the Aral Khan arrived at Khiva, and finding the Russians had given in returned home again.†

Our next notice of Khiva is in 1731, in the reign of the Empress Anne, when we are told Colonel Erdberg was sent there as an envoy, but was pillaged on the way and returned home again.‡

I do not know how Shirghazi came to his end, nor have we any more information about this crooked period of Khivan history.

ILBARS KHAN.

A few years later we begin to have a more detailed notice of the Khanate, and then find it subject to the Kazak prince Ilbars, whose parentage I do not know. When in 1739 Nadir Shah returned from India, Abulfaiz, the Khan of Bukhara, sent to congratulate him, and received a courteous letter and presents from him, of which he informed Ilbars Khan, but the latter sent him a churlish answer, upon which Abdul Kerim remarks, "You cannot make a damned soul enter heaven even by force."§ Ilbars was a truculent person, and during Nadir's absence in India had ravaged the borders of Khorasan, an outrage which the great conqueror was hardly likely to submit quietly to.

While Nadir was at Charbekr he sent an envoy and two Khojas of Juibar to Ilbars Khan to summon him to his presence, and apparently also to obtain the release of the Persian prisoners in durance at Khuaresm. When this embassy arrived at Khankah and Hazarasp they found Ilbars encamped there with 20,000 Yomuds and other Turkomans, Kazaks, and Uzbegs, an army whose strength intoxicated him with a great sense of his own importance. In his letter Nadir reminded him that he was master of Iram as far as Adem, of Basrah and Muscat, of Khorasan, India, Kabul, Kandahar, Balkh, Badakhshan, Kunduz, and Khulm, as far as the Siah Posh Kaffirs, and of Bukhara, Samarkand, and Ferghana, and that his arms had been everywhere successful and favoured by heaven. It was necessary that the ruler of Khuarezm should also go to

---

* *Id.*, 208; Rytschkof, 1-19.   † Muller, op. cit., 208.   ‡ Michell, op. cit., 541-2.
                        § Schefer, op. cit., 96-7.

his stirrup, be clothed in a robe of honour and otherwise rewarded. He had not accepted his invitation to accompany him to India, and had thus failed to share in his Royal largess. Instead of behaving amicably towards his son, Riza Kuli Murza, whom he had left in charge at Meshed, he had organised several predatory raids of Yomuds and had ravaged the environs of that Holy City. Each time he had been defeated and forced to retire to Khiva, where he had not been pursued, because Riza Kuli had received no orders from his father to march against him. When he, Nadir, returned from India, "accompanied by victory, the divine aid, and good fortune," and had gone as a guest to visit Abulfaiz Khan, the most illustrious descendant of Jingis Khan, whom he venerated as a father, it was becoming that this short-sighted chieftain (*i.e.*, Ilbars) should have gone to his presence, where his past faults would have been pardoned and he would have been duly rewarded, but instead of going to him at Bukhara 3,000 of his Yomuds had marched against Charjui. They had been scattered like "the stars in the Great Bear," and most of them killed or made prisoners, and his anger had naturally been aroused, but Abulfaiz had interceded for him, and he had consented to send an envoy accompanied by two persons in the confidence of the Bukharian Khan. He therefore summoned him to his presence, promising him pardon if he went, and if he did not go he threatened "to tread under his country with his horses' hoofs and to hang his head like a ring from a gibbet."*

When Ilbars read this letter he fell into a violent rage and ordered the three envoys to be killed.† Hanway says two of them were killed and the third sent back with his nose and ears cut.‡ Nadir thereupon divided his army into two divisions and ordered one to cross the Oxus, while the other marched down its right bank to escort a flotilla of boats he took with him. The Persians speedily arrived at Hazarasp, where Ilbars and his people were planted. Nadir ordered his troops to pass Hazarasp by and to make straight for Khankah. Ilbars noticing this threw himself rapidly into the latter place, which was speedily bombarded. In three days he asked permission to capitulate, which was granted him. He presented himself with a sword and cord fastened about his neck, and was kindly treated by Nadir; but the sons of the Khojas whom he had killed having demanded his death, his execution and that of twenty of his officers was ordered.§ Thereupon the various towns of the Khanate except Khiva surrendered.

When Ilbars was threatened by the Persian Shah he sent an invitation to the famous Abulkhair of the Little Horde to go to his help. Abulkhair accordingly went with a body of Kazaks and Uzbegs and occupied Khiva. At this time the Russian engineer officers, Gladishef, Muravin, and Nazimof, had gone at Abulkhair's invitation to examine

* Schefer, op. cit., 101-104.   † Id.   ‡ Hanway's Travels, ii., 395.   § Schefer, 105-6.
4 T

the site for a Russian fortress at the mouth of the Sir, and had surveyed
the Kazak steppes.* Not finding the Khan at his camp they went on
to Khiva. On Nadir's approach Abulkhair sent Muravin and some
sultans with his submission, and asked to be allowed to retain Khiva.
The Russian officer was well received and given presents of robes and
money. Abulkhair was ordered to repair to the great conqueror's camp,
where he should be treated graciously as a dependent of the Russian
empress, with whom he wished to be on good terms. Whether suspicious
of Nadir's intentions or otherwise, Abulkhair refused to obey this summons, and withdrew again to his steppes.† The citizens nevertheless
determined to resist the Persians who beleagured the place, and after a
four day's bombardment compelled it to surrender. Nadir having selected
4,000 young Uzbegs, sent them to recruit his army in Khorasan, and
released the Persian and Russian slaves. There were then 12,000 of the
former in the Khanate. They were sent home and settled at a new town
built by the Shah, near Abiverd.‡

TAGIR KHAN.

Nadir now appointed Tagir Khan, a cousin of the ruler of Bukhara,
who had been his faithful friend, as Khan of Khuarezm, and having
arranged the affairs of the Khanate returned to Charjui. His reign was
very short, however, for we are told that while Nadir was engaged in a
war in Daghestan, in August, 1741, a band of Uzbegs and Aralians
sought the assistance of Nurali, the son of Abulkhair Khan, who marched
to Khiva, killed Tagir and some other chiefs, and occupied the Khanate.§
The leader of the rebels was called Ertuk Inak, and it seems they
momentarily placed Nurali on the throne, but having heard that Nadir
was preparing an army to revenge himself, Nurali left the Khanate and
rejoined his Kazaks. The Persian army duly went under the command
of Nasrulla Murza. Whereupon Ertuk Inak grew repentant, went to
meet it to Merv, and asked pardon. Nadir granted this in consideration
of the 500 faithful Uzbegs he had with him.‖

ABUL MUHAMMED KHAN.

Nadir now nominated Abul Muhammed, the son of Ilbars, who had
sought refuge under the shadow of his banners, to the Khanate. The
brother of Ertuk Inak and other chiefs joined the Persian army, probably
as hostages, while a number of prisoners were again released. Ertuk was

* Lervhine, op. cit., 291.   † Id., 295.
‡ Histoire de Nadir Shah, Sir Wm. Jones's Works, 396-7.   § Id., 345.   ‖ Id., 356.

appointed first minister. The latter was, however, shortly after killed by some rebel Uzbegs and Yomuds.[*] The Khan also seems to have disappeared.

ABULGHAZI KHAN II.

The rebels apparently placed Abulghazi, who is called Abulghagi by Jones, at their head. The Persian general, Ali Kuli, now marched to Khuarezm, where he defeated the Yomuds near Urgenj, and made them retire to Mount Balkhan. We are told that having regulated the district and given a ruler to the Khanate he returned to Khorasan. This was in 1745.[†]

KAIP KHAN.

In 1750 the Khan of Khiva was Kaip, the son of Batir, who had previously been set up by a section of the Little Horde as a rival to Nurali Khan.[‡] His father, Batir, seems to have ruled over the Karakalpaks. In 1750 an envoy named Irbek went to Russia to ask that the caravans going to Khiva should pass through Batir's territory and not through Nurali's. He seems to have received a courteous but evasive answer.[§]

The same year Aichuvak, brother of Nurali Khan, with a band of Kazaks made an attack on the Aralians, and carried off a large number of prisoners, cattle, etc. As these last were subjects of the Khivan Khan he laid hands on the people of Nurali then at Khiva, and in order to release them the plunder taken from the Aralians had to be restored.[||]

As Kaip forbade his subjects to traverse Nurali's territory when visiting Orenburgh, the latter grew angry, and in 1753 ordered a Khivan caravan to be plundered, and offered to subject Khiva to the Russians if they would send him 10,000 men and some artillery. The latter refused, and insisted on the captured merchandise being restored to its owners.[¶] Notwithstanding those good offices Kaip, in 1754, allowed a Russian caravan to be detained at Khiva, and it was only released a year later. The Kazaks under Erali sultan asked permission to punish this, and strangely enough Kaip at this time having sent an envoy to the Russian authorities the latter proved faithless to his master, and reported that the Uzbegs wished to be rid of him, and asked the assistance of the Russians to help them. The Russians would not act directly, but allowed Nurali Khan and his son Erali to undertake an expedition on their own account, and promised to ransom the latter if he was captured. The chiefs of the Little Horde thereupon summoned a council to discuss the matter, but having asked a Khoja for his blessing on the undertaking, he turned round on them

---

* Id., 378.　† Id., 389.　‡ Levchine, 219.　§ Id., 219-220.　Michell, op. cit., 542.
|| Levchine, 222.　¶ Id., 223.

and forbade it.* Eventually, at what date is uncertain, Kaip was
driven out by his own people for his rapacity and cruelty, and once more
went to live among the Kazaks of the Little Horde,† and he took part in
the various attacks made by the Kazaks on the Torguts during their
famous flight in 1770.‡ He was subsequently elected Khan by a section
of the Little Horde. This was in 1786.§ He married a daughter of
Abulfaiz, Khan of Bukhara,‖ and died about the year 1791.¶

ABULGHAZI KHAN III.

We must now try and realise the strange form of government that
ensued at Khuarezm. Probably on account of the hard treatment which
they had received at the hands of their Khans, the Uzbegs seem to have
determined to control their authority very considerably, but as it was a
matter of conscience with them to be nominally at least superintended by
a scion of the house of Jingis Khan, they, on the death or removal of
their sovereign, sent for a fresh one from among the Kazaks or Karakalpaks, who preserved the Imperial strain among them. These sovereigns
were merely titular rulers, however, and the real authority was in the hands
of the Inaks, or prime ministers, who were the senior bis of the Uzbeg
tribe of Kunkurat, or Kungrad, the most aristocratic among the Uzbegs as
it was among the contemporary tribes of Jingis Khan. These bis held the
hereditary post of Inak and were governors of Hazarasp. They became,
in fact, the Mayors of the Palace to the Rois faineants, and thus it came
about that both at Bukhara and Khiva there were at this time and during
the rest of the century double sovereigns, one titular and the other real.
The Khan himself, the titular sovereign, was kept in seclusion with his
family. He was fed on dainty food, and dressed in robes of gold
brocade. Every day the Inak and grandees had an audience with him,
and he never acted without the intervention of the former. Every Friday
the courtiers went to the palace, where the Inak sat beside the Khan,
and when the time for prayer arrived he assisted him to rise and supported him on his way to and from the Mosque.

After some years the Khan was generally exiled, and another one sent
for. As Abdul Kerim says, it was a system of playing with a Khan.**

The earliest of these Inaks mentioned by Muravief was Ishmed
bi.†† He was succeeded by his son, Muhammed Amin, who became
Inak in 1755, and continued to fill that post for seventeen years.
During his administration the Khanate prospered. It had no
coins, and the Khutbeh was said in the name of the nominal Kasak

---

* Id., 227.   † Id., 255 and 272.   ‡ Id., 256.   .§ Id., 277, ante, 667.
‖ Meyendorf, op. cit., 208.   ¶ Levchine, 285.   ** Schefer, op. cit., 179 and 180.
†† Voyage en Turcomanie, 271.

Khan. The money of Bukhara and Persia was used there.* On his seal, Muhammed Amin had the phrase : "Thanks to God, the prophet has a slave on whom he may rely." He was on terms of close friendship with the Atalik Danial bi of Bukhara, with whom he once sought refuge, and who assisted him to regain his authority in Khuarezm. I do not know the names of the Khans who occupied the titular throne after the eviction of Kaip. Muhammed Amin was succeeded as Inak by his son Ivaz, who is described as a person of great sagacity, and at the same time simplicity of character, but the Khanate seems to have suffered considerable decay in his hands. The Yomud Turkomans, who generally broke out into revolt at each change of Khan, refused to obey him as did those of Mangushlak and the Kasaks. The Kunkurats of Aral, under their leader Tureh Sufi, who was a relative of his, also refused to obey him.†

During Ivaz Inak's rule, Khuarezm was visited by Mahmud Shah, of Afghanistan, who was then a fugitive. He received him with great honour, set apart a large sum and bountiful provisions for his entertainment, and had a daily interview with him.‡ After living there four months Mahmud went to Asterabad, and was accompanied there by an escort of various nomades supplied by Ivaz.§

It was during the latter's rule also, that the Russian doctor Major Blankennagel visited Khuarezm.

He arrived at Khiva in October, 1793, and was confined closely in a house near the town. A few days later he was sent to see Fazil bi, who had grown blind.∥ Abdul Kerim says Fazil was Muhammed Amin's son and the brother of Ivaz Inak, and that his father and brother always consulted him on grave matters. He also tells us he became blind when old; that he was still living in 1818, and had built a splendid medresseh at Khiva.¶ Blankennagel soon saw the case was nearly hopeless. He was charged with being a charlatan and a spy, and some were for killing him, but after an interview with his patient matters became more comfortable, and he was invited to stay the winter.** His medicine luckily produced a strong reaction in the old man, and he got much better, which secured a great reputation for the Doctor, who soon had as many as 300 patients. As he prescribed to them for nothing he speedily won over a large number of partisans. They at length allowed him to leave the place, and presented him before he did so with a kaftan, belt, cap, horses, and ninety pieces of money, and also gave his companions kaftans, but they appropriated the good horses he had taken with him and gave him some very inferior ones in exchange. He despaired of persuading the Khivans to trade more freely with Russia at Mangushlak, and found them very jealous of her approach. He tells us the whole population of the place

* Schefer, op. cit., 176-7.   † Id., 18a.   ‡ Id., 52 and 55.   § Id., 55.
∥ Voyage, &c., 86.   ¶ Schefer, 178,   ** Blankennagel, 88 and 89.

was not more than 100,000, of whom 41 per cent. were Uzbegs, 15 Sarts, 10 Karakalpaks, 5 or 6 Yomuds, and the rest slaves. The army comprised some 12,000 to 15,000 men, of whom only about 2,000 had guns, the rest being cavalry armed with swords, spears, and bows and arrows. The Yomuds and Karakalpaks were reckoned the best of the soldiers, then the Uzbegs, and lastly the Sarts.

The Khan when Blankennagel was at Khiva was Abulghazi, son of Kaip. He is mentioned by Levchine, who tells us Kaip left two sons, Abulghazi and Burkan,* and from his account he seems to have also controlled a section of the Little Horde.† Blankennagel tells us the Khan was kept in seclusion, and only shown three times a year to the people.

Ivaz Inak died in 1219, i.e., 1804.‡

On the death of Ivaz his eldest son, Kuth Murad Bek, was pointed out as his successor by the suffrages of the people and of his brothers, but he would not accept the honour and resigned it in favour of his brother Iltazar, and he was unanimously proclaimed Inak. For six months he duly paid his daily devoirs to the Kazak Khan who ruled at Khiva, when one night he summoned his brother, Kutlugh Murad, and reminded him that Timurlenk, Nadir Shah, and Muhammed Rahim of Bukhara were none of them Khan's sons, but men like themselves who had earned their own fortunes. "Thanks to God," he continued, "I have judgment, courage, and soldiers. How much longer must I support this puppet? I wish to become Khan myself, and ask your advice. I will give the Kazak Khan a sum of money, send him home, and then rid myself of the Yomuds." Kutlugh Murad approved of this view, and duly recited the fatiha. The next day Iltazar had the Kazak Khan led out from the fortress and sent back to his own people.

ILTAZAR KHAN.

Iltazar told the departing Khan he was going to send for another to fill his place, but he proceeded to raise and equip a considerable force, and soon had a body of 10,000 Uzbegs by him clad in armour. He then summoned the ulemas and other religious notables, the ataliks, inaks, etc., and told them he had himself become their ruler and they had no longer any need of a Kazak Khan. All present assented and called down divine blessings on him except Bek Pulad, the Atalik of the Uighur tribe. The latter said, "This conduct is not worthy of you. Imitate the example of your father and ancestors. It may not be God's pleasure that you should bring so grave a matter to a happy conclusion." But as

---

* Op. cit., 285.   † Id., 287.   ‡ Schefer, 182.

the rest were unanimous he at length acquiesced. This opposition rankled in Iltazar's mind, but he postponed his vengeance and distributed robes of honour among the grandees, the ulemas, and aksakals or elders of the tribes. His name was duly recited in the Khutbeh, and he was congratulated by the Uzbegs, Karakalpaks, and Turkomans, except the Yomuds, whose *rôle* in the history of the Khanate recalls that of the janissaries in Turkey. Iltazar busied himself in preparing his army. Every day a grand band played before his palace, and he had a tugh or standard made which cost 1,000 gold miskals. When he rode out on horseback he was preceded by twenty couriers, and he was surrounded by his prætorians and body guards. He now prepared a campaign against the Yomuds, who lived on the road towards Asterabad and Gurgan. He had one of these robbers, who had plundered an Uzbeg, led round the market place by a rope through the nose; and he told them plainly if they would abandon their life of brigandage, live at peace, and pay the dues on their camels, sheep, and crops paid by the other tribes, they might have peace, if not they must take their departure. Robbers by instinct and profession, they would not submit to this order, and Iltazar marched against them. They were attacked, 500 of them killed, 500 made prisoners, and the rest driven into the recesses of the desert. Iltazar then prepared an expedition against Tureh Sufi, whose people occupied the so-called island of Aral, but he was unsuccessful, and returned to Khiva. He then wished to march against Bukhara, but Bek Pulad urged that it would be very imprudent to do so. This aggravated Iltazar's feeling towards him, and one day when the various amirs came one after another to the palace Bek Pulad was seized and cut down as he left the audience. His family and tribe, the Urghurs, rose in revolt. There were two encounters, and eventually Bek Pulad's sons fled to Bukhara and several of their chief supporters perished. The rest, in the graphic language of Abdul Kerim, "secured the kind of peace imposed by the wolf."* In order to secure his power for his descendants, Iltazar now united himself with the daughter of Akhteh Khoja, a seyid of illustrious lineage who lived at Urgenj, and whom he seized and married forcibly against her father's wish. He then determined to attack Bukhara, and first sent an envoy with proposals of peace to the Yomuds, inviting them to return home again, and couched in very friendly terms, and offered them further an opportunity of pillage in his new venture. This readily won them over. They accordingly returned, were granted lands at Urgenj, and largely increased Iltazar's power, who oppressed the people even more harshly than before.† In 1805 he marched against Bukhara. At this time Abdul Kerim was at Urgenj, on his way from Bukhara to St. Petersburg as the envoy of the Bukharian

---

* *Id.*, 187.   † *Id.*, 189.

Khan. He at once returned to Karshi and warned its governor of the preparations he had seen. He compares Iltazar to a bat, which only comes out and disports itself after twilight and retires again to its hiding place on the approach of day, and adds the further graphic illustration, "When the forest is deserted by the lion it is occupied by dogs and abject foxes."* A month later Iltazar ravaged the environs of Bukhara and carried off 50,000 sheep and several thousand camels. The Amir now awoke from the lethargy in which he was plunged, and began to make preparations. Meanwhile Iltazar renewed his incursions, and Muhammed Niaz bi was ordered to march against him with 30,000 Uzbegs. When Iltazar heard of their approach he armed 12,000 men of the tribes Teké, Yomud, Salor, Chaudor, Amir Ali, Buzeji, Uzbeg, Kunkurat, Kankali, Mangut, and others, and marched along the Oxus. He speedily surprised a son of the Dad khah of Bukhara and 500 followers, who had unwarily trusted themselves too far. They were bound with cords and taken to the door of Iltazar's tent, who with his people had cut off the retreat of the main army of Bukhara. The latter thereupon determined to attack him, and did so with such vigour that they were dispersed and many of them drowned in the river. Iltazar himself gained a boat, but many of his companions clambering into it, it sank, and he was drowned. His brothers Hassan Murad Bek and Jan Murad Bek also perished, Kutlugh Murad Bek was made prisoner, while another brother, Muhammed Rahim, escaped and made his way back to Khuarezm. The famous tugh or standard already mentioned was captured, and 1,000 people of distinction were made prisoners.† This was in 1806. Abdul Kerim tells us Iltazar struck money but he had no time to issue it. It bore the inscription, "Iltazar, heir of the kings of Khuarezm, has by the grace of God impressed his name on the gold and silver."‡ M. Veliaminof Zernof has, however, published a coin struck at Khuarezm in 1716 hej, i.e., 1801-2, but without a khan's name, which must have been issued by him.

MUHAMMED RAHIM KHAN.

The news of the victory was received with great rejoicings at Bukhara. The prisoners were relieved of their chains and pardoned, and the Amir summoned Kutlugh Murad Bek and his chief people, who were rewarded with robes of honour. The former said he was the slave and dog of the Amir Haidar and ready to do his bidding. A week later all the prisoners were released.§

Kutlugh Murad was nominated governor of Khiva, with the style of Inak, and left for that place with the other prisoners, but before his

* Id., 160.   † Id., 166.   ‡ Id., 181.   § Id., 167.

arrival the Khuarezmians had already installed his younger brother, Muhammed Rahim, as Khan. Kutlugh Murad acquiesced in this nomination and contented himself with the position of Inak, and then wrote to the Bukharian Amir saying he could not do otherwise than he had done as the people had forced his hand, and hoping he would excuse him carrying out his engagement with him.*

The two brothers now concerted measures for restoring prosperity to the Khanate. They organised an expedition against the Aralian Uzbegs, which was not very successful, but the borders of the sea of Aral were wasted. Some time after Muhammed Rahim's uncle, Muhammed Riza Bek, revolted at the head of a band of Uighurs. They began to pillage, but he was captured and executed. When peace was restored the Khan summoned sixty grandees of the tribe under pretence of rewarding them, but having got them into his power he had them put to death. During the winter the Khan organised an expedition against the Kazaks of Chekly, of Turt Kara, and of Chumeky.† The two former were ruled by Shirghazi Sultan, and the tribes of Chumeky, Jebas, etc., by Bulki Sultan.‡ These Kazaks had for many years infested the borders of Khuarezm, and had plundered the caravans which went there. Muhammed Rahim ordered the Yomuds and Uzbegs to attack them; they accordingly fell on the tribes of Chumeky and Chekly, harried them, and returned with their plunder to Urgenj.§ The subjects of Shirgazi Khan were forced to pay one per cent. of their sheep which they annually took to Khiva. Shirghazi himself went there in 1819 and died while Muravief was there, whereupon Rahim nominated his son as his successor, in which the Kazaks acquiesced.‖ The next year the tribes of Turt Kara and Oi were similarly punished, and in the winter "the isle of Aral," where the Kunkurats had been for so many years independent and whence they had made raids on the Khanate, was attacked. The Khuarezmians approached it over the ice. Tureh Sufi Murad still ruled over the Aralians. The struggles that ensued were apparently indecisive, when a Khivan fugitive who had long lived with Tureh Murad deemed it a good opportunity to make peace with his old sovereign. He and his son were the body attendants of the Aralian Khan. They assailed him with their swords when he was asleep, killed him, and put his head in a sack. They then took the grim trophy to Muhammed Rahim, who rewarded them and took them into his service. The Aralians having learnt the death of their chief submitted humbly, and the Khan returned to Khiva with the family and treasure of Tureh Murad and appointed his own deputy at Aral, while he married Sufi Tureh's daughter.¶ This doubtless greatly added to his prestige, since it connected him with the old royal stock of Khuarezm. According to

---

* Id.   † Id., 194.   ‡ Id., 195.   § Id., 197.
‖ Muravief, op. cit., 281.   ¶ Id., 198-9.

4 U

Muravief, he also married one of Iltazar's widows, who was the daughter of a Seyid, and two other maidens of the same aristocratic descent.* He describes him as a monster of cruelty, and tells us how he had the pregnant Aralian women ripped open and their unborn children hacked in pieces.† His measures produced at least tranquility, for those who were dangerous to him either became exiles or were put to death. He also stamped out brigandage and the arbitrary collection of taxes, for which he adopted a fixed rate, and instituted a custom-house and mint where gold and silver pieces were struck.‡

In 1813 he prepared an expedition against Khorasan with a force variously estimated at 12,000 and 30,000 and seven pieces of artillery. He invited the Tekke and Göklan Turkomans to join him, but they refused. He then turned to the Yomuds, who had recently suffered severely at the hands of the Persians and who gave an evasive answer. Nevertheless he marched on to Busreh, near the Gurghen, where he met a Persian army under the command of six khans. The Persians were strongly posted, and an ineffectual artillery fire followed. After four days spent in skirmishing the two armies returned to their respective homes.§ On his way back Muhammed Rahim fell upon the Göklans and carried off many prisoners. He also assailed the Tekkes, whose cultivated land he annexed to Khiva, and drove them to take refuge in sterile mountains, where they had to buy their grain at a high cost from the Khan and to pay him heavy dues. A number of these Turkomans migrated within the Khanate and were given lands along the canals.‖ In this expedition his men lost many cattle, etc., but the value of the dead camels and horses was returned to them on their tails being produced.¶ He also conciliated the Chaudor Turkomans who encamped about Mangushlak and who acknowledged his supremacy. Many of them also settled at Khiva.** This policy was a wise one, for it secured a safe passage for his caravans and for the trade of Khiva with Russia without the risks of the Kazak steppes. He also seems to have encouraged strangers to settle in his dominions; so that notwithstanding his tyrannical disposition the Khanate greatly prospered, and in fact he may be said to have been its creator as an important power.

Frazer describes a campaign undertaken by Muhammed Rahim in Kurdistan, which he dates about 1815. He took advantage of the disturbed state of Khorasan, crossed the desert, and beleagured the fort of Dereguz. The Kurds assembled from various quarters, and the Khivan Khan growing anxious about his retreat entered into a parley and suggested that they should join hands and make common cause against the hated Khajars. He raised the siege and the Kurds withdrew

---

* Voyage, etc., 277.   † Id., 278.   ‡ Id., 279-80.   § Id., 286.
‖ Id., 287.   ¶ Frazer, op. cit., 621.   ** Muravief, 289.

meanwhile sending a body of well-armed men to attend him as a body guard. Their chiefs would not trust themselves in his hands, but they urged him to advance on Meshed, promising him their assistance. He in turn became suspicious, seized the horsemen they had furnished him with, made an ineffectual attempt to capture Dereguz, and then retired towards Khiva with his prisoners. His men and camels suffered severely during the retreat, and he also treated his Kurdish prisoners harshly, except their leader, Bedr Khan, who being a good chess player he constantly had him to play with him.* Two or three years later the Kurdish chiefs being threatened with destruction by the Persians, sent an envoy to ask his help and offering to put their country in his hands. The Persians growing afraid of such a coalition agreed to retire and make peace with the Kurds, who thereupon, not being really anxious for an Uzbeg yoke, gave fresh instructions to their envoy informing him of what had happened and declaring their unwillingness to expose Muhammed Rahim to the risks of such a campaign. He saw through their subterfuge and imprisoned the envoy, but released him again on receiving a plausible message that if he would postpone his expedition till the death of Futeh Ali Khan he might easily conquer such parts of Khorasan as he wished, and that they would help him.†

In the earlier part of his reign Muhammed Rahim had no open war with Bukhara, although he seems to have ordered the Turkomans several times to pillage the Bukharian caravans. In the spring of 1820, however, he marched with a considerable force against the fortress of Charjui, which he besieged for a month. His heavy baggage and provisions were transported thither in boats. During the siege his people did not fail to plunder the Tekke Turkomans, who nomadised in the neighbourhood. While the Khan was absent on one of these raids the son of the Amir of Bukhara crossed the Oxus and took up a strong position in a defile between the fortress and the absent Khivans. A three day's battle ensued, which ended in favour of the latter, whose artillery decided the day, but each side returned home after the struggle.

The next year the Khivan Khan renewed his attack. This time Mir Haidar went against him. His guns stopped the Khivan flotilla, the water on the Oxus being very low, and when Muhammed Rahim sent his brother, the Inak Kutlugh Murad, across the river against them, he was defeated and lost several of his boats and many men, whereupon the Khivans again went home.

In 1822, being informed by a spy that Mir Haidar had gone against the Kitai Kipchaks, Muhammed Rahim crossed the Oxus at Hasarasp, surprised the town of Vardausi, whence he carried off many prisoners, and secured Chaidir, peopled by Khivans who had migrated

* Fraser's Khorasan, Appendix, 62 and 63.   † Id., 63-4.

from their own country. He then overran the country as far as Karakul, and returned without meeting the Bukharian army.° He seems to have had some remorse in his latter days for these attacks upon his co-religionists, and Burnes tells us that on his deathbed he counselled his relations to heal the differences with Bukhara, and before he died he sent an envoy to solicit the Amir's pardon for the quarrels he had so perseveringly promoted and the injuries he had inflicted on the commerce of his kingdom.†

In 1819 General Yermolof, the Governor of Georgia, having determined to enter into relations with the Turkomans east of the Caspian and with Khiva, organised an expedition thither. Captain Muravief was chosen to lead the expedition. He took letters with him from the Russian commanders. Having visited the Turkomans he afterwards landed at Krasnovodsk on the 19th of September. He describes with some minuteness the steppe intervening between the Caspian and Khiva, and the manners of the Turkomans living there. These nomades had been ordered to pay half a tilla, or eight francs, to the Khivan Khan for each camel in their caravans, and when he passed, there was much discontent about this and a conference was to take place with the Khan at Ak Serai to arrange matters.‡ He speaks in enthusiastic terms of the fertility of the land along the banks of the canals. He arrived near Khiva on the 6th of October, having been met outside the city by two officials, one of them named Al Chapar Alla berdi, who became his host with the double motive of squeezing some presents out of him and of gaining the Khan's favour by becoming his executioner if necessary. He was a Persian by birth, and distinguished by a long beard and a surprising greed for money. Muravief was afterwards sent to lodge at a fort named Il Gheldi, a private stronghold possessec by a rich grandee named Khojash Mehram, who placed his family and treasures there out of reach of the marauding Turkomans. Here he was kept a prisoner, was given tea, sugar, pilaf, and fruit for his meals, and allowed to take exercise in a small court and garden.§

He was looked upon as a Russian spy, and a council was summoned to discuss what was to be done with him, where various motives for his journey were discussed and it was determined to keep him confined. It is strange to read that Muravief consoled himself in his solitude by reading Pope's Homer.‖ At length, after being detained for some weeks, during which the Khan was absent hunting, and whose monotony was relieved by the visits of various natives prompted by curiosity and otherwise, he received orders to go to Khiva,¶ where he was lodged in the house of Mekhter Agha Yusuf, the first vizier of the Khan, and was supplied with immense dishes full of different meats, with tea, sugar,

° Baer and Helmersen, Beitrage, etc , ii., 60-63.   † Burnes, op. cit., ii., 384.
‡ Muravief, Voyage en Turcomanie, etc., 196-7.   § Id., 124-5.   ‖ Id., 131.   ¶ Id., 159-60.

and fruits.* He tells us the Khan worked at night and slept in the day time. Thus it came about that he had to send the letters and presents he had with him after nightfall. Among the latter were damask and other cloth, lead, powder and flints, and sugar, and some glass goblets which were a rarity there. He also sent the Khan's brother, Kutlugh Murad Inak, some presents.† He was at length summoned to an interview, and having put on his uniform, except his weapons, he was preceded by certain Yessauls, or heralds, who opened a way for him through the crowd, among whom, he tells us, he heard the voices of Russian prisoners.‡ He entered through a handsome brick gate into a court yard surrounded with mud walls, where sixty-three Kazak envoys were seated, waiting to take part in a feast, and who before leaving each received a piece of cloth with which to make a kaftan. In a second court, which was the arsenal, were seven cannons with their wheels, etc., broken. The third court was occupied by the council. A fourth court, rudely formed, contained the Khan's kibitka. Muravief was introduced in the usual form by a Russian malefactor who had escaped from Siberia and had had his nose mutilated.§ The Khan was seated in his kibitka, dressed in a robe of red cloth which Muravief had given him, and fastened round the neck by a silver brooch. His turban had a white band about it, and he was seated on a Khorasan carpet. He was about fifty years old, stout, six and a half feet high, and it was said that his horse could not carry him for more than two hours together. He had a thin beard of a light colour and an agreeable face, and looked more like a Russian than an Uzbeg, especially on account of his light complexion, his compatriots having dark hair, and he spoke easily with a dignified manner. He asked the envoy why he had gone there. The latter replied he had gone to tender the respects of his master the governor of the Caucasus, to open up close intercourse with him, and to divert if possible the trade from Mangushlak, which involved a steppe journey of thirty days to Krasnovodsk, which only required seventeen days journey across the desert. The Khan replied that the inhabitants of the former place were his subjects while those of the latter were subject to the Khajar rulers of Persia, and it would therefore not be safe for his caravans to go there.| He reciprocated the friendly expressions of the envoy, said he would send back some of his people with him, and then retired. Presently the Khan sent him a robe of gold brocade, an Indian scarf, and a dagger with a silver sheath. These he duly put on, as well as a kind of jacket with short sleeves made of Russian cloth of gold, while his cap was changed for an inferior one which the Khan had sent him. He was then summoned to another interview, where he was again cordially treated, a grey Turkoman horse was given him, and with two Turkomans

holding the stirrups and others the bridle he had a triumphant march
to his lodgings through the crowd.* Other robes of inferior quality
were given to his followers. Before setting out on his return Muraviof
distributed presents among the courtiers, especially remembering the
three principal grandees of the court, the Mekhter Aga, the Kush begi,
and Khajash Mekhrem.†

Having purchased some horses and other necessaries he set out on
his return by way of Il Gheldi, and again remarks on the numbers of
Russian slaves he noticed in the crowd, who cried out to him to bring
their fate before the Emperor, their common master.‡ The Yuzbashi
and two other Khivans, named Ashnazer and Yakubbi, accompanied him
as envoys from the Khan. He duly reached the Caspian, where a
Russian corvette was waiting for them.

The Khan's character seems to have been very moody. Abdul Kerim
says he was generous and religious, was fond of the ulemas, and was not
a tyrant. After this abstract statement he gives us a more concrete one
from which we may judge for ourselves.

One of his ministers, Yar Muhammed, who had served him many
years, was charged by some females with having made presents to one of
the Khan's wives, the daughter of Sufi Murad ; others charged a young
relative of Yar Muhammed's with having entered her apartments. In
vain the minister replied that the young lady, who was but fourteen years
old, had gone to his house unbidden, and that he had given her presents
to show her honour. He was seized with all his family, thirty-six
persons, young and old, down to infants in the cradle, and they were all
put to death, as was the daughter of Sufi Murad.§

Bedr Khan described the Khan as most capricious and as a
perfect madman, one day loading a person with favours, at another putting
him to death without any adequate cause. A good swordsman, spearsman,
and horseman, he says he was personally brave, but unskilled in war.
His troops also he described as brave but undisciplined, while the fortifications of his towns were contemptible. The Khan's royal equipage was
mean and poor.‖ This poverty is otherwise confirmed. We are told
that the rations for the Khan's horses and wives were duly weighed out,
and the latter were in the habit of sending the remains of their meals
to the bazaar for sale, so as to secure themselves a few copecks for pin
money, etc.¶ Mollah Murad Ali, a Kurdish envoy, who lived at his
court for two years, also describes him as of a violent and inconsistent
temper, although not so bloodthirsty as commonly reported. He was
quite ignorant or careless of the most commonly received international
amenities. The characters of stranger or guest had no sanctity for him,
and as he felt he was tolerably safe from attack the slightest suspicion

---

 * Id., 178-9.   † Id., 181.   ‡ Id., 187-90   § Schefer, op. cit., 200, 201.
     ‖ Frazer, 64 and 65.   ¶ Blankennagel, note. 8.

secured imprisonment, captivity, or death, without trial, examination, or appeal.* On this Frazer has some philosophical (!) comments. He says: "The lawless description of the community and the narrow theatre in which the Khan's character was formed, the necessity of strong measures to coerce such men as his subjects for the most part were, and to support a usurped authority with the ignorance arising from inexperience to compass these ends by other means than those of rigour and even cruelty, account in some measure for the capricious, inconsistent, and blood-thirsty character of the Khan without necessarily supposing anything unusually malignant in his disposition."†

Muravief reports him as formerly addicted to debauchery and drink, but as having become more temperate. He no longer became drunk and had but seven wives in his harem. Instead of brandy he drank vinegar and water, and he forbade his people to smoke or drink spirits under pain of punishment. Besides his native tongue he spoke and wrote Arabic and Persian, and knew something of astrology and medicine. He wore a simple dress made of Bukharian silk, and his food consisted of pilaf, of a kind of gruel made of buckwheat, soup thickened with saffron, and roast meat without butter.‡ Although he had fixed houses for his wives he spent most of his time in a moveable kibitka and was very fond of hunting and hawking. During his absence his brother, the Inak, or one of his favourites controlled affairs.§

He slept little and chiefly during the day, and did his business at night, a scheme suggested probably by his suspiciousness, and he was very fond of watching people play at chess.‖ On Friday his friends and the clergy met at his residence to say their prayers in common. He had two brothers, the Inak Kutlugh Murad and Muhammed Nasr.

The Khan bore the title of Taksir, i.e., "Error," probably with the meaning of corrector of errors; he was also styled Khan Khesret, Lord, and Khan Khoja. His power was supreme, and matters were arranged so that he and his favourites could get the most profit possible out of the state. Any patriotism or care for the common weal was out of the question. Each man's kibitka or house being his country, each one strove to conceal his wealth. Fear of punishment was the motive power in the Khanate, and as this diminished with the distance from the capital so did the tyranny. In this community of slaves the Khan was assisted by a council which judged civil causes and capital crimes. The council consisted of his favourites and merely did his bidding, while it served to screen him from the popular murmurs. When Muravief was at Khiva its president and state treasurer was the visier Yusuf Mekhter Aga. A Sart by origin he favoured his countrymen who belonged chiefly to the mercantile class. As he was also of the dependent race he was more subservient than an

---

* Frazer, 65.   † Id., 65, note.   ‡ Op. cit., 292.   § Id., 292-3.   ‖ Id., 293.

Uzbeg would be.* The second vizier, or Kush begi, was an Uzbeg, and was well spoken of for his resolute and obliging character. The third official, the Khojash Mekhrem, was the son of a slave of the Khan; he presided over the Customs. He was a Persian by origin and chiefly employed his compatriots. The Sarts and slaves praised him while the Uzbegs hated him; like most parvenus, he crouched before his master and was arrogant to those over whom he had authority. He was rich and retained the Khan's good favour by continual presents. He was no however a member of the council. The most potent members of it were Rahim's brother Kutlugh Murad and the Kazi or head of the Faith. The ministers of religion had their authority sharply controlled, and Muravief says "they had merely the unlimited right to appeal to God for his blessing and pity on the Khan and other true believers."† At the council also assisted the heads of the four Uzbeg tribes, who sat according to seniority, but their position was merely an honorary one. The council met weekly on Fridays in a hall with a thatched roof, with a round opening to the sky, and without windows or floor. It was dignified with the name of Ghernush Khanah or Hall of Secret Audience.‡ The Khan generally presided and the sitting began with a meal of pilaf. The members of the council received no regular pay, but had concessions of land or the right° to dig canals. The local courts were presided over by inferior Kazis. Among the punishments in vogue were hanging by the feet until death ensued, and impalement, which was rendered more cruel by the prisoner being first pinioned, and when the stake was in his body his legs and arms being loosened.§ The bastinado was freely used, and in some cases, as for instance as a punishment for smoking, the mouth was slit open on either side as far as the ears; infidels were buried alive so that their blood might not soil the sacred land, and Muravief declares that Bekovitch was himself flayed alive and his skin made into a drum cover. Slaves were too valuable to be killed and were punished by being mutilated, nailed to the door post for a while, etc. These diabolical cruelties prove what a charnel house and focus of brutality the Khanate was and how necessary that it should be trampled under. Among the Khan's favourites, who were nearly all foreigners, much to the chagrin of the lordly Uzbegs, was a fugitive from the borders of China and a Russian renegade. The latter was styled Tangri Kuli, i.e., servant of God.‖

The money current in the Khanate consisted of gold tillas, silver tengas, and copper puls; Bukharian, Persian, and even Dutch coin was also current, and Muravief says that in the ruins of Old Urgenj sacks of money often occurred which were claimed by the Khan as treasure-trove. The Uzbegs and Turkomans paid no taxes, but in lieu of them gave military service and furnished themselves. The latter

* Id., 297-9.   † Id., 302.   ‡ 303.   § Id., 310.   ‖ Id., 305-6.

in fact received state pay. The most important tax was the house or cauldron tax, which was collected by the elder of each clan or family, who was an elected official. Besides the produce of the royal demesnes, which were cultivated by his slaves, the Khan drew a tax from all sales of grain ; the price of this he also insisted upon fixing. He was also the owner of several canals whose water he farmed out. All articles entering the Khanate paid customs duty and all shops a licence tax. In case of raids or barantas made on Persia, etc., the Turkomans and others had to surrender one-fifth of their plunder to the Khan.* He also drew a large revenue from the presents made to him by those expecting favours or protection.

The Sarts were the chief merchants, and with them trade meant the art of deceiving and cheating. Muravief calculates the state revenue at 4,000,000 francs annually. There was little opportunity for amassing money, as the Khan had to secure his position by continual largess. His chief wealth consisted in precious stones, horses, and cannons. Muravief describes in detail the products and commerce of the Khanate. In the slave market Russian men obtained the largest price, but their women were not so costly as those of Persian blood.† The best proof of the unsettled condition of affairs was the number of forts scattered about the country, where the great proprietors maintained garrisons to protect their labourers and produce from sudden attacks of robbers. These were generally square and made of earth, and contained a reservoir of water, dwellings, mills, oil presses, stables, shops, etc.

The Khan had several hunting lodges fortified in the same way, the chief being Akserai, Mai Jenghil, Khan Kalassi, etc.‡ There was no regular army, and the general levy of Uzbegs and Turkomans consisted of about 12,000, which could be doubled in case of necessity by arming the Karakalpaks and Sarts. This army was ill-organized and disciplined but the men were unsurpassed as skirmishers or scouts. As it consisted entirely of cavalry it could only fight on level ground, and was much embarrassed when attacking fortifications. It received no pay, therefore a month or six weeks was almost the limit during which it could be kept under arms. The Khan maintained a cannon foundry, overlooked by a Turk from Constantinople. The guns were served by Russian prisoners. I must remit my readers to the narratives of Muravief and other recent travellers for an account of the manners and customs of the inhabitants of the Khanate, and must now on with my story. Muhammed Rahim died in 1241, i.e., 1825. M. Vel Zernof has published one of his coins, on which he styles himself Muhammed Rahim Behadur Khan, and which was struck at Khiva in 1236 hej, i.e., 1820-1. Other coins with other dates are extant.§

---

* *Id.*, 323.   † *Id.*, 342.   ‡ *Id.*, 350.
§ Coins of Bukhara, etc.

ALLAH KULI KHAN.

Muhammed Rahim was succeeded by his eldest son, Allah Kuli, who, having received a well filled treasury, soon began to dissipate it in a war with Bukhara. The Kazaks, who had been retiring south before the Russian advance, were claimed as subjects both by Bukhara and Khiva, and there were perennial struggles between them ; and we are told that even when Khiva was threatened by the famous armament under General Perofski, the Bukharian Amir extended his forays as far as Hazarasp.[*]

In 1832, Allah Kuli marched with all his army to Merv, and levied contributions from the Tekke Turkomans. He fixed a custom house there and at Sirakhs, where the Salor tribe had its camp, and he afterwards levied duties on the caravans which passed those places. The road from Khiva to Merv is over a very sterile country, and the Khivans had to dig wells at every stage of their march. The Khan commanded the expedition in person and gave out that he had marched to oppose the Shah Abbas Murza, who threatened him from Meshed. He took a vast number of camels with him, and 2,000 of these beasts perished *en route*. Burnes says that in Rahim Behadur's march over the same country he had had to leave his guns on the road, and that one still remained there when he wrote.[†] It was doubtless on this occasion that the Khan captured the fort of Muzderan, razed its fortifications, and transplanted its inhabitants. A large number of them took refuge in a cave, " and," says Burnes, " as they issued like bees from a hive they were put to death, or sent in perpetual exile across the desert."[‡]

Burnes, on his return to Persia, went past the Khivan camp on the Murghab. The Khan himself had returned to Khiva a few days before. Before they reached the camp a Yuzbashi with some attendants visited the caravan to exact the dues. Burnes describes him as an elderly man with a large tilpak stuck on his head. He was received with obsequious politeness by the merchants, who presented him with tea and tobacco, silks, cloth, raisins, and sugar, and then displayed their merchandise. " Every person made an offering," he says, " and we sent two handfuls of raisins and a bit of sugar as our homage."[§] The Yuzbashi demanded the usual tax of one in forty, refrained from opening the bales and accepted their statements as to the contents, invoking the wrath of the Khan, his master, upon any one who dared to deceive him.[‖] The total dues amounted to 200 golden tillas, and the merchants escorted the polite publican to his horse. On reaching the Uzbeg camp they found a party of 350 Turkomans just setting off on an alaman, and heard the Yuzbashi give them his parting blessing, " Go and bring the Prince Royal of Persia,

[*] Vambery's Bukhara, 377.   [†] Burnes's Travels, i., 385-6.   [‡] Op. cit., ii., 70.
[§] Op. cit., ii., 30.   [‖] Id.

Abbas Murza himself, to the feet of the Khan Huzrut,"* he said. The caravan went past Sirakhs, the headquarters of the Salor Turkomans who paid a sparing and doubtful allegiance to Khuarezm and Persia, and at this very time detained a Persian envoy in chains, while they refused to grant a share of the transit dues to the Khan.†

At Sirakhs, Burnes met the alamans on their return. They dropped in, he says, by twos and threes, with their horses lame and jaded, and by evening upwards of a hundred had arrived. They had made a descent on Meshed four days before, about ten in the morning, and had ridden right up to the walls of the town, driving men and animals before them. They were not opposed, and when a few miles from the city having counted their gains found they had 115 human beings, 200 camels, and as many cattle with them. They had already divided the booty, one-fifth being given to the Khan of Urgenj. Burnes appositely compares these raids made in the name of religion against the heretic Kizilbashis with the similar raids made by the Spaniards upon the Mexicans and Peruvians, where the butcheries of the natives were defended and even blessed by the priests, and where the King of Spain was also presented with a fifth of the spoil.‡

Let us now turn to the intercourse between Khiva and Russia. At this time there was a very thriving trade carried on by the caravan route leading from Bukhara by Urgenj and Mangushlak to Astrakhan. About 1820, during the late Khan's reign, when Khiva and Bukhara were at war, the Russians tried to open a new trade route by the eastern shores of the Sea of Aral. The route having been surveyed and found practicable a caravan set out duly escorted by 500 soldiers and two guns. It seems the Khivan Khan was afraid that this contingent of troops might be used against himself, and sent word to the Russian commander that he could not allow reinforcements for the enemy to march across his territory, but that the Russians were free to go to Khiva whenever they pleased and he promised them his protection there. The Russians disregarded this message and tried to force their way, and when the Turkomans and Kazaks assailed them they stockaded themselves. They had not much difficulty in defeating their nomade opponents, but they had to retire eventually after burning and losing their merchandise.§ This aroused an ill feeling between the two countries, and led to mutual raids being made.

The Russians had been long suffering enough, crowds of their countrymen were held in bondage in Khiva, and their caravans were being constantly plundered. At length, in 1835, they determined to build a fort to command the landing places at Mangushlak and to overawe the Khivans. This greatly irritated Allah Kuli Khan, who threatened to make reprisals, and a party of 120 Russians having soon after gone out

---

* *Id.*, 38 and 39.   † *Id.*, 51.   ‡ *Id.*, 64.   § Burnes, i., 428.

reconnoitring they were captured and sold as slaves at Bukhara and Khokand, notwithstanding the remonstrance of the Emperor. In 1836 the Emperor Nicholas ordered an embargo to be laid on all Khivan merchants at Orenburgh, Astrakhan, etc., and their release was forbidden unless the Russians held in bondage were released and depredations in Russia ceased. The Khivans returning from the Great Fair at Nishni Novgorod, who are said to have numbered forty-six, were accordingly detained in August, 1836; and General Perofski, the Governor of Orenburgh, wrote to the Khan to tell him that his actions were bad, that bad seed produces bad fruit, that he must return the prisoners, cease his life of rapine and interfering with the Kasaks, and give the Russians in his country the same privileges accorded to Khivans in Russia. In January, 1837, an envoy arrived to say the Khan was ready to release the Russians if the Khivan traders were allowed to go and the fort of Novo Alexandrofsk was razed. The latter demand was ignored, and in regard to the former the release of the merchants was promised when the Russian prisoners should be set free. In November of the same year Kabul bi, whose son was among the detained Khivans, arrived at Orenburgh as the Khan's envoy, escorting twenty-five prisoners, and taking considerable presents. The Khan also promised to send back others. It seems he was afraid he would be asked for the kun or blood money for the life of Prince Bekovitch and of the Russians who had died in captivity, and for compensation for the plunder of the various caravans. A reply was sent back that Russia could not abate her claims nor release the Khivans until all the prisoners were set free. After waiting two years scarcely 100 men were restored, while in 1839 about 200 fishermen were seized on the Caspian.* It was therefore determined to adopt more active measures, and on the 26th of November, 1839, a proclamation was issued setting out the grievances of Russia.† In the beginning of 1840, General Perofski left Orenburgh with about 6,000 infantry, 10,000 camels, and an army of drivers. The winter was chosen as affording a more certain supply of water. But the weather proved unusually severe and the thermometer fell to 40° below zero; snow was piled up in drifts, and a terrible wind swept over the naked steppes. Several thousand soldiers were frostbitten and lost their legs and arms, and a great number of men and animals perished before they reached Akbulak on the Russian and Khivan frontier.‡ Meanwhile, the Kushbegi left Khiva with several thousand men to oppose the enemy. They found the snow 5 feet deep and had to drive a herd of Kazak ponies before them to open a way and then rode with a wall of snow on either side. An advanced body of Turkomans made a raid on the Russian cattle, but were hotly pursued and lost forty of their men. The Uzbeg general in a letter to his master described the Russians as half-starved, pig-eating, idol-worshipping sons

---

* Michell, 547-8.   † Id., 549.   ‡ Ferrier, Afghans, 422.

of burnt fathers. He spoke of them as soldiers in contemptuous terms, and as the Khan could easily dissipate them at any time he requested permission to retire to winter quarters to Kunkurat. His men had suffered terribly from the frost—feet, ears, noses, and even men's tongues, which were protruded while sleeping, had been frostbitten and lost.[*]

Perofski finding the elements too much for him determined to retire, which he accordingly did after losing the greater part of his army. This untoward event was not ungrateful to the English diplomacy of that time, and Major Todd, who was then at Herat as agent, sent the Kazi Muhammed Hassan on an embassy to Khiva to draw closer the bonds between the two countries. At this time the Vizier Yakub Mekhter was very hostile to the English, and the Kazi met with a rude reception from him. He had an audience with the Khan, who reproached him for having introduced the English who were Kaffirs into a Mussulman land. To this he replied that Allah Kuli had himself refused to assist his senior brother, Shah Kamran, and had forbidden his subjects to furnish him with provisions, and that the Bukharians and Muhammedzis had followed his example and joined the Khajars, whereupon the English came to the rescue with their corn, gold, blood, and intellect to defend the ramparts which were crumbling under the balls of Muhammed Shah, and protected the true Mussulmans against the heretics, and he ended up by asking who were Infidels, the Persians whom he had supported or the English who had protected the true believers, and might ere long be needed to stem the invasion of Russia.[†] At this point, seeing the impression he had produced, the Kazi drew from his pocket a letter from Major Todd, and assured him that its words were so many precious pearls which he had woven into a wreath of friendship, etc. It was contained in a silken bag embroidered with gold. The Khan greedily broke the seal and read the letter containing the proposals for an active alliance against Russia. The Khan was much pleased with the letter and with the optical instruments and splendid arms which accompanied it, while Yakub Mekhter, whose insolent behaviour had reached the Khan's ears, was temporarily disgraced.[‡] The draft of a treaty was arranged, and the Kazi set out on his return. He was waylaid near Merv by Niaz Muhammed Khan, the uncle of Yakub Mekhter, from whose minions he escaped with difficulty. When the Kazi had reported the success of his mission to Major Todd that officer despatched Captain Abbott to Khiva. He was instructed to obtain the liberation of the Russian prisoners, and then to go to Astrakhan, and, if possible, secure the release of the Khivan merchants. Abbott set out in the spring of 1840, directly after the disaster to General Perofski's column.[§] En route he sent on a messenger to acquaint the Khan with his approach, who found the latter seated in his black tent, whereupon he took off his shoes, raised the

---

* Abbott's Journal, 91-2   † Ferrier, op. cit., 424-5.   ‡ Id.   § Id., 426.

curtain, entered, crossed his hands, and said, Salaam Alikum, and stated
his mission. The Khan treated him kindly and sent out a lordly escort
to meet Abbott, who was assigned quarters in one of the Vizier's palaces
outside the town.* Abbott entered the city in his embroidered uniform and
gold epaulettes, attended by the master of the ceremonies and a brilliant
escort with bejewelled bridles and handsome matchlock guns, who discharged their pieces, and wheeled their horses at full speed *more Asiatico.*†
He entered the town through a crowd of people, and then repaired to his
lodgings. He was assigned two tillas a day, or twenty-eight shillings for
his maintenance, which he, however, refused to accept, much to the profit
of the Vizier.‡ He had pheasants, melons, grapes, etc., for his meals, and
fared sumptuously. It was not long before he was summoned to an audience
with the Khan, and he tells us the housetops on his way were crowded with
women. The palace, a poor brick building at a corner of the city wall,
had some brass guns near one of its gates. Having entered an outer
room he mistook the vizier for the Khan and duly saluted him ; he says
he was a dark, high featured, long bearded man, who reminded him of
the knave of clubs, and was dressed in a large Uzbeg cap and a quilted
chintz robe. He was first offered some refreshments, then after
remaining for about an hour kneeling in the recognised constrained
attitude, he was summoned to the Khan's presence, presented his
credentials and gifts, and stated the object of his mission as being to
cultivate a mutual friendship between England and Khiva, and doubtless
also to thwart the ambition of Russia.§

Abbott describes Allah Kuli, whom he calls the Khan Huzrut or Supreme
Khan of Khuarezm, as about 45 years old, of an ordinary stature and
very agreeable countenance, and as having more beard than most of the
Uzbegs, due to the mixture of Persian blood in his veins. He says he
was amiable and just, with a sound judgment, but with a hard disposition. Major Gens says he knew Russian, which he had learnt from an
Astrakhan captive named Phoma, *i.e.*, Thomas.‖ Like his countrymen he
was fond of sport, and spent several months in the winter in hawking and
coursing. He had strictly but four wives, but, says our author, as he
was an admirer of beauty these were occasionally changed, so that the
total number claiming the position was twelve, several of whom had
families. Their title was Babi, and they were chiefly of Uzbeg race
chosen from among the branches of the royal family. The Khan's
brother, Rahman Kuli, held the office of Inak of Hazarasp. He was a
tall and powerful person with a vigorous mind and much consulted by
his brother. The Khan's eldest son, or the Tureh, acted generally as
regent when his father was away hunting, otherwise he took no part in
affairs. Of the officials the Mekhter was the most important. The

* Abbott, i., 61-4.   † *Id.*, 64.   ‡ *Id.*, 67.   § *Id.*, 77.
‖ Baer and Helmersen, Beitrage, i., 63.

former holder of the office, Yusuf bi, was remarkable for his humanity
and talent and had held the post under five successive monarchs. From
respect to his memory the office was given to his son Yakub bi, whose
incapacity and irresolution are inveighed against by Abbott. The
Kushbegi had also succeeded his father in his office. He commanded
the force sent against the Russians, in which campaign we are told he
exhibited neither courage nor military skill. The government of the
country was purely autocratic, the monarch himself transacting all important business and giving special orders on all important affairs, the
prime minister, or mekhter, having little more authority than an English
under secretary. The Kushbegi, or Grand Falconer, who was commander-
in-chief, discharged alternately high military functions and the meanest
of a civil character. Even the priesthood had small influence.[*]

When Abbott was presented he found the Khan seated on a
carpet and supported by several cushions. He was dressed in a
green cloak fringed and lined with dark sables and showing at the
waist a gold chain; a large Uzbeg cap of black lambskin was
on his head, a dagger with a golden sheath in his belt. The
dark tent in which he sat was about 24 feet in diameter and
contained no furniture but the carpet and cushions just mentioned; a
fire burnt in its midst, and the smoke went out at a hole in the ceiling.
The Khan, it seems, was devoted to smoking, which was said to be his
only vice, as he neither snuffed nor drank and had but four wives.[†] The
audience over, Abbott sent a letter and rifle he had brought with him to
the Khan's brother, the Inak of Hazarasp. He also received permission
to ride out about the place and send his people out as he pleased.[‡] He
was soon summoned to another audience where he was questioned as to
the relative power of Russia, England, and other European countries; as
to his capacity for discriminating whether gold was found in certain neigh-
bourhoods, and as to his knowledge of medicine. The Khan had a sore
ear for which he asked the English Elchi to prescribe, and the latter
prudently recommended him to wash it with soap and water and to sit
facing the wind.[§] Abbott then urged the Khan to use his good offices for
the release of Colonel Stoddart, but he replied that he was on terms of
defiance with the Amir, who he said was a madman, and ended by
inquiring what ransom the English would give for him.[‖] Soon after
he had an audience with the Vizier and discussed with him the recent
Russian expedition. He urged on that official the necessity of the
release of the Russian prisoners before the Khivans could expect any
assistance from England, and was assured the Khan meant soon to
release them all. The Khan now sent a messenger to the Amir of
Bukhara to solicit the release of Colonel Stoddart.[¶]

---

* Abbott's Journal, ii., 332-34.   † Id., 178.   ‡ Id., 79 and 80,   § Id., 84.
‖ Id., 85.   ¶ Id., 95.

In another audience Abbott presented the Khan with a map of Europe, the names being written in Persian, and pointed out to him the interest England naturally felt in Central Asia from her relations with India, and the necessity there was both for her and the Khivan Khan to restrain the ambition of Russia. He also explained her policy towards the Afghans, etc.* In another interview the discussion turned on the recent Russian expedition and the release of the prisoners. The Khan was evidently afraid of Russia, and produced a six-pound shot polished like silver which had been carried off by his people in the recent skirmish, and Abbot concluded from the effect of this shot on the Khan's nerves that "so long as it remained in the royal pavilion it would keep ajar the door of reconciliation."† He now prepared for his journey to Russia, to secure the assent of that power to the terms for the exchange of prisoners he had arranged. The Khan suggested he should go by way of Mangushlak, as the district about Mount Balkhan was in the hands of the Yomuds, who were in revolt against him.‡ It is curious to find the Khan in discussing the power of various nations describing China as the most powerful of empires,§ showing how long the tradition of its strength survived in Central Asia. Abbott's departure was constantly delayed on the plea that the Caspian was frozen and the steppes were deep in snow, and he was sharply interrogated about various embarrassing matters—for instance, as to the Russians being idolators, and as to Christians believing in more than one God. In regard to the latter point Abbott neatly escaped the difficulty. "Do you believe Christ to be the son of God?" he was asked. "What do you call him?" he said. "He was the son of Huzrut Mariam." "And his father?" They could not answer this. "But what do your books call him? Do they not call him Ru Allah, the Spirit of God?" On their not having a reply he said, "Will you explain this—the spirit of a spirit? I will then inform you why we call him, as he called himself, the Son of God."‖ He was asked if he had ever seen the mountains of Kaf through the chink in which the first dawn shows itself on Bab ul Mandeb, where an angel stands whirling a fiery sword, etc. The most embarrassing questions were generally about the pig, and Abbott had to show considerable ingenuity to avoid confessions on this crucial matter. He did this by affecting not to know what was meant by khuk, i.e., pig, and neatly turned the table on the Uzbegs by asking if they meant that animal with long ears and a sweet voice, the ass, and saying, "No, we never eat anything so unclean." The wild ass was an Uzbeg delicacy.¶

Such traps and pitfalls were laid for him at every corner, and it was necessary for him to be cautious, for only shortly before, two Europeans

* Id., 96.   † Id., 105.   ‡ Id., 114.   § Id., 117.
          ‖ Id., 121.   ¶ Id., 110.

who appeared in the Khanate without credentials were executed as Russian spies, and the Khan chuckled over their fate.* The Vizier, who was a very avaricious person, extorted our traveller's watch as the ransom of an Afghan dependent of his who had been imprisoned, and other useful articles on other pleas, and he tried to thwart him in various ways. One of his needs was what he called warming medicine, a euphemism for brandy, which Abbott, who was a total abstainer, could not of course supply him with.

On one occasion Abbott was invited to a feast at the palace. He was told to change his white turban for an Uzbeg cap, probably to avoid scandal to the priesthood, who alone wore white turbans there. When he entered the saloon he found sixty or seventy people, chiefly priests; the Sheikh ul Islam was at one end, then followed the rest, kneeling in a row, with their backs to the wall. Abbott's seat was separated from that of the last of the priests by a member of the royal family. He saluted the assembly on entering with the Salaam Alikum, and had a conversation with the chief Mollah. He amusingly describes the torture to his legs and ankles caused by the constrained position in which he knelt for a while, and how astonished the assembly was when he ventured to proclaim his pain and to change his position to the squatting attitude adopted by tailors. After sitting an hour in solemn silence, the Persian envoy entered and sat on the opposite side of the room, three places below Abbott's. He had gone to Khiva to obtain the release of 30,000 Persian slaves, equal in value to £48,000, as a return for guaranteeing the Khan from the Russians. Soon after he entered, the Sheikh ul Islam pointedly asked him what those were who denied the title of the three first Khalifs, i.e., the Shias; and the embarrassed envoy, amidst the titters of the audience, had to say Kaffirs, a confession which Shia casuistry readily excuses when made under compulsion. An hour after the Persian envoy, came the Inak and his cousin, the eldest son of the late Khan. Several long pieces of chintz were now brought in and spread on the floor; on these were ranged flat cakes of bread, then earthenware basins of mutton broth, with clumsy wooden spoons, swimming in fat; and lastly, some poor pilafs and cups of mixed butter and grape juice. Afterwards the cloth was removed and cold water poured over their hands, when they dispersed.† Among his greatest triumphs Abbott counted an order he obtained from the Khan for the release of twenty-two daughters of Afghans who were prisoners at Khiva, which was done as a peace offering to the Queen of England, while a double-edged dagger, with its ivory hilt studded with jewels, a small head-stall for a horse decorated with gold inlaid with rough rubies and emeralds, and an Ispahan sabre were selected as presents for the Russian Emperor. The letters sent with these written in

---

* *Id.*, 131.　　　† Abbott's Journal, 136-144.

Turki were enclosed in sarcenet bags flowered with gold. He obtained permission for a Russian official to visit Khiva to take back to Russia all the captives he could find who wished to return, on condition that the Khivan traders were released.* Abbott's epaulets seem to have produced some impression upon the Khan. At Khiva military rank was conferred by the Khan himself, a commander of a thousand horse receiving a dagger with a golden, and one of a hundred with a silver scabbard.† Abbott was thwarted at every step by the Mekhter, who, it would seem, affected to believe him a Russian spy. In one of their angry conferences, when he spoke about his destiny, Abbott suggested that this might be to lose Khiva to the Russians. "Oh!" he said fiercely, "if we fall fighting the Kaffirs we pass straight to paradise." "And your women," replied the sarcastic officer, "what kind of paradise will your wives and daughters find in the arms of Russian soldiers?" A repartee to which no answer was made.‡ The Persian envoy left Khiva some days before Abbott. In answer to the Shah's request for the release of prisoners and promise of aid Allah Kuli sent the boorish answer, "Tell Muhammed Shah that he is still a child, his beard is not yet grown; why does he not first drive the Russians out of Persia?"§ At his final audience with the Khan the latter summoned the chief of the Chaudor Turkomans who wandered between Khiva and Mangushlak, and who, having heard of the liberality of Abbott, wished to be his guide, and ordered him to conduct him safely to Mangushlak and then to obtain him means for the transit to Astrakhan. Before he retired he reminded the Khan that as his dominions formed a barrier between two rival empires, it would be well for him to behave with prudence. "It is very hard," said the Khan in reply, "that they cannot find in all the world some other battle-field than just my dominions."‖ His profuse liberality had left the English envoy very bare of money, and he failed to persuade the officials at Khiva to find him any, so that he could not ransom the female slaves and others whom he had intended sending to Herat. He set out with a quaking step under the escort of the powerful and unprincipled Turkoman chief. The rest of his adventures I must rapidly condense. The whole story of his sufferings is told in graphic terms in his very picturesque narrative, assuredly one of the most brilliant books of travel ever written.

He duly reached the port of Guedik, where, however, he could find no ship, this having been previously arranged by the treacherous Vizier. He, therefore, determined to go to Dash Kaleh, a post occupied by the Russians, four days further south. His escort refused to accompany him, and he had to go on with his servants. En route and within ten hours of his goal he was attacked by a party of Uzbegs, was seized and stripped, and in the melee he lost two fingers and received a gash on the head. In

* Id., 163.   † Id., 134.   ‡ Id., 172.   § Id., 173.
‖ Id., 179.

this state he was carried off to a nomade camp some distance away, where he was treated with great cruelty and his servants were reduced to slavery.*

Meanwhile Major Todd had despatched a most faithful Afghan named Akhud Zadeh to Khiva with some money for Abbott, and Ferrier has described the loyalty and perseverance with which when he heard of that officer's fate, although he did not know the Tartar language, and had to suffer great privations, he eventually found him in destitution. He was armed with a special firman from Allah Kuli and speedily obtained his release. Abbott now made his way to the Russian outpost and thence to Astrakhan, while Akhud Zadeh returned to Khiva.†

A report having reached Herat that Abbott was dead, Major Todd despatched Lieutenant Shakespear to make inquiries and to complete the negociations. He arrived there the same day as Akhud Zadeh and from him learnt the particulars of what had happened. He then proceeded with his business and won a favourable opinion from the Khan. In one of his conversations with him the latter said, " How is it your nation, which is so distant from mine, should wish so much for an alliance with me ? " To which Shakespear neatly replied, " We possess India, a vast garden, and for fear of a surprise we wish to surround it with walls ; those walls are Khiva, Bukhara, Herat, and Kabul."‡ The Vizier Yakub Mekhter, who tried continually to thwart him, having sneered at him for being an infidel, he replied tartly to that intriguer, " Which of us is the infidel—you, who, driven by insatiable avarice, daily put slaves to the torture, tear the daughter from her father, the wife from her husband, and sell them to the highest bidder in your bazaars ; or those who, like myself, seek the deliverance of so many unhappy beings, and wish to send them back to their country and their families ? " The Khan, who felt keenly this jibe, turned to the Vizier and asked him when he would cease to expose their vices to strangers, and to one who would make them known to all the world, and Yakub remained in disgrace for some days. To conciliate the Khan, Shakespear gave him a bill of exchange endorsed by the Kazi of Herat which was to be paid him if the long-delayed caravan was not released. He then collected all the Russian prisoners he could find, to the number of 424, and hiring camels for their transport duly arrived at Old Urgenj, and thence went on to Astrakhan and St. Petersburg, where he was very courteously received by the Tzar Nicholas and was afterwards knighted.

Ferrier justly animadverts on the contrast between these rewards and the neglect which was the portion of Abbott and Akhud Zadeh, who had prepared the way, and instances it as a case of the grim comedy of the world§ Abbott himself, who must have been a singularly amiable person, in referring to the same contrast, says that no one could more

---

* *Id.*, 428.   † *Id.*, 431.   ‡ *Id.*   § *Id.*, 433.

patiently bear hardship than himself, and no one was more deserving of
a laurel wreath than Shakespear. Among the released prisoners some
had occupied high positions at Khiva. One, William Laurentief, had been
chief of the artillery; and another, Ann Kostin, a soldier's wife, had been
housekeeper to the Khan. In July, 1840, Allah Kuli issued a proclamation abolishing the trade in Russian slaves and prohibiting inroads into
the Russian dominions.[*] The English influence at Khiva was only short-
lived. Meanwhile the Shah seems to have again pressed for the release of
his countrymen. The Khan very naturally replied they had been bought
for hard cash from the Turkomans, who could not be made to disgorge
what they had paid for them; that many of the slaves had redeemed
themselves, married, and settled at Khiva, and if he attempted to
send them back there would be an outbreak in the Khanate.[†] Thereupon
the English once more offered their services, and Captain Conolly was
sent to Khiva to try and settle the differences, and was accompanied by
Allah Dad Khan Papolzye, an envoy from the Afghan ruler Shah Shuja.
At Meimeneh he met Akhud Zadeh, who also went with him. Conolly
was well received by the Khan, but he refused to release the prisoners.
After he had been at Khiva four months Yár Muhammed, the Afghan
governor of Herat, turned Major Todd out of that town and sent to
advise the Khivan Khan to do the same with Conolly. Instead of this,
he presented him with a robe of honour, begged him to consider Khiva
as his country and the Royal Palace as his own house. As he could
not secure the release of the slaves in a direct way he now proposed
to ransom them, and sent Akhud Zadeh to Kabul to suggest this to Sir
William McNaghten. The departure of that official, who, as the son
of the Kazi of Herat, had great authority and who was much attached to
the English, opened the way for fresh intrigues, and Yakub Mekhter's
influence was soon in the ascendant. The Khan speedily became more
exacting, asked for a subsidy, and also for English officers to organise
his army and to cast some guns for him. Conolly made excuses and
especially urged that such a policy would endanger the life of Colonel
Stoddart. The Khan became more and more disagreeable, and ended
by letting Conolly know that he was in his way, and that he should not
be very sorry if he were to leave.[‡] He thereupon made up his
mind to go to Khokand to explore the route thither as he 'had been
instructed. His subsequent adventures I have detailed elsewhere.[§]

Meanwhile the intercourse between Khiva and Russia continued
intermittently. In 1840 Lieutenant Aitof returned to St. Petersburg
before the arrival of the other prisoners, and was accompanied by a
Khivan envoy named Athanias Khoja Reis Mufti, who took a letter for the
Emperor and returned in 1841. Three other envoys followed him, but
none went to the Russian capital. One of these, named Shinar Mahmet

* Michell, op. cit., 550.   † Ferrier, 434.   ‡ Id., 435-6.   § Anio, 798, &c.

Niaz, returned home with Captain Nikiforof, who tried in vain to negotiate a treaty. Colonel Danilefski went to the Khanate in 1842 and succeeded in making the first treaty between the two countries. While he was at Khiva the Khan Allah Kuli died. This was in 1842. Several of his coins, on which he styles himself Allah Kuli Behadur Khan, are extant. It is curious to find on these coins the revival of the old name of the Khanate, Khuarezm, which occurs on them as a mint place.*

RAHIM KULI KHAN.

Rahim Kuli succeeded his father in 1842. His reign began with a struggle with the Jemshidis, an Iranian tribe living on the left bank of the Murghab, of whom 10,000 had been transported to Khuarezm and planted as a colony on the bank of the Oxus near Kilijbay. The Sarik Turkomans who encamped about Merv also began hostilities. His younger brother, Muhammed Amin, was sent against them with 15,000 men, but they suffered very severely in the terrible country that intervenes between those two towns. As the Amir of Bukhara was at this time besieging Hazarasp, the Inak turned his arms against and defeated him, and concluded a peace.† Rahim Kuli died in 1845.‡ M. Vel. Zernof has published one of his coins.§

MUHAMMED AMIN KHAN.

Rahim Kuli Khan was succeeded by his brother Muhammed Amin. Vambery says he is looked upon as the greatest of the Khuarezmian Khans of modern times. Directly after mounting the throne he marched against the Sarik Turkomans and after six campaigns captured the citadel of Merv, as well as a fort named Yolöten in its neighbourhood. Scarcely had he returned, however, to Khiva when the Sariks rebelled and killed the officer he had left in command at Merv, as well as the garrison there. He again fought against them and had as his allies the Jemshids, old rivals of the Sariks, under their chief Mir Muhammed. The allies were successful and afterwards entered Khiva together in triumph. The Tekke tribe next proved rebellious and he had to march against it, and after three campaigns, in which many men and cattle perished, they were in part subdued, and a body of Uzbegs and Yomuds was left among them to overawe them. A quarrel having ensued between the leaders of these two contingents, the Khan had the Turkoman chief hurled from the top of a lofty tower at Khiva. This exasperated the Yomuds against him and they allied themselves secretly with the Tekkes.|

---

* Vel Zernof, Coins of Bukhara, etc., 444, etc. † Vambery, Travels, 355-6.
‡ Schuyler, op. cit., i., 387. § Coins of Bukhara, etc., 453. | Vambery, op. cit., 357.

I have shown how the Khivan Khans began to dominate more or less over the neighbouring Kazaks. The Kazaks of the Lower Sir or Jaxartes afterwards became the objects of rivalry between the Khivans and the Khokandians, and when the latter built some forts on that river they received notice from the former to demolish them. As they did not do so, the Khivans during the reign of Allah Kuli Khan built several strong-holds on the left bank of the river Kuvan for the collection of ziaket or dues from the Kazaks and from the caravans that passed that way. This was about 1830.[*] In 1846 the Khivans built their frontier fortress of Khoja Niazbi, so called from the name of its first governor.[†] The Khivan rule there was a harsh one, and the Kazaks were especially punished for the raids of Jan Khoja, who destroyed Bish Kaleh.[‡]

Meanwhile the Russians, who also claimed suzerain rights over the Kazaks, were naturally anxious about these encroachments, and they speedily advanced their foot also. In 1847 they built several forts in the Kazak steppe,[§] and in that very year the Khivans replied with a demonstra-tion in its neighbourhood.[‖] The same year the fort of Raimsk or Aralsk was founded on the Sea of Aral. This was accepted as a menace by the Khivans, who crossed the Sir to the number of 2,000, and harried more than a thousand families of Kazaks owing allegiance to Russia. The Russians attacked and punished the marauders and released the prisoners. Three months later the Khivans made a raid into the Karakum steppe, where they murdered many old men, carried off women and children, and robbed two caravans, but on hearing that the Russians were in motion they hastily withdrew. In 1848 they made several inroads across the Sir; on one occasion 1,500 of them proceeded to pillage the Kazaks for nearly twenty-four hours, while 300 Turkomans approached within gunshot of the Russian fort and visited their landing wharf. They soon found they were no match, however, for the troops of the white Tzar, and contented themselves with asking for the demolition of the forts of Aralsk and Novopetrovsk.[¶]

In 1853 General Perofski attacked the Khokandian forts on the Lower Sir as I have mentioned.[**] In order to prevent the Khivans from giving assistance, he made a demonstration towards their fort of Khoja Niaz.[††] It was to oppose this that, as I have said, the Khan Muhammed Amin sent a division of his army. At this time, however, the Russians did not go beyond inciting their Kazak allies to scour the country right and left.

In the beginning of 1855 Muhammed Amin undertook a campaign against Sirakhs. The terrified inhabitants sent to ask assistance from Feridun Murza, the ruler of Meshhet. He quickly marched to Ak Derbend, about 70 versts distant, with 7,000 Khorasan troops, 3,000 others and 10 guns. He sent on an advanced division of 500 men under

---

* Michell, op. cit., 318-19.   † Id., 385.   ‡ Id., 380.   § Id., 320.
‖ Russische Revue, i., 123.   ¶ Id., 383.   ** Ante, 633 and 634.   †† Michell, 332.

Muhammed Hassan. Near Sirakhs these were joined by several hundred others, and together they fell on the first Khivan division, defeated [it, captured six cannons, and compelled Muhammed Amin to retire. The Khan had carelessly pitched his camp some distance from his people, and a volunteer from Merv offered to guide Muhammed Hassan to it. He did so, and succeeded in capturing Muhammed Amin. Out of 200 Khuaresmians who were near some were killed and the rest fled. The Khan was at once decapitated. The Persians speedily relieved Sirakhs, and the Khivans, who had lost their Khan, withdrew, losing many prisoners in the retreat; 270 heads, including those of Muhammed Amin and of fourteen of his relations, were sent as a ghastly trophy to the Shah at Teheran, who ordered the Khan's head to be buried and a small mausoleum to be built over it.* This mausoleum was afterwards demolished because the Shah feared the Shias might mistake it for the tomb of an Imaum Zadeh, and it might thus give rise to a sinful act.† Muhammed Amin was killed in 1855. M. Vel. Zernof has published one of his coins, on which he styles himself Muhammed Amin Behadur Khan.‡

ABDULLA KHAN.

The retreating army raised Abdulla, the son of Ibadulla, the son of Kutlugh Murad, who was brother to the last Khan's grandfather, to the throne. Scarcely had he reached the capital when Seyid Mahmud Tureh, a brother of Allah Kuli Khan, who had superior claims to the throne, in the presence of all the mollahs and grandees, threatened to kill the new Khan. He was, however, imprisoned.

Then the Yomuds, who had latterly been so persecuted, intrigued in favour of two other princes, one of whom was apparently called Ata Murad.§ The insurrection was, however, nipped in the bud, both the young princes were strangled, and the Khan marched at the head of several thousand troops to punish their supporters, the Turkomans. They were prudently repentant, and their aksakals went to him submissively, with bare feet, and swords suspended round their necks. He pardoned them, but two months later they again began to rebel, and according to Veliaminof Zernof, invaded the Khanate with 15,000 men. The Khan marched against them, and a battle ensued near Kizil Teker, in which the Uzbegs were beaten. Abdulla was among the killed, and his body was thrown into a common grave with a number of others.‖ A coin of Abdulla's, on which he calls himself Seyid Abdulla Khan, and struck in 1855, has been published by M. Vel. Zernof.¶

---

* Vel. Zernof, Coins of Bukhara, etc., 457-8.   † Vambery, Travels, 358, note.
‡ Op. cit., 454:   § Vambery, op. cit., 358; Michell, 33.
‖ Vambery, op. cit., 358-9; Vel. Zernof, 458.   ¶ Coins of Bukhara, etc., 454.

KUTLUGH MURAD KHAN.

The Khivans now raised Abdulla's brother, Kutlugh Murad, who was only eighteen years old, to the throne. He had fought in the late battle, and been badly wounded there. He, however, prepared to make head against the Yomuds, who set up his father's second cousin, Niaz Muhammed bi, as a rival. They overran the Khanate, and a large number of its towns fell into their hands. Meanwhile the Karakalpaks also rebelled, and nominated Yarlik Tureh as their Khan. Kutlugh Murad issued a general summons to his people to march against the Turkomans, but these nomades forestalled him. Their *protegé*, Niaz bi, gained admission to the palace under pretence of paying homage, and thereupon murdered him and seven of his ministers. During the tumult that followed, the Mekhter ascended the wall of the citadel, and announcing the murder from the battlements, called upon the Khivans to put to the sword every Yomud inside the city. These Turkomans were thereupon savagely attacked, and very few of them escaped. Vambery says it took six days to clear the streets of corpses.* Coins of this Khan, on which he styles himself Kutlugh Murad and Murad Muhammed Behadur Khan, have been published by M. Vel. Zernof.†

SEYID MUHAMMED KHAN.

On the death of Kutlugh Murad, we are told, the crown was tendered to Seyid Mahmud, the son of Muhammed Rahim Khan, a devotee to opium, which rendered him unfit to rule, and in consequence he abdicated in favour of his younger brother, Seyid Muhammed, who was then thirty years old.‡ He began his reign by attacking the rebellious Turkomans and Karakalpaks. He routed a body of the latter who were on their way from Kunia Urgenj to dispute his succession, in which struggle Yarlik, who had been chosen as their chief by the Karakalpaks, was killed. A section of that tribe thereupon submitted to Bukhara.§ These civil broils caused great devastation and distress in the Khanate, whose towns were terribly desolated; and while the Yomuds and Uzbegs destroyed one another, the Jemshidis from the Murghab plundered the country from Kitsj to Fitniek and returned home again with much spoil and 2,000 Persian slaves whom they had released.‖

The frontier fortress of Khoja Niaz, where blackmail was levied on the caravans going between Bukhara and Russia, was generally garrisoned by about 100 men and several guns. Khoja Niaz, from whom it took its name, was succeeded as its governor by his son Irjan,

---

* Vambery, op. cit., 359-60; Michell, op. cit., 53; Vel. Zernof, op. cit., 439.
† Coins of Bukhara, etc., 454-5.   ‡ Vambery, op. cit., 360; Michell, 552.
§ Michell, op. cit., 34.   ‖ Vambery, 360-1.

who in 1856 went to Khiva with forty of the garrison. Thereupon the Kazaks in the neighbourhood proceeded to expel the officers left in charge, spiked and dismounted the guns, destroyed their carriages, and plundered the Khivan property there. They followed up their success by causing disturbances on the Russian frontier. Meanwhile the Khokandians laid claims to the fort. They had twice taken it during the previous ten years, and the last time the Khivans had had to pay the Khokand Governor of Ak Mejid a large quantity of cattle for permitting them to return. The Russians having now conquered Western Khokand, naturally claimed a reversion in the fort, and sent a detachment to occupy it, but finding it virtually dismantled and situated among marshes and sterile wastes, with no water and little fuel near, they determined to abandon it again.*

The disturbances which had so long taken place at Khiva caused a famine there. In 1857 this was aggravated by an epidemic, which was apparently cholera. The same year the Khan sent Fazil Khoja, the Sheikh ul Islam of the Khanate, to St. Petersburg to announce his accession, his condolence on the death of the Tzar Nicholas, and bearing his congratulations to his successor, Alexander.† In May, 1858, a mission was sent to Khiva by General Ignatief, whose journey has been described by M. Kühlewein. It crossed the Ilek and Yemba and went along the western shore of Lake Aral to the Gulf of Aibugir. Near Cape Urga the Russians were met by four deputies from the Khan, viz., the Karakalpak prince Istlu, the Kazak bi Azbergen, Murad bek, and a son of the Governor of Kungrad. About half way to the latter town a customs officer took an inventory of their heavy baggage, afraid apparently that they might have some cannon with them.‡ They entered Kungrad in state amidst the shouts of "Urus, Urus," and were there welcomed by the Divan baba. The governor of the town was not very civil, and speeded their departure, as he had to pay their expenses out of his own pocket. This town was the former capital of the Aralians, and only submitted to Khiva about 1814. Thence the mission proceeded in boats towards Khiva—a tedious journey, averaging but ten miles a day. They found almost all the villages and towns ruined; the auls or camps of the Karakalpaks containing only old men and children, the rest of the inhabitants having been sold as slaves at Khiva and on the Persian frontier. The towns of Kipchak and Khojeili had met the same fate.§ At New Urgenj, then the second town in the Khanate, they were welcomed by Darga, one of the Khan's ministers, a portly, handsome old man, in a cashmere robe, whose portrait is given in Michell's work. On reaching Khiva the mission encamped in a garden outside the town. At their audience they found the Khivan infantry at the gates and the bodyguard marshalled in front of the palace. They were first received

* Michell, 385-388.   † Id., 34.   ‡ Id., 26.   § Id., 29.

4 X

by the Mekhtar, who like the other great officials had an apartment in
the palace, and then by the Khan. The latter was seated on a raised
divan with a dagger and pistol lying before him, while behind him floated
the state banner. The Kush begi, the Mekhter, and Divan begi were
in front, and the chamberlain at the door. The imperial letter was carried
in on a red cushion by the secretary of the mission, and handed to the
Mekhter, who passed it on to the Khan.*

Kühlewein tells us there were two kinds of gold coins or tillas issued
in the Khanate, one worth about twelve and the other about six shillings.
The silver coins were the tenga, worth about sevenpence, and the shahi,
about threepence. Puls or karapuls were the copper coins; forty-
eight of these made a tenga. The army consisted of 1,000 sarbaris or
infantry and 20,000 cavalry. In time of war the troops received four times
their ordinary pay. The revenue had greatly fallen off, chiefly because
of the migration of the Kazaks and the secession of the Turkomans.†
There was peace in the Khanate during the stay of the Russian mission,
but after it left the Kungrads and Karakalpaks making a league with the
Turkoman chief, Ata` Murad, killed their ruler Kutlugh Murad, with
many of his party. He was succeeded by Muhammed Fanah, nephew
of Tura Sufi, who I have mentioned as the ruler of these Aralians in
the early part of the century, and who submitted to Khiva in 1814.
Muhammed Fanah was apparently countenanced by the Russians. He
actually styled himself Khan of Khuarezm, and struck coins bearing his
own name. In the course of another year, however, he was killed, and
the Aralian Kungrads again acknowledged the Khan of Khiva as their
master.‡

In 1863 Khiva was visited by Vambery. He found the Chaudor
Turkomans in open rebellion against the Khan. The Kushbegi and
the Khan's brother had, in fact, taken the field against these marauders,
and he had to make a detour to avoid them. He speaks in glowing
terms of the beauty of the capital, and how he and his Haji companions
were presented with bread and dried fruits as they entered its gates,
amidst shouts of welcome and kisses bestowed upon their rags. At the
caravanserai they had to pass a rude inspection under the eyes of
the Mekhrem, during which suspicious tongues whispered freely
Jansiz (spy), Feringhi, and Urus, his European countenance peering
through every disguise. At this time there was living at Khiva a certain
Shukrullah bi, who had been to Constantinople as an envoy from the Khan,
and on whom Vambery called. His knowledge of Turkey made him
easily pass himself off as an effendi from Stambul, who was a dervish by
profession, and had visited Khiva on his way to Bukhara by order of his
Pir or spiritual chief. He was heartily welcomed by the quondam envoy
who inquired about his various friends in the West. Vambery, with

* Id., 32.   † Id., 43-4.   ‡ Id., 33.

the other hajis, his companions, put up at a tekkie or convent, where travelling dervishes generally stayed. It was called Töahibaz, or Tört Shahbaz, meaning the four falcons or heroes, from the four kings who were buried there.* The day after his arrival he was summoned to the Khan's presence by a yasaul, who also took him a small present. His newly-found patron Shukrullah bi accompanied him. He found a crowd of people of every age, class, and sex waiting to present petitions, who readily made way for the dervish who had come to bless their Khan. He first had an interview with the Mekhter, before whom he spoke the usual prayer, those present duly saying amen and stroking their beards. He then presented his printed pass sealed with the Sultan's tamgha, whereupon the Mekhter kissed it reverently, rubbed it on his forehead, rose to place it in the Khan's hand, and, returning, conducted the dervish into the hall of audience. The Khan was seated on a dais with his left arm supported by a round silk velvet cushion, and holding a short golden sceptre in his right hand.† Vambery describes him as very dissolute in appearance, and as presenting in every feature the picture of an enervated imbecile and savage tyrant. The pseudo dervish raised his hands in the recognised fashion and was followed by the Khan and his companions. He then recited a short Sura from the Koran, then two Allahumu Rabbenna, and concluded with a loud amen, when there was a general stroking of the beard. While the Khan was still stroking his, each one exclaimed Kabul bolgay, i.e., " May thy prayer be heard." Having approached the Khan and duly executed the Musafeha or greeting prescribed by the Koran, accompanied by the reciprocal extension of both hands, he retired a few paces and the ceremonial was at an end.‡ The Khan inquired about his journey, and he diplomatically replied that all its sufferings had been richly rewarded by the sight of the Huzrats Jemal, i.e., the beauty of his majesty, and he expressed a wish that he might live 170 years. He asked leave to visit the shrines of the Sunni saints within the Khanate, and then to be allowed to speed on his way. He declined the Khan's proffered money with all the unctuous humility of a "haj," but accepted his present of an ass to ride upon, which he asked might be a white one, that being the prescribed colour for pilgrimages. The traveller returned to his lodgings amidst the greetings of the crowd. He complains of the exacting nature of the hospitality he received, a good appetite being a proof of good breeding, and "to be able to eat no more" being deemed incredible. On one occasion he calculates that his companions each consumed two pounds of rice, a pound of fat from a sheep's tail, besides bread, carrots, turnips, and radishes, washed down by from fifteen to twenty large soup plates full of green tea. He also had to run the gauntlet of a large number of anxious students who wished to be informed of all the details

---

* Vambery, Travels, 124-5.   † Id., 128.   ‡ Id., 128-9.

of a holy man's life in that centre of culture, Stambul;[*] at other times he had to dispense some of the Khaki Shifa or "health dust" collected in a house at Medina, said to have been the prophet's, or to breathe a Nefez or holy breath to cure diseases. Among the acquaintances he made was one Haji Ismael, who had lived twenty-five years in Turkey, where he had followed the professions of tutor, proprietor of baths, leather cutter, caligraphist, chemist, and conjurer, but was then chiefly famous as a mixer of aphrodisiacs and love potions.[†] Some time after he had a second interview with the Khan, and at his request exhibited to him a specimen of his caligraphy, in which he professed his own incapacity, but happily said that "every failing that pleases the Khan is a virtue." On withdrawing he was conducted to the apartments of the State Treasurer, and in a courtyard close by found some 300 Chaudor Turkoman prisoners in rags and suffering from hunger, etc. These were divided into two sections. Those under forty, chained together in parties of ten to fifteen, were to be sold as slaves. Those over that age, being the Aksakals or grey beards, awaited a severer punishment, and he saw eight aged men place themselves on their backs on the ground, where they were bound hand and foot; the executioner then gouged out their eyes, kneeling to do so on the breast of each of the victims, and after each operation he wiped his knife dripping with blood upon the white beard of the hoary unfortunate.[‡] This was partially in revenge for similar cruelties practised by the Turkomans, and partially from a Draconic code which was patronised by the Khan, who, as a great patron of religion, was a most exacting judge, and apparently affixed the punishment of death to many new offences. Inter alia to cast a look at a thickly veiled lady was to incur that doom: the man being hung and the woman buried in the ground to her breast, and then killed with a volley of keziaks or balls of baked clay. Vambery found the treasurer sorting out the robes of honour, which consisted of gaily-coloured silk gowns flowered with gold, for the successful officers in the late campaign. The value of these depended on the number of heads which the recipient could claim to have cut off, and our traveller next day saw a number of the heroes return dragging prisoners at their horses' tails, and also carrying sacks containing human heads. These they allowed to roll out on the ground like so many potatoes until there was a heap composed of several hundreds. Each one got his receipt, and a few days later was duly paid. It is necessary to remember this ghastly brutality, and to insist upon it, for it points a grim moral when we discuss the necessity of the stamping out of such dens of iniquity, even by such hard heels as those of Russia. Before leaving, Vambery imparted another blessing to the Khan, who asked him to visit him again on his return from Bukhara, that he might send an envoy back with him to the new Sultan to obtain

* Id., 132.   † Id., 134-5.   ‡ Id., 138.

from him the usual investiture of his Khanate.* Seyid Muhammed died in 1865, and was succeeded by his son Seyid Muhammed Rahim Behadur Khan.

SEYID MUHAMMED RAHIM KHAN.

His reign has proved a singularly disastrous one for the Khanate of Khuarezm. It was doubtless inevitable that some time or other the Russians would plant their heavy foot upon it. The disasters of Bekovitch and Perofski were grim shadows that invited retribution sometime, and the lawless subjects of the Khan afforded ample excuses of other kinds for interference in his affairs. Yet the disaster came somewhat before its time. Russia, like all vast empires whose means of communication are backward, and which profess to have a strong centralised authority, is much too often at the mercy of its border commanders. They necessarily have to be invested with the discretionary powers of satraps Where they are ambitious they can easily force the hand of the central authority, and when so forced even against its will and contrary to its policy, it has to condone what has cost treasure and blood to secure. It cannot in the face of a victorious army and the prestige it has secured sacrifice the fruits of victory even when thus obtained, and even when to do so lays it open very naturally to the charge of Machiavellianism.

Such an ambitious person was General Kaufmann, who, in 1867, immediately after his arrival at Tashkend, wrote to inform the Khan of his appointment and claiming the right to send detachments across the Sir Daria or Jaxartes to punish marauders. The Khan, we are told, was then but twenty years old, and was more occupied with falconry than with business. His answer, which arrived a few months later, repudiated the Russian claim to rule both banks of the Sir. In it he undertook to keep the peace south of the river.† It must be remembered that the Kazaks who owed allegiance to Russia were in the habit of wintering largely south of the Sir and on the Kuvan and Yany Daria, and notwithstanding the Khan's letter, Russian detachments continued to cross the former river to punish those who assailed them. Meanwhile on the other side of the Khanate the Russians were enlarging their influence in the Caspian. In November, 1869, to overcome the Turkomans, and probably also as a future base against Khiva, a detachment landed at the bay of Krasnovodsk and proceeded to build a fortress there, and shortly after another was planted at Chikishlar. At this time there occurred a widespread rebellion in the steppes. The Don Cossacks who resented the new regulations which were being imposed upon them, the Kalmuks and the Kazaks, were all in a state of ferment; the Kazaks in the neighbourhood of Turgai alone being quiet. The Valley of the Volga and the Ural were

---

* Id., 143.   † Terentief, Schuyler, ii., 426.

thus in a state of confusion, the terrified inhabitants fled, and the caravans ceased to pass. This rebellion continued all through the summer of 1870, and the Kazaks succeeded in burning the fort of Novo Alexandrofsk on the Mertwyi-Kultuk inlet of the Caspian. The small station of Nikolai, with the neighbouring lightships, were also destroyed, and a detachment under Colonel Rukin was overwhelmed.* When the Russian troops went to put down the rebels the latter affirmed that they had been instigated by the Khivan Khan, and the latter also was accused of scattering inflammatory proclamations and of assisting the rebels with men and money.† He was also charged with harbouring outlaws and robbers, with keeping a number of Russians in durance, and with detaining the Russian envoy, Sultan Daulet Bushaef, a Kazak whom he accused of having been treacherous both to Khokand and Bukhara.‡

As a set-off to the building of the fort at Krasnovodsk, the Khan, sent a detachment to poison all the wells on the way thither, by throwing dead dogs into them. He had a new citadel built in his capital, and armed it with twenty guns, and ordered the Taldik channel of the Oxus to be diverted and several canals to be cut to make it impassable for Russian ships.

A small fort was built at Cape Urga, and the Russian Kazaks migrating to Khiva were freed from all taxes on condition of supplying troops in case of war.§ General Kaufmann in January, 1870, wrote the Khan a peremptory letter, repeating his former complaints, and threatening vengeance unless things were altered. This letter was speedily answered in two others, one from the Kush begi and the other from the Divan begi. They insisted on the right of the Khivan tax collectors to levy dues from the people in the Bukan mountains, of which complaint had been made, and as to the captives they had been taken to Khiva by the Kazaks, who would have illused them in revenge for injuries they had themselves sustained had "not he, who sits under the shadow of God, cooled with the waters of prudence their flaming hearts." They should be returned if the Russian troops were forbidden to cross the frontier, and the Kazaks were indemnified for the property they had lost on April 6th. General Kaufmann replied to this note claiming that the Emperor of Russia ruled wherever his subjects lived (a very convenient and elastic principle), and that therefore the Yany Daria as far as lake Akchakul, where the Russian Kazaks wandered, as well as the Bukan mountains, and all the road from Kizil kum to Irkibai· on the Yany Daria, in accordance with the treaty made with Bukhara, had been and would always be considered Russian. All this while disturbances continued in the steppe, as I have mentioned, and were attributed to the intrigues of Khiva. General Kaufmann had, in fact, accumulated a very plausible number of grievances, and he now prepared to use them. Troops having been sent to the Ust urt and the Barsuk sands to keep the steppes quiet, a force was prepared in Turkestan for a campaign; meanwhile the Khivan Khan sent Baba bi to Bukhara to secure the Amir's alliance, who on a hint from the Russians was duly arrested.[*] Presently the Amir tried to mediate. He released Baba bi, and sent Haji Urak as his spokesman, urging the release of the Russian prisoners, the discontinuance of marauding, and that the Khan should send an envoy to Tashkend, but he found the latter obdurate and unwilling to treat unless the Russians ceased crossing the debateable frontier with their troops.[†] He was moved by other and more forcible arguments, however. In the spring of 1872 a strong detachment under the command of Colonel Markozof, with the nominal object of exploring the old bed of the Oxus, left Krasnovodsk and advanced to the springs of Ortaku, 300 versts east of the Balkhan mountain. He then turned southward, and having punished the Turkomans in the district of Ushamala went to the fort of Kizil Arvat.[‡] He was obliged to retreat, however, after being attacked by the Turkomans and losing many camels. About the same time other detachments from Turkestan explored the Kizil Kum sands as far as the Khivan frontiers, while Ming Bulak and the Bukan mountains were also surveyed.[§] These demonstrations seem to have frightened the Khan, who now sent two envoys, Murtaza bi and Baba Nazar Atalik, one to Tiflis and the other to Orenburg, thus ignoring the Governor-General of Turkestan, with whom alone he had been ordered to correspond.[‖]

In a letter addressed to the Grand Duke Michael he complained of the invasion of his borders by several recent Russian expeditions, and offered to send back the eleven Russian prisoners he held if that would prevent this recurring, otherwise he should neither send them back nor stop the pillaging, and he ended up with the phrase, "If these prisoners serve you only as a pretext for war against us, with the aim of extending your dominions, then the will of the Almighty be done."[¶] The envoys were stopped, one at Timur Khan Shura, the other at Orenburg, and were told that no letters would be received till the prisoners were released and an embassy sent to Tashkend. Whereupon the Khan despatched some representatives to the Viceroy of India, Lord Northbrook, to ask for help against Russia. He, in the words of Mr. Terentief himself, "as was to be expected, advised them to make peace with Russia, obey her demands, and give no cause for further dissatisfaction;"[**] a loyalty which has hardly been imitated by Russian viceroys in recent years.

The chief difficulty of a campaign against Khiva is in reaching it. As Mr. Schuyler says, it is a small oasis in the midst of a desert,

* Schuyler, II. 422.   † Id., 422.   ‡ Hellwald, 134.
§ Schuyler, II., 332.   ‖ Id., 423.   ¶ Id.   ** Id., 424.

lying 600 miles from Tashkend, 930 from Orenburg, and 500 from Krasnovodsk, and it was at this time impossible to approach it by water, as the Aral flotilla was too weak and the mouths of the Oxus too shallow.*

The plan of campaign decided upon was to despatch three columns. The main one, from Turkestan, under the command of General Kaufmann himself, which consisted of 3,420 infantry, 1,150 cavalry, and 677 artillerymen, with 20 guns, 2 mitrailleuses, and 8 rocket stands, was divided into two divisions; one marched by way of Jizakh, under General Golovatshof, and the other by Kazalinsk, under Colonel Golof.† Eight thousand camels were employed for the transport of the trains. They were hired chiefly from the Kazaks, who were to receive 50 roubles for every one that died. Four steamers with barges in tow were to attempt to mount the Oxus and co-operate. The second column was to start from Orenburg and was to advance by way of the Yemba and the western bank of the Aral. It comprised 3,461 men and 1,797 horses, with several guns and rocket stands, and was under the command of the Cossack Ataman Verefkin.‡ The third column was divided into three sections, the first of which, under Colonel Lomakin, was to advance from Mangushlak by way of Bish Akty, Ilte idahe, and Tabin Su to the Aibugir Gulf, and there to co-operate with the Orenburg column. The other two divisions, numbering altogether about 2,000 men, under the command of Colonel Markosof, were to march respectively from Chikishlar and Krasnovodsk,§ at each of which points the Russians had a fortress. Schmidt has described the equipment, order of march, etc., of these detachments in detail—a description of the highest value to those who wish to study campaigning in a very difficult country, as it embodies the experience of some of the most skilled of the Russian officers.‖ It forms, however, no part of our present purpose, and we will turn to the narrative of the campaign itself.

The Kazala column was the first to move, and reached Irkibai on the Jany Daria in twelve days, having lost but few of its camels. There a fort was built and named Blagoweschtschensk. Setting out thence the column in three days reached Kizil Kak. Here it encountered very severe weather; the midday sun melted the crust of ice on the surface and made the road difficult for the camels, while the men suffered severely from the total want of firewood. Thence in two days it reached the Bukan mountain,¶ and thence, marched by way of Yuskuduk, Kokpatas, and Mingbulak, to Tamdy. The main division, which marched from Jizakh, went by way of Uchma, Farish, Sintab, Timur Kabuk, and the springs of Balta Saldir, thus skirting the Bukharian frontier by the northern spurs of the Karatau and Nuratau mountains. The cold was very severe, and many of the camels, which were weak to begin with,

* Op. cit., ii , 335. † Id., 336-7. Schmidt, Russische Revue, iv., 324-5.
‡ Schmidt, op. cit., 325. § Id., 325-6. ‖ Vide op. cit., 326-39. ¶ Id., 389.

the Kazaks who doubted being eventually paid for them, perished. At Timur Kabuk the Beks of Nurata and Siauddin met the expedition with 100 camels and some provisions sent by the Amir of Bukhara, who thus paraded as a fair-weather friend of the Russians.* Here the army divided into two columns, on account of the scarcity of water; one marched by way of the springs of Bishchaghan, Jani Kasgan, and Kideri, and the other by those of Koshbaigi, Baiman tanti, Maschi, and Aristan-bel-Kuduk. At this last place was the general rendezvous, and there about the 12th of April the two Jizakh columns were united.† Meanwhile the Khivan Khan grew frightened. He sent back twenty-one Russian slaves and some envoys with a friendly message to Kazala, but it was too late, and the expedition was already on its way. Schuyler was at Kazala when these slaves arrived. He describes them as looking well. They reported that they had been carried off as prisoners by the Kazaks, had been bought by the Khan, and been employed by him chiefly as gardeners. They had been treated like the Persian slaves, and fed chiefly on fruit, rice, and an occasional bit of mutton or tallow, and described the Khan as personally good-natured and affable.‡ It had been originally meant to advance from Aristan-bel-Kuduk by the well-known route of Ming Bulak and Shurakhana, but it being reported by the Bukharians that the road by Khalata and Uch Uchak was shorter and less sterile the direction of the march was altered. This is the official explanation given by M. Schmidt. Schuyler gives another explanation less creditable to General Kaufmann, who, it appears, would not be entitled to the cross of St. George unless he had prepared the full plan of campaign, which he had not done in this case.§ The troops rested nearly a fortnight at Aristan-bel-Kuduk. There they spent Easter, ate the Paschal or Easter cake of the Russians, and, according to the testimony of M. Schmidt himself, fired three rockets (doubtless supplied for the destruction of the Khivans) into the air to commemorate the Ascension of the great Peace Messenger himself.‖

Having obtained 800 fresh camels from the Kazaks of the Kizil Kum the expedition once more set out, and on the 6th of May reached Khalata. *En route* they were joined by the Kazala column, which had had a very severe march from Tamdy through deep sand, diversified by pits of bitter water.¶ The old ruined Bukharian fort of Khalata was restored and renamed Fort St. George. Here, as Schuyler says, began the real difficulties of the situation. I shall condense his graphic account. The eighty miles of good road, he says, which had been supposed to exist between Khalata and the Amu Daria turned out to be 120 miles of shifting sand, where apparently the only water was at the wells of Adam Krilgan, *i.e.*, "Man's destruction," about twenty-four

* Id., 390. Schuyler, ii., 398.   † Schmidt, 391.   ‡ Op. cit., i., 49.
§ Op. cit., 339.   ‖ Op. cit., 392.   ¶ Schmidt, op. cit., 389-4.

4 Y

miles from Khalata. This place was an utter desert, with a few bad wells and without a sign of vegetation. After a day's rest there, it was determined to send the troops on by a march with three halts of six hours each to Uch Uchak on the Amu Daria ; the sands, however, were so heavy and the heat so intense that the advance guard could not get beyond thirteen miles, and fresh water had to be sent for to Adam Krilgun. "Affairs were now desperate. It was impossible to advance, and it seemed shameful to retreat, while the small quantity of water at Adam Krilgan rendered it ruin to remain, for the supply which had been brought was nearly exhausted." "Finally a hope of safety appeared in the shape of a ragged Kirghiz who had joined the Kazala detachment on the march from Irkibai, and whose excellent qualities the Grand Duke Nicholas and Colonel Dreschern had been the first to discover. He said that a few miles to the right of the road were the wells of Alti Kuduk. General Kaufman handed him his pocket flask and offered him a hundred roubles reward if he would bring it back filled with water. This was done, and a portion of the troops was immediately sent to Alti Kuduk, where the wells were found to be few, and, what was worse, deep, but there was water. The pontoons were then unloaded and filled with water, to serve as drinking troughs for the remaining horses and camels. The expedition was preserved, and after a halt of several days pursued its way in small detachments and by slow stages to the Amu Daria, which it reached on May 23rd, in eleven days instead of two." "Of the 10,000 camels with which the expedition had been provided but 1,200 remained. The whole road from Khalata was strewn with camp equipage, officers' baggage, and munitions of war. Ammunition and stores had in several places been buried in the sand, with the expectation that subsequent detachments would be sent out from Khalata for the purpose of recovering them. An officer who passed over the road a few weeks subsequently told me, says Schuyler, that the whole distance was covered with the skeletons and decaying bodies of camels and horses, the stench from which was intolerable, while the articles strewn along the road made it appear almost like a bazaar." *

On the news of the Russian preparations a general levy seems to have been made in the Khanate. One part of the army so raised marched towards Kungrad to the fort of Jani Kala, near Cape Urga, to protect the Khanate on the side of the Ust Urt, while a body of 6,000 or 7,000 men went to Daukara to cover the approach by the eastern shores of the Aral. These were apparently the only quarters where danger had been suspected.† When General Kaufmann's approach was ascertained a force of 3,500 Turkomans, Kazaks, and Naukers were assembled at Uch Uchak; 1,500 of these had been posted there under the Divan beg Muhammed Nias, and were afterwards joined by 2,000 more under the

* Op. cit., ii., 340, 341.   † Schmidt, op. cit., 386.

Divan beg Muhammed Murad, the Khan's vizier. These troops were concentrated at the Lake Sarda ba kul, east of Uch Uchak. The Russians had already had a skirmish with one of their outposts. They now encountered the main body, which was soon dispersed by a few rounds of grapeshot.[*]

The Russians now continued their march along the right bank of the river towards Shurakhana, and in four days reached Ak Kamish. Nearly opposite here was the fort of Sheikh Arik, guarding a ford, where the enemy had concentrated in force; a few shells sufficed to disperse them, and their camp was speedily taken by the Russians, some of whom crossed the river breast-high, while others went over in boats captured from the enemy and in pontoons. Only rice and salt were found in the camp. The Russians lost but two horses, which were speedily eaten by the hungry soldiers.[†]

On May 28th a deputation went from Shurakhana to the Russian camp complaining of the ill-usage it had received from the Khivans and Turkomans, and soliciting protection. The deputation was received with due honour, as being the first Khivans who had submitted, and a detachment of Cossacks went to the town and stayed there four days.[‡] The people, reassured by the Russian proclamation, now brought provisions, cattle, meal, grapes, forage, etc., into the camp, and after their late hardships the troops might well suppose, in the words of Schmidt, that they had crossed the river Lethe in crossing the Oxus.

Let us now shortly examine the progress of the other detachments. The story of that of Colonel Markosof has been told in detail by Schmidt.[§] He had been ordered to march by way of Bugdaili and Aidin to the Uzboi, or old bed of the Oxus, and then by Topiatan, Igdy, Ortakuya, and Dandur to the ruined fort of Zmukshir, forty miles west of Khiva, and there await the arrival of the Turkestan division. He reached Igdy, about half of the journey, in safety, and had a successful encounter with the Tekke Turkomans, from whom he captured a large booty. Between Igdy and Ortakuya lies a terrible waste of sand, through which Markosof tried to hurry his men in order to capture Khiva before the other columns arrived, and thus secure the honours of the campaign for the army of the Caucasus; but the terrible heat and the want of water at length compelled a halt, and as the deserts beyond Ortakuya were still more extensive it was resolved to retire to Krasnovodsk. Many of the troops through illness and weakness had to be carried on camels, and were harassed by the Turkomans. They at length reached Krasnovodsk, but "almost the whole expedition was ill. Sixty men died of sunstroke. The troops returned without their arms. The camels, the booty of the Turkomans, and various

* Id., 403-5. † Id., 406-7; Schuyler, ii., 342. ‡ Schmidt, 408; Schuyler, 342.
§ Russische Revue, v., 1, etc.

provisions were abandoned in the steppe.   One staff officer threw away
a full service of silver plate and all his conserves."[*]   Some of the
cannon were buried in the sand but were afterwards recovered, and many
rifles were brought in subsequently by the Kazaks and friendly Turkomans.[†]   The expedition, though thus a failure, yet effected a certain
diversion by keeping the Tekke Turkomans employed, and thus preventing
them from joining the Khivans.   The division under Colonel Lomakin
marched across the Ust Ust plateau.   It left Kinderli in three sections,
on the 27th, 28th, and 29th of April, and suffered great hardships from
the fierce sun and the want of water.   It marched by way of the brooks
Kaundy and Senek to Bish Akti, where a detachment which had been sent
out under Major Navrozki defeated a body of Kazaks, and secured a
welcome supply of camels and horses.   Thence the column advanced by the
wells of Kamisty, Karastchik, Sai Kuyu, and Bussaga.   The column, as
before, was broken into sections, which marched after each other at
intervals so as not to exhaust the water in the wells.   The next stages
were the wells of Karakin, Kinir, Alpai Mas, and Ak Metschet, Ilte Iji,
Bailiar, Kizil Agir, and Baichagir, Mendali, Alan, and lastly Itibai, at the
south-west corner of the Aibugir gulf.   Near Alan they passed the ruins
of a fort built by Prince Bekovitch.   Having communicated with General
Veretkin, the detachment now crossed the Aibugir, passed through
Kungrad, and a few hours later safely joined the Orenburg detachment.
This march across the Ust Ust was a wonderful feat ; 400 miles of
desert country, with scarcely any water or provisions, were compassed in
twenty-nine days.[‡]

The Orenburg column left the Yemba on April the 11th, and traversed
a road which had been frequently explored, and accomplished its march
with little difficulty.   It first went eastward as far as the Barsuk sands,
and then followed the western shores of the Aral as far as the well-
known promontory of the Ust Ust called Urga.   General Verefkin now
issued a proclamation to the nomadic Karakalpaks and Turkomans,
bidding them remain at home, and to the Russian Kazaks who had sought
refuge on Khivan territory to go on with him to Khiva.   Several of the
chiefs of the latter accepted the invitation, and proved of service as guides
and from their knowledge of the language in the subsequent operations.
Crossing the Aibugir, General Verefkin occupied the fort of Janikala,
which he destroyed, and then advanced on Kungrad.[§]   A considerable
force of Khivans which had been posted near it fled, and the town was
speedily occupied.   Its ruined walls and houses spoke eloquently of the
destruction caused during the struggle between the Khivans and
Turkomans fifteen years before.   General Verefkin caused the so-called
Khan's palace, where the Beg of Kungrad lived, and the house of the Jesaul

* Schuyler, 344-5.   † Id., 345-6.
‡ Schmidt, op. cit., iv., 411-22 ; Schuyler, ii., 346-7.   § Schmidt, 419-22.

Mamit, the commander of the Khivan advance guard, to be destroyed. The only booty secured in the town was about 1,000 pounds weight of bread, made of rice and chugara. The people had fled, but they returned again speedily as they became reassured, and supplied the army with some welcome provisions.*

There it heard bad news of the Aral flotilla. This had left the mouth of the Sir Daria on the 29th of April, and had two days later anchored at the island of Takmak ata off the Aibugir gulf. Having remained there for some days, it, on the 9th of May, entered the western branch of the Ulkun Daria, called the Kichkin Daria, and appeared before the small fort of Ak kala. This was bombarded, and the garrison driven out, the Russians having some men wounded by a shot from the fort. The flotilla then mounted the Ulkun Daria to within about 50 versts from Kungrad, where it anchored from want of water. Thence a small surveying expedition was sent on to examine the country and communicate with General Verefkin. It was, however, betrayed by its Kazak guide, and its members were murdered. Their mutilated bodies were afterwards found by a detachment from the Orenburg column, and buried under eleven Italian poplars at Kungrad.† The Orenburg column now advanced towards Khojeili, and after two unimportant skirmishes encountered the main body of the Khivans, between 3,000 and 5,000 strong, with several guns, under the command of the Uzbeg Yakub Bi, about 30 versts from that town. Schmidt has described in detail how this force, which offered little resistance, was driven before it by the Russians, who speedily entered Khojeili, where they were well received by the inhabitants.‡ Thence they advanced on Mangut ; *en route* they fought another engagement with a considerable body of Yomud Turkomans under Janubi bey. Mangut speedily surrendered. The retiring enemy was not allowed much rest, and while General Verefkin with his main body pursued one section of them towards Kitai on the Karagös canal, another was followed towards Kilij Niaz bi by Colonel Skobelef. Advancing still further, the columns passed through Gurlen, the Khan's army, in which the Khivans had placed much reliance, making the feeblest show of resistance to the disciplined serried ranks of the Russians.

The Khan now began to see that his cause was hopeless, and he sent General Verefkin a letter asking for a three or four days' truce, saying that he had sent a similar one to General Kaufmann, that he wished only for peace with Russia, and hoped the General would continue to punish the Turkomans, who were very unruly subjects.§ The letter was treated as a mere excuse to gain time, and the advance was continued by way of Kat and Kashkupir towards Khiva, fighting

---

* Schmidt, op. cit., v., 12-14.   † *Id.*, 14, 15.   ‡ *Id.*, 18-21.
§ *Id.*, 30.   Schuyler, op. cit., 348.

skirmishes and crossing several canals on the way. In one case a
pontoon 189 feet long was thrown over the canal of Kilij Niaz Bi in less
than twenty-four hours. At length, on June 7th, the Russians encamped
in a garden belonging to the Khan, scarcely three miles from
Khiva. The fortifications were now reconnoitred, a difficult operation,
as the environs of the town were much broken with gardens, etc. A vigorous and well-directed fire was kept up from the ramparts, and one shot
severely wounded General Verefkin in the head. This fire was returned
by the Russian artillery, and presently a deputation of the citizens came
out asking for peace, saying the Khan had fled and that great confusion
reigned inside. The Russian general ordered them to return and stop
the firing from the walls, and then to repair to the camp of General
Kaufmann, of whose approach he had heard, and who alone had
authority to make peace. He also threatened that unless the firing
ceased in two hours the town should be bombarded.* On the return of
the deputation the fire from the walls continued. This was explained by
a second deputation from the burghers as due to the Turkomans, whom
they could not control. The bombardment began and continued till ten
at night, when a three hours' respite was granted. Meanwhile a letter
arrived from General Kaufmann to say that he was only sixteen versts
from Khiva on the Yanghi Arik, and that he was then negotiating for
the surrender of the city, and bidding General Verefkin meet him at a
bridge three miles from the east gate of the town.

We left the Turkestan column at Sheikh Arik. Near there a short
and decisive engagement was fought with a body of Turkomans, and
General Kaufmann also received a letter from the Khan complaining
naively of the invasion of his borders, and expressing himself ready to
carry out the General's wishes. The latter replied that peace must be
made at Khiva.†

On the 5th of June the column again set out and in a few hours
reached Hazarasp, where a few shots were fired at the advance guard
of the Russians, but when their main body drew near, the defenders
abandoned the town. This was the strongest fortress in the Khanate,
being protected on three sides by water and on the fourth by a wall
thirty feet high and three fathoms thick half way up. It might have
offered a serious resistance. It was now surrendered by the citizens, and
the Russians found in it four mounted brass cannons of good workmanship, some carriages for falconets, a great store of shot and powder,
1,000 puds of wheat, 800 puds of chugara for the horses, and 680 puds
of rice. On the 6th of June General Kaufmann heard news of the
Orenburg division, and the next day received the congratulations of the
Khan of Bukhara. On the 9th he again set out, and on the 10th reached
the lake of Yanghi Arik. There he received a letter from the Khan,

* Schmidt, op. cit., 36-7.   † Id., 41.

the bearer of which was the latter's cousin, the Inak Irtasali. In it he acknowledged himself as- the subject of the Tzar, complained of his inability to restrain the Yomuds, and promised to come in person to the Russian camp the following morning.*

Meanwhile anarchy prevailed inside the city ; the parties of resistance and submission were arrayed against one another, and the Khan, who was helpless between them, fled before his cousin had returned. The Divan begi Mat Murad headed the militant party. The Khan's brother Atajan Tiura, who had been imprisoned for seven months, was nominated Khan, and his uncle Seyid Amir Ul Umara was given joint authority with him. They were the nominees of the party of peace, and the next morning went to General Kaufmann's camp with Irtasala already mentioned and other notables, and offered their submission.†

Meanwhile General Verefkin having sent a large section of his contingent to join that from Turkestan, the Turkomans reopened a fire from the walls on those who remained. The bombardment was there-upon renewed, the Shahabad or north gate of the city was battered in and stormed, and Colonel Skobelef advanced through the streets to the palace. While this was taking place, General Kaufmann approached the Hazarasp gate and entered the town in triumph with colours flying and music playing. A guard was placed at the palace to protect the Khan's harem and the property there. The walls of the town were occupied, and orders given for the disarming of the inhabitants. Having assembled the troops in the great square and thanked them in the Emperor's name for their exertions, the General repaired to the audience hall of the palace and received the various deputations who brought him more or less hollow congratulations.‡ As Seyid Muhammed had sought refuge among the Yomuds, Atajan Tiura, who had been nominated Khan during the late disturbances, was temporarily confirmed. General Kaufmann now wrote to ask him to return, offering to restore him to his former position. A few hours later he appeared at the headquarters.

Mr. McGahan has described General Kaufmann's first interview with the Khan ; how he rode to the garden of his own palace on a richly caparisoned horse, and dismounted at the end of a short avenue leading up to the General's tent, taking off his hat as he approached and kneeling before Kaufmann, who sat on a camp stool, and who does not seem to have behaved with the chivalrous courtesy due to a fallen enemy. Presently the Khan took up his position, kneeling in Khivan fashion on a carpet. Our traveller describes him as about thirty years· old, with a not unpleasant countenance when not clouded by fear, with a large face, rather oblique eyes, aquiline nose, a very thin black beard and moustache, and a sensual mouth. He was a giant in size, being fully six feet three inches

---

* *Id.,* 44.   † *Id.,* 44-5.   ‡ *Id.,* 46-8. Schuyler 350-1.

high, and broad shouldered in proportion. He was dressed in a long khalat or tunic of bright blue silk, and the usual tall black sheepskin hat.[*] General Kaufmann used some ironical phrases, told him he had gone to see him as he had promised, and when his modest guest said it was the will of Allah, replied severely that Allah would not have willed it if he had done as he (Kaufmann) had advised him. The Khan used language of humble courtesy in reply, and the Russian general promised that he should be reinstated. He proved very docile and tractable and, Mr. McGahan says, showed a great deal of intelligence and good sense in the direction of affairs.[†] His habits were very simple, and the only luxury he indulged in was a stable full of fine Turkoman horses and an occasional new wife.[‡] Although such a stalwart man he had little personal courage, and never commanded his forces in person. He had only four wives, the number allowed by the Koran, but had besides about one hundred concubines, some from each of the races in his dominions. These women spent most of their time in making clothes, beds, and carpets for the family, and in household work. The Khan smoked all day. While the Russians were there he used to ride to their camp every morning and hold a divan with Colonel Ivanof, where he spent an hour or two, and then returned to his palace for breakfast, after which he administered justice for two or three hours. hearing all kinds of cases, trivial and important—an eastern patriarchal custom, which has the advantage of making an autocrat know what is passing among his humblest subjects, and is an improvement on those despotisms where the ruler never hears anything except from the lips of courtiers and sycophants. In the afternoon, when he had taken tea, the Khan went to the harem to sleep, and in the evening rode out with a body of attendants to see General Kaufmann, or to visit the country round.[§]

The whole revenue of the Khanate was about 90,000 tillas or £45,000, but a large portion of this did not reach the Khan's hands. The revenue was derived from the Custom's dues on foreign merchandise, a line of licence tax on shopkeepers and traders, and the land and house tax. The Karakalpaks paid a sheep in every hundred, a bullock in every twenty, and a camel in every six. The Kazaks who visited the bazaar paid a shilling for every camel or every ten sheep; besides this there was a harvest tax answering to our tithe. The roads and canals were kept up by the Government. The population of the Khanate, excluding the Nomades of the Kizil Kum, was about 500,000.| This is not the place to describe the internal economy of the country or the manners and customs of its people, but I am tempted to quote a passage from Captain Burnaby's work, in which, describing its judicial arrangements, he tells us that when a person appeared from the evidence of witnesses to be

---

* McGahan, op. cit., 274-5.   † Id., 275.   ‡ Id., 280.
§ Id., 288. | Id., 280-1.

guilty and yet refused to confess, he was beaten witn rods, salt was put in his
mouth, and he was exposed to the sun until he confessed.* In the Khan's
treasure house situated behind the hall of audience at the palace, which is
described as a low vaulted room, the walls and ceiling of which were
covered with rude frescoes representing vines and flowers, there was a
large square old chair, broad and low backed, and covered with leather.
This was the Khan's throne. It showed, says Mr. McGahan, some very
skilful carving and incrusting, reminding one of the old throne of the
Tzars at St. Petersburg. It had a silver plate on the back, with the
inscription—" In the time of Muhammed Rahim, shah of Khuarezin, in
the year 1231, made by the unworthy Muhammed." There were several
iron chests with heavy locks. In one was about £30 worth of Khivan
silver. In another a saddle, bridle, and harness covered with gold
plating and set with rubies, emeralds, and turquoises. Leaning against
the wall or lying in heaps on the floor were swords, daggers, guns,
pistols, and revolvers of various kinds, several splendid old matchlocks
with crooked stocks and long slender tapering barrels, beautifully inlaid
with gold and silver, also a double-barrelled English hunting rifle, a
present from Lord Northbrook, whose letter already referred to was
found with it. Among the other weapons were several sabres and
pistols of European fabric, a number of Khorasan blades inlaid with
gold, and slender Persian scimitars with scabbards set with turquoises
and emeralds; short thick knives and poniards from Afghanistan,
richly mounted and well jewelled sheaths; beautiful carpets, silk
coverlets, cushions, pillows, and khalats, cashmere shawls, etc. Close by
this room was another containing several suits of armour inlaid with
gold, and 300 volumes † These have been described by M. Kuhn. He
says the greater part of the MSS. were historical works, chiefly
translations from the Persian into Turki, and they had been written for
the most part during the domination of the present Kungrad dynasty.
Among them, however, were native works, such as a history of the
Khivan Khans, by Yunus Mirab, which must be very valuable, as it
contains a history of the dynasty from the reign of Iltazar Khan.
Besides these books were a considerable number of diplomatic documents
letters of the Khan, writings relating to internal administration, taxes,
&c. There were also twenty gold and five silver seals belonging to the
Khans, and about two hundred dies for striking money.‡

Let us now complete our account of General Kaufmann's proceedings
A council was appointed to assist the Khan, consisting of three Russians
Lieutenant-Colonels Ivanof, Posharof, and Khoroshin, and three
Khivans, namely, the Divan beg Mat Nias (the ablest of the native
officials), the Inak Irtasali, and the Mekhter (or Finance Minister),
Abdulla bi. The Khan himself was the nominal, but Colonel Ivanof

---

* Op. cit., 317.   † McGahan, op. cit., 249-50.   ‡ Russische Revue. iv., 73.

4 Z

was the real, president. The Khan was given the right to administer
the Shahriat and to appoint the local governors.* Mat Murat and his
confidante, Rahmet Ulla, who had been very hostile to Russia, were sent
prisoners to Kazala and thence to Russia, while the quondam Khan Atajan
entered the Russian army. A difficult and not very wisely considered
reform was now attempted. It was determined, in order to satisfy
Russian sentiment, to liberate 30,000 Persians who were held as slaves
in the Khanate, the victims of Turkoman robbery; many of them
had long settled in Khuarezm, tilled a large portion of its land and
were its most valuable citizens. They were ordered to assemble at the
various bazaars in the Khanate, whence, after having been duly
identified, they were to go to Krasnovodsk in parties of 500 and 600.
But two such parties actually went, one of which was attacked by
Turkomans, when most of the Persians were either killed or re-enslaved,
and hundreds of others were apparently slaughtered after the Russians
departed.† At length a treaty of peace was signed between General
Kaufmann and the Khan, by which the latter undertook to be a faithful
servant of the Emperor, and to make no treaties of commerce, etc.,
with neighbouring powers, nor to undertake any military expeditions,
without the knowledge and consent of the Russian authorities.

The boundary between the two empires was to be the Amu Daria,
following its most western branch as far as the Sea of Aral, thence
along the latter sea to Cape Urga, and along the northern edge of
the Ust Ust and the ancient bed of the Oxus. All the territory on
the right bank of the Amu Daria, with all its nomade and settled
inhabitants, were ceded to Russia, and if the latter power chose to
make a portion of it over to Bukhara the Khan was to acquiesce. The
Russians were to have the *exclusive* right of navigating the Oxus. The
Bukharians and Khivans were only to do so with the consent of the
Russian authorities. The latter were to have the right of planting quays
and jetties, factories, depôts, and farms wherever they pleased on the left
bank of the river, and the Khan was to be responsible for their safety.
All the towns and villages of the Khanate were to be open to Russian
traders, and their caravans were to have free passage and to be
guaranteed security, nor were they to pay transit or other dues.
Russian merchants were to be allowed to have agents at Khiva and the
other towns of the Khanate, and to possess landed property there, which
was only to be taxed with the consent of their officials. Contracts
between Russians and Khivans were to be conscientiously carried out
and grievances speedily remedied, those committed by Russians at the
hands of the nearest Russian authorities, and those by Khivans by
Khivan officials. Russian criminals were to be apprehended and
surrendered, and no one was to be allowed to enter the Khanate from

---

* *Id.*, v., 150.   † Schuyler, op. cit., ii., 354.

Russia without a passport. The edict of the Khan abolishing slavery was to be maintained, and finally an enormous fine of 2,200,000 roubles (£274,000) was imposed on the Khan for the expenses of the war, to be paid either in silver or Russian paper, by instalments, 100,000 roubles for the first two years, and to be gradually increased till 1881, when the sum was to be 200,000 roubles.* Thus was the Khanate laid prostrate, and one of the most memorable campaigns of our century brought to a successful issue. As a mere military feat the conquest of Khiva was nothing, for the forces of the Khan proved to be contemptible ; but as an engineering campaign, against difficulties of a physical kind, it is worthy to rank among the most notable in history. The treaty which was made by General Kaufmann, and published in the *Turkestan Gazette* before the authorities at St. Petersburg had an opportunity to revise it, was another instance of the power of provincial satraps in an unwieldy empire like Russia. To reconcile it with the frank and volunteered statements of Count Schouvaloff in London requires the casuistry of a practised diplomat; more ingenuous people must shake their heads. But if we take higher ground than the ephemeral jealousies of England and Russia, and the questionable fruits which follow such ploughing and sowing, we shall perhaps not be sorry that the death-knell of Khivan independence has been sounded, and a stop been put to a rule which was a stain on our century.

Note 1.—The various dignitaries that form an Eastern court are so numerous and confusing that it will be convenient to tabulate those of any importance in a typical Khanate like that of Khiva :—

1. The Inaks—literally, younger brothers—who were four in number, two being the nearest relatives of the Khan, and two others merely of the same race. The chief inak was *ex officio* Governor of Hazarasp.

 The Nakib, or spiritual chief, who must always be a Seyid. Vambery says he holds the same position as the Sheikh ul Islam at Constantinople.

3. The Bi, who in battle was always at the right hand of the Khan.

4. The Atalik, a kind of councillor of state, who must be an Uzbeg. The number of ataliks was arbitrary; there was generally one in each town. On this office, see *ante* 869, note 1.

5. The Kushbegi, whose original office was that of chief falconer or huntsman, but who became the head officer, prime minister, or vizier of the Khanate.

6. The Mekhter, or finance minister, who also had control of home affairs. He was generally a Sart.

7. Yesaulbachis, guards of the chamber, who introduced strangers. There were two of these officials at the court.

---

* L'Année Géographique, 1873. 7-10. Schuyler, op. cit., 363-4.

8. Divanbashi, the secretary or accountant. ·

9. Mekhrems, chamberlains, also two in number.

10. Mingbashi, commander of 1,000 horsemen.

11. Yuzbashi, commander of 100 horsemen.

12. Onbashi, commander of 10 horsemen.

These formed the class of officials, properly so called, and were styled sipahi. Some were irremovable, some had a fixed stipend, and some were employed only in time of war.

The Ulemas, or priests, of whom the Nakib was the head, are thus divided:—

1. Kazi Kelan, supreme judge in the Khanate.

2. Kazi Ordu, chief provost-marshal or judge while the army was on a campaign.

3. Alem, the chief of the five muftis.

4. Reis, inspector of schools and general supervisor of religion.

5. Muftis, of whom there was one in each principal city.

6. Akhond, professor or teacher.

The first three belonged to the higher rank of officials and were paid by the Khan, the others were mainly paid from the Vakf, or fund for pious uses.*

Note 2.—We will now describe the principal towns in the Khanate which have been of historic importance during the Uzbeg domination. The readers of Abulghazi will have noted that he frequently mentions the town of Vezir as the residence of the Khan, and evidently as one of the chief places in the Khanate, yet he will search in vain for such a place upon the map, and, in fact, its site has been for a long time and until recently unknown. The earliest mention of it (*so nomine*) known to me is in a Jagatai work which was apparently the foundation of the Sheibani Nameh, and which is quoted by my friend M. Lerch; there it is called Shehr Vezir, *i.e.*, the town of Vezir, probably a corruption of Shehr i Vezir, the town of the Vezir or Vizier.† M. Lerch happily identified this form of the name with the Sellizure of Jenkinson, who makes the latter as Abulghazi makes Vezir, the residence of Hajim Khan. Abulghazi tells us it was situated six agatch or parasangs from Urgenj.‡ From the narrative of Abulghazi§ and also of Jenkinson it is clear that it was situated to the west of Urgenj. It was also situated close to the Kir or Ust Ust;∥ and further, Abulghazi tells us it was possible to go thither from Urgenj by water, *i.e.*, by the old channel of the Oxus. From all these facts we have no difficulty in fixing its situation at the ruins of Deu Kisken. These ruins were visited by Glukhofski in 1873, and are described as situated on an outlying promontory of the Ust Ust, close to the Chink or bounding cliff of the plateau. The extent of the ruins there excited the surprise of the Russians, as also the fine appearance of the arches, arcades, façades, and gables, the good masonry and the glazed tiles.¶

Jenkinson tells us the country south of Sellizure was very fertile, and in confirmation of this we find the Russian explorers describing the Urun Daria or old Oxus bed, between here and Lake Sari Kamish, as dotted with ruins,

* Vambery, op. cit., 335-7.   † Lerch, Khiva, etc . 41.   ‡ Op. cit., 235.
§ *Id*, 236, 247.   ∥ *Id.*, 236.   ¶ Petermann, Mittheilungen, 1874, p. 25.

while on either side are remains of numerous irrigation canals.* M. De Goeje in his learned pamphlet on the Oxus has, I think, identified with every probability the Vezir of later writers with the Git or Kit of Ishtakhri and Ibn Haukal.†

Abulghazi says there were formerly several towns dependent on Vezir, each having its own governor, but the district had been so much ravaged that when Ilbars Khan founded the new Khanate there only remained two, Yani Shehr and Tersek.‡ Yani Shehr, or Shehr el Jedid (both names meaning the same thing, i.e., New Town), occur on coins of Abdulla Khan of the Golden Horde in 765 and 766 of the hej Fraehn.§ I have identified it in a previous note as M. Goeje has also with Yanghi Kent at the mouth of the Sir,‖ but this is a long way from Vezir, and it may be that its site is to be looked for among the various ruins on the old course of the Oxus, near the latter town.

As to Tersek, it is mentioned among the towns captured by Sheibani in his early expedition to Khuaresm. He first captured Tersek, which he fortified, and then took Buldumsaz, whose ruins, according to M. Lerch, are situated at the end of the canal of Kilich Niazbi.¶

East of Vezir, on the Kunia Daria, are the ruins of the famous city of Urgenj, so long the capital of the oasis. They are now known as Kunia Urgenj, to distinguish them from New Urgenj, near Khiva. This is the site of the famous Al Jorjania, which was the capital of Khuarezm in the time of the Arabs. It was also called Gurganj.** Formerly there were two towns of this name close to one another—one called Great (Kubra) Urgenj and the other Little (Sughra) Urgenj.†† Mokadessi describes it, under its name of Jorjania, as growing in size and as having four gates. Near the pilgrims' gate was a palace built by Al Mamun. Mamun's son Ali also built himself a palace there, in the square where the sheep market was held.‡‡ This old city was destroyed by the Mongols during the famous siege which I have described.§§ It was called Ornas by Carpini, Civitas Ornarum by Benedict of Poland, and Arnach or Ornach by some Russian chroniclers.‖‖ It was the site of a bishopric subordinate to the metropolitan of Sultania, which is referred to as sedes Vernensis by Wadding, who reports how, in 1393, Antonio Pietro de Malliano succeeds Boniface there as bishop, the latter having been promoted to Sultania.¶¶ Ibn Batuta, who visited it in his famous journey, found it a flourishing city. In 1379 Urgenj, which is called Khuarezm by Sherifuddin, was devastated by Timur.*** It was visited by Jenkinson in 1557, who tells us its walls of earth were by estimation about four miles in circumference. Its buildings were made of earth, but were chiefly in poor condition. He tells us it had a long covered street, i.e., a bazaar. It had recently been won and lost four times in civil war, and had but few merchants.††† A few years later its final decay was ensured by its being forsaken by the river Oxus, which, as Abulghazi tells us, took a fresh

---

* Id. † Op. cit., 64, 65. ‡ Op. cit., 212. § Fraehn, Catalogue of Puch Collection.

‖ Op. cit., 65. ¶ Op. cit., 41. ** Jihan Numa De Goeje, op. cit., 114.

†† Khiva, by Suavi Effendi, 35. ‡‡ De Goeje, op. cit., 104.

§§ Ante, i., 85; ii., 33, 34. ‖‖ Fraehn Ibn Foslan, 162.

¶¶ Wadding Annales Minores, ix., 120; D'Avesac, 509.

*** Ante, 234-5. ††† Jenkinson in Hackluyt, i., 368.

course about 1575, and caused the environs of the town to become more or less desolate.* In 1603 it was plundered by the Ural Cossacks, as I have described.† Glukhofski tells us it was again ravaged, at the end of the seventeenth century, by the Kalmúk chief Aĕomka, i.e., Ayuka.‡ It is now a mere collection of ruins. These ruins were visited by Glukhofski in 1873. He describes a stately tower or minaret as remaining then, which has the shape of a truncated cone, and is built of beautiful burnt bricks and ornamented with four convex rings, containing inscriptions, the letters being of the height of a man. Inside it is a winding staircase, reaching to the roof. Its interior is tenanted by many pigeons and bats. Besides this is a fine ruined palace, containing a large round hall with a vaulted cupola, the upper part of which is ruined. This hall has a double row of windows, one about six feet from the ground, consisting of four, and the other near the dome, of sixteen windows, and its walls are decorated with reliefs and arabesques, on which are remains of gilding and colour. Lastly, there is a fine mosque, with an appendant gable to it, containing the tombs of famous people in Khuarezmian history. Among these tombs are two surrounded by a copper trellis-work, and especially remarkable for the excellence of their Oriental style and workmanship.§ Urgenj, under its name of Khuarezm, occurs as a mint place on coins of the Golden Horde, from the reign of Mangu Timur, in 674 hej, to that of Pulad, at the end of the sixteenth century.

A sister town to Urgenj, and generally held with it, was Tuk. The site of Tuk, so often mentioned by Abulghazi, is not certainly known. M. Schmidt tells us that in a private communication he has received from Mr. Sobolef the latter claims to have found the sites both of Tuk and of Kara Uighur Tughai, another desideratum,|| but this has apparently not yet been made available. Abulghazi tells us Urgenj could be seen in the distance from the ramparts of Tuk, and that Urgenj lay to the south-west of it, and it apparently took several hours to go from one to the other.¶ From these unsatisfactory data it is perhaps not altogether rash to identify Tuk with the important town of Khojeili, whose present name is merely derived from its being the residence of a large colony of Khojas. In this identification I am at one with M. Goeje.** Tuk does not occur in any of the older writers, and it is probably a comparatively modern town, a fact to which I shall revert in the next note.

Another famous site in the Khanate of Khuarezm is Kat, which is evidently a very old city, and is spoken of by the early Arabic geographers as, in fact, the metropolis of the country. It is so styled by Ishtakhri. He tells us how its old site had been overrun by the river and was then in ruins, and how its citizens had removed it some distance to the east, and that they feared the river might again damage the new citadel. It then contained the palace of the Khuarezm Shah, a large mosque, and a prison, and was watered by the Canal Jardur, on whose banks was the great market place which was a third of a parasang square.†† Mokadessi tells us its citizens called it Shahristan (i.e.,

* Op. cit., 312.   † Ante, 894.   ‡ Petermann, Mittheilungen, 1874, p. 25.
§ Petermann, op. cit., 25. || Russische Revue, vi., 235.   ¶ Abulghazi, op. cit., 247.
** Op. cit., 56.   †† Goeje, op. cit., 87, 88.

the capital). He says it was as large as Nishapur and larger than Bukhara. Its chief mosque was supported by pillars of black stone as high as a man, above which were wooden planks. It was a prosperous town, and many learned and rich people lived there, while its shops were provided with many luxuries. Its architects were men of taste, and its readers famous for their voices and for a peculiar intonation like that of Irak; on the other hand, it had the reputation of being dirtier than Ardebil, and many drains emptied themselves in its streets, which were also marked by foul odours. The manure was collected in holes, whence it was transported in sacks to the fields (assuredly a very early instance of utilizing town sewage). Mokadessi remarks how the inhabitants brought in this filth on their shoes even into the mosques.[*] Kat suffered terribly in Timur's campaigns.[†] It became one of the principal towns of the Uzbeg Khanate. It was generally the home of an appanaged prince, and is frequently mentioned by Abulghazi. It was visited by Jenkinson, who tells us he arrived there after crossing the main arm of the Oxus. It is now in ruins and deserted. Sobolef found the ruins of Kat on the right bank of the Oxus, near the modern village of Sheikh Abbas Vali, and nearly opposite New Urgenj.[‡] These ruins were also visited by Mr. Kuhn in 1873; he also places them near Sheikh Abbas Vali.[§] The modern Kat is on the left bank of the Oxus. It would seem that by the city of Khuarezm, Kat was sometimes also designated.[‖]

With Kat is generally named the still famous city of Khiva. We are told by Yakut the natives called it Khivak.[¶] Its importance dates chiefly from the times of the Uzbeg domination. It is mentioned by Ishtakhri;[**] by Mokadessi, who calls it a large town built on a canal of the river, and containing some handsome mosques;[††] and by Yakut.[‡‡] It fills a notable place in the pages of Abulghazi, and since the accession of the Kungrad dynasty it has been the capital of the Khanate.

The present appearance of Khiva has been graphically described by Mr. McGahan. As he approached it, he says, he was impressed by its heavy mud walls, high and battlemented, with heavy buttresses and a ditch, partly dry, partly filled with water, over which could be seen the tops of trees, a few tall minarets, domes of mosques, and one immense round tower that reflected the rays of the sun like porcelain. He entered the town through the gate of Hazarasp, a heavy arched and covered gateway, ten feet wide by twenty deep, arched over with brick and flanked by heavy towers with loopholes—a little fortress in itself.[§§] " Picture to yourself," says Vambery, "three or four thousand mud houses, standing in different directions in the most irregular manner, with uneven and unwashed walls, and fancy these surrounded by a wall ten feet high, also of mud, and you have a conception of Khiva."[‖‖] The mud houses, some more pretentious than others and having porticoes in front of them, are relieved occasionally by trees. Inside the city is the citadel, which has an encircling wall of its own, pierced by four gates, and is a mile long by a quarter wide. Within the citadel are most of the public buildings of

* De Goeje, 101, 102. † Vide ante, 234. ‡ Russiche Revue, vi., 236. § Id., iv., 64. De Goeje, 113. ¶ Id. ** Id., 96. †† Id., 105. ‖ Id., 113. §§ Op. cit., 231. ‖‖ Vambery, Travels, 329.

Khiva. Its wall is much older than the wall encircling the outer city, and probably marks the limits of the older town. The outer wall was only built in 1842, when Allah Kuli was at war with the Amir of Bukhara. The diameter of the latter varies, for it is in shape like an oyster shell, with the narrow end elongated and squared. The longest diameter is a mile and a half, and at the shortest a mile. The wall is on an average twenty-five feet high, and in places higher. It is twenty-five feet wide at the bottom and only two or three at the top, and is girdled by a wide ditch. The space between the two walls is occupied at one place almost completely by tombs in another place by gardens, a number of small canals permeating it and watering elms and fruit trees. Although made of mud, the houses are not uncomfortable inside. They generally consist of an open court, with a number of rooms opening upon it. One of these courts visited by Captain Burnaby he describes as containing some carved stone pillars, supporting a balcony, which looked down on a marble fountain or basin, the general appearance of the court being that of a patio in some nobleman's house in Cordova or Seville. A second apartment had a raised dais at each end, covered with handsome rugs. There were no windows, glass being a luxury, but the opening for light was covered with trellis-work. The doors were handsomely carved, and the room was warmed by a charcoal chafing-dish.*

The chief square in Khiva is bounded on one side by the Khan's palace, a huge rambling structure with mud battlements and walls about fourteen feet high. Opposite this is a new medressi or college, which was not finished when Mr. M'Gahan was there. The other two sides are filled up with sheds and private houses, while at the south-eastern angle of the palace rises beautiful and majestic the sacred tower of Khiva. This is about thirty feet in diameter at the bottom and gradually tapers to the top, a height of about 125 feet, where it seems to have a diameter of fifteen feet. It has neither pedestal nor capital, nor ornament of any kind, and is merely a plain round tower. Its surface, however, is covered with burnt tiles, brightly coloured in blue, green, purple, and brown, on a white ground, arranged in a variety of broad stripes and figures, the whole producing a most brilliant and beautiful effect. The tower is also covered with verses from the Koran, and is held in great reverence by the Khivans. From its top a mollah in a shrill voice summons the citizens to prayer every morning. The two towers flanking the palace gate, which are surrounded by domed roofs, are similarly decorated with coloured tiles.† Near the middle of the open space McGahan describes a hole ten feet square and six feet deep, where criminals were executed. Passing through the palace gateway, which was encumbered with heavy brass cannons, the traveller just mentioned entered a long, narrow, irregular court, which branched off to the left leading to the stables, while on the right were two heavy wooden doors which led to the harem, while right in front were a mass of low, irregular mud structures. Passing through a low corridor and two or three low ill-lighted rooms he emerged into the grand court of the Palace, which was about forty feet square, paved with brick, and only shaded

---

* Op. cit., 299.   † McGahan, 233-4.

by a small elm tree in one corner, and was shut in by walls twenty feet high, over which on the northern side rose the square mud tower of the harem; on the south side was the Khan's audience chamber. "Fancy," says our traveller, a kind of porch entirely open to the court, thirty feet high twenty feet wide, and ten feet deep, and flanked on either side by towers ornamented with blue and green tiles in the same way as the large tower in the square, a floor raised six feet above the pavement of the court, the roof supported by two carved slender wooden pillars, the whole resembling much the shape of a theatre, and you will have a very good idea of the grand hall of state."*

Mr. McGahan had an extraordinary adventure in the harem of the palace, for a description of which I must remit my readers to his volume. I can only extract two or three paragraphs descriptive of its appearance. He tells us the great court of the harem was 150 feet long and 40 wide, and contained a succession of high porches along one side, while in its centre were three or four very large kibitkas or tents set on circular platforms of brick. The scene by moonlight was naturally very picturesque. Passing through one of the porches he was conducted by one of the Khan's wives, whom he had surprised, into a room where was a pile of cushions, and which contained five or six lamps on the walls. The ceiling of this room was painted in rude designs and in harsh colours. One wall was covered with shelves crowded with cups and bowls of all sizes and colours; many of these were of Oriental porcelain, others of more gaudy and cheap Russian pottery. Its floor was a medley of carpets, cushions, coverlets, shawls, robes and khalats, guitars, arms, household utensils, etc., evidently prepared for hasty removal.†

The most beautiful and sacred structure in Khiva is the Mosque Pehlivan Ata. Its fame depends on its containing the tomb of the renowned saint and patron of Khiva, Pehlivan Ahmed Zemchi. Vambery tells us it is four centuries old, while McGahan says it was built by Muhammed Rahim Khan in 1811. It is built of kiln-burnt bricks, and has a dome about sixty feet high, covered with the same kind of tiles as those of the great tower already spoken of, burnt of a brilliant green, and surmounted by a gilt ball. The interior of the dome is covered from bottom to top with tiles, adorned with a delicate blue tracery interwoven with verses of the Koran. These are so deftly joined that the whole appearance is that of an immense inverted vase of Chinese porcelain.‡ Inside the nave of this mosque, in niches in the walls and protected by copper lattice-work, are the tombs of former Khans. Here lie the bodies of Muhammed Rahim, Abulghazi, and Shirghazi Khan. In a kind of side chapel is the tomb of Allah Kuli Khan. That of Pehlivan is contained in a small dark chamber, lit only by one window; its walls, as also the tomb, are covered with grey tiles. The tomb itself is in the middle of the floor, is seven feet long, four feet wide, and three feet high, and its tiles are so closely joined that it looks like solid grey marble.§ Behind the mosque were a number of rooms occupied by the blind, containing a few cooking utensils, a sheepskin thrown on the floor with a coverlet or two for a bed, and a stone water jug. These places were scrupulously clean, and the inmates were daily

* Id., 235.   † Op. cit., 461-2.   ‡ McGahan, op. cit., 297.   § Id., 298.

5 A

supplied with tea, bread, and rice, and two or three times a week with fruit, melons, sugar, etc. The institution was supported partly by a donation of the sainted Pehlivan, by gifts from the Khan, and by alms. On a platform round the central dome of this mosque and approached by a narrow crooked stair, and disposed in an irregular fashion, was a jumble of little cells and rooms inhabited by the mollahs.*

Besides this mosque there are others in Khiva, as the Jüm a Mesjidi, which is attended by the Khan on Fridays, and where the official Khutbeh is read; the Khanmesjidi, inside the citadel: the Shaleker, the Atamurad Kushbegi, and the Karayüzmesjidi.†

Next in importance to the mosques are the Medressis, or colleges. The most renowned of these is the Medressi Medemin Khan, i.e., of Muhammed Amin, built about 1842 by a Persian architect after the model of a Persian medressi of the first class. On its right is a massive tower, which owing to the death of the builder is incomplete. Other medressis are named after their founders—Allah Kuli Khan, Kutlugh Murad Inak, Arab Khan, and Shirghasi Khan.‡

McGahan describes another one built by the present Khan, as made of burnt bricks, two storeys high, and one hundred feet square, with an elevated portal fifty feet high, to be ornamented when finished with blue and white tiles. Inside this, as in other medressis, is a large court, round which are ranged the rooms. Each mollah has two rooms, one for a kitchen the other for a study, the former provided with a small fireplace, sewer, etc., and about six feet by eight feet in size. These rooms are dark, being only lighted by a crevice over the door. Mollahs and students live here in communities, each one cooking his own food. The medressi just described could accommodate one hundred people.§ That of Muhammed Amin has 130 cells and room for 260 students. It enjoys a revenue, says Vambery, of 12,000 Khivan batmans of wheat and 5,000 tillas (i.e., £2,500) in money. Its officers consisted of five akhonds or professors, receiving yearly 3,000 batmans and 150 tillas; one imaum, 2,000 batmans and 40 tillas; one muezzin and one barber, each 200 batmans; two servants, the same; two muttewali, or inspectors, who were paid a tithe of the whole revenue; the balance was divided among the students, according to three classes, receiving respectively 60 batmans 4 tillas, 30 batmans 2 tillas, and 15 batmans 1 tilla.‖

The basaars at Khiva are like those in other Oriental towns. Mr. McGahan describes their cool dark shade as a great relief from the blinding glare of the streets. "A pleasant compound scent of spices and many other agreeable odours greet your nostrils," he says; "the confused noise and hum of a large crowd assails your ears; and an undistinguishable mass of men, horses, camels, donkeys, and carts meets your eyes. The roof is formed by beams laid from wall to wall across the narrow street, supporting cross timbers, and the whole covered with earth. Apricots, peaches, plums, grapes, and melons of a dozen different kinds lie about in heaps." "Properly speaking," he says, "there are no shops. An elevated platform runs along one side, and men are seated among heaps of wares, with no apparent boundary line between them; on the other side are a few barbers, butchers, cobblers, and smaller traders. The following wares are to be seen in the bazaars and shops: Ripe and dried fruits, wheat, rye, jugera, clover seed, bread in small rolls, Russian sugar, green tea (which comes from India through Bukhara), domestic Russian and Bukhara stuffs of cotton and silk, bed-covers, boots and shoes, copper ware and iron vessels, tea-pots, tea-cans, and tea-cups; also from Russia a good deal of silk, which is manufactured in Khiva; and formerly, of course, there was also a busy traffic in slaves. Besides the ordinary bazaars already named is a more stately building, called the Tim, which is a double arcade or passage 100 yards long by 40 feet wide, built of brick in a succession of arches. The roof is about 40 feet high, and each arch ends in a kind of dome funnel with a round hole at the top which serves to light and ventilate the place.* Around the Tim are the Nan bazari (bread market), Bakal bazari (grocers), Shem bazari (soap and candle makers), and the Sertrash bazari (barbers' shops), where the heads are shaven—not the beards, of course, which are sacred with Muhammedans.†

While the retail trade is done in these bazaars the wholesale is chiefly transacted in the Caravanserai, which was built in 1823 by Muhammed Rahim Khan, and consists, as usual, of a quadrangular paved court, with shops like alcoves ranged round its four sides. These shops have arched ceilings towards the court, and receive light through the doors only. In them are stored the wares of the rich merchants of Khiva.‡

From Khiva we will turn to Hazarasp, which is also a very old town. It is mentioned by Ishtakhri and Mokadessi, by Abulfeda and Yakut,§ and has been an important bulwark to Khuarezm during its occupation by the Uzbegs.

Hazarasp is described by Mr. McGahan as looking very picturesque, from its crooked and irregular walls, high and battlemented, and surrounded by water. The main entrance of the fortress is approached by a long, narrow, covered street, with shops on either side. The gateway is heavy and massive, and flanked as usual with towers. It is built of brick and plastered with mud. The gates are pierced in one or two places by holes, evidently made by cannon balls in some old siege. The town itself is mud-built, and entirely encompassed by the walls of the fortress, which enclose about three acres, to which a kind of addition or wing has been built. It is ten miles from the river and forty from Khiva. Its houses are poor, and it contains a palace which has not apparently anything remarkable about it.‖ Its strategic position, as the outpost against Bukhara, and its strength as a fortress, have always given it an important position in Khivan history, and, as we have seen in the previous pages, it was frequently the seat of a separate appanaged prince, and in later times the heritage of the Inak.

Note 3 —The topography of Khuarezm in early and mediæval times has given rise to a large literature, in consequence of a problem of physical geography of the highest interest, both scientifically and politically, involved in it, namely, the ancient course of the river Oxus. That the Oxus, or a

* McGahan, 304. † Vambery, 331. ‡ McGahan, 308.
§ De Goeje, 96, 105, 112, 114. ‖ McGahan, 196-202.

branch of it, once fell into the Caspian, is patent not only from the testimony of many writers of credit, but from the existence to this day of the old bed through which it flowed. When this flow took place, whether it was continuous or intermittent, and how far the divergence of so great a river affected the Aral lake, are questions which have exercised much patient inquiry. Sir Henry Rawlinson, Sir Roderick Murchison, Colonel Yule, and Major Herbert Wood have written about it recently in England; M. de Goeje has published an elaborate essay on the subject in Holland, and M. Paquier a more recent one in France, while in Russia it has naturally been the subject of much research. The problem occupied the early geographers as well as the more recent ones, and may be said to be still in many aspects a *lis pendens*. This is not the place to discuss the whole question, but it is necessary, if we are to understand aright the history of Khuarezm in late times, that the recent history of the Oxus should be clearly apprehended, and notwithstanding the mass of material which has been accumulated there still remains room for discussion.

Let us first follow the story told by Jenkinson. He says that on the 27th of August he reached a cape, and he should have made the port of Mangushlak, but being driven by a storm he had to land on the opposite side of the bay, where no boats had previously landed. This place was twenty-five days' journey from Sellizure, i.e., Vezir. There can be no doubt, as Professor Lenz has argued, that he landed on the northern shore of the bay of Kara Kichu. Having discharged his boat he went to Mangushlak, where he was entertained by the governor. We must remember that he was not a mere casual traveller, but that his caravan numbered 1,000 camels, that he would therefore follow the usual route of travellers, and that his destination was Vezir. He tells us that on leaving Mangushlak he travelled for twenty days across a wilderness from the sea-side without seeing a town or habitation, during which his people found no water save what they drew out of old deep wells, very brackish and salt. At length, on the 5th of October, he reached a gulf of the Caspian, where he found fresh water. He adds that into this gulf the great river Oxus once fell. Leaving there on the 4th of September he arrived three days later at Vezir. By the older commentators it has been supposed that Jenkinson on leaving Mangushlak went southwards along the shores of the Caspian until he reached the Bay of Karaboghaz or the Gulf of Balkhan, and thence followed the track of the old bed of the Oxus into the Khanate; but putting aside the utterly purposeless journey of a large caravan along the barren shores of the Caspian for twenty days, which would have to make a wide detour if it went this way in order to reach its goal, the explanation becomes quite impossible when we examine the dates. It is physically impossible that the travellers could have reached Vezir from the Bay of Karaboghaz in three or at the most five days.

The route actually followed by our traveller, and which he describes graphically enough, was across the Ust Ust plateau, where the great caravan route in the seventeenth century passed; and, as M. de Goeje has remarked, Ishtakhri reckons the distance from the Caspian to the Aral many centuries before as a journey of twenty days, which agrees well with Jenkinson's notes.

The question still remains, Where did he emerge from the wilderness? M. Goeje will have it that he came out at the Aibugir Gulf, which he identifies with Jenkinson's Gulf of the Caspian. In this I cannot agree. Jenkinson says he found sweet water there, which could never be the case in a gulf of the Aral; and as we know, the Aibugir Gulf contains very salt water.

I believe he came out at Lake Sari Kamish, where an old itinerary in fact terminated. This agrees admirably with the distance from Vezir. It agrees also with the statement that the Oxus once fell into it; and no doubt, in the days of Jenkinson, when it was probably the outlet of the Laudan as well as of the overflow of the Urun Daria, it was a much larger sheet of water and extended much further west towards the Caspian; and it would in fact appear to travellers as a gulf of that sea, which the Aibugir never could. It is true the water of the Sari Kamish is not now sweet; but formerly, when much larger and when the outlet for two arms of the Oxus, it was very probably so, and has become salt, as all lakes in the Asiatic steppes do, from partial desiccation in contact with the nitrous soil of the surrounding country. I take it, therefore, that Jenkinson came out at Sari Kamish, and thence proceeded to Vezir. Vezir was then as he describes it, and as the remains of buildings and irrigation canals all along the course of the Urun Daria testify, the centre of a fertile district. The Oxus certainly flowed past it, although, as he says, it did not then, i.e., in 1557, reach the Caspian, and Abulghasi expressly tells us it was possible to go from Urgenj to Vezir by water. Glukhofski explored the Urun Daria from Sari Kamish to Kunia Urgenj. He found fresh water pits in several places in the old channel, while the wells supplied fresh water except when he approached the meridian of the Aibugir Gulf, when the well water was not only salty but bitter.[*] The water was also bad in the rivulet of Dekcha, which flows some twenty-four versts above where the Urun Daria falls into the Sari Kamish lake. The course of the Urun Daria is marked by a succession of saksauls (Anabasis Saxaul), tamarinds, thorns, etc. It ends in the Sari Kamish, which now consists of two lakes joined by a stream about ten versts long. Both lakes are deep, and their water is salt and not palatable. Glukhofski remarks that it is quite obvious that the lake has shrunk, and we are told its old banks can be easily traced, in some instances twenty versts from the present lake, in others one hundred saschines. *Only the former lake margin is lined with vegetation,*[†] which shows the shrinkage has taken place recently and that the water was once fresher.

Along the whole course of the Urun Daria as far as the lake are to be seen the mouths of former canals, which themselves spread out into a network of smaller canals, etc. The size of these canals and the number of ruins on their banks are a proof not only of the old cultivation of the district, but of the amount of water which must once have flowed this way. These ruins date from two epochs—one more ancient, with buildings of a higher class of taste, and a more modern one of which the remains are more ordinary. From the report of the inhabitants, Glukhofski concluded that the water had flowed

---

* Petermann's Mittheilungen, 1874, 24.   † Id., 25.

along the Urun Daria as far as Sari Kamish but eleven years before his visit, i.e., in 1862, while even six years before it reached the dam at Igbenkylich, sixty-two versts above Kunia Urgenj.* It would seem that the river-course has been laid dry through the efforts of the Khivans in the struggle they had with the Turkomans during the reign of the late Khan, when they dammed up the mouth of the Laudan. Before this the banks of the river were occupied by a thriving population of the Ata Murad tribe of Yomuds, who have since had to migrate nearer Khiva.† It was then possible to go by boat as far as the town of Deksha, near Sari Kamish. Before the diversion the Laudan had two outlets, one along the Urun Daria, while the other fell into the Aibugir Gulf.‡ The latter still flowed when Boutakof made his survey.

Reverting again to Jenkinson, we find him reporting that on leaving Kunia Urgenj he followed the river for one hundred miles, when he crossed another great river, called the Ardock. He describes this as very great and swift, and as running out of the Oxus and going north, and after a course of 1,000 miles underground as falling into the Lake of Kitai. On crossing this river he reached Kat.§ From this narrative it seems clear that he followed the bed of the Kunia Daria, which was then doubtless a considerable river, and reached the Artock, i.e., the branch of the Oxus now flowing into the Sea of Aral south of the modern town of Gurlen and almost opposite Kat, where in fact the Kunia Daria—which means "Old River"—still has its entrance. This was, in fact, the main route from Vezir to Bukhara.

On turning to Abulghazi we find him reporting that he was born in the year 1605, i.e., 1014 of the hej, and adding that thirty years before his birth, i.e., in 1575, the Amu carved itself a road from the point called Kara Uighur Tukai, below Khast Minaressi, and taking the way of Tuk Kal'assi entered the Sea of Sir, whereby the environs of Urgenj were converted into a desert. Nevertheless the humbler inhabitants of Urgenj continued to live there. In spring the Khan and his troops moved to the bank of the river, where they dwelt in the district most easily cultivated, and returned to Urgenj after the harvest.‖

The exact nature of this revolution in the river bed I do not profess to explain, any more than previous inquirers. In order to do so we must know with certainty the localities mentioned by Abulghazi, and also the details of the topography of the Khanate more minutely than we do. I only conclude that, by some means or other, the water was in the main diverted from the Kunia Daria, which previously flowed by the city, and thus probably increased the flow of the river flowing into the Sea of Aral. It would seem that Kunia Urgenj was not deserted entirely, and, in fact, with people so competent to make canals as the Khuarezmians this would be hardly likely. I believe myself that the occasion when this diversion took place was the time when the channel known as the Laudan was formed, and which many inquirers have taken for the old river bed, but of which Major Wood says, " It may be doubted whether the Laudan was ever more than a large irrigation canal, which passed its superfluous waters into Aibugir during high floods of the Amu."¶

There was a gap, therefore, in the time during which the water did not flow

* Petermann's Mittheilungen, 1874, 26.   † Id., 26.   Russische Revue, iv., 60.   ‡ Id., 61.
§ Hacklayt, i., 369.   ‖ Abulghazi. Ed. Desmaisons, 312.   ¶ Op. cit., 1.

into the Urun Daria, between the diversion of the river and the cutting of the Laudan, and perhaps separating the two series of ruins on the banks of the former, already named, one dating no doubt from the prosperous days of the Khanate, and the other from the time of the Turkoman domination. In regard to the Aibugir gulf, I look upon it as of very recent origin. Not only is it not mentioned by the older writers, but its aspect, as described by various travellers, shows it has been created by the overflow of the river Laudan and by the two outlets of the Kunia Daria, called Kiat Jargan and Kat Daria by Admiral Boutakof.

If the Laudan itself is of as recent origin as I have argued, and the lower part of the Kunia Daria has also a very recent history, as I shall argue presently, it follows that the Aibugir lake—which has gradually become desiccated as its feeders from those rivers have ceased to flow—is, in fact, a new feature in the physical geography of this part of Asia.

Having considered the branch of the Amu Daria which flowed past Urgenj, let us now turn to that which runs northward; that branch, in fact, which falls into the Sea of Aral, and which is now the main arm of the river. Opposite Khojeili this branch of the Oxus throws off what is now a comparatively insignificant stream known as the Kuwan Jerma, to which I shall revert presently. Below this point it breaks into a complicated series of channels which form, in fact, its present delta. The topography of this delta is constantly altering from the singularly easy and frequent change which the course of the river is continually undergoing. One of these recent changes has been well described by Major Wood, and I shall quote his account. Speaking of the Chartambye channel, he says, "I was informed on the spot that it had no existence a few years ago, and it has probably been formed by the efforts of the Amu to get rid of the increased discharge caused by the closing of the Laudan. While passing on a caique immediately to the north of the Kashkanatao hills, I was also told by a Kirghiz Mollah, born and bred in the locality, that a dozen years previously he had walked over cultivated fields, which at that moment formed the bed of the stream on whose surface our boat was floating. There is no doubt also that Boutakof, in his explorations of the lower Amu, passed over dry ground, which was traversed by the writer (i.e., Wood) in 1874, but Boutakof himself noted in 1859 the commencement of the flooding caused by the closing of the Laudan canal, since in some places he remarked the limpidity of the water (which was consequently almost stationary), and which allowed fields and irrigation channels to be seen through it.* What is true of the Chartambye channel is true also of the Yghan, Telia bye and Oguz channels, whose very recent origin is, perhaps, best proved by the absence of old settlements along their banks, and also of irrigation canals. If we put these minor streams aside, we have remaining the main channel of the Oxus, which bears the significant name of Kunia Daria, and communicates with the sea of Aral by two mouths, the Taldik and the Ulkun Daria.

The latter of these is now the larger and more important of the mouths, but for the reasons already cited, namely, the absence of old settlements and irrigation canals, I am convinced that the Ulkun Daria is only a recent branch

* Notes on the Lower Sir Daria, etc., Journ. Geog. Soc., 1875, p. 7.

of the river. Having eliminated these newer channels, we are now reduced to
the Kunia Daria, or old river, with its outlet by the Taldik mouth; and this
I look upon as the only one of its lower branches which has claims to be
deemed old. Here are situated the fort of Old Nukus, the town of Kungrad,
the forts of Kulikul and Kopakul, and the ruins of Mulla Perm.

When I say that I deem this to be the old bed of the river, I speak
relatively only, however.

Some time ago, in a letter to the *Geographical Magazine*, I called attention
to the fact that the names in the delta of the Amu Daria are modern;
that they are clearly due to its Uzbeg inhabitants, most of them being
merely the names of Uzbeg tribes, and dating therefore from a period at the
earliest not later than the latter part of the sixteenth century. The only
explanation of this, when we consider the former wealth and prosperity of
Khuarezm, is that the river did not then flow where it does now. If it had
done so its waters would have been utilised for irrigation, and its banks made
to produce rich crops. Now, on turning to the sixth volume of the *Russische
Revue* I find Mr. Schmidt reporting, on the authority of Mr. Sobolef, that west
of the Kushkani Tau mountains, and north of Chimbai, all the ruins of forts
and of graves prove them to be of quite recent date. East of Chimbai, on the
other hand, we have ruins of older towns, as those of Ak Kaleh, situated ten
versts from Chimbai (formerly the seat of the Uzbeg tribe Massyd), which was
devastated by Nadir Shah. Twenty versts farther east, on the canal Naupyr,
are the remains of Baghdad, which was also ruined by Nadir.[*] Reverting
therefore, to the outlet of the Oxus, opposite Khojeili, which is called Kegeilee,
and also Kuk Uzak or Blue River, which flows past Chimbai and formerly
watered these old towns, we shall find its whole course marked by numerous
and elaborate canals, proving that it was once a famous river. Like the other
branches of the Oxus, its bed has no doubt shifted a good deal, and has formed
at least one divergent stream of some consequence, called the Kuvan Jerma,
which falls into Lake Dowkara, and thence into the Caspian by the Yany Su.
But both these names, Kuvan Jerma and Yany Su, meaning new river, prove
that this channel is in fact of recent origin. The old course of the river was
along the Kegeilee and the Berdin Uziak.

This is, if we are to follow the evidence, a much older channel than the lower
Kunia Daria, and, as I believe, was formerly the main, if not the only outlet of
the Oxus into the sea of Aral. The origin of the lower Kunia Daria itself may
perhaps be traced in a passage of Abulghazi, where he tells us that a year
before his own birth his father caused a canal to be made which began above
Tuk, i.e., Khojeili, and which a few years later had the breadth of an arrow
flight; it passed by way of Knighun, and then fell into the sea.[†]

Our analysis may be carried still farther. The places mentioned on the
Kegeilee are old only relatively; that is, we do not find them mentioned in the
earlier history of the Khanate, or in the pages of the Arab geographers.
Again, it is very strange and curious that the towns on the main branch of the
Oxus itself, beginning with Tuk, and comprising Kipchak, Mangut, Gurlen and
Rahman Berdi Bi, all bear new names. Tuk is not mentioned, so far as I

---

* Op. cit., vi., 285.　　　　† Op. cit., 301.

know, by any author earlier than Abulghazi, while the others are apparently of Usbeg origin, and are also not named in early times. When we pass Rahman Berdi Bi, we come to Shah Baz Vali, the ancient Kat, a very famous site in old days. Can the explanation of this be that in early times the river did not pass along its present course, but that from Kat it found its way northwards through some defile or passage in the Sheikh Jaili Hills, which would account for the statement of Jenkinson about its passing underground, and account also for the apparent ignorance of Abulghazi as to its lower reaches; the Sheikh Jaili Hills forming a frontier to his kingdom. This is only a conjecture, but it seems a reasonable one.

Note 4.—Genealogy of the Khans of Khuarezm:—

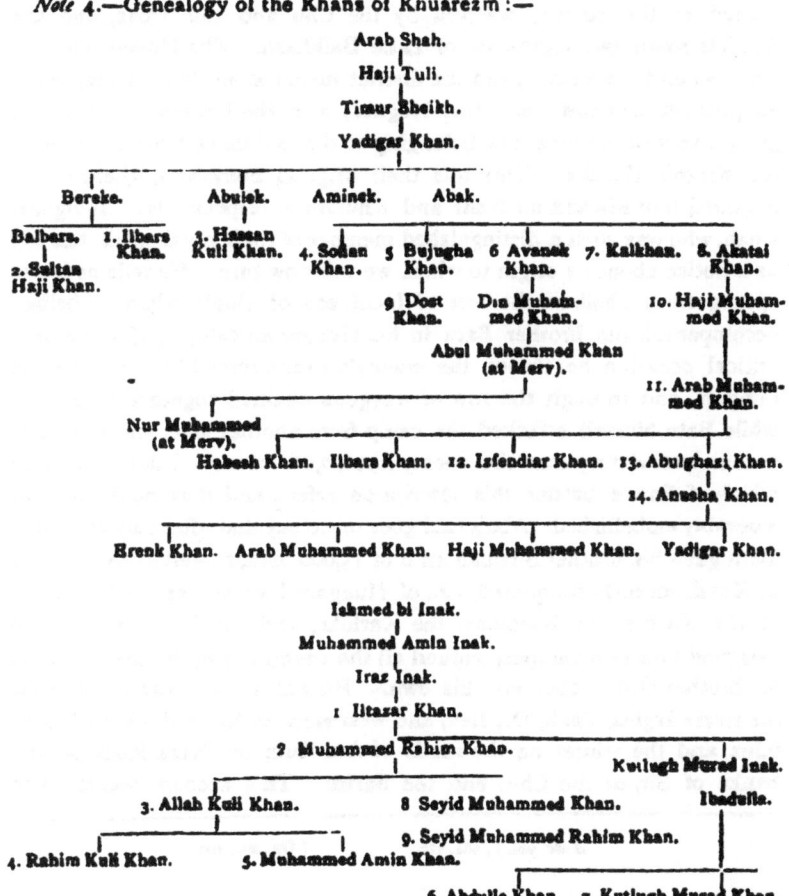

CHAPTER XI

THE SHEIBANIDS OF TURAN.

IN the former volume of this work I described how the Kalmuks, at the beginning of the seventeenth century, spread over and occupied the country lying between the Yemba and the Ural in the west, and the Altai Mountains in the east. This migration took place in the earlier part of the seventeenth century, and was largely due to the pressure of the Mongols under Altan Khan in the east.[*] I agree with Müller that before the year 1600 there were virtually no Kalmuks west of the Altai. Until about that year the vast area just referred to was occupied by the Uzbegs, the Kazaks, and the Nogais. The Kazaks were in the main limited to the country watered by the Chu and the Talas, and the districts south and south-east of Lake Balkhash. The Nogais lived on the Ural and the Yemba, and the district surrounding those rivers, which was afterwards known as Great Nogaia; and the Uzbegs occupied the greater part of the area now belonging to the middle and little hordes of the Kirghiz Kazaks. This was their original homeland, whence they migrated into Mavera un Nehr and Khuarezm respectively. Abulghazi Khan, who was such a distinguished member of their royal stock, has left us a notice about its origin to which we will now turn. He tells us it was sprung from Sheiban, the son of Juchi, son of Jingis Khan. Sheiban accompanied his brother Batu in his Hungarian campaign, where on a critical occasion he turned the enemy's camp, forced his way over the rampart, and through the row of waggons chained together behind it, while Batu himself attacked the camp from another side, and won such a complete victory that the enemy lost 70,000 men.[†] I don't know to which of Batu's battles this description refers, and it is no doubt considerably embellished. Abulghazi goes on to say that after this campaign Batu gave his brother Sheiban an il of 15,000 men, as well as the country of Kurel, recently conquered, i.e., of Hungary! as well as the four uruks of the Kuchis, the Naimans, the Karluks, and the Buiruks, while he assigned him as a camping ground all the country lying between that of his brother Orda Ichin and his own. He was to pass the summer on the rivers Irghiz, Sauk, Or, Ilek, and westward as far as the Ural Mountains, and the winter on the sands of Ara Kum and Kara Kum, on the banks of Sir, of the Chu, and the Sarisu. This account seems to be

---

perfectly reasonable, and in unison with what we know elsewhere. Abulghazi adds that the descendants of Sheiban were also said to have ruled over the land of Kurel, or Hungary, "but," he adds the prudent ejaculation, "this country is a long way off, and God alone knows whether what they say is true or not."[*] I need not say that this report was wholly unfounded. We don't know how long Sheiban lived, and are merely told he left twelve sons, namely, Bainal or Yasal, Behadur, Kadak, Balka, Cherik or Jerik, Mergen or Surkhan, Kurtugha or Kultuka, Ayachi or Abaji, Sailghan or Sasiltan, Beyanjar or Bayakachar, Majar, and Kunchi or Kuwinji.[†]

According to the authority followed by Von Hammer (? Rashid), Behadur had four sons, Marakul, Yeltimur, Taniklejar, and Yesubuka. Abulghazi gives him two sons only, Jujibuka and Kutlugh Buka, the former of whom succeeded him. We know nothing more of him. Jujibuka, according to Abulghazi, had four sons, Badakul, Bektimur, Nikchar, and Isbuka, the eldest of whom, Badakul, succeeded him. He was in turn succeeded by his only son, Ming Timur, or Mangu Timur, who, on account of his bravery, was called Kutlugh Ming Timur. He was perhaps the Kutlugh Timur who is mentioned as a great commander in the reign of Uzbeg Khan, and who was appointed by him his deputy in Khuarezm.[‡] When Ibn Batuta passed through Khuarezm, he tells us it was ruled by Uzbeg's deputy. It was perhaps through his influence that his tribes adopted the name of his suzerain, and became afterwards known as Uzbegs.

We now reach a very important epoch in the history of the Golden Horde. The family of Batu became extinct, and a struggle ensued for the Khanate between the families of Orda, Sheiban, etc., as I have shown.[§] The first of these families to put a prince on the Imperial throne on the extinction of the family of Batu was, as I have shown, that of Sheiban, in the person of Khizr Khan,[‖] who was doubtless a relation of Mangu Timur. It is a noteworthy fact that Khisr Khan struck coins at Khuarezm. But to continue our story. Abulghazi tells us that Mangu Timur had six sons, Ilbak, Janta, Fulad or Pulad, Suyunich, Timur, and Tunka Bek Kundi. Fulad, or Pulad, was no doubt the Pulad Timur and Pulad Khoja who reigned in the Kipchak. Coins of his are extant, on which he is styled son of Nugan, which is read doubtfully, and which ought doubtless to be Mangu. I have previously described his reign. He seems to have been killed by Aziz Khan, of Kipchak, about the year 1367.[¶] Pulad left two sons, Ibrahim and Arabshah, the latter of whom made a famous invasion of Russia in 1376.[**] Ibrahim was the ancestor of the khans of Khuarezm and Arabshah of those of Bukhara, as I have shown in the previous two chapters.

---

[*] Op. cit., 191. [†] Id. Von Hammer, Golden Horde. Table. [‡] Golden Horde, 303.
[§] Ante, c. iv., v. [‖] Ante. 195-8, [¶] Ante, c. iv. [**] Vide ante, 212.

Mangu Timur had other powerful sons besides Pulad. One of them, Ilban or Ilbak, coined money on which he styles himself son of Mangu Timur. Ilban's son also coined money.[*] Another son of Mangu Timur, as I have said, was called Bek Kundi Oghlan, or, as he is called in another passage of Abulghazi, Tunka-Bek-Kundi.[†] Tunka bek's son was Ali Oghlan.[‡] Ali Oghlan had a son Haji Muhammed Khan, who was possibly the Alchi Khan of Petis de la Croix and the Alaji Oghlu (*i.e.*, El haji Oghlan), of Langles, who tells us that on the death of Merdud, son of Khizr Khan, Alaji Oghlan, a prince of the blood royal, settled on the Volga, and many Tartars went over to him.[§] I was once disposed to identify him with Azis Khan. Haji Muhammed, according to Khuandemir, had two sons, Sediak and Ibak.[‖] Sediak, *i.e.*, Seyid Akhmed, I believe, was the Seyid Ahmed who invaded Russia with Ahmed of the White Horde, and fills such a notable place in the history of the Golden Horde.[¶] It will be noticed that several of these princes are expressly called khans, and there can be no doubt that they ruled over their own clans, and were largely independent of the head of the house of Sheiban. That house was for a long time ruled, as I have shown, by the great Abulkhair Khan, the ancestor of the Khans of Bukhara, and during his reign the other princes were more or less submissive to him, but on his death they broke out into rebellion. Among others, we are told by Khuandemir, were Sediak and Ibak Khan, the sons of Haji Muhammed. Ibak, it seems, fought against Sheikh Haidar Khan, the son of Abulkhair, and defeated him, and the latter's grandsons, Muhammed Sheiban and Makhmud, had to take refuge at Astrakhan, with Kasim Khan, where they were shortly after beleaguered by Ibak, in alliance with Ahmed Khan of the Golden Horde, Kasim's uncle.[**] Khuandemir, as I have said, makes Ibak the son of Haji Muhammed and ignores Mahmudek, who is made the son of Haji Muhammed and father of Ibak by Abulghazi, which, judging from the number of generations on his pedigree as compared with that of his contemporaries, is probably right, and it is probable that Abulghazi has made a mistake.[††] Ibak especially distinguished himself, as I have described,[‡‡] when in 1481, in concert with the Nogai chiefs Musa and Yamgurchi, he fell upon and slaughtered Ahmed Khan of the Golden Horde, who had probably given his support to the family of Abulkhair. The Russian Annalists call him Tzar of Sheiban or Nogai.[§§] On this occasion, we are told, that having returned to Tiumen he sent to inform the Grand Prince that his enemy no longer lived. He boasted, we are told, of his descent from Jingis Khan, and claimed to have better rights to the throne of Batu than Ahmed and his sons, who were only the

---

[*] *Vide ante*, c. iv.   [†] Op. cit., 186, 192.   [‡] Abulghazi, 186.   [§] Op cit , 378.
[‖] Vel. Zernof, ii., 233.   [¶] *Ante*, 272, 292, 305.   [**] *Ante*, 316.
[††] Vel. Zernof, Khans of Kasimof, ii., 233, etc.   [‡‡] *Ante*, 326.
[§§] Vel. Zernof, op. cit., ii., 240.

descendants of Timur Kutlugh, while the title of Tzar of the Musselmans belonged to him alone. He courted the friendship of the Tzar Ivan, whom he treated as an equal.*

He apparently was obeyed over a wide area, and was acknowledged as their overchief by the petty princes of Siberia,† and by the Bashkirs. In the traditional Saga about the origin of the Siberian Khanate, he is called Upak tzar, of Kazan, and he is said to have married his sister to Mar the Siberian ruler, whom he afterwards killed.‡

It was apparently by this conquest that he acquired the style of Tzar of Tiumen, which belonged of right to the Siberian Khans. Ibak also exercised some kind of patronage over the Khanate of Kazan. There was at this time a struggle there between the two brothers, Ali and Muhammed Amin, and the Russians first put one brother on the throne, and then another.§ It seems that in 1487, Ibak and the Nogai Murzas Alach, Musa and Yamgurchi, and the latter's wife sent letters to Moscow asking for the release of Ali. "You are my brother," writes Ibak to the Grand Prince ; "if you would live on good terms with me release Ali ; what advantage is it to you to keep him in irons. Remember that by treaties concluded with that prince you promised to shew kindness and friendship towards him." The Nogai princes wrote in more modest language. They sent the emperor a profound salutation with a small present, and said they would submit to his wishes, for their fathers had always been friends of Muscovite monarchs. Circumstances, they said, had constrained the Horde of Ibak to migrate to a distance from the Russian borders ; but now that prince, who had vanquished his enemies, had once more drawn near and desired an alliance with the Grand Prince. They also asked that the Nogais might be allowed to trade in Russia without paying dues. The Tzar replied that he would not release Ali, who had been deposed for his perfidies and perjuries, but he would consent to be friendly with them if Ibak would punish Ali's subjects who had sought refuge with him, and who ravaged the borders of Russia, and those of Muhammed Amin ; if he restored the property these freebooters had carried off, and in future prevented the repetition of such crimes. Meanwhile he retained one of the envoys, and dismissed the others, telling them not to enter Russia again by way of the country of the Mordvins, as they did on this occasion, but by way of Kazan and Nijni Novgorod.‖

I don't know when Ibak Khan died, but he does not occur after the year 1493.¶ According to the Saga about the origin of the Khanate of Siberia, when Ibak killed Mar, the ruler of Siberia, the latter's grandson Mamut, with his people, retired to the Irtish, where they built themselves a new city ; eventually Mamut returned and killed Ibak.**

---

* Karamzin, vi., 199.   † Vel. Zernof, ii., 388.   ‡ Id., 387, etc. See also next chapter.
§ Ante, 374-5.   ‖ Karamzin, vi., 234-5.   ¶ Vel. Zernof, ii., 391.   ** Id., 386, etc.

MURTAZA KHAN.

According to Abulghazi, Ibak had a son named Murtaza Khan,* who
doubtless succeeded to his heritage.   During his reign the greater part
of the Uzbegs migrated into Mavera un Nehr and Khuarezm, under
Sheibani, Ilbars, etc , pushed on in some measure by the Kalmuks, who
were being themselves hard pressed by the Mongols, and in a measure
attracted by the decrepitude into which the empire, founded by Timur,
had fallen.   Those who remained behind were apparently subject to
Murtaza, and were probably only a small section of the race.   I only find
one reference to his doings.   When the Nogais put his son Kuchum to
death, they proposed to do so in revenge for the way in which his father
had harried them.†   I know nothing more of him than that he seems to
have survived till about the year 1565.†

KUCHUM KHAN

A much more famous person than Murtaza was his son Kuchum, who,
by the way, is expressly referred to as a grandson of Ibak in a letter of
the Tzar Feodor Ivanovitch.§   Kuchum was a collateral relative of the
princes of Bukhara, and it is not impossible that he took part in
Sheibani's campaign in Mavera un Nehr for many facts make it
probable that he was brought up in that seat of Mussulman
learning and religion.   His first appearance in history was about 1556,
when we find Yadigar, the Khan of Siberia, complaining to the Russian
Tzar that he could not send the amount of tribute agreed upon because
his country had been suffering from the incursions of the Tzarevitch of
Sheiban.   This date agrees with the· statement of Abulghazi that
Kuchum reigned forty years, which counting back from 1595 brings us
to 1555.‖ Yadigar was still reigning in 1563, however, and Vel. Zernof
from several somewhat vague data concludes that it was in that year
that Kuchum displaced him.¶   In 1569 we find him styled Tzar of
Siberia by the Russian ruler, who made a treaty with him by which he
took him under his protection on condition that he paid annually 1,000
sable and 1,000 squirrel skins.   This treaty, sealed with a golden seal,
was taken to Siberia by the Russian officer Chabukof.**

According to the Kemesofian annals, two years after his accession
he went to Kasan, where he married a daughter of its Khan Murad,
in whose wake a great number of Russian and Chuvash slaves went to
Siberia.††   No such person as Murad occurs among the Khans of
Kazan, which at this time was a part of the Russian empire, and the
notice, if authentic, must refer to some petty prince whose name has

---

* Op. cit., 186.   † Müller, op. cit., vi., 488.   ‡ Vel. Zernof, ii., 304.   § Id., 394.
‖ Müller, op. cit., vi., 186, 222.   ¶ Op. cit., ii., 396.   ** Karamsin, ix., 165-6.
†† Müller, vi., 186.

otherwise escaped notice. We are told that besides the one just
named Kuchum had two other wives, each with her separate yurt, one
the daughter of the Murza Devlet bey, who lived on the Panin bugor at
Bizik Tura, and the other on the Irtish, six miles below Tobolsk. The
latter was called Susge whence the place Susgunskoi Muis got its name.[*]

The dominions of Kuchum included the various Tartar hordes of the
Irtish and the Tobol and the Barabinski Tartars. The Russians on their
invasion found an independent or quasi-independent prince at Tiumen.
Kuchum's dominions on this side did not apparently extend beyond
the mouth of the Tura, and the Tartars at Tarkhanskoi ostrog were the
furthest who paid him tribute.[†] A portion of the Bashkirs and the
Ostiaks in the immediate neighbourhood of the Tobol, etc., also probably obeyed him. Kuchum was the first to systematically introduce
Muhammedanism into Siberia. His religious innovations were not
universally popular, and were resisted by many of the professors of the
old faith. He had to send to his father Murtaza for reinforcements. The
latter sent him his eldest son Akhmet Ghirai, an achun (i.e., a reader or
Muhammedan doctor), several mollahs, and a certain number of abisses.
The Kesemofian Annals report that other teachers were obtained from
Kazan. The Siberians were now compelled to be converted, and those
who were refractory received hard treatment.[‡] Notwithstanding this,
Kuchum's efforts were not completely successful, and there were Tartars
even in the neighbourhood of the Irtish who remained attached to their
old faith. A bi of the Yaalinishian Tartars, who lived at the mouth of
the river Tara, assured Müller that from his youth he with his parents
and subjects and the people in the neighbourhood had always been
heathens. It is also well known that some Tartars who lived between
Tobolsk and Demianskoiyam in a place called Lebauzkie yurt, and the
majority of those near the town of Turinsk, remained heathens until
they were eventually baptised with the Ostiaks. Many of the Barabinski
remained so until the last century, although Muhammedanism had been
introduced among them long before, and doubtless in the time of Kuchum,
by missionaries from Tobolsk and Tura.[§] Fischer says some families of
Turinsk Tartars who were settled on the river Nitza were still idolators
in 1639. Evangelists of that creed had made desultory attempts before,
and some are even said to have suffered martyrdom. We are told that
during the reign of Kuchum an aged Sheikh went to Siberia from
Bukhara, and reported that he had been supernaturally informed that
many holy men who had lost their lives in propagating the faith were
buried in Siberia, and that they deserved to be commemorated by an
annual feast. He accordingly made researches, and found the burial
places of seven, which were thenceforward looked upon as sacred, and
were so considered even when Müller wrote.[||]

* Müller, vi., 187.   † Id., 188-9.   ‡ Müller, op. cit. 190.   § Id., 193-4.
|| Op. cit., vi., 191.

There were several Bukharian families settled at Tobolsk, Tiumen, Turinsk, Tara, and Tomsk, who claimed that their ancestors went to Siberia with Kuchum; especially is this told of a family of Seyids settled near Tobolsk, at the villages of Sabanak and Tadsim aul, one of whose leading men, Din Ali Khoja, a native of Urgenj, was specially attached to the fortunes of Kuchum, and is even said to have married his daughter, named Nal Khanish.   He had three sons, Sultamet Khoja, Seyid Memet, and Ak Seyid, who lived at Tara.   Sultanet had two sons, Yusuf Khoja and Ayub Khoja, who lived at Tobolsk.   Ayub's sons, Sultamet Khoja and Yahya Khoja, were living when Müller was in Siberia.*

Kuchum, according to the "Collection of Annals" quoted so often by Vel. Zernof, had two older brothers, Jan Girai and Akhmed Girai.†   Of the former we know nothing; Akhmed went to Siberia, as I have mentioned.   Müller tells us he married a daughter of Shigai, who has been identified very probably with the Kazak chief Shigai, previously mentioned.‡   He goes on to say that having ill-treated his wife, her father determined to avenge her, and he despatched a man to waylay him.   The latter went to the Irtish and saw Akhmed on the other side engaged in hawking, and shouted to him to go over to him, as he had a letter for him from his father-in-law.   Akhmed accordingly trusted himself on the other side, where he was fastened like Mazeppa to a horse.   His body was afterwards found on the banks of the Turba, a tributary of the Tobol.§

Russia had its backwoodsmen at an early date—adventurous hunters and dealers in peltries who formed small settlements about the Ural Mountains.   Among these were the Stroganofs, a family who probably sprang from Novgorod.   Nicholas Witzen has a curious tale as to its origin.   He says it sprang from an illustrious murza of the Golden Horde, who had been baptized under the name of Spiridon, and it was he who taught the Russians the method of calculating by means of the abacus.   The Tartars, vexed with him, captured him in a fight, and bastinadoed him till he died—whence the name Stroganof given to his son from the Russian word "strogat," to beat.   He was succeeded in turn by his descendants, Cosmas, Lucas, Feodor, and Anika.   Lucas contributed to the ransom of Vasili the Blind, when a prisoner at Kazan.‖   The family had enriched itself by the salt mines on the Viuchegda, which belonged to them, and the Tzar granted to the two brothers, Gregory and Yakub, all the country on the banks of the Kama from Permia to the river Sylva, as well as the banks of the Chussovaia, and permitted them to build forts to protect themselves from the Siberian and Nogai Tartars, to employ soldiers and artillery, to have

---

* Op. cit., 197-8.   † Hist. of the Khans of Kasimof, ii.; 337.   ‡ Ante, 634.
    § Müller, op. cit., 196-7.   ‖ Müller, op. cit., 212, note.

a special jurisdiction in their own territory, to build villages, work
salt mines, and to sell fish and salt for twenty years without paying
duty, etc.* In 1558 the-Stroganofs founded the little town of Kankor
on the Chussovaia, in 1564 the fortress of Kerghedan, and a few
years later some other settlements on that river and the Sylva. They
thus attracted many vagabond and bohemian adventurers, and in 1572
defeated an insurrection of the Cheremisses, Ostiaks, and Bashkirs, and
made them submit once more to the Tzar.† This progress of the
Stroganofs was not pleasing to Kuchum, and we are told that in July,
1573, he sent Mahmetkul to destroy the new settlements. M. Vel. Zernof
has devoted an interesting note to the discussion of the question of the
parentage of Mahmetkul, whom some authors call the son and others
the nephew of Kuchum, and he has shown pretty clearly that he was
in fact Kuchum's nephew, and that his father was called Altaul.‡

Mahmetkul found the Russian positions too strong, and contented
himself with killing some Ostiaks who had submitted to the White
Tzar and carrying off their wives and children. He also put to death a
Russian named Tretiak Chebukof and some Tartars who were on their
way to the Kazaks.§ Karamzin says that Kuchum had recently grown
inflated in consequence of the union of his son Ali with the daughter of
the Nogai Murza Din Akhmet, and suggests that he had something to
do with the Cheremis revolt ‖

The Stroganofs now appealed to the Emperor to be allowed to punish
the invaders. They received permission to plant colonies on the
river Tobol, to build towns and fortresses there, to employ artillery,
and to enlist a kind of militia, called Pishchalniki. Permission was
granted them during a limited time to dig for iron, tin, lead, and sulphur,
and they were ordered to protect the tributary Ostiaks and Voguls, and
to endeavour to subjugate the Tartar Khanate on the Irtish to the Russian
crown. This permission was granted by a brief dated the 30th of
May, 1574, which further gave them the privilege of trading freely and
without paying dues with the Bukharians and Kazaks.¶ The campaign was however postponed, as the Stroganofs found they were
scarcely strong enough for such an enterprise. During the next six
years the two brothers Gregory and Yakub died, and were succeeded in
their great wealth by their younger brother Simeon, who, seconded by
his nephews—Maxim, the son of Yakub, and Nicetas, the son of Gregory—
at length brought the matter to a successful issue.**

The Cossacks of the Don were at this time a very lawless body. They
were in the habit of plundering the Persian and Bukharian caravans,
and even went so far as to attack an embassy taking presents from the
Tzar to the Shah, while the districts on the Lower Volga were held in

---

* Müller, op. cit., vi., 206.   † Karamzin, ix., 477.   ‡ Vel. Zernof, Khans of Kasimof, 3, note 6.
§ Müller, op. cit., vi., 229, 307.   ‖ Op. cit., ix., 478.   ¶ Karamzin, ix., 480.   ** Id.

terror by them. In 1577 the Tzar Ivan sent some troops against them, under the Stolnik Ivan Murashkin, who punished them severely and scattered them. One body of them fled towards the Kama under the leadership of an ataman named Yermak Timoveef. Yermak is a diminutive of Yermolai, or Hermolaus.[*] They arrived at Orel Gorodok, belonging to the Stroganofs, which had only been recently built. Maxim Stroganof, who was then the head of the family, received these strangers well and took them into his service, with a view doubt-less of completing the family venture in Siberia.[†] The strangers were, it seems, ordered to proceed along the Chussovaia, and reached the river Sylva on the 8th of October, 1578, where they planted a fortress, whose site is still known as Yermakovo Gorodichi. There Yermak spent the winter, during which he sent 300 Cossacks to the Vogul country, who returned, after having explored the frontiers of Siberia, laden with booty. He had three priests and a monk with him, and is said to have built a church in his new settlement dedicated to Saint Nicholas, and traditions survive of the method in which he drowned some of his refractory Cossacks in the river there.[‡]

It was now deemed an opportune time to prosecute the campaign in Siberia. Stroganof provided Yermak with three cannons; to each of his men he supplied three pounds of powder, three pounds of lead, three puds of rye flour, two puds of groats and oats, one pud of biscuit, one of salt, two and a half puds of butter, and to each two men half a salted pig. Each hundred men were provided with a flag with a sacred image on it. Night and day they worked at the preparations, and eventually had to leave some of their stores behind, as the boats could not carry them all. Besides the more useful articles, Yermak also secured a store of musical instruments of various kinds. He was the commander-in-chief of the whole. Under him were Ivan Kolzof and Ivan Gross, and the Piatidesiatnik Bogdan Briaga, or Briasga. There were also four yesauls, who acted as adjutants, and the Cossacks were divided into bodies of ten and a hundred.[§]

Let us now consider the approaches to Siberia. There were at this time several routes from Russia to the river Ob; the merchants making use of the various rivers on either side of the Ural as the chief means of transport. From Wytschegda one route followed the river Wischera, a tributary of the Kama. Thence the road was by the Loswa, the Tawda, and lastly the Tobol. Another route went from the river Wym to the Wychegda, thence by the Ishma to the Petschora. From the Petschora there were three ways to the Ob; one followed the Schokur and the Sigwa or the Lapina, another followed the Olesh, the Ilitsb, and the Soswa. The third went along the Ussa and the Sob. The routes by the Sigwa and the Soswa were the most frequented, and had been the longest known.[‖]

---

* Müller, op. cit., 232 3.   † Id., 234-6.   ‡ Id., 239-45.   § Id., 249-50.   ‖ Id., 224-5.

Yermak and his people now set out. According to the accounts followed by Müller, they were at first about 5,000 strong; the Sagas of Siberia fix their number at only 840. It was a strangely romantic expedition, fitly compared by Karamzin with the similar venture of Pizarro in Peru, and was the initial step of that vast conquest by which the whole of Siberia was secured for Russia through the indomitable perseverance and skill of a mere handful of Cossacks. It is told in an old Siberian tale that often at midday at the outfall of the Tobol into the Irtish two wild animals used to appear; one came from the side of the Irtish—a great hairy white wolf; the other from the Tobol—a small black hound. These two had several struggles, in which the hound got the best of it, after which both beasts retired. When Kuchúm heard of this he took counsel with his medicine-men and soothsayers and it was concluded that by the wolf was meant the Khan, while the dog represented a Russian chieftain who would shortly deprive him of his kingdom.* This characteristic *ex post facto* tale condensed the fate of the Tartars.

Yermak set out on the 5th of July, 1579, taking with him some Zirianians as guides. He is said to have deposited some of the treasures he did not wish to take with him in a cavern in a rock, still named Yermakof Kamen. It is situated on the Chussovaia, near the village of Kopchik, and there have been some persevering efforts to secure the supposed, and no doubt altogether fabulous, treasure.† After a weary progress along the Chussovaia, whose upper waters are very shallow, the Cossacks reached the river Serebrenka, where they wintered, and where the ruins of their settlement still remained when Müller wrote, and were known as Yermakovo Gorodichi. It was situated on the north bank of the Serebrenka, and at the mouth of the little brook Kokui. This district was peopled by Voguls, who, notwithstanding that they behaved very hospitably, were ruthlessly plundered by the Cossacks. This brought down upon the latter many serious difficulties, for it aroused alarm among the tribes through whose land they passed; and we are in fact told that a party of Cossacks who left the winter quarters to explore, and went along the Tagil to the Neiwa, were attacked by some Tartars and Voguls under a Murza, and that hardly any of them escaped. The place was afterwards known as Mursinska ‡

In the spring Yermak set out again, and having crossed the low spurs of the Urals reached the Barancha, in the water-shed of the Tobol, and only ten versts from his winter quarters. Before he set out he called a muster of his men, and, according to Müller, disease and other causes had made such ravages among them that only 1,636 remained. He set out on the 12th of May, 1580, and soon reached the Tagil where he built himself fresh boats. He delayed there some weeks, and the place

---

* Müller, op. cit., 187-8.   † *Id.*, 231.   *Id*, 237-8.

was also afterwards known as Yermakovo Gorodichi." From the Tagil
he soon reached the Tura. There, where the little town of Turinsk was
afterwards built, lived a Tartar prince named Yepancha, or Yapansa,
who also ruled over the neighbouring Voguls. He fired a shower of
arrows into the boats, but his people dispersed at the sound of the
Russian firearms, and the invaders speedily occupied and plundered
his quarters. Turinsk was afterwards also known as Yapancha.† The
Cossacks now advanced, plundering, along the Tura, and occupied the
town of Chingi, or Tiumen, with very little trouble.‡ They apparently
went into winter quarters in the fertile district of Tiumen. During the
winter, parties of them went out in various directions and secured
ample booty, and also yassak or a tax of skins from the neighbouring
Tartars. One of these parties went as far as the village of Terkhan
Kalla, afterwards known as Terkhanskoi Ostrog, which was situated
at the outfall of the Tura into the Tobol and on the frontiers of Kuchum
Khan's dominions. This village was the residence of a Terkhan, and
at this time there happened to be there a tax collector of Kuchum's,
named Kutugai The Cossacks carried the latter off, and he was
graciously received by Yermak, who made many inquiries about his
master, and eventually sent him back with presents for the Khan, his
wives, and princes, and the various murzas.§ This was meant
apparently to put Kuchum off his guard and make him believe the
Cossacks were on a peaceful errand. Kutugai returned with his
presents, and appeared before Kuchum in a Russian costume, but the
suspicious Khan was not reassured, and ordered a muster of his people
to resist the Cossacks. In May, 1581, Yermak advanced once more
along the Tura and the Tobol. At the outfall of the former he met a
body of Tartars under six princes, three only of whose names are
recorded, namely, Kashkara, Warwara, and Maitmas. A sharp fight
ensued, with at first varying success, but the Cossacks were at length
victorious, and having slaughtered a great number of the enemy secured
so much booty that they could not carry it all in their boats, but had to
bury some of it in the ground.‖

Yermak's force was now reduced to 1,060 men, with whom he continued his march along the Tobol. At a point where the river has a
high bank planted with birches, called Berezof yar, he had another fight
with the Tartars, whom he dispersed. A little lower down the Tobol,
where it was narrow, Kuchum had caused an iron chain to be put
across the river, and had ordered one of his yesauls, Alishai, to attack the
Russians while their boats were delayed by the chain. Yermak arrived
at this point, which was called Karaulnoi, on the 16th of July, and he
speedily forced his way through. We are told that he dressed up a

* Müller, op. cit., 258-9.   † Id., 260-1.   ‡ Id., 260.   § Id., 264.   ‖ Id., 266.

number of bundles of birch poles in his Cossacks' uniforms to deceive the people on the banks, and leaving only sufficient men to watch the boats he landed the remainder, attacked the body lying in wait from behind, and dispersed it.[*] At length the Cossacks reached the mouth of the Tawda, whence a trade route went to Russia, and which was apparently the original goal of the expedition; but it was now determined to prosecute the campaign further. Having halted therefore for eight days, and learnt further particulars about Kuchum's dominions from a Saissan whom he met there, Yermak went on. Meanwhile the Khan, having collected all the Tartars, Ostiaks, and Voguls he could, sent them under Mahmetkul to meet the Russians. He made a new ditch about his capital of Sibir, ordered the neighbouring princes to fortify their towns, and raised some intrenchments on the Irtish close to the mountain Chuvash.[†] Advancing from the Tawda, the Russians encountered Mahmetkul and his army at a village called Babasanski yurti, from a Tartar murza named Babasan.

Karamzin says Mahmetkul had about 10,000 cavalry with him. The Russians, although so inferior in numbers, inflicted a severe defeat on the Tartars. This struggle apparently lasted for five days, and was probably the most severe of the whole campaign. Bows and arrows, however, were no match for firearms. A little further down the Cossacks came to a place called Dolgei Yar, at the mouth of the Turba, where they were again assailed by a shower of weapons, but had little difficulty in dispersing the enemy. A saga reports how a vision was seen by the Tartars, in which a lordly king with a naked sword in his hand, and sitting on a throne which was borne on the shoulders of a number of his champions, appeared on the Tobol, and now he drove the Tartars before him, whose bowstrings snapped while their hands were paralysed, and that in panic they fled to Kuchum to inform him.[‡] This only proves—as the campaign of the Spaniards in America proved—the fantastic legends that speedily gather round such adventures as the one we are describing. About sixteen versts from the outfall of the Tobol into the Irtish there is a small lake called Karachinskoi osero, so called from a Tartar named Karacha, who was one of Kuchum's privy councillors. At first the Cossacks seem to have been afraid of the numbers of Tartars collected there, and they even began a retreat towards Russia, but being reassured by a Vogul elder they turned again and captured the place.[§] This fortress was taken on the 12th of August, 1581, and the Cossacks secured a large booty of gold, silver, pearls and precious stones, corn, cattle, and honey. At this time of the year the Greek Church prescribes a fast of fourteen days, but to secure the Divine favour Yermak ordered that the fast should last for forty days, during which he stayed at Karachinskoi.

---

* Müller. op. cit., 268. † Id., 271. ‡ Id., 274-5. § Id., 276-7.

The Siberian annals now insert another story; how on the site of the future Tobolsk a town with churches and bell-towers was observed to rise, and even the bells were heard to ring; how the two animals already mentioned re-appeared, engaged again in deadly combat, until the wolf, which represented the Tartars, seemed to be killed, but that when they went to see its corpse it rose with a roar and threw itself into the water; whence they argued that their cause, although then overwhelmed, was not hopeless, and that the time would come when their fortunes might revive.[*]

On the 26th of September Yermak once more advanced. On entering the Irtish he arrived at a Tartar settlement named Saostrofnie, belonging to a small chief named Atik, which he captured, and where he transported the baggage, etc., from his boats. Their numbers had been greatly reduced, and the Cossacks again discussed whether it was prudent to go on any further; but it was pointed out to them that it matters very little where one dies when death is inevitable, and that if they returned to Russia it would be to be punished for their misdeeds on the Volga, while the way thither was long and arduous and the winter was upon them, etc. It was therefore determined to go on.[†] They were now approaching the kernel of the Tartar Khanate. Kuchum at the head of his people planted himself in the intrenched position of Chuvash, already mentioned, which Müller suggests derived its name from some Chuvash captives who were probably settled there.[‡] The Cossacks determined to attack this intrenched position, and were led by Yermak himself and Kolzof to the cry of "God is with us," while the Tartars clustered round their chief, Kuchum, who it seems was blind, and who, surrounded by his imaums and mollahs, invoked the aid of Muhammed. His people rushed out on the serried Russian ranks through three openings in the ramparts, and the battle was a severe one. At length, however, Mahmetkul was wounded, and was removed by the murzas in a small boat to the other side of the Irtish. This disconcerted his people, who began to break; the Ostiak chiefs took to flight and were followed by the Tartars, while Kuchum himself fled with some of his treasures towards the river Ishim.[§] The Russians had 107 killed in this fight, whose memory was long after sacredly preserved by a special service in the cathedral of Tobolsk.[||] It seems Kuchum had with him two iron cannons, each two ells long and which fired 40-lb. shot; these, which he had doubtless obtained either from Bukhara or Kazan, he now threw into the Irtish, and they were afterwards fished out by the Cossacks and preserved as trophies.[¶] The principal Tartars from the towns of Chuvash, Bizik, Susgan, and Abalak accompanied Kuchum in his flight,[**] during which he seems to have stayed awhile at Yalutura on the Tobol.[††]

---

* Müller, op. cit., vi., 279-80. † Id., 281-4. ‡ Id., 284, note. § Karamzin, ix., 49-3.
|| Müller, op. cit., 286. ¶ Id., 287-8. ** Id., 290. †† Id., 293.

Yermak at length, on the 7th of November, 1581, entered the town of Sibir, the capital of the Khanate, which was apparently very small and had barely room within its bounds for the Khan's residence and those of his dependents. It was bounded on one side by the river Irtish, on another by the brook Sibirka, and on two others by a rampart. No traces of its buildings, which were probably of wood, remained when Müller wrote.[*] According to Karamzin, a great booty of furs and other precious things was made by the Cossacks, who, however, found no food there.[†]

Three days after the occupation of the town an Ostiak chief from the river Demianka, named Boyar, went with a number of his people to pay his respects to Yermak, and took him presents of furs, fish, etc. In the same way there went to him many Tartar families from the Irtish and the Tobol. They were well received, and sent home again after a small tribute had been exacted from them.[‡] Meanwhile the Cossacks, dreaming not of danger, passed the time in resting and amusing themselves; but their enemy was not asleep. A party of twenty Russians having gone to fish to the village of Abalak, on the lake of the same name, were suddenly attacked by Mahmetkul, and were all killed except one, who fled with the news to Yermak. The latter marched to the rescue. He overtook Mahmetkul and his people at the village of Shamshinski yurti, on the Irtish, and exacted a bloody revenge, only a few Tartars escaping with their chief. Yermak carried off the bodies of his dead companions and buried them on the promontory of Sauskan, a few versts from Sibir, where the Khans had their burial-place.[§] This victory was followed by the submission of two chiefs; one named Ishberdi (a Tartar name) came from beyond the Yeskalbinian bog, probably from the Tawda, and became a faithful subject of and helped the Russians to subdue some other petty princes;[‖] the other was called Suklem, and was probably a Vogul. Like the rest, they were ordered to pay a tribute or yassak of furs. Ivan Kolzof was now despatched to Moscow with the news of the defeat of the Siberian Khan, and with a submissive letter from Kuchum for the Tzar.[¶] He set out in the middle of winter, travelling on snow shoes with *narten* or long narrow sledges drawn by dogs and reindeer. Ishberdi acted as his guide and showed him the way over the mountains from the Tawda to Cherdin, known as the "Wolfs' Road."[**]

While Yermak had been prosecuting his bold adventure so successfully, the Voguls of the Upper Tawda, under a chief who lived at Pelim, and was thence called Pelimskoi kniaz, broke over the Yugorian mountains and plundered the newly-built towns of the Stroganofs on the Kama. The next year they renewed their attack, and attacked Cherdin itself. About this time news reached Moscow of the journey

* Müller, op. cit., 494-6.　† Op. cit., ix., 494.　‡ Id., 498-9.　§ Id., 500-1.
‖ Id., 502.　¶ Id., 504.　** Id., 505-6.

of Yermak. The commander of Cherdin, Vasili Pelepelizin, wrote to complain of the shelter which the Stroganofs had given to the rebellious Don Cossacks, and attributed the inroad of the Voguls to revenge for the way in which their homes had been recently ravaged.[*] Thereupon, on the 28th of November, 1582, the Tzar Ivan wrote a sharp letter to the Stroganofs denouncing Yermak and his doings. Soon after, however, Kolzof and his companions arrived at Moscow, and the Tzar speedily relented. We are told that he sent the deputation back with a present of two costly suits of armour, a silver drinking cup, one of his own fur cloaks, and a piece of cloth for Yermak, and other presents for the Cossacks. They were apparently also accompanied by a number of adventurers, who were a welcome reinforcement for the little heroic band. Let us, however, revert to Yermak. Early in 1582 he learnt through a friendly Tartar murza, called Senbachta Tegin, that Prince Mahmetkul was encamped with an inconsiderable force on the river Vagai, a tributary of the Irtish which falls into it about 100 versts from Sibir. He accordingly despatched sixty active men to try and surprise him. They came up with him near the lake Kular, not far from the Irtish and where the Kularofskaia Sloboda is now situated, surprised his camp at night, killed most of his men, and made him prisoner.[†]

This capture was very welcome to Yermak, who in Mahmetkul had a valuable hostage whom he could use in his future dealings with Kuchum. He received him well, and assigned him a residence at Sibir. Meanwhile Kuchum, who as I have said had retired to the country of the Ishim, was attacked by Seidiak, the son of Bekbulat, the former ruler of Siberia, who it seems had returned from Bukhara and was now in alliance with the Kazaks. Kuchum was also deserted by Karacha, who was the most powerful of the murzas, and whom we have mentioned before. The latter withdrew with a great number of people to the neighbourhood of the river Tara, to a lake called Chulimskoi osero.[‡]

During the spring of 1582 Yermak sent the piatidesiatnik, Bogdan Briasga, with fifty Cossacks, to exact tribute from the Tartars and Ostiaks on the Irtish. They had a sharp encounter with a body of Tartars at the outfall of the Arimdsyanka and stormed their fortress. They were still pagans, and we are told swore fealty by kissing a bloody sword. Briasga duly sent his master a goodly store of skins and provisions;[§] he then went on to the Nazzinskian and Karbinishan Volosts, which, warned by the fate of their neighbours, duly submitted. The tribes which lived at the Turtasian Volost, on the river Turtas, as well as the neighbouring Uwatian Tartars, also agreed to pay tribute after a slight skirmish. These were the last villages in this direction

---

* Müller, op. cit., 307-9.   † Id., 318-4.   ‡ Id., 326-7.   § Id., 327-9.

inhabited by Tartars, and lower down the river the country belonged to
the Ostiaks. Briasga duly subdued the villages of the Ugrian·people
along the Irtish and made them tributary. The story is told in detail
by. Müller,* but is no part of our subject. He followed the Irtish to
its junction with the Ob, and then he once more returned to Sibir,
having, according to Müller, not lost a single man on the way, although
he had had several struggles.†

Yermak spent the summer of 1582 at Sibir, and later in the year he
sent a second embassy to Moscow, escorting Prince Mahmetkul and
taking a quantity of tribute. After this, in the spring of 1583, following in the steps of his lieutenant Briasga, he made a progress down
the Irtish to the Ob.‡ In the autumn of the same year he made an
excursion along the Tawda where there were two Tartar settlements, at
Krasnoyar and Nalimsk, which were subject to a prince named Labuta.
These Tartars gathered together at a place called Pachenka, on a stream
of the same name, and the fight was so fierce that not one of them
survived, while a lake close by became so foul with corpses that it was
afterwards called Pogannoe osero, or the unclean lake.§ Among the
dead was a leader named Pecheneg. Moving on, Kuchum reached the
settlements of the Voguls, who were speedily made tributary.‖

Meanwhile the Tzar Ivan sent Simeon Dimitrovich Bolkhofski to take
possession of the new conquests. He set out with 500 Cossacks on the
22nd of May, 1583, and arrived at Sibir in November of the same
year. The arrival of this reinforcement was followed by a famine
in Siberia. In a thinly peopled country a ruthless campaign speedily
causes want, and we are told that many of the Cossacks died of hunger,
and this was accompanied by a scourge of scurvy, which so often attacks
men who herd together without proper sanitary precautions, and
with indifferent diet, in cold damp countries. Among the victims was
Bolkhofski himself.

Meanwhile a messenger came from the Murza Karacha, whom we have
previously named, asking that a body of Cossacks might be sent to him
to protect him against the attacks of the Kazaks. Yermak, who wished
to win over this chief, accordingly sent him the Ataman Ivan Kolzof,
with forty Cossacks. But it soon appeared that what Karacha meant
was to inflict a severe blow upon the Russians, for Kolzof and his forty
followers were treacherously killed, and Karacha, who had his emissaries
in various directions, speedily secured a general outbreak among the
Tartar and Ostiak tributaries. Several Cossack tax gatherers were put
to death.¶

Karacha now marched with a body of supporters, whom he collected
from all sides, and sent them to beleaguer the city of Sibir. Driven to

---

* Müller, op. cit., 322-342.   † Id., 342.   ‡ Id., 345-7.   § Id., 349-50.
‖ Id., 350-4.   ¶ Id., 361-2.

bay, the small Cossack detachment determined upon a desperate effort.
Leaving Yermak in command of the town,.a large body of them went
out under the command of Matthew Mecheriak, in the night, and
proceeded to surprise Sauskan, where Karacha had his camp This
they captured, and killed a great number of Tartars, including two of
Karacha's sons, while that chief himself fled beyond the lake. Meanwhile,
however, reinforcements came up, and the Tartars again rallied and
pressed the Russians hard. The latter made themselves a rampart out
of the enemy s carts, and resisted the assault bravely, and when the
enemy drew off, after considerable loss, they again repaired to Sibir.[*]
This struggle, which proved how strong the Russians were, brought back
the neighbouring Tartars and Ostiaks once more to their allegiance, and
they again furnished supplies of food, etc.

At this time it would seem that caravans from Bukhara were in the habit
of visiting Sibir, doubtless along a very old trade route, and Yermak was
one day informed that Kuchum Khan was meditating an attack upon one
of these caravans. He therefore set out with 150 men to protect it, and
went as far as the mouth of the Vagai, but he could hear nothing of it.
Near the outfall of the Vagai is a lake, called Begishefskoe Osero, so
named from a Tartar prince, Baish or Beguish, who had a stronghold
close by, and whose son Tobosi is supposed to have given his name to
the neighbouring lake of Tobosi Kul.[†] Yermak having attacked this
stronghold, the Tartars offered a stubborn resistance, and in the
assault most of them were killed. He now marched to Shamsha,
Kianchik, Sala, and Kaurdak, the last three of which settlements were
still to be found on the Irtish when Müller wrote. Shamsha he identifies
with Shamshuiski Yurt (in Tartar Shangshiaul), situated about twenty
versts from Abalak

At Sala there was a slight skirmish, while at Kaurdak the inhabitants
sought shelter in the thick woods close by.[‡] At Tebenda or Tuwenda,
afterwards called Tebendinskoi Ostrog, lived a Tartar chief named
Yeligai, who agreed to pay tribute, and wished to marry his beautiful
daughter (whom Kuchum had desired for one of his sons) to the Cossack
leader. The latter declined the proffered civility, but promised that he
should be protected.[§] At the mouth of the Ishim there was another
struggle, in which five Cossacks fell, and which gave rise to a Tartar legend
styled "the Khan's tears," and beginning with the words "Yanim,
Yanim, bish Kazak," i.e., "Heroes, heroes, five Cossacks." Having
buried their companions, the little party under Yermak again advanced
along the Irtish.

West of the Irtish, on a lake called Aussaklu, there was a famous
Tartar fortress named Kullara, which was used as a frontier defence
against the Kalmuks by Kuchum. Having assaulted it in vain for five

---

[*] Müller, op. cit., 362-4.   [†] Id., 370-1.   [‡] Id., 373-4.   [§] Id., 374-5.

days, Yermak passed on, determined to return to it on his home journey. He next approached the little town of Tasharkan, situated on lake Kularchok, east of the Irtish. Its inhabitants had felt the weight of the Cossack weapons at the fight at Chuvash, and submitted without a struggle. Müller says that at this place there was a stone as big as a sledge load, of a violet blue colour, which the Tartars said had fallen from heaven, and that out of it came cold, rain, and snow.* It is well known that jade is constantly used by the Tartars as a rain-stone.

The Siberian annals now take Yermak to Shish tamak, a Tartar village, situated where the Shish falls into the Irtish. Here lived a number of poor Tartars who were called Turalinzi, and who were subjects of Karacha. On account of their poverty, Yermak did not exact tribute from them, but only a present.† This seems to have been the last Tartar settlement on the Irtish, and Yermak determined to retrace his steps. When he arrived at Tashatkan, he again heard news of the Bukharian caravan, and that it had arrived at the Vagai. He accordingly hastened thither, and went as far as a mound on its western bank known as Atbash, i.e., Horse's head. But he could get no intelligence of the merchants. He therefore determined to return to Sibir, and duly reached one of his former camping places, where he had cut a ditch, which was afterwards called Yermakova Perekof. Near by was a mound called Zarewo Gorodichi, and by the Tartars Kyssim Tura, i.e., the Maiden city, or fortress, from a tradition that the earth which formed it was carried thither by a number of maidens in the skirts of their dresses.‡

Unaware that the enemy was close by, and fearing no danger, Yermak and his companions lay down to sleep, without posting sentinels or taking other precautions. Others affirm that a storm of rain came on which disguised the enemy's approach. Meanwhile Kuchum was close by with his troops. He sent out spies, who returned with three guns with their cartouche cases, as a proof of the ease with which he might surprise the Russians. He accordingly hastened on and fell upon them. Yermak cut his way through to the river, where he expected to find a boat, and finding none threw himself in. His armour—doubtless the suit sent by the Emperor—weighed him down however, and he was drowned. This was on the night of the 17th–18th August, 1584. Thus perished one of the most adventurous characters in history. Karamzin has the patriotic ejaculation: "The waters of the Irtish did not drown him. The memory of Russia, the page of history, the annals of the Church, these guarantee to Yermak an eternal memorial."§ "His exploits," says the same historian, "are written not only in the annals, but also in the sacred temples, where to this day prayers for the repose of his soul and those of his brave companions are offered up." His name, like

---

* Müller. op. cit., 377. † Id., 378. ‡ Id., 367, 380. § Op. cit., ix., 517.

that of our own Arthur, is the theme of much legend and romance, and
has been attached to many localities.   In the huts of the poor may be
seen portraits of the prince hetman, whose success wiped out his
character of criminal and outlaw.   He was of middle stature, with
projecting muscles, wide shoulders, a flat but agreeable face, a black
beard, black and curled hair, and piercing eyes.[*]   He may well claim,
with Columbus, to have discovered a new world, for although the
immediate conquest he made had to be made again, it was none the
less by his work that Siberia was eventually added to the Russian
realm, and thus a bright rainbow was thrown across the darkest sky
in Russian history, that which overshadowed the closing years of Ivan
the Terrible.

On the 25th of August the dead body of Yermak was discovered at
the Tartar village of Yepanchinaki, twelve versts above Abalak.   We are
told that a grandson of Beguish, called ' Yanish, who was fishing,
noticed a man's feet in the water.   He drew the body ashore, examined
its suit of costly armour, and it was speedily recognised as that of
Yermak.   A murza named Kaidaul took off the armour from
the body, when fresh blood ran from its mouth and nose, to the
surprise of the Tartars, for the body was rigid.   Kuchum and the
various Tartar and Ostiak leaders now collected together, and having
placed the body on a stand, fired arrows into it, and fresh blood
again flowed from the wounds.   The legend affirms that the birds of
prey refused to touch the corpse, and that at length, in consequence
of some lugubrious visions, the Tartars determined to bury it, and
that they laid it in the cemetery of Beguish, under a crooked
gnarled pine.   Thirty oxen and ten sheep were consumed at the funeral
feast.   One part of his coat of armour was offered to the Ostiak
idol at Belogorsk ; another was given to the murza Kaidaul.   His gown
was given to Prince Seidiak, and his sword and girdle to the murza
Karacha.[†]   Miracles are said to have been performed by his relics,
while it was reported that for awhile a blue flame appeared over the grave
on Saturday evenings.   The Muhammedan clergy, who discouraged the
popular superstitions about the famous hero, contrived to keep the
people away, and eventually the site of the grave was entirely lost.[‡]   It
is strange to read that in '1650 a letter arrived at Tobolsk from the
Kalmuk chief Ablai, asking that the suits of armour which the emperor
had sent to Yermak, and which had afterwards fallen into the hands of the
murza Kaidaul and of Alach, the chief of the Kodzkish Ostiaks, might be
sent to him.   Orders were accordingly given that they should be obtained
from the heirs of those chiefs, and sent to the Taisha.   Only the former was
recovered.   It was a coat of chain-mail 2 ells long and an ell and a half
across the shoulders, and on the breasts and shoulders there were gilt

---

* Müller, op. cit., 384.   † Id., 387-8.   ‡ Id., 388.

imperial eagles.* This request is explained by the magical properties which were supposed to attach to things belonging to the hero. Diseases were healed with earth from his grave, and Ablai carried some of the latter with him as a kind of charm. As he was about to undertake a campaign against the Kazaks, he wanted the coat of mail for the same purpose.† Let us now return to the Russians. Only one of Yermak's companions, it seems, escaped, and he hastened away to Sibir, where the news was received with natural trepidation. The Cossacks had been reduced in numbers to ,150, and the vengeance of the Tartars, as well as want and hunger, now faced them. They accordingly determined to return home, and left Sibir on the 27th of August, 1584.

Kuchum did not molest the retiring Russians, whom he was too glad to see turning their faces westwards under Ivan Glukhof, but he sent his son Ali with some troops to occupy Sibir. The latter was shortly after driven out by Prince Seidiak, of the old Siberian stock. The Cossacks deemed it best to return home, not by the way they went, but by the Irtish, the Ob, the Yugorian mountains, and the river Petchora, a route which was not only frequented by the Zirianians but also by Russians from Solwychegodzka, who exacted tribute from the Ostiaks and Samoyedes in the modern district of Berezof. Meanwhile, news of the disaster seems to have reached Russia, and one hundred Cossacks under Ivan Mansurof were sent to the rescue. When they reached the Tobol, hearing that Sibir was no longer in Russian hands, they turned aside, followed in the footsteps of their brothers, and arrived safely in Russia.‡ Meanwhile Kuchum failed to regain his old authority. His rival, Seidiak, ruled at Sibir, while many of the small Tartar communities on the Irtish, etc., became more or less independent.

The ease with which Yermak had prosecuted his campaign naturally invited a repetition of it, and when Glukhof reported at Moscow the history of his adventures it was determined to send a fresh expedition. An advanced party of 300 Strelitzes and Cossacks was therefore despatched, under the Voivodes Vasili Borissovich Sukin and Ivan Miasnoi, which left Moscow in the spring of 1587. They invaded Siberia from the side of the Yugorian mountains and the river Ob. On the 10th of July, 1586, Sukin arrived at the old Tartar fortress of Chingi, on the river Tura, where he proceeded to build a new town, to which the Tartar name of Tiumen was given § It was situated on the south bank of the Tura, and was named apparently from a small stream which fell into the Tura there, named the Tiumenka. It was laid out on an ambitious plan, and close to the old fortress of Chingi ruins of, whose mounds and ramparts still remained when Müller wrote. The site was a very fertile one, and the new town was duly furnished with a church.‖ This was the first permanent Russian settlement east of the Ural mountains.

---

* Müller, op. cit., 39a.   † Id., 390-a.   ‡ Id., 393-40ª.   § Id., 410-12.   ‖ Id., 413.

The Cossacks had little difficulty in subduing the neighbouring Tartars, who had now no powerful supporter to lean against, and we are told that those who lived on the Tura, the Pishma, the Iset, the Tawda, and even the Tobol, became tributary to the commander at Tiumen,[*] who was not long, as I shall show in the next chapter, in subduing Sibir and its khan, Seidiak. A new town was now built on the Loswa, a tributary of the Tawda, which was named Loswinskoi, or Na Loswi gorodok, which was to be an entrepôt on the route from Cherdin and the river Wischera to the Loswa and the Tawda, and thence to the Tobol. This town had, however, but a very short-lived existence, and seems to have decayed in two or three years.

In the summer of 1590 Kuchum, who had been living for some time with some Nogai clans in the Barabinski steppe, marched to the neighbourhood of Tobolsk. According to one account he harried some of the neighbouring Tartars; another says he plundered the Tartar settlements of Kaurdak and Salinsk. This was doubtless in revenge for the people there having submitted to the Russians. The new voivode of Tobolsk, Kniaz Kolzof Mosalskoi, set out with a body of Tobolsk troops and some Tartars in July of the following year, and came up with the Khan on the river Ishim, near the lake Chilikul, and having defeated his people carried off two of his wives, one of his sons, called Abulkhair, and much booty.[†]

In order to overawe the district of the upper Irtish and the Tartars who lived in the Barabinski steppe, and to restrain Kuchum, who was constantly violating the new settlements, it was determined in 1594 to build the town of Tara.[‡] Kniaz Andrew Vasilivitch Yelezkoi was appointed to carry out this task. He was accompanied by 145 strelitzes from Moscow, 100 Kazan and Sviashkishlan Tartars and 300 Bashkirs, 50 Poles, and 50 Polish Cossacks. A contingent was also suppplied from Tiumen, consisting of Lithuanians, Circassians, and Cossack exiles, Tartars of Tiumen and Werkhotura, Tartars from the lake Andrew (thirty versts from Tiumen), from the Belakofka (a tributary of the Pishma), with some Tabarinski and Koshuki Tartars, etc. From Tobolsk there went 100 Cossacks, 100 Tartars in the Russian service under the Ataman Cherkas Alexandrof and two petty Tartar leaders, Baiseit and Baibakhta, 300 tributary Tartars, and 150 of the same race to drag and work the boats. Most of these troops were cavalry, and their numbers prove that some trouble was expected from Kuchum. The enumeration of the various kinds of Tartars thus employed, in effect against their old chief, is interesting, as showing how speedily the Russians had made their peace with the indigines. The force was duly supplied with artillery, ammunition, and other requisites. The town was not actually planted on the river Tara, as originally intended, but

* Müller, op. cit., 415-16.   † Id., 429.   ‡ Id., 452.

on a neighbouring feeder of the Irtish, the Agarka; it, however, retained its originally intended name of Tara.* According to instructions from Moscow, letters were now sent to Kuchum inviting him to come to terms. He was promised that if he would acknowledge the supremacy of Russia, and send one of his younger sons with two or three leading Tartars as hostages to Moscow, his eldest son, Abulkhair, and the other distinguished captives at Moscow, should be returned to him.†

Karamzin tells us that a letter was also written to the old chief in the same sense by Abulkhair, who praised the generosity of the Tzar Feodor, who had made rich presents both to him and Mahmetkul. Kuchum, who had been abandoned by two of his sons, who were allies of the Nogai Chin murza, and who had gone over to the Russians with Mahmetkul's mother, replied bravely to the Russian request: " I did not cede Siberia to Yermak, although he conquered it; but, wishing peace, I demand as a frontier the banks of the Irtish."‡

In 1595 a new voivode was appointed to command at Tara, in the person of Feodor Yelezkoi, who seems to have at once prepared to attack Kuchum and his friend the Nogai Ali, who were living in the Barabinski steppe. Reinforcements were sent for from Tobolsk and Tiumen, and five field pieces were also secured for the campaign.§

In the winter of 1595 ninety Cossacks were despatched along the Irtish, and returned on the 20th of December with twenty-eight Ayalinsk Tartars, whom they had captured while fishing at the lake of Busukof, afterwards called Bolskhoi osero.‖ Kuchum had recently tried to transport these Tartars to the upper Irtish, where he lived. His henchman, the Nogai Ali, had carried off 150 of them, who in conjunction with a number of Malagorodzi had built themselves winter quarters at a place called Chernoi Ostrof. It was a party of these emigrants whom the Russians had carried off. It seems Kuchum was at this time encamped in a so-called " waggon town," two days' journey beyond the outfall of the Ob.¶

Müller identifies the Chernoi Ostrof of this notice with a place on the Irtish named Chernoi Gorodichi, where traces of Tartar buildings still remain.** A fresh expedition was organised against this settlement, and although some of the Tartars escaped, sixty of them, with the yessauls Mamik and Seitkul, the kniases Ilgului and Temsenek, and the son of the kniaz Kolkildei, were carried off to Tara, and the place was destroyed.††

In the spring of the next year a more ambitious expedition set out for the steppe of Barama. This comprised 483 men, and was commanded by the Pismennoi Golova Domosherof. They set out on the 29th of March, on lishi or snow shoes. They speedily subdued the villages of

---

* Müller, op. cit., 459. † Id., 460-1. ‡ Karamzin, x., 36. § Müller, op. cit., 469.
‖ Id., 471-2. ¶ Id., 473. ** Id., 473-4. †† Id., 475.

Changui (now called Tunuskaia), Lugui, Luba, Kelema, Turash, Barama (or Ulugh Barama), and Kirkipi. Where there was resistance, as at Changui, the place was mercilessly plundered; otherwise the Tartars were merely made tributary.

About this time, as I have said, the mother of the Tzarevitch Mahmetkul, with the Nogai Murza Chin and his family, and thirty-eight Tartars, went to Tara and put themselves under the Russian rule.[*] Kuchum himself remained obdurate, and it was determined to finally crush him. A body of 700 Russians and 300 Tartars was collected at Tobolsk and Tara, which set out, according to Müller and Fisher, on the 19th of May, 1598, under the command of the Voivode Ivan Mosalskoi.

Karamsin, quoting as his authority the letters of the Voivodes of Tara, written in September, 1598, and preserved in the archives of the College of Foreign Affairs, says they set out in August, 1598, under Andrew Voyeikof, who commanded 397 Cossacks, some Lithuanians and inhabitants of the country. They marched towards the Ob, where amidst corn fields surrounded by marshes, Kuchum and his family, with 500 faithful retainers, had found refuge. Voyeikof made forced marches to reach him, and abandoned some of his baggage en route. On the 2nd of September, before sunrise, he attacked Kuchum's camp. The battle lasted all day, and was fatal to the fortunes of the Siberian Khan. His brother and his son, the Tzariviches Illiten and Kan, six princes, ten mursas, and 150 of his best soldiers were killed. Towards evening the Tartars were driven from their fortifications and pushed towards the river. There more than a hundred were drowned, and fifty made prisoners, while a few others escaped in boats. Eight wives, five sons and daughters of the Khan, and five princes, together with a considerable booty, fell into the hands of the Russians. Burning what he could not carry away, Voyeikof retired to Tara with his illustrious prisoners, and sent word to the Tzar Boris Godunof that the Russians were now undisputed masters of Siberia.[†] The news was very grateful to the usurper Boris, who ordered a grand feast to be made, and rewarded the Cossacks who escorted the Tartar prisoners with valuable presents.[‡] Meanwhile, the Khan himself had escaped. Accompanied by two supporters, he went along the Ob to the country of Chata.

In vain the Russian voivodes sent him word that by submitting and joining his family at Moscow he would be treated by the emperor with kindness and generosity. A Muhammedan priest named Tul Mahmet, sent by Voyeikof, found him in a wood on the banks of the Ob among the dead bodies of a number of Tartars whom the Russians had killed. The blind old man was seated under a tree, with three of his sons and thirty faithful attendants by him. He listened to the messenger who offered him the Imperial clemency. "I did not go to

* Müller, op. cit., 482.   † Karamsin, xi., 25-7.   ‡ Müller, op. cit., 485.

him," he said, "in happier days, when I was rich and strong; shall I go now to find a disgraceful death? I am blind and deaf, poor, and alone. I do not mourn for the loss of my riches, but I grieve for Asmanak, my cherished son, captured by the Russians. With him I should have been content to live on without kingdom or fortune, without my wives or any other children. Now I shall send the rest of my family to Bukhara, and will go to the Nogais." He had neither warm clothes nor horses, and asked for some as alms from the Chats, who were formerly his subjects, but had now submitted to the Russians. He then returned to the field of battle, where in the presence of Tul Mahmet he spent two days in burying the dead, and then mounting a horse, says Karamzin, he disappeared from history.*

This is, however, a slight rhetorical exaggeration. It would seem he fled along the Irtish until he reached the lake of Nur Saissan and the country of the Kalmuks, where he lingered on awhile, and then moved back to the district of the Ishim to try and collect his scattered people again. Having stolen a number of horses belonging to the Kalmuks, he was pursued by them and overtaken at the lake of Kargalchen, near the Ishim. Here the small body of people who still followed him was dissipated. Kuchum thereupon fled to the Nogais or Manguts. The chronicle of Kemesof tells us that the Nogais had suffered much ill-usage at the hands of Kuchum's father, Murtaza, which they now revenged by putting the old Siberian chief to death.† His captured family made a solemn entry into Moscow in January, 1599. It was a great day of triumph for the usurper Boris, who may be said to have completed the task of conquering Siberia.

We are told the wives, daughters, granddaughters, and the sons of Kuchum, named Asmanak, Shaim, Babaja, Kumush, and Mollah, entered the city riding in beautiful sledges, the women dressed in pelisses made of velvet, satin, and cloth of gold, and decorated with gold and silver embroidery and with lace; the Tzarevitches in long red robes, trimmed with rare furs. They were preceded and followed by a number of the feudal soldiery I have called Bayard-followers, dressed in sable pelisses. The streets were filled with crowds of people. The princes and princesses were lodged in the houses of the nobles and great merchants, and were given moderate pensions. The wives and daughters of the Khan were allowed to go and live at Kasimof and Beyetsk, with Uraz Makhmet and with Mahmetkul.‡ Mahmetkul himself entered the Russian army. He took part in a fight with the Swedes in 1590, and in 1598 went with the Tzar Boris to Serpukhof to oppose the Krim Tartars.§ Abulkhair, Kuchum's son, adopted Christianity in 1591, and was re-named Andrew.‖ Among the captives were the wife of Ali, son of Kuchum,

* Karamzin, xi., 28. † Müller, vi., 487-8. Abulghazi, 186. ‡ Karamzin, xi., 30.
§ Müller, op. cit., 357-8. ‖ Karamzin, xi., 31.

5 E

named Khanzadeh (she was the daughter of the Nogai chief, Din Akhmed), and his two sons Alp Arslan and Yasur.* The former of these two became Khan of Kazimof, as I have shown.†

ALI KHAN.

At the battle in which Kuchum was finally beaten, in 1598, several of his sons took part, and eventually escaped. Of these the leader was Ali. Deprived of their settled homes, they continued to live a nomadic life in the steppes, gathering round them many Siberian Tartars, etc., who looked upon them as their legitimate rulers, and duly plundered the borders of the Ishim, the Jrtish, and Tobol, and carried their depredations as far as the Jaik and the neighbourhood of Ufa.‡

In the year 1600 we find four of Kuchum's sons, namely Ali, Kanai, Asim, and Kubei Murat, with 250 Sirianzi and Tabinzi from the neighbourhood of Ufa and Tiumen, on the upper Ishim. Some parties of Cossacks and Tartars from Tobolsk and Tiumen went out against them, but meanwhile Ali sent envoys with his submission to the Russian authorities. It seems he was then living at the Chebar Kul lake, called Piestroye osero by the Russians.§ Soon after, he sent his younger brother, Kubei Murat, to see on what terms they would treat with him. He was sent on to Moscow, as was Ishim, another son of Kuchum's, who had sought refuge with the Russian authorities at Ufa. Word was sent to Ali to tell him to repair in person to Tobolsk, or in default to send one of his brothers, Kanai or Asim. These messengers went as far as the river Obaga, now called Abuga, which falls into the Tobol, but could not meet with the Sheibanid princes, so they returned again to Tobolsk.‖

Meanwhile Ishim on his own account sent some of his people from Ufa to tell his brothers to repair thither. They found Kanai and Asim with 650 men in winter huts in a small wood between the Abuga and the Ishim, their camp being protected by a laager of waggons. Ali and his younger brothers with 300 men were five days' journey distant in the valley of the Tobol. Ali had adopted the style of Khan. Meanwhile Kanai's mother, who came originally from Sabran, had written to tell her son to go and seize that town.¶ Ali and Kanai seem to have been more or less rivals. In 1603 the former was encamped on the so-called lake of the five woods; with him were the Sirianzi already named, while the Tabinzi had gone over to Kanai, who lived on lake Narim.** At this time a body of 700 Nogais, who were in this part of the country under their chief Urus, joined Ali, who had 400 men of his own.

* Vol. Zeraof, op. cit., iii., 3.   † Ante, 437.   ‡ Müller, Op. cit., viii., 55-6.
§ Id., 56-7. Fischer, Sib. Gesch., i., 348-9.   ‖ Müller, op. cit., 58.
¶ Id., 59-61.   ** Id., 63.

With the combined force he meditated an attack on the district of Tiumen. The Russians had sent back some of Kuchum's wives, and also his son Kanchuvar; but this did not appease Ali, who during the years 1603-4-5-6 constantly molested the Russians. In 1605 Asim with 300 men was encamped at the outfall of the Suyer into the Tobol, 160 versts from Tiumen.[*]

In 1606 the Kalmuks appeared for the first time in the district of Tara, and it is not improbable that they had been invited to go thither by Kuchum's dispossessed family; at all events, they seem to have acted in alliance with them against the Russians.[†] In alliance they crossed the Tara and proceeded to plunder the Russian settlements. The Voivode Matfei Mikhailovitch Godunof marched against them, and although he did not overtake the marauders he succeeded in capturing Ali's mother, with whom he withdrew towards Tiumen.

In July, 1607, Asim, Ishim, and Kanchuvar invaded the district of Tiumen with a swarm of Kalmuks, surprised a number of Tartars at Kinirskoi Gorodok, situated on a tributary of the Tura, called the Kinirka, and carried off their wives and children prisoners. At this time Ali was encamped on the brook of Lipkina, between Kobucha and Kinirskoi Gorodok. Kanai, in alliance with a Nogai murza and 200 men, also made a raid on the neighbourhood of Tobolsk. To revenge this the Russians sent out a force under Nazarei Mikhailof Sin Isyedinof, which, during the absence of the princes in an expedition against Tara, surprised their camp in the wood Shamshi. Ali's wife and two sons, and two wives of Asim with two daughters, as well as a sister of Ali's, were captured and carried off to Tiumen.

The Tartars, meanwhile, having returned from their raid, in turn pursued the Russians, and a two-day's struggle took place near the lake Kibirli.[‡] Although nothing is said of Ali himself in the narrative, M. Vel. Zernof concludes that he was captured on this occasion, and sent to Russia. The prisoners were so sent in December, 1608. To avoid the supporters of the Second False Dimitri, they did not go straight to Moscow, but to Vologda, and thence to Novgorod.[§] At Moscow Ali became a pensioner.

He occurs for the first time in official documents in 1615, and for the last time in 1638. He lived at Yaroslaf, as did his brother Altan or Altan, and was there kept under surveillance, not being allowed to ride out into the neighbouring villages without the emperor's consent. His son, Kanchuvar, was present at a battle at Smolensko, where he deserted, and tried to find his way to the Krim, but being captured by the Cossacks, was sent to Solvichigodsk, and thence to Ustiuge, and at last during the reign of Alexis Mikhailovitch, was at his father's request allowed to return to Moscow.[‖] We don't know when Ali died.

* Müller, op. cit., 66.　　† Id., 69.　　‡ Id., 69-70.
§ Müller, 73. Vel. Zernof, iii., 293-4.　　‖ Id., 797-8.

I would here remark that some of the Kuchum princes were at this time apparently growing weary of the struggle, for we read that in November, 1607, Yulubai, the father-in-law of Chuvak, who is called Asim's brother (*i.e.*, doubtless by the same mother), with eleven Tartar families, went to Tiumen, and reported that he had left Prince Asim on the river Kobucha. In July, 1608, Prince Altanai also surrendered himself at Tiumen.[*]

ISHIM KHAN.

We do not read of the Sheibanid princes for some years. At length we are told that Ishim was living in 1616 with two Kalmuk princes, Salbar and Koshur, near Semipalat, on the upper Irtish, whence he harried the neighbourhood of the Siberian towns and of Ufa. He wrote at the time to say that he intended going to offer his submission to the Russians. In the Russian archives he is styled Tzar, and he had doubtless on the withdrawal of his brother Ali adopted the style of Khan.[†] His offer of submission came to nothing, and in 1618 we find him in alliance with the Kalmuks, again at issue with Russia, and sustaining a severe defeat in the steppes of the Irtish and the Tobol, in which a number of his people were killed and others captured. Among the booty were many camels, of which fifty-eight were sent on to Moscow.[‡]

In 1620 Ishim, in alliance with a Kalmuk Taisha named Saichak, went to lake Shuchie, and brought word that the Kalmuks, having been terribly beaten by the Mongols, were in full flight westwards.[§] Shortly after we read how Ishim married the daughter of the Torgut chief Urluk, of whom we wrote in the former volume, and that he was then living with his father-in-law.[||] At this time the Kalmuks were swarming all over the steppes of Western Siberia, south of the Russian borders, and virtually occupying them. In 1622 Ishim was living at Khama Karagai, on the Tobol, seven days' march from Tiumen.[¶] Shortly after we find him at the outfall of the river Ui, near the town of Ufa, where he had gone to recover the Tabinzian Tartars who had deserted him.[**] This is the last mention I can find of him.

ABLAIGIRIM.

Again it is some years before we hear of the Sheibanid princes. In 1629, however, we are told that Ablaigirim, the son of Ishim, in alliance with the Kalmuk chiefs Kokshul, Urluk, and Baibagish, made the Barabinski Tartars tributary to the Kalmuks, and strove to gain the goodwill of their Taishas, of the Telengut prince Obak,

---

[*] Müller, op. cit., viii., 75 4.   [†] Id., 88.   [‡] Id., 90-1.   [§] Id., 283.   [||] Id., 288.
[¶] Id., 288.   [**] M., 292.

and of the Kurchakish Taisha Keshesh, who, although a Kalmuk, was living among the Telenguts.* He had a following of 300 men, and was encamped on the river Yulus.† He also won over the Chaskian Murza Tarlaf, who was son-in-law to the Telengut chief Obak, and who lived at Chaskoi Gorodok.‡ Having gained a number of adherents in the Barabinski steppe, Ablaigirim seems to have ventured on attacking some Murzas who were in alliance with Russia, and destroyed their settlement of Mursin Gorodok.§ A party of Cossacks was sent against him, and a struggle ensued on the river Shagarka, in which his people were terribly punished, and according to the report of the Ostiaks the line of retreat from the battlefield for twenty versts towards the Barabinski steppe was strewn with dead bodies and abandoned baggage.∥

This victory seems to have effectually detached the wavering chiefs of the Barabinski from their alliance with Ablaigirim. At this time we meet with another Sheibanid prince, named Devlet Girai, the son of Chuvak, who with a number of Tartars made a cruel raid on the upper Irtish. This attack was unexpected and took place when the greater number of the fighting men were absent hunting, and only old and disabled people with women and children were at home. The villages of Tebendinsk and Kaurdask were wasted, the men there put to death, and the women, children, and cattle carried off, such of the cattle as could not be moved were killed and left for the wild beasts. The villages of Kretchetnikof and Kapkaninskaia were also desolated.¶ When news of this reached Tobolsk, troops were sent after the marauders, who were overtaken at the wood called Kosh Karagai, near the Ishim. Most of the Kalmuks were killed and the prisoners were released.**

In 1632 Ablaigirim with but thirty men attacked a village on the Iset called Alibaieve Yurti, which was plundered and many women and children carried off. He had previously made fair promises to its defenders, and had assured their safety by a Kalmuk oath, consisting in licking an arrow and planting it in the ground with its point to the stars. He kept the oath to the letter, and carried off such property as he seized, including boys and girls, in the guise of *tribute*.†† In the summer of 1633 a force of 1,380 men was sent from Ufa to inflict punishment on Ablai, and his brothers or cousins, but none of the pestilent family were met with.‡‡ The same year Devlet Girai made a descent on the Iset, and plundered the Ufa-Katai Volost and a place in the district of Tiumen called Baishevi yurti. He threatened that he would soon return with his relative Ablai, and a few months later a large Kalmuk body duly made an attack on the town of Tara, and laid in ashes all the neighbouring villages. Those who did not find shelter in

* Müller, op. cit., viii., 300-3.   † Id.   ‡ Id., 306-8.   § Id., 310.   ∥ Id., 310-11.
¶ Id., 315-16.   ** Id., 317.   †† Id., 347.   ‡‡ Id., 348.

the town were killed or made prisoners and a large booty was carried off.[*] In 1634 the Sheibanid princes and Kalmuks made a similar raid upon the environs of Tiumen with similar success.[†] In the spring of 1635 Ablai made another plundering raid along the Iset. At this time he and Devlet Girai lived together on a lake called Chabtatli beyond the Ishim, at the foot of the Itik mountains.[‡] Later in 1635, still in alliance with the Kalmuks, the two princes burnt the villages of Verkhna-Nizinskaia, and Chubarofa. These persistent attacks on the part of the borderers of the Siberian towns, reminds one of the similar warfare which the backwoodsmen in America have had to wage so long with the Indians, and explains, if it does not excuse, much of the cruel revenge that was sometimes taken. Men whose houses are burnt, their wives ravished, and their children enslaved, are not good scholars for philanthropists. The Russians had another difficulty at this time in that they might array against themselves at any moment the combined force of the Kalmuks, many of whom were ready enough to join the martial descendants of Ḳuchum Khan.

In 1635, an expedition set out from Tobolsk and the neighbouring towns, which did little beyond slaughtering some Kalmuks. Another expedition set out from Ufa in 1636. The Cossacks followed the course of the river Ufa to its source, where they found a Kalmuk encampment, in which Ablai and his brother Tevka were then living. Many of the Kalmuks were killed, and the two princes with fifty-four Kalmuks were captured and taken to Ufa.[§] Ablai was sent on to Moscow, and in 1650 news was sent to his cousin Devlet Girai that he had died there.[|]

DEVLET GIRAI.

On the retirement of Ablai there still remained in Siberia a representative of the family of Kuchum, in the person of his cousin, Devlet Girai, who, we are told, had his camp at the lake Akushli, at the foot of the mountain Munchak, on the Ishim. He had less than a hundred people with him, which, as Müller says, was rather a small following for one who aspired to recover the throne of Siberia.[¶] He kept up communication with Bukhara, and we are told how on one occasion ten of his followers escorted his sister, who was married there.[**] In 1637 he sent a messenger to Tara in the company of twenty-two Bukharian merchants with a deferential message, but the authorities suspected, doubtless justly, that he was a spy.[††]

In 1640, Devlet Girai, in alliance with the Kalmuks, plundered the neighbourhood of Tarkhanskoi Ostrog. In 1641, the Russians sent a

---

[*] Müller. op. cit., viii., 333-4.　　[†] Id., 335-6.　　[‡] Id., 357.　　[§] Id., 340.　　[|] Id., 438.　　
[¶] Id., 343-4.　　[**] Id., 344.　　[††] Id., 345.

body of 272 men to punish these marauders, who were severely handled. Many of them were killed, and others captured. Among the latter were a nephew and niece of the Torgut chief, Urluk.* The next year we find Devlet Girai trying to incite the Kalmuk Taisha Ishkep to attack the Russians, and assuring him how from what he had seen the year before, the settlements about Tiumen might be easily ravaged.†

In 1645 Devlet Girai again made friendly overtures to the Russians. At this time there are mentioned with him two other princes of his family, Bugai or Abugai, a son of Ishim, and Kuchuk, the son of Ablai. In 1646, Abugai, with a number of Kalmuks, made a descent on the Russian frontiers.‡

Abugai and Kuchuk again molested the neighbourhood of Ufa in 1648; in fact, their depredations were almost constant.§ In March, 1649, the Kuchumian princes, in alliance with the Kalmuks, plundered the settlements on the Iset.‖ The next year an envoy went to Devlet Girai from Moscow, who found him nearly dead from want and hunger. He had had but one sheep to support himself and his followers upon during a month, and was supplied with provisions by a Tartar from Ufa.¶ In 1651, Devlet Girai and Abugai, with some Kalmuk Tartars, burnt the monastery of Dolmatof Uspenskoi, and plundered other places on the Iset.** Bugai also attacked the village of Burgamakova, on the Tara.††

A few months later Devlet Girai, with a son who is not named, and a son-in-law called Garu Bagashaef, burnt the Tartar village of Chiplarova.‡‡ The plans of the Russians who were sent in pursuit miscarried, and they did not overtake him. A similar fate overtook the expedition sent from Tiumen in 1653 against Devlet Girai and Kanchuvar.§§ In November, 1653, Bugai, Kuchuk, and Kanchuvar were living on the Tobol.‖‖ In 1655 some envoys from Tobolsk to the Kalmuk Taishas, Dor and Karacha, met *en route* with Bugai and his brothers, who a month later, made their annual raid on the district of the Tobol.¶¶

In 1656, Bugai, with his cousins Kanchuvar and Chuchelei, the sons of Ablai, set out from their camp on the Ishim, where they lived together with Devlet Girai, for a new baranta.*** In 1659, Bugai, Kuchuk, Kanchuvar, and Chuchelei, with a number of Kalmuk Taishas and a force of 1,000 men, set out on a more ambitious campaign. They destroyed the villages of Tunuskaya, Lubaiskaya, Kulebinskaya, Choiskaya, and Barabinskaia, killed fifty-nine men and two women, and carried off as prisoners 358 males and 375 females.††† Most of these prisoners were afterwards released at the instance of the Kontaish of the Sungars.

---

* Müller, op. cit., viii., 354.   † Id., 357.   ‡ Id., 360-1.   § Id., 363-4.   ‖ Id., 437.
  ¶ Id., 438.   ** Id., 439.   †† Id., 441.   ‖‖ Id., 443.   ¶¶ Id., 448.
  ‡‡ Id.   ¶¶ Id., 449.   *** Id., 450.   ††† Id., 451-2.

Neither Müller nor Fisher afford us any further light on these Kuchumian princes, nor do I know their later history.   For a long time previously to this date their authority had been merely nominal, and the Kalmuks were the actual rulers of the country beyond the Jaik, and they and their followers were doubtless absorbed by them.

Note 1.—We have argued that the steppes of the Middle and Little Hordes of the Kazaks are the original homeland of the Usbegs.   These steppes are strewn with many ruins, doubtless of various dates and origins.   Levchine speaks of some as the remains of Lama pagodas, and doubtless relics of the Kalmuks.   Others resemble Muhammedan mosques, others again are so ruinous that their original destination is not obvious.   Some are built of stone, some of bricks, the latter being in many cases glazed.   The Kazaks know nothing certain about these ruins, and attribute them to those who occupied the country before them.   Some of them they call Nogai ruins and Nogai tombs. The name Nogai, with them as with the Khivans and Bukharians, has not the specific application it has with us, being applied generally to all the Russian Tartars.[*]

The most important of the ruins in the Kazak steppe are those of Ablaikitak and Semi Palat, which are of Kalmuk origin, and have already occupied us. In the mountains Ken Kozlan, on the Kizil Su, which falls into the Taida, in a beautiful site, is a cruciform building, of granite.   The vaulting has fallen in, but it was evidently once painted red, while the walls were covered with stucco.   On the upper storey of the building was a gallery, and a kind of entablature supported by four wooden pillars, which were protected from the weather by a covering of mastic.   Around this building are some dwellings in ruins whose walls are fringed with vegetation.

At the Psikaz of Karkalinski, in a gorge of the mountains through which flows the Jirim Su, is a vast wall of granite, built no doubt to command the pass.

Ninety-five versts from the fortress of Troitzkaia, beyond the river Tooiusa, are the ruins of a mosque, near which are other remains.   On the river Aiagaz, which falls into the Balkhash, is a building terminating in an acute angle, beautifully built.   This structure contains three statues, which the Kazaks affirm represent the two lovers, Baian Khan and Kuz Kurpiach (about whom they have many songs), and their servant.   Those who think thus, take offerings and deposit them there.[†]   On the Kara Kinghir, which falls into the Sarisu, eight versts from its mouth, are the ruins of a town known as Juvan Ana.   Here are the remains of five mosques and of a considerable building, and the Kazaks affirm that a famous Nogai chief once lived there.[‡]

On the Sarisu, half-a-day's journey from its outfall into the lake Telegul,

---

* Levchine op. cit., 107-8.   † Levchine, 109-10.
‡ Rytschkof, Orenb. Top., i., 210. Levchine, op. cit., 110.

are the ruins of another town, known as Belian Ana, which was once six versts long and a verst wide. Here are also the remains of five mosques. The Nogais affirm that this town was named from a woman whose memory they greatly reverence.

On the river Nura, which falls into lake Kargaljin, and at twenty-seven versts from its outfall, are the remains of a town called Totagai or Botagai. It was once ten versts in circumference. *Inter alia*, there are remains of a quadrilateral palace, resembling a castle. It is 300 fathoms in circuit. Here also are a mosque and a crowd of ruined stone houses. The Kazaks affirm the Nogais* once lived there.[†] The environs of the Nura are rich in such remains. On the right bank of this river fifty-five versts from lake Kargaljin are some considerable ruins, which have been described by M. Changhin. There are also some fortifications near the mountain Kart, and the remains of a tower on the upper Nura, near an old copper mine.

On the Yakshi Kun are ruins of two buildings explored by the same traveller. These are thirty versts asunder, one of stone and the other of brick, and both covered with cupolas and having double entrances, one to the north and the other to the south. The Kazaks assign these buildings to the Kalmuks, which is not their probable origin. They hold them sacred, and present prayers and offerings there. On the little river Ak Koriak are a series of six elliptical fortifications, separated by intervals in which are square forts. A peninsula on the lake of Yakti Yanghiz is protected by a strong rampart, made of polygonal blocks of porphyry.

On the Turgai are a number of old tombs of stone and brick; one of these consisting of an immense mound, is, in the traditions of the Kazaks, the grave of a hero of enormous size. A little further along the Turgai are the remains of a large square town, whose walls are nine saghimes high. Around it are the tombs of its inhabitants. In the district of Baitak, on the Great Kobda, there was formerly, according to the Kazaks, a great town, and there are still remains of buildings, of canals, and of cultivated fields there. In 1750, some of the buildings were still in decent preservation, and were seen and described by Lieutenant Righilmann. This place is held in great veneration by the Kazaks.

There was another town on the river Ouil, near the districts of Mavli Berdi and Mavlum Berdi, and in the middle of the last century there were still thirty or forty brick buildings, canals for irrigation, etc., there.[‡]

Levchine describes a series of ruins on the old route from Seraichuk to Urgenj, across the Ust Urt. These, however, form no part of our present subject.

Similar ruins exist on the Yemba, the Saghiz, and the Ilek, near lakes Barbi, on the Tobol, and in various parts of the steppe.[§]

Some of them are no doubt attributable to the Uzbegs, who ruled over this wide area during the most flourishing period in the history of Kipchak.

---

* *Vide antr.*   † Rytschkof, op. cit., 210.   ‡ Levchine, 114.   § *Id.*, 112-13.

5 F

Note 2.—Genealogy of the Sheibanids of Turan :—

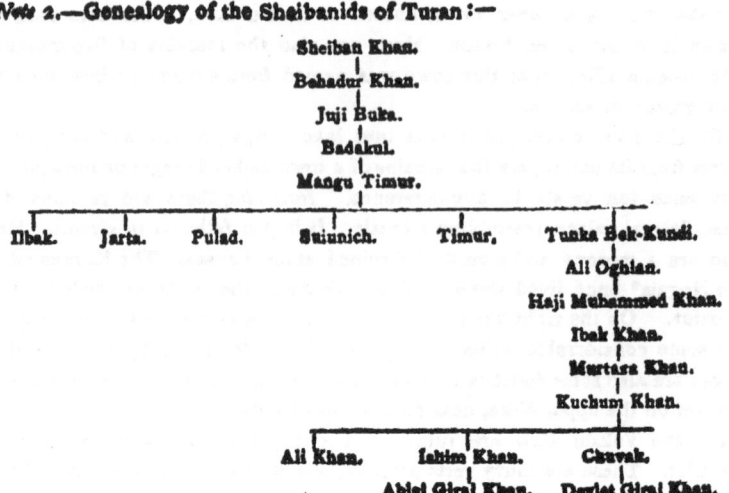

In this table I have followed Abulghazi, except that I have not inserted Mahmudek between Haji Muhammed and Ibak, for a justification of which I must refer to the text of this chapter. I have followed the statements of Abulghazi in Desmaison's edition, but I would add that in the copy of Abulghazi followed by Müller, Mahmudek, who is called Maamut by him, is made the brother of Ibak and the father of Murtasa,* which may not improbably be right. Munshi gives the first descents differently. He makes Sheiban be succeeded by Kabghay Sultan, he by Khakai(?) Sultan, he by Behadur Kazak Sultan, he by Neteghul Sultan, he by Khoja Bugha Sultan, and he by Mangu Timur Sultan,† but I much prefer the authority of Abulghazi.

---

* Op. cit., vi., 285.   † Senkofaki, supplement, 17, and table.

CHAPTER XII.

THE NOGAIS, KARAKALPAKS, AND SIBERIAN TARTARS.

THE appearance of a new tribal or race-name among the Mongols is by no means an unfrequent occurrence. When a great conqueror left his tribe as a heritage to his family, we often find the portion allotted to one or other of the sons assuming his name. When a chief made himself a great reputation by his conquests or by his zeal in religion this result often ensued. The Ottomans and the Uzbegs are well known cases. We have now to deal with a similar instance. The Nogais, the well known nomadic Tartars of Southern Russia, derive their name from a famous prince of the royal family of the Golden Horde, called Nogai.

Teval, the seventh son of Juchi, the founder of the Golden Horde, had two sons, Tartar and Mongkadr. The former had one son, who was called Nogai, and who became the head of his grandfather's ulus. I have already said that the Mongol divisions were tribal and not territorial. In dividing his heritage among his children, a great Mongol chieftain, the head of a race of unsettled and nomadic herdsmen, whose pastures had no definite limits, gave to each a certain number of clans or tribes, which thenceforward looked to him as their chief, no matter how scattered and widely separated they became. We must never lose sight of this fact, and especially in treating of the Nogais, who afterwards became a very disintegrated and sporadic race.

When the division of Juchi's appanage took place, the position of Teval, and afterwards of Nogai, was, if we are to judge from the tribes who still bear the latter's name, confined to the more nomadic tribes previously called Pechenegs—a wave of Turkish invaders who preceded the Kipchaks proper in the steppes of Southern Russia—and it would seem that the Pechenegs, wherever situated, were assigned as a portion to Teval and his family.

Nogai distinguished himself at a very early age. He is first heard of in 1259, in conjunction with Tulabugha, leading a Mongol army to the ravage of Poland.* On the death of Batu and the accession of Bereke, Nogai became the chief commander of the Mongol forces, and when war broke out between Bereke and Khulagu, the Ilkhan of Persia, Nogai commanded the army of Kipchak, as I have described.† This

---

* Ante, 109.　　　　　† Ante, 115-26.

war was doubtless largely due to the religious zeal of Bereke, who resented the atrocities committed by the Ilkhan and his followers upon the faithful.

This war was renewed in 1265 between Bereke and Ababa, who had meanwhile succeeded his father.* An army under the orders of Nogai again invaded Persia, and a severe fight ensued on the banks of the Aksu, in which he was wounded in the eye by an arrow, and his army was forced to give way. It was pursued across the Kur by Abaka. The latter, however, halted, and retired at the approach of Bereke, who had marched with a large reinforcement for his general. While the armies were in view of one another, Bereke died. His corpse was removed to Serai and his army withdrew. Nogai went to his yurt in Southern Russia.†

It was situated apparently on the river Bug.‡ Here he rapidly grew very powerful, chiefly in consequence of the unsettled succession to the Khanate of the Golden Horde. His alliance was sought by the Emperor Michael Palæologos, who had in 1261 recovered Byzantium from the Latins, and who was then at war with the Bulgarians. He invited Nogai's Tartars to ravage the Bulgarian towns on the Black Sea, namely, Mesembria, Ankhialos, Sisopolis, Agathopolis, and Kaistritza. He also sent the Tartar chief many costly gifts of pearls, jewels, and precious stuffs, and Nogai for a while discarded the sheep and dog skins in which he was formerly clothed. The ingenuous Tartars asked the envoys if these clothes would prevent their wearers from growing weary at their work, and if the jewels would ward off thunderbolts ?§ The Emperor had sent his natural daughter Maria to join the harem of the Ilkhan Khulagu ; he now sent another natural daughter, called Euphrosyne, to become the wife of Nogai.‖

This was perhaps not the only intermarriage between the royal house of Nogai and those of the Christians. In an ancient saga we read that Feodor Rostislovitch, the black grandson of Mitislaf Davidovitch, of Smolensko, being at the Horde, so won the heart of the Tartar queen that she determined to give him her daughter in marriage. He had acquired some rights to the throne of Yaroslavl by marrying Maria, the heiress of its former prince. Maria died while he was at the Horde, and the people of Yaroslavl having refused to acknowledge him he determined to remain with the Tartars and to marry the Tartar princess, who was baptised accordingly with the name of Anne, and the marriage was authorised by the Patriarch of Constantinople. His father-in-law meanwhile had a splendid palace built for him at Serai, and gave him the towns of Chernigof, Cherson, Kazan, and Bolghar, and eventually also secured for him the principality of Yaroslavl, where

* Ante, 123.   † Von Hammer, Golden Horde, 253.   ‡ Raschid ud Din in D'Ohsson, iv., 761.
§ Pachymeres Stritter, iii., part 2, 1066 to 1067 ; Golden Horde, 253.
‖ Stritter, op. cit., 1046, 1062.

his wife built a church in honour of St. Michael the Archangel. This saga, which is by no means contemporary, is clearly a very exaggerated narrative, and Karamzin suggests that if it be true in part it refers to Nogai, whose chief wife was a Christian and who was himself apparently not a Muhammedan, rather than to the Khan Mangu Timur,[*] but Von Hammer seems to think differently.[†]

When the Tartars returned unsuccessfully from Lithuania in 1275 we are told that Nogai sent a fresh army through Gallicia, the troops of which province were also ordered to march. The Gallicians laid siege to Grodno, while the Tartars attacked Novogrodek; but the allies secured little by their campaign, save a considerable amount of booty at a great loss in men.

Some time after we find Nogai interfering again in Bulgaria. Lakhanas had raised himself from the position of a swineherd to be the ruler of that country, and had persuaded a large number of his countrymen that God had chosen him to deliver their land from the Tartar yoke. Michael Palæologos had given him the hand of Maria, the widow of Constantine, the King of Bulgaria, whose husband Lakhanas had killed, and through her he had obtained the throne of that country. But having been defeated in battle by the Tartars, Terteres, who was the rightful sovereign, was seated on the throne, while the quondam swineherd took refuge with Nogai. The Emperor Michael now sent Asanes, who had married a sister of Euphrosyne, Nogai's wife, to ask him to render Lakhanas no assistance against the rightful sovereign of Bulgaria. Nogai received them both well, and heard his story. He then ordered Lakhanas to be put to death at a feast, while Asanes was sent home again.[‡]

Nogai's power increased daily, and on the death of Mangu Timur in 1282, he begins to appear as the rival rather than the first subject of the Khans of the Golden Horde, claiming that the country he ruled, and which bore his name, had been won by himself and not the Khan.[§] As I have shown he espoused the cause of Dimitri, who was at issue with his brother Andrew, the protege of the Khan Tuda Mangu, both being candidates for the grand principality of Russia, and by his assistance Dimitri was put on the throne.[||] Shortly after this Nogai was engaged in a war in Thessaly. This war was undertaken by him in 1283 in support of his father-in-law, the Emperor Michael, against whom John, entitled the Sebastokrator, had rebelled. Nogai supplied a contingent of 4,000 men. Michael's army was encamped near Lysimachia, and was ready to move when the Emperor was taken suddenly ill. News thereupon came that the Tartar contingent was at hand. The

* Karamsin, iv., 135-6.　　　† Golden Horde, 257, note 6.
‡ Stritter, iii., 1067-9 ; Golden Horde, 257 ; Karamsin, iv., 157.　§ Stritter, iii., 1048.
|| Ante, page 135.

messengers of Nogai were admitted to his sick room, and he thanked
them for so promptly coming to his assistance. Michael's days,
however, were numbered, and he died almost immediately, and was
succeeded by his son the elder Andronicus, who it would seem did not
wish to prosecute the war. There was a difficulty, however, with the
Tartars, who were very unwilling to return home empty-handed. By
the general advice of the notables, Andronicus accordingly ordered
Michael Glaba, his master of the horse, to lead them into the country
of the Triballi, *i.e.*, of the Serbians, who were old enemies of the empire,
and to plunder it. A year later, in 1284, a body of 10,000 Tartars, who
were encamped about the Danube, crossed into and plundered Bulgaria, then ruled by Terteres, and entered Macedonia and Thrace.
They were attacked and defeated by the Curopalates, Umpertopulos, the
Governor of Mesembria.* The next year we find that the Vlakhs, who wandered between Byzantium and Bizye, were suspected of being in alliance
with the Bulgarians, and a great number of them were transported into
Asia.† Terteres, the Bulgarian king, was also constrained to give his
daughter Seki in marriage to Nogai's son.‡

   During the reign of Tuda Mangu, who was a devotee and a mere
titular sovereign, the real power being in the hands of Tulabugha,
Nogai had become practically independent. He undertook a famous
campaign with the latter in the winter of 1285-1286. This was
against Hungary, where Ladislas the Fourth, the son of Stephen
the Fourth, then reigned. He was known as the Kumanian, from his
mother having belonged to that Turkish race. The Tartar column
we are told covered a space eleven miles wide, and advanced to
the Danube, but it was much impeded, and lost many men in consequence of the heavy rains and snows which filled the rivers, and
converted the country into a vast quagmire. Karamzin says also, that the
Tartars were misled by their Russian guides. They suffered heavy losses
in their retreat, and according to the hyperbole of one annalist, Tulabugha
fled on foot with only one woman and one sumpter-beast.§ As they
passed through Transylvania they fought a sharp battle at the castle of
Turusko, in the district inhabited by the Szeklers of Aranysos, in which
1,000 of them were made prisoners. They however destroyed the Saxon
fortress of Nukud, the town of Bistritz, the monastery of Sarivar, and
other unfortified places.∥ The invaders did not all leave the country,
but some of them settled under the name of Neugais or Nogais, in
villages along the Theiss, where there still remain places called Tartar-
Falva, Tartar-Szent-Miklos, Tartar-Szent-Gyorg, Tartaros, and
Tartarszallasa,** and in the letter addressed by Pope Honorius, abusing
the Hungarian king for allying himself with the infidels, there occurs the

---

* Pachymeres and Nicephorus Gregorius in Stritter, iii., 1073-5.
† *Id.*, Jirecek Gesch. der Bulg., 282.   ‡ Jirecek loc cit.
§ Karamzin, iv. 281.   ∥ Wolf, 412-13.   ** Golden Horde, 268.

phrase "Te cum Tartaris, Saracenis, Neugeriis paganis conversatione damnata confœderare." The policy of the Hungarian king at length in 1290 cost him his life, for it is not improbable that the Tartar invasion of Hungary was made at his instigation. It seems from Karamzin that the misfortunes of the Tartars in this war caused a quarrel between Nogai and Tulabugha. The camp of Nogai was the haven where the discontented fugitives from that of Tulabugha found refuge. Among these the most important were the sons of Mangu Timur, led by Toktu, whose intrigues at length led to the deposition and death of Tulabugha, as I have described.* Toktu was put on the throne by the influence of Nogai, and shortly afterwards that king-maker, who doubtless presumed on his close connection with the Imperial family of Byzantium, sent his wife Bilak Khatun to his court with the message, "Thy father salutes thee, and wishes thee to know that there remain on thy throne much ordure and many thorns." "Which are they?" asked Toktu. She then named twenty-three military chiefs who had supported Tulabugha against him. Toktu sent them to Nogai, and they were put to death. This demand was followed by other signs of patronage, which were no doubt resented by Toktu, and led after a while to a rupture between the two chiefs. Matters were brought to a crisis in this way. Kelmish, the sister of Mangu Khan, had been married to the Kuakurat Saljidai Gurkhan. They had a son Yailak, and a daughter Olju. Yailak married Katak, the daughter of Nogai, and Olju was the wife of Mangu Timur and the mother of Toktu. Thus Yailak was Toktu's uncle.

It would seem that when the other princes of the Golden Horde became Muhammedans, Nogai remained a Shamanist, and it was this which probably attracted to him a considerable amount of support. His daughter Katak some time after her marriage having become a convert to Islam was ill-treated and despised by her husband, who remained a Shamanist. She accordingly complained to her people. Nogai sent word to Toktu bidding him remember the obligations he was under to him, and telling him that if he wished the relations of father and son to continue between them he must send Saljidai to his camp. Toktu replied that Yailak had been his foster-father, and he refused to give him up. Nogai sent a second embassy with no better result, and he then ordered his sons to march against the Khan. This is Rashid's account.† Marco Polo makes out that Toktu was incited to the war by two sons of Tuda Mangu, who had been deposed by Tulabugha. (He says killed by Nogai and Tulabugha in concert.) Novairi says the cause of the strife was, that several chiefs who feared that Toktu would do them harm had taken refuge with Nogai, and that when Toktu demanded their return this was refused. He thereupon sent his exacting patron a hoe, an arrow, and some earth. The meaning of this

* Ante, 139, 140.   † D'Ohsson, iv., 759; Golden Horde, 570.

enigmatical message was interpreted thus by Nogai himself: The hoe means, if you bury yourself in the ground I will drag you out; the arrow, if you climb up into the sky I will bring you down; and lastly, the earth, choose a battle-field. "Tell Toktu," he said in reply, "that our horses are thirsty and that we will go and water them in the Don." Novairi has mistaken the Don for the Volga, for he says it was on the river on which Serai was built.[*] Upon this message Colonel Yule has the following very apposite note: "What a singular similarity we have here to the message that reached Darius eighteen hundred years before, on this very ground, from Toktu's predecessors, alien from them in blood it may be, but identical in customs and mental characteristics."

I quote the message from Professor Rawlinson's translation: "At last Darius was at his wits' end; hereon the Scythian princes understanding how matters stood despatched a herald to the Persian camp with presents for the king: these were a bird, a mouse, a frog, and five arrows. The Persians asked the bearers to tell them what these gifts might mean, but he made answer that he had no orders except to deliver them and return with all speed. If the Persians were wise, he added, they would find out the meaning for themselves. So when they heard this they held a council to consider the matter. Darius gave it as his opinion that the Scyths intended a surrender of themselves and their country, both land and water into his hands. This he conceived to be the meaning of the gifts because the mouse is an inhabitant of the earth and eats the same food as man, while the frog passes his life in the water; the bird bears a great resemblance to the horse, and the arrows might signify the surrender of all their power. To this explanation of Darius, Gobryas, one of the seven conspirators against the Magus, opposed another which was as follows: Unless, Persians, ye can turn into birds and fly up into the sky, or become mice and burrow under the grounds, or make yourselves frogs and take refuge in the fens, ye will never escape from this land, but die pierced by our arrows. Such were the meanings which the Persians assigned to the gifts."[†] Mr. Rawlinson quotes another version of the story from Pherecydes of Leros, whose date is uncertain, but who may have lived as early as the days of Herodotus. This is very like the story just quoted, but it adds a plough to the other things sent.[‡] When Muravief reached the court of Khiva in 1820, it happened that among the Russian presents offered to the Khan were two loaves of sugar on the same tray with a quantity of powder, shot, and flints. The Uzbegs interpreted this as a symbolical demand: Peace or War.[§]

Novairi dates the beginning of the strife between the two Khans in the year 697 (i.e., A.D. 1297). It was in that year, this author tells us, that the two rivals fought a battle at Yaksi, between their two countries (? on

* Novairi D'Ohsson, iv., 735-4.   † Op. cit., iii., 198.   ‡ Id., note 6.
§ Voyage en Turcomanie, 165; Yule's Marco Polo, ii., 500.

the Ozy or Uzy, *i.e.*, the Dnieper), Nogai having an army of 200,000 men. Toktu, he tells us, was beaten, and returned to the Don, in which river many of his men were drowned. Nogai forbade a pursuit, and retired with the captives and spoil he had made.* Rasohid ud Din has a different story. He says Toktu appeared in the year 698 (*i.e.*, 1298) on the Ozy, that is, the Dnieper, with an army of thirty tumans (*i.e.*, of 300,000 men), but the river not being frozen that winter he could not cross it, and retired to spend the summer on the Don. Nogai did not then pursue, but the next year he crossed the Don with his family under the pretence of persuading Toktu to submit their differences to a Kuriltai. He really wished to surprise him while his army was scattered. Toktu assembled his people hastily, and a struggle ensued at Tejesmari (?) on the Don, in which Toktu was defeated, and retired to Serai.† Polo describes this fight in very general terms. He tells us the two sons of Tuda Mangu fought on Toktu's side, and that like himself they escaped after the defeat.‡

Toktu was not long in raising a fresh and more numerous army, and Nogai deemed it prudent to repass the Dnieper, but pillaged the town of Krim *en route*, and carried off a great number of prisoners. These having been released his troops were greatly discontented, and made secret overtures to Toktu to pass over to him, and to surrender Nogai if he would pardon them. Upon hearing of this intrigue Nogai's sons fell upon the guilty parties. They in turn persuaded Taga or Teke, Nogai's second son, that they intended to recognise him as their sovereign. When he accordingly joined them, they put him under arrest. Chaga, his elder brother, then marched against and defeated them, and soon after Teke escaped in the night with the 300 men who had been nominated to watch him. Toktu determined to take advantage of these disturbances. He crossed the Dnieper with sixty tumans (*i.e.*, 600,000 men !) and encamped on the borders of the river Berka, *i.e.*, the Bug, "where his enemy's yurt was," and whither Nogai repaired with thirty tumans of araba suwar (*i.e.*, nomades in carts). Pretending to be ill, he reclined in his araba, and sent word to Toktu that he and his army had long been faithful to the Khan, and that he had passed his life in his ancestors' service. That he was now borne down with old age. If any fault had been committed it had been done by his sons, and he asked pardon. While he thus parleyed, he treacherously ordered his son Chaga to cross the river some distance away, and to surprise his rival. Toktu having ascertained this from a spy whom his outposts had seized, ranged his men in order of battle. The fight was fiercely contested, and Toktu won. Nogai's sons thereupon retired with 1,000 men to the country of the Kelards and the Bashkirs (*i.e.*, the Hungarians). Nogai having been wounded in his flight by a Russian,

---

* D'Ohsson, iv., 754.   † *Id.*, 760.   ‡ Yule's Marco Polo, ii., 500-1.

asked to be taken before Toktu, but he died *en route*, while Toktu returned to Serai.*

From Novairi's narrative we may add a picturesque episode. He tells us that while his sons fled, the old chief himself would not move. He was then very old. His long eyebrows hung over his eyes. He was accosted by a Russian soldier in the service of Toktu. "Take me to Toktu," he said, "I am Nogai." The Russian thereupon cut off his head and carried it to his master, who was much affected and ordered the soldier to be put to death, saying it was not right that a simple soldier should put a prince of the blood to death. The death of Nogai occurred, according to Novairi, in the year 699 (*i.e.*, 1299).† The great chief had lived on terms of friendship with the Ilkhans Abaka and Argun. His son Buri, whom he had sent to Persia, married a daughter of Abaka's. When the strife broke out between him and Toktu he sent several embassies to Gazan to ask his aid, and offering to become his vassal. Toktu, although at feud with Gazan, also sent envoys to counteract the effects of Nogai's advances. The Ilkhan thereupon summoned the envoys of both sides. He told them he should not mix himself up with their quarrels, and counselled them to live peaceably together, and to prevent all misunderstanding he did not as usual go to winter in Arran, but remained in Mesopotamia.‡

Nogai fills a notable place in history. The important person he was in the Russian Steppes is best shown by the fact that the tribes over whom he there ruled still call themselves by his name. Madame de Hell disputes this etymology, but the matter is beyond doubt, and as we have already seen the colonies he left behind in Hungary were called Nogais, even during his life. He dominated over the Steppes from the Don to the Danube, and was suzerain also over the kings of Bulgaria. His chief camp, as I have said, was on the Bug. Pachymeres has a curious story that one of Nogai's right-hand-men, named Kuximpaxis (which he says means chief of the Magi, and who was probably a chief Shaman), on his master's death took ship with his wife and children and set sail for Persia, but, in consequence of contrary winds, he fell into the hands of the Romans at Heraclea Pontica, and having asked for pardon, and promised to become a Christian, he with all his household were baptised.§ Von Hammer calls him Kasimbeg.

Nogai left three sons—Chuke, the Tzakas of the Byzantines, Teke, and Buri—and two daughters, one called Togulja, whom he married to Taz, the son of Munjuk, an officer of Toktu's, and who had a son named Aktaji,‖ and a second called Kayan, who was married, as I have already mentioned, to the Kunkurat Yailak. Chuke, whose mother was called Alakka,¶ succeeded his father over a much diminished heritage. He soon distinguished himself in Bulgaria. Terteres, the king of that country, had fled from the attacks of Nogai, who had put Smiltzos on

---

* Rashid in D'Ohsson, iv., 761.   † D'Ohsson, iv., 754.   ‡ Rashid, D'Ohsson, iv., 760.
§ Stritter, iii., 1085, 1098.   ‖ Novairi, D'Ohsson, iv., 753-4.   ¶ Pachymeres, Stritter, iii., 1080.

the throne in his place, and had taken refuge at Adrianople, where he was concealed, the Emperor not daring to give him an open asylum. Chuke had married the daughter of Terteres, and had thus certain claims to the throne; he accordingly entered the country, which he speedily conquered, and put Osphentisthlabus, his wife's brother (who is called Sairuja by Novairi), on the throne at Tirnova, which was then the Bulgarian capital.*

A war soon after arose between the sons of Nogai. Teke and his mother, and the mother of Buri, tried to persuade Chuke to make peace with Toktu, his father's enemy. This so enraged the latter that he had them put to death.† The murder seems to have raised up a party in the Horde against him, headed by his brother-in-law Taz, and his general Tunguz, who made an incursion into Bulgaria and Russia.

They determined on their return to siege Chuke, but he escaped with 150 horsemen to the country of As (i.e., to the Kuban), where 10,000 of his troops were encamped. The Alans were subject to Nogai, according to De Guignes.‡ His camp was pillaged by Tunguz and Taz; but his troops rapidly increased in numbers, and he at length marched at their head against these two chiefs and defeated them. His sister Togulja fought against him on this occasion. The defeated party demanded assistance from Toktu, who sent his brother Buzluk with a contingent.

Chuke, feeling himself overpowered, fled to Bulgaria, which is called Vlakh by Abulfeda,§ to his brother-in-law, Osphentisthlabus, who had him removed to his capital, Tirnova. Fearing the revenge of Toktu this ignoble person had his benefactor executed by some Jews—who were accustomed, we are told, to execute state officers—and his head was sent to the Krim. The patriarch Joachim, who was suspected of intriguing with the Tartars, was also executed.‖ These events took place in the year 1300. The appanage of Nogai was now divided by Toktu among his own family, his brother Seraibuka receiving a large share. Only a small following apparently remained with Turi or Buri, the surviving son of Nogai and the son-in-law of the Ilkhan Abaka, who determined in 1301 to avenge the deaths of his father and brother, and persuaded Seraibuka to rise in rebellion against Toktu. The plot was disclosed to the latter by another of his brothers, named Buzluk, who had been asked to join. The Khan had both Seraibuka and Buri seized and put to death, and gave Seraibuka's portion to his own son.

After the death of Buri, Kara Kijik, the son of Chuke, with two of his relatives, called Jirek timur and Baltatlu, and about 3,000 followers, fled

---

* Pachymeres, Stritter, iii., 1880-81.   † Rashid, D'Ohsson, iv., 762.

‡ De Guignes, iv., 350.   § Annales, v., 177.

‖ Abulfeda, v., 177; Novairi in D'Ohsson, iv., 756; Pachymeres, Stritter, op. cit., 1061; Von Hammer, Golden Horde, 273.

to the country of Shemshemen, and halted at a place called Badul, near Gaeuk, where they were well received by Shemshemen, and settled in his country, whence they made many incursions into the country of Toktu, during the rest of the latter's life.* I can make nothing of these names except the last, which is clearly the Jaik or Ural; they probably refer to some portion of steppe beyond the Jaik, where the Nogais were so powerful at a later era.

Here the continuous story of their history for a while ends, and we can only resume our march with certainty at a later period. It is however possible to fill up the gap with certain conjectures which are at least plausible. During the reigns of Toktu's successors, Uzbeg and Janibeg Khan, the power of the central authority at Serai was too firmly settled for any discontented rebels to make their influence felt. When, however, "the hump of the camel was broken," in the person of Berdibeg, the son of Janibeg,† matters assumed a different aspect. The family of Batu Khan was extinct, and there was room therefore for a bold venture upon the crown. This was at first occupied by Khizr, of the family of Sheiban, but we are told by Abul Ghaffar how Zenkireh Nogai, jealous of the intrusion, and claiming himself to be the best heir to the throne, drove away Khizr, and installed his son Kara Nogai as Khan. I have told the story of these princes so far as it is known in the fourth chapter of this volume. They were probably descended from Nogai himself. At all events they seem to have ruled over Nogais. Their names are singularly suggestive of their having done so. This line of princes being entered in the lists as Khans of the Golden Horde, and some of them having coined money, I have classed them as Khans of the Golden Horde,‡ and have already considered their reigns, and may now pass them by and continue the story at another point.

As I have suggested, the effect of Toktu's victories was to drive the greater part, if not the whole of the Nogais, beyond the Volga into the country of the Jaik and the Yemba. There, as I believe, they were divided into two important sections ; one of them occupied the southern part of this country, which was afterwards called Great Nogaia, and became more or less sophisticated by Muhammedanism. The other settled on the borders of the Bashkirs, retained its old religion and customs, and founded the so-called Khanate of Siberia, to which I shall revert presently.

We will now limit ourselves to the Nogais proper. When Urus Khan and Toktamish were struggling as rivals for the throne of Kipchak, we are told that Idiku, a Beg of the Manguts, entered the service of the famous Timur otherwise known as Timurlenk. It is from this Idiku that the various Murzas of the Nogais claim to descend. Speaking of

---

THE NOGAIS, KARAKALPAKS, AND SIBERIAN TARTARS. 1021

him, Abulghazi says that one called Kutlugh Kaba, of the tribe of the Ak Manguts, had a son and a daughter. The son was Idiku. The daughter became the wife of Timur Bek Oghlan, whose son was Timur Kutlugh Khan.* It is not improbable that Kutlugh Kaba was descended from the line of princes founded by Zenkireh Nogai, above named. Sherifuddin tells us that when Toktamish was defeated by Urus Khan, and sought refuge at Samarkand, Idiku, who was in the service of the latter, also went there, and announced to Timur the approach of an army which Urus had despatched in pursuit of Toktamish.† I have described in the fourth chapter the struggle which ensued, in consequence of which Toktamish secured the throne of Kipchak. After this we are told by Abulghazi that Idiku separated from him and rejoined Timur Kutlugh. The latter was very jealous of Toktamish, and desirous of securing the throne for himself. Toktamish therefore determined to kill him, and accordingly Timur Kutlugh repaired to the court of the great Timur, and was followed six months later by Idiku.‡ It was doubtless the hospitality extended by Timur to his rival that caused Toktamish to assail the empire of the former, and to thus bring about his own ruin.

In the famous campaign which ensued, and which I have descr ibed, Idiku, or Idiku the Uzbeg, as he is called by Sherif ud din, was one of the principal advisers and guides of Timur,‖ while his elder brother Isa beg is named among the commanders of the army of Toktamish.¶ After the defeat of Toktamish, Guneji Oghlan, Timur Kutlugh Oghlan, and Idiku Oghlan were rewarded with precious kaftans and robes with jewelled girdles, richly caparisoned horses, etc. They then requested from Timur that they might be permitted to return to collect their tribes and ulusses which had been scattered and dispersed in the recent troubles. Timur granted their wish, and also gave each of them a diploma exer pting their subjects from any capitation tax. They acccordingly returned home. Guneji alone returned to his patron, the other two had other ambitions. Timur Kutlugh was determined to secure the Khanate of Kipchak for himself and Idiku to become its Warwick.**

The latter is next found supporting Timur Kutlugh in his struggle with Toktamish and Vitut,†† and after the great defeat of the latter, he sent a joint letter with Timur Kutlugh to Timurlenk, in which both offered

---

* I have taken this sentence from the old French translation of Abulghazi, published at Leyden in 1726. In the edition of Desmaison, which is here doubtless founded on a faulty MS., Timur Kutlugh Khan is made the father of Idiku, which is quite impossible. Vide Leyden ed. 46a; Desmaisons, 170-72.   † Sherifuddin, ii., 281.   ‡ Op. cit., 171
§ Ante, 239, etc.   ‖ Sherifuddin, ii., 73.   ¶ Charmoy, Mems. St. Pet. Acad., iii., 435.
** Sherifuddin, iii., 122.3; Exped. de Timur by Charmoy, Mems. St. Pet. Acad., iii., 437, 467.
†† Vide ante, 261-2.

their homage,* and we are told that thenceforward he treated the Khan
of Serai rather as an equal than as his master.† On the death of Timur
Kutlugh in 1399 or 1400, the throne of the Golden Horde was practically
at his disposal, and he placed Shadibeg, the brother of Timur, upon
it. Shadibeg was deposed in 1407, and Idiku put Puladbeg in his
place.‡ He now undertook an expedition into Russia, which I have
already described.§ From this he was recalled to assist Pulad, his
protege, who had been attacked in his absence by Timur, the son of
Timur Kutlugh, but he arrived too late, and was himself obliged to seek
refuge among his Nogais, who then wandered in the steppes north of the
Black Sea. During the reigns of the four sons of Toktamish, who ruled
successively at Serai, he remained apparently in retirement there, and is
heard of only in connection with his perennial struggle against Vitut and
the Lithuanians. At length we again find him nominating a Khan at
Serai, namely, Chekre, who is called a relation of his by Abul Ghaffar,‖
but the new protege had only a reign of seven months, when he and his
patron were both driven away by Ulugh Muhammed. In 1431 we find
Idiku struggling with Kadirberdi, a son of Toktamish,¶ but this was his
last performance, for he was sharply attacked by that Khan. Some say
he was then killed, others that he escaped, and was drowned in the
Sihun. Abul Ghaffar reports that having been wounded in the battle he
hid away among the reeds, where he was discovered, and killed by Ulugh
Muhammed. For twenty years he had more or less dominated over the
Khans of the Golden Horde as patron and protector. Von Hammer
says he was a crafty, artful, and enterprising man. He had a very
dark complexion and a square countenance; he was a patron of
learning and a benefactor to the poor, and was a faithful observer of the
laws of Islam. His name became the generic one of the Nogai
Hordes.** Ibn Arabshah says he left twenty sons (the history of Kazan
thirty), to each of whom he left a large army.††

The next page in our story is singularly confused. On Idiku's death
two of his sons, namely, Gazi Nurus and Mansur, found refuge in Russia,
while two others, Keikobad and Nuruddin, escaped at the same time to
Turan.‡‡ These four princes we shall revert to presently, but they and
their following did not constitute the whole of Idiku's people. As we
have seen he left other sons. We have no definite information to lead
us to their identification. It is at least probable that many of their clans
joined in forming the new Khanate of Krim, and that Shirin, Barin, and
the other begs who put Ulugh Muhammed on the throne of Krim§§ were
sons of Idiku. Nurus and Mansur were the rulers of two Nogai tribes,
which still bear their names, and which have been closely united in their

---

* Vide ante, 261-2.   † Von Hammer, Golden Horde, 366.   ‡ Ante, 265-6.   § Ante, 266-8.
‖ Ante, 271.   ¶ Ante, 274-5.   ** Hist. of Krim Khans, Journ. As. xii. N.S., 380.
†† Von Hammer, Golden Horde, 384.   ‡‡ Langles, op. cit., 391-2.   §§ Ante, 449.

history.   We are told they were accompanied to Muscovy by Ghayas ud
din, the son of Shadibeg, and by 3,000 brave and determined Tartars.
Not feeling at home in Russia they determined to return.   They elected
Ghayas ud din as their leader, and undertook to fight under his banner
until they had secured him the crown.   They accordingly attacked
Shirin beg, who had supported Ulugh Muhammed, and who was the
ancestor of the Shirin begs, so well known in the history of Krim.   The
struggle was severe, but Ghayas ud din was successful, and Ulugh
Muhammed's people fled.   Haidar beg, the leader of the Kunkurats,
alone stood firm with a number of his slaves, but having been wounded
he also withdrew and joined his master in the Krim.*   Ghayas ud din,
according to Langles, reigned only a year and a half.   On his death he
says that "Kuchuk Muhammed, who was very young, was put on the
throne by Mir Mansur, who was one of the greatest of the Tartar chiefs,"
but who threatened to depose him if any one more fit appeared.†

Meanwhile Borrak Khan, the son of Urus, was living in the neigbour-
hood of Azak, and Mansur sent envoys to offer him the crown.   When
Borrak had mounted the throne he proceeded to put Mansur to death.
This caused great troubles among the Tartars, and Gazi Nurus and other
grandees fled to Kuchuk Muhammed, who had been deposed.   After
killing Mansur, Borrak exiled all his supporters to the mountain
Kakhan.   Their privations were very great, and driven to despair
they also joined Kuchuk Muhammed.   A fiercely contested battle now
followed, in which Borrak was killed and his people fled.‡   Borrak was
apparently killed in 831 of the hej., i.e., 1427-8.

Josafa Barbaro confirms this story, and tells us how, when Kuchuk
Muhammed invaded the Kipchak, he was supported by Nurus, the son
of Idiku.§   Kuchuk was supported also by Seyid Ahmed,‖ whom I
have ventured elsewhere to identify with the brother of the Sheibanid
Khan Ibak.¶   Seyid Ahmed had great influence with the Nogais, and is
said to have imported a large number of them into Europe,** and they
doubtless formed the main portion of the so-called Horde of Seyid
Ahmed, also called the Blue Horde.††   When he was captured and
imprisoned in Lithuania, they were largely left without a leader and were
apparently incorporated with the Krim Tartars.

Let us now revert to the tribes of Mansur and Nurus.   Of the
descendants of Mir Nurus himself I have no information, and it would
seem that his tribe was afterwards subordinate to that of Mansur.
Mansur's descendants are enumerated in a well-known table published
by Butkof, but it is a mere arid list of unimportant names (vide note,
end of chapter).   The most important fact it contains is that Idaik

---

* Langles, op. cit., 393-3.   † Id., 394.   ‡ Id., 395-6.   § Ante, 395.
‖ Ante, 392-3.   ¶ Ante, 980.   ** Ante, 393.
†† Vol. Zernof, Khans of Kazim of, i., note 49.

sultana, the daughter of Musek, son of Asek, son of Temsurba, son of Mansur, married Feth Girai, the son of Mengli Girai of Krim, and became the mother of Safa Girai, the famous chief of Kazan, of whom I have had much to say.* This alliance no doubt brought the Mansurs into much closer intimacy with the Krim Khans, and we find that Sahib Girai, the uncle of Safa Girai, employed Baki bey, an Amir of the Mansur tribe, to rid him of his kalga, Islam Girai, who had proved rebellious.† To recompense Baki bey for his services on this occasion Sahib Girai gave him the tribe of Atai Khoja, in addition to that of Sijivit, and raised him above the other chiefs.‡

The Mansurs come prominently forward again during the reign of Muhammed Girai the Third, of Krim, when they were governed by a chief called Kantemir, i.e., blood of iron.§ We are told he was very powerful, and had the right to use horsetail standards, like the Turkish Pashas. He lived near Akkerman, and was not disposed to submit to the Krim Khan. An open feud shortly arose. It would seem that a large part of the tribe Mansur then lived in the Krim, where Kantemir formerly also lived. Shahin Girai, the brother of the Krim Khan Muhammed, proceeded to murder the latter's family in the most cruel manner, as I have described.‖ He then ravaged the towns on the Danube, and was eventually defeated in a severe struggle by Kantemir, who marched against him at the head of 30,000 men from the Dobruja.¶ Kantemir afterwards invaded the Krim, and made two unsuccessful attempts to capture Bagchi Serai.**

The struggle was renewed during the reign of Inayet Girai, as I have shown,†† and it was only in the reign of Behadur Girai Khan, who reigned from 1637 to 1641,‡‡ that the Mansurs were finally subdued and pacified. It would seem that they then migrated largely to the Krim. Peyssonel tells us the second of the four great clans in the Krim was called Mansur Oghlu, and that its chiefs intermarried with those of the Krim Khans; he adds that a branch of the Mansur Oghlus still lived among the Nogais, and bore the name of Karacha.§§ The former followed the fate of the other Krim Tartars, whose history I have described in the seventh chapter. The latter apparently remained with the Nogais of Akkerman, otherwise called the Bujiak Tartars. When in 1770, as I shall show presently, a large migration of Nogais took place from the steppes of Southern Russia to the Kuban, the Mansurs, and Nurusses, who had lived with the Bielogorodian or Akkerman Tartars, went there also. They lived, when Klaproth wrote, beyond the Kuban, in permanent villages, the houses of which, like those of the Circassians, were

* Ante, 388, 400.   † Nouv. Journ. Asiat., xii., 366.   ‡ Id., 368.
§ Von Hammer, Krim Khans, 116.   ‖ Ante, 542.   ¶ Id.   ** Id., 543.   †† Id., 544.
‡‡ Nouv. Journ. Asiat., xii., 440.   §§ Op. cit., ii., 272-3.

composed of wicker work, covered with clay or plaster.* The Mansurs
or Mansurofs were also definitely called Manguts. Pallas tells us they
were governed by their Prince Murfakgirei ; they were removed in the
year 1790, together with the Nogais of the Kassaiaul, to the banks of the
Kuma during the expedition entrusted to Lieutenant-General Bibikof.
" Of these people there still remain," says Pallas, " fifty-seven nobles and
eighteen hundred subjects within the line of Caucasus ; they all are at
present governed by the commandant of the fortress of Constantinogorsk,
in whose district they possess their pasture grounds.   The remainder
of this tribe, who continue on the opposite bank of the Kuban, lead a
wandering life between the Laba and the Urup."†

Pallas mentions another section of the Nogais whom he classes as
belonging to the Horde of Kassai, who were probably, from their
chiefs' names, also Mansurs.   He says they lived among the Abassins
on the banks of the Great Selenchuk and the Urup or Warp.   A
great part of these Nogais, he says, " were removed to the banks of
the Kuma during the expedition commanded by General Tokelli in the
year 1787, when they inhabited what is commonly called the Mount of
Serpents, in the promontory of the Beshtau, under their Prince Arslanbek
Mansur.   In the summer of 1793, however, they left their former
habitations and emigrated to the source of the Kalaus.   They lead a
wandering life, like all the tribes of the Nogais, yet do not neglect the
cultivation of millet, though their flocks afford them the principle means
of support.   Three brothers of the before-mentioned Prince Mansur
have settled with their Ulussians beyond the Kuban, and occupy the
narrow defile of the mountains of Urup, where the rivulet Inal falls into
the passage on the right, as well as the banks of the two rivulets Tegen
which flow into the Urup on its left side."‡   It would seem that i
is in reference to these Nogais that Klaproth has the following
notice.   He calls them Mansurs, and says they consisted, when he
wrote, of 450 families, and formerly resided in the country contiguous
to the lower part of the Great Injik, about twenty-five versts from .
the Russian boundary line, but were then removed to the river Chotz,
which empties itself thirty versts below the conflux of the Great and Little
Laba into the left of that river, but as they led a roving life and had not
room enough there, " it is not improbable," he adds, " that they will
soon return to their former pastures."   Their princes were Akhmet Girai,
Mansur Oglu, and the two nephews of Colonel Atashuka Shamursin, by
his sister, Musa and Murza Bek Mansur Oglu, who lived peaceably with
their subjects.   As all their princes belonged to the tribe of Mansur
Oglu, they were called by the Russians Manssurowzi, and by the
Circassians Mamzirru'ko.   Among them resided Bekmurza Mansur
Oghlu, a brother of Arslan Bek, who lived on the Russian side.   Bek-

---

Klaproth, Travels in the Caucasus, 161,   † Pallas, op cit., i., 405   ‡ Id., 421.

5 H

mursa himself originally resided among the Russians, but fled with his
subjects, and committed many murders and depredations; but after
the death of his brother Kelman-Bek he joined his nephew. When
Klaproth wrote, he led a peaceable, roving life. . . . Those Nogais
dwelling beyond the Kuban, on the two rivers Injik, might have
been easily persuaded to return to the Russian side before they removed
to the Chotz; but the incapacity and avarice of the officers on the
frontiers proved incessant obstacles. The road to them was very good
in spring or autumn, and their cattle grazed on the Little Injik, only
seven versts from the boundary line. In summer they kept them in the
Black Mountains, and in winter at their auls. They lived in felt yurts,
and often changed their place of abode. They maintained a good
understanding with the Abasses of Lou and Dudaruk, as also with
the Beshilbai.*

In regard to the Nurus Nogais, Pallas says they consisted when he
wrote of only thirty-six murzas or nobles and about four hundred of the
lower order of people, who lived under the protection of Russia near
the Beshtau. The tribe formerly comprised 2,000 families.† Klaproth
says they consisted of 650 families and were of the Akkerman horde.
They resided near the Lower Laba, opposite to the fortress of Kaukaskaya
and Ust-Labinskaya, and were akin to the Nurus, who were settled
on the Russian side. Their chief princes were Kara Murza, Ibash
Oglu, Bahatir Shah Kassai Oglu, Roslan-beg-Achmat Oglu, and
Kelmik Adshi (or Hadshi) Oglu. After some disputes among them,
Roslan-beg and Bahatir Schah placed themselves under the authority
of the Beslenie, and the others under that of the Temirgoi, both
Circassian tribes. They were extremely addicted to plunder, and their
most courageous leader was Arslan Girai Urus Oglu. They had
pastures on both sides of the Laba, where their cattle were kept in
enclosures. In autumn and spring they left the Laba and drove
their flocks and herds to the Chalmik, or Chelbok.‡

When Mengli Girai of Krim finally crushed the power of the rulers of
the Takht Il, or the main branch of the Golden Horde, he seems to have
transplanted a considerable number of Nogais from the district of the
Volga. Many of these were settled between the Danube and the Dniester,
in the district generally known as Bessarabia, and called Bujiak by the
Tartars. Thence they were known as Bujiak Tartars. They were also
called the Akkerman or Bielogorodian Horde, from the town of Akkerman
(i.e., White Town) or Bielegorod, which was their headquarters. Peyssonel tells us that Mengli Girai compelled them to abandon their nomadic
habits and build themselves houses. He granted land to their Murzas,
and administered the district very much in the same way that the Krim
was governed, their chiefs drawing a tax from their subjects as

* Klaproth, op. cit., 292-3.   † Op. cit., i., 420-3.   ‡ Klaproth, op. cit., 296.

they did in the Krim.[*] We have only fragmentary notices of these Tartars. In 1637, after the famous rebellion of Kantemir, in which they probably shared, we are told that Inayet Gerai transported the Bujiak Tartars to the Krim, and made them swear to be 'obedient to the Khan in future.[†] This transportation can only have been partial, however. About the year 1660 we are told that Muhammed Girai of Krim marched against the Nogais who lived close to the Turkish frontier, i.e., the Bujiak Tartars, who refused to obey him. The Turks, on whom these Nogais now immediately depended, resented this, and the Khan was deposed.[‡] It would seem that these Nogais had been specially granted a settlement near the Danube by the Porte, which even went further, and in order to break down the power of the Krim Khans transferred to them, their own protegés, the crown lands on the Dniester which had formerly belonged to the Khan.[§] This settlement in the south of Bessarabia, however, only lasted for three years, for on the complaints of the voivodes of Moldavia and Wallachia as to their predatory habits, they were remitted back once more to their steppes.[||] This seems to have led to an open revolt, and we are told that the Nogais living near Akkerman having rebelled against the Porte, Selim Girai Khan, who mounted the throne in 1668, was ordered to transport them to the Krim. The Khan accordingly crossed the Dniester and transplanted them, but they gradually found their way back again.[¶]

In 1701, when Devlet Girai Khan was at issue with his brothers, as I have mentioned,[**] one of them, named Gazi Girai, fled from the Krim, went to the Nogais, with whom he made a raid on Poland, and then passed into Bessarabia. The Khan having marched against him, a large number of Nogais determined apparently to settle in Bessarabia and Moldavia, in the so-called refuge of Khalil Pasha. Among these Nogais the clans of Ormit and Orak are named. They each compounded for their tithes by a payment of 1,000 piastres and of 800,000 aspres for the current year. A few months later 800 families of these Nogais were transported from Bessarabia to the Krim.[††] Two years later we read of an outbreak among the Nogais caused by the extortions of Yusuf Pasha, the Governor of Otchakof. We are told he marched into their country and oppressed them very cruelly for three months, compelling each household to furnish ten kilos of wheat, ten of barley, and an ox. A commission was appointed to inquire into this, consisting of the Judge, Mollah, and Mufti of Babatagh, the Judges of Kili, Ismael, and Akkerman, who were told to restore to the Tartars in the neighbourhood of Tomorofa, Ismail, and Kili the property of which they had been plundered.[‡‡]

* Op. cit., ii., 309.   † Von Hammer, Osm Gesch, iii., 265.   ‡ Nouv. Journ. Asiat., xii., 442.
§ Von Hammer, Osm Gesch, iii., 584. || Id., 584-5.   ¶ Nouv. Journ. Asiat., xii., 443.
** Ante, 564.   †† Von Hammer, Osm Gesch. iv., 54-5.   ‡‡ Id., 49.

In 1707, 6,000 Nogais from the Bujiak assisted the Krim Khan Kaplan Girai in his campaign against the Circassians.[*] In 1711, we are told that the Porte ceded to the Nogais a strip of country thirty-two leagues long and two wide between the Pruth and the Dniester.[†]

In 1727, we find the Kalga Adel Girai arousing a revolt against the Khan Mengli Girai the Second of Krim. The latter, with the Governor of Otchakof, had an interview with the murzas of these Nogais, the Kowais(?), and the Karachas (i.e., a section of the Mansurs), and the result was that they were again granted the district between the Dniester and the Pruth which had been made over to them in 1711 and confirmed to them in 1721,[‡] and they agreed to pay a fine of 1,000 purses to the Porte for their recent outbreak. The next year, those Nogais who had settled in the so-called refuge of Khalil Pasha in Bessarabia, were at the request of the Moldavians, whose borders they had molested, transported to the neighbourhood of Ismail and Akkerman, and their pastures were duly separated from the Bujiak Nogais proper.[§]

During the reign of Hakim Girai Khan the oppression of the Nogais of Bujiak by the Krim Tartars caused grave discontent and several revolts, which I have already described.[‖] These disturbances led eventually to the deposition of the Khan, and it was largely through the influence of the Nogais that his successor, Krim Girai, mounted the throne.[¶]

A few years later the Nogais were visited by Baron de Tott. This was during the reign of Maksud Girai, who mounted the throne in 1767. I shall abstract his account, which chiefly relates to the Great Nogais, further on. We now reach the period when Peter the Great was so successful in his wars with Turkey. These wars were largely fought in the district of Bessarabia, and apparently put an end to what little independence there had been among the Bujiak Nogais. Many of them gradually migrated to Turkey, and settled in the Dobruja, and others, doubtless, went to the Kuban, in company with the Great Nogais, when they returned thither in 1770. Bessarabia was finally annexed by Russia in 1812.

THE GREAT NOGAIS.

Having collected the broken history of those subjects of Idiku who remained west of the Volga, we will now turn to a much more important branch of them who were known as Great Nogais. When that chief fell it would seem that the greater part of his people fled to the east

---

* Von Hammer, Osm Gesch, iv., 93.　　† Id., 241.　　‡ Id., 241.　　§ Id., 242.
‖ Antr, 583.　　¶ Id., 524.

of the Volga, and encamped on the Jaik and the Yemba, and we are told that two of his sons, named Nur ud din and Kaikobad, went to Turan. Nur ud din became the founder of the power of the Great Nogais. He was the father of Okas, or Vakas, which, as M. Vel. Zernof says, is an Arabic name. The author of the Sheibani Nameh tells us Okas was a contemporary of the great Abulkhair Khan.[*] Okas was the father of Musa, Yamgurchi, Aisan or Hassan, and of a fourth son named Khuarizmi bek, who was killed in the struggles of Sheibani and Musa with Burunduk Khan. Musa and Yamgurchi were the sons of one mother.[†]

It seems that during Abulkhair's reign these princes were subject to him. On his death, Khuandemir tells us that among the leaders of the revolt against his house were the Manguti, Abbas (? Okas), Musa, and Yamgurchi.[‡] They apparently followed the lead of Ibak, the ancestor of the Sheibanids of Turan, in alliance with whom Yamgurchi and Musa, as I have described,[§] fell upon and killed Ahmed Khan of the Golden Horde, who was Yamgurchi's brother-in-law.[‖]

We now find the Nogais acquiring considerable influence at Kazan. There was a struggle in the Khanate for supremacy between the two brothers Muhammed Amin and Ali Khan.[¶] The latter was supported by the Nogais, while the Russians, who somewhat dreaded an alliance between them and the Kazan Khan, naturally supported Muhammed Amin.[**] In 1487 Ali Khan was attacked by the Russians, who carried him off with them. Two years later, we are told, the Tzar Ibak, i.e., the ruler of Tiumen, together with the murzas Alach (? Okas, or perhaps his son Hassan), Musa, and Yamgurchi and his wife, sent letters to Moscow to try and obtain his release. Yamgurchi, as I have said, was brother-in-law to Ahmed Khan, and his wife was therefore a princess of the Golden Horde. I have described the answer of the Grand Prince elsewhere.[††] Ivan permitted Musa, who is here called the grandson of Idiku, to give his daughter in marriage to Muhammed Amin, but he would not allow the latter prince to unite his sister in marriage to Yamgurchi's son. The latter s people, in alliance with the inhabitants of Astrakhan, were in the habit of plundering the Russian fishermen on the Volga.[‡‡]

Another Nogai chief who is prominent at this time was Timur, who is called the uncle of Musa by Karamzin,[§§] and who was therefore the brother of the Okas above named. He was a close ally of the Astrakhan Khans, and is styled the Amir ul umera of Kassim Khan by Khuandemir.[‖] Timur's daughter, Nursaltan, was a famous person in the politics of this period, having married successively Khalil and Ibrahim, Khans of Kazan, and Mengli Girai of Krim.[¶¶]

* Vel. Zernof, ii., 243.   † Id., 245.   ‡ Id., 235.   § Ante, 326.   ‖ Golden Horde, 408.
¶ Ante, 374.   ** Karamzin, vi., 228.   †† Ante, 376, 981.   ‡‡ Karamzin, vi., 236.
§§ Id.   ‖ Vel. Zernof, op. cit., ii., note 31.   ¶¶ Vide ante, 376, et seq.

In 1499 we read how Yamgurchi and Musa, who had attacked Abdul
Latif, the Khan of Khazan, doubtless, as the champions of his brother,
Muhammed Amin, were defeated by the Russians.[*] This is the last
mention I can find of Yamgurchi, who probably died soon after.
According to the genealogical table already cited, he left three sons,
Urastla, Aguish, and Kujash. Musa took an active part in the affairs
of the Sheibanids. We are told by Abulghazi[†] that a strife arose between
him and the Kujash Murza, by whom, Kujash, the son of Yamgurchi, is
doubtless meant. Victory declared itself for the latter, upon which Musa
took counsel with his people, and it was determined to appeal for aid to
Bereke sultan, the famous rival of Sheibani, to whom he accordingly
went. I have already described the issue of the struggle which
followed,[‡] how Kujash was killed, and his camp plundered. When
Sheibani was engaged in his early struggles with Burunduk Khan, we are
told by Khuandemir that he was visited at Sighnak by an envoy from
Musa, inviting him to go to the Desht Kipchak, assuring him that his
master would side with him, put him over the Khanate, and serve him
faithfully. He accordingly went, and was well received by Musa.
In alliance they fought against Burunduk Khan, and defeated him,
whereupon Sheibani called upon Musa to fulfil his promise, but
the latter would not on the ground that the Mangut amirs were not
agreeable.[§]

In the year 1505 we find Muhammed Amin, the Khan of Kazan,
invading Russia with a force of 40,000 Kazan people, and 20,000 Nogais.
I have described these events elsewhere,[‖] and will only add here that
during the siege a prince of the Nogais, who was Muhammed Amin's
brother-in-law, and therefore a son of Musa, was killed.[¶]

At this time the Nogais sent several kindly emisssaries to Russia, who
generally took presents of horses, and negotiated for liberty of trading.
In 1507 the Grand Prince wrote to Hassan and other Murzas, telling
them they must not assist Muhammed Amin, the Tzar of Kazan, and
reminding them of his good nature in setting free one of their young
princes who had been captured by the Russians.[**]

In 1509 Timur, who was in the service of Vasili, and is probably the
same Timur already mentioned, went to the camp of Musa, and of
Hassan, the son of Yamgurchi (? his brother), to try and persuade them
to organise an expedition for the rescue of Sheikh Ahmed, his relative
and friend, who was then a prisoner in Lithuania.[††]

We do not again read of Musa. According to the genealogical table,
he left five sons—Shigai (who was killed at Astrakhan), Idiak (i.e.,
Sediak), Sheikh Mamai, Doru, and Isup or Yusuf. A fifth, named
Ismael, was afterwards famous, and Herberstein mentions a sixth, named
Cossum (? Hassan).

---

* Karamsin, vi., 360.   † Op. cit., 201-2.   ‡ Antt, 878.
§ Vel. Zernof, ii., 242.   ‖ Antt, 379.   ¶ Karamsin, vi., 423.
** Karamsin, Germ. ed., vii., note 15.   †† Karamsin, vii., 220; antt, 345-7.

In the first years of the sixteenth century we find Sheikh Ahmed, the chief of the Golden Horde, having a fierce struggle with Mengli Girai, of Krim, and we are told that the former was assisted by "Mamai bey, one of the descendants of Idiku,"* who was no doubt the Sheikh Mamai of this account.

In 1509 Muhammed Girai defeated Aguish, Akhmed Ali, and Sediak murzas of the Nogais, who, in alliance with Abdul Kerim Khan, of Astrakhan, had attacked the dominions of the Krim Khan.† Aguish was the son of Yamgurchi, while Akhmed Ali and Sediak are probably the sons of Musa, called Sheikh Mamai and Idiak in the above list.

We now reach the date when Russia was visited by the famous Herberstein, who went there in 1517 and 1526 as an envoy from the German Court to the Grand Prince Vasili Iranovitch. He tells us the Nogais then lived beyond the Volga, in the neighbourhood of the Caspian, chiefly by the river Jaik. They had no kings, but were ruled by chiefs or dukes, *i.e.*, by murzas. When he was in Russia, he says three brothers gained possession of these duchies, and divided the provinces equally between them. The first of them, Shidiak, held the city of Seraichuk, with the district immediately adjacent to the river Jaik. The second, Cossum (? Hassan), had the territory between the Kama, the Jaik, and the Volga, while the third, Sheikh Mamai, held a portion of Siberia, with the country immediately surrounding it.‡

Sediak was clearly the senior prince of the three. He is mentioned as having had a struggle with a Kazak chief named Ahmed Khan, who, we are told, was killed by the hand of Uruk Murza. Uruk is said to have been the brother of Kil Muhammed, both of them having been sons of Alchaghir (?), the brother of Sediak.§

In 1522 Muhammed Girai, of Krim, in alliance with Sheikh Mamai, marched against the Khan of Astrakhan, and drove him away.‖ Presently Mamai grew suspicious of his ally, and fancied he meant to subdue the Nogais. We are told he was thus addressed by his brother (really his cousin) Aguish : " What are we doing, idiots that we are, assisting a neighbouring and ambitious power whose aim it is to subdue us one after another. It is time to alter our policy, or we shall be too late." Mamai listened, and persuaded the Krim Khan that his soldiers would suffer in discipline if allowed to remain in the town, and recommended him to have them camped outside. Muhammed consented. He also gave himself up to pleasure, and took no pains to protect his camp against surprise. The conspirators suddenly surrounded his tent, and put him, his son Behadur, and several grandees to death. The Nogais then made a general assault on the camp, and pursued the

---

* Nouv. Journ. Asiat., xii., 354.   † Karamzin, vii., note 10.   ‡ Herberstein ed. Hack., ii., 73-4.
§ Vel. Zernof, ii., 275-6.   ‖ *Ante*, 851 ; Karamzin, vii., 136.

Tartars to the Don, where many of them were drowned. They still followed, entered the territory of Krim, and laid much of it waste, and when the chiefs there mustered a force of 12,000 men to oppose them, completely defeated them also. This happened in 1522.[*]

In 1530 Safa Girai, the Khan of Kazan, whose mother was a Nogai princess, descended from Mansur Murza, the son of Idiku,[†] and who had himself married Mamai's daughter, was assisted by his father-in-law with a contingent of 30,000 men in resisting a Russian attack on Kazan.[‡]   Shortly after, Safa Girai was expelled from Kazan by a popular outbreak, and we are told Mamai's daughter was sent back to her father.[§]   Safa Girai was succeeded by Jan Ali, a boy of only fifteen, and we are told how in 1533 a deputation of the grandees of Kazan went to Moscow to ask permission for their young chief to marry the daughter of Yusuf, a powerful murza of the Nogais, so as to secure peace with that Horde.   Vasili consented to the match.[‖]

Yusuf, as we have seen, was the brother of Mamai. The daughter who married Jan Ali fills an important rôle in the subsequent history of Kazan, as I have described.[¶]   Her name was Suyunbeki (? Eaalei).[**]   Jan Ali did not like her.[††]   He was killed in an insurrection in 1535, whereupon Safa Girai was recalled from the Krim, and married his widow, Yusuf's daughter.

During the same year we have several notices of other Nogai chiefs. In May, 1535, the Murza Sediak (i.e., the brother of Mamai, already named), sent Tik Duvan and Koshdaulet as envoys to the Grand Prince to complain of the robberies of the Tartars of Gorodetz (i.e., of Kasimof), who had *inter alia* waylaid Barak and forty others who were under his protection, and plundered Sultanah, his envoy, who was returning from Kazan. At this time the Nogais dominated over the Khanate of Astrakhan; and we find Sediak boasting in his letter, just named, that the children of Timur Kutlugh, (i.e., of the Tzar of Astrakhan,) had submitted to him, as had Ibakof (? the ruler of the Sheibanids, of Turan), with all his friends and dependents.[‡‡]   The Kazaks were also becoming very powerful, and we find Daniel Gubin, the Russian agent among the Nogais, reporting that news had reached Sheikh Mamai from Urgenj that the Kazaks, who had subdued the Kalmuks, meant to attack him. Sheikh Mamai, with Yusuf, and some other murzas, was then encamped on the Yemba, and they were preparing for the Kazak attack.[§§]

In September of the same year, Gubin again wrote, reporting that the Kazaks were then at peace with the Nogais, and that Sediak had received an envoy from Kesteniora (?), brother of Izkander and uncle of Abdulla Khan, of Bukhara, who was betrothed to his daughter, who

* *Ante*, 476; Karamsin, vii., 158.   † Bethof, Gen. Tab. of the Nogais.
‡ Karamsin, vii., 189; *ante*, 391.   § Karamsin, vii., 194.   ‖ Vel. Zernof, i., anno 93.
¶ *Vide* chap. vi.   ** Karamsin, viii., 99.   †† Vel. Zernof, i., 118.
‡‡ *Id.*, ii., 323.   §§ *Id.*, 326.

had warned him against fighting the Kazaks. Meanwhile, however, the Tashkendians, who were hard pressed by the same robbers, wrote to ask the Nogais to assist them.* In October, of the same year, complaints about the Kasimof Tartars were sent to Moscow by Ismael Murza, another brother of Yusuf. On the other hand, we find the Grand Prince writing in 1534 and 1536 to Sediak and to Mamai Murza, promising to discover and to send back any of their subjects who had been carried off either to Russia or to Goredek, *i.e.*, to Kasimof.†

This is the last mention I can find of Sheikh Mamai, who, according to the genealogical table already referred to, left several sons, namely, Kasim or Kassai Murza, Khan Murza, who died childless, Bey Murza, Bi Murza, Bek Murza, and Ak Murza.

On the death of Sheikh Mamai, his brother Yusuf became the senior chief of the Nogais. In 1537 news was sent to Russia that he had defeated the Kazaks. In 1540 the Nogais made a raid into Russia, and burnt several villages. The Tartars of Kasimof thereupon attacked them, killed many of them, and rescued the prisoners they were carrying off.‡ About this time we find Kosh Muhammed and Kel Muhammed, Murzas of the Nogais, complaining of the attacks of the Kasimof Tartars.§

In 1546 Safa Girai was driven from Kazan for the second time. This is mentioned in a letter addressed by the sons of Yusuf Murza—Yunus Murza and Ali Murza—written to the Grand Prince Ivan the Fourth, in which they describe the revolutions that had recently taken place at Kazan, and their intercourse with Safa Girai.‖

Safa Girai died in 1549, and was succeeded by Utamish, the son of his favourite wife the Nogai Suyunbeka.¶ He was speedily deposed by the Russians, and carried off to Russia with his mother.** This seems to have moved her father, Yusuf, who was a chief of great influence, and was styled Prince of Princes by the Sultan,†† to try and obtain her release. He wished to marry his daughter, the widow of two Khans, to the new ruler of Kazan, Shah Ali, and to secure the freedom of her son Utamish, and a correspondence ensued between him and the Russian Grand Prince. The latter consented to Suyunbeka marrying Shah Ali, but Utamish was retained as a State prisoner in Russia.‡‡

It is quaint to read how Yusuf discoursed in his letter to the Tzar on the vanity of human grandeur, citing passages from the Koran and the Gospel in support of his position; how he implored the Russian sovereign not to shed human blood, and to become his friend; charged his late relative Safa Girai with perfidy and cruelty, and severely blamed the seditious spirit of the principal grandees of Kazan.§§

---

* Vol. Zernof, ii., 330-1.   † *Id.*, i., note 100.   ‡ *Id.*, 63-4.   § *Id.*, note 110.
‖ *Id.*, note 118; *ante*, 404.   ¶ *Ante*, 405-6.   ** *Ante*, 409   †† Karamzin, viii., 204.
‖‖ *Ante*, 409; Vol. Zernof, i., note 134.   §§ Karamzin, viii., 205.

In 1551 Ali Murza (no doubt the son of Yusuf), above named, who is described as a descendant of Idiku, and one of the principal chiefs of the Nogais, threatened to invade the Krim. Sahib Girai collected his people, marched against, and defeated him.* Meanwhile matters again became disturbed at Kazan.

In 1552 Shah Ali withdrew thence, his people being weary of his ill-government.† This was followed by an invitation to Yadigar to mount the vacant throne. He was a declared enemy of Russia, and the latter power determined to crush Kazan, which, as we have shown, was captured in October, 1552.‡ The annexation of Kazan seems to have had a very powerful effect upon the neighbouring Tartars, who began to fear for their independence, and Yusuf was apparently not loath to listen to the advances of the Turkish Sultan, Suliman, and his *protégé*, the Krim Khan, who urged him to rally to the threatened cause of Muhammedanism.§ He also allied himself closely with the Khan of Astrakhan, and his son Ak Murza (really his nephew, for Ak Murza was the son of Sheikh Mamai) married Abdulla, the cousin of Yamgurchi, who was then Khan there.‖

At this time we find the power of Yusuf somewhat on the wane, and that of his brother Ismael beginning to assert itself. In 1551 Ismael wrote to the Tzar offering him his alliance if he would allow his son Muhammed Murza to marry the daughter of Shah Ali, the Khan of Kazan and Kasimof. It seems Shah Ali had no son, and his niece, the daughter of Jan Ali, was the only available princess of the family, and the Tzar seems to have made some efforts to secure a union between the young Murza, whom Ismael had appointed to be his heir, and the latter princess, but the negotiations came to nothing.¶

Ismael, however, remained faithful to the Russians, and when Yusuf allied himself with Yamgurchi, he became the patron of Dervish Ali, who aspired to the throne of Astrakhan. In December, 1553, envoys went to Moscow from Ismael, with whom it was arranged that a Russian army should march upon Astrakhan in alliance with him to punish Yamgurchi, and also Yusuf, the latter of whom had imprisoned a Russian envoy. The envoy was named Suyunduk Kul Yusufof. The Tzar at the same time ordered the Nogai envoys, who happened to be at Kasimof, and the appanages to be sent on to Moscow.** The Russians sent three armies, which speedily captured Astrakhan, and drove Yamgurchi away, supplanting him by Dervish Ali.††

Yamgurchi, assisted by Yusuf Murza, by the Krim Tartars, and some Janissaries, tried in vain to regain the throne.‡‡

We next, *i.e.*, in 1555,§§ hear of Ismael as murdering his brother Yusuf,

---

* Nouv. Journ. Asiat., xii., 367.   † Ante, 412.   ‡ Ante, 422.
§ Karamsin, viii., 229.   ‖ Ante, 354.   ¶ Vel. Zernof, i., 93-6.   ** Id., 79.
Ante, 354-5.   †† De Guignes, ii., 384 ; Karamsin, viii., 248.   ‡‡ Vel. Zernof, i., 79.

and addressing the Tzar thus from Seraijuk: "Your enemy no longer
lives; my nephews and sons have unanimously put the reins of power in
my hands. I rule over all the clans."[*]   The sons of Yusuf were called
Yunus, Ali-Akran, Boram, Jan, and Akhmet.[†]   Ismael persuaded the
Russians to build a fort on the delta of the Volga, and another on the
Irgiz, in the present government of Saratof, where certain Nogai Murzas
refused to submit to him. The Czar confirmed these friendly communications by presents, but would not accept the title of brother or father
which Ismael wished to give him, considering these epithets incompatible
with his dignity.[‡] De Guignes tells us that Ismael now occupied the
country of the Nogais, that Kassai Murza took Teshovit, and Arslan
Murza took Murudin(?).   Kassai was apparently a son of Sheikh Mamai.
The Tzar sent envoys to congratulate Ismael, and bearing presents, who
were accompanied by Ignatius Zagriaski. He also ordered the various
officials along the Volga to take precautionary measures against the sons
of Yusuf.[§]

Presently Dervish himself seems to have begun to act treacherously,[∥]
and *inter alia* we are told he allowed Yusuf's sons to cross the Volga, where
they defeated Ismael, and killed Kassai Murza.[¶]   Kassai was probably
the Kassaim, eldest son of Sheikh Mamai, mentioned in the genealogical
table. His sons were Kariamalei Murza, Yar Arslan Murza, Uruz Murza,
and Torga Murza. Ismael, who now apparently quarrelled with these
princes, collected his clans.

To allay the disorders among the Nogais, the Tzar sent Andrew Tyiz-
kin and Gregory Velin to secure that Ismael, Arslan and Bassa (?Kasam)
should be faithful to Russia, and to promise them assistance. This was
in 1556. Meanwhile, Dervish having killed all the murzas favourable to
the Tzar, had fled and sought refuge in a small town on the Volga.
Ismael now drove Yusuf's sons entirely out of the Nogai country,
whereupon they drew nearer to Dervish. The Nogai chiefs were
much divided in their sympathies, and so hard pressed was Ismael
that he asked permission to retire to Kazan or Astrakhan, to save
himself from the threatened attack of the sons of Sheikh Mamai, with
whom he had also quarrelled. Presently he killed Arslan, and made his
peace with the family of Yusuf, and at length, no doubt chiefly by his
influence, the various murzas of the Nogais agreed to abandon the cause
of Dervish and to submit to Russia. They also asked permission to
be allowed to enter the Krim. They proved faithful for a while to their
promises, and went in pursuit of Dervish, captured his artillery, and
drove him to take refuge at Azof, and eventually at Mekka. The Tzar
informed Ismael and the other murzas that he had given orders to
Cheremisinof and his other officers on the Volga to defend the Nogais

---

[*] Karamzin, viii., 253.   [†] Bathel, op. cit.   [‡] Karamzin, viii., 255-4.
[§] De Guignes, ii., 384-5.   [∥] Anto, 357.   [¶] This last statement seems to me very doubtful.

against the Cossacks and the Crimean Tartars, and to grant them the right of trading freely. The various murzas thereupon repaired to Astrakhan, and again took the oath of allegiance. Nine of them seem to have been more or less discontented, and went to live with Devlet Girai, of Krim, with whom however they were not long in quarrelling. They returned home again, and afterwards fought against him.[*]

In 1556 an Astrakhan tzarevitch named Tokhtamish, who had lived in the Krim a long time, and whom some of the Tartars wished to set up as a rival to Devlet Girai, went to live with Ismael. The Tzar Ivan, who probably wished to utilise him against the Krim Khan, accordingly wrote to Ismael and his son Muhammed Murza, bidding them send their guest on to Moscow, and adding that this was also the wish of Shah Ali, who was a relative of Tokhtamish. Ismael sent him to the Tzar, with a suggestion that he would let him have some authority at Astrakhan, a request which was naturally refused. His envoy Bigchura and a murza named Semen or Sain accompanied Tokhtamish. In August, 1557, the Tzar sent to ask that the wife of the latter, who was then living with her father, Kutum Murza, might also be sent to Russia.[†]

We now reach the period when the famous traveller Jenkinson was on the Volga. He tells us that all the land on the left bank of that river as far as Astrakhan, and following the Caspian as far as the land of the Turkomans, was called the country of Mangut or Nogai. Its inhabitants were Muhammedans, and he says they were all destroyed in the year 1558, when he was at Astrakhan, through civil wars among them, famine, pestilence, and such plagues, so that there perished in that year above 100,000 of them. "The like plague was never seen in those parts, so that the said country of Nogay, being a country of great pasture, remaineth now unreplenished, to the great contentation of the Russes, who have had cruel warres a long time together."

"When they prospered," says Jenkinson, "the Nogais were divided into diverse companies, called Hordes, and every Horde had a ruler whom they obeyed as their king and who was called a Murza. Town or home they had none, but lived in the open fields, every murza or king having his hordes or people about him, with their wives, children, and cattle, who having consumed the pasture in one place removed to another, and when they moved they had houses like tents set on waggons or carts, and drawn from place to place with camels, in which they carried their wives, children, and valuables. Each man had at least four or five wives, besides concubines. They did not use money, and bartered their cattle for apparel and other necessaries." "They delight," says our traveller, "in no arte or science except the wars, wherein they are experts but for the most part they are a pasturing people, and have great store

---

[*] De Guignes, IF., 388.7.   [†] Vel. Zernof, i., note 155.

of cattle, which is all their riches.   They eat much flesh, and especially the horse, and they drink mares' milk, wherewith they be sometimes drunk. They are seditious and inclined to theft and murder. Corn they grow not, neither eat bread, mocking the Christians for the same, and disabling our strength, saying we live by eating the top of a weed and drink a drink made of the rain, allowing their great devouring of flesh and drinking of milk to be the increase of their strength."[*]

On his journey towards the Caspian Jenkinson went by a place called Perovolog, where the Tartars used formerly to transport their boats from the Volga to the Don and exact blackmail from the travellers of both rivers. This place was doubtless the district about Tzaritzin. After leaving there he passed a great horde of Nogais pasturing. "It consisted of about a thousand camels drawing carts with houses upon them, like tents of a strange fashion, seeming to be a far-off town." This horde belonged to a great murza called Smille (*i.e.*, Ismael),—"the greatest prince in all Nogai, who hath slain and driven all the rest, not sparing his own brethren and children, and having peace with the Emperor of Russia he hath what he needeth and ruleth alone, so that now the Russes live at peace with the Nogaians, who were wont to have mortal wars together."[†]

When Jenkinson was at Astrakhan in 1558, there was, as we have seen, a great famine and plague among the Nogais, who repaired in large numbers to that place for relief; "but they were but ill entertained or relieved, for there died a great number of them for hunger, which lay all the island through in heaps dead and like to beasts unburied, very pitiful to behold, many of them were also sold by the Russians and the rest were banished from the island." "I could have bought many goodly Tartar children if I would have had a thousand of their own fathers and mothers, a boy or a wench for a loaf of bread worth sixpence in England; but," says the old trader naively, "we had more need of victuals at that time than of any such merchandise."[‡]   On his way Jenkinson passed the mouth of the Jaik, a day's journey up which was Seraichuk, which he says was subject to the Murza Smille.[§]

In September, 1563, we find the Tzar Ivan writing to Ismael in reply to the complaints of the latter, that exorbitant dues were levied upon his people who happened to go to Russia. The Tzar said it was an old custom that those who went to Moscow paid him a certain tax, and those who went to Riazan and Kalomna paid dues to the Governor of Kolomna, whence his (Ismael's) people had got the impression that two tolls were levied on them. He said that a similar levy was made at Vladimir, and it would be better in order to avoid this that the Nogais should repair to Gorodok, *i.e.*, to Kasimof, where Tzars and Tzarevitches had long lived.

The Tzar reminded him that these princes, as well as the princes of Shirinsk, had to pay toll. Ismael had complained also that the people of Shah Ali of Kasimof had taken the best horse from his people, who were on their way to Moscow, and claimed it as a present for their khan. The Tzar seems to have inquired into these matters, and in consideration of the grievance remitted the usual payments due from envoys on such occasions.[*]

Ismael only survived this correspondence a very short time. He died apparently in the end of 1563 or the beginning of 1564; his eldest son Muhammed had preceded him to the grave, having died in 1562.[†] He was a great friend to the Russians, a friendship which conferred reciprocal benefits, since it no doubt enabled him to secure a much more stable position among his very unruly subjects.

According to the genealogical table above mentioned, his sons were Muhammed Murza, Din Akhmed Murza, Kulbai Murza, Din bey Murza, and Uruzli Murza. Muhammed, as I have said, died before him, and Ismael was succeeded by his second son, Din Akhmed, who was also on friendly terms with the Tzar.[‡] In 1564 he wrote to Ivan Vasilivitch to complain that one of his people having married a maiden at Kasimof, she had been detained by Shah Ali.[§] During his reign Kuchum Khan of Siberia became very powerful, and we read that in order to secure the alliance of his neighbours the Nogais, he married his son Ali to the daughter of Din Akhmet || Her name was Khanzadeh, and she was captured with the rest of Ali's family by the Russians in 1598.[¶]

In 1569 we find the Tzar sending Simeon Malkhof as his envoy to the Nogai Murza Uruzli, the brother of Din Akhmet.[**] We do not read of them again till July, 1577, when we are told that the Kazaks attacked the camps of Ak Murza and Bek Murza, the sons of Sheikh Mamai, drove off a number of their flocks and some of their men, and sent a messenger to Din Akhmet and to Ulus (i.e., his brother Uruzli) Murza, who told them that his master Ak Nazar, who then ruled over the Kazaks, was at peace with Russia and Tashkend, but that he desired to wage war against the Nogais on the Jaik and the Volga.[††]

This is the last mention I can find of Din Akhmet, and his brother Uruzli now succeeded to the overchieftainship of the Nogais.

Christopher Burroughs, who was at Astrakhan in 1580, tells us how on the 26th of February of that year the town of the Nogais, which he calls their Yurt, situated about three-quarters of a mile from Astrakhan, got on fire, and half of it was burnt. These Nogais, according to him, numbered about 7,000 men, women, and children, and were subject to the Russian emperor.

---

[*] Vel. Zernof, i., 93.   [†] Id., 94.   [‡] Karamsin, ix., 51.   [§] Vel. Zernof, i., 94.
[||] Karamsin, viii., 478.   [¶] Vel. Zernof, iii., 1, 2.   [**] Id., ii., 323.   [††] Id., 337.

On the 7th of March, 1580, a combined army of Krim Tartars and Nogais appeared before Astrakhan. Two of the Krim Khan's sons were with them. They sent word to the governor that they intended paying him a visit, whereupon he said he was ready to receive them, and "taking a great shot or bullet in his hand, willed the messenger to tell them that they should not want of that gear so long as it would last." After blockading the town for a few days, the allies broke up their camp, and went northwards into the country of the Nogais.*

It was apparently during this very year that the Cossacks of the Ural or Jaik founded their formidable power. I have described how after the capture of Astrakhan the Don Cossacks plundered the borders of the Volga, and laid violent hands not only on the merchants who passed that way, but even on the Tzar's envoys. Accordingly Ivan the Terrible sent an army under Ivan Murashkin, which defeated and dispersed them. One section of them went northwards, as we saw in the former chapter, under Yermak, and eventually founded the Khanate of Siberia. Another section went to the banks of the Terek, and founded a Cossack colony there, while a third body, marching eastwards along the shores of the Caspian, reached the mouth of the Jaik. There they heard from their prisoners an account of the famous Nogai capital, Seraichuk. They proceeded to attack it, and having captured it, set fire to its buildings, laid violent hands on its inhabitants, and even dragged the corpses out of their tombs. This happened in 1580, and details of it are preserved among the correspondence of the Tzars with the Nogai Murza Urus during the year 1581.† This terrible raid, and the settlement of the Cossacks on the Lower Ural, must have been a serious blow to the Nogais, who doubtless had to move their camps further north. In 1583, we are told that, incited by Muhammed Girai of Krim and by Kuchum Khan of Siberia, they ravaged the borders of the Kama.‡ The Cossacks built themselves a capital, well-known under the name of Uralsk. This was about 1584. They surrounded it with earthen ramparts, and became the terror of the Nogais, especially, says Karamzin, of Urus, son of Ismael, who ceased not to complain to the Tzar of their brigandage. The latter replied that they were vagabonds and fugitives, and beyond his control, which met with the retort from Urus: "A town of such importance, could it exist without your countenance? Some prisoners whom we have taken say they are subjects of the Tzar."§

The capture of their capital, Seraichuk, by the Cossacks of the Ural, and the settlement of those unruly vagabonds in the very heart of their country, tended still more to disintegrate the Nogais, and we now find their clans scattered in various directions. In 1594, Kuchum, the

* Hackluyt, i., 473.
† Levchine, Cossacks of the Ural; Journ. Asiat., 1st ser., xi., 267-8; Karamzin, ix., 481.
‡ Karamzin, ix., 539.   § Id., x., 99.

Sheibanid ruler of Siberia, was in alliance with some Nogais, under
their Murza Ali, who was probably Ali, the son of Yusuf.[*]   It would
seem that the villages of Meraloi Gorodok, Turash, Kirpiki, and
Malegorodzi, situated on the Barabinski steppe and on the Irtish, were
tributary to Ali.[†]

About the year 1595, Muhammed Kul, a son of Hajim Muhammed
Khan, of Khuarezm, having been defeated by the Bukharians, took
refuge with the Nogai Murza Kuchuk, who was his wife's brother.
By Kuchuk he was given up to the Russians.[‡] This Kuchuk was
apparently the son of Muhammed, the eldest son of Ismael. He is
mentioned in the Russian archives in the years 1574-8, and then lived
with his older brother, Seyid Ahmed. They had about 20,000 subjects,
the ulus of their father, and encamped in summer near Kazan, and in
winter on the Volga.[§]

In 1601 we are told that the Nogais were divided into two
sections, one subject to Urus (i.e., the Great Nogais), and another to
Kassai (i.e., the Little Nogais).[∥] In that year Alta Ulishaim and Yan
Arslan, the sons of Urus, prepared to make an attack on their uncle
Kassai, but before doing so, they proposed to put their wives and
children in safety, and to transport them to the river Iset; and
after the war to emigrate themselves, to the number of 7,000 men,
to the district between the Iset and the Mias. This plan was not
carried out,[¶] and other dissensions apparently broke out among the
Nogai princes. We read how the above-named Yan Arslan was at feud
with Ishterek, the son of Din Akhmet, and when the Tzar Boris issued
an order that they should live at peace together replied : "The
Tzar desires a miracle. He wishes the lambs to make a treaty of
peace with the wolves, and that they should drink at the same fountain."[**]
It would seem that the feuds of the various Nogai princes were in
some measure instigated by Boris, who wished in this way to prevent
them creating a homogeneous power.[††] One section is now found
molesting the Russian frontiers in Siberia, and we are told how this body,
numbering 300 men, under a prince named Urus (probably a brother of
Yan Arslan), settled on the rivers Abuga and Ui, whence he plundered
the Tartars, who were subject to Russia, and allied himself with the
Kuchumian prince Ali.[‡‡]

In 1608 this section of the Nogais made an inroad into the district of
Tiumen, and plundered many settlements on the river Pishma. The
plunderers were pursued by a Russian force under the Ataman Drushina
Yurief. They were overtaken on the other side of the Iset, were defeated,
and compelled to release their prisoners.[§§]   In 1610 these Nogais

---

* Müller, op. cit., vi., 461.   † Id., 465.   ‡ Abulghasi, 289-90.
§ Vel. Zernof, iii., note 7.   ∥ Vide ante.   ¶ Müller, viii., 6a-3.
** Karamsin, xi., 107.   †† Id., 106 ; De Guignes, iii., 387.
∥∥ Müller, op. cit., 64-5.   §§ Id., 74-5.

attacked the Bashkirs, on the river Mias, and afterwards returned in safety to the Iset.* This was, however, only a detached section, and we must revert to the main Horde.

We read that in November, 1604, the Boyard Simeon Godunof arrived at Astrakhan with full powers from the Tzar to settle the differences among the Nogais. Their principal chiefs having here assembled, they declared the Ishterek above named the senior or eldest prince, and the Russian commissary accordingly caused him to swear an oath binding himself and all the descendants of Ismael to fight to the death against the enemies of Russia, to grant no one the titles of prince or regent without the Tzar's confirmation, to cease the internal broils in the tribe, and to have no intercourse with the Shah, the Sultan, the Khan of Krim, the Tzars of Bukhara and Khiva, the Kazaks, the Shevkal of the Kumuks, or the Circassians. Ishterek also undertook to encamp near the Caspian, in the steppes of Astrakhan on the Terek, the Kuma, and on the Volga near Tzaritzin, and to subdue the people of Kassai, who occupied Little Nogaia. So that from the Black Sea to beyond the Caspian there should only be the Horde subject to himself.†

In accordance with this compact he harried the borders of the Azof Nogais, so that many of them were reduced to poverty, and sold their children at Astrakhan.‡

This treaty did not secure a long peace, however, for in 1613 we find the Nogais under Ishterek ravaging the whole Ukraine, and even crossing the Oka and assaulting the neighbourhood of Kolomna, Serpukhof, and Moscow. The motive of this attack was that he disapproved of the accession of Michael Romanof.§ He had, in fact, apparently supported the cause of the second false Dimitri, whose last foothold in Russia was on the lower Volga, where his Polish henchman retired in 1614, with his wife Marina and her son. They were all captured by the Muscovites on the Jaik, i.e., in the country of the Nogais.‖

My materials for Nogai history now become very fragmentary, and I cannot avoid regretting not having access to the Russian archives, where a long series of Nogai diplomata are preserved. The nation, however, seems to have reached a climax in its fortunes about this time. The Kalmuks swept over the steppes of the Jaik, broke it to pieces, and scattered it hither and thither.

They had probably made temporary raids west of the Altai before, but their first movement of any importance thither was in 1606, when they invaded the district of Tara, doubtless at the instigation of the Siberian princes. An army was sent against them in the spring of 1607, which was only partially successful.¶ This encounter was followed

---

* Müller, op. cit., 80.   † Karamsin, xi., 107-8.   ‡ Id., 109.   § De Guignes, iii., 387.

‖ Kelly's Russia, i., 212.   ¶ Ante, vol. i., 614.

by others during the next four years.* About 1620 the Kalmuks
suffered a terrible defeat at the hands of the Mongols, as I have
shown.† As they at the same time were hard pressed by the
Kazaks, they poured in great numbers into Siberia under their chiefs,
Karakula, Dalai, and Mergen, and settled on the Chumish, the Ob,
and the Tobol.‡ These immigrants were soon at issue with the Nogais,
who, doubtless, resented the invasion of their pastures.§

The Kalmuks, however, continually pressed westwards, and soon
reached the country of the Bashkirs. The Nogais seem to have been
driven forward, and we read how Uruslan Taisha, a Kalmuk chief,
demanded that the Bashkirs should pay him the tribute they had
formerly paid to the Nogais.‖ In 1624 there were rumours that the
latter had been again punished by them.¶

It was the Torguts who chiefly pressed upon them, and their chief,
Urluk, had much intercourse with them. The Nogai chief at this time
was Kanabei Murza, who was detained as a hostage at Astrakhan,
but who, we are told, was to be released in the spring. It would seem
he suggested that Urluk should send him some troops, and that they
should make a joint attack on Astrakhan.** This was about the year
1632. These overtures came to nothing, and in fact apparently led
to a quarrel, for we are told that in 1633, Urluk and his son Daitshing,
with the assistance of a rebellious Nogai murza named Saltania,
marched against Kanai (i.e., the Kanabei above named), and pressed
him so hard that he appealed to Moscow for help, and orders were
accordingly issued to the commanders of Tobolsk, Tiumen, and Tura, to
punish Urluk, but these towns were too far off to render any assistance.††
Kanai bore the patronymic of Tambaief; that is, he was the son of Ten
bai or Din bei, the son of Ismael. We are told that his brothers
and nephews, as also the sons of Urus and Din Akhmet, joined in the
appeal to Russia for help. Saltania is called an Altaulian murza, and we
are told that he was an unruly person, and had for many years molested
the district of Astrakhan.‡‡

In 1643, Urluk, with his sons and grandsons, moved to the neighbourhood of Astrakhan, and endeavoured to detach the Nogai princes from
their allegiance to Russia, whereupon the Russians marched against
him and killed him, with some of his sons and grandsons.§§

Not long after this, Urluk's sons, Yeldeng and Loosang, crossed the
Yaik, and entered the steppe of the Volga, where they subdued the
Nogais of the three tribes, Kitai Kipchak, Mailebash, and Etissan or
Yedissan, as well as the Turkomans of the Red Camel Horde (Ulan
tuman), living south of the Yemba.‖‖ Bell refers to this event, and

* Ante, vol. i., 614-5. † Ante, 615. ‡ Müller, op. cit., viii., 280, etc. § Id., 286.
‖ Id., 290-2. ¶ Id., 293. ** Id., 322-3. †† Id., 330. ‡‡ Id., 331.
§§ Id., 358. ‖‖ Pallas Saml. Hist. Nach., i., 59.

says that the Torgut chief, Chorluk, *i.e.*, Kho Urluk, in his march westwards to the Volga, "defeated Eyball Utzick, a Tartar prince, who lived in tents beyond the Yemba. Advancing forward, he met three other Tartar chiefs, named Kitta-haptzay, Malebash, and Etzan, whom he also defeated, and at last settled to the east of the Volga, under the protection of the Russians."[*] The greater part of the *Volga* Nogais now became subject to the Kalmuks, and followed their fortunes. The famous Torgut chief, Ayuka, who mounted the throne in 1672, also tried to detach the Nogais of the Little Horde and the mountain Circassians from their dependence on the Krim Khans, while he exacted hostages from the hordes of Kassai and Yedissan.[†] In 1673, when Ayuka did homage to the Russians, he also promised obedience on behalf of his dependents, the murzas of the Nogai hordes of Yedissan, Yembulad, Mailebash, and Keletshin.[‡] The Russians employed various methods for conciliating the great Kalmuk chief, and, *inter alia*, apparently used the good offices of the Mamadamim Urussof (*i.e.*, son of Urus), a chief of the Yedissan Nogais, and the Murza Kan Mambet, who found Ayuka encamped at a place called Kara Tepe, in the Kuman steppe.[§] During the remainder of Ayuka's reign the Nogais of the Great Horde, except a small section, which encamped near Astrakhan, were his faithful subjects. The greater part of them abandoned the steppes of the Jaik and Volga, and removed to those of the Kuban and the Kuma. In 1701 it would appear that the chief camp of the Yedissans was at Jinjik, near the country of the Circassians. | They were then partially, if not altogether subject to the Krim Khans, and we read how in 1707, in his war against the Circassians, Kaplan Girai, of Krim, was assisted by a large contingent of Nogais, of the tribes Istuakoghli (? Ishterek Oghli), Yuvarlak, Kitai Kipchak, and Yedissan, who were together known as Yaman Sadak, and who supplied a force of 20,000 men.[¶] During the confusion that succeeded the death of Ayuka, which took place in 1724, the Nogais of the Great Horde, who lived in the Kuban, and had been dependent on him, deemed it a good opportunity to break their yoke, and we are told that the Yedissan and Yembulad tribes migrated across the Krim steppes, and joined the so-called Belgorodian or Akkerman Tartars, who were under Russian protection.[**] Von Hammer tells us that the chief cause of this migration, besides the fear the Nogais had of the Kalmuks, was the fact that the tribes Yedissan and Yembulad were on bad terms with their neighbours, the Circassians, and also with the Kassai or Little Nogai Horde. After these two tribes had migrated, they were followed by the Kitai Kipchaks, who were a section of the Yedijeks.[††]

---

* Pinkerton's Voyages, vii., 281.   † Pallas, op. cit., i., 60. 1.   ‡ *Id.*, 61.

§ *Id.*, 64. | Von Hammer, Osm Gesch, iv., 34-5.   ¶ *Id.*, 94.

** Pallas, op. cit., i., 72.   †† Von Ham., op. cit., 242.

When Peyssonel wrote, the Yedissan Horde was encamped between the Dniester and the Dnieper, and that of Yembulad, between the latter river and Azof. The former was governed by a Seraskier, and the latter by a Kaimakan, appointed by the Krim Khan.[*]

During the reign of Mahsud Girai these Nogais were visited by the Baron de Tott. He tells us the two tribes of Yedissan and Yembulad were then very discontented in consequence of the Khan having recently transferred to the sultan the Ishetirack, or grain tax, which they paid.[†] They were then governed by the Khan's son, who bore the title of Seraskier, or General. He also tells us the pastures of the Yedissan tribe were separated from Besserabia by the Dniester.[‡]

"They were settled in tribes in valleys of fifty or sixty feet deep, which intersect the plain from north to south, and are more than thirty leagues in length by half a quarter of a league in breadth, the middle of which are occupied by some muddy rivulets and terminate towards the south by small lakes that communicate with the Black Sea. The tents of the Nogais were on the banks of these rivulets, as well as the hovels to shelter the numerous flocks of the pastoral people during the winter. Every proprietor had his particular mark, which was made with a hot iron on the thigh of the horses, oxen, and dromedaries; the sheep, marked with colour on the fleece, were kept in sight and strayed very little from the habitations, but all the other kinds collected in particular herds were driven in the spring to the plains, where the proprietor abandoned them till winter. At the approach of that season he went in search of them, to bring them back under his hovels." "It is very remarkable," he says, "that a single Tartar thus employed, in an extent of plain which is never less than from ten to twelve leagues wide by more than thirty leagues in length from one valley to the other, is ignorant even on what side to bend his steps, nor does he reflect about it. He puts thirty days' provisions, consisting of millet flour roasted, in a little bag; six pounds of flour are enough for his consumption. His provision made, he mounts, never stops till sun-set, puts shackles on his horse, leaves him to graze, sups on his flour, goes to sleep, and awakening in the morning continues his journey. In his way, however, he observes the marks of the herds he meets with, retains them in his memory, communicates his discoveries to the different Nogais employed in the same business, tells them what he is looking after, and in return receives such useful information as terminates his expedition." "It is undoubtedly to be feared," says De Tott (who was evidently a bad prophet), "that so patient a people, endowed with such qualities, may one day furnish a very formidable military force."

He relates his entertainment among the Nogais so graphically that I am tempted to deviate from my rule, as to describing the manners and

---

customs of the Tartars, to give it. He says of one of their tents: "It is like a large poultry basket built in lattice work, and formed in a circular enclosure, over which is a dome open at the top; a felt of camel's hair covers the whole on the outside, and the hole at the top intended occasionally as a vent hole for smoke; pieces of raw leather are used for fastening the lattice work together, and a kind of felt screen is put at the top of the smoke hole at right angles to the wind to create a draft."

His host, a murza, supplied two sheep and a kettle. The former were speedily killed and put in the latter, while spits were prepared for roasting such parts as it would not hold. A jar full of mare's milk, a little bag of roasted millet flour, some small white balls, of the size of an egg and as hard as chalk, and another pot, were also provided. Into this pot about three quarts of water were poured, then six ounces of roasted millet flour, which was carefully stirred. "The cook then asked for one of the white balls," says the Baron, "which was cheese made of mare's milk, saturated with salt, and dried; breaks it in small pieces, throws it into his ragout, contriving to stir it round in the same direction. The contents begin to thicken, and he still keeps stirring, but with difficulty at last, until the whole is of the consistence of bread without yeast." He then drew out his flat knife, emptied the kettle on his hand, and presented De Tott with a cylinder of puff-paste in a spiral form. "I was anxious to taste it," says the latter, "and I was really better pleased with the mess than I expected. I tasted also the mare's milk, which, perhaps, I should likewise have found good, but for a sort of prepossession I could not overcome.

"Whilst I was employed by so much luxury about my supper, a more interesting scene was preparing for me.

"I have already said that on my arrival the Nogais retired each of them to his hut, but showing no curiosity to see me, and I had already made a sacrifice of my vanity on that head when I perceived a considerable troop of them advancing towards me; the tranquillity, the slowness even with which they approached, could give me no uneasiness. We could not, however, conceive the motives which brought these Nogais on our side until we saw them stop at a distance of four hundred paces; and one of them advancing alone till he came near the Murza, who conducted me, communicated to him the desire the chiefs of his nation had to see us, adding, that unwilling in the smallest degree to disturb our rest, he was deputed to inquire if their curiosity would not displease me, and in case it should not, which would be the place where his companions would the least incommode me? I answered the ambassador myself, and assured him that they were all at liberty to mix with us; that amongst friends there was no distinction of place, much less any particular line of separation. The Nogai insisted on the orders he had in that respect, and the Murza rose up to point out to him the spot to which the spectators might advance, which was soon occupied by the curious troop. I approached also to take a nearer view of them, and to have the pleasure of making acquaintance with these gentlemen. They all rose upon me coming within reach, and the most remarkable amongst them, to whom I addressed myself, saluted me by taking off his cap and making an inclination of his body. I observed that the deputy had used the same ceremonial to the Murza, which surprised me the more, as the Turks never uncover their heads, but to be more at their ease, and that only when they are alone or amongst very familiar friends. It is for this reason also that the European ambassadors and their retinue go to the Grand Signor's audience with their hats on, and it would be a breach of decorum to present oneself otherwise before a Turk."* As he travelled over the steppe De Tott came across a group of Nogais collected round a dead horse which they had just been skinning. "A young man, naked, of about eighteen years old, received on his shoulders the skin of the animal. A woman who performed the office of tailor began by cutting the back of this new coat, following with her scissors the shape of the neck, the fall of the shoulders, the semi-circle which joins the sleeve, and the side of the habit, which came down below the knee. It was unnecessary to support a stuff which from its humidity already adhered to the skin of the young man. The woman tailor proceeded very smartly to form the cross lapels and the sleeves, after which the mannikin who served as a mould, sitting down squat, gave her the opportunity of stitching the pieces together; so that, clothed in less than two hours in an excellent brown bay coat, nothing remained for him but to tan this leather by constant exercise, which was accordingly the first thing he did, and I saw him presently mount a horse bare-backed to join his comrades who were employed in collecting the horses. The Tartar horses were dispersed, as we have seen, over the plains in particular droves, and distinguished by the mark of the proprietor; but as there are occasions when each individual must contribute to the public service, there is also a particular drove of horses for that purpose belonging to the whole community. This drove is kept near and within sight of their dwellings; but these animals at liberty in an open country are not easily got hold of; it is evident likewise that the choice which must necessarily be made of different horses for draught and for the saddle increase the difficulty. The Nogais succeed in this by a method which furnishes the young men destined for that sort of hunting with the opportunity of becoming the most intrepid and most skilful horsemen in the world. For this purpose they provide themselves with a long pole, at the end of which is fastened a cord, the extremity of which terminated in an eye-let, passed through the pole, forms a running knot, open enough easily to admit a horse's head. Furnished with this implement the young Nogais, mounted on horses bare-backed, the lounge of the halter passed through

* De Tott's Memoirs, i., 328-336.

the horse's mouth, ride up to the drove full gallop, observe the animal which suits them,· follow him with extreme agility, come up with him, notwithstanding his shifts, to which they accommodate themselves with wonderful address, gain on him by swiftness, and seizing the moment that the end of the pole reaches beyond the horse's ears, they slip the running knot over his head, slacken their speed, and thus retain their prisoner, whom they conduct to their depository."[*]

De Tott says he had been told that the steppes north of the Black Sea were formerly covered with forests, and that the Nogais had torn up even the smallest stumps to avoid possibility of a surprise. "But if this precaution effectually secures a nation so transportable as to move off with everything in less than two hours, it deprives the Tartars of the fuel which is so necessary in that climate. To provide against this want, each family carefully collects the dung of the cattle, which they knead, with a sort of sandy earth, and produce a turf which unfortunately smokes the Tartars more than it warms them.

"No people live more soberly. Millet and mare s milk are their usual diet. The Tartars, however, are very carnivorous. A Nogai might lay a wager that he would eat a whole sheep and win it without having an indigestion. But their taste in this respect is restrained by their avarice, and that avarice is carried to such an extent that, in general, they retrench every article of consumption of which they can dispose. It is only therefore when one of their animals is accidentally killed that they regale themselves with its flesh; but never unless they arrive in time to bleed the dead animal. They observe the precepts of Mahomet also with respect to sick animals. The Nogais watch all the periods of the disorder in order to seize the moment when, finding their avarice condemned to lose the animal, they may at least gratify their appetite by slaying at a moment before its natural death.

"The fairs of Batta and some others on the frontiers of the Nogais country procure them a sale for the immense droves they are possessed of. The grain, which they collect in abundance, finds a vent likewise by the Black Sea, as well as wool in general, and that kind called pelades, i.e., wool removed from the skin of dead animals with lime. To these articles of commerce must be added some bad leather and a great quantity of hare skins. These different articles combined procure the Tartars very considerable annual returns, which they will only receive in Dutch or Venetian ducats; but the use they make of them destroys every idea we might be led to form of their wealth from this prodigious quantity of specie.

"Perpetually accumulating, and no part returning into circulation by any kind of barter, avarice takes possession of and buries all the riches, and the plains they are concealed in offer not a trace to aid

* Op. cit., 344-5.

those researches which they otherwise might tempt. Several Nogais dying without communicating their secret have already deprived the world of considerable sums. It is also to be presumed that these people are persuaded that if they were forced to abandon their country they might safely leave their money without forfeiting their property, and, in fact, it would be of the same use to them five hundred leagues distance. They derive no other enjoyment from it than the mere pleasure of possession; but this has so many attractions for them that a Tartar frequently takes a thing for the sole pleasure of possessing it a moment—compelled soon after to restore it, he must pay likewise a considerable penalty, but he has enjoyed it in his way and he is contented. The avidity of the Tartars never calculates eventual losses. They are satisfied with the enjoyment of momentary advantages."[*]

The Great Nogais continued to live in the district between the Bug and Azov until the year 1770, when, dissatisfied with their patrons, the Krim Tartars—who, as we have seen, had ever treated them harshly—they were permitted by the Russians to again return to the Kuban. M. Bernet, who in 1836 published an account of his journey over the Nogai steppes, tells us that when Dolgoruki attacked the Krim in 1771 a section of the Yembulad tribe was settled on the Lower Manitch and another section on the Upper, the Horde of Yedishkul on the Lower Kuban, and the Akkerman or Bielogorod Horde about Taman and Temruk.[†] At length, in the year 1779, says Pallas, after they had sufficiently evinced their predatory and turbulent disposition towards the Kalmuks, as well as the Circassians and other inhabitants of the lines of the Caucasus, some Russian troops were sent against them under the command of General Suvarof, who was empowered by the Government to re-conduct these refractory hordes to the steppe near the Dnieper. But being little accustomed to subordination, numbers of them fled across the river Kuban, and were, in the year 1788, after many struggles, completely dispersed, so that a considerable part of these fugitives became a prey to the mountainous nations. One section were settled on the steppe between the Berda and Moloshnye Vody; another one was encamped, when Pallas wrote, near the rivers Kuma and Podkuma and the mountain Beshtau; while another branch crossed the Kuban and put themselves under the protection of the Turks. Many of the last were taken prisoners at Anapa, transported to the Taurida, and distributed among the nobles of that country.[‡] The first section consisted apparently entirely of Great Nogais. It was about 1791 that they were transported from the Kuban to their new quarters between the Berda and the Moloshna. The Yedissan tribe, comprising 3,425 men, was in 1793 ruled by Bayazid bey, and had its pastures on the Moloshna; the Yembulad, with 1,103

---

‡ *Id.*, 349-52.　　† Op. cit., 81.
* Pallas, Travels in the Southern Provinces of Russia, i., 421-2.

persons, wandered on the Karsak; and the Yetishkul, with 533, on the Berda. They were attached to Melitopolsk, a district subject to the Tauridan government. They had no princes nor any other titles of distinction than those of murza, of whom the two families of Suban Kazi and Edei Oghlu had assumed the style of bey and were held in the highest estimation.[*] The Russian governor of Taurida, Privy Councillor Von Shegulin, had distributed corn among these Nogais and otherwise encouraged them to become agriculturists, a plan which was largely successful, and furnished a considerable amount of wheat for exportation from the Krim. These Nogais in summer migrated with their flocks northwards along the banks of the rivulets, sowing wheat and millet in remote places, and neglecting all further cultivation till harvest time. On the return of winter they again moved towards the Sea of Azof, where they found grass preserved for forage, and perhaps a remaining supply of the hay they previously made in the valleys.[†]

The Nogais who were removed to the Krim on the capture of the fortress of Anapa consisted, when a census was taken, in 1793, of 4,331 males and 3,593 females. They were at first distributed among the Murzas, but afterwards by order of the Court were considered as Russian subjects, and lived in their own villages, where they speedily became rich.[‡]

Klaproth tells us that the eastern part of the steppe of the Caucasus between the Kuma and the Caspian was partly inhabited by Nogais of the tribes Yedissan and Yembulad, and partly by hordes of Kara Nogais or Black Nogais and Nedishkuls (i.e., Yedishkuls).

All these Nogais are Muhammedans and strictly nomades, and each horde has its regular district for its summer and winter camp. Among them is still found the curious disease mentioned by Herodotus of the Scythians. I take the following notice from Klaproth's Journey in the Caucasus. Quoting Herodotus, he says : " When the Scythians were masters of Asia, they went thence towards Egypt ; but when they had reached Syria and Palestine, Psammetichus, King of Egypt, went to meet them, and by presents and entreaties prevailed on them not to advance. They returned therefore by way of Askalon into Syria, and left the country without doing any further mischief, excepting that some, who remained behind, plundered the temple of Urania. This temple, from all accounts that I have been able to collect, was the most ancient which this goddess ever had, and that in Cyprus owes its origin to it according to the admission of the Cyprians themselves; their temple of Cythera was likewise erected by Phœnicians, natives of Syria. The goddess hereupon sent a feminine disease among those Scythians who had plundered their temple at Askalon, and this punishment was perpetuated for ever among their posterity. The Scythians say that this disease was

---

* Pallas, i., 533.   † Id., 532-3.   ‡ Id., ii., 345-4.

a chastisement for the sacrilege; and strangers who visit the country of
the Scythians witness it in the state of those who are called by those
people Enaraeans." Hippocrates, in his "Treatise on Air and Vapour,"
in which he gives many particulars concerning the Scythians, also speaks
of these Enaraeans. " There are likewise among the Scythians," says he,
"persons who come into the world as eunuchs, and do all the work of
women; they are called Enaraeans, or womanish. The people of their
country consider this defect as a visitation of the gods, and pay respect to
these Enaraeans in order to divert a similar misfortune from themselves.
For my part, I believe that this evil is no more sent by the deity than
anything else we see, for I think that every effect has its cause, and that
nothing can happen without one." "Reineggs is the first modern who
found this kind of infirmity among the Nogais, only with this difference,
that they are not born with it, but it arises from incurable debility after
diseases, or from increasing age. The skin then grows wrinkled, the
scanty beard falls off, and the man assumes a completely feminine
appearance. He becomes incapable of copulation, and his sentiments
and actions lose the masculine character. In this state he is obliged to
shun the company of men, and to associate with women, whom he
perfectly resembles. Reineggs, however, is mistaken when he says that
these persons also wear female apparel, as they would in that case have
to dress in red clothes and veils. It is indeed common for old Nogai
women to go with nothing but an untanned sheepskin thrown over their
wrinkled hides, and a cap of the same on their heads; and thus
equipped they are not to be distinguished from those women like
individuals of the other sex."[*]

THE LITTLE NOGAIS.

By the so-called Little Nogais were originally meant the Nogais who
encamped about the Sea of Azof. They were also known as the Horde
of Kassai. Kassai was the brother of Urus, the overchief of the Great
Nogais. This we gather from the fact that the sons of Urus are
described as his nephews.[†]

It is about the year 1584 that we first meet with this tribe, when
we are told by Karamzin that the Hordes of Krim, the Azofians and the
nomade Nogais of *Kasief* (*i.e.*, of Kassai), burnt the dwellings in the
districts of Bielef, Koselsk, Vorotinsk, Meschofsk, and Massalsk. They
were defeated on the banks of the Oka by the Russian voivode Michael
Besnin.[‡] At this time the Nogais (no doubt the Little Nogais) took an
active part in the affairs of Krim. In 1584 Islam Girai mounted the
throne of that Khanate,[§] and four months after his ascension, Saadet

---

* Klaproth, op. cit., 160-1.   † Müller, op. cit., viii., 62.   ‡ Karamzin, x., 196.
§ Ante, 519.

Girai, the son of Muhammed Girai, marched against him at the head of the Nogais. The invaders were at first successful, but in a subsequent fight on the plains of Andal they were defeated, and Esni bey, the leader of the Nogais, with some other chiefs of equal rank, were killed.[*] Saadet withdrew to the Nogai steppe, but returned the following year, when a fresh fight took place, in which his brother, Mobarek, together with the bravest among the Nogais, fell. After this Saadet retired again to the steppe, and lived among the Nogais for eight years, and eventually died there.[†] It would seem that at this time the Nogais also made raids upon Bessarabia and Moldavia.[‡] The Turkish work cited very often by Von Hammer for the history of the Krim Khans, and known as the Seven Planets, written by the Mollah Sherif Muhammed Riza, here gives the names of the several Hordes of the Nogais, as Mansur, Oruk, Mamai, Ur Muhammed, Kassai, Tokus, Yedijek, and Yembulad.[§]

The history of the Krim Khans, translated by Kazimirski, gives the name Yedissan, and does not mention that of Ur Muhammed.[||] Karamzin criticises in one of his notes the statement of Prince Stcherbatoff that in May, 1594, Kassai, prince of the Nogais, with 8,000 of his people, and the Tzarevitch Yaruslan (really Yan Arslan), with 12,000 people of Azof, laid siege to the town of Schatzk, commanded by the voivode Massalski, who defeated them and drove them towards the river Medveditsa.[¶] Karamzin declares that Kassai no longer lived, and that the camp or Horde of Kassai alone survived, but in this the Russian historian is apparently mistaken. Kassai was probably alive some years after, for we are told by Müller that about the year 1601, Ulishaim and Yan Arslan, sons of Urus, and nephews of Kassai, marched against the latter.[**]

This is the last mention I can trace of the founder of the Horde. Two or three years later we find his ulus ruled by a prince named Barangazi, and are told he was dependent on the Turks and the Krim Khans, and that although he had often promised to be faithful to Russia, he had constantly broken his word, and pillaged its borders. Boris Godunof therefore determined to crush him, and ordered the Don Cossacks to unite with Ishterek, the ruler of the Great Nogais, in attacking him. He sent Ishterek a jewelled sabre, with a note to tell him it would either chastise the enemies of Russia, or Ishterek himself. The latter accordingly greatly oppressed the Nogais of Azof, so that a great number of them were reduced to poverty, and sold their children at Astrakhan.[††]

From this time only very fragmentary notices of these Nogais are available to me, and I shall merely mention a few prominent facts in their history. Inayet Girai, who succeeded to the throne of Krim in 1635,

---

[*] Nouv. Journ. Asiat., xii., 379.   [†] Id., 380.   [‡] Von Hammer, Krim Khans, 65.
[§] Von Hammer, Osm Gesch, ii., 550, note 10.   [||] Nouv. Journ. Asiat., xii., 380.
[¶] Karamzin, x., note 185.   [**] Müller, op. cit., viii., 62.   [††] Karamzin, xi., 108-9.

had a fierce struggle with the Nogais of the tribe Mansur, during which, apparently to secure himself allies, he removed the Horde of Oruk, which previously dwelt on the Don, to the Krim. The next year the immigrants assisted the Mansur begs in deposing the Khan.[*]

I know nothing important about these Nogais until the disturbances which occurred on the death of Ayuka, the great chief of the Kalmuks, when we are told that one of the reasons why the Yedissan and Yembulad hordes, who were Great Nogais, and had settled, as I have shown, on the Kuban, wished to migrate westwards, was that they did not agree with the Kassai or Little Nogais and the Circassians. Pallas tells us that the Kassai tribe had among it a princely family which had considerable authority among all the hordes. He says that Kasbulad was its founder—that is, in all probability, the Kassai already mentioned. He was the father of Arslan bek, from whom the descent was as follows :—

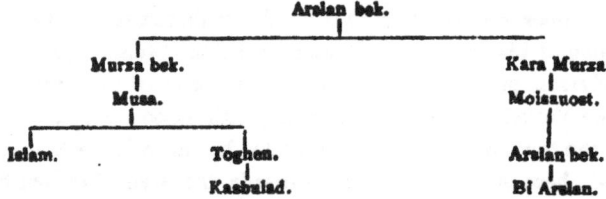

Arslan Bek, the father of Bi Arslan, was a famous freebooter, and was known as Sokur haji, or the blind pilgrim. He committed great ravages in the Astrakhan steppes, until he was defeated in 1771 by General de Medem, and did homage to Russia. His stock ended with his son Bi Arslan. Kasbulad, of the collateral branch, was held as a hostage by the Russians, and baptised under the name of Dimitri Vasilovitch Taganof. He commanded at Mozdok during the visit of Pallas.[†]

Pallas says the Kassais, together with the Nurusses and the families attached to the nobles of Islam and Akhlof, were removed to the banks of the Kuma, between the rivulets Tanglik and Psemuka, but the greater number of them deserted across the Kuban. The whole of this tribe formerly consisted of 8,000 families. In addition to those properly-styled Kassai there was a section of the race named Kasbulad, doubtless from the progenitor of the ruling stock among the Kassais already named. Of this section there were left when Pallas wrote, seventy-two murzas and 4,300 of the ordinary Tartars, who lived under the protection of Russia, within the lines of the Caucasus; a third section, named Kanchak, of whom the Russians controlled sixty-five murzas and 2,500 men, seems also to have formed a part of the same Horde.[‡] The senior chief of the Kassai Horde when Guldenstadt wrote, was called Ismael.[§] In regard to the

---

* Nouv. Journ. Asiat., xii., 438-9.   † Op. cit., i., 425.
    ‡ Id., 423.   § Beschreibung der Kauk. Länder, 174.

Nogais living north of the Caucasus generally, I find the following résumé of their recent history in Wahl's "Land of the Tsar." He says the Nogais of the Kuban are divided into five tribes, i.e., the Tokhtamishes, Mansurofs, Kipchaks, Kara Murzas, and Nurusofs. "There are now," he adds (i.e., in 1874), "about 16,500 individuals of this tribe in Russia, who are all Muhammedans, and occupy themselves with the breeding of cattle and horses. In 1860 they were still living, to the number of 40,000, in the north western part of the Azof country, but these, together with the Crimean Tartars (80,000), have since emigrated to Turkey. It is said, however, that many of them have since come back."[*]

In the wars of Russia with the Krim Khans at the end of the century a large section of the Nogais sided with the former and formed their advanced guard. They were afterwards allowed to settle on the Sea of Azof and were granted certain privileges. Some of them lived in kibitkas and others in underground huts. In 1801 they were put under the superintendence of Count Dumaison, who caused houses to be built for them, and endeavoured to introduce settled habits among them. Other Nogais who had submitted to Russia were planted on the steppe between the Molochna and Perekop. In 1804 German colonists began to settle here, and the land was divided into farms. The Nogais in this district now ceased their nomadic life and became settled Russian subjects.[†]

When the Russians overthrew the Khanate of Astrakhan, a considerable number of Nogais detached themselves from the Great Horde, and settled about that town. Their subsequent history was that of the Tartars of Astrakhan. They are apparently divided into the two sections of Yurtofs and Yemeshnis, and now number about 10,000.[‡] Another small section of the Nogais settled on the Samara, where it adopted the manner of living of the Bashkirs.[§]

THE KUNDURS.

As I have shown, some of the subjects of the Great Nogai Khan encamped in the plains north of the Caucasus, doubtless in company with the Alans, who were also subject to him. It was thither that after his death one of his sons repaired, and it is not improbable that the clans which had been subject to him remained more or less subject to his family. The focus and centre of this Horde was the town of Majar, which, according to Guldenstadt, was formerly occupied by Nogais.[||] I am now strongly of opinion that Mamai, who filled such a notable place in the history of the Golden Horde as a king maker, etc., and whose history I have detailed elsewhere,[¶] was a Nogai. The form of his name, "Mamai," is

* Op. cit., 175.   † Schlatter, op. cit., 881-89.   ‡ Vide ante, 357-8; Wahl, 18.
§ Georgi Besch. Aller Nat., 158. || Klaproth, Caucasus, 238.   ¶ Ante, ch. iv., passim.

exactly that which the name Muhammed takes among the Nogais.
Now we are told that the Tartars who rove about in the neighbourhood
of the ruins of Majar, relate that this place was the residence of the
Khan Mamai, while the Russians in the vicinity give this place the
name of Mamaiski Gorod.*

I may here add, that Bell, of Antermony, tells us that he passed
near Simbirsk a mound of sand which was pointed out to him as Mamai's
grave.†

Majar and its district were terribly ravaged in Timur's campaigns,
and we do not hear of it again for a long time. At length, on the
collapse of the Golden Horde, we find a remarkable movement among
the Circassians. Led by a race of martial princes, they migrated
largely from their old haunts about the Beshtau, and occupied the two
Kabardas and the neighbouring districts. This was apparently about
the end of the fifteenth or the beginning of the sixteenth century. This
movement thrust out the old Tartar inhabitants, who had, as I have
argued, been subject to Nogai, and forced them into the mountains,
where they were divided into several sections. The most important of
these is called Tartar Kusha (i.e., Mountaineer Tartars), by the
Circassians. The Georgians call them Bassiani, and they live near the
sources of the Kuban, Baksan, Chegem, Nalchik, Cherek, and Argudan.‡

"Their elders report that they long ago lived in the steppe of
the Kuma, as far as the Don. They assert that the ruins of Majar
are the remains of their former capital; that when driven thence
they retired to the Kabarda, whence again they were driven by the
Circassians, to whom they are now subject."§ They are divided into
three main sections, named from the rivers where they live, the Baksans,
Chegems, and Balkars. Their manners and customs have been minutely
described by Klaproth.

Another large section of these Mountain Tartars are called Karachais,
or more properly, perhaps, Karaaghachi.

They are mentioned by Father Arch. Lamberti, who visited Mingrelia
about the middle of the seventeenth century. He says : " The Karacholi
also are seated to the north of the Caucasus. They are called by some
Karaquirquez, that is, Black Circassians. Their complexions are very
fair, so that this name was probably given them only because the
atmosphere of their country is always gloomy and overcast with clouds.
They speak Turkish, but so fast that it is difficult to understand them.
I have sometimes been puzzled to conceive how they could have
preserved the Turkish language in its purity among so many different
nations."‖ " They assert," says Klaproth, " that they removed from Majar
to the district they now inhabit before the migration of the Circassians,

* Klaproth, Caucasus, 299.   † Bell's Travels, Pinkerton, vii., 279.
‡ Klaproth, Caucasus, 260.   § Id., 281.   ‖ Id., 286, note.

to whom they are also subject." He says, "they live dispersed at the north of the Elbruz, which is called by them Mingi tau, on the rivers Shursuk, Kuban, and Teberde. To the east they are separated by the mountains of Kanjal, Chalpak, and Urdi; and to the north by the mountains of Avarsech, Kechergan, Baramut, and Mara, from the Circassians and Abasses. To the west they have the Abassian tribes of Tramkt, Lo'u, and Klich. Their two principal villages are Karachai, at the influx of the Kursuk into the right of the Kuban, which contains about two hundred and fifty houses, and another of about fifty houses, situated to the west of the Upper Kuban, on the little river, Teberde. The latter is of recent date, having been founded by refugees from Karachai, who quitted the principal villages for fear of incursions of the Kabardians. The road to them, which is extremely incommodious, and cannot be travelled with carriages, runs along the Kuban and Baksan."° Klaproth writes their name Karachai, *i.e.*, Black rivulet; others derive it from Kara Aghach, Black wood or forest. What is chiefly important for us is, that these Mountain Tartars are Nogais by descent. In addition to what has above been said, I may add that Pallas calls them a tribe of Nogais;† while Klaproth gives a more striking proof in comparing their language with that of the latter ‡ The history of these Mountain Nogais is very obscure, and we must limit ourselves to one incident in it. Donduk Ombo was perhaps the most powerful of the rulers of the Volga Kalmuks. *Inter alia*, he in 1736 undertook an expedition against the Krim and Kuban Tartars. On this occasion he removed about 8,000 of the Mountain Tartars we are describing, and who, by Pallas, are called Kundur Mankuts, to the Kuban, when he exacted tribute from them; but on his death they once more returned to their mountains, except about eight hundred and fifty families, whom his successor Donduk Taaishi settled on the Akhtuba.§

When the Torguts made their famous flight in 1770 these Kundur Tartars sought refuge on the islands of the Volga under the fortress of Krasnoyarsk, and thus escaped being carried off. They afterwards returned once more to the Akhtuba, where they became free subjects of Russia.‖ There lived with these Kundurs a body of Buruts or Black Kirghises, who were carried off to the Volga with some Sungarian fugitives in 1758.

In confirmation of the Nogai origin of the Kundurs I may mention that Pallas found them using the peculiar arabas which are characteristic of the Nogais.°° The Russians call the Kundurs, Kundrofa. Wahl puts their present number at 11,000, which doubtless includes many Tartars of other descent. He calls them Nogais, and says of them,

° Klaproth, Caucasus, 384. † Op. cit., i., 626. ‡ Op. cit., 282.
§ Pallas, Hist. Nach., etc., i., 76-9. ‖ Id., 94.
¶ Georgi Beschreibung, etc., 121. °° Pallas, Travels in Southern Russia. i., 122-4.

"They live now in the governments of Krasnoyarsk and Astrakhan, surrounded by Russian peasants, Kalmuks, and Kirghiz, and call themselves 'Karagatch' or 'Kara-agatch' (black tree). They are nomadic, and keep camels and oxen like the Nogais; they are not cleanly, though hospitable, and have little compassion for the poor and wretched. Being but lukewarm readers of the Koran, their mollahs are held in little respect.

"The price of a wife is from fifty to one thousand roubles—an exorbitant sum when one considers the simplicity of their habits, but not difficult to explain. A family of five persons cannot do with less than £15 per annum, to which sum must be added £3 for Goverament taxes. In order to make up the sum of 115 roubles he must sell a camel (25 roubles), 2 horses (50 roubles), 1 ox (25 roubles), 5 goats (5 roubles), and 5 sheep (10 roubles)."

Having considered the Nogais, properly so called, we will now turn to two other branches of the same race, known under other names.

THE KARAKALPAKS.

Karamzin, in describing the Nogais at the beginning of the seventeenth century, tells us how they were then divided into three Hordes, one of which, called Altaul, occupied the steppes near the Sea of Aral, and had close relations with Bukhara and Khiva.† It is probable that this Horde derived its name from Alta, the son of Urus, chief of the Great Nogais, who is mentioned by Müller.‡

This horde drifted gradually eastwards, and we do not hear of it for many years. When it occurs again the notices of it reach us through the Kazaks, and we find it referred to as that of the Karakalpaks or Black Caps, so called from its head gear, as its members were also known to their neighbours under the name of Manguts, from their flat noses. There can be no doubt that the Karakalpaks were Nogais. Rytschkof, in reporting their traditions, tells us how one of them sets out that when the Tartar Tzar Mirtamurom, i.e., Mir Timur, or Timurienk, destroyed their town of Bolghar, they wandered to the mouth of the Sir, which proving to be a convenient place, they settled there. As the sun was very hot, or according to others, as a token of sorrow for having to leave their old homes, they began to wear black hats, whence their name of Karakalpaks.§ Klaproth, no doubt, in following this legend, dated the migration of the Karakalpaks in the reign of Timur, which was much too soon.

Another story reported by Murad Sheikh, and the other Karakalpak envoys to Orenburg, was that their people once lived on the hilly bank of the Volga, between Astrakhan and Kazan. They moved away when Russia conquered the two Khanates just named, being afraid that they would otherwise be plundered and subjected.* These two stories both point to no other conclusion than that the Karakalpaks were a section of the Nogais. To this may be added the further fact that their indigenous name was Kara Kipchak,† while Kara Kijik was the name of a grandson of Nogai Khan. I have little doubt, therefore, that the Karakalpaks are descended from the Alta Horde of Nogais above named. They still retain the characteristic flat faces, which gave their original name to the Manguts, and Vambery quotes a Tartar proverb, which says, " Karakalpak, Yüze yalpak, Uzi Yalpak," i.e., " Karakalpak, has a flat face, and is himself totally flat."‡ The first mention of the Karakalpaks, eo nomine, known to me is in the narrative of the traveller, Bell, of Antermony, who was on the Volga in 1715, and who tells us that Samara was a small place, fortified only with a ditch and palisades, with wooden towers at proper distances, mounted with cannon sufficient to defend it against the incursions of the Tartars, called Karakalpaks or Black Caps, who inhabited the desert east of that place.§

The Karakalpaks were formerly divided into two sections, known respectively as the Upper and Lower Karakalpaks. The Upper Karakalpaks, when Rytschkof wrote, were settled on the lower Sir Daria, from its mouth as far as Tashkend, where they lived in fixed yurts in the winter, and nomadised in summer. Although they had Khans, yet these had but small authority, the chief power being in the hands of the Khojas, of which sacred family there were many among them. They were a numerous race, but not very warlike, being to some extent agriculturists, and they had accordingly suffered considerably at the hands of the Kazaks, who had driven them from their old haunts. In consequence of this many of them, especially those who lived near the towns of Turkestan and Tashkend, had put themselves under the protection of the Sungarian Kalmuks.‖ The Lower Karakalpaks were apparently a much less numerous tribe, who lived on the Sea of Aral and the Kuvan Daria.¶ This latter section had intercourse with Russia at the beginning of the last century. About 1732 Abulkhair, the Kazak Khan, removed his camp to the neighbourhood of the Sir, or Jaxartes, whereupon the Karakalpaks, who had been much oppressed, made overtures through Tevkelef, the Russian agent, and Abulkhair, to submit to Russia, and swore fidelity to that power. Abulkhair himself, who wished to gain the favour of Russia, and to induce his own people to accept the Russian suzerainty, seems to have encouraged this submission,** which was useful to the Russians in their subsequent claims upon the district of the Lower Sir. For some years after Tevkelef's

* Rytschkof, op. cit., i., 139.   † Id., 140.   ‡ Sketches of Central Asia, 294.
§ Op. cit.; Pinkerton, vii., 279-80.   ‖ Rytsch., op. cit., i., 20-21.   ¶ Id., 20.
** Levshine, 171-2.

mission, however, there does not seem to have been any intercourse with
the Karakalpaks. At length, in 1741, Dimitri Gladyschef was sent from
Samara to the camp of Abulkhair, where he arrived in the April of the
following year. There he met some elders of the Karakalpaks, who
nomadised between the Sir and the Adamat, and who were named
Abeidulla, Murad Sheikh, Urasan Batir, Tokumbet bi, Ubilei Sultan,
and Khoja Mersen, together with three other khojas, went to him, and
offered the eternal submission of all the Lower Karakalpak Horde,
which numbered 30,000 families. He accordingly induced them to swear
allegiance, to kiss the Koran, and to append their names, those of their
families or tribes, and their seals to the formula. They also sent a letter
by him excusing their not having as yet visited Orenburg on the ground of
their civil commotions, and promising to go there with Abulkhair the
following year. This was signed by Gabai Abdulla Sultan, Murad
Sheikh, and other influential elders, and the seal was marked with three
stamps. The deputies who submitted to Gladyschef represented
about 12,000 families.* In the spring of 1742, Mamut Batir and Kushan
Batir duly accompanied Abulkhair to Orenburg, and there renewed the
oath on behalf of their people. Gladyschef was now again despatched
to secure the release of a number of Russian slaves who were held
captive by the Karakalpaks, and also to try and persuade the latter to
settle near Orenburg. When he reached their camp he was visited by
Kaip Khan (who is called the son of Ishim Khan, by Rytschkof, but who
was really his descendant),† with his two sons, Uruzkul Khan with his
son, and Gabai Abdulla, the brother of Kaip Khan, with his three sons,
who duly swore allegiance. The Lower Karakalpaks were therefore at
this time subject to Kazak princes. The elders and commonalty also
joined in the oath, which specially mentioned their three sections, the
Knuraskoi, Abinskoi, and Khitaiskoi. On his return Gladyschef was
accompanied by eight distinguished Karakalpaks and by two freed
slaves, one a Russian, and the other a Meshcheriak. In their letter the
princes spoke of their people as comprising four sans, i.e., 40,000 persons.
They asked that the Kazaks might be prevented from ravaging their
land, and waylaying their messengers. They promised on their own
behalf to send a stately embassy, to despatch 30,000 merchants to
Russia, and to set free the Russians they held as slaves. Of these
envoys, three named Maman Batir, Ablak Sheikh, and Pulad Yesaul,
were sent on to Saint Petersburg with Gladyschef.‡

· About the same time, Philat Gordeyef, who understood Tartar well,
together with the interpreter Mansur Delnoi, were sent from Orenburg
with some presents of latten and other ordinary wares for the Karakalpak
Khan and elders. They were met en route in November, 1743, by
messengers from Kaip Khan and Uruzkul, headed by the elder, Khalwet

---

* Rytschkof, i., 129-30.   † Anis, 652-3.   ‡ Rytschkof, i., 131-2.

Sheikh, the son of the above-named Sheikh Murad. The envoys who went to Saint Petersburg were well received there, and a ukaz, dated in August, 1743, set apart a certain sum for the redemption of the Russian prisoners, who it would seem were valued at no more than from five to six roubles each.   They were also received in audience by the Empress Elizabeth, who in person received their oath of submission, and promised them protection.* Gladyschef accompanied them on their way back, and bore an Imperial letter for the Karakalpak Khans and elders. Meanwhile, however, the inconstant Abulkhair, who doubtless suspected and disapproved of this intercourse between the Karakalpaks and Russia, collected a number of his people, and accompanied by his sons, Nurali and Erali, and by Janibeg Terkhan, fell unexpectedly on the Karakalpaks, killed a number of them, carried off some into slavery, and greatly harried their country. *Inter alia*, they drove off 20,000 cattle, and as many sheep, and captured one of their Khans, the Uruskul, already named, with his wives and children. He was detained as a hostage by the Kazak Khan.† The latter offered as an excuse for the raid that the Karakalpaks had refused to send him as usual a large quantity of winter provisions, on the plea that they were now Russian subjects. He also suspected that Khalwet Sheikh, who had been for some time at Orenburg, and was not on good terms with him, and whose father, Murad Sheikh, was held in great veneration by his compatriots, was planning a scheme by which the Kazaks might be crushed between the Russians and the Karakalpaks.‡ When Gladyschef and his companions reached the Little Kazak Horde on their way home, the Imperial letter was appropriated, and the Karakalpak envoys sent on alone.§ The Kazaks continued to press hard upon the Karakalpaks, and to desolate their country, and intercourse now practically ceased between them and Russia. Their fate did not improve with the death of Abulkhair in 1748. His murderer and rival, Barak, also attacked and plundered them.‖ These attacks must have been the main cause of the desolation which overspread the valley watered by the lower course of the Sir, where many canals and remains of settlements testify to the former culture of its inhabitants—a culture doubtless extending to the time of the Karakalpaks, who were an agricultural and peaceable people. When Gladyschef visited the latter in 1742 he found the stone walls and towers of Yanghi Kent more or less intact. The Khan of the Karakalpaks was then encamped within them.¶ Kaip was apparently succeeded as chief of the Karakalpaks by his son Batir, who continued his father's strife with the family of Abulkhair.** Batir's son Kaip was elected their ruler by the Khivans,†† and doubtless in consequence a large number of Karakalpaks began to settle on the lower Oxus, where they afterwards became an important element in the population.

---

* Rytschkof, 134-5.   † *Id.*, 137.   ‡ *Id.*, 137-8.   § *Id.*, 138 ; Levchine, 202.
‖ Levchine, 211.   ¶ *Id.*, 114.   ** *Id.*, 219.   †† *Ante*, 925.

The strife with the Kazaks still continued, and about the year 1750 we are told the Karakalpaks were attacked by Erali, the son of Abulkhair, who, however, was killed, while most of his companions shared the same fate.* During the next few years there was almost constant strife between Nurali Khan of the Little Horde of the Kazaks and Batir and his son Kaip.† It was probably in consequence of this that, in 1760, a large number of Karakalpaks migrated from the Lower Sir to the neighbourhood of Tashkend, attaching themselves to the Great Horde, which then dominated there.‡

At length, driven by the oppressions of the Kazaks, the Karakalpaks towards the end of the last century abandoned the Lower Sir altogether, advanced up the river, occupied the lands near the present outlet of the Jani Daria, and betaking themselves to agriculture excavated a large canal, which ultimately formed a branch of the river Sir, and is known as the Jani Daria, or New River.§ Thereupon the Lower Sir fell entirely into the hands of the Kazaks.‖ From this time the Karakalpaks may be said to have ceased to exist as an independent power. Some settled in the Khanate of Bukhara, but the greater number of them migrated to Khiva. Of the latter Vambery speaks as follows :—

"They inhabit the further bank of the Oxus, opposite Görlens, far away, close up to Kungrad, in the vicinity of extensive forests, where they occupy themselves with the breeding of cattle; they have few horses and hardly any sheep. The Karakalpaks pique themselves upon possessing the most beautiful women in Turkestan; but on the other side, they are themselves described as being the greatest idiots, and I have heard many anecdotes confirming this assertion. Their numbers are computed at 10,000 tents. From time out of mind they have been subject to Khiva. Forty years ago they rebelled under their leader, Aidost, who invaded Kungrad, but were at a later date defeated by Muhammed Rahim Khan. Eight years have hardly elapsed since they rose again under their chief, Zarlig (this was in 1855¶), who is said to have had under him 20,000 horsemen, and to have committed great devastation, until they were utterly routed and dispersed by Kutlugh Murad. Their last insurrection took place three years ago under Er-Nazar, who built himself a stronghold, but was nevertheless overcome."** Kühlewein, who was at Khiva in 1858-9, tells us the Karakalpaks in the Khanate then numbered 15,000, and that they led a partially nomadic life. They were burdened with taxes heavier than those imposed on any of the other tribes, the result being to completely impoverish them.††

After the Russians had occupied the mouths of the Oxus, there were rumours that the Turkomans had made a league with the Karakalpaks, who, according to Mr. Schuyler, up to this time had

* Levchine, 222.   † Vide ante, 66a, etc.   ‡ Levchine, 16a.
§ Michell's Russians in Asia, 305.   ‖ Id., 313.   ¶ Id., 33-4.
** Vambery, Travels in Central Asia, 348-9.   †† Michell, op. cit., 40.

been comparatively peaceable. Coloned Ivanof therefore summoned their Bis to meet him at Chimbai. The Bis were so frightened at being called that they assembled the next day, when they were told that they must furnish lists of the population. This, upon various pretexts, all but two declined to do, whereupon they were immediately surrounded by Cossacks and arrested. Being told they would not be freed until the lists had been presented, they agreed to furnish them, and on the next day handed them in. Colanel Ivanof informed them that the lists represented less than the actual population, and then the Bis—expecting death, as the Cossacks had their rifles pointed at them—immediately added more names. Unquestionably they would have made additions as long as the Russian officer desired. " By this arrest we not only did not attain our purpose, but we excited the ill-feeling of the population against us, as they greatly reverenced their Bis." The last sentence is a quotation from the *Golos*. With it we conclude our account of the Karakalpaks.

THE SIBERIAN TARTARS.

We must now devote a few paragraphs to the concluding subject-matter of our chapter and volume, namely, the Siberian Tartars. On the dispersal of the family of Nogai, I believe that one portion of his subjects migrated to the neighbourhood of the Bashkirs, and founded the Khanate of Siberia. Müller long ago pointed out that this area contains several traces of having been formerly dominated by the Nogais. In the neighbourhood of Ufa is a district through which the road to the Siberian Khanate formerly passed, which is known as the Nogai way, and when Müller himself travelled up the Irtish he heard the western part of this district called the Nogai Steppe by every one.[*] The ruins that still remain there are assigned by the Kasaks to the Nogais. The people of Khiva and Bukhara still apply the name of Nogais to the Muhammedan Tartars of Orenburg and Kazan, while the Bashkirs affirm that they themselves were originally one people with the Nogais.[†]

In addition to this may be added that one of their traditions makes the Siberian Khans descend from a Nogai chief.[‡] I have not much hesita-tion, therefore, in concluding that when the Nogais withdrew, as I have described,[§] to the frontiers of the Bashkirs, that they became the founders of the Siberian Khanate.

Let us now turn to the native Saga in regard to this Khanate. M. Veliaminof Zernof, in describing the traditions of the origin of the Khanate of Siberia, says the one preserved in the Stroganofski and

---

* Op. cit., vi., 171.   † Lehrberg, 72.   ‡ Fischer, Sib. Gesch., 148.   § Ank., 1019-20.

Esipoffski annals is alone of any value. This begins with a certain king On, a tzar of the Muhammedan persuasion, by birth a Tartar, who lived near the river Ishim, and who was killed by one of his own subjects "from among the common Tartars" called Chingis or Chingy, who made himself tzar in his place. On's son, Taibuga, escaped, but after a while Chingis knowing of the existence of Taibuga, called him to him, overwhelmed him with marks of kindness, and gave him a principality. Taibuga became a zealous adherent of Chingis, conquered many countries for him, and at last, with his assent, retired to the river Tur, and founded the city of Chingy or Chingidin.* This story is clearly but a dim legend about the Kerait chief, Wang ou Unk Khan and Jingis Khan himself, and has doubtless been built up out of Chingin or Chingidin, the name of the town. Chingi Tura simply means the largest city, the metropolis, whence the Russians named its succcessor Velika Tiumen, *i.e.*, the Great Tiumen.†

We may therefore discard On and Chingis from our view altogether. Taibuga seems to be the real traditional stemfather of the Siberian Khans, who are referred to as of the race of Taibuga, and it is not improbable that he was the descendant of Buri, who ruled over the colony of Nogais, which had found shelter in Siberia, as I have mentioned, a contention which is strengthened by the fact that the Siberian Khans were still pagans when conquered by Kuchum, Nogai Khan and his sons having been so also. Taibuga is said to have been succeeded by his son Khoja, and he by his son Mar. Mar, we are told, married the sister of Upak, Tzar of Kazan, *i.e.*, of Ibak, the Uzbeg chief of Turan, of whom we spoke in the last chapter, by whom he was put to death. Thereupon Ibak siezed and appropriated his kingdom.

Mar left a son named Obder or Ader. Obder died during Ibak's reign, leaving two sons, Yabolak or Abalak, and Mamuk or Makhmet.‡

We are told in the Saga about the origin of the Khanate that Mamuk having collected some of his people, marched against Ibak, whom he killed, and thus secured the patrimony of his ancestors. He did not settle at Tiumen, however, but built himself a new capital on the Irtish, about twenty versts above Tobolsk, in a place formerly called Kashlik, by the indigenes, which the Tobolsk Tartars call Izker, and which is otherwise known as Sibir, a name probably given it by the Permians or Sirianians, from whom it passed to the Russians.§

The date of these events is not known, but as we do not hear of Ibak after 1493, it was probably soon after that year. In May, 1496, Muhammed Amin, the Khan of Kazan, informed the Tzar, Ivan Vasil-ovitch, that he had been attacked by Mamuk, who is called the Tzar of

* Vel. Zernof, Khans of Kazimof, 386.
† Lehrberg, Untersuchungen zur Erläuterung der Altere Geschichte Russlands, 73-4.
‡ Müller, op. cit., vi., 178-9; Lehrberg, 79, 80; Vel. Zernof, ii., 387, etc.
§ Müller, op. cit., vi., 180; Lehrberg, 80.

Sheiban, and further that the Kazan princes, Kalimet, Urak, Sadir, and Agish, had proved treacherous to him   The Grand Prince sent an army to the assistance of his *protégé*, whereupon the rebellious princes fled to Mamuk, who deemed it prudent to retire.   When Mamuk heard that the Russian troops had withdrawn, he once more advanced at the head of a *great Nogai army*, and in alliance with the four princes above-named, whereupon Muhammed fled and retired to Moscow, where he arrived in November, 1496.[*]   Mamuk now became the ruler of Kazan.[†]   His rule there, however, was a short one.   He behaved very harshly, and *inter alia*, imprisoned his allies, the Kazan princes, who had rebelled against the late ruler.   He then marched to besiege Arsk, which held out bravely.   Meanwhile the gates of Kazan were closed against him, and the princes there wrote to the Grand Prince to ask him to appoint them a ruler other than Muhammed Amin.   He accordingly nominated the latter's brother, Abdul Latif, to the Khanate, and Mamuk withdrew, and died on his way home.[‡]   He was no doubt the Khan of Siberia, son of Obder, above-named.

It would seem that the Siberian Khan was obeyed by the Voguls, Ostiaks, and other Ugrian tribes of the Urals, and when in 1499 the Grand Prince sent an army to subdue the latter the attack was resented by their suzerain.   At all events, we read that in that year Abalak, or Agalak, the brother of Mamuk, in alliance with the Kazan Prince Urak, marched against Abdul Latif.   The Russian Grand Prince despatched an army, under Feodor Belski, to the latter's assistance, whereupon Abalak retired.[§]   It may be noticed that in the Siberian narrative Abalak is called the brother of Obder, while the Russians, who are probably right, style him Mamuk's brother.   Abalak is doubtless the right form of the name.   A village of Abalak, twenty-six versts above Tobolsk, on the right bank of the Irtish, and two neighbouring villages of Yebalatskoi and Abalatskoi Selo, probably derive their name from him.

The Siberian chiefs no doubt intermarried often with those of the Southern Nogais, and we are expressly told how, in 1505, Abalak's imperial kinsman, the Tzarevitch Ak kurd, father of the Tzarevitch Ak daulet, settled in Russia.[‖]   Ak kurd, *i.e.*, the White Wolf, is otherwise expressly called a Nogai prince.[¶]

Abalak was apparently succeeded by his son Aguish, who was in turn succeeded by Mamuk's son Kasim, and he by his sons Bekbulat and Yadigar.   Their reign coincided with the great conquests of Ivan Vasilovitch in the East.   As we have seen, Kazan was subdued in 1552, and Astrakhan in 1554.   In 1555 the Bashkirs recognised their dependence on Russia.   We are told that in that year one named Mitka (*i.e.*, Demetrius) Kurof, who had been sent as an envoy to Siberia, returned

---

* Lehrberg, 85.   † *Ante*, 377.   ‡ Lehrberg, 85-6 ;   *ante*, 377.
§ Lehrberg, 89 ; Karamsin, vi., 360; *ante*, 378.   ‖ Vol. Zernof, ii., 392.   ¶ *Id.*, i., 35.

to Moscow, with a representative of the Khan Yadigar, named Boyanda, bearing a tribute of 700 sable skins. This was not the whole tribute due, however, and Yadigar excused himself in respect of the rest on the ground that he had recently been attacked by the Tzarevitch of Sheiban (i.e., by Kuchum Khan), who had taken many of his people from him. This excuse did not avail, as Mitka reported that Yadigar might have sent more skins than he actually did. Boyanda was thereupon committed to prison and his property impounded, and two Tartars, named Devlet Kosa and Sabana Kasanof, were sent to the Siberian Khan to order him to send the full tribute. They returned the following year, and took with them another envoy from Yadigar, named Istimur, who brought the full tribute of 1,000 sables, as well as 100 sables for tolls, and 69 sables in lieu of squirrel skins. Yadigar also sent a letter of submission, and promised not to fail with his tribute again. Boyanda was thereupon released.*

Lehrberg says Bekbulat is not named in the Russian annals, only Yadigar.† On the other hand, Müller tells us that these annals mention two other Siberian princes at this time, namely Sembakhta, a son of Mamak, and another named Sauskan. The former name occurs in a legend in which the Tartars, with prevision of their doom, are said to have frequently seen over the site where Tobolsk now is, a Christian town with churches and bell towers, and that in the days of Senbachta the water in the Irtish and the fields on either side became blood-red in colour, and afterwards changed to black, while the high ground on which Tobolsk stands assumed a golden and silvery sparkle, whence it was afterwards called Altia Arginak, while afterwards, in the time of Prince Sauskan, fiery clouds appeared in the heavens and reached to the earth. This Prince Sauskan seems to have given its name to a place on the river near Tobolsk called the Sauskanian Curve.‡

To revert to Yadigar. He apparently ruled over Siberia until the year 1563, when we find him sending an envoy, named Chegeben, to Moscow with tribute,§ but while the latter was still at Moscow, Yadigar was attacked and killed by Kuchum Khan, as I described in the previous chapter.

Kuchum now possessed himself of the Siberian Khanate, which he held for many years.

Of the details of the conquest of Tiumen by him we know nothing.

In the Siberian Saga already referred to we read that during the reign of the Siberian princes Yadigar and Bekbulat, Kuchum invaded the land with an army, killed the two princes, and seized their country. Seidiak, the son of Bekbulat, escaped and fled to Bukhara. Another account says that on the death of his father and grandfather, Seidiak succeeded them at Sibir, where he reigned till driven away by Kuchum, when he went to Bukhara.[*]

A third legend of no value reports that Yadigar left behind him a widow of an ungainly appearance, whose offspring the Tartars did not wish to rule over them, so they sent to the Khan Murtaza in Great Bukharia, asking him to send them one of his sons as a ruler. Murtaza thereupon sent his middle son Kuchum with a considerable following into Siberia, where he was well received, and accepted as Khan. Meanwhile, Yadigar's widow repaired to Bukhara, where a Seyid had compassion on her. There she was delivered of a son, whom she named Seidiak, which the legend explains as meaning the little Seyid.[†] This last story was evidently manufactured to account for the name Seidiak, and it seems clear from all the facts that Kuchum invaded the country as a conqueror, and took it from Yadigar Khan.

For many years Kuchum Khan was undisturbed master of Siberia. I have described the terrible struggle he had with Yermak and his Cossacks, and how on the death of their leader in 1584 they with-drew westwards. Thereupon Kuchum sent his son Ali to re-occupy Sibir, but we are told he was almost immediately driven out thence by Seidiak.[‡]

In 1586 the Russians once more crossed the Urals, and, as I have shown, at once proceeded to build themselves a town near Sibir, to which they gave the name of Tiumen.[§]

Seidiak, who ruled at Sibir, had at this time with him the Kazak prince, Uraz Makhmet, who afterwards became Khan of Kasimof.[||] The latter had probably been captured by Kuchum in one of his raids upon the Kazaks, and had fallen into Seidiak's hands on the capture of Sibir. This seems probable from the fact that Uraz Makhmet is described as a prisoner in Seidiak's hands, and from other considerations.[¶] With Seidiak also lived at this time the Murza Karacha. The Cossacks did not feel strong enough to attack him, and sent to Moscow for reinforcements, and we read how in the summer of 1587 a further detachment of 500 Cossacks reached Tiumen. The Pismennoi Golowa Danilo Chulkof was now ordered to march to the Irtish, and to proceed to build a new town near Seidiak's capital. Chulkof set out, and during the year 1587 laid the foundations of the famous city of Tobolsk, on the eastern bank of the Irtish, opposite the outfall of the Tobol. A wooden fort and a church were the first buildings erected of the renowned city.[**]

During the summer of 1588 Seidiak, with the Kazak Tzarevitch, the Murza Karacha, and 500 followers, were one day hawking on

---

[*] Müller, Saml. Hist. Nach., vi., 185.   [†] Id., 184.   [‡] Müller, vi., 395.   [§] Antè, 927.
[||] Antè, 436.   [¶] Vel. Zernof, Khans of Kasimof ii., 384-399.   [**] Müller, op. cit., vi., 418.

the river Irtish, when they approached the new town, and were
duly invited by its governor to a feast, at which a treaty might be
arranged. The invitation was accepted, and the three chiefs, with 100 of
their followers, were admitted, the rest remaining outside. While drunk
with a liberal supply of brandy they were arrested, and their followers
were put to death.* When the news of this reached the body which was
encamped outside, it immediately fled, as did the Tartar inhabitants
of Sibir. They withdrew to the steppes, and thenceforward Sibir
remained uninhabited.† The three captives were sent on to Moscow
in September, 1588.

The so-called Turalis seem to be the descendants of the true Siberian
Tartars. Tura means a town in the Turkish dialects of Siberia, and
Turali, according to some, simply means the dwellers in towns. Their
name, however, is more probably derived from the river Tura, on which
they live. They occupy its banks from its sources to its outfall into the
Tobol, as well as the country between the Tawda and the Iset. Their
oldest town was the capital of the Siberian Khanate, Chingi Tura.
Many of the Turali now live in an outskirt of the city of Turinsk;
others at Tiumen; others scattered about in villages. Georgi, who
gives details about their habits, has the following interesting paragraph,
inter alia, about them: " They are the unmixed descendants of the old
indigenes of this part of the country, and apparently form a separate
stock, although they know nothing of their origin. They differ from the
Tartars, in having stout, strong bodies, and big heads and faces, like the
Kalmuks." ‡

Note 1.—Klaproth has quoted a curious passage from what he describes as a
history of the Tartars, written in the Nogai dialect, which he procured at
Mosdok, and which describes the residences of the ancient Tartar Khans.
Most of it under its present orthography is unintelligible to me, but such as it
is, it deserves a place here. It runs as follows:—

   " ACCOUNT OF THE PLACES OF ASSEMBLY AND HABITATIONS."

   "The habitations of the Khans were stone buildings.§ The residence of
one Khan was Urish (? a corruption of Urgenj), and the residence of another
Khan was Khurssan (? Khorasan). Thus the residence of the Amir Khoja
Khan was Uich Osen (?) and Toktamish Khan's residence Jam Jaik, between
Shermishen (?) and Timsadak (?) ; Jan Beg (*i.e.*, Janibeg) Khan's residence
was Ak Adil, with the name of Sarai Aldi ∥ ; Bus Agash (?) was Kara Khan's
residence ; Burn Khan's residence, Ack Thubah (*i.e.*, Akhtuba); Kuchum

------
* *Id.*, 421-2.   † *Id.*, 422.   ‡ Bosch, etc., 112.
   § Klaproth says the word used for stone buildings here is Majar.
   ∥ This was doubtless the New Serai descri ed above, page 98.

Khan's residence was on Mount Tura (i.e., Chingi Tura, in Siberia). The abode of Ubar-durg-Khan was the hill Ushal(?); Hirid Hakim Khan's was Seraichuk; Jaik Khan's was Majar. There were three other vice-Khans. Ajdrukhan (i.e., Astrakhan) was the place of abode of Timur Kutlugh Khan; Borki (i.e., Bereke) Khan's residence was at Kathatur (?); and Sheikh Ali Khan's at Kasan."[*]

Note 2.—I ought here to mention that several clans in the country of the Kuban, when Klaproth wrote, were subject to princes descended from the Krim Khans and bore the name of Girai. Thus he tells us that near the Nogais who lived on the river Khotz lived also Selim Girai Ademeyef, an atalik of Major-General Sultan Mengli Girai, descended from the Khans of Krim. His subjects consisted of forty families, with whom he was constantly engaged in plunder. He afforded protection in his aul to the notorious robber, Roslan Beg Taganof, and his brother Jambulat Taganof, who did not live with him, but among the little Abasses; yet, whenever the former went out on an expedition against the Russians, the latter repaired to the aul of Selim Girai, and there remained till the party returned, and the booty was divided.[†]

Again, after mentioning various other tribes, Klaproth tells us that there were in the regions beyond the Kuban some descendants of the Krim Sultans, who, however, had few followers. They were comprehended by the Tartars and the Circassians under the general appellation of Sultanie, and he mentions—

Murad Girai Khas Girai, who lived on the Laba, above the Naurus Aul, whose subjects were only forty families, and his brother, Devlet Girai Khas Girai, who was settled among the Abasek, in the Black Mountains, on the river Kudshups, and whose dependents were also about forty families.

The children of the Sultan Arslan Girai, and the brothers of Major-General Sultan Mengli Girai, who lived among the Nogais, on the Great Selenchuk, near Akhmet Girai Mansurof. They were in very indigent circumstances.

Another Sultanie family consisted of the children of Sultan Kasilbeg, who were dispersed in several places, and wandered from tribe to tribe. One of them, Gerik Kasilbeg Oglu, accompanied the notorious Jambulat Taganof in his predatory excursions. Both had formerly lived between the Temirgoi and the Abasek, but had fled to the Shapshik, among whom they resided when Klaproth wrote.

" They had but the empty title of Sultans, with scarcely any power. They could not compel any man to attend them in their expeditions, but were accompanied by volunteers alone."[‡]

Note 3.—The title of Murza, which is so characteristic of the Nogais, is said by Fischer to be derived from the Arabic, Amir Zadeh.[§]

* Travels in the Caucasus, 239.   † *Id.*, 252.   ‡ *Id.*, 263-4.
§ Siberische Geschichte, 194, note 14

Note 4.—Genealogy of the Nogai chiefs:—

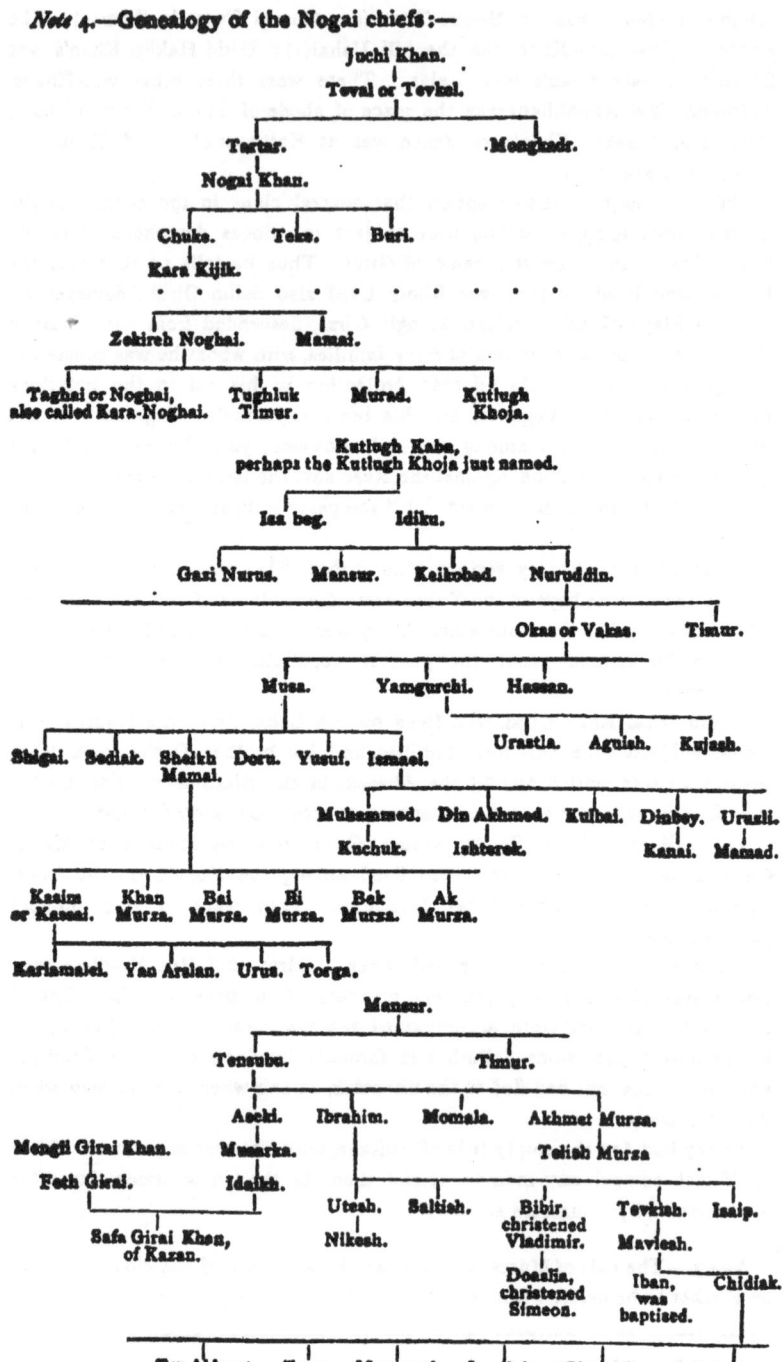

NOTES, CORRECTIONS, AND ADDITIONS.

I FEEL naturally somewhat ashamed of the following long list of corrections. They are due to several causes, the chief being that I have not been able to afford to pay for a sufficient number of revisions to free the text from the results of the infirmity of my much-enduring assistant, the printer, who has had to do his work under great difficulties in a provincial town. The subject itself is again very difficult and complicated, and at every turn there is a pitfall in the varying orthography of my authorities, while the multitude of proper names has been another embarrassment.

Page 4, line 32. A Pecheneg is mentioned as fighting in the army of Mamai against the Russians (see page 215).

Page 4, line 43, note ‡. The work by Zeuss, here referred to, is his " Die Deutschen und die Nachbarstämme."

Page 10, line 3. In reference to the area controlled by the Khans of the Golden Horde, I would remark that Alaktagh is distinctly said to have been within the jurisdiction of Batu Khan (see page 79). As to Uzbeg's zeal in the cause of Islam, I would refer to the statement of Uzbeg himself to the Egyptian Sultan, as reported by Novairi (see page 149).

Page 15, line 36. The Inkirasses are called Angirasses by others, and I have so called them on page 14.

Page 26, line 20. " The Tarikhi Mekim Khani," translated by Senkofski, says, that before the pillage of the caravan at Otrar, the Khuarezm Shah had sent Behauddin Shah as an envoy to Jingis Khan, who was then at Tamghadj. This envoy, on his return, reported that when he neared the river of Tamghadj he saw an elevated mound ten parasangs in circumference, whose surface was white, and at first he thought it must be covered with snow ; but as this could not be in that latitude, he inquired from the inhabitants, and was told it was due to the bones with which the place was covered. The Mongols had fought a battle there, and killed an incredible number of people, whose corpses had been devoured by wild beasts, and nothing remained of them but their bones. He afterwards crossed a plain, five parasangs in extent, whose soil was black and unctuous, and exhaled an intolerable odour. This was due also, as he was told, to the decomposition of the bodies of those who had been slain in the recent fight, and the air was so tainted in a circumference of sixty parasangs. On reaching the town of Tamghaj, he found its ditch also filled with bones, and was told that the citizens, afraid their wives and daughters would be violated by the Mongols who were attacking the town, had thrown them down, to the number of 10,000, from a high tower.

Jingis Khan received the envoy affably, and sent him back with presents for his master, who interpreted the politeness as a confession of weakness.*

Page 27, line 12. Berezin writes his name and title in full, as " Hal Sultan Inaljuk, Gair Sultan."†

Page 27, line 28. Ye lu chu tsai says several envoys of Jingis and several hundreds of merchants were killed on this occasion. The Yuen chao pi shi says that Wu hun, Jingis's envoy, together with 100 men, were killed.‡

According to the Yuen shi, the envoys were murdered in the summer of 1219.§

Page 29, line 15. For " Kutulkan " read " Kultukan."

" 29, " 33. For " Kankalis " read " Merkits."

" 30, " 15. For " whom " read " which."

" 33, " 1. For " them " read " the inhabitants."

" 38, " 15. On this and the succeeding paragraph, see note 1 at the end of Chapter I.

Page 38, line 44, note 1: For " Eerman " read " German."

" 39, " 2 and 26. For " Bejak " read " Bujek."

" 39, " 7. Pallas identifies with some probability the Kalka, upon which this famous battle was fought, with the small river Berda, called Kayalik by the Tartars, and which falls into the Sea of Azof at Petrofsk. Others with less probability identify it with the Kaletz, which falls into the Kalmius beyond Mariupol.‖

Page 41, line 15. Kolomna is no doubt the Iga of Rashiduddin, so named by him from the river Oka, on which it stands.¶ This is clear, since he tells us Kulkan was killed there.

Page 42, line 33. See on the Marimes or Merims, further on, page 104.

" 42, " 41. St. Martin calls him Mukan, Mems, sur l'Armenie, 268.

" 43, " 16. For " Sviattosaf " read " Sviatoslaf."

" 49, " 19. For " archbishop " read " archdeacon."

" 50, " 17. For " Moldavia " read " Wallachia."

" 57, " 16. Insert a comma after "Frangipanni."

" 59, " 35. Insert " not " between " should " and " have."

" 62, " 6. For " of " read " for."

" 64, " 28. This is a mistake. Jingis did not displace his son entirely ; he displaced his eldest son in favour of his second one.

Page 72, line 29. For " Ordu " read " Orda."

" 78, " 25. Erase the comma between "Yaroslaf" and "Yaroslavitch."

" 83, " 1. Insert " in " between " repeated " and " the."

" 86, " 5. For " He " read " Rubruquis."

" 91, " 27. Insert " the " between " in " and " cause."

" 91, " 31. Instead of "did not live until long " read " lived long."

" 92, " 28. Instead of " to " read " of."

" 92, " 30. Instead of the full stop put a semicolon.

" 92, " 43. In note ** put a comma after Fræhn, and a full-stop after Bull (i.e., Bulletin).

---

* Senkofski Supplement, 16-17.   † Brstschneider, Notices, etc., 60, note 88.
‡ Id., 54, note 79.   § Id., 60.   ‖ Travels in Southern Russia, i., 519, 520.
¶ D'Ohsson, ii., 625.

Page 101, line 5. For "Abulghazi" read "Abulfeda."

„ 101, „ 8. In the Catalan map, given in "Cathay, and the Way Thither," *Berchiman* is placed between Sarra and Borgar.

Page 101, line 33. For "most the southern" read "the most southern."

„ 102, „ 1. For "sons" read "descendants."

„ 110, „ 19. Insert "to" before "which."

„ 110, „ 33. Insert "of" after "consequence."

„ 112, „ 44, note *. In this and other notes where this work is referred to, the "c" in "Resc" ought to be erased.

Page 116, line 17. For "equally" read "correspondingly."

„ 117, „ 10. For "Tulubaka" read "Tulabugha."

„ 121, „ 18. Insert "in value" after "amounted."

„ 124, „ 16. Erase "that."

„ 125, „ 3. The Kipchak was called the steppe of Bereke Khan by the Amir Abu Muhammed Mustapha.*

Page 129, line 8. For "the" read "his."

„ 131, „ 38. Erase the comma between "stock" and "fish."

„ 134, „ 6. For "Tukta" read "Toktu."

„ 142, „ 1. Insert "the" before "Tsarevitch."

„ 157, „ 10. For "loose" read "lose."

„ 162, „ 30. For "there" read "at Moscow."

„ 164, „ 12. For "ingenious" read "ingenuous."

„ 164, „ 40. After "Sultan" read "(*i.e.,* Uzbeg Khan)."

„ 172, „ 6. For "Muhammud" read "Muhammed."

„ 172, „ 39, note †. For "ans" read "ass."

„ 173, „ 4. For "Western" read "Eastern."

„ 177, „ 7. For "Zarporogian" read "Zaporogian."

„ 177, „ 14. For "its" read "their."

„ 178, „ 18. For "metropolitan" read "patriarch."

„ 178, „ 33. Langles says Ashraf had abandoned Muhammedanism and become a Guebre or Fire Worshipper.

Page 178, line 42. For "Trebis" read "Tebriz."

„ 180, „ 9. For "Urjenj" read "Urgenj."

„ 180, „ 40. Langles, who calls Berdibeg the brother of Janibeg, says he abandoned the government of his kingdom to Taughly Tuli Bai, his first minister, by whose counsel he put to death the various princes of the royal blood.†

Page 183, line 8. Insert "after Berdibeg" after "them."

„ 193, „ 13 and 14. For "have shown in the introduction" read "shall show in Chapter XII."

„ 193, „ 18. Jullad was apparently attacked by Timur in his famous campaign. Fraehn says it was situated in the Little Kabarda, south of Ekaterinograd.‡

Page 193, line 24. On Mokshi (see also pages 43 and 103). It is possibly, as D'Ohsson suggests,§ to be identified with Mokhatahla, on the Cherek, a tributary of the Terek.

---

* See Charmoy, Mems. St. Petersburg Acad., 6th series, iii., 503. † Op. cit., 372.
‡ Golden Horde, 359, note 1. § Abul Casim, 23, note 3.

Page 195, line 26. In this line, and in several other places, I have by some hallucination written the name of this chronicler " Abdul Ghassar" instead of " Abdul Ghaffar."

Page 197, line 1. For "Nigni" read " Nijni."

„ 197, „ 20. I am now satisfied that this Bazarji was no other than the Azis Khan mentioned lower down. While the former name does not occur in the Russian chronicles, that of Azis Khan is not mentioned by Khuandemir and Abdul Ghaffar, who alone name Bazarji. The date at which each occurs favours the identification; so does the fact that no coins occur with the name Bazarji. So again does the fact that just as Bazarji owed his position to his wife Taidula, who was a person of great distinction, so also the wife of Azis Khan was a princess, treated with especial honour (vide page 205). The name Bazarji is apparently connected with Bazarchi, a place near Bukhara (see page 785). I believe Azis Khan or Bazarji to have been a relative of Mamai's.

Page 199, line 34 and 36. For "Oreng" read " Ureng."

„ 200, „ 17. For "Usbeg" read " Uzbeg."

„ 200, „ 30. For "Abdul Ghassar" read " Abdul Ghaffar."

„ 200, „ 31. The origin of this "Zekireh (i.e., Zechariah) Nughai" is a great puzzle. I have here tentatively made him and Mamai descendants of Tuka Timur, but it is not improbable, as Zekireh's second name suggests, and as I have elsewhere argued (page 1020), that both these chiefs were descended from Nogai Khan.

Page 201, line 2 and 31. For "Abdul Ghassar" read "Abdul Ghaffar."

„ 201, „ 19. Langles says Tughai reigned for three years and died in 726 hej—of course, an impossible date. He makes him be succeeded by his brother Toglu Timur, who, he says, reigned for seven years. Tughluk Timur is called the brother's son of Tughai by Khuandemir, as I have stated in the text. If Tughluk Timur be the same person as the Khan Talu beg, the nephew of Mamai, mentioned on page 213, as is not improbable, this is another proof that Zekireh Nogai and Mamai were brothers, as argued on page 203. It must be noted that the identifications in this very difficult part of the history only profess to be tentative.

Page 202, line 10. I am not so sure as I was that Merdud and Murad were not the same person.

Page 204, line 1–7. This is a mistake, as I have shown further on (page 979). Pulad was no doubt the descendant of Sheiban, and Nugan is a corruption of Mangu, which was his father's name.

Page 204, line 24. For "Abdul Ghassar" read "Abdul Ghaffar." Here again I have to modify my opinion. The Alaji Oghlu, or El haj Oghlu, here named, was not the same person as Azis Khan, but was a descendant of Sheiban (vide page 980). De la Croix calls him Alchi Khan, and says he was the father of Dervish, mentioned on page 272. He was probably also the Ali beg of Abdul Ghaffar.

Page 206, line 1. For "Bukharias" read "Bukharians."

„ 206, „ 15. An Abdulla is said, in the legends about the foundation of Kazan, to have ruled there, and to have been killed by Timur. He was perhaps a brother of Tughai.

Page 206, line 35. Erase the comma between "Karach" and "Haidar."

" 206, " 40. In the note ‖, read 204 for 202.

" 207, " 2-6. In the legends about the foundation of Kazan mention is made of Alin bek, son of Abdulla. This Alin was perhaps the Ali beg here named. I may add that Abdul Ghaffar calls Hassan the father of Ulugh Muhammed, a near relative of Toktamish.

Page 207, line 3. For "Abdul Ghassar" read "Abdul Ghaffar."

" 207, " 26. Tulun bek was not improbably the Tunka bek Kanish, son of Mangu Timur and brother of Ilban, or Ilbak, of the house of Sheiban, mentioned by Abulghazi.

Page 207, line 34. Ilban is called Ilbak by Abulghazi. I have here followed the orthography of his father's name given by M. Soret. I have elsewhere called him Mangu Timur (see page 979).

Page 208, line 20 and 21. This is very doubtful, as it would make him the same person as Ulugh Muhammed. Bulak is another form of Pulad.

Page 209, line 43. For "Khakan" read "Khan."

" 215, " 9. Vladimir was brother of the Grand Prince Dimitri.

" 216, " 31, 35, 36, 39, and page 217, line 11. For "Ghassari" read "Ghaffari."

Page 221, line 6. It is very possible that the Afghan tribe of "Mongol" or "Mangal" is descended from the subjects of Sasibuka.

Page 221, line 11 and 32, note ¶. For "Ghassari" read "Ghaffari."

" 222, " 35. On the parentage of Idiku (see further, page 1021).

" 223, " 25. For "their" read "the."

" 225, " 32. For "Ghassari" read "Ghaffari." I am not so sure that this author is after all not right in making Toktamish a descendant of Orda, and a relative of Urus Khan.

Page 228, line 8. Insert "while" before "the other."

" 228, " 14. For "Khans" read "Khan."

" 228, " 39. For "there" read "at Serai."

" 229, " 16. For "Noresmen" read "Norsemen."

" 231, " 1. For "kinsman" read "kinsmen."

" 232, " 39. For "rulers" read "ruler."

" 238, " 17. For "Azak" read "Ayuk."

" 240, " 21. For "has" read "had."

" 242, " 31. For "dear" read "near."

" 246, " 6. For "his" read "Toktamish's."

" 254, " 6. For "summoning" read "summoned"

" 254, " 44. Here and elsewhere the reference to De la Croix is to Sherifuddin, of whose work he was the translator.

Page 258, line 7 and 8. This statement about the Karakalpaks is a mistake. They did not migrate till a later time (see page 1056).

Page 258, line 39. Insert "the" before "Ordu."

" 259, " 12. Munshi makes Timur Kutlugh a son of Bughai Sultan, son of Urus Khan, and tells us that when Timur invaded the Kipchak, he went to Astrakhan, where he was proclaimed Khan.*

---

* Senkofski, 31.

Page 259, line 19.   Insert a comma between " retreat" and " on."

„ 262, „   27.   For " Tumen" read " Tiumen." It is very improbable that Toktamish was killed in Siberia, and much more likely that he fell somewhere in Russia.

Page 262, line 36.   For " Timurlenk " read " Timurlenk."

„ 263, „   4.   For " Ghassar " read " Ghaffar."

„ 264, „   8.   For " their country " read " Novgorod."

„ 265, „   32.   Dorn says* that prayers were offered at Shirvan in the name of Shadibeg and in the presence of Idiku as late as 1406, and Savilief has published a coin of Shadibeg's struck at Shemakhi.†

Page 266, line 1.   Langles also makes Pulad the son of Shadibeg.

„ 268, „   24.   For " Abdul Ghassar " read " Abdul Ghaffar." Timur was the son of Timur Kutlugh.

Page 269, line 18.   For " Abdul Ghassar " read " Abdul Ghaffar."

„ 270, „   32.   He is called Kubuk by Abulghazi, who tells us Toktamish had eight sons, and thus enumerates them—Jelal ud din, Jabbar Berdi, Kubuk, Kerim berdi, Izkander, Abusaid, Kucbuk, and Kadirberdi.‡

Page 271, line 8, 9, and 14.   For " Abdul Ghassar " read " Abdul Ghaffar."

„ 272, „   16.   At this point the story is very confused, and after much subsequent deliberation I have come to a conclusion different to that contained in the text at several points.   In the first place, I believe the Muhammed here mentioned was not Ulugh Muhammed or Great Muhammed, as Von Hammer says, but Kuchuk Muhammed, the descendant of Urus Khan, who had good claims to the succession.   The Kuidat of the Russian chroniclers was not Kibak at all, but Ghayas ud din, to whom I shall refer presently.

Page 272, line 29 and 35.   For " Abdul Ghassar " read " Abdul Ghaffar." Seyid Ahmed is made a son of Tash Timur, by Miechof, but it is more probable, as I show in another place (see page 980), that he was a brother of the Sheibanid Prince Ibak.

Page 273, line 3.   Alchi was the Sheibanid Haji Muhammed Khan, about whom see page 980 ; see also note to page 204.

Page 273, line 8, etc.   At this point I should have done better to have followed the guide of Abdul Ghaffar, as reported by Langles, whose account is the most reasonable and clear.   After naming Dervish Khan, he tells us how Kadir berdi, son of Toktamish, returned from exile and attacked Idiku, and how the former was killed and the latter was wounded.   After the fight, Mir Shirin, Mir Barin, Chekre, and other chiefs, met together, and there being no descendants of Toktamish left, they selected Ulugh Muhammed, son of Hassan Jefai, who was a near relative of Toktamish, and who had hitherto lived in obscurity, and made him their ruler.   He at once proceeded to search for Idiku, who, after his defeat, had hidden away in the reeds, and having found him, put him to death.   Two of Idiku's sons, named Nuruz and Mansur, fled to Russia with Ghayas ud din, the son of Shadibeg, who was no doubt the Kaidat of the Russian chroniclers, and who was not a protégé of Idiku's at all, as I have argued in the text, but belonged to the rival family of Urus Khan.

---

* Versuch. einer Gesch. d. Schirwan, 572.   † Schiltberger, ed. Hack., 141, note by Bruun.
‡ Op. cit., 187.

The refugees in Russia numbered 3,000 active men. They put Ghayas ud din at their head, and marched against Shirin Beg and his associates, who were defeated. Haidar Beg, a chief of the Kunkurats, stood his ground for a while, but he also at length fled, and joined Ulugh Muhammed in the Krim. Ghayas ud din reigned for a year and a half, during which he fought against Borrak, as I have mentioned (page 273). On his death, he was succeeded by Muhammed. Not by Ulugh Muhammed, as I have stated, however, but by Kuchuk Muhammed, who struck coins at Astrakhan. Kuchuk Muhammed, we are told, was very young, and Mir Mansur, Idiku's son, who was his chief supporter, threatened to depose him if any one more fit to reign appeared. Thereupon, Borrak Khan, who, it seems, had retired to Azak after his defeat by Ghayas ud din, was offered the crown by Mir Mansur. This he seems to have accepted, and at once proceeded to put his patron to death, and to exile his supporters. Mansur's brothers thereupon fled to Kuchuk Muhammed, who fought a serious battle against his rival, in which Borrak was killed, and his people fled.[*] Ulugh Muhammed, who had fled to the Krim, now returned, and attacked Kuchuk Muhammed. After several struggles, the two agreed to divide the Khanate between them, Ulugh Muhammed retaining the Krim, and Kuchuk Muhammed the country of the Volga and the Jaik.[†] This view of the various revolutions which occurred at this crooked period is more reasonable than that in the text, in which I have followed Von Hammer and other authorities. It necessitates some alterations: thus, the paragraph headed "Kibak restored," on page 273, should be headed "Ghayas ud din," and the actions there assigned to Kibak should be transferred to the latter. The next paragraph, headed "Ulugh Muhammed Khan," should be assigned to "Kuchuk Muhammed," who was no doubt the Muhammed who struck coins at Astrakhan in 1419, and who was defeated by Borrak Khan.

Page 274, line 26. For "Khandemir" read "Khuandemir." I now prefer, with this author, to make Devlet Berdi a son of Tash Timur, who was the brother of Ulugh Muhammed.

Page 274, line 32. The Muhammed here mentioned was Kuchuk Muhammed.

Page 274, line 36. The ephemeral reign of Kadirberdi, who is named among the sons of Toktamish by Abulghazi, I would now place, with Langles, before that of Ghayas ud din or Knidat (vide note to page 273).

Page 275, line 9. For "Kipchaks" read "Kipchak." Chekre is mentioned by Langles among the chiefs who originally put Ulugh Muhammed on the throne.

Page 278, line 9. Alter the comma after "times" to a full-stop.

    „   285,   „   5.   For "river" read "ruin."
    „   285,   „   25. The second "Taran" in this line should be "Turan."
    „   286,   „   20. For "Teraz" read "Terez."
    „   286,   „   25. These were the same people otherwise called Khilj.
    „   288,   „   32. For "there" read "then."
    „   288,   „   45. For "He" read "Mazarof."

---

* Langles, op. cit., 389-96.   † Id., 397.

Page 289, line 3. Lerch says Sighnak had only been abandoned within ten years previous to 1858, and its ruins still remain east of the Russian fort of Julek, near the Karatau hills.*

Page 291, line 8. Lerch tells us its site is strewn with potsherds and mutton bones, and it is threaded by canals. There are no traces of violent destruction, and the place has evidently been abandoned, and has then decayed. The Kazaks find excellent bricks for their tombs among its ruins. In one of Lerch's excavations he found a tomb with a cupola, decorated with enamelled tiles and remains of enamelled lattice-work for windows. In another, bricks decorated with arabesques. One of the mounds is reputed to be the grave of the famous nomade hero, Janjarkhan, who on account of his jealousy had his capital destroyed by serpents. Lerch found a grave-stone dated in 763 of the hej (i.e., 1362), and also many coins of the Golden Horde, chiefly struck at New Serai, and dating from the fourteenth and fifteenth centuries.†

Page 291, line 21. Lerch says the only place between these two forts showing traces of an old population is the Kirghiz Kazak cemetery of Khorkhut, near the last post station before reaching Fort Number Two. Most of the Kazak tombs here are built of burnt earth, and the Kazaks have only lately begun to erect small tombstones with inscriptions. Among these tombs one comes across pieces of dressed stone, with Arabic characters in relief, very like those on old sites such as Sabran. There are also hillocks near here like those about Yanghikeut. Lerch fixes the site of Jend at this place.‡

Page 292, line 18. I have later on identified him with the Sheibanid Prince Seyid Ahmed, a brother of Ibak (see page 980).

Page 294, line 44. For " i." in note ‡ read " v."

  „ 295, „ 31. Ulugh Muhammed at this time, as we have seen, ruled in the Krim.

Page 300, line 9. Transpose "many" and "so."

  „ 305, „ 29. He also had a fifth son, Chuvak, the ancestor of the Astrakhanid Khans of Bukhara (vide page 743).

Page 305, line 40. In note ** for " Ross " read " Koss."

  „ 310, „ 31. For " he " read " Casimir."

  „ 317, „ 10 and 12. For "him" and "his" read "me" and "my."

  „ 326, „ 23 and 33. For "Tumen" read "Tiumen." On this Ivak or Ibak see later on, page 980.

Page 327, line 7. Erase "and" after "sons."

  „ 327, „ 18. Insert a full-stop after "them."

  „ 327, „ 19. Erase the comma after "another."

  „ 333, „ 20. For "Gernadius" read "Gennadius."

  „ 334, „ 5. The date ought to be 1488.

  „ 336, „ 18. For "conduct" read "conduct."

  „ 345, „ 11. For "endowers" read "widowers."

  „ 347, „ 12. For "Seyid Ahmed" read "Sheikh Ahmed."

  „ 349, „ 22.. I ought to add to this list of Russian customs inherited from the Tartars some others enumerated by Mr. Schuyler. He says that until his visit to Central Asia he held the view of M. Solovief, that the Mongol influence in this respect had been very small, but he was afterwards struck in Central Asia with many little things, such as the customs about funerals, which made him alter his view. He says : " The style and ceremony of the Court in Old Russia were modelled after Asiatic forms. Among other things the word ' above ' (verkh), which was constantly used of the residence of the Tzars in the Kremlin, and is even now a not uncommon expression for the Winter Palace, is to this day used in Bukhara (yukhari) to denote the residence of the Amir." Kalita, the *sobriquet* of the Grand Prince Ivan, whose history I have told above, is derived from "halta," Turkish for a purse or bag. " The Russian nobles shaved their heads and dressed in the fashion set by their conquerors. They wore little skull-caps, exactly like those now worn in Central Asia. That of the murdered Tzarevitch Dimitri is still preserved in the Cathedral of the Kremlin, and the crown called ' the cap of Vladimir Monomakh ' is nothing but a Kirghis cap ornamented with precious stones. The names for many articles of dress, as shoes (bashmak), boots (ichetof), belt (kushak), are Tartar. Asiatic stuffs were common in Moscow under their original names. The stables for the best horses of the Tzar were, even in the seventeenth century, called those of the *Argamaks*, still the best breed of horses in Central Asia. . . . . The word for ' treasury,' or ' crown property,' still in use (*kasna*), should be a Tartar word, coming from the Arabic, and that for ' treasurer' (*kasnachi*) should be a purely Tartar form. This word has come to us in a very different way—through the Spanish in the form *magasine*. . . *ambar, sarai* and *cherdak* (garret and storehouse) are Eastern words." Mr. Schuyler, however, denies the Mongol paternity of the severe punishments which prevailed in Russia in the Middle Ages, which he says were introduced from Constantinople with the ecclesiastical law. While as to the seclusion of the Russian women, he contrasts it with the manner in which the Mongol women appeared in public on all occasions.*

Page 351, line 6.	Shigaviei was also called Sheikh Avliar.

„	351,	„	11.	For " fratris" read " frater."

„	351,	„	17.	" Shidiak" was also called " Seidiak."

„	352,	„	22.	" Abdul Rahman " ought rather to be written " Abdur Rahman."

Page 354, line 31.	" Shumbeka " was more correctly called " Suyunbeka."

„	358,	„	6.	For " there " read " they."

„	359,	„	6.	For " It " read " The name Astrakhan."

„	359,	„	8.	For " Phanagona " read " Phanagoria."

„	361,	„	2.	For " Shidak " read " Seidiak."

„	361,	„	43.	A longer account of these Lithuanian Tartars is given in the first chapter. I may here add that in a note to the account of the Krim Khans translated by M. Kasimirski we are told that many of these Lithuanian Tartars took part in the bloody battle of Grünwald, fought in 1407 between the Poles and the Teutonic knights, when they were enrolled in the Polish army.†

---

* Schuyler, i., 152-3.			† Nouv. Journ. Asiat., xli., 357-8.

Page 362, line 1. My friend M. Schefer has suggested to me the addition of the family names of Bakhmatief and Sherametef.

Page 364, line 5. The authority followed by Langles makes him the son of Hassan Jefai (see page 449).

Page 365, line 7. This Haidar was perhaps the Haidar, leader of the Kunkurats named in the note to page 273. . It is chronologically impossible he could have been the son of Mengli Girai, as suggested in the text.

Page 377, line 5. Mamuk is so called by the Russians, but he was not really a Sheibanid, but the ruler of the Siberian Khanate (*vide* pages 1062-3).

Page 377, line 23. For " lord " read " Lord."

   „ 378,   „   3. On Agalak (see page 1063).

   „ 381,   „   8. Insert " they " before " reasoned."

   „ 382,   „ 17. For " Alexander " read " Vasili."

   „ 404,   „ 27. The letter was written by the sons of Yusuf, the Nogai chief, to Ivan the Fourth.

Page 412, line 37. For " they " read " their followers."

   „ 436,   „ 16. For " Odanovitch " read " Ondanovitch."

   „ 436,   „ 28. For " Odan " read " Ondan."

   „ 445,   „ 20. For " Siyunbeka " read " Suyunbeka."

   „ 449,   „   2. For " Veliammof " read " Veliaminof."

   „ 449,   „ 44. note |. For " Sarmatics " read " Sarmatiis."

   „ 453,   „ 34. Azapes is no doubt a corruption of Sipahis or Spahis.

   „ 455,   „ 22. For " the nephews " read " his nephews." About them see page 350.

Page 456, line 16. For " Kostof " read " Kozlov " or " Gosleve."

   „ 464,   „ 16. For " horns " read " teeth."

   „ 466,   „ 29. For " luggage " read " baggage."

Page 468, line 28. For " Muhammed II.'s brother " read " Muhammed's second brother."

Page 471, line 44, note †. For " *Id.*" read " Karamzin VII."

   „ 473,   „   3. For " intrepidation " read " trepidation."

   „ 487,   „ 40. Add " in addition to the Sijuvits " after " he gave him."

   „ 487,   „ 43. In note ‡, for " Osm Reich " read " Osm. Gesch."

   „ 488,   „ 43. In note §, read " Osm. Gesch. ii., 181."

   „ 491,   „   1. For " Sumbeka " read " Suyunbeka."

   „ 491,   „ 14. For " his " read " this."

   „ 498,   „ 32. For " it " read " the Order."

   „ 518,   „   5. This Khan was Islam Girai *the Second*.

   „ 532,   „ 32. For " its " read " his."

   „ 534,   „ 27. Insert a comma after " wished."

   „ 538,   „ 17 and 18. According to Blau he was the son of Adil.*

   „ 543,   „ 27. For " Janibeg Khan " read " Janibeg Girai Khan."

   „ 544,   „ 13. For " Khan Timur " read " Kantemir."

   „ 544,   „ 30. It may be that this Orak gave its name to the Nogai clan, Orak.

Page 544, line 35. For " Menghi " read " Mengli." .

---

* Op. cit., 65.

Page 547, line 21. Goslove was otherwise called Koslov.

„   550, „ 32. For " usual " read " unusual."

„   555, „ 21. For " 1559 " read " 1659."

„   558, „ 40, note ‡. For "Osm. Gesh., 584," read "Osm. Gesch., iii., 584."

Page 560, line 20. For " rhe " read " the."

„   561, „ 36. This fortress is generally called " The Seven Towers."

„   563, „ 17. Krim Girai was apparently not a Khan, and ought to be styled Krim Girai Sultan ; yet he is styled Khan on the coins of Saadet Girai II.* He was the son of Selamet Girai.

Page 565, line 28. For " Devlet " read " Kara Devlet."

„   566, „ 13. For " Behln " read " Behlu."

„   567, „ 29 and 41. For " saiks " read " caiques " or " kayaks." They were pinnaces or longboats.

Page 576, line 35. For " Polkuls " read " Potkuls."

„   576, „ 39. The Kasai were the Little Nogais (see page 1050).

„   579, „ 22. For " has " read " had."

„   581, „ 26. Selamet II., as we know from his coins, was the son of Haj Selim Girai.†

Page 581, line 34. Selim Girai the Second was the son of Kaplan.‡

„   583, „ 10. Hakim or Halim was the son of Saadet.§

„   596, „ 36. For " Batatagh " read " Babatagh."

„   600, „ 30. For " Kazak " read " Kassai " (see page 1050, etc.).

„   608, „ 24. For " kaki " read " kadi." This office of kadi asker is by some called kadi lesker, and also kazi lesker, as I have called it in lines 26 and 30 of this page.

Page 621, line 4. This place is mentioned by Schiltberger under the name Karikeri, and he says the infidels called it That. Bruun adds that Murtad is Turkish for a renegade, and Pallas says the Krim Tartars call the Tartars of the scuth coast Tadd, as they do not deem them of pure blood, but mixed with Greeks and Genoese.‖

Page 624, line 45. Schiltberger describes Kaffa as surrounded by two walls, the inner containing 6,000, and the outer 11,000 houses. It was then the most important town on the Black Sea, and besides Italians, Greeks, and Armenians, contained many " infidels," who had a temple of their own. It also contained two kinds of Jews (i.e., Talmudists and Karaits). There were four towns on the coast dependent on it. These Bruun decides were Lusce, now Alushka ; Gorzum, now Gurzuf ; Partenice, now Partenite ; and Jalita, now Yalta. At these places only, besides Kaffa, were there Genoese consuls.¶

Page 625, line 34. I have overlooked a famous town, which was once almost as important as Kaffa as an entrepôt of trade. This was Tana, known to the Tartars as Azak, situated on the left bank of the Don, about six miles above its mouth. Its position made it a most important mart, and the Venetians had a settlement there at the beginning of the thirteenth century, which speedily grew in importance and became a rival to Kaffa. The

---

* See Blau, 67.   † Blau, 73.   ‡ Id.   § Id.
‖ Schilt., ed. Hack, 176.   ¶ Id., 491.

Venetians of Tana were patronised by the great Khans, Uzbeg, Janibeg, Berdibeg, and Kutlugh Timur. They granted them a site for a factory, where their consul lived.[*] It is no part of our story to relate the fierce struggle for supremacy in the Euxine trade which ensued between Genoa and Venice, during which Tana continued to grow, and became the seat of a bishop,[†] until it was terribly wasted by Timur in 1395, as I have described (see page 255). The Venetians, however, seem to have soon returned again, and Clavigo speaks of six Venetian galleys arriving at the great city of Constantinople to meet the ships coming from Tana. De Lannoy states in his "Voyages et Embassades" that in 1421 four Venetian vessels arrived thence at Kaffa. Schiltberger, who visited it about this time, calls it "Asach, which the Christians call Alathena" (i.e., Alla Tana), and says that large galleys full of fish were sent thence to Venice, Genoa, and the islands in the sea.[‡] Josaphat Barbaro went to Tana in 1436, and lived there about sixteen years. He gives no definite description of it, but from his allusions it must have been a place of great importance. In 1475 Tana fell into the power of the Ottomans, as I have described (page 454), and it speedily became their most important fortress and arsenal north of the Black Sea, where they kept a garrison to overawe the Tartars and threaten the Russians.

Page 625, line 35. Note 4 really begins with this line.

    „ 627, „ 23. Insert "and" after "Borrak."

    „ 627, „ 35, note §. The reference ought to be Vel. Zernof, ii., 264.

    „ 629, „ 1. Shahibeg was a title of Sheibani.

    „ 629, „ 11. For "Sheihani" read "Sheibani."

    „ 629, „ 33. For "Kainu" read "Kasim."

    „ 629, „ 38. Mr. Schuyler suggests for "Berkin" read "Bikema."

    „ 630, „ 9. Hakim was a pupil of the famous Khoja Ahmed Yassavi.

    „ 630, „ 15. For "Tarez" read "Taraz."

    „ 630, „ 39. For "he" read "Kasim."

    „ 631, „ 16. The biographer of Uraz Makhmet says he was buried at Seraichuk,§ but he probably confused him with Kasim Khan of Astrakhan.

Page 632, line 33. For "they" read "the Kazaks."

    „ 632, „ 41. In note §, for "235" read "325."

    „ 633, „ 14. For "Taras" read "Talas."

    „ 635, „ 34. There is still a vivid tradition of Shigai Khan's bravery. We are told he died far away from his native land. His tombstone is to be seen at Kumish Kent, which, according to M. Khanikof, is a small settlement near Bukhara. He was buried at Avlie Ata (i.e., at Taraz).‖

Page 636, line 16. For "Issevi" read "Yassavi."

    „ 643, „ 32. Pulad and Bulat are both the same name.

    „ 652, „ 39. For "Kiap" read "Kaip."

    „ 656, „ 9. For "hides" read "skins."

    „ 667, „ 39. Erali was the brother, not the son of Nurali.

    „ 672, „ 2. For "1712" read "1812."

---

[*] Von Hammer, Golden Horde, 255.   [†] Cathay, and the Way Thither, 233.
Schilt., ed. Hack., 49.   [§] Vel. Zernof, ii., 125.   [‖] Id., 276, and note 39.

Page 683, line 20.   M. Leech says that in this mosque are also buried the Uzbeg chief, Suiunich Khoja Khan, who died in 931 hej, i.e., 1524-5, his two sons, his daughter, and grandson.*

Page 687, line 37.   Vambery says mosaic pictures, but this ought probably to be porcelain tiles.

Page 703, line 34.   For " Siraks " read " Sirakhs."

  „   703,   „   35.   For " Murzas " read "the Murzas."

  „   704,   „   36.   Erase "the" before "reading."

  „   706,   „   3.   For " Kassim " read " Kasim."

  „   729,   „   5.   For " him " read " them."

  „   729,   „   13.   For " Kerminek " read " Kermineh."

  „   751,   „   11.   Ferrier says the Uzbegs took Kandahar in 1620 from the Persians, and were not driven out again till 1634.†

Page 752, line 2.   For " Audhud " read " Andkhud."

  „   764,   „   29.   For " submission " read " defeat."

  „   767,   „   11.   Erase the stop between Ibrahim and Sultan.

  „   770,   „   15.   For " piece " read " fierce."

  „   770,   „   43.   In note * for " id." read " Schefer, op. cit."

  „   785,   „   1.   For " new thing " read " suggestion."

  „   786,   „   10.   For " marke " read " market."

  „   786,   „   12.   Insert a comma between " this " and " Orenburgh."

  „   786,   „   26.   For " compliments " read " complements."

  „   789,   „   30.   For " he " read " Ayaz."

  „   790,   „   42, and 791, 43, notes ‡ and †.   For " Wolf " read " Wolff."

  „   798,   „   11.   For " he " read " Stoddart."

  „   799,   „   31.   For " Zadek " read " Zadeh."

  „   801,   „   29.   For " counties " read " countries."

  „   803,   „   25.   For " Zadek " read " Zadeh."

  „   810,   „   3 and 8.   For " Osenburgh " read " Orenburgh."

  „   816,   „   3.   Insert " the " before " chief."

  „   824,   „   27.   Insert " of " before " others."

  „   829,   „   7.   Insert " were " after " brothers."

  „   830,   „   33.   Insert " their " before " refusing."

  „   833,   „   35.   For " increased " read " intense."

  „   845,   „   37.   I have followed the usual orthography of Uratippa, which ought perhaps more properly to be written Ura teppeh, " the fire hill."

Page 849, line 9.   For " Keningbez " read " Kenegbez."

  „   852,   „   17.   For " flows " read " flow."

  „   855,   „   36.   For " him " read " Moorcroft."

  „   857,   „   24.   For " Kilich " read " Kilij."

  „   860,   „   15.   For " the Sighan " read " Sighan."

  „   866,   „   7.   For " Bulkh " read " Balkh."

  „   866,   „   12.   For " Khulm " read " Kundus."

  „   866,   „   20.   For " Gazanfer " read " Kasanfer."

  „   869,   „   17.   For " Sirfal " read " Sirpul."

* Rapp. Com. Arch., 1867-8, xxlii., etc.   † Travels, 135.

Page 873, line 36. Insert " is " between " there " and " called."

„ 874. I have most stupidly headed the second genealogical table on this page with the words " Janids or Manguts," instead of " Janids or Astrakhanids."

Page 876, line 17 and 24. For " Vesir " read " Vezir."

„ 877, „   6. For " were " read " was."

„ 879, „   4, etc. Balbars may as rightly be styled Bilbars.

„ 880, „   6. For " Ismal " read " Ismael."

„ 880, „ 29 and 34. For " Avanek " read " Aminek."

„ 881, „ 2, 9, and 22. For " Avanek Khan " read " Aminek." The four sons of Aminek, mentioned in line 9, were of course the brothers of Sofian Khan.

Page 884, line 1. For " Avanek " read " Aminek."

„ 884, „ 25. Kalkhan is called Kahl Khan in the Leyden edition of Abulghasi. He was the son of Aminek, not of Avanek Khan.

Page 885, line 29. For " Kalk " read " Kal."

„ 888, „ 31. Erase " his."

„ 892, „ 35. For " we " read " he."

„ 892, „ 39. Put "(i.e., Hajim)" after " Azim Khan."

„ 893, „ 26. Insert " he " before " reached."

„ 893, „ 31. Insert " who " before " assigned."

„ 905, „ 18. For " son " read " brother."

„ 912, „ 36. For " Iram " read " Iran."

„ 914, „ 37, note *. For " Lervhine " read " Levchine."

„ 919, „ 28. For " Urghurs " read " Uighurs."

„ 921, „ 22. For " Shirgasi " read " Shirghazi."

„ 922, „ 36. According to Riza Kuli Khan, this campaign took place in 1233, i.e., 1817. He says that at the instigation of the Kurdish tribes, who had risen against Feth Ali Khan, Muhammed Rahim marched towards Asterabad, with 30,000 men and some artillery, under pretence of imposing tribute on the Turkomans of the Atrek and the Gurgan. The Sirdar Zulfekar Khan marched against him with the levies of Damighan and Semnan, and completely defeated him at Pusserek, where he was intrenched. The only piece of cannon he carried off was the one he abandoned at Kara Eteklik.*

Page 927, line 30. Khesret is generally written Hasret or Huzrut.

„ 930, „ 10. Riza Kuli tells us Allah Kuli built a castle at Merv, which he armed with several cannons, and put the uncle of his first minister there as governor, but the inhabitants rebelled, killed him, and seized the cannons.†

Page 936, line 10. For " Abbot " read " Abbott."

„ 939, „ 5. See further about Akhud Zadeh, ante 799, etc.

„ 941, „ 19. According to Riza Kuli Khan, he died in 1263 hej, i.e., 1847.

Page 941, line 21. During the last few weeks M. Schefer has presented me with his translation of the account of the embassy of Riza Kuli Khan, who was

---

* Schefer Relation, etc., 66-7, note 2.   † Id., 159.

sent as an envoy from Nasir ud din, Shah of Persia, to Muhammed Amin in 1851, and whose narrative is very interesting. It unfortunately arrived too late to be utilised in the text, and I can only here extract a few passages. It seems that on his accession the ruler of Khuarezm sent a prince of the Persian royal stock, named Muhammed Vali Khan Kajar, who had been made prisoner by the Turkomans, with presents and news of the event to Teheran.* The Persian Shah Muhammed sent an envoy in return, but presently a coolness arose between the two princes. Some time after the accession of Nasir ud din to the Persian throne, Muhammed Amin sent a fresh envoy, Ata Nias Mahrem, with some Turkoman horses and two falcons, and with offers of renewed friendship. It was in answer to this last mission that Riza Kuli was despatched. He took with him a double-barrelled gun and two pistols as presents for the Khivan Khan, and was told to try and secure the release of the Persians detained captives at Khiva. He went in company with Ata Nias Mahrem. The envoy describes in detail his journey through Mazanderan to Sari, near the Caspian, near which he was joined by a number of Khuarezmians and Khokandians returning from Mecca,† and then went on by way of Ashraf and Asterabad, and across the Turkoman steppes, where he suffered considerable hardships. On the 30th of May our traveller quitted the desert and entered the district of cultivated land at Pei Shakri. The next day he entered Khiva, where he was duly welcomed by Rahmet Ullah, Divan Khal Mehter (who was the Khan's Chancellor of the Exchequer), and by the Nazir Mehter Aga, and was eventually lodged in a villa belonging to the late Khan Muhammed Rahim.‡ He describes this in detail, as also his entertainment at the house of his late companion, the Khivan envoy.§ At this time the Khan was absent on an expedition towards Merv, and Tangri Kuli Tureh, a son of Muhammed Rahim, was in command at Khiva with the title of Naib.‖ During the festival succeeding the fast of Ramazan, it was customary to give Persian slaves in the Khanate a three days' holiday, during which they repaired in great numbers to the capital, Khiva, and had intercourse with one another. The Persian envoy entertained many of them, and tells an affecting story of the meeting of two cousins who had been separately carried off as slaves, and had come together under these strange circumstances.¶ The Khan returned on the first of August. He was dressed in a rose-coloured robe, and had an aigrette on his head and on that of his horse. The envoy meanwhile was attacked with fever, and it was some days before he had an audience. At this interview the Khan feigned not to understand Persian, while Riza Kuli refused to speak in Turki. They eventually communicated through an interpreter, and the envoy reports how he described the power and resources of Persia, and the great qualities of his master, the Shah. The Khan complained of the demonstration which the Persians had recently made at Sirakhs, and was told that it was not meant as a menace to him, but to repress the turbulent Turkomans. The conversation now turned to more dangerous topics, and the Khan enlarged on his duty as a good Sunni to persecute the heretic Shias. The envoy then spoke out like a statesman on

* Schefer, xlv. † Id., 34. ‡ Op. cit., 72. § Id., 72-7.
‖ Id., 77. ¶ Id., 853, etc.

the folly of Muhammedans destroying one another for these differences o
creed, and recited how Nadir Shah and others had tried to heal the schism;
and the conversation, which is reported at length, is both very interesting
and graphic. The Khan seems to have been moved. He argued that it was
not his own people, but the Turkomans who were to blame for the alarums
into Persia; and on being asked why he did not forbid the selling of Persian
slaves, he replied that if the Khivans ceased to buy them the Bukharians
would not. He was asked to restore the prisoners at Khiva as a graceful
offering to the Shah, and replied that he could not take them from their
owners, who had bought them with gold. The envoy asked him to redeem
them, and in return suggested that the Persians would help him to conquer
Merv. The Khan summoned his councillors to discuss the matter, but it was
decided that the time was inopportune, and that the Persians should be
misled by diplomatic answers.* Orders were at the same time secretly sent
to the Turkomans of the tribes Tekke, Akhal, Salur, and Saruk, to fall upon
the Persians as they retired from Sirakhs, while a body of 8,000 cavalry
menaced Khorasan. A great number of Persians were captured, and sent to
be sold at Khiva. We are told that two or three thousand Khivans of the
tribes Jemjid, Ak Derbendi, and Jami, took part in the raid of the Tekkes.†

Riza Kuli now began to prepare for his return home again. The Khan
sent him a present of a kaba of embroidered satin, and a gubbeh of beautiful
silk threaded with gold. He also sent him 500 tumans in ashrafis or gold
coins, and in tenghas or silver coins, which were stamped with the name of
Muhammed Amin Khan. As these were not current beyond the Khanate, Riza
Kuli employed them in buying himself camels, horses, etc., for his journey. He
also redeemed a number of the Persian slaves. The Khan also bade him
escort Seyid Ahmed Nakib, of Bukhara, together with several learned men
and doctors, from Kashgar, Ferghaneh, Khokand, and Khiva, who wished to
make the pilgrimage to Mekka, as far as Teheran. He returned by way of
Kunia Urgenj, and arrived at home again on the 3rd of November, 1852.‡
He digresses at several places, and describes the topography of Khuaresm
and the neighbouring districts in very interesting detail, and also gives a
valuable notice of many customs that prevailed in the Khanate. Among the
presents which the Khivan Khan sent the Shah, were two trained falcons,
a gun made at Khiva, Russian pistols, and European porcelain. He also sent
two gold watches for the Shah's ministers. Ahmed Nakib Khoja, on his own
account, presented two eagles and two trained merlins. After staying some
time at Teheran, Muhammed Amir's envoy, Muhammed Sherif Bey, returned
home again, taking with him a snuffbox enriched with diamonds, as a present
from the Shah to the Khan.

For some time there was no intercourse between the two sovereigns.
Meanwhile the Khivan Khan was not quiet. He marched his troops against
Sirakhs and Merv, and incited the Turkomans to ravage Khorasan. The
governors of these frontier districts complained to the Court, and accordingly
Feridun Mirza, formerly governor of Fars, and uncle to the Shah, was

---

* Op. cit., 95-112.   † Id., 113.   ‡ Id., 206.

nominated governor of Khorasan and guardian of the famous tomb of Ali
Riza, at Meshed, and Murza Fazhl Ullah Vizier Nizam was appointed his
first minister. The Turkomans of Merv and Sirakhs, weary of the exactions
of the Khivan Khan, accepted a governor at the hands of Feridun.[*] At this
time the Turkomans of Kariab, incited by Muhammed Amin, blockaded the
route to Merv, and fell on a small detachment which went to its relief. They
were, however, defeated, lost several hundred men, and a quantity of flour
which they were taking to Kariab. On news of this reaching Khiva, the Khan
determined to attack Merv and Sirakhs, and to take them from the Persians.
Some troops, with a quantity of grain, were thereupon sent to reinforce the
Merv garrison, while a division was despatched to punish Jafer Agha Jelari,
the governor of Kelat, who had treacherously sided with the Khivan Khan.
Feridun Murza having made a tour of inspection of several frontier posts, and
dispersed some Turkoman raiders, returned to Meshed. Meanwhile, Jafer
Agha pressed the Khivan Khan for succour, and at length the latter gave him
1,000 Kariabi horsemen with whom to recover Kelat. A few hours' combat
ensued, in which the Agha was defeated and lost many men, and he once more
appealed to his patron, who now sent to Meimeneh, Herat, Akhal, and the various
Turkomans for assistance, and then sent 3,000 men towards Merv under Shah
Murad Uinak and the Kush begi. He followed himself, with the full determination to conquer Khorasan. When Feridun Murza heard of this, he set
out from Meshed with 10,000 men for Ak Derbend. He despatched a small
detachment to the succour of Sirakhs, which arrived as the people of the
town were being attacked by the Khivans. The reinforcement turned the tide
of victory, and six cannons and 600 great muskets were captured by the
troops of the Khorasan.[†] This defeat stirred the Khan to fresh efforts, and he
drew near Sirakhs. Muhammed Hassan Khan was sent against him with two
regiments of Ferahan and one of Guerrus (the latter were a tribe of Northern
Kurdistan), four pieces of artillery, and 1,000 picked cavalry, with which he
defeated 2,000 Khivans he met *en route*. Another body of 2,000 Khorasan
troops was sent off from Ak Derbend under Mehdi Kuli Murza, and others.
According to the exaggerated notice of Riza Kuli, Muhammed Amin had
mustered a force of 40,000 men of the tribes Jemjid, Kariabi, Teimeni, and of the
people of Menneneh and Shiburghan, and from the Salur Surak, Tekke,
Goklan-Yomud, and other Turkomans.[‡] He arrived before Sirakhs the same
day as the Persian troops. His tent, which was of a green colour, was pitched
on a hill, called in Turki Kanli-Teppeh, *i.e.*, the bloody hill. There he was
surrounded by his ministers, relatives, and grandees, and he urged his men by
various means to an immediate attack. A terrible fight ensued, in which the
citizens of Sirakhs and the Khorasan troops at length defeated the enemy,
who began to withdraw. Their booty comprised 3,000 heads, a great
number of horses and camels, a cannon of the calibre of seventeen pounds,
and sixteen smaller pieces, as well as a great number of muskets. The
fugitives were pursued to the foot of the "Bloody Hill." Muhammed Amin,
who had witnessed the rout of his men, called for his horse, with its saddle

* *Id.*, 212-13.　　　　† *Id.*, 215.　　　　‡ *Id.*, 216.

broidered with gold, a gold ball hanging from the crupper, and an aigrette on
its head. His own costume also made him conspicuous. He had an aigrette
and a gold plate on his head. The upper part of his headgear was covered with
red cloth, which he alone in the Khanate was allowed to wear. On seeing
him, the troopers of Khorasan made a rush. Kurban Kal struck him with his
sabre, and gashed him from the mouth to the ear. The Khan cried out, " I
am the Khan Hazret. I am a great person ; conduct me to the King of
Persia," but no one listened ; a struggle ensued among the troopers for the
right of beheading him, and twelve of them were in consequence killed.
Eventually Sihat Niaz Khan, son of Erazh Khan, of Sirakhs, cut off the
head. This took place on the 7th of March, 1855. Besides the Khan, a
great number of officers were killed ; the names of the chief of them are given
by Riza Kuli. Their heads were put on lances, and carried in triumph to
Ak Derbend. The news reached Teheran on the 24th of March, the Shah's
birthday. The Khan's head and his headgear were duly verified by Riza Kuli.
The Shah ordered the heads of the Khan and his grandees to be buried
outside the city gate, called Dervazehi Daulet, and a tomb was built there.
Readers of the Koran were nominated to it, and a distribution of water and
soup to the poor took place. Muhammed Amin was thirty-five years old
at his death, and had reigned about nine years.[*]

Page 945, line 8. I have elsewhere called " Ak Mejid " " Ak Musjid."

„   946,   „   12. For " Sarbaris " read " Sarbasis."

„   964,   „   33. For " Ust Ust " read " Ust Urt."

„   968,   „   46, note *. For " op. cit." read " Burnaby's Ride to Khiva."

„   971,   „   41. A town of some note in the Khanate, of which I have
omitted a notice, was Khankah, which was deemed one of the strongest places
in the country. It was captured by Nadir Shah, and Ilbars Khan was killed
there. It was situated between Hazarasp and Khiva.

Page 974,   „   19. For " Artock " read " Ardock."

„   977,   „   3. For " Shah baz Vali " read " Sheikh Abbas Vali."

„   978,   „   26. The battle referred to was no doubt the fight on the
river Sayo (see page 51).

Page 979, line 6. On Sheiban's death, see further, page 79.

„   994,   „   12. For " allegianee " read " allegiance."

„   997,   „   33. For " 1587 " read " 1585."

„   998,   „   41. For " indigines " read ' indigenes."

„   1001,   „   33. For " Bayard " read " Boyard."

„   1009,   „   16. For " verts " read " versts."

„   1016,   „   44, note §. For " Turcomaine " read " Turkomanie."

„   1017,   „   26 and 38. For " Chaga " read " Chuka."

„   1020,   „   1. A country of Sem Sem is mentioned in the account of
Timur's campaign in the Caucasus, which may possibly be this place (see page
256). There is, however, a place in Siberia called Shamsha (page 994).

Page 1020, line 18, and 1021, 5. For " Zenkireh " read " Zekireh."

„   1022,   „   23. M. Berezine, in his " Yarlik Toktamysha," 61, says that

---

[*] *Id.,* 222.

Idiku was killed by a Tartar of the Barin tribe, from whom his head was stolen by a friend, who, having presented it to Ulugh Muhammed, received in reward that chief's daughter in marriage.[*]

Page 1022, line 15 and 21.   For "Abul" read "Abdul."

   „   1025,   „   21.   Put marks of quotation before " They lead."

   „   1025,   „   33.   For " Chotz " read " Khotz."

   „   1026,   „   7.   For " Chotz " read " Khotz."

   „   1028,   „   14.   For " refuge " read " ordu or camp."

   „   1030,   „   2.   For " Khazan " read " Kazan."

   „   1030,   „   8.   For " the Kujash Murza " read " Kujash Murza."

   „   1031,   „   14.   For " Iranovitch " read " Ivanovitch."

   „   1032,   „   18.   For " Suyunbeki " read " Suyunbeka."

   „   1035,   „   12.   The name in De Guignes is " Muradin."

   „   1035,   „   20 and 25.   For " Kassaim " and " Kasam " read " Kassim."

   „   1048,   „   18.   M. Bernet was not the author of this work, but only the reviser of the text, It was written by M. Daniel Schlatter.

Page 1062, line 19.   The mention of Buri here is a mistake.   He was killed by his brother Chuke.   It was Kara Kijik, the son of Chuke, who fled eastwards on his father's death.

---

[*] Schiltberger, ed. Hack., 145, note by Bruun.

WS - #0052 - 030125 - C0 - 229/152/25 - PB - 9780282360733 - Gloss Lamination